Communication Theories

Communication Theories

Perspectives, Processes, and Contexts

Katherine Miller
Texas A&M University

Boston   Burr Ridge, IL   Dubuque, IA   Madison, WI   New York   San Francisco   St. Louis
Bangkok   Bogotá   Caracas   Kuala Lumpur   Lisbon   London   Madrid   Mexico City
Milan   Montreal   New Delhi   Santiago   Seoul   Singapore   Sydney   Taipei   Toronto

McGraw-Hill Higher Education ⅋

A Division of The **McGraw-Hill** Companies

1 2 3 4 5 6 7 8 9 0 DOC/DOC 0 9 8 7 6 5 4 3 2 1

Library of Congress Cataloging-in-Publication Data
Miller, Katherine
    Communication theories : perspectives, processes, and contexts / Katherine Miller.
        p. cm.
    Includes bibliographical references and index.
    ISBN 0-7674-0500-5
        1. Communication—Philosophy. I. Title.

P90 .M479 2001
302.2'01—dc21   2001026629

Sponsoring editor, Holly J. Allen; production editor, Jennifer Mills; manuscript editor, Amy Marks; text designer, John Edeen; cover designer, Jean Mailander; art editors, Rennie Evans and Emma Ghiselli; illustrator, Lotus Art; manufacturing manager, Randy Hurst. This text was set in 10.5/12 Goudy by Black Dot Group and printed on 45# Highland Plus by R. R. Donnelley & Sons Company.

Cover: Circles, by Johannes Itten. © 2001 Artists Rights Society (ARS), New York/ProLitteris, Zürich. Photo © Alinari/Art Resource, NY.

Text credits appear on a continuation of the copyright page, page 328.

♲ Printed on recycled, acid-free paper.

www.mhhe.com

Contents

Preface   xv

P A R T **1** O N E

Perspectives on Communication Theory   1

C H A P T E R

1

Conceptual Foundations:
What Is Communication?   2

Defining Communication   3
Conceptualizing Communication: Points of Convergence   5
Conceptualizing Communication: Points of Divergence   8

Moving Beyond Definitions   11
Conceptual Domains of Communication Studies   11
Disciplinary Domains of Communication Studies   12
The Domain of This Textbook   15
Summary   17

C H A P T E R

2

Philosophical Foundations:
What Is Theory?   18

The Nature of Theory   19
Conceptualizing Theory: What Is Theory?   19
Conceptualizing Theory: What Should Theory Do?   21
Summary   23

Metatheoretical Considerations   23
Ontological Considerations   24
Epistemological Considerations   25

Axiological Considerations   27
Summary   29

Theory in the Communication Discipline   29
Communication Theory as a Pluralistic Enterprise   29

CHAPTER

**Post-Positivist Perspectives
on Theory Development**   32

Philosophical Roots: Positivism   33
Classical Positivism   33
Logical Positivism: The Vienna Circle   33
The Demise of Positivism   34

Post-Positivism in Social Research Today   35
Metatheoretical Commitments   35
Structure and Function of Post-Positivist Theory   37
Criteria for Evaluating and Comparing Theories   40
The Process of Theory Development   41

Post-Positivism in Communication Research   44

CHAPTER

**Interpretive Perspectives
on Theory Development**   46

Historical Background   46

Foundational Theoretical Positions   47
Hermeneutics   47
Phenomenology   49
Symbolic Interactionism   50
Summary   51

Interpretive Theory in Communication   51
Ontology of Interpretive Theory   52
Epistemology of Interpretive Theory   52
Axiology of Interpretive Theory   53

Structure and Function of Interpretive Theory   53
General Interpretive Theories   54
Grounded Theory   56

Summary   58

CHAPTER

5 Critical Perspectives on Theory Development 60

Historical Roots of Critical Theory 61
The Influence of Marxism 61
The Frankfurt School 63

Contemporary Critical Theory 64
Ontological Commitments 65
Epistemological Commitments 66
Axiological Commitments 67
Summary 69

Critical Approaches in Communication 69
Cultural Studies 69
Feminist Studies 71

Summary 72

PART TWO

Theories of Communication Processes 75

CHAPTER

6 Theories of Symbolic Organization 76

**Social Scientific Approaches to
Symbolic Organization** 76
Schema Theory 77
Attribution Theory 81
Summary of Social Scientific Approaches 83

Humanistic Approaches to Symbolic Organization 84
Narrative Theory 84
Dramatism 88

Comparison and Commentary 92

CHAPTER

7

Theories of Message Production   95

Constructivist Theory   96
Metatheoretical Foundations of Constructivism   96
The Construct System   97
Person-Centered Communication   97
Linking Constructs and Communication   98
Message Design Logics   99

Action Assembly Theory   101
Metatheoretical Commitments   103
Structures in Action Assembly Theory   103
Activation and Assembly Processes   104
Action Assembly Theory: Evidence and Extensions   105

Planning and Goals   106
Explicating Relevant Constructs   107
Berger's Theory of Planning   108

Comparison and Commentary   109

CHAPTER

Theories of Message Processing   113

Three Classic Models of Persuasion   114
Cognitive Dissonance Theory   114
Theory of Reasoned Action   115
Social Judgment Theory   116
Summary   117

Elaboration Likelihood Model   118
Central and Peripheral Routes to Persuasion   118
Which Route Do You Take?   118
And Where Does It Get You?   119
Critiques of the Elaboration Likelihood Model   119

Inoculation Theory   122
Components of the Inoculation Process   123
Tests of Inoculation Theory   125

Problematic Integration Theory   125
What Is Being Integrated in Problematic Integration?   126
When Is Integration Problematic?   126
Communicative Implications of Problematic Integration   128

Comparison and Commentary   130

CHAPTER

9

Theories of Discourse and Interaction   132

Speech Act Theory   132
Original Formulations of Speech Act Theory   133
Applications and Challenges   135

Coordinated Management of Meaning Theory   136
Metatheoretical Foundations   136
Central Concepts of Coordinated
    Management of Meaning Theory   137
Evidence for and Critiques of Coordinated
    Management of Meaning Theory   140

Communication Accommodation Theory   141
Central Concepts—What Happens in Interaction?   141
Antecedents to Accommodation   142
Consequences of Accommodation   145
Evidence for and Critiques of Communication
    Accommodation Theory   146

**Expectancy Violation and Interaction
Adaptation Theories   146**
Original Statement—Expectancy Violation Theory   147
Tests and Development of the Theory   149
Interaction Adaptation Theory   150

Comparison and Commentary   150

CHAPTER

10

Theories of Communication in Developing Relationships   153

Social Penetration Theory   153
Original Statement of Social Penetration Theory   154
Meanwhile, in the Field of Communication . . .   158
Developments and Tests of Social Penetration Theory   160
Summary and Evaluation of Social Penetration Theory   162

Uncertainty Reduction Theory   163
Original Statement of Uncertainty Reduction Theory   163
Berger's Extensions to Uncertainty Reduction Theory   166
Tests and Critiques of Uncertainty Reduction Theory   167
Expanding the Scope of Uncertainty Reduction Theory   170
Summary and Evaluation of Uncertainty Reduction Theory   171

Comparison and Commentary   172

CHAPTER

11 Theories of Communication in Ongoing Relationships   174

Relational Systems Theory: The Palo Alto Group   174
The Players: Gregory Bateson and Colleagues   174
The Concept: Shifting the Focus
    from Individual to System   175
The Book: *Pragmatics of Human Communication*   176
Developments from the Palo Alto Group
    in Communication   179

Theories of Relational Dialectics   182
Philosophical Roots   183
Central Concepts in Dialectics   185
Relational Dialectics: Contradictions   186
Relational Dialectics: Praxis   188
Research on Dialectics   189

Comparison and Commentary   191

PART 3 THREE

Theories of Communication Contexts   195

CHAPTER

12 Theories of Organizational Communication   196

Weick's Theory of Organizing   197
The Process of Organizing   198
Tests and Applications of Weick's Model   201

Structuration Theory   201
The Duality of Structure   202
Key Concepts   202
Structuration Theory in Organizational Communication   204

The Text and Conversation of Organizing   205
The Core Concepts: Text and Conversation   207

Unobtrusive and Concertive Control Theory   210
Control   210
Identification   212
Discipline   212
Research Applications of Concertive Control Theory   213

Comparison and Commentary   214

CHAPTER

13

Theories of Small Group Communication   216

Formative Research in Group Interaction   216

Functional Theory   218
Formative Influences of Functional Theory   218
Assumptions and Predictions of Functional Theory   220
Empirical Tests, Critiques, and Revisions of
    Functional Theory   222

Structurational Approaches   224
Structuration Theory Revisited   224
The Structuration of Group Arguments   226
Adaptive Structuration Theory   227

Symbolic Convergence Theory   229
Theoretical Precursors and Original Development   230
The Symbolic Convergence Framework   230
Explanations for Convergence in Small Group
    Communication   232

Comparison and Commentary   233

CHAPTER

14

Theories of Media Processing and Effects   236

The Development of Media Effects Research   236
The Bullet and the Needle   237
Alternatives to Strong Effects   238

Social Cognitive Theory   239
Key Concepts in Social Cognitive Theory   240
Social Cognitive Theory and the Communication Media   241
Summary   242

Uses and Gratifications Theory   242

What Gratifications Are Sought and Obtained
from Media?   243

How Are Media Used in the Gratification Process?   244

Extensions and Critiques of the Uses and Gratifications
Approach   245

Media Systems Dependency Theory   246

Media Systems Dependency Theory: The Basic Framework   247

Tests and Extensions of Media Systems
Dependency Theory   249

Theories of the Media and Emotion   250

Excitation Transfer Theory   251

Empathic Reactions to Media Content   252

Social and Developmental Factors   253

Comparison and Commentary   254

CHAPTER

15

Theories of Media and Society   257

Agenda Setting Theory   257

Defining Agenda Setting   258

Agenda Setting: The Core Proposition   259

Theoretical Developments in Agenda Setting   261

Critiques of Agenda Setting Theory   263

Spiral of Silence Theory   264

Major Components of Spiral of Silence Theory   264

Evidence for and Extensions of Spiral of Silence Theory   266

Critiques of Spiral of Silence Theory   268

Cultivation Theory   269

Historical Background   269

Assumptive Base of Cultivation Theory   270

Testing Cultivation Theory   271

Critiques and Extensions of Cultivation Theory   272

Comparison and Commentary   274

CHAPTER

16 Theories of Culture and Communication 276

Speech Codes Theory 278
Formative Influences 278
A Seminal Study: "Talking Like a Man in Teamsterville" 280
The Speech Codes Framework: Current Commitments 281
Research in the Speech Codes Tradition 284

Theories of Face and Culture 284
Dimensions of Cultural Variability 285
The Concept of Face 286
The Concept of Facework 288

Theories of Co-Cultural Groups 289
Standpoint Theory 289
Muted Group Theory 291
Co-Cultural Communication 292

Comparison and Commentary 293

Bibliography 297
Credits 328
Index 329

Preface

When I began writing this textbook several years ago, I thought I had a pretty clear understanding of what I was getting myself into. I had been in the field of communication for a number of years, had worked in several high-powered departments with active scholars in a variety of areas, and had taught communication theory at several levels. However, while writing this book, I was both humbled and amazed by what I still had to learn, for theory within the communication discipline is wide-ranging and complex, encompassing huge differences in scholarship in terms of topic areas and in terms of philosophical foundations and approaches to the theory development process. This book, then, is my attempt to understand—and help students understand—the burgeoning world of communication theory.

I had several goals in writing this book. The first of these was to help students understand the intricacies and nuances of theories that were developed by communication theorists or that have been used extensively by communication researchers. Because I wanted the coverage of theories to be comprehensive and current, I was faced with the task of limiting the number of theories considered. As I explain in Chapter 1, three criteria guided me in making these choices about theory inclusion. First, I included only work that could be clearly distinguished as a theory. That is, I did not include individual research efforts or areas of interest in communication that had not been codified into coherent theoretical statements. Second, I included only theories that have been developed by scholars working in the communication discipline or widely used and extended by scholars in the field. Finally, I concentrated on theories that would be largely considered social science theories. This is not to say that all theories with rhetorical roots are ignored, but those that are highlighted have had a strong influence on a wide range of communication scholars.

My second goal in writing this book was to help students to think critically about the theories they encounter. For me, critical thinking is enhanced through processes of analytical comparison and through the application of an appropriate critical lens. To facilitate critical thinking, then, I grouped theories in sets of two to four per chapter, with each chapter covering an important substantive area in communication scholarship. This grouping allows students to compare and contrast theoretical approaches regarding similar communication phenomena. More important, though, I tried to enhance critical thinking by giving extensive coverage to the theoretical perspectives and frameworks that undergird theories in communication. Thus, the first five chapters of this book deal not with specific theories of communication but with the conceptual and philosophical frameworks within which these theories were developed. I consider general definitions of communication and theory as well as specific perspectives on theorizing rising from post-positivist, interpretivist, and critical traditions.

My third goal in writing this text was to make communication theories—and the process of theorizing—accessible to students. Thus, I have tried to write in a style that is understandable and conversational without losing the complexities of the theories at hand. I have included numerous examples that will help to clarify theoretical issues for students, as well as extensive tables, key terms, and discussion questions for each chapter.

Features

To reach my goals, I have built into the textbook a number of key features:

- **Organizing Framework:** The book is organized into three parts. Part One (Perspectives on Communication Theory) provides strong foundational chapters that will help students understand the scope and nature of theory development processes generally and within the field of communication more specifically. These chapters cover conceptualizations of communication, the nature of theory and metatheoretical considerations that guide theory development, and the three major theoretical perspectives of post-positivist, interpretivist, and critical theory. These perspectives are discussed in terms of their historical roots and their current commitments, and they provide a framework for understanding theories in the remainder of the book.

  In Part Two (Theories of Communication Processes) and Part Three (Theories of Communication Contexts), the text moves to a consideration of specific theories developed and used by scholars in the communication discipline. As noted earlier, these theories were chosen with specific criteria in mind, and this selective coverage of theories allows for greater depth of coverage and an opportunity for enhanced understanding and critique of each theory's complex features.

- **Spotlight on the Theorist:** I have tried to show the human side of theorizing by including boxes that spotlight the specific theorists that students encounter in this book, giving them a human face and describing some of the tribulations and rewards of the theory development process. In short, I want students to see the connections between theories and theorizing and communication in their everyday lives.

- **Current Research and an Extensive List of References:** The coverage of these theories is current, and extensive references are included for further research.

- **Comparison and Commentary Sections:** Theories are grouped into sets of two to four per chapter, based on the topic areas addressed. These groupings allow students to compare and contrast related theories, and this process is facilitated by the "Comparison and Commentary" sections at the end of each chapter.

- **End-of-Chapter Pedagogy:** Each chapter closes with key terms and discussion questions to point students to critical issues raised throughout the text.

- **Instructor's Manual:** This textbook is accompanied by an instructor's manual that includes a number of features that will help instructors in their pedagogical tasks. Specifically, the instructor's manual includes sample syllabi, possible paper assignments, key terms and chapter outlines, and extensive test items (in true/false, multiple-choice, fill-in-the-blank, and essay formats). The manual also includes suggestions for Web sites and video resources that can enhance the educational process.

Acknowledgments

The writing of this textbook spanned several years—and two university campuses—and many people have helped immensely along the way. My first thanks go to Holly Allen of Mayfield Publishing, who approached me with this project and was incredibly patient with my fits and starts along the way. Thanks go, also, to the rest of the Mayfield/McGraw-Hill team, especially my production editor, Jen Mills, and my copyeditor, Amy Marks. Through several drafts of this book, I have been assisted by the insightful reviews of scholars throughout the communication discipline. I thank the following reviewers for the time they took to carefully read the manuscript and provide detailed and productive critiques of my work: Patricia Amason, University of Arkansas; Sandra Ball-Rokeach, University of Southern California; Stanley Baran, Bryant College; Brant Burleson, Purdue University; Deborah Cai, University of

Maryland; Kenneth N. Cissna, University of South Florida; Stanley A. Deetz, University of Colorado; Steve Duck, University of Iowa; Elizabeth Graham, Ohio University; Radha Hegde, Rutgers University; Bill Henderson, University of Northern Iowa; Michael Holmes, University of Utah; Joann Keyton, University of Memphis; Elizabeth J. Natalle, University of North Carolina, Greensboro; Elizabeth Perse, University of Delaware; Diane Prusank, University of Hartford; and Bryan C. Taylor, University of Colorado.

I have also been ably assisted by students in my Communication Theory classes at both the University of Kansas and Texas A&M University. I thank them for reading and commenting on chapters from this textbook at various stages of preparation. In addition, special thanks go to Ircka Birch and Stephanie Roe for their dogged library research and endless photocopying and to Dan and Jen Ryan for their assistance with the preparation of the final manuscript. Finally, I am ever grateful for the loving support and encouragement of my husband, Jim Stiff, and for the joy that our daughter, Kalena Miller, brings to my life on a daily basis.

P A R T   O N E

Perspectives on Communication Theory

A perspective is a way of viewing or seeing a particular phenomenon. An artist's perspective encompasses concerns such as distance, angle, lighting, and filter—all factors that can influence the way a particular object is viewed. The notion of perspective in communication theory, then, suggests that there is a lens through which communication processes can be viewed and appreciated.

It is important to note that we are not talking about *perspective* in the singular but about *perspectives* in the plural, for there is clearly not a single or correct lens through which communication phenomenon can be viewed. Rather, different theorists look at communication from different angles, using different filters and lighting processes. These varying perspectives lead to different types of theory and to different ways of understanding communication processes in our everyday lives.

In Part One, then, we consider various perspectives we can use in approaching communication theory. We begin with two chapters that provide grounding in the concept of communication (Chapter 1) and the concept of theory (Chapter 2). These two foundational chapters are followed by a consideration of three major perspectives on theory development in the communication discipline. These are the post-positivist perspective (Chapter 3), the interpretivist perspective (Chapter 4), and the critical perspective (Chapter 5).

1 Conceptual Foundations

What Is Communication?

In the classic movie *Cool Hand Luke*, Paul Newman was the recipient of a now famous line: "What we have here," he was told, as he stood with insouciant charm, "is a failure to communicate." Though this comment was delivered over 30 years ago, the sentiment is a timeless one and still has traction as we enter the 21st century. In today's society, such a failure would seem a serious—or perhaps fatal—problem because the central concerns in our lives are predictably connected to the ubiquitous concept of communication. We are told that open communication is the key to a good relationship. We are told that the Internet and World Wide Web are part of a global communication revolution. We are told that the communication industry is instilling negative values in our children. We are told that productive organizations are those that communicate effectively with both employees and customers. With all these messages ringing in our ears, it is little wonder that anyone accused of a failure to communicate would be highly concerned.

Communication, then, is seen as central to our everyday ideas about what makes life worth living. Thus, it is not surprising that academics have attempted to unravel the secrets of the **communication process.** This desire to study and understand communication is not new. Indeed, Pearce and Foss (1990) trace the systematic study of communication back to the sophists in the 5th century B.C.; through the times of Plato and Aristotle; through the Middle Ages, the humanistic revival of the Renaissance, and the scientific study of the Enlightenment; and through to the establishment of communication as an academic discipline in the 20th century. In other words, scholars have sought a systematic understanding of the communication process—communication theory, that is—for several thousand years.

Our concern in this book rests primarily with contemporary views of communication theory that have emerged in the communication discipline since the 1950s. Even this limitation is far from straightforward, however. What we now think of as the discipline of communication has incredibly diverse roots. For example, scholars in rhetoric and public communication might trace their forebears to English departments in the early part of the 20th century and the subsequent creation of speech departments. Other scholars might trace their lineage through early studies in mass communication in departments of sociology and political science. Still others might see their roots in the work of social and industrial psychologists. In spite of these diverse histories, we can now identify a discipline of communication. We examine in this book the theorizing and theories of this community of scholars—this discipline of communication.

This textbook considers several important ways to approach communication theory, and it analyzes a wide range of theoretical statements that have sprung from such approaches. Before moving into these important discussions, however, we must draw a map of the terrain. That is, before we start discussing the wide variety of ideas that make up the body of communication theory, it is important to establish an understanding of what communication theory *is*.

Drawing this map of communication theory requires two distinct but interrelated tasks— understanding the nature of communication and understanding the nature of theory. We undertake the task of understanding the nature of theory in Chapter 2. In this chapter, we consider the first term in the phrase "communication theory" by exploring definitional controversies that have been raised regarding what communication is, by considering the implications of these debates for the disciplinary study of communication theory, and by previewing the contents of subsequent chapters in our consideration of communication theory.

■ DEFINING COMMUNICATION

In 1998, political pundits reacted with derision to President Bill Clinton's comment in a deposition that "it all depends on what your definition of the term 'is' is." Though this comment was seen as ludicrous by some, it hits on a central truth of both academia and everyday life: People define terms in different ways, and those differences in definition can have a profound impact on the extent to which we understand each other and can move forward with both academic and everyday pursuits. Given the variety of ways in which words are used and understood, we are often ill-served to search for the single, so-called correct definition of a term. Rather, it is typically more useful to consider the appropriateness and usefulness of particular definitions for the specific context in which those definitions will be employed and to consider the extent to which interactants converge on definitions of

relevant terms. In other words, it is better to evaluate definitions in terms of their utility rather than in terms of their correctness. This is not to suggest that "anything goes" with regard to definitions. However, we should not assume that there is always a single *right* way to define a concept.

Nowhere is this cautionary note more appropriate than in considering the nature of communication. Conceptualizations of communication have been abundant and have changed substantially over the years. In the middle of the 20th century, defining communication was a popular sport among communication scholars. Consider the following titles of articles published in the mid-1960s: "On Defining Communication: Another Stab" (G. R. Miller, 1966) and "On Defining Communication: Still Another View" (Gerbner, 1966). So widespread was the sport of defining communication that Dance and Larson (1976) reported over 126 definitions that had been proposed in the literature. To illustrate the variety of definitions proposed during this definitional heyday, a sampling is included in Table 1.1.

As Table 1.1 illustrates, however, a great deal of variation existed among these definitions. Some take a very abstract view of communication, whereas others are extremely specific. Some include myriad situations and contexts in which communication might occur, whereas others are very narrow in their specification. For example, consider two of the early conceptualizations put forth in the middle of the 20th century that offer vastly different views of what communication is:

> [Communication is] the process by which an individual (the communicator) transmits stimuli (usually verbal) to modify the behavior of other individuals (the audience). (Hovland, Janis, & Kelley, 1953, p. 12)

> [Communication is] all of the procedures by which one mind can affect another. (W. Weaver, 1949, p. 95)

Hovland, Janis, and Kelley provide a relatively narrow view of communication, defining

Table 1.1 Sample Definitions of Communication	
Definition	**Source**
[Communication is] all of the procedures by which one mind can affect another.	Weaver (1949)
Communication means that information is passed from one place to another.	Miller (1951)
From a communication point of view, the event may be observed in the employment of symbols (act), under specific circumstances (scene), by an individual or individuals (agent), using selected media (agency), for defined ends (purposes).	Babcock (1952)
[Communication is] the process by which an individual (the communicator) transmits stimuli (usually verbal) to modify the behavior of other individuals (the audience).	Hovland, Janis, & Kelley (1953)
Communication is the process by which we understand others and in turn endeavor to be understood by them. It is dynamic, constantly changing and shifting in response to the total situation.	Andersen (1959)
[Communication] is a process that makes common to two or several what was the monopoly of one or some.	Gode (1959)
Communication does not refer to verbal, explicit, and intentional transmission of messages alone. . . . The concept of communication would include all those processes by which people influence one another.	Ruesch & Bateson (1961)
Communication means, fundamentally, the stimulation in the minds of others of essentially your awareness, understanding, and sense of importance of the event, feeling, fact, opinion, or situation you are attempting to depict.	Oliver, Zelko, & Holtzman (1962)
Communication among human beings is the art of transmitting information, ideas and attitudes from one person to another.	Emery, Ault, & Agee (1963)
Communication is a process by which a person reduces the uncertainty about some state of affairs by the detection of cues which seem to him to be relevant to that state of affairs.	Lewis (1963)
Communication: The transmission of information, ideas, emotions, skills, etc., by the use of symbols—words, pictures, figures, graphs, etc. It is the act or process of transmission that is usually called communication.	Berelson & Steiner (1964)
Comunication is social interaction through symbols and message systems.	Gerbner (1966)
In the main, communication has as its central interest those behavioral situations in which a source transmits a message to receiver(s) with conscious intent to affect the latter's behavior.	Miller (1966)
Human communication is the eliciting of a response through verbal symbols.	Dance (1967)
Communication cannot be understood except as a dynamic process in which listener and speaker, reader and writer act reciprocally, the speaker acting to provide direct and indirect sensory stimulation of the listener; the listener acting on the stimulation by taking it in, investing it with meaning by calling up images in the mind, testing those images against present information and feelings and sooner or later acting upon those images.	Martin & Anderson (1968)

Table 1.1	Sample Definitions of Communication (continued)
Definition	**Source**
Communication [is] the sharing of experience, observable as the extent to which the responses of a generator and perceiver (both of which are necessarily living organisms) are systematically correlated to a referent stimulus.	Goyer (1970)
Communication [is] patterned space-time behavior with a symbolic referent.	Hawes (1973)

Source: All definitions are drawn from Appendix A of Dance & Larson (1976).

it as a one-way activity encompassing primarily verbal signals used to modify another's behavior. In contrast, Weaver's definition is incredibly broad, including all the procedures by which one "mind" could have an effect on another. For example, if one person decided to plant a flower and another person noticed it, this would count as communication. For most contemporary scholars investigating communication processes, neither of these definitions would pass muster in terms of utility. The Hovland et al. definition excludes too many activities that we normally think of as communication (e.g., just chatting to pass the time of day), whereas the Weaver definition includes practically everything and thus doesn't help us distinguish communication from other forms of human activity.

Through all this definitional turmoil, however, a number of conceptual features have emerged as important points of discussion throughout the years. Some of these features are widely accepted as appropriate to definitions of communication, and we consider these as points of convergence. These concepts—communication as a process, as symbolic, and as transactional—are not considered in detail because they have really become truisms about communication rather than issues of theoretical contention. Other conceptual dimensions, in contrast, have met with a great deal of discussion and debate in the literature. These features are considered in more detail as points of divergence in the conceptualization of communication. Because this textbook serves as an introduction to a wide range of theoretical positions regarding

communication, we do not settle on any singular, specific definition to guide our investigations here. However, it is important to lay out the issues of contention in order to draw a map of the conceptual terrain.

Conceptualizing Communication: Points of Convergence

Communication Is a Process Perhaps the most widespread point of convergence in definitions of communication is the notion that communication is a *process*. A process-oriented conceptualization of communication suggests that it is continuous and complex and cannot be arbitrarily isolated. That is, communication unfolds over time. David Berlo (1960) popularized this idea over 40 years ago, stating:

> If we accept the concept of process, we view events and relationships as dynamic, on-going, ever-changing, continuous. When we label something as a process we also mean that it does not have a beginning, an end, a fixed sequence of events. It is not static, at rest. It is moving. The ingredients within a process interact; each affects all others. (p. 24)

Think, for instance, of a relatively simple interaction between a child and a parent in which the child is reprimanded for not cleaning up after play. When we see communication as a process, we realize that this interaction is really not all that simple. Rather, the interaction is influenced by the past behavior of these two individuals (e.g., Does the child habitually fail to clean up? Is the parent under other kinds of stress?), by relationships each has had with others (e.g., perhaps an older child was excessively neat, setting up parental expectations for this child), and by the situation surrounding the interaction (e.g., perhaps grandparents are arriving for a visit and neatness is seen as an important priority). Further, this so-called simple interaction will affect subsequent interactions between the child and the parent. In short, when we look at communication as a process, we see that even simple interactions are influenced in complex ways by the past and will also have important implications for the future.

In early conceptualizations of communication, this process was seen as a primarily linear one, in which communication moved from a source to a receiver. For example, Lasswell's (1964) classic model of communication asked a series of linear questions: Who? Says what? To whom? Through what channel? With what effect? Though this conceptualization can be seen as a process (i.e., a sequence of steps), most communication scholars today do not accept this simple linear model, or even one that incorporates a feedback loop from receiver to source. Rather, most communication researchers now take a transactional approach to communication. This point of convergence is considered next.

Communication Is Transactional   A second point of widespread convergence in conceptualizations of communication is the notion that communication is **transactional** and hence highly complex. In unpacking the concept of transaction, it is useful to contrast it with the related ideas of action and interaction (see Dewey & Bentley [1949] for an early explication of this distinction).

If we considered communication to be strictly action, we would look at a source presenting a message to a receiver or an audience. We would not consider the reaction of the audience or feedback from it. This linear and one-way approach to communication (e.g., like Lasswell's model discussed earlier) has been labeled the hypodermic needle model or magic bullet model of communication (see Forsdale, 1981). This action model (which we revisit in our discussion of historical models of media effects in Chapter 14) suggests that communication is a simple process of injecting our messages into receivers.

In contrast, if we view communication from an interaction perspective, we move beyond the hypodermic needle and magic bullet to consider the importance of feedback from the receiver. That is, in an interaction model, we look at not only the message of the source but also the reaction of the receiver. An interactional view is clearly a move forward because it acknowledges that communication is not strictly a one-way process with direct and linear effects. However, this model is still relatively simplistic in its isolation of a source and receiver and its consideration of limited influence between them.

Most communication scholars today, however, conceptualize communication in a transactional sense. A transactional view of communication, like an interactional view, includes the important role of feedback. However, a transactional view goes further, in seeing communication as a process in which there is constant mutual influence of communication participants. As Burgoon and Ruffner (1978) note:

> People are simultaneously acting as source and receiver in many communication situations. A person is giving feedback, talking, responding, acting, and reacting continually through a communication event. Each person is constantly participating in the communication activity. All of these things can alter the other elements in the process and create a completely different communication event. This is what we mean by transaction. (p. 9)

Consider, again, our exchange between a parent and a child regarding picking up after play. If we view communication as an interaction, we look first at what the parent says, then consider what the child says, and so on. When looking at the exchange as a transaction, we need to look simultaneously at both parties involved. The parent, for instance, might vary the content or tone of the reprimand based on ongoing nonverbal feedback from the child. At the same time, the child might respond to the parent's cues by adjusting messages and behavior.

A view of communication as transactional also emphasizes the importance of *context* in the communication process. That is, not only do participants constantly influence each other, they are also influenced by the context in which they interact. For example, a comment made in an organization can take on very different meaning depending on whether it is heard in a formal performance appraisal meeting or in casual conversation in the cafeteria. A television show depicting violent acts might be viewed very differently by children alone as compared with children in the company of parents discussing the program's content. In short, a transactional perspective of communication recognizes the inherent complexity of the communication process and will enhance our understanding of a variety of communication exchanges.

Communication Is Symbolic   A third area of convergence in conceptualizations of communication is the belief that communication is *symbolic*. To explore this concept, it is useful to talk briefly about the more general concept of **sign,** investigated by the field of *semiotics* (for treatments in the field of communcation, see A. A. Berger, 1989; Leeds-Hurwitz, 1993). Semioticians see a sign as consisting of two inextricably linked parts—the *signifier* and the *signified*. Consider the word *book* and the object made of paper and glue that you hold in your hand right now. In this case, the signifier is the word *book* and the signified is the physical object. In semiotics, a sign is the relationship between the signifier and the signified. This relationship is obviously not a perfect one-to-one correspondence and is often an arbitrary relationship in that there is no natural correspondence, for instance, between the letters *b-o-o-k* and the object to which they refer.

Once this basic semiotic notion is understood, a number of further elaborations can be made. First, many theorists follow I. A. Richards

(1936), an early scholar in the field of semantics, in distinguishing between a sign and a **symbol.** This distinction deals with the arbitrariness of the connection between the signifier and the signified. For example, Langer, in her book *Philosophy in a New Key,* conceptualized a sign as something that signals the presence of something else. In this sense, smoke is a sign of fire and tears are a sign of sadness. Of course, even with these signs there is not a perfect match because tears can be shed in joy as well as sadness. However, a natural match exists between the signifier and the signified in this case. Symbols, in contrast, "are not proxy of their objects, but are *vehicles for the conception of objects*" (Langer, 1942, p. 61). Thus, symbols hold an arbitrary, rather than natural, relationship to what is symbolized, and a symbol has no inherent meaning.

What then is the relationship between the symbol and the referent? Ogden and Richards (1946) explained this relationship in terms of a semantic triangle in which the three points of the triangle are the *symbol* (e.g., the word *book*), the *referent* (e.g., the physical object), and the *reference* (e.g., what you mean by *book* when you use the symbol). In this triangle, the link between the symbol and the referent is typically represented with a dotted line because this relationship is arbitrary. That is, you might be quite clear about what you mean when you use the term *book*, but that symbol might have different meanings for different people. Not only are there a wide range of physical objects that could be described as books, but individuals also have a wide range of other concepts and emotions associated with the symbol. For some, books are sacred objects that are cherished and saved throughout a lifetime. For others, books are objects that weigh down the backpack and should be sold back as soon as the end of the semester arrives.

However, with most symbols, some degree of shared meaning exists between interactants. This is true because the symbols are developed through shared social experience and exist within a system of other symbols. However, this imperfect relationship between symbol and referent suggests that there will always be gaps in understanding. These gaps will be smallest for individuals who have shared experiences (e.g., growing up in the same culture, being of the same generation, having professional similarities). They will be largest for those who have had radically divergent social experiences.

So, when theorists say that communication is symbolic, they mean that it requires signs and symbols that have relationships to referents that are to some extent arbitrary. These symbols can be verbal (e.g., the use of language) or nonverbal. Nonverbal symbols can be seen in a wide range of communicative activities and in many contexts. Some nonverbal behavior actually serves more as a sign than a symbol. For example, Ekman and Freisen (1975) have found that facial expressions are widely seen as unarbitrary indicators of emotion that are recognized across cultural bounds. Other nonverbal communication clearly has the arbitrary form of a symbol. Consider, for example, some communication examples in the organizational context. When you dress in a suit for a job interview, that suit could symbolize many things—your respect for the company, your willingness to conform, or your sense of organization and decorum. When a manager chooses to send a message by means of a paper memorandum rather than by phone, e-mail, or interpersonal channels, that choice could symbolize many things—the formality of the message or perhaps the need to file the message for future reference. In short, the nonverbal messages we send and receive are characterized by their symbolic nature, and because of the possible gaps between symbol and referent, "perfect" communication is unlikely.

The ways in which symbols function in communication have come under some scrutiny in recent years. This debate has considered not only the issue of whether communication is symbolic (but see Andersen, 1991, for a contrary definitional view) but also the ways in which symbols are attached to referents in the real world—in essence the extent to which we can say that symbols hold any stable meaning. A number of theorists have argued recently that

symbols do not have any stable connection to the world and that meaning is, instead, a function of power relationships, ideology, situational context, or history (e.g., Bochner, 1985; Deetz, 1973; Lannaman, 1991; Stewart, 1986). In contrast, others (see, especially, Ellis, 1995) have argued that though symbols do not have single, correct meanings, those symbols can be seen as having purposeful and significant attachments to referents. As we see in later chapters, this debate is one strand of the ontological discussions that mark important differences among post-positivist (Chapter 3), interpretive (Chapter 4), and critical (Chapter 5) approaches to communication theory. This debate over the stability of meaning, however, does not detract from agreement that communication is a symbolic process.

Conceptualizing Communication: Points of Divergence

As noted earlier, most contemporary communication scholars agree that communication can be conceptualized as a process that is symbolic and transactional, though different aspects of these conceptualizations will be emphasized depending on the theoretical needs of the researcher. However, communication scholars have less agreement in several other areas. One of these areas involves the social nature of communication processes, and another involves whether communication should be conceptualized as a purely intentional behavior. These points of divergence are taken up in this section.

Communication as a Social Activity The first point of some divergence is whether communication necessarily involves two or more people (e.g., is a social or interpersonal activity) or whether communication can occur within one individual (i.e., **intrapersonal communication**). That is, can you communicate with yourself? Though the colloquialism of "talking to yourself" is frequently used in modern society, many communication scholars would prefer to label this phenomenon as cognition or thinking and leave the term *communication* for situations in which two or more people are involved. Other scholars see intrapersonal communication as distinct from thinking, and divisions within professional associations and numerous publications (see, e.g., C. V. Roberts & Watson, 1989; Vocate, 1994) now acknowledge the importance of intrapersonal communication.

In some ways, though, this issue may be a red herring in the conceptualization of communication. Even scholars who see communication as a clearly social process (e.g., involving two or more people) also acknowledge the importance of internal states such as cognition and emotion on communicative interaction. Indeed, we will see that many theories of message production (Chapter 7), of message processing (Chapter 8), and of discourse and interaction (Chapter 9) highlight the role of planning and other cognitive processes on the creation of messages in social situations and the regulation of behavior during conversation. Further, theories that look specifically at those intrapersonal and perceptual ways of understanding the symbolic world (Chapter 6) are central to our understanding of communication processes.

The more important point in conceptualizing communication as a social process is in the function that communication serves as a social vehicle. That is, when we see communication as something that occurs between people, the question arises of what communication is doing in that relationship. We deal more thoroughly with this issue in our discussion of speech act theory in Chapter 9. However, it is worth making some initial distinctions here among the various ways we can look at language:

- The *semantic* level of language study considers the links between signs and referents. Our brief discussion of semiotics in the preceding section dealt primarily with this level of analysis.
- The *syntactic* level of language study considers the rules that govern language use by considering various grammars.
- The *pragmatic* level of language study looks at language in use. That is, a pragmatic

view looks at the ways in which we "do things with words" (Austin, 1962).

When we conceptualize communication as a social activity, we are then looking primarily at the pragmatic level. That is, communication, in this social sense, is a vehicle through which we are trying to do something. What we are trying to do with communication could vary greatly— we might be trying to get others to understand or appreciate our internal thoughts or emotions, or we might be trying to understand those internal states in others. We might be trying to coordinate behaviors with others or to have others behave in a specific desired way. In other words, we don't just seek to communicate. Instead, from the pragmatic viewpoint, we seek to do specific things in communicating.

In summary, then, in conceptualizing communication as a social activity, we are not discounting the importance of cognitive and internal psychological states in the communication process. Rather, we are emphasizing the point that communication is a critical part of social commerce and that through communication we seek to have an impact on the people around us.

Communication and Intention Perhaps the most active debate in the area of defining communication revolves around the issue of **intentionality.** Many years ago, Watzlawick, Beavin, and Jackson (1967) wrote a highly influential book, *The Pragmatics of Human Communication.* We deal extensively with their ideas in our discussion of communication in ongoing relationships (Chapter 11). However, this book has probably been cited more for one phrase than for the rest of the book combined. This is Watzlawick et al.'s dictum that "you cannot not communicate," suggesting that meaning is inherent in all human behavior. For example, an individual who pulls on an old pair of blue jeans and wears them to class may do so simply because everything else in the closet is dirty. Following Watzlawick et al., however, this behavior is communication because others might derive a variety of meanings from it (perhaps disrespect for authority or conformity to peer pressure). As Motley (1990, p. 1, emphasis in original) summarizes, Watzlawick et al.'s dictum "favors a broad approach to communication phenomena, making *communication* synonymous, or nearly synonymous, with *behavior*."

Even in early conceptualizations of communication, many theorists disagreed with the idea that you "cannot not communicate," arguing that only intentional behaviors should count as communication (e.g., Burgoon & Ruffner, 1978; G. R. Miller, 1966). In this view, communication occurs only when there is clear intent on the part of the source to communicate. G. R. Miller's (1966, p. 92) definition is a case in point: Communication occurs in "those situations in which a source transmits a message to a receiver with conscious intent to affect the latter's behavior." It should be noted that definitions such as Miller's did not suggest that the intent needed to be successfully realized in order for communication to occur (that is, the attempt doesn't have to be competent or effective in order to be communication) but rather that intent on the part of the source is a defining feature that moves us from the concept of behavior to the concept of communication.

In the early 1990s, this debate flourished once again, with Peter Andersen (1991), Janet Beavin Bavelas (1990), Wayne Beach (1990), Theodore Clevenger (1991), and Michael Motley (1990, 1991) all weighing in with varying positions on the issue. One of the most important underlying threads in the revival of this debate was the distinction between a source perspective on defining communication and a receiver perspective. Motley (1990, 1991) represents the source position, arguing that a source must have a "receiver-based intention" (either conscious or unconscious) in order for communication to occur. In contrast, Andersen (1991) represents the receiver perspective in arguing that any behavior that is received (either through active attention or incidentally) counts as communication.

Consider, again, our example of wearing old blue jeans to class. From a source-based perspective (Motley, 1990, 1991), this behavior is not communication because there is no receiver-directed intent to communicate, either con-

scious or unconscious, on the part of the person putting on the blue jeans. From a receiver-based perspective, this behavior might be communication, depending on whether the professor (or perhaps other students) receive, either incidentally or through purposeful attention, a message from that wardrobe choice. If a message is received, the wearing of blue jeans is communication. Otherwise, communication has not occurred.

A second critical issue highlighted in this debate is the distinction between *verbal messages*, *analogic messages*, and *symptomatic behavior* (Andersen, 1987, 1991; Motley, 1990, 1991). Motley (1990, pp. 14–15) describes the distinction among these three categories:

> Symptomatic behaviors (e.g., stomach growls, observable autonomic responses, scratching, etc.), at least in their pure form, exemplify behaviors whose source is something other than an effort to influence a receiver. Verbal behaviors, on the other hand, are typically intended for receivers, as are analogic behaviors; i.e., intentional imitations of symptomatic behaviors—or "ritual" behaviors in the terms of Cronkhite (1986)—and other nonverbal "behaviors purposively displayed to receivers." (Andersen, 1987)

To illustrate this distinction, imagine that you are talking to a friend on the phone and you are exhausted. Because of your fatigue, you might let out an uncontrollable yawn. This is **symptomatic behavior.** Or you might tell your friend that you are very tired and need to get off the phone. This is **verbal behavior.** Or you might emit a fake yawn to communicate your exhaustion to your friend. This is **analogic behavior.** These distinctions are important for several reasons. First, by highlighting the role of analogic communication in much interaction, these distinctions emphasize the importance of nonverbal messages in our conceptualization of communication. Second, they emphasize that a wide range of consciousness is possible in communication, even when considering receiver-directed and intentional behavior. This issue has been further emphasized in discussions of the "mindlessness" of much communication (see, e.g., Langer, 1989). For example, Kellermann believes that communication is both "inherently strategic" and "primarily automatic" (Kellermann, 1992, p. 288). That is, she argues that though our communication is receiver directed and intentional, it is also often unconscious and guided by cultural scripts and ingrained habits.

In summary, early questions of "Is communication intentional?" have evolved in recent years to include sophisticated debates about receiver perception, strategic intent, automatic communication, and the nature of meaning. It is unlikely that these debates will be resolved to the satisfaction of all involved (see, e.g., the positions expressed by Ellis, 1991, p. 221; Mumby, 1997, p. 21). But perhaps these debates should not be resolved for, as noted earlier, definitions are not right or wrong but are more or less useful for the purposes at hand. It is important, however, to be familiar with these issues as we embark on the study of a variety of communication theories. As Andersen (1991) emphasizes, "These perspectives launch scholars down different theoretical trajectories, predispose them to ask distinct questions, and set them up to conduct different kinds of communication studies" (p. 309). Thus, definitional choices about communication influence—and are influenced by— the theoretical and research commitments of communication scholars.

▪ MOVING BEYOND DEFINITIONS

It appears, then, that we do not have—and probably never will have—an undisputed definition of communication. As noted earlier, this is not necessarily a bad state of affairs because varying definitions can usefully serve different theoretical and practical purposes. Utility depends on the scholar, the research context, and a host of other factors. However, this lack of a singular definition of "what we study" makes it even more important to understand the varying ways that communication is approached by scholars. In the remainder of this chapter, we consider two procedures for "dividing up" communication studies. One of these procedures is

the consideration of varying conceptual approaches to the study of communication. The other procedure involves the subdisciplinary domains that typically define our academic departments and professional associations. Following our discussion of these two frameworks, we consider the domains of communication that are included in this textbook.

Conceptual Domains of Communication Studies

A recent essay by Robert Craig (1999) makes a compelling case for the importance of considering distinctions among varying conceptual domains in communication theory. Craig argues that typical discussions of the concept of communication distinguish between a **transmission model of communication** and a **constitutive model of communication.** According to Craig, within the transmission model, "communication is a process of sending and receiving messages or transferring information from one mind to another" (p. 125), whereas the alternative is "a model that conceptualizes communication as a constitutive process that produces and reproduces shared meaning" (p. 125). In a constitutive model, communication "is not a secondary phenomenon that can be explained by antecedent psychological, sociological, cultural, or economic factors; rather, communication itself is the primary, constitutive social process that explains all these other factors" (p. 126).

Craig believes that seeing communication theory as a choice between a transmission and a constitutive model is problematic. First, he argues that a fair fight is rarely provided because "the transmission model, as usually presented, is scarcely more than a straw figure set up to represent a simplistic view" (p. 127). Second, Craig argues that the transmission view of communication does resonate in many practical settings. That is, in everyday life we often think about communication as the sending and receiving of information rather than as the creation and re-creation of social realities. For example, we talk about "sending that guy a message" or "picking up my e-mail" in ways that are clearly oriented toward transmission. Hence, from a point of view that values practical theory, the transmission view should not be totally rejected. Finally, Craig argues that the simple contrasting of these two models fails to account for the rich variety of ways in which scholars have often thought about the communication process.

To deal with these conceptual issues, Craig proposes that we recast the constitutive view of communication as a "metamodel," or an overarching way of thinking about communication theory, rather than as a definition of communication. As Craig argues:

> That is, the constitutive model does not tell us what communication really is, but rather implies that communication can be constituted symbolically (in and through communication, of course) in many different ways, including (why not, if it is useful to do so for some purpose?) as a transmission process. (p. 127)

Craig then goes on to define seven different conceptual traditions in communication theory. These seven traditions are presented in Table 1.2, along with the ways in which each tradition theorizes communication and problems of communication. It should be emphasized that these traditions all stand within the larger metamodel of communication as a constitutive process. That is, the traditions are not radically different—and incommensurate—paradigms of theory and research. Rather, these traditions are different ways of constituting and talking about communication. For example, a scholar working within the semiotic tradition might consider the ways in which specific linguistic choices are constituted within interaction. In contrast, a proponent of the critical tradition would take a broader view in looking at the means through which the cultural icons communicated in television advertising control the perceptions and actions of the viewing public.

Craig hopes that by establishing this constitutive metamodel, space will be opened up for more dialogue among the various ways of thinking about communication theory and research. As Craig summarizes:

> The scheme I am proposing divides the field according to underlying conceptions of communicative practice. An effect of this shift in perspective is that communication theories no longer bypass each other in their different paradigms or on their different levels. Communication theories suddenly now have something to agree and disagree about—and that "something" is communication. (p. 135)

Though this conceptual matrix has not yet been widely adopted in the field, it surely will be in the future (Craig's article recently won a "best article award" from the International Communication Association). Because Craig's argument is both elegant and insightful, we rely on some of his points in our presentation of communication theory. For example, many of the arguments made by theorists in the sociopsychological and cybernetic approaches to communication theory resonate with the post-positivist approaches to theory we consider in Chapter 3. Similarly, the ideas of phenomenological and sociocultural theorists are largely represented in the interpretive ideals of Chapter 4, and critical theory is considered in Chapter 5.

Useful as these conceptual distinctions are, however, they do not reflect the way the field is typically segmented in academic departments or in presentations of communication theory. Craig admits this ("the structure of the matrix differs radically from conventional ways of dividing up the field," p. 132) and argues that this reconceptualization is critical to the development of communication theory. However, it is also important to look at the ways in which the field of communication is typically divided within academic departments and within pedagogical treatments of communication theory and research. These divisions within the field are considered in the next section.

Disciplinary Domains of Communication Studies

There is little doubt that communication is a fragmented discipline. This fragmentation can, not surprisingly, be seen in the way we label ourselves and talk about ourselves. For example,

Table 1.2	Conceptual Domains of Communication Theory	
	Communication theorized as:	**Problems of communication theorized as:**
Rhetorical	The practical art of discourse	Social exigency requiring collective deliberation and judgment
Semiotic	Intersubjective mediation by signs	Misunderstanding or gap between subjective viewpoints
Phenomenological	Experience of otherness; dialogue	Absence of, or failure to sustain, authentic human relationship
Cybernetic	Information processing	Noise; overload; underload; a malfunction or "bug" in a system
Sociopsychological	Expression, interaction, and influence	Situation requiring manipulation of causes of behavior to achieve specified outcomes
Sociocultural	(Re)production of social order	Conflict; alienation; misalignment; failure of coordination
Critical	Discursive reflection	Hegemonic ideology; systematically distorted speech situation

Source: Adapted from Craig (1999).

Kellner (1995) notes the wide array of labels used by departments that study communication issues and even notes that there are idiosyncratic preferences for the terms "communication" or "communications" when referring to the discipline. Within the major professional associations of the field (the National Communication Association and the International Communication Association), a wide array of subdisciplines are represented in the divisions and commissions (see Table 1.3). These subdisciplines vary across the different associations (e.g., the National Communication Association has a larger and more diverse structure than the International Communication Association, with more emphasis on pedagogical issues), and they vary within associations in terms of definitional criteria. That is, some divisions are defined in terms of levels (e.g., interpersonal communica- tion, group communication, mass communica- tion), some in terms of a process (e.g., language and social interaction, communication technol- ogy, communication apprehension and avoid- ance), and others in terms of contexts (e.g., instructional, political, health). Even these dis- tinctions are overly simplistic given that a term such as *organizational communication* could imply both a level and a context in which interaction occurs.

The debate regarding disciplinary divisions can be seen within a broader context as well. For instance, when considering the history of the field, we see that wide differences exist between those who look at the development of speech communication (e.g., H. Cohen, 1994) and those who consider the communication disci- pline as it developed from sociology and social psychology (e.g., E. M. Rogers, 1994). Craig

Table 1.3	Subdisciplinary Domains in Communication
Divisions and interest groups in the International Communication Association (ICA)	**Divisions and commissions in the National Communication Association (NCA)**
Communication and Technology	African American Communication and Culture
Communication Law and Policy	American Studies
Feminist Scholarship	Applied Communication
Gay, Lesbian, Bisexual, and Transgender Studies	Argumentation and Forensics
Health Communication	Basic Course
Information Systems	Communication and Aging
Instructional/Developmental Communication	Communication and Law
Intercultural/Developmental Communication	Communication and the Future
Interpersonal Communication	Communication Apprehension and Avoidance
Language and Social Interaction	Communication Assessment
Mass Communication	Communication Needs of Students at Risk
Organizational Communication	Environmental Communication
Philosophy of Communication	Experiential Learning in Communication
Political Communication	Family Communication
Popular Communication	Feminist and Women's Studies
Public Relations	Freedom of Expression
Visual Communication	Gay, Lesbian, Bisexual, Transgender Studies
	Health Communication
	Instructional Development
	International and Intercultural
	Interpersonal and Small Group Interaction
	Intrapersonal Communication/Social Cognition
	Language and Social Interaction
	Latina/Latino Communication Studies
	Mass Communication
	Organizational Communicaiton
	Peace and Conflict
	Performance Studies
	Political Communication
	Public Address
	Public Relations
	Rhetorical and Communication Theory
	Semiotics and Communication
	Spiritual Communication
	Theatre
	Training and Development
	Visual Communication

(1995) argues that this fragmentation is evidence of the tenuousness of the communication discipline:

The rationale for our field's existence, at core amounts to scarcely more than a single, culturally very potent symbol, "communication," a *word* still trendy enough to attract students, legitimate enough to keep skeptical colleagues at bay for awhile, and ambiguous enough to serve as a lowest common denominator for our otherwise largely unrelated scholarly and professional pursuits. Any further theoretical analysis of "communication," any attempt to define the field that goes much beyond the magic word itself, threatens to elevate some traditions over others and so upset our delicately balanced system of alliances." (p. 178)

Communication is not just fragmented within the discipline, it is also characterized by a high level of interdisciplinary pursuits. Clearly, the history of communication is an interdisciplinary one (see H. Cohen, 1994; Craig, 1995; E. M. Rogers, 1994) given that its development was shaped by fields such as journalism, sociology, psychology, theater, rhetoric, and English. Further, communication remains highly interdisciplinary, as many academics creating scholarship on communication do not reside in communication departments. For example, the study of concepts that we might see as communication is often a mainstay of departments of psychology, sociology, journalism, management, or anthropology.

Is all of this fragmentation a good thing or a bad thing? Commentators differ on this issue, and several representative views can be found in the 1993 "Future of the Field" issue of *Journal of Communication*. In this issue, Rosengren (1993) laments fragmentation, arguing that "it is as if the field of communication research were punctuated by a number of isolated frog ponds—with no friendly croaking between the ponds, very little productive intercourse at all, few cases of successful cross-fertilization" (p. 9). In contrast, B. J. O'Keefe (1993, p. 75) notes that she is "struck by increasing interconnections between previously separate disciplines and by projects that deliberately attempt to forge connections," and she argues (following Bochner & Eisenberg, 1985) that we should not have a coherent discipline in which all agree on theoretical and methodological choices but should instead strive for cohesion in which there is room for subdisciplinary dialogue and in which proponents of those subdisciplines respect and protect each other. For some, the issue comes down to whether we should maintain our allegiance to the *concept* of communication or to the *discipline*

of communication. Beninger (1993, p. 18), for instance, argues that we should "embrace the subject, not the field" by looking at communication in a broad conceptual sense rather than in what he sees as a narrow disciplinary way.

The Domain of This Textbook

This chapter so far has discussed a wide range of issues with regard to the definition of communication, the conceptual domains of communication, and the somewhat fragmented and interdisciplinary nature of communication as a field of study. It is little wonder, then, that students of communication theory may learn very different things, depending on the predilections of their professors and the authors of their textbooks. Indeed, when J. A. Anderson (1996) analyzed the contents of communication theory textbooks, he found 249 distinct theories. Of these, only 22% appeared in more than one book and only 7% appeared in more than three books.

It appears, then, that writers of communication theory textbooks face a number of choices in order to delimit the topics under consideration and give some sense of coherence (or at least cohesion) to the subject matter of communication. Some of these choices are necessary for purposes of clarity and expediency—not *everything* can be covered in one book. All choices on domain must be made with a clear conceptual justification. Given the necessity of defining a domain, the following choices have been made with regard to *this* textbook.

First, this book strives to give comprehensive and up-to-date coverage of the major theories considered rather than just considering thumbnail sketches. In order to evaluate theories and examine their usefulness for both scholarship and everyday life, it is critical that the theories be discussed in detail and not glossed over. This initial choice, then, means that it is impossible to consider all theoretical statements that might be included under the huge and multifaceted umbrella of communication. Thus, three major criteria were used to delimit the domain of this book.

Criterion One   I first decided to include only work that can be clearly distinguished as a specific theory of communication, given the descriptions of theory that are presented in Chapters 2 through 5 of this book. It should be emphasized that this criterion does not preclude the inclusion of a variety of approaches to theory or types of theory: critical theories, interpretive theories, post-positivist theories—all are included in this book. However, this book does not cover individual research efforts on particular topics within the communication discipline that have not been codified into coherent theoretical statements. These research efforts will sometimes be briefly considered in order to provide context or support for theories under consideration, but the major emphasis of the book will be on the description and analysis of ideas that have been codified into coherent theoretical statements.

Criterion Two   I next decided to include only theories that have been either *developed by* scholars working within the communication discipline or *widely used and extended by* scholars in the communication discipline. To some extent, then, I chose to embrace the field rather than the broader subject of communication (contrary to the recommendation of Beninger, 1993). I made this choice in order to concentrate on the work done by communication scholars that is largely (though certainly not always) published in communication journals. In other words, I have decided to define *communication theory* as "theory done by communication scholars."

Criterion Three   Finally, I limited the scope of this book to theories that would be largely considered social science theories within communication or that have had a major impact on work in the social science portions of the discipline. In other words, theories of a purely rhetorical nature are not included in this text. This is not to say that all theories of rhetoric are ignored. Indeed, Chapter 6 highlights two very influential rhetorical theories (narrative and dramatism). And other theories such as symbolic

convergence theory (see Chapter 13) and concertive control theory (see Chapter 12) have clear roots in the rhetorical tradition of the communication field.

In grouping these chapters, I have followed the trend of professional associations in communication (the National Communication Association and the International Communication Association) of considering both communication processes and communication contexts as organizing factors. Theories are grouped into chapters that take on a relatively coherent topic area of explanation. However, it is clear that many theories could fit well into multiple chapters. For example, communication accommodation theory could find a home either in theories of interaction or in theories of intercultural contexts. Indeed, structuration theory was so difficult to place that it wound up as a central feature of three chapters (Chapters 5, 12, and 13). In spite of these classification difficulties, a (more or less) coherent structure for organizing the chapters emerged.

- The remainder of Part One (*Perspectives on Communication Theory*) considers the philosophical background that is essential for understanding the theory development process (Chapter 2) as well as the three dominant perspectives on theory development in communication and other social research disciplines: the post-positivist perspective (Chapter 3), the interpretive perspective (Chapter 4), and the critical perspective (Chapter 5). We talk more about the selection and structure of these perspectives at the end of Chapter 2.

- Part Two (*Theories of Communication Processes*) reviews representative and influential theories that have considered major aspects of communicative behavior. This section includes theories of symbolic organization (Chapter 6), theories of message production (Chapter 7), theories of message processing (Chapter 8), theories of discourse and interaction (Chapter 9), theories of communication in developing relationships (Chapter 10), and theories of communication in ongoing relationships (Chapter 11).

- Part Three (*Theories of Communication Contexts*) reviews influential theories that have been important for developing an understanding of communication in more specific situations and contexts. This section includes theories of organizational communication (Chapter 12), theories of small group communication (Chapter 13), theories of media processing and effects (Chapter 14), theories of media and society (Chapter 15), and theories of culture and communication (Chapter 16).

Each of the chapters in Parts Two and Three opens with a brief discussion of the communication process or context under consideration. Then, two to four specific theories are considered that have attempted to enhance our understanding of the communication process or context. Each theory is described in detail, including consideration of metatheoretical roots, assumptions and structure, underlying theoretical mechanisms, empirical support, critiques of the theory, and basic and applied extensions. However, because the theories differ in terms of domain, level, context, application, and philosophical foundation, application of a cookie-cutter format for description and evaluation would not be productive. Instead, the description of each theory has been designed to provide the most insight into key issues for understanding that theory. Each chapter closes with a brief comparison of the theories in the chapter and commentary about theoretical strengths, weaknesses, and future directions.

Summary

In this chapter, we have explored the terrain surrounding the concept of communication. Some might say the terrain is rather treacherous, given the widespread definitional squabbles, conceptual quagmires, and disciplinary feuds that have

sprung from the study of communication. It is hoped, though, that you will see this terrain not as treacherous but as ripe for challenging exploration. In the next chapter we explore the concept of theory and then, in Chapters 3, 4, and 5, analyze three different approaches for the development and analysis of communication theory. We will then be ready to consider the wide and varied range of theories that have been used to describe, explain, understand, and even change communication processes.

Key Terms

communication process
transactional
sign
symbol
intrapersonal communication
intentionality
symptomatic behavior
verbal behavior
analogic behavior
transmission model of communication
constitutive model of communication

Discussion Questions

1. How does viewing communication as a transaction make it more complex than when taking an action or interaction view?
2. Besides the examples of fire and tears offered in this chapter, what other signs can you think of? What makes these signs different from symbols?
3. Defend or attack Watzlawick, Beavin, and Jackson's statement that "you cannot not communicate." Does this idea make sense when you consider your interactions with friends and family?
4. In our everyday lives, do we typically view communication using a transmission model or a constitutive model? What are the implications of this distinction for our interactions?

2. Philosophical Foundations
What Is Theory?

Sir Karl Popper, a philosopher instrumental in shaping 20th-century views of knowledge, said that "theories are nets cast to catch what we call 'the world'" (Popper, 1959). Popper was primarily interested in investigating the ways in which we come to understandings of the natural and physical world, but his views are also highly appropriate in a consideration of how we come to know about the human and social world in which we live and communicate. We are faced every day with puzzles about communication and social life. Why does one friendship flourish and another flounder? Why do disciplinary tactics have different effects on different children? How can we manage workplace conflict in constructive ways? What effect will increasing use of the Internet and the World Wide Web have on our daily lives? In addressing these puzzles, we attempt to make sense of our social worlds, and that sense making often involves casting out the net of what we might think of as common-sense theory.

Consider, for example, the first puzzle mentioned in the preceding paragraph: Why does one friendship flourish and another flounder? We may have very practical reasons for gaining an understanding of this issue (e.g., we want to enhance the chances of a successful friendship with a particular individual), or we may simply be curious about the vagaries of social life. In either case, making sense of friendship develop-

ment will involve creating and testing a variety of informal theories. Perhaps the success of friendship is based purely on the similarity of the two individuals involved in the relationship. Perhaps friendship development depends more on the specific communicative choices made by individuals as they get to know each other. Or perhaps events both inside and outside the relationship mark turning points that are influential in the process of relational development. All of these possibilities represent common-sense theories in that they enhance our understanding of how relationships develop and they are all somewhat abstract representations of relational development. In other words, these understandings move beyond the specific and concrete observation that "Bob and I are good friends because we both like country and western music" to the abstract statement that "friendship development is enhanced by the similarity of relational partners."

Everyone tries to make sense of their lives by developing and testing these common-sense theories. Indeed, we talk further about this concept of humans as "naive scientists" when we discuss attribution theory in Chapter 6. However, people who make sense of communication as part of an academic career are communication researchers and theorists. And though the explanations and understandings of communication developed by these scholars have a great deal in common with our everyday theories about communication (e.g., scholarly theory development also involves the consideration of both observations of the social world and abstract understandings of those observations), they are also different in a number of important respects.

This chapter explores the nature of theory by looking at what we mean by *theory* in the scholarly world and by looking at the foundations we bring to the development and use of theory. We first examine the basic questions of what theory is and how theory functions in fields of social research. We then consider metatheoretical assumptions that we bring to the theory development process, particularly assumptions about ontology (the nature of the world and reality), epistemology (the nature of knowledge), and axiology (the nature and role of values). Finally, we look at these ideas within the context of the communication discipline, building an argument for communication theory development as a pluralistic process.

■ THE NATURE OF THEORY

Understanding the nature of theory in the scholarly world involves a consideration of two issues. First, it is important to develop a shared understanding of what a theory is. A variety of approaches to this issue have been proposed over the years, and although we will not reach any sense of closure about the "right" way to define *theory*, we will consider issues regarding the conceptualization of theory that guide our investigations throughout this book. Second, it is critical to look at how theory functions as a vehicle toward enhancing our understanding of the social world. Thus, we then consider the general question of what a communication theory should do.

Conceptualizing Theory:
What Is Theory?

In discussing the problem of defining *theory* in social scholarship, D. C. Phillips (1992) argues, "There is no divinely ordained *correct* usage, but

we can strive to use the word consistently and to mark distinctions that we feel are important" (p. 121). This point is certainly well-taken, as in all problems of definition. Indeed, we talked about this issue extensively in Chapter 1, as we considered the various ways in which scholars have defined *communication*. As was pointed out in that discussion, we are seeking not the *right* definition of a particular term but one that is most useful for our purposes (see G. R. Miller & Nicholson, 1976). That is, definitions should be judged in terms of their utility rather than in terms of their correctness.

Unfortunately, the search for a definition of *theory* that has high and broadly based utility is a difficult one. Phillips (1992) notes that we can define *theory* either in a *stipulative* way by setting forth a group of characteristics that must be present in any theory (that is, we stipulate a definition of *theory* and judge what is and is not a theory based on this definition) or in a *reportive* way by looking at entities that have been called theories in the past and analyzing the nature of those entities (that is, we report on common usage of *theory*). Neither of these approaches is entirely satisfying. The first approach seems overly restrictive in that only entities meeting our stipulations will count as theory, and the second approach seems overly inclusive in that anything that has been called a theory in the past will count as a theory now. Thus, combining these two approaches seems a reasonable compromise. A search for a workable conceptualization of theory necessarily involves a consideration of both what we think theory should look like (stipulative approach) and what it has looked like during the history of social research (reportive approach).

One final point about defining *theory* must be emphasized and will become increasingly apparent as we consider approaches to theory development in communication throughout this book. Specifically, different schools of thought will define *theory* in different ways depending on the needs of the theorist and on beliefs about the social world and the nature of knowledge. That is, the post-positivist approach to theory presented in Chapter 3 defines *theory* in very different ways than either the interpretive approach (Chapter 4) or the critical approach (Chapter 5). To the extent possible, though, this chapter presents points of convergence among these various approaches to theory development.

So, what is a theory in this most general sense of the term? As we noted at the beginning of this chapter, theories help us understand or explain phenomena we observe in the social world. They are the "nets with which we catch the world" or the ways in which we make sense of social life. Thus, a theory is necessarily an **abstraction** of the social world. A theory is not the communicative behavior itself but an abstract set of ideas that help us make sense of that behavior. Abstractions might take on a variety of forms and may be put together in a variety of ways, but it must be stressed that theories are at an abstract or higher level than actual observations and theories have the goal of "explaining and systematizing lower-level findings" (Rosenberg, 1986, p. 342). In providing this abstract understanding of observations, a theory must go beyond or "look behind" phenomena in the social world (Hempel, 1966). In doing this, most theories include

- descriptions of phenomena in the social world
- relationships among these phenomena (sometimes in the form of rules or laws)
- an underlying and abstract storyline that describes the mechanisms at work in these relationships
- links between the storyline and the observed phenomena and relationships (sometimes called correspondence rules or bridge principles; see Phillips, 1992, p. 130)

Several points about the parts of a theory should be emphasized. First, in moving beyond a mere description of the social world, we are distinguishing between a taxonomy (or typology) and a theory. That is, a theory is more than a cataloging of the social world: It is an attempt to provide an abstract understanding or explanation of that social world. Second, theories could be formulated at a variety of levels of generality. For example, we will encounter some theories (e.g., structuration theory in Chapter 12 or coordinated management of meaning in Chapter 9) that are of broad scope and can apply to a wide range of communication situations. Other theories we will encounter are much narrower (e.g., uncertainty reduction theory in Chapter 10 or spiral of silence theory in Chapter 15) but still are important theoretical statements that help us explain or understand a portion of social life.

To highlight the various parts of a theory, we briefly preview a theory we consider in much more detail in Chapter 10—social penetration theory. Earlier in this chapter, we discussed enhancing our understanding of relational development and friendship formation through the proposal of informal theory. Social penetration theory is a formal and widely used theory that tackles this topic area. Social penetration provides a description of the relationship formation process (i.e., social penetration is a process through which we enhance the depth and breadth of our relationships over time through communication), an explication of the concepts and relationships that are part of the social penetration process (i.e., a consideration of the stages of relational development and self-disclosure processes), an explanation of the mechanisms that move the process of social penetration (i.e., we develop relationships because of our desire to enhance outcomes with reference to future alternatives and past comparisons), and a consideration of the links between observed interaction and the social penetration process (i.e., there are appropriate ways to define relational stages and instances of self-disclosure).

Of course, this is only one example of how these various parts can be seen in an actual theory, and we find very different ways of developing understanding in other theories. Various perspectives on theorizing tend to use these concepts in different ways, and in Chapters 3, 4, and 5 of this book, we consider some of the specific forms that theories can take when considered within the post-positive, interpretive, and critical schools of social theory. However, it makes sense to follow the lead of Richard Miller (1987, p. 135), who is "prepared to accept as a theory an explanatory . . . story even though it might not be as precise as we would often like" and to appreciate the variety of ways in which these theoretical understandings can be constructed.

Regardless of the precise form that theory takes, this consideration of what theory is emphasizes the clear distinction that should be made between the abstract world of theory and the empirical world of observation. We use an abstract theory to understand empirical observations. In the area of relational development, we understand our empirical observations and experiences with friends (and others) in the social world by invoking an abstract explanation involving the importance of similarity in the friendship formation process. This distinction, then, between abstract theory and empirical observation leads to the classic "chicken-or-the-egg" question of social theory: Which comes first, the theory or the observation? A **deductive approach** to theory building (e.g., Dubin, 1978; Hage, 1972) tends to give primacy to theory. That is, abstract theories are developed early after initial sensitizing observation, then empirical observations are used to test those theories. For example, in considering our theory of relational development and friendship formation, a deductive theorist might first formulate specific propositions about attitude similarity and relational development and then test those propositions with empirical data. The movement is from the general proposition to the specific instances seen in the research.

In contrast, an **inductive approach** to theory building (e.g., Glaser & Strauss, 1967) gives primacy to observation. In this approach, theoretical abstractions are based on—or grounded in—empirical observation. For example, an inductive approach to the study of relational development would advocate a great deal of observation of (and often participation in)

developing relationships before any propositions or hypotheses are formed. Only after the scholar has been immersed in the process of developing relationships could he or she come to any conclusions about the abstract processes involved in the relational development process.

Not surprisingly, neither of these pure types are reflective of how theory development is most typically practiced in social research. Rather than working in a purely deductive or inductive mode, social theorists most often "tack" between observations and abstractions, using observations to hone previously developed theoretical statements and theory to guide subsequent empirical observation. The distinction then becomes whether theory is given primacy—as in the deductive theorizing of post-positivist approaches—or whether observation is given primacy—as in the inductive theorizing of interpretive approaches.

In summary, then, the question of what a theory is can be answered by considering some ways in which we form abstract understandings and explanations about the way the observed social world works. These understandings can be formed at a variety of levels and through a variety of inductive and deductive processes, but they share the common feature of attempting to answer questions regarding how and why communicative processes work in the ways they do.

Conceptualizing Theory: What Should Theory Do?

A second issue in conceptualizing theory involves considering the function of theories. That is, what should theories do? Confronting the functions we want theory to play will help us consider the appropriate forms that theories can take and the standards by which we can evaluate the quality of a particular theory of social and communicative life.

Bernard Cohen (1994) draws on the work of Larry Laudan (1977, 1982) in proposing that the central function of theory is to solve problems. Laudan (1977) notes that "the first and essential acid test for any theory is whether it provides acceptable answers to interesting questions; whether, in other words, it provides satisfactory solutions to important problems" (p. 14). This approach suggests that theories can be evaluated both in terms of the importance or significance of the problems being addressed and in terms of the quality of the solution the theory provides. Cohen (1994) argues that questions of importance and significance are specific to particular disciplines and are often determined by values—and sometimes only in hindsight. However, determining the success of theoretical solutions to problems is an issue that is directly germane to the determination of what theories should do and how we should evaluate the quality of various social theories.

Theories can be used to address a number of types of problems. Laudan (1977) begins with two types: empirical problems and conceptual problems. An **empirical problem** is "anything about the . . . world which strikes us as odd, or otherwise in need of explanation" (Laudan, 1977, p. 15). For example, a communication researcher might notice that interactants from Eastern cultures (e.g., Japan, Korea, or China) behave differently in business meetings than interactants from Western cultures (e.g., North America or Western Europe). A theoretical explanation similar to the theories of face and culture that we will consider in Chapter 16 could then be forged to enhance our understanding of this phenomenon.

Laudan's second problem type, the **conceptual problem,** can be internal or external. An internal conceptual problem exists when a particular theory exhibits inconsistencies that need to be clarified. For example, a theory of group decision-making may include statements that would lead to different predictions depending on whether a group were described as a decision-making group or an information-gathering group. If a group were involved in both of these activities, a conceptual problem within the theory (e.g., how to deal with dual-function groups) would need to be resolved. Conceptual problems can also be external, in which case a particular theory conflicts with an explanation provided by another theory. For example, in Chapter 10 we consider related theories of communication during initial interaction (uncertainty reduction theory and predicted outcome value theory) in which the underlying mechanisms proposed lead to conflicting predictions and explanations of relational development.

To empirical and conceptual problems, Cohen (1994) adds the category of the **practical problem,** arguing that "utility in solving practical problems has historically played a major role in both assessing and promoting theory construction" (pp. 70–71). Indeed, Kurt Lewin's (1951) oft-stated comment that "there is nothing so practical as a good theory" (p. 169) highlights the role of theory in solving practical problems. Within the field of communication, the role of theory in dealing with practical or applied problems is particularly important. Communication scholars often confront applied issues such as how to improve the provision of health care, how to enhance the effectiveness of problem solving within organizational groups, or how to develop persuasive campaigns to promote desirable behavior. Practical problems exist at a much more abstract level as well, and communication theorists struggle with the challenge of creating and maintaining democratic workplaces and communities or enhancing the process of development on a global basis. Addressing these practical problems can be guided by existing communication theory and can serve as an impetus for more abstract theory-building (Seibold, 1995). Indeed, Gerald Miller (1995, p. 49) argues that "[a]ll nontrivial communication research addresses social issues and problems" and that those social issues and problems can best be tackled through theory-driven and theory-building efforts.

Thus, theory functions to solve empirical, conceptual, and practical problems. Within this framework, the quality of a theory can be assessed by answering three related questions (Cohen, 1994, p. 72):

- Does the theory solve the problem, regardless of whether that problem is empirical, conceptual, or practical?

- Does the solution compare favorably with alternative solutions?
- Is the solution progressive in that it represents an improvement over its predecessor (similar to the second question) and opens up new avenues for solving new problems?

At this point, we will not address specific criteria for answering these questions because different approaches to theory development will provide different explications of these criteria. For example, the adequacy of explanation is evaluated very differently in post-positivist, interpretive, and critical theories, as are judgments about comparative worth in theory development efforts. These questions can serve, however, as a general foundation for understanding how theories from a variety of perspectives can be evaluated.

Summary

In this section, we have considered formative ideas about what a theory is and what a theory should do. A theory is an abstract statement that provides an understanding or explanation of something observed in the social world. A theory functions to answer empirical, conceptual, and practical questions, and the quality of a theory can be assessed—in a very general sense—in terms of the answers provided to those questions. In the next section we take a step back from these questions of theory to examine some of the larger assumptions that guide any theorist during the theory development process.

▉ METATHEORETICAL CONSIDERATIONS

Throughout the preceding discussion of theory form and function, frequent mention was made of the fact that different schools of social thought have very different ideas about what theory is and what theory does. In other words,

the theory development process does not exist within a vacuum. Rather, a philosophical framework exists in which theory development and testing occurs. That framework strongly influences beliefs about what counts as theory and how theory should function within the academic community and within larger society. Indeed, Chapters 3, 4, and 5 are devoted to detailed discussions of three of these theoretical frameworks: post-positivist, interpretive, and critical approaches to theory development.

Some of the important distinctions among the philosophical frameworks that influence these schools of thought on theory development can be traced to their metatheoretical foundations. **Metatheory,** as the term implies, is theory about theory. That is, metatheoretical considerations involve philosophical commitments on issues such as what aspects of the social world we can and should theorize about, how theorizing should proceed, what should count as knowledge about the social world, and how theory should be used to guide social action. These metatheoretical themes have traditionally been the province of philosophers of science, but in recent years social theorists and social researchers have paid increasing attention to metatheoretical issues (see, e.g., edited volumes in the social sciences such as Fiske & Shweder, 1986; Guba, 1990b; M. Martin & McIntyre, 1994; and volumes specific to the communication discipline such as Dervin, Grossberg, O'Keefe, & Wartella, 1989).

These discussions of metatheoretical issues may have had their genesis in Thomas Kuhn's (1962) landmark publication, *The Structure of Scientific Revolutions*. Though Kuhn was writing primarily about the development of theory and knowledge within the so-called hard sciences such as physics, his book has probably been even more widely read and cited within social research disciplines. We discuss some of Kuhn's more specific ideas about theory development and the cumulation of knowledge in Chapter 3, but one clear impact of his writing was to spur discussions about metatheory—and the theoretical approaches defined by metatheory—within social and behavioral scholarship. In the next few sections, we consider three specific areas of metatheory—ontology, epistemology (and related issues of methodology), and axiology—that help map the terrain for different schools of thought in social research. In these sections we attempt to merely draw and define the boundaries and contours of the map. The specific placement of approaches to theory on this map will be left for our discussions in Chapters 3, 4, and 5.

Ontological Considerations

The study of **ontology** within philosophy involves investigations into the nature of being. In metatheoretical discussions within social research, questions of ontology involve issues such as "What is the nature of reality?" and "What is the nature of the knowable?" (Guba, 1990a, p. 18). In other words, questions of ontology address the nature of the phenomena that we address in our scholarship—the *what* of our theorizing. For researchers in social fields such as communication, this involves considering the nature of the social world and the entities that populate that world.

Many typologies have been proposed to describe various ontological positions, and these typologies are the subject of much debate in social research (see, e.g., Phillips's [1992] chapter titled "Objectivity and Subjectivity"). Space does not permit a full discussion of these debates here. However, it is important to distinguish among several important ontological positions that can be adopted in social scholarship. Few theorists take the pure or extreme versions of these positions but instead use these positions as landmarks in describing their own individual ontological positions.

Burrell and Morgan (1979) label one position on the ontological map as a **realist stance**. Many scholars take a realist stance with regard to the physical world (i.e., they believe in the hard reality of rocks, trees, planets, and so on), but views of the social world are more important for communication theorists. According to a social

realist, "The social world external to human cognition is a real world made up of hard, tangible and relatively immutable structures" (Burrell & Morgan, 1979, p. 4). A social realist sees both the physical and the social world as consisting of structures that exist "out there" and that are independent of an individual's perception. That is, for a realist, an individual can have varying levels of a concept called *communication competence* just as one could possess a car or a house or have hair of a certain color. In this view, communication competence is a real entity that can be recognized and possessed.

At the other end of the ontological spectrum is the **nominalist stance**. "The nominalist position revolves around the assumption that the social world external to individual cognition is made up of nothing more than names, concepts and labels which are used to structure reality" (Burrell & Morgan, 1979, p. 4). Thus, for a nominalist, there is no world "out there"—only the names and labels of entities that are created by individuals. *Communication competence* is merely a label that an individual might apply to a specific experience of self or other in social life; it is not a real and objective thing.

A third—some would say intermediary—point on the ontological map is a stance that has been highly influential in social research since the late 1960s. This stance is often called a **social constructionist position** (e.g., Berger & Luckmann, 1967). According to this position, social reality cannot be construed as either totally objective (the realist position) or totally subjective (the nominalist position). Rather, social reality is seen as an intersubjective construction that is created through communicative interaction. As Leeds-Hurwitz (1992) states, "In this view, social reality is not a fact or set of facts existing prior to human activity. . . . [W]e create our social world through our words and other symbols, and through our behaviors" (p. 133). However, most social constructionists would argue that these intersubjective realities are then reified or objectified because individuals treat the social constructions and are affected by the social constructions as if they were objective features of the social world. For example, the competence of communicators can be seen as socially constructed when different groups of individuals come to see different kinds of communication as competent during the course of one or more interactions. What is competent in a high school classroom might be very different from what is competent in a court of law or in the surgical suite of a hospital.

To further illustrate this point, these three ontological positions can be contrasted with regard to an additional concept. Consider, for example, the notion of *hierarchy* that is central to communication in organizational settings. A realist would contend that the existence of hierarchical levels in organizations is a very real thing that affects individuals every day. This hierarchy is demonstrated in a number of ways: the printed organizational chart that is distributed in organizational publications, the chain of command that governs organizational activities and communication, and the like. For a realist, hierarchy is a social fact of organizational life. In contrast, a nominalist would contend that the attribute of *hierarchy* is simply a social label created by individuals as they make their way through the social world. This label might be a convenient one to assist in interaction—especially for those wielding power in organizations—but it has no inherent reality or meaning outside the name. Finally, a social constructionist would argue that the concept of hierarchy is one that has been imbued with meaning through many communicative interactions, both historically (e.g., looking at how organizations have worked over time) and in current experience (e.g., the way things work in the organization at which you are employed). As the hierarchy concept becomes part of our social fabric, it influences subsequent communicative interaction (e.g., we always follow the chain of command in organizational communication) and also has the potential to be transformed by those interactions (e.g., we can try to buck the system by going over the boss's head). This illustrates the ways in which a concept is created through social interaction, enables and constrains communication, but may become so naturalized that we don't even notice its influence on us.

In summary, a central metatheoretical issue is the ontological stance one takes with regard to the social world. A social theorist's ontology might be realist by positing a hard and solid reality of both physical and social objects. Or a theorist's stance might be nominalist in proposing that the reality of social entities exists only in the names and labels we provide for them. Or a theorist's stance might be social constructionist in emphasizing the ways in which social meanings are created through historical and contemporary interaction and the manner in which these social constructions enable and constrain our subsequent behavior.

Epistemological Considerations

The study of **epistemology** within philosophy involves questions about the creation and growth of knowledge. Typical questions of epistemology might be "What counts as knowledge of the social world?," "What can we know?," "What is the relationship between the knower and the known?," and "How is knowledge about the social world accumulated?" Like questions of ontology, epistemological debates have recently come to the fore in social research. Indeed, many debates about epistemology have their roots in debates about ontology because our conceptions of the nature of the social world necessarily influence our beliefs about how we can come to know about that social world. For example, if you see communication competence as a hard fact of social life, you could come to know about an individual's competence through standardized instruments and procedures. In contrast, if you believed competence was socially situated, knowledge of competence would have to be based on an understanding of specific settings and interactions. As in our discussion of ontology, in this section we merely map out a few crucial epistemological positions and the distinctions among them as a way of setting the stage for discussions of approaches to theory development in communication in the next three chapters.

The epistemological position that has dominated thought in both the physical and social sciences throughout much of the 20th century is an **objectivist position.** Though this stance has many variants, several aspects of an objectivist epistemology are particularly important. First, objectivists believe that it is possible to understand and explain the social world and that explanations about the social world accumulate through the work of a community of scholars. Second, objectivists believe that knowledge about the social world can best be gained through a search for regularities and causal relationships among components of the social world. Third, objectivists believe that regularities and causal relationships can best be discovered if a separation exists between the investigator and the subject of the investigation (i.e., between the knower and the known). Finally, objectivists argue that this separation can be guaranteed—or at least enhanced—through the use of the scientific method. We talk more about the scientific method in Chapter 3. In short, the methods of science emphasize observable evidence, clear definitions, distinctions between the observer and the observed, and, as much as possible, control over the phenomenon being studied. In the objectivist epistemological stance, the scientific method is necessary because "scientists, like all men and women, are opinionated, dogmatic, ideological. . . . That is the very reason for insisting on procedural objectivity; to get the whole business outside of ourselves" (Kerlinger, 1979, p. 264). Methodological choices like this are tightly linked with issues of epistemology in social research.

In contrast, a **subjectivist position** rejects many of these foundational principles. For the subjectivist, "the social world is essentially relativistic and can only be understood from the point of view of the individuals who are directly involved in the activities which are to be studied" (Burrell & Morgan, 1979, p. 5). Thus, subjectivists eschew the notion of a separation between the knower and the known and with it the scientific method that tries to enhance that separation. Instead, subjectivists support "inquiry from the inside" through the use of ethnographic methods in which understandings of motives and contexts are favored over causal and law-like explanations. Because knowledge is situated and relativistic, a subjective epistemology also largely rejects the concepts of knowledge generalization and of knowledge cumulation, preferring instead local understandings that emerge through situated research. Table 2.1 summarizes some of the key issues that distinguish objectivist and subjectivist epistemological positions in social research.

To contrast these two positions, consider an objectivist and a subjectivist scholar, each interested in studying children's responses to televised violence. The objectivist scholar might choose to use either experimental or survey research methods in which a premium is placed on standardized instruments, random sampling, and control over procedures. Because this scholar hopes to add to the accumulation of knowledge on this topic, the objectivist would probably design the research project to test current media theories and would look for evidence that could either confirm or falsify (i.e., refute) those theories. The type of explanation sought by the objectivist scholar would probably be a causal one, investigating, for instance, the extent to which viewing violent cartoons will lead to explicit instances of verbal or physical aggression in children's interaction. These epistemological and methodological choices would likely spring from a realist ontological stance and involve the deductive process of proposing hypotheses at an abstract level and then testing those propositions with empirical data.

In contrast, a subjectivist scholar would argue that an understanding of children's responses to televised violence could be understood only from the inside—that is, by finding out more about the experiences of children while watching (and after watching) violent television programming. Thus, this researcher might choose to observe children watching car-

Table 2.1	Objectivist and Subjectivist Positions in Epistemology	
	Objectivist stance	Subjectivist stance
Kind of knowledge gained through theory	Explanation of social phenomena based on causal relationships	Understanding of social phenomena based on situated knowledge
Methodological commitments in search for knowledge	Separation between knower and known through use of the scientific method	Inquiry from the inside through ethnography and reports of social actors
Knowledge goals for theory development	Cumulation of general knowledge through testing of the community of scholars	Emergent and local understandings of situated social life

toons over a number of Saturday morning sessions and might even become an active part of the viewing experience. This participant observation might be supplemented with in-depth interviews (with the children and perhaps their parents) designed to elicit each child's experience in television viewing. These observations could then be used to ground theoretical ideas about television violence and children within a particular context for a particular group of children. These epistemological and methodological choices demonstrate an adherence to a nominalist or social constructionist ontology and an inductive approach to theory in which the details of observed behavior are used to generate more abstract ideas about the communication process.

In summary, epistemological foundations involve a theorist's ideas about what knowledge is and how knowledge can be constituted in the social world. To the objectivist, knowledge should consist of causal statements about the social world and should be generated through the efforts of a community of scholars using established scientific methods. In contrast, a subjectivist's epistemological stance posits that knowledge is situated within the local situation and thus must be garnered through experience or through extended interaction with insiders.

Axiological Considerations

A final set of metatheoretical issues that should be considered involve **axiology,** or the study of values. The classical scientific view of this topic is that values should have no role in the practice of researchers. As Phillips (1992) argues, scholars holding this view believe that "social science must expunge any trace of values" because "if we allow any chink through which values can enter, then objectivity will escape through the very same crack" (p. 139). Most philosophers of science—and most social researchers—have rejected this hard-line position, however. Indeed, it is probably safe to say that no social researcher today believes that values can be totally expunged from the processes of research and theory development. As G. S. Howard (1985) states, "The controversy is no longer about *whether* values influence scientific practice, but rather about *how* values are embedded in and shape scientific practice" (p. 255). In this section, we briefly consider three positions that represent important and influential points of view on this issue.

One school of thought contends that the role of values in social research can best be sorted out by distinguishing among different types of values and among different aspects of the scholarly process. For example, George Howard (1985) distinguishes between nonepistemic values (i.e., emotional, moral, and ethical values) and epistemic values (i.e., values regarding what constitutes good theory and research). Howard argues that epistemic values are important in allowing scholars to make choices about what theories should be accepted as reasonable accounts of the world but that nonepistemic values "should not influence the conduct of science and that often when they do intrude, it is to the detriment of the undertaking" (p. 256).

A similar argument has been made by differentiating between the *context of discovery* in which research problems are chosen and formulated and the *context of justification* in which research hypotheses are checked, tested, and critically evaluated. Karl Popper (1976) argues that we cannot (and should not) eliminate values from the context of discovery but that within the context of verification we must have mechanisms that will "achieve the elimination of extra-scientific values from scientific activity" (p. 97). For example, values might influence a social researcher's choice to study the ways in which physicians interact differently with representatives of different cultural groups: Indeed, this choice of research area might be spurred on by a scholar's encounters with the medical community. However, once the study begins, the scientific method should exclude the influence of values in the testing of theoretical propositions. Thus, according to these positions on axiology, values do have a role in research, but that role is constrained in terms of when values of various kinds influence scholarship.

A second position on the relationship between values and theory argues that it is impossible to eliminate the influence of values from any part of the research endeavor. This position argues that "some value orientations are so embedded in our modes of thought as to be unconsciously held by virtually all scientists" (Phillips, 1992, p. 142). For example, Sandra Harding (1987) argues from a feminist perspective that there is a male bias in fundamental aspects of scientific thought, and Stephanie Shields (1975) found that a great deal of

research on sex differences in the 20th century was influenced by historical biases (e.g., ideas about natural and social differences between men and women). These values may enter the research and theory development process in either overt or very subtle ways.

More generally, N. R. Hanson's classic work, *Patterns of Discovery* (1965), argues that observation is always influenced by the observer's theoretical perspective and background knowledge. For example, Gould (1981) examines the ways in which intelligence has been studied over time and finds that values and theoretical perspectives have influenced the scientific process in a variety of ways. For example, intelligence has been measured using techniques that will lead white men to come out on top, or with statistical techniques that will favor a particular value about how intelligence is structured in individuals. Thus, according to this second axiological position, values and theoretical perspectives constitute lenses through which we view the world, and these lenses cannot be eliminated in any portion of the scholarly process.

A third position on the role of values in scholarship goes beyond the argument that we cannot expunge values from the research process to contend that we should not separate values from scholarship. This position, which we discuss extensively in our consideration of critical perspectives on theory in Chapter 5, argues not only that values guide choices of research topics and influence the practice of research but also that scholarship involves active participation in social change movements. Thus, a scholar in this tradition interested in workplace participation would be influenced by values in the choice of research problem; in the formulation of theoretical positions; in the conduct of research; and in recommendations for social, structural, and communicative change that could improve the quality of life for organizational members. This axiological position goes beyond the acknowledgment of the role of values in research to a pointed consideration of *whose* values are given precedence. As Guba (1990a) summarizes, "If the findings of studies can vary depending on the values chosen, then the choice of a *particular* value system tends to empower and enfranchise certain persons while disempowering and disenfranchising others. Inquiry thereby becomes a *political act*" (p. 24).

Metatheoretical positions on axiology, then, consider the role of values in the process of theoretical development and testing. Though few social researchers would now suggest that theory development and testing can be a value-free process, many still advocate a very limited role of values. Other scholars, however, believe that values are so entrenched in our world views that we cannot avoid having them seep (or flow!) into our research. Finally, many scholars believe that values should play a very active role in our research, directing our scholarship in the paths of social change.

Summary

Theory arises within a context bounded by and influenced by the assumptions of social researchers. We have considered several areas of important metatheoretical assumptions that guide the theory development process, including issues of ontology (the nature of reality), epistemology (the nature of knowledge), and axiology (the role of values). As we will see in subsequent chapters, these metatheoretical foundations have a strong influence on how theory is developed and assessed. We will also see that there are links—though not necessary ones—among these metatheoretical areas.

■ THEORY IN THE COMMUNICATION DISCIPLINE

In the first two chapters of this book, we have developed two conceptual maps. The first map, presented in Chapter 1, charted the landscape of conceptualizations of communication by identifying key points of definitional convergence and divergence among communication scholars and

by discussing the domain of communication in both conceptual and disciplinary terms. The second map, presented in this chapter, introduced the terrain of the theory-building enterprise by defining theory and how it functions and by considering important metatheoretical entailments regarding ontology, epistemology, and axiology. It should be clear from these discussions that any consideration of communication theory will be a complex and multifaceted endeavor. In the final few pages of this chapter, then, we briefly consider communication theory as a pluralistic activity and highlight some of the approaches to developing and working with communication and theories that we discuss throughout the remainder of this book.

Communication Theory as a Pluralistic Enterprise

In the early to middle part of the 20th century, there was widespread agreement among social researchers—including communication scholars—about the proper road for the development and testing of theory. This position held that social research disciplines would flourish if they followed the lead of the physical sciences with their realist ontology, objective epistemology, and value-free methodology. Though some communication scholars have retained aspects of this vision as an ideal (see discussion of postpositivists in Chapter 3), others have turned to alternative frameworks that emphasize the socially constructed nature of reality and an accompanying subjective epistemology (see discussion of interpretivists in Chapter 4) or that emphasize the role of values in social theory and active contributions to relevant societal change (see discussion of critical theorists in Chapter 5). Do we need to decide among these options for theorizing? Are they mutually exclusive and competing options for social theory and research? Or can a variety of approaches to communication theory coexist?

This book takes the position that a variety of perspectives on communication theory can and should coexist. Of course, there are clear points of tension—and even conflict—among these perspectives. As we will see in subsequent chapters, a post-positivist theorist and an interpretive theorist construct and evaluate their theories in very different ways. And critical theorists differ from both of these perspectives in their view of the role of theories and theorists in the social world. However, all these perspectives share a commitment to an increased understanding of social and communicative life and a value for high-quality scholarship. That is, all communication theorists would agree with the statements "It is important to study and understand communication processes" and "Our scholarship should be careful, rigorous, and well-grounded."

This does not suggest that communication scholars typically endorse the "anything goes" view of epistemology often attributed to Paul Feyerabend (1970), an influential—and some say anarchist—philosopher of science. Indeed, within each guiding approach to communication theory, clear metatheoretical entailments lead to commitments regarding judgments of quality in theory and research. However, the view of communication theory adopted in this book suggests that the development of theory within the communication discipline can best be viewed as a pluralistic process in which a variety of viewpoints make valued contributions. This pluralistic enterprise requires an ability to communicate across these approaches, for as Jacobson (1991) argues, "As inquiry moves along the continuum from physical toward social and political topics of research, analysis must increasingly rely on dialogue among scholars" (p. 148). A pluralistic approach also endorses an active stance toward the development of communication theory. As Rosenberg (1986) notes, "Given a range of alternative accounts of knowledge, the only way to decide which will really be fruitful for social science, which will make the potentials for knowledge considerable, is by actually employing them in the work of social scientists" (p. 341).

Perhaps the most persuasive case made for such an approach is presented by Fay and Moon (1977) when they ask the question "What

would an adequate philosophy of social science look like?" They compare traditions in social research that value science and causal explanation, that value interpretation, and that value social change. As we will see, these positions are representative of the post-positivist, interpretive, and critical approaches to theory. Fay and Moon argue that none of these approaches—in isolation—provides a satisfying approach to social research. Instead, they present an argument for the importance of social research that deals effectively with questions of interpretation, explanation, and critique. Similarly, a volume in the subdiscipline of organizational communication (Corman & Poole, 2000) takes on the explicit goal of finding common ground among the approaches to theory and research presented in this book. As Poole and Lynch (2000) note in the final paragraph of their book,

> While it seems unlikely that any position will win the day, the many options discussed can give us guidance in the practice of scholarship, as we are confronted with problems that indicate the need to combine, work between, or even integrate perspectives. This rich set of approaches greatly increases the possibility that the fruits of research . . . will be substantial, rather than just a smile hanging in the air, with no cat at all behind it. (p. 223)

The remainder of this book, then, will be spent in an examination of the pluralistic field of communication theory. In Chapter 1, we briefly reviewed upcoming chapters and considered the criteria used to select the theories covered in Parts Two and Three. Here, however, we briefly discuss the approaches to theory development that will be considered in the remaining three chapters of Part One. The first of these, the post-positivist perspective on theory development considered in Chapter 3, maintains many positivist ideals of theory development that have flourished in the physical sciences but adapts these ideals in ways that take into account the role of values in theory and social construction processes. The interpretivist perspective on theory development considered in Chapter 4, takes a stance encompassing a nominalist—or social constructionist—ontology and a subjectivist epistemology. Because this perspective emphasizes the situated nature of social life, theory development is most likely to proceed in a way that is grounded in the insider's experience. Finally, in Chapter 5 we examine the critical perspective on theorizing. This perspective shares some of the ontological and epistemological commitments of the interpretivist school but embraces an activist stance with regard to the role of values in social theory. These three perspectives were chosen for consideration because—under various labels—they are consistently seen as the most dominant approaches to theory development within the philosophy of social science (e.g., Braybrooke, 1987; Fay & Moon, 1977), within other fields of social research (e.g., Guba, 1990b), and within the field of communication (e.g., Corman & Poole, 2000).

Within each of these three chapters, historical background is provided regarding the perspective under consideration and its ontological, epistemological, and axiological entailments. Then, the structure and function of theories within each perspective is considered, and we discuss how theory can be evaluated within that particular approach to theory building. Finally, each of these chapters introduces founding theoretical perspectives—metatheoretical or "grand theory" approaches that have informed the development of communication theory within each tradition. In discussing each of these approaches to theory development, an effort is made to avoid caricatures of the perspectives. It is easy to present any of these metatheoretical approaches simplistically and in ways that set them up as "straw person" approaches for subsequent critique (see K. I. Miller, 2000, for development of these ideas). These temptations are assiduously avoided as we explore the various perspectives that contribute to the pluralistic enterprise we call communication theorizing.

Key Terms

abstraction
deductive approach
inductive approach
empirical problem
conceptual problem
practical problem
metatheory
ontology
realist stance
nominalist stance
social constructionist position
subjectivist position
objectivist position
epistemology
axiology

Discussion Questions

1. Of ontology, epistemology, or axiology, which is the most important to consider when examining a theorist's metatheoretical assumptions? Justify your position.

2. Do positions along the ontological map correspond with certain positions on the epistemological or axiological maps? In what ways? Or can these various metatheoretical positions be seen as independent? What are the implications of relationships among ontology, epistemology, and axiology?

3. What are the most crucial differences between the naive theories we construct about everyday life and the theories that social researchers develop?

4. In your own communication experiences, what would you say are some practical problems and some empirical problems that theory could usefully address? What might a theory addressing those problems look like?

3 Post-Positivist Perspectives on Theory Development

It is natural for people starting out on a new venture to emulate those who have gone before. Robert Frost may have advocated taking the road "less traveled," but when faced with new territory, people often prefer to embark on a well-trod path, for such paths will provide routes and signposts to make the journey less arduous. So it has been for scholars who, during the 20th century, embarked on the study of human and social behavior. Because understanding how people think, behave, and interact was largely uncharted territory, the pioneers often turned to more established research disciplines—those in the physical sciences—for guidance. As a result, social researchers, including scholars in the discipline of communication, have often modeled themselves after the naturalistic ideals found in fields such as physics and biology.

D. C. Phillips (1992, pp. 42–48) has sketched out a number of ways in which values held by scholars in the natural sciences have made their mark on the social sciences. For example, social researchers occasionally take concepts and findings from the physical sciences and use them as a basis for social research (e.g., using evolutionary theory to guide investigations of psychology and group behavior). More typically, social researchers have maintained allegiance to metatheoretical assumptions from the physical sciences such as a realist

ontology and an objectivist epistemology. These metatheoretical assumptions have then guided scholarship regarding social and communicative behavior. Other social researchers have argued for the superiority of the structural features of theory as embodied in the natural sciences and for the centrality of the scientific method within social research.

Most of these strategies that emulate scholarship in the natural sciences are discussed in this chapter as we look at post-positivist perspectives on theory development in communication. We first consider the roots of the post-positivist approach by looking at the historical development of positivism. We then examine the nature of post-positivist theorizing within social research by discussing metatheoretical entailments of post-positivism, the structure and function of post-positivist theories, and the development of knowledge within the post-positivist tradition. We conclude by looking specifically at how post-positivist theorizing is exemplified within the communication discipline. Before considering these issues, however, it is useful to briefly examine the issue of terminology. A variety of terms have been used to label the general perspective we discuss in this chapter, including *functionalism*, *empiricism*, *naturalism*, and *positivism*. We use the term **post-positivism** to emphasize that though communication theorists today can trace their roots to the important movement of positivism, they have also moved beyond those roots in important and substantive ways.

■ PHILOSOPHICAL ROOTS: POSITIVISM

The term *positivism* is now widely used as a term of derision within fields of social research. However, this usage often sets up positivism as a straw person that can be easily batted down by those preferring an alternative philosophy of science. Indeed, Phillips (1992) argues that the term *positivism* "has ceased to have any useful function—those philosophers to whom the term accurately applies have long since shuffled off this mortal coil, while any living social scientists who either bandy this term around, or are the recipients of it as an abusive label, are so confused about what it means that, while the word is full of sound and fury, it signifies nothing" (p. 95). Thus, in this section we take a very brief look at the history of the positivist movement by first distinguishing between two "brands" of positivism—**classical positivism** and **logical positivism**—and then discussing the reasons for the decline of the positivist school in the middle of the 20th century. Much of this discussion is drawn from presentations of the positivist movement by Phillips (1992) and Diesing (1991).

Classical Positivism

The term *positivism* was coined by St. Simeon (*Concise Routledge Encyclopedia of Philosophy*, 2000), and the classical positivist position was developed by Auguste Comte (1970), a French philosopher who argued that branches of knowledge must pass through three intellectual stages, "the theological or fictitious state, the metaphysical or abstract state, and the scientific or positive state" (p. 1). This progression contends that religious and metaphysical explanations are less acceptable than those based on scientific evidence and that, as a result, fields such as physics are at a higher level than fields that do not fully comport with scientific ideals. In classi-

cal positivism, the foundation of knowledge was to be found in empirical or observable phenomena and understood through formal logic embodied in scientific laws. It is through a "well-combined use of reasoning and observation" that it is possible to come to "a knowledge of the final causes of phenomena" (Comte, 1970, p. 2). Thus, classical positivism was a foundationalist position that advocated the primacy of empirical data and formal theory in the generation of knowledge about the physical and social world.

Logical Positivism: The Vienna Circle

The logical positivist movement was embodied by a group of scholars who met during the 1920s and 1930s near Vienna, Austria. Known as The Vienna Circle, these scholars included Moritz Schlick, Rudolf Carnap, Otto Neurath, Herbert Feigl, Friedrich Waismann, Kurt Gödel, and Victor Kraft. Later influential members of the logical positivist movement included Hans Reichenbach, Carl Hempel, and Alfred Ayer. The logical positivists began by making a critical distinction between *science* and *metaphysics* via the "verifiability principle of meaning." This principle stated that "a statement is held to be literally meaningful if and only if it is either analytic or empirically verifiable" (Ayer, 1960, p. 90). Analytical statements are mathematical or logical statements that can be seen as meaningful through the force of reasoning. The only other statements deemed as meaningful by logical positivists were those that could be verified by the senses. As Phillips (1992) more colloquially puts it, "If it can't be seen or measured, it is not meaningful to talk about" (p. 100). Thus, **scientific statements** are analytical or empirically verifiable, and all other statements—those labeled by logical positivists as **metaphysical statements**—are meaningless.

After making this clear distinction between metaphysics (which wasn't meaningful) and science, the logical positivists turned their attention to explicating the syntax and semantics of scientific language. For example, a great deal of attention was spent in constructing an ideal language for science, in describing various kinds of scientific statements (e.g., observation statements, theoretical statements, and correspondence rules), and in clarifying the relationships among them (see Diesing, 1991, pp. 6–10). Logical positivists also considered the question of what counts as confirmation and disconfirmation of scientific statements and theories. Consider the statement "All leopards have spots." Clearly, one cannot prove this statement true because one cannot observe all the leopards in the world. This led some (e.g., Popper, 1959) to argue that the goal of science should be **falsification** rather than **verification,** though many logical positivists felt that there were problems with a falsifiability principle, as well (e.g., Carnap, 1937). The concept of falsification is discussed in more detail later in this chapter.

Throughout all these efforts, the logical positivist movement was one of accounting for an ideal of science—science as logical positivists believed it was meant to be. As Diesing (1991) summarizes,

> This movement approaches science from far above, from the ideal of perfect knowledge. . . . Thus the treatment of testing begins with the idea of complete verification. . . . Explanation is defined first as deduction from true, verified laws with all relevant circumstances specified. . . . Theory is defined first as a fully axiomatized structure of axioms, postulates, definitions, and theorems. . . . Actual sciences are interpreted as approximations to the ideal. (pp. 24–25)

The Demise of Positivism

The work of positivists thrived in the early decades of the 20th century. Indeed, this school was so well-entrenched that the terms *philosophy of science* and *positivism* were virtually synonymous. However, by the 1960s, positivism was all but dead and new views of the philosophy of science had ascended. What happened? What factors led to the demise of positivism? Several explanations help shed light on the downward spiral of this intellectual movement.

First, the very logic of the logical positivist movement came under question. Recall that logical positivists began with the notion—expressed in the verifiability principle—that all statements were empirically verifiable, analytic, or metaphysical (i.e., nonsense). If one takes a reflexive look at the verifiability principle, it is clear that this statement, itself, is not analytically true (i.e., not true by the force of logic). Thus, if it is not a metaphysical statement (nonsense), then the only alternative is that it should be empirically verifiable. However, the verifiability principle clearly is not subject to verification, which creates a clear problem for logical positivists. Internal inconsistencies like this one that arise when looking reflexively at logical positivism served to render the philosophical status of the movement problematic.

Second, scientists and philosophers of science began to increasingly accept the theory-laden nature of observation. As discussed in Chapter 2, this position argues that all observations—in the physical and social sciences—are influenced by the theoretical stance of the observer and that "some value orientations are so embedded in our modes of thought as to be unconsciously held by virtually all scientists" (Phillips, 1992, p. 142). If one accepts the position that all observations—in the physical and social sciences—are influenced by the theoretical stance of the observer, it is impossible to maintain the clean distinction between observational and theoretical statements that was so important to logical positivists. Furthermore, the theory-laden nature of observation cuts to the heart of the verifiability principle of meaning, for it is no longer possible to allow sensory experience to be the final arbiter of meaningfulness. A rejection of the verifiability principle means in essence a rejection of the entire logical positivist movement. As Diesing (1991, p. 15) explains,

> Once the two languages [observational and theoretical] had been distinguished, it proved difficult to keep them apart. Some philosophers argued that most scientific observations nowadays are made through instruments, and the instruments embody a theory by which we

interpret the observed fuzzy lines and patches as moons of Jupiter, microbes, or Brownian motion. Thus even "observation terms are themselves for the most part theoretical terms whose credentials we have come to accept at face value."(Rozeboom, 1962, p. 339)

Consequently, there could be no pure and direct observation language.

Finally, the logical positivist movement was seen as more and more detached from the workings of science. Logical positivists concentrated on the syntax and semantics of science, not its pragmatics. In other words, in their quest to map out an ideal for science, the logical positivists had little to say about what scientists actually did or what theories actually looked like. Other philosophers of science began to take a different tack by addressing how science proceeds as hypotheses are proposed and tested, theories are built and modified, and research programs thrive or degenerate (e.g., Agassi, 1975; Feyeraband, 1962; Kuhn, 1962; Lakatos, 1970). These investigations were seen as far more relevant than the quibbling over syntax that occupied the attention of most logical positivists, and this move from prescribing what science should be like to describing what scientists do marked an important shift in the philosophy of science.

■ POST-POSITIVISM IN SOCIAL RESEARCH TODAY

If positivism, in its classical and logical forms, is largely rejected, what philosophical foundation should take its place as a framework for social research? Very different answers to this question have been proposed. Some social researchers argue that flaws in the positivist foundation require a radically different philosophy of science, one in which the realist ontology, objective epistemology, and value-free axiology of positivism are vehemently rejected and replaced with forms of inquiry that honor nominalism, subjectivism, and omnipresent values. The positions of these scholars are discussed in great detail in Chapters 4 and 5 as we consider interpretive and critical perspectives on communication theory. However, some scholars believe that a rejection of positivism does not require a total rejection of realism, objectivity, and the scientific goal of value-free inquiry. However, these scholars reject the notion of absolute truth, reject the unassailable foundation of observation, and reject the assumption of an always steady and upward accumulation of knowledge. In these rejections, scholars have forged a new philosophy of science that D. C. Phillips (1987, 1990, 1992) has called post-positivism. The metatheoretical tenets of this position are discussed in the next section.

Metatheoretical Commitments

Ontology   In Chapter 2, we discussed three ontological positions: the realist, the nominalist, and the social constructionist. To summarize, a realist believes in a hard and solid reality of physical and social objects, a nominalist proposes that the reality of social entities exists only in the names and labels we provide for them, and a social constructionist emphasizes the ways in which social meanings are created through historical and contemporary interaction. Both the realist and the social constructionist positions make contributions to the ontology of post-positivist researchers in the communication discipline. Researchers in the post-positivist tradition can be seen as realists in that they support the position that phenomena exist independent of our perceptions and theories about them (Phillips, 1987). However, this realism is tempered by the argument that humans cannot fully apprehend that reality and that the driving mechanisms in the social and physical world cannot be fully understood. As J. D. Smith (1990, p. 171) states, "Realism is essential . . . because it poses 'at least in principle, a standard by which all human societies and their beliefs can be judged: they can all have beliefs about the world which turn out to be mistaken'" (Trigg, 1985, p. 22).

Phillips argues, however, that a post-positivist ontology does not deny the notions inherent in approaches advocating a "social construction of reality" (Berger & Luckmann, 1967). Rather, Phillips (1990) draws the distinction between beliefs about the reality and the objective reality (pp. 42–43). Making this distinction allows a post-positivist scholar to appreciate (and investigate) multiple realities that are constructed by social collectives through communicative interaction. For example, a post-positivist scholar could study the ways that beliefs about the imminent end of the world influence the behaviors of mountain survivalists, members of cults, and fundamental religious groups. However, the fact that a social group has arrived at certain beliefs about the world does not make those beliefs about the social or physical world necessarily true. As Phillips (1990) notes, "It is clear that Freudians believe in the reality of the id and superego and the rest, and they act as if these are realities; but their believing in these things does not make them real" (p. 43).

It could be further argued that post-positivism is consistent with social constructionist views in two important ways. First, many post-positivists would argue that the process of social construction occurs in relatively patterned ways that are amenable to the type of social scientific investigation undertaken by post-positivists. Individuals have free will and creativity but they exercise that creativity in ways that are often (though not always, certainly) patterned and predictable. In the field of mass communication, Barbara Wilson (1994) argues convincingly for this point regarding her own study of children's responses to the mass media:

> I believe that children's interpretations and responses are as richly individualistic as snowflakes. However, I also believe that there are common patterns that characterize a majority of young viewers and that those patterns are as predictable and explainable as the basic process by which all those unique snowflakes are formed from water. (p. 25)

Second, many post-positivists would argue that social constructions are regularly reified and treated as objective by actors in the social world. Thus, it is reasonable to study the impact of these reified constructions on our communicative lives. Tompkins (1997) has made this argument with regard to his organizational communication research with the National Aeronautics and Space Administration (NASA):

> The engineers, scientists, managers, bureaucrats, and other kinds of members did *not* believe in a socially constructed world. They believed the rockets they made did in fact go to the moon. Moreover, they believed that NASA and the contractor firms who worked for them were real. They believed that these organizations could succeed or fail by objective criteria and that their bosses could hire or fire, reward or penalize individuals—actions with *real* consequences. (p. 369)

Thus, a social constructionist ontology is consistent with a post-positivist position that emphasizes both the patterned nature of the social construction process and the regular and predictable effects that reified social constructions have on social actors. Thus, the ontology of post-positivism is not necessarily the belief in a hard, immutable, and unchanging social world implied in a strict realist stance. Rather, a post-positivist ontology entails a belief in regularity and pattern in our interactions with others. The ways in which these regularities and patterns are studied within post-positivist theory are considered in the next section.

Epistemology and Axiology Post-positivist assumptions about the grounds of social knowledge and the role of values in the production of social knowledge are also based largely on the objectivist tenets we discussed in Chapter 2. These assumptions include the three interlinked notions that (a) knowledge can best be gained through a search for regularities and causal relationships among components of the social world, (b) regularities and causal relationships can best be discovered if there is a complete separation between the investigator and the subject of the investigation, and

(c) this separation can be guaranteed through the use of the scientific method.

As they have done with ontological assumptions of realism, however, most post-positivist scholars in communication today have tempered these epistemological and axiological bases to what Guba (1990a) has termed modified objectivist. Post-positivist theorists generally hold to the first assumption mentioned in the preceding paragraph. That is, the search for knowledge remains centered on causal explanations for regularities observed in the physical and social world. This is clearly consistent with the ontological position outlined previously. It should be noted, though, that the regularities and causal relationships studied by post-positivist scholars today are rarely simplistic and often involve a multiplicity of factors and over-time relationships (see K. I. Miller, 2001, for examples in organizational communication).

Beyond this first assumption, however, post-positivists have largely rejected the second assumption, regarding the necessary distinction between knower and known. Instead, many post-positivists have concluded that "the hope for a formal method, capable of being isolated from actual human judgment about the content of science (that is, about the nature of the world), and from human values seems to have evaporated" (H. Putnam, 1981, p. 192). Because this assumption of value-free inquiry is rejected, post-positivists have similarly rejected blind obedience to the scientific method. Instead, objectivity is seen as a regulatory ideal. In other words, a post-positivist will use methods that strive to be as unbiased as possible and will attempt to be aware of any values that might compromise neutrality. However, because the possible fallibilities of the scientific method are recognized, the post-positivist will also rely on the critical scrutiny of a community of scholars in order to safeguard objectivity and maximize the growth of social scientific knowledge. Thus, though no claims to absolute truth and value-free inquiry are made, the belief exists that progress can be made if researchers exercise care in their theorizing and research and are critical of theoretical assertions and empirical justifications. As Phillips (1990) summarizes,

The ideal that is embraced seems to be this: Seekers after enlightenment in any field do the best that they can; they honestly seek evidence, they critically scrutinize it, they are (relatively) open to alternative viewpoints, they take criticism (fairly) seriously and try to profit from it, they play their hunches, they stick to their guns, but they also have a sense of when it is time to quit. It may be a dirty and hard and uncertain game, but with no fixed algorithms to determine progress, it is the only game in town. (pp. 38–39)

Structure and Function of Post-Positivist Theory

Thus, post-positivist scholars attempt to build theory and conduct research in ways that will enhance the objectivity of the research and lead to accurate explanations of the social world. What does theory look like from this post-positivist point of view? And what is the function of post-positivist social theory? The next two sections address these issues.

The Structure of Theory   When we looked at definitions of theory in Chapter 2, we emphasized the point that theories are abstractions. The abstract quality of theory is particularly germane in post-positivist approaches to theory because post-positivist scholars believe that theories must provide general explanations that go beyond the observation of individual events. A post-positivist scholar would also want the general statements in a theory to be logically organized and to have clearly established links to the observable world. Of course, all theories—even within the post-positivist tradition—will take somewhat different forms. But a perusal of a textbook on theory construction helps to provide some parameters about what post-positivists think theory should look like. A slightly modified version of the advice from Robert Dubin's (1978) classic *Theory Building* is used as an example here. Though this book was written by a sociologist (along with many other textbooks from this era written on theory construction processes—e.g., Blalock, 1969; Hage, 1972), it is quite representative of classic theory construction in the post-positivist tradition within communication.

Dubin argues that a theory must start with **units**—the concepts or constructs that make up the subject matter of the theory. After defining the units of interest, the theory must specify the **laws of interaction** among these units and must specify the conceptual **boundaries** within which the theory is expected to hold. Then, as Dubin states (1978), "Once these . . . basic features of a theoretical model are set forth, the theorist is in a position to derive conclusions that represent logical and true deductions about the model in operation, or the propositions of the model" (p. 8).

The units, laws, boundaries, and propositions make up the abstract portion of the theory. However, a theorist should also specify how the theory connects with the empirical or observable world. Thus, a theory should also include **empirical indicators** for each theoretical term. These are sometimes known as correspondence rules or operational definitions because they define the operations through which each theoretical unit is to be measured. Finally, the empirical indicators can be substituted for the theoretical units in the propositions, and this substitution will yield **hypotheses** that can be empirically tested to provide verification or falsification of the theory.

It is useful to illustrate these terms by describing how they might work in a theory of communication. Consider, for example, a theory we might propose about empathic communication, or communication involving the cognitive or affective connection between individuals who are interacting. This theory is based on work by K. I. Miller, Stiff, and Ellis (1988) and Stiff, Dillard, Somera, Kim, and Sleight (1988), but keep in mind that we are just using this as an example of how theory can be put together in the post-positivist tradition. The example is illustrative, but it does not do justice either to the complexities of theory construction or to the research on empathic communication.

A theory of empathic communication might start with basic units (i.e., concepts that play a part in our explanation) and definitions of those units. For example, our theory might include the concepts of empathic concern, emotional contagion, and communicative responsiveness. The first step in our theory construction process would be to define these three concepts. We could define *communicative responsiveness* as "the ability of an interactant to understand the needs of another and respond appropriately," *empathic concern* as "a nonparallel emotional response in which one person 'feels for' another," and *emotional contagion* as "a parallel emotional response in which one person 'feels with' another." After the units of the theory are defined, the post-positivist theorist would specify laws of interaction among those units and derive propositions based on those laws. For example, our theory of empathic communication might propose that empathic concern should enhance communicative responsiveness and that emotional contagion should detract from responsiveness. These propositions would be based on an underlying logic that sees parallel emotion ("feeling with") as a force that counteracts effective communication and nonparallel emotion ("feeling for") as a force that will enhance effective listening and message production. The theorist would also set up the boundaries within which these relationships should hold. Finally, the theorist would propose ways to measure the units (perhaps through self-report measures on a survey or through the observation and coding of natural conversation) and then derive hypotheses that could be tested with empirical research. This mini-theory of empathic communication is presented in Table 3.1.

Thus, the structure of theory in the post-positivist tradition requires that theories provide abstract explanations of empirical phenomena in the form of specific concepts and definitions, specific relationships (often causal) among those concepts, and explicit links between the abstract concepts and empirical observations of phenomena. This structure emphasizes a deductive approach to theory in which abstractions of the world are formed and then tested against observations in the social world.

The Function of Theory In their most basic sense, theories function to impose some kind of

Table 3.1	A "Mini-Theory" of Empathic Communication
Theoretical units	**Communicative Responsiveness:** The ability of an interactant to understand the needs of another and respond appropriately **Empathic Concern:** A nonparallel emotional response in which one person "feels for" another **Emotional Contagion:** A parallel emotional response in which one person "feels with" another
Laws of interaction	**Law One:** Empathic concern should enhance ability and desire to be communicatively responsive. **Law Two:** Emotional contagion should interfere with ability and desire to be communicatively responsive.
Boundaries	These units and laws should hold only for adults in interpersonal communication situations.
Propositions	**Proposition One:** Higher levels of empathic concern will be associated with higher levels of communicative responsiveness. **Proposition Two:** Higher levels of emotional contagion will be associated with lower levels of communicative responsiveness.
Empirical indicators	Theoretical units can be assessed through self-report measures.
Hypotheses	**Hypothesis One:** A positive correlation will exist between the self-report measure of empathic concern and the self-report measure of communicative responsiveness. **Hypothesis Two:** A negative correlation will exist between the self-report measure of emotional contagion and the self-report measure of communicative responsiveness.

order on unordered experience (Dubin, 1978). At a more detailed level, a wide range of functions of theory have been proposed in the literature (e.g., Littlejohn, 1996, identifies nine functions of theory). However, the three functions of theory that are most typically identified by post-positivist theorists are the interlinked functions of explanation, prediction, and control (e.g., G. R. Miller & Nicholson, 1976).

The function of **explanation** suggests that theories answer questions of why things occur. That is, in moving from the empirical world to the abstract world, a theory attempts to go beyond observation to illuminate the mechanisms behind the phenomenon. A variety of types of explanations are possible in theory. For example, some scholars have differentiated between contextually based explanations, in which causes for human behavior are seen in the external environment, and individually based explanations, in which causes for human behavior are seen in internal abilities, desires, and motivations. Indeed, the same observable behavior might be readily explained in different ways in different theories. The key point is that, for post-positivists, theories should provide an explanation for observed behavior, and the explanation typically takes the form of cause-and-effect relationships. For example, our mini-theory of empathic communication explained the responsiveness of interactants in terms of the causal forces generated by the internal characteristics of emotional contagion and empathic concern.

The second function of theory, **prediction,** follows from the notion of explanation. That is, if the theory provides an abstract explanation of a particular phenomenon, we should be able to use that abstract explanation to predict what will happen in a similar situation. Again, let us turn to our mini-theory of empathic communication. Our explanation of why certain people are responsive in interaction and certain people are not responsive would allow us to predict (e.g., from scores on self-report measures of empathic concern and emotional contagion) which individuals would be most effective in comforting a troubled friend. We can sometimes predict phenomena even in the absence of explanation. For example, some weather forecasts are very accurate about predicting meteorological events even if there are no clear explanations for why the events occur.

Finally, the third function of theory in the post-positivist tradition is **control.** Again, this function is a natural offshoot of explanation and prediction. That is, if one can explain and predict phenomena, it is also sometimes possible to use that information to control future events. For example, if our mini-theory of empathic communication received widespread empirical support and was confirmed as a reasonable explanation of the role of empathy in interaction, we might use that knowledge to train individuals to be more responsive in interactions with others, or, perhaps, to select individuals for sensitive communicative employment opportunities (e.g., as a counselor or a hospice worker) by measuring their level of empathic concern and emotional contagion before the hiring decision is made. In both of these instances, we have used our theoretical knowledge about empathic communication to control aspects of the social environment.

Criteria for Evaluating and Comparing Theories

If explanation, prediction, and control are the functions of post-positivist theories, how are we to judge the goodness, or effectiveness, of a particular theory? And, if multiple theoretical explanations exist for a particular communica-

tion phenomenon, how are we to choose among these competing theories? These questions address the issue of establishing criteria for evaluating and comparing theories. In Chapter 2, we discussed several general ways to evaluate the quality of a theory, including the extent to which a theory is successful in solving empirical, conceptual, or practical problems; the extent to which the theory is better than other available solutions; and the extent to which the theory is progressive in opening up new avenues for solving new problems. However, it is also possible to propose more specific standards for the evaluation of particular types of theories. Thomas Kuhn (1977) has presented one set of criteria that would probably be widely endorsed by post-positivist social theorists and researchers:

- A theory should be *accurate*. That is, within the theory's conceptual boundaries, empirical observation should be in agreement with the predictions of the theory. An implication of this criterion is that a theory must be *testable*. That is, determining the accuracy of a theory requires the scholar to put it to empirical test through the evaluation of observations of the social world.

- A theory should be *consistent*, both internally and externally. In an internal sense, the various propositions and laws of the theory should not contradict each other. In an external sense, the theory should not contradict other widely held theories in the relevant domain.

- A theory should have *broad scope*. This does not mean that theories (especially in the social sciences) should be universal in applying to all people or all situations. However, the boundaries of a theory should be construed in terms such that predictions will extend to a wide range of empirical situations.

- A theory should be *simple*, or in the term used by some theorists, *parsimonious*. Remember that at the most basic level, theories try to impose order on unordered experience. Thus, a high-quality theory will be one that provides a clean and uncluttered explanation of the observed phenomena. Of course, social and communicative life is complex, and theories of behavior will necessarily reflect and attempt to model this complexity. However, a good theory will make sense of our complex social world in a way that provides a coherent—and, it is hoped, parsimonious—underlying explanatory mechanism.

- A theory should be *fruitful*. This criterion is sometimes known as the heuristic function of theory, and it suggests that a high-quality theory should stimulate new research and lead to new discoveries. That is, though the explanations of a theory in some way provide closure in our understanding of a particular phenomenon, they should also open up new roads of investigation for current and future social scientists. For example, a theory of initial interaction in interpersonal contexts might open up and inform programs of research in intercultural adaptation or organizational socialization.

This is not an exhaustive list of ways in which theory can be judged, nor are the criteria on this list mutually exclusive. For example, a theory that is broad in scope is also most likely to be fruitful. There will also be times when contradictions exist among the criteria. A theorist who strives for simplicity and parsimony, for instance, may do so at the expense of predictive accuracy or broad scope. In essence, this list summarizes a set of values that many post-positivists have for theory, though the application of these values may lead to conflicting decisions about theory quality. As Kuhn (1977) argues,

[These criteria] function not as rules, which determine choice, but as values, which influence it. Two [scholars] deeply committed to the same values may nevertheless, in particular situations, make different choices as, in fact, they do. But that difference in outcome ought not to suggest

that the values scientists share are less than critically important either to their decisions or to the development of the enterprise in which they participate. Values like accuracy, consistency, and scope may prove ambiguous in application . . . but they do specify a great deal: what each scientist must consider in reaching a decision, what he [sic] may and may not consider relevant, and what he [sic] can legitimately be required to report as the basis for the choice. (p. 331)

The Process of Theory Development

Most post-positivists believe that researchers and theorists embark on the development of social and communication theory in order to learn more about the world in which we live. Indeed, the functions of theory discussed in the preceding section and the criteria proposed for evaluating theory suggest that if theory development is successful, we will gain new and broadened understandings of the social world. But how does this process of theory development and knowledge accumulation work? How do post-positivists believe we come to know more about the social and communicative world? We now turn to these questions regarding the theory development process.

Use of the Scientific Method The first key factor in the development of theory and growth of knowledge in the post-positivist tradition is a straightforward one. Post-positivists develop theory and accumulate knowledge about the world through the process of empirically testing theories. When an abstract theory about communication is developed, it must be tested against observations of communicative behavior. According to post-positivists, those empirical observations must be of a special kind. Specifically, in order to test and develop theories, we must make our observations through the use of the **scientific method.** Table 3.2 lists some of the defining features of the scientific method.

Table 3.2 clearly illustrates that scientific observation and testing is very different from everyday, or so-called naive, observation. For example, scientific observation requires clear

Table 3.2	Hallmarks of the Scientific Method

Differences between scientific method and naive observation methods

Selecting abstract concepts to represent observable phenomena
Defining concepts both conceptually and operationally
Linking concepts through propositions
Testing theories with observable evidence
Controlling alternative explanations through study design
Making definitions and procedures public for scrutiny by the scientific community
Using unbiased evidence in making truth claims
Reconciling theory and observation objectively

Source: Adapted from Watt & van den Berg (1995).

definitions of constructs at both the abstract (conceptual) and the empirical (observational) levels. In our naive theories, we rarely define constructs with much precision. Scientific testing involves controlling for alternative explanations through controlled study design. In our naive theories, we often base our conclusions on casual—and uncontrolled—observation. Scientific testing requires the scrutiny of a community of scholars to check on our theories and conclusions. Again, this widespread dissemination of ideas is rarely a feature of naive theorizing about communication processes.

Why is the scientific method important? Why do post-positivists insist on this kind of observation? A number of answers could be given to these questions, two of which are highlighted here. First, we have already mentioned on several occasions the theory-laden nature of observation, and post-positivists largely accept the impossibility of totally bias-free inquiry. However, post-positivists still see bias-free inquiry as a goal and the scientific method as a crucial tool for eliminating the influence of bias from observation, to the extent possible. The scientific method imposes standards of control that reduce the influence of the researcher's values and biases on the process of observation and interpretation and hence enhance the objectivity of the research enterprise.

Second, we have noted that post-positivists seek to explain social phenomena through their theories, and these explanations often take a causal form (see Cook & Campbell, 1979). In order to test causal explanations, a researcher must attempt to satisfy John Stuart Mills's so-called canons of causality. These canons state that one variable (x) can be said to cause a second variable (y) if (a) x precedes y in time (that is, x comes before y), (b) x and y covary with each other (that is, a correlation exists between x and y), and (c) alternative explanations for the observed covariation can be ruled out (that is, other viable causes for y have been eliminated). For example, it is possible to reach the conclusion that television violence causes aggressiveness in children only if (a) it can be shown that children's television viewing came before their aggressiveness, (b) it can be shown that as television viewing increases, aggressiveness increases, and (c) alternative explanations for the aggressiveness (e.g., age of child, socialization factors, ingestion of candy) can be ruled out. In order to satisfy these three conditions, a good deal of control needs to be exercised over research procedures. For example, in conducting a scientific experiment, the research controls the time-ordering of relevant variables and controls for alternative explanations through procedures such as randomization and control over study procedures. In short, the use of the scientific method enhances the exercise of control and hence increases our ability to assess causality, a critical feature of post-positivist explanation.

Theory Verification   The scientific method is thus crucial in the testing of a theory. As this testing process proceeds, then, how is the scholar to know that a theory is verified? Can we ever say that a theory is "true"? As suggested earlier in our discussion of logical positivism, these questions have garnered a great deal of attention on the part of philosophers of science. Since the time of the logical positivists, scholars have largely rejected the notion of the total confirmation of a theory because we are always observing only a small part of the world and hence can never know if the theory holds in every observable instance. This has come to be known as the *problem of induction*.

Karl Popper—in response to this conundrum—proposed the notion of falsification, in which, instead of searching for instances of support or verification, a theorist should actively look for facts that are inconsistent with the proposed theory. If no falsifying instances are found, the scholar can conclude that the theory is corroborated (not confirmed) and should be retained for the time being. If we observe a falsifying instance, "we know that some part of our theory is false and in need of correction, and we have some unexpected observations that can suggest a correction" (Diesing, 1991, p. 31). Popper does not, however, suggest giving up a theory after a single falsifying instance. Rather, in noting the counterbalancing human tendencies of criticism and tenacity, he advocates a balance between giving up a theory too readily and holding on to a theory too tightly.

Of course, Popper proposed this method—his procedure of "conjecture and refutation"—as an ideal for the practice of science, but it is hard to argue that researchers work this way in all (or even most) instances. Rather, when we look at the practice of researchers, we find that scholars tend to look for confirmation of their theories, not falsification. This is not particularly surprising. Scientists are, of course, human, and they will tend to cling tenaciously to their own creations—their theories. How, then, are we to accomplish the falsification of theories and move scientific work toward more accurate explanations? It is at this point that the community of scholars must work together. One scientist might propose a theory, and others work to falsify it and develop alternatives. In Popper's ideal scientific community, scholars will have a variety of opinions and a willingness to be refuted (Popper, 1962). In such a community, scholarly debate over theories will flourish and theories will grow toward a state of *verisimilitude* in which, though absolute truth is not obtained, we enhance the quality of our explanations of social phenomena.

The Evolution or Revolution of Research Programs   Finally, in considering the development of theories and theoretical knowledge, it is important to look at the big picture. The classic view of science from the positivist point of view is one in which scholars in the so-called positive disciplines (i.e., those using the scientific method such as the natural sciences) will steadily accumulate knowledge about a given topic area. This view of a steady **evolutionary growth of theory** has been rejected or greatly modified by current philosophers of science and by many post-positivists. For example, Lakatos (1970) argues that progress in science occurs as scientists work on long-term research programs that are built on the foundation of strongly held assumptions about the nature of the world. When programs produce occasional verifications, they are progressive research programs. Programs that receive no empirical support are degenerative. But both kinds of research programs—progressive and degenerative—can survive for a long time as researchers within a program work on specific theories and hypotheses while protecting the hard core of assumptions that undergird the research program as a whole.

An even more radical (and more influential) restatement of the notion that scientific knowledge accumulates through a gradual evolutionary process was Kuhn's (1962) book *The Structure of Scientific Revolutions*. Kuhn's work was based on historical studies of the natural sciences, but his ideas have been seized on by scholars across a wide range of social disciplines. Kuhn argued that when a discipline begins its research, it is in the "protoscientific" or "preparadigmatic" stage. Researchers at this stage work relatively independently on widely disparate research problems. Eventually, as data are gathered and theories are disputed, one theory or set of theories will come to dominate, heralding the arrival of a paradigm. A variety of meanings have been attached to the term *paradigm* (by Kuhn and others) including a world view, an exemplar study, or a set of standard theories and methodologies. When a discipline is working within a paradigm, scientists proceed in a normal science mode to solve specific puzzles raised by the paradigm and write textbooks that codify the teachings of the paradigm. Eventually, however, observations will be made that do not fit neatly into the reigning paradigm's theories. Such observations are called *anomalies*. These anomalies will produce new and widely divergent theories and will begin a period of *crisis* within the discipline. Eventually, a new paradigm will win out, either through the (not necessarily rational) persuasion of its proponents or through the death of the leaders of the old paradigm. In this view, knowledge growth is revolutionary, not evolutionary, and may not even be progressing toward better knowledge or theories.

How should we reconcile Kuhn's account of the **revolutionary growth of theory** with the workings of social researchers? Several different positions have been taken on this issue. First, many scholars have concluded that the social research disciplines (including communication) are protosciences (i.e., preparadigmatic) and are still waiting for the emergence of an overarching and unifying paradigm. Other scholars see the positivist approach to research as the old paradigm and herald interpretive and critical approaches (see Chapters 4 and 5) as the new paradigms that will overthrow positivism. Still other scholars see paradigms lurking everywhere: Each new theory, each new methodology, each new point of view is seen as a new paradigm that will change the way we approach social and communication research.

But Kuhn wasn't even writing about the social sciences, so perhaps debates about whether we do or do not have a paradigm are misplaced. Regardless of the paradigmatic status of the communication discipline, however, several important implications can be drawn from Kuhn's writing. First, Kuhn's book illustrates that science and research occur in fits and starts. Hopeful beginnings sometimes conclude in dead ends. And tiny findings sometimes blossom into productive research programs. The implication here is that we should not necessarily expect our knowledge to accumulate in a steady fashion but should anticipate a variety of turns in the road and speed bumps along the way. Second, Kuhn emphasizes for us the huge effect that our theoretical assumptions—our paradigmatic ways of thinking—have on the way we view the world and the way we do research. For post-positivists, the impact of paradigms highlights the importance of understanding the metatheoretical framework in which research occurs, the attempt to make research as objective as possible, and the need to work within a scientific community so that the critical scrutiny of other scholars can be brought to bear on the work being accomplished.

■ POST-POSITIVISM IN COMMUNICATION RESEARCH

There is little doubt that the post-positivist perspective on theory can be seen in a great deal of the work that is ongoing in communication studies. For example, in his lament "Why are there so few communication theories?" Berger (1991) clearly envisions the future development of theory as proceeding in a post-positivist manner. In noting that graduate students learning to build a theory "should be required to explicate theoretical constructs and to begin to build theories that explain communication phenomena" (p. 109), Berger sets forth a blatantly post-positivist agenda for future theory development efforts.

There have been notable debates within this dominant post-positivist tradition, however (see, e.g., Corman & Poole, 2000). One of the most important of these debates arose in the early and mid 1970s as scholars debated the proper logic to be used in theory building. In this debate, the theoretical approaches of laws, systems, and rules were pitted against each other (see, e.g., *Communication Quarterly*, Vol. 25, No. 1, 1977). The rules approach was one based largely in the interpretive tradition (see Chapter 4), but both the laws and the systems perspectives were firmly grounded in the post-positivist tradition. For example, these perspectives largely agreed on issues of axiology (the goal of value-free inquiry), ontology (a largely realist perspective), and epistemology (the search for regularities through the scientific method). However, systems and laws approaches differed on the specific logics that should be used to explain communicative phenomena. The precise details of this debate are not important to consider at this point. What is crucial, though, and a telling conclusion to this chapter, is what this debate demonstrates about post-positivism within the field of communication studies. That is, though many communication scholars are still committed to post-positivist values in the development and testing of theory, there is still room for debate about precisely how theories should be developed and tested. It is this ongoing room for debate that leads to much of the vibrancy we note in communication theories throughout this book—vibrancy that encompasses even those theories firmly entrenched in the traditions of post-positivism.

Key Terms

post-positivism
classical positivism
logical positivism
scientific statements
metaphysical statements
falsification
verification
units
laws of interaction
boundaries
propositions
empirical indicators
hypotheses
explanation
prediction
control
scientific method
evolutionary growth of theory
revolutionary growth of theory

Discussion Questions

1. What distinctions can be made between post-positivism and the movements that preceded it (e.g., classical positivism and logical positivism)? Is post-positivism merely watered-down positivism?
2. What are the appropriate methods for constructing a post-positivist theory? Are these methods largely inductive or deductive?
3. What are the appropriate criteria for evaluating a post-positivist theory? How do these criteria differ from those presented for evaluating theory, in general, in Chapter 2?
4. How is the community of scholars involved in the growth of knowledge in the post-positivist tradition? Do you think social scientists work in this way, or is the community of scholars an idealistic vision of how research proceeds?

4 Interpretive Perspectives on Theory Development

We are confronted on a daily basis with both puzzling and not so puzzling communicative interactions, situations that may be mundane or profound. We make choices about how best to talk with an instructor about a bad grade on an exam. We try to make sense of the myriad political commentators discussing the news of the day. We mourn for a grandparent suffering from Alzheimer's disease, who no longer recognizes cherished family members. In all of these everyday situations, we seek an understanding of how and why communication works in the way it does. In this chapter, we consider theorists who puzzle over issues such as these as well as a host of others. Interpretive theory grew out of a dissatisfaction with post-positivist theories, when many scholars saw such theories as too general, too mechanical, and too detached to capture the intricacies, nuances, and complications of human interaction. Interpretive theorists seek an understanding of how we construct meaningful worlds through interaction and how we behave in those worlds we have created. In seeking this type of understanding, interpretive theorists approach the world and knowledge in very different ways from post-positivist theorists.

In this chapter we consider interpretive theory first by charting the historical roots that undergird the perspective. We then look at three important foundational frameworks that have influenced much of interpretive theory in communication today. Following these historical and foundational considerations, we discuss the ontological, epistemological, and axiological positions that guide interpretive theorists. Finally, we examine the form and function of two different kinds of interpretive theories: general interpretive theories and grounded theories.

■ HISTORICAL BACKGROUND

Charting the historical roots of any intellectual movement can turn quickly into a slide down a slippery slope as influences on thinking are traced through time. At the risk of sliding down that slope, however, it is instructive to ground an understanding of the interpretive perspective on theory development by harkening back to ideas of the Enlightenment, particularly the philosophical positions of René Descartes (1596–1650). In 1644, Descartes published the *Principles of Philosophy*, in which he argued that all explanation can be based on the observation of matter and motion (Descartes, 1963). In this and other philosophical work, Descartes established both a foundationalist approach to knowledge that served as a basis for the positivist and post-positivist schools discussed in Chapter 3 and a clear distinction between the external world of objects and the internal world of the subject. This distinction, often referred to as **Cartesian dualism,** is reflected in realist ontologies and positivist epistemologies. Cartesian dualism suggests that clear differences exist between the outside world and inside perception and that the distinction between the two—object and subject—allows for the unbiased observation of the social world. Similarly, Cartesian dualism argues for a distinction between mind and body that privileges rational thought processes over emotional or bodily experience. Descartes is perhaps most famous for his dictum "I think, therefore I am," and in this phrase the Cartesian privileging of rationality—clearly seen in positivist and foundationalist philosophies—is established.

In the middle of the 18th century, however, objections were already being raised to these Enlightenment notions of objectivity, rationality, and foundational knowledge grounded in external observation. Most influential during this time period was Immanuel Kant (1724–1803), a philosopher central in what is now known as **German idealism.** Kant argued that humans have a priori knowledge that is independent of the outside world. Following from this argument, and in contrast to a Cartesian position, German idealism posits that an understanding of the human condition should begin with consideration of the subjective spirit and the intuition that guides it. As Burrell and Morgan (1979) note, "It is this basic, uncomplicated assumption which underlies the whole of German idealism" (p. 227).

German idealist philosophy encountered some rough times in the middle of the 19th century, as foundational approaches once again gained ascendency. Idealism was "forced into a secondary place by the 'practical' achievements of sociological positivism" (Burrell & Morgan, 1979, p. 227). However, interest in German idealism was revived in the late 19th and early 20th centuries and gave rise to the neo-Kantian movement. We discuss in the next section several scholars who were prominent in this movement (i.e., Wilhelm Dilthey with regard to hermeneutics and Edmund Husserl with regard to phenomenology). However, another scholar who is representative of this intellectual tradi-

tion is Max Weber (1864–1920). Weber is often associated with his Theory of Bureaucracy, but this theory represents only a small portion of his work. In other writings, Weber was concerned with developing theory and method that would be appropriate for gaining an understanding (**verstehen**) of the subjective *lebenswelt*, or life world. In Weber's view, the positivist procedures of the natural sciences were not appropriate methods of *verstehen*, and he advocated a move toward an interpretive social science that could account for the subjective meanings of individuals involved in social action.

Thus, at the turn of the 20th century, many social thinkers were dissatisfied with the foundational grounds that began with Descartes in the Enlightenment and were continuing to be developed in classical positivist and logical positivist positions. These scholars, instead, believed that an understanding of social life must account for the subjective and personal meanings of individuals. In the next section, we consider several philosophical positions that have strongly influenced interpretive theory within communication and other social sciences. Though these theoretical frameworks (hermeneutics, phenomenology, and symbolic interactionism) do not reflect a comprehensive list of interpretive thinking during this time period, they are representative and illustrative of work that continues to influence researchers who take an interpretive position today.

FOUNDATIONAL THEORETICAL POSITIONS

Hermeneutics

Hermeneutic philosophies were originally concerned with the interpretation of the Bible and other sacred texts, but during the late 19th and early 20th centuries **hermeneutics** evolved and flourished as a method for understanding a wide variety of textual material. Wilhelm Dilthey (1833–1911) was an important early proponent of hermeneutics. He argued that hermeneutics provided a methodological path for studying social creations, or the "objectifications of mind" (Burrell & Morgan, 1979, p. 236). The hermeneutic school was further developed by theorists such as Karl-Otto Apel and Paul Ricoeur, but hermeneutics as an approach for understanding social life has perhaps been most thoroughly developed and is most consistently associated with Hans-Georg Gadamer (e.g., Gadamer, 1975, 1989).

At the core of the hermeneutic tradition is the concept of a text. Though, as noted earlier, hermeneutics began with a consideration of sacred texts such as the Bible, Gadamer and others have extended the application of hermeneutics to any human action, product, or expression that can be treated like a text. That is, the subject of study for hermeneutics could include a classic work by Plato, a speech made by a contemporary politician, the rites and rituals of a particular organizational or national culture, or drunken behavior observed at a fraternity party. In short, both the process and the product of communication are relevant for hermeneutic inquiry, and thus hermeneutics serves as an important foundational basis for interpretive theory within the communication discipline.

Hermeneutic analysis involves a consideration of the text in light of the researcher's theoretical knowledge and information about the type of text, the source of the text, and the situation in which the text was produced. As Diesing (1991) explains,

> The hermeneutic maxim here is: No knowledge without foreknowledge. That is, we form an expectation about the unknown from what we "know." Our foreknowledge may be mistaken, or partial or misleading, or inapplicable to this text; but in that case the interpretation will run into trouble. If our foreknowledge is weak, we may begin with two or more contrary expectations and see which one works out better, or more likely we will simply fail to see what is going on. Our initial hypothesis, based on foreknowledge, directs our attention to certain passages in the text as the important ones. (p. 108)

Thus, the hermeneutic scholar does not blindly interpret the text with which he or she is pre-

sented. Rather, hermeneutic analysis involves a process of tacking, or going back and forth between theory, tacit knowledge the researcher takes into the project, and the textual data (Radnitzky, 1970). For example, consider a hermeneutic scholar studying transcripts of a hostage negotiation. In studying such a text, the scholar would likely be interested in enhancing our understanding of how interactants' motives and the context in which the negotiation occurs contribute to the specific text enacted and the relationship of that text to our extant knowledge regarding negotiation in general and hostage negotiation in particular. In proceeding with hermeneutic analysis, the researcher would consider the transcript itself, the situation in which the negotiation took place, the biographies of the parties in the negotiation, theoretical and empirical knowledge about the process of negotiation, and the researcher's own political and personal views relevant to the situation. This process of tacking among these various issues has come to be known as the *hermeneutic circle* and is central to the development of theory within this tradition.

The contributions of hermeneutic scholarship to contemporary interpretive theory in communication can be summarized through several central ideas. First, hermeneutics emphasizes the importance of understanding (as opposed to explanation, prediction, and control) as a goal of social analysis. That is, social researchers should consider issues of meaning and subjective significance rather than engaging in a scientific search for universal laws and causal relationships. Second, hermeneutics emphasizes the central concept of text and proposes that a wide variety of actions and created objects in social life can be regarded as a text. Cheney and Tompkins (1988) expand on this argument for the communication discipline in their discussion of the concept of text as the basis for human communication research. That is, texts analyzed in communication research could include speeches, television shows, business meetings, intimate conversations, nonverbal behavior, or the architecture and decoration of a home. Third, through the development of the hermeneutic circle, these scholars argue against the distinction between the knower and the known that is a founding principle of the post-positivist traditions discussed in Chapter 3. Indeed, Gadamer argues that *verstehen* involves at its core "the interchange of the frames of reference of the observer and the observed" (Burrell & Morgan, 1979, p. 238). That is, texts and social actions are interpreted using experiential and theoretical lenses developed through the personal and professional background of the observer. As Diesing (1991) emphasizes, "The hermeneutic approach does not require detachment or neutrality of the scientist. . . . Indeed, it even denies that neutrality is possible" (p. 122).

In summary, hermeneutics points scholars to the importance of texts in the social world and to methods of analysis that emphasize the interlinked influence of text, author, context, and theorist. Thus, hermeneutics provides a path away from the emphasis on explanation and control found in positivist research and toward the subjective understanding of social life. Another path toward such interpretive scholarship is considered in the next section.

Phenomenology

Like hermeneutics, phenomenological scholarship is not a totally coherent intellectual movement. Rather, it reflects the thinking of a number of philosophers including Edmund Husserl, Maurice Merleau-Ponty, Martin Heidegger, and Alfred Schutz. In this section, we consider two lines of thinking in the phenomenological movement, **transcendental phenomenology,** as represented in the work of Edmund Husserl, and **social phenomenology,** as represented in the work of Alfred Schutz. Though these two schools have different theoretical goals and methods, they share the phenomenological framework that Deetz (1973) has outlined within the communication discipline. The first and most basic principle of phenomenology—clearly related to the German idealism discussed earlier in this chapter—is that knowledge is not found in external experience but in individual conscious-

ness. Thus, phenomenology revolves around a search for subjective understanding rather than a search for objective causal and universal explanation. Second, meaning is derived from the potential for a particular object or experience in a person's life. That is, the meaning of a tree growing in a backyard could revolve around beautiful leaves, desired shade, noisy birds that inhabit the tree, or an unwanted impediment to pool construction. In essence, the meaning ascribed to any object or experience will depend on an individual's background and current life events. Third, phenomenologists believe that the world is experienced—and meaning is developed—through language. This assumption follows from the social constructionist ontology discussed in Chapter 2. These three foundations of phenomenology, however, take on different levels of importance depending on the particular school of phenomenology being considered.

Transcendental phenomenology (sometimes called classical phenomenology) was founded by Edmund Husserl (1859–1938), a physicist and mathematician who became concerned with foundational issues of how we come to know the world. Central to his concern was the thesis that in our daily activities in the life world, the essence of objects and experience becomes obscured by taken-for-granted concepts that come to be known as common sense. For example, our interactions at the dinner table might say a great deal about who we are as family members, but we typically take for granted these interactions—and the meanings they may hold. Because of this obfuscation of the essence of experience, Husserl believed that "the central endeavour of phenomenology is to transcend the natural attitude of daily life in order to render it an object for philosophical scrutiny and in order to describe and account for its essential structure" (Natanson, 1966, p. 3).

This goal of transcendence, according to Husserl, was to be reached through the method of *époche*. This method involves bracketing, or setting aside, the natural attitudes of taken-for-granted life in order to gain a purer understanding of the phenomenon under investigation. Thus, an understanding of the individual experience of receiving a negative performance review from your supervisor can be achieved only by bracketing related experiences, attitudes, and beliefs and isolating the performance review phenomenon for consideration. According to transcendental phenomenology, true understanding of a phenomenon can be achieved only if personal biases, histories, values, and interests can be transcended (i.e., set aside in brackets) for the period of the investigation.

Based on these foundations of transcendental phenomenology, other philosophers moved to a more active consideration of the social world of everyday experience. In the area known as social phenomenology, the writings of Alfred Schutz (1899–1959) have had a particularly strong influence on the work of sociologists and communication scholars. Schutz accepted many of the foundational principles established by Husserl, but instead of advocating a bracketing of the life world through which transcendence can be achieved, he discussed ways in which that intersubjective life world can be approached and understood. In other words, Schutz advocated the intense study of *lebenswelt*, not its bracketing. According to Schutz, this everyday life world can be understood in terms of the so-called typifications used to organize the social world. These typifications are interpretive constructs that vary based on an individual's biography, his or her cultural group, and the specific social context under consideration. For example, typifications for dating behavior will vary considerably based on national and ethnic culture, individual personality, and the specific relational context. As such, specific behaviors (e.g., the woman requesting the date, the couple splitting the tab for dinner, or physical contact occurring during a first date) might be seen as appropriate in one typification but not in another. Schutz saw these typifications as organized into a stock of knowledge that is incredibly complex, and he believed that describing and understanding this stock of knowledge is the central task of social researchers. "To see this world in its massive complexity, to outline and explore its essential features, and to trace out its manifold relationships were the composite parts of his

central task . . . a phenomenology of the natural attitude" (Schutz, 1962, p. xxv).

Thus, phenomenology points to several important foundations for interpretive scholarship. Both transcendental and social phenomenology emphasize the importance of the everyday life world as an object of study, and both note that our understanding of that life world is often obscured by its very "everydayness." To overcome this, social phenomenology provides an approach and vocabulary for interpreting that life world and coming to an understanding of how the natural attitude of everyday life is played out.

Symbolic Interactionism

Interestingly, the man typically credited as the father of **symbolic interactionism,** George Herbert Mead (1863–1931), never used the term. However, his work has influenced a wide range of scholars who emphasize an understanding of the social world grounded in the importance of meaning as produced and interpreted through symbols in social interaction. Theorists in the symbolic interactionist tradition are typically divided into *the Iowa school* and *the Chicago school* (Meltzer & Petras, 1970). Scholars in the Iowa school, though grounded in the philosophical positions of symbolic interactionism, adhere largely to the epistemology and methodology of the post-positivist tradition. Hence, they are not discussed here in detail. Instead, we concentrate on scholars within the Chicago school who have taken a more interpretive approach to the founding work of Mead. Particularly noteworthy is Herbert Blumer, who has been called "Mead's foremost apostle" (Littlejohn, 1996) and who has most fully articulated this strand of symbolic interactionism.

The title of Mead's most famous work, *Mind, Self, and Society* (Mead, 1934), delineates three critical concepts that are necessary for organizing a discussion of the symbolic interactionist movement. What should be noted first is that these three concepts reciprocally influence each other within symbolic interactionism. That is, human thought (*mind*) and social interaction (the *self* with others) serve to interpret and mediate the *society* in which we live. As Douglas (1970) notes, "Meaning arises out of interaction, and not the other way around" (p. 295). At the same time, mind and self arise within the social context of a society. This interplay among society, individual experience, and interaction thus becomes the fodder for theorizing in the symbolic interactionist tradition. As Holstein and Gubrium (2000) summarize,

> Symbolic interactionism orients to the principle that individuals respond to the meanings they construct as they interact with one another. Individuals are active agents in the social worlds, influenced, to be sure, by culture and social organization, but also instrumental in producing the culture, society, and meaningful conduct that influences them. (p. 32)

Mead and his followers use a number of concepts to flesh out the ways in which meaning arises through interaction in social groups. For example, Mead talks of *significant symbols* that have shared meaning within a society. Without a shared symbolic system, coordinated action is impossible. Other important concepts within symbolic interactionism are *significant others* (i.e., influential people within your life), the *generalized other* (i.e., your concept of how others perceive you), and *role taking* (i.e., modeling behavior after the behavior of others). These concepts are woven together in symbolic interactionism to provide a complex picture of the interplay of individual perception and psychology, symbolic communication, and societal norms and beliefs in the social construction of society.

Consider, for example, the question of what it means to be a *mother*. Clearly this term constitutes a significant symbol for which there is some degree of shared meaning in society (i.e., a mother is a female parent). However, the meaning associated with *motherhood* goes far beyond this basic level. For a particular woman, the meaning of motherhood will depend on cultural norms and the values and behaviors of significant others (e.g., her own mother and father, sib-

lings, spouse, children, and friends). A woman enacting the motherhood role will engage in role-taking behavior (e.g., choosing to do things like—or perhaps unlike—her own mother) and will develop perceptions of how others see her in the motherhood role. She may develop an idealized view of how a generalized other believes motherhood should be enacted. Through these complex processes, the meaning of *mother* is shaped and shifted both for individuals and for larger social and societal groups.

Summary

Though a variety of other influences have contributed to interpretive theory in communication (e.g., ethnomethodology, theories of sociolinguistics), this brief consideration of hermeneutics, phenomenology, and symbolic interactionism provides a number of framing concepts that continue to influence interpretive theorists today. The three frameworks we examined are, of course, different in terms of assumptions, emphases, and methods. However, taken together, they highlight principles that are central to an interpretive theoretical frame. These principles include the importance of subjective experience, the intersubjective creation of meaning, the goal of understanding in social research, and the interconnections between the knower and the known. In the next section of this chapter we discuss the ways in which the fundamental frameworks of hermeneutics, phenomenology, and symbolic interactionism influence interpretive theory within the field of communication today.

■ INTERPRETIVE THEORY IN COMMUNICATION

As in our discussion of post-positivism in Chapter 3, we consider here a number of metatheoretical principles that frame theory within the interpretive school of thought. These metatheoretical commitments are considered in terms of ontology, epistemology, and axiology. It should be emphasized, though, that interpretive theory is not a monolithic enterprise and that this discussion represents general trends rather than the framework of any particular interpretive theorist. Further, connections among ontology, epistemology, and axiology are unavoidable because beliefs about reality, knowledge, and values are inextricably meshed together. Thus, the division of metatheoretical commitments into these three categories is a somewhat artificial one.

Ontology of Interpretive Theory

In Chapter 2, we discussed a number of ontological positions regarding the nature of the social world, ranging from realist to nominalist and including social constructionism. Interpretive theorists in communication reject a realist interpretation of the social world, espousing instead a nominalist or—more often—social constructionist position. The ontological position of most interpretive theorists in the communication discipline holds that social "realities exist in the form of multiple mental constructions, socially and experientially based, local and specific, dependent for their form and content on the persons who hold them" (Guba, 1990a, p. 27).

These nominalist and social constructionist ontological positions have several important implications. First, a nominalist position embraces the notion of multiple realities, none of which can be seen as more true or false than another. That is, one social group's belief in the power of pagan ritual is just as real as another group's belief in Christian doctrine. Second, the social constructionist aspect of interpretive ontology emphasizes the processes through which social realities come to be understood and acted upon by social actors. As L. L. Putnam (1983) explains, "Collectivities are symbolic processes that evolve through streams of ongoing behavior instead of through static social facts. Such concepts as roles, norms, and values are artificial creations, ways of classifying and making sense of social actions" (p. 35). Finally, the ontology held by most interpretive theorists highlights the notion that reality cannot be understood except through a consideration of the mental and social processes that are continually constructing that reality. This third ontological implication leads to the epistemology of interpretive theorists and researchers.

Epistemology of Interpretive Theory

The epistemological bases of interpretive research are predicated both on beliefs about reality (**nominalist ontology** and **social constructionist ontology**) and on perceived shortcomings of the scientific research methods that have dominated social research for much of the 20th century. In the discussion of post-positivist epistemology in Chapter 3, we noted the widespread rejection of the belief that knowledge can be generated in a manner that is totally free of the scholar's values and theoretical beliefs. We further noted that post-positivist theorists deal with this shortcoming by still striving to be as value-free as possible and by relying on the scholarly community to safeguard against bias that emerges in the research process.

Interpretive theorists reject these post-positivist moves, arguing that the theory-laden nature of observation makes objective investigation impossible. As a result, interpretive theorists advocate a **subjective epistemology.** Consistent with a nominalist or social constructionist ontology, a subjective epistemology proposes that there are no universal laws or causal relationships to be deduced about the social world. Instead, interpretivists strive to gain local understanding of specific social collectives and specific events. Because reality is socially constructed, interpretivists believe that this understanding can be reached only from the actor's point of view. That is, "interpretivists formulate interpretations . . . that account for the way that subjective meanings are created and sustained" (L. L. Putnam, 1983, p. 41). In order to gain this understanding, an interpretive scholar attempts to minimize the distance between the knower and the known, and resultant research findings are the creation of the interaction between the researcher and the community. This requires "inquiry from the inside" (Evered & Louis, 1981) in which the researcher immerses himself or herself in the social setting, combining interviewing and observation with his or her own personal experiences in the field. Theory—like the social reality being theorized about—is created inductively (Glaser & Strauss, 1967) through the interaction of the investigator and the social collective.

Axiology of Interpretive Theory

In Chapter 2, we discussed a variety of positions regarding axiology, or the role of values in theory development and research. As can be inferred from our consideration of epistemology in the preceding section, interpretive theorists eschew the notion that social research can be totally separated from the values of the researcher, the research community, and society. However, beyond this overall rejection of value-free inquiry and theory, interpretive theorists vary a bit on axiological issues.

In our discussion of phenomenology, we considered the concept of bracketing—the idea that a social researcher should set aside preconceived beliefs and values in the investigation of social life. This concept suggests that interpretive scholars should try to minimize the influence of values on the research process. In line with this, Max Weber advocated the building of "an objective sociology upon the foundations of subjective meaning and individual action" (Burrell & Morgan, 1979, p. 231). This axiological position is also largely consistent with the beliefs of the Iowa school of symbolic interactionism. However, this approach to the role of values in theory development—that those values should be bracketed for more objective study of the everyday life world—is not shared by most contemporary interpretive theorists.

Instead, most interpretive theorists in communication today tend to follow the lead set by hermeneutics and the Chicago school of symbolic interactionism in arguing for the impossibility of separating values from scholarship. In this view, personal and professional values are a lens through which social phenomena are observed. This lens can be examined and dis-

cussed in terms of its influence on the research project, but it can never be eliminated (or even bracketed) from the scholarly endeavor. For example, in this axiological view, a woman studying sexually harassing messages in the workplace could never totally eliminate the influence of gender and workplace experiences on observation and analysis—nor should she even try to. Indeed, some interpretive theorists would advocate a celebration of the connection between knower and known, arguing that "the research product is a joint construction" involving values and experiences of both researchers and participants (Foss & Foss, 1994, p. 41) and that the joint construction process should be appreciated to the fullest extent possible.

■ STRUCTURE AND FUNCTION OF INTERPRETIVE THEORY

When we discussed the structure and function of post-positivist theories, we found that theorists in that tradition relied largely on variants of practices established in the natural sciences. Because of post-positivists' epistemological foundations concerning the primacy of causal explanations and the ability to generalize across people and settings, a reliance on formal and well-specified theory makes sense. Thus, a post-positivist theory attempts to explain communicative behavior, typically through an organized set of lawlike statements.

Interpretive theory, in contrast, is grounded in ontological and epistemological beliefs that contrast sharply with those of post-positivist theorists. As discussed earlier in this chapter, interpretive theorists favor local understanding over general explanation, and, as a result, theories based on the model of the natural sciences are not adequate or appropriate for the interpretive scholar. Instead, interpretive theories aid in our understanding of a world that is socially constructed through communicative interaction, and these theories aim to reflect the complexity of both the social world and the social construction process.

In this section, we make a distinction between *general interpretive theories* and *grounded theories*. Both kinds of theories clearly fall under the rubric of interpretive scholarship, but they are very different in both form and function. What we will call general interpretive theories attempt to provide an understanding of the processes through which communication functions in intersubjective interaction. These theories often propose that these processes of social construction and interaction can be discussed across situational boundaries—hence the *general* label used here. In contrast, grounded theories concentrate on local and emergent communication phenomena. Instead of illuminating general processes of intersubjectivity and social construction, these theories aid in our understanding of specific situations and contexts. For both general and grounded theories, we will consider theoretical form and function as well as standards for evaluation.

General Interpretive Theories

Theoretical Function and Form   The heart of an interpretive ontology is the belief that we socially construct our world through communicative interaction. Thus, meaning is created intersubjectively, as individuals bring subjective understandings into interaction, and these understandings evolve, develop, and sometimes become reified through communicative behavior. Given this ontological base of interpretive scholarship, a key question is, How does this intersubjective process work? How is meaning created symbolically in interaction? How do we come to have our individual subjective understandings, and how are these understandings shared and developed in the communities in which we live and function? Questions such as these stimulate the development of general interpretive theories.

Clearly, theoretical goals regarding understanding the processes of social construction and interaction are isomorphic with the goals that stimulated the theorists we discussed when we considered some foundational work that under-

girds interpretive theory. For example, Mead, the founder of symbolic interactionism, was motivated by a desire to understand the ways in which meaning is produced and interpreted through symbols in social interaction. Schutz, the founder of social phenomenology, sought to understand the typifications that guide our behaviors in the intersubjective and everyday life world. Thus, these founding theorists laid the groundwork for theories that seek an understanding of how meaning is created and how behavior is guided through intersubjective symbolic interaction.

Communication scholars in the interpretive school have built on these foundational frameworks in formulating theories that enhance our understanding of the ways in which communicative behavior both shapes and is shaped by intersubjective understandings. For example, constructivist theory (Chapter 7) looks at the interconnections between individual cognitive structure and the creation of symbolic meaning in interaction. Constructivist scholars seek a general understanding of cognitive and interaction processes but ground that general understanding in the ontological assumptions of interpretive scholarship. Similarly, coordinated management of meaning theory (Chapter 9) considers the ways in which communicative behavior is guided and interpreted in terms of social rules for both meaning and activity. Again, this theory stems from a social constructionist ontology but aspires to provide understanding of the social constructionist process on a cross-situational basis. Finally, speech code theory (Chapter 16) looks at how particular ways of speaking characterize the cultures of specific speech communities. These theories provide understandings of the general processes through which meaning is created and re-created through interaction.

A final note on the functions of general interpretive theory is in order. In Chapter 3, we discussed post-positivist theorists as guided by three interrelated goals: explanation, prediction, and control. It is useful to consider these goals as they relate to the formulation of general interpretive theory as well. Though interpretive theorists working in this area are interested in general processes of interaction, they would largely state their goal as one of **understanding** rather than **explanation.** That is, interpretive theorists are looking at interactional processes from the point of view of the social actor rather than looking for external causal influences. This distinction is found in Schutz's distinction between **"genuine-because"** motives (i.e., explanations) and **"in-order-to"** motives (i.e., understandings) (see R. J. Bernstein, 1976, pp. 153–156, for further discussion). This distinction between the search for explanation and the search for understanding represents a fundamental distinction between post-positivist and interpretive theories.

Consider, for instance, a person who uses a threatening message to gain compliance from a friend. An explanation (based on "genuine-because" motives) might consider causal factors such as personality or relational development in theorizing about this phenomenon. Such an explanation would be typical of post-positivist scholarship. In contrast, an understanding of the behavior (based on "in-order-to" motives) would consider the contingencies of the particular situation, the interactional goals of the participants, and the rules that influence that type of interaction. This understanding would involve the local goals and contingencies of interactants. Because interpretive theorists are more interested in understanding than in explanation, they also tend not to have the goals of prediction and control in mind when developing theories about human interaction.

Thus, a general interpretive theory seeks to provide an understanding of intersubjective meaning processes. Theories of this nature are typically stated verbally (rather than mathematically) and are often quite formal in their presentation. Thus, a general interpretive theory will attempt to describe carefully the processes of social and symbolic interaction under consideration. Further, because interpretive theorists of this type are looking to elucidate general

processes of interaction and social understanding, general interpretive theories are often stated in relatively abstract terms. That is, a general interpretive theory will look for essential elements of communicative interaction and meaning development and discuss these elements in a way that can be applied across specific communicative contexts. For example, constructivism (Chapter 7) has been used to understand a wide range of communicative functions, including persuasion, comforting, and conflict management; and speech codes theory (Chapter 16) has investigated ways of talking in a variety of speech communities.

Criteria for Evaluation What constitutes a good theoretical understanding of general interpretive processes? To some extent, the criteria developed in Chapter 3 for post-positivist theorists can also be applied here. That is, general interpretive theories will, to a large degree, be judged in terms of their accuracy, consistency, scope, simplicity, and fruitfulness. However, because these general interpretive theories specifically aim for an understanding of the everyday life world, it is important to ask an additional important question in evaluating theory. Collin (1985) has situated this question in terms of a comparison between theoretical understanding and common-sense understanding. That is, most people can provide a common-sense explanation for why children raise their hands for attention in a classroom, why different people comfort grieving friends in particular ways, or how disputants come to a common understanding in a conflict. Given the existence of these naive theories of the everyday life world, an important additional test for a general interpretive theory is whether the theory can provide a depth of understanding that goes beyond those common-sense understandings. As Collin (1985) suggests, the quality of a general interpretive theory can be judged in terms of "whether we can attain . . . systematic, integrative knowledge of human action of a kind from which we may derive more powerful interpretive accounts of action" (p. xvi).

Grounded Theory

In our discussion of interpretive epistemology, we emphasized several crucial benchmarks for the generation of knowledge within interpretive scholarship. Interpretive scholars reject universal laws and instead strive to gain local knowledge. Interpretive scholars reject the primacy of a priori social structures and believe that meaning emerges from interaction. Interpretive scholars reject the desirability or possibility of separating the knower from the known both in everyday life and in social research. Interpretivists' fundamental allegiances to these related concepts of local, emergent, and intersubjective knowledge have led to a kind of theorizing that is in sharp contrast to the work of post-positivist theorists and is even quite different from the general interpretive theories described in the preceding section. The term **grounded theory** was coined by sociologists Barney Glaser and Anselm Strauss (1967), and since then the grounded theory approach has gained currency in a number of social science disciplines (see, e.g., Lincoln & Guba, 1985; Strauss & Corbin, 1997). In this section, we consider both the function and form of grounded theory and the ways in which it is generally evaluated.

Theoretical Function and Form   In their original explication of the grounded theory approach, Glaser and Strauss begin by arguing that most social researchers (e.g., scholars in the post-positivist tradition) are typically far more interested in theory verification than in theory generation. They suggest that this emphasis is an unfortunate one that has hampered the development of knowledge about a variety of social processes. Allegiance to existing and often grand theories, Glaser and Strauss contend, can blind researchers to important processes in social life. To remedy this situation, Glaser and Strauss argue that "to generate theory . . . we suggest as the best approach an initial, systematic discovery of the theory from the data of social research" (Glaser & Strauss, 1967, p. 3). In this statement, we see the two

critical facets of grounded theory: First, it is driven by empirical observation or grounded in data (hence the label), and second, it is produced in a systematic way.

Because the creation of grounded theory is an empirical endeavor, the theory creation process is intimately connected with methodological issues of data collection and analysis. Space does not allow a full explication of grounded theory methods (see Glaser & Strauss, 1967, and, especially, Corbin & Strauss, 1990), but a few key points about grounded theory methods can be highlighted here. Not surprisingly, these issues reflect the epistemological stance highlighted earlier—that knowledge generation is a local, emergent, and intersubjective process.

First, the development of grounded theory depends on the consideration of multiple data sources. These data sources might include interviews, participant or nonparticipant observation, archival data and records, surveys, popular press accounts, past theory and research, and the theorist's own insights and evaluations. It should be noted that all these components are treated as data within a grounded theory investigation. For example, in a grounded theory investigation of adolescent communicative attempts to resist drugs, data for the study could include

- interviews with teens about their experiences in being offered drugs
- observation of real or simulated drug resistance interactions
- past theory and research on compliance gaining, compliance resisting, and adolescent behavior
- popular press and fictionalized accounts of drug resistance among adolescents
- the theorist's (and others') personal experiences with drug resistance attempts

A grounded theory investigation will not see all of these data sources as necessarily equal in the generation of theory. Indeed, in the development of grounded theory, all data sources must be evaluated in a systematic and careful manner. However, no particular source of data (e.g., past theory and research) is given primacy in the analysis and no particular source of data (e.g., personal experience) is purposefully excluded from analysis.

How, then, is theory generated in the grounded theory method? Theorists in this tradition place a strong emphasis on the notion of a *comparative process*. Both terms in this phrase are crucially important. First, grounded theory involves multiple points of comparison: Indeed, the development of grounded theory is often referred to as a constant comparison method. Data are never considered in isolation but rather in reference to other data and to conceptual categories that have emerged from those data. Specific activities of comparison include open coding, axial coding, selection coding, theoretical sampling, the creation of conditional matrices, and the creation of memos and diagrams (see Corbin & Strauss, 1990, for a full discussion of these procedures). Second, the generation of grounded theory is clearly an ongoing process in which there is a continual intertwining—even a blurring—of data collection, analysis, and theorizing. Orona (1990) describes in great detail how interviews, observation, coding, memo writing, diagramming, and conceptualizing were constant and integrative parts of her development of a theory of temporality and identity loss among Alzheimer's patients. Thus, as Glaser and Strauss (1967) originally stated, the "strategy of comparative analysis for generating theory puts a high emphasis on *theory as process*; that is, theory as an ever-developing entity, not as a perfected product" (p. 32).

The product that comes out of this process (i.e., a grounded theory) can take a variety of forms. It could take a form similar to that of a post-positivist theory (e.g., a well-codified set of propositions). Or a grounded theory could be presented in a narrative form, a running commentary that weaves together relevant conceptual categories and how they fit together. Most typically, a grounded theory will take the less formal and narrative tack, and Glaser and Strauss think this is appropriate. "The discussional form of formulating theory gives a feeling

of 'ever-developing' to the theory, allows it to become quite rich, complex, and dense, and makes its fit and relevance easy to comprehend" (Glaser & Strauss, 1967, p. 32).

Grounded theory could consider a wide variety of topical issues, though these theories will not be grand theories that attempt to understand an extremely wide range of communicative behavior. Within communication, a distinction could be drawn between *context theories* (e.g., a theory about decision-making groups or a theory about pornographic material on the Internet) and *process theories* (e.g., a theory about conflict management or identity formation). Grounded theories in either of these areas are valuable. Indeed, many theorists in this tradition cross context and process in considering, for instance, the social construction of identity in online Internet communities (Markham, 1998). By beginning with this relatively specific type of grounded theory, the scholarly community can then work to generate related theories of identity construction (i.e., a process theory) and computer-mediated communities (i.e., a context theory).

Criteria for Evaluation Because research methods and theory development are intimately connected in the grounded theory approach, it is impossible to evaluate theory without considering the research process itself. As Glaser and Strauss (1967) argue,

> The adequacy of a theory for sociology cannot be divorced from the process by which it is generated. . . . We also believe that other canons for assessing a theory, such as logical consistency, clarity, parsimony, density, scope, integration, as well as its fit and its ability to work, are also significantly dependent on how the theory was generated. (p. 5)

Thus, evaluating a grounded theory involves evaluating both the process through which it was generated and the form in which it is presented to the scholarly community. Indeed, in a book entitled *Grounded Theory in Practice* (Strauss & Corbin, 1997), the editors comment on each theoretical contribution by assessing both the process of theory development through

Table 4.1	Criteria for the Empirical Grounding of a Grounded Theory
Criterion #1: Are concepts generated?	
Criterion #2: Are the concepts systematically related?	
Criterion #3: Are there many conceptual linkages and are the categories well developed? Do they have conceptual density?	
Criterion #4: Is much variation built into the theory?	
Criterion #5: Are the broader conditions that affect the phenomenon under study built into its explanation?	
Criterion #6: Has process been taken into account?	
Criterion #7: Do the theoretical findings seem significant and to what extent?	

Source: Adapted from Corbin & Strauss (1990).

research and the presentation of the theory in the written monograph. For example, in evaluating one contribution, the editors note,

> She has used several aspects of grounded theory—namely, constant comparative analysis, development of theoretical concepts and statements, and theoretical sampling, as well as the usual supporting techniques of theoretical coding and memoing. She has woven in as necessary presentational elements much factual detail, both illustrative and persuasive, and a fair amount of quoted material. (Strauss & Corbin, 1997, pp. 1–2)

Beyond this general idea that the evaluation of process and product cannot be divorced in a grounded theory investigation, scholars have developed a number of specific criteria that are useful in the assessment process. Corbin and Strauss (1990) provide seven criteria that relate specifically to methodological issues in the development of grounded theory (p. 253) and also a series of more general questions that can be asked about the quality of both the process and the product of grounded theory. This set of criteria is presented in Table 4.1. These criteria suggest that a good grounded theory is one that is conceptually rich, with well-developed con-

cepts and categories, and connections developed between the concepts and categories. Such a grounded theory is situated, in both time and space, by considering the relationship of concepts to broader conditions and to change over time. Finally, a good grounded theory is meaningful to the individual theorist, to other researchers, and to the larger social system in which the theory is generated.

■ SUMMARY

In this chapter, we considered both the historical roots of interpretive theory and the way interpretive theorists work in enhancing our understanding of communicative interaction. The contemporary works of general and grounded theorists are in sharp contrast both in form and in function, as theorists in the general mode attempt to gain an understanding of the processes through which communicative interaction functions and theorists in the grounded mode seek local understandings of emergent communicative processes. However, all these theorists begin from the same base—a philosophical belief in the importance of communication as an intersubjective creator of symbolic meaning. It is these ontological foundations—a belief in social constructionism and the central role of communication in the social construction process—that joins theorists under the interpretive umbrella.

Key Terms

Cartesian dualism
German idealism
verstehen
hermeneutics
transcendental phenomenology
social phenomenology
symbolic interactionism
nominalist ontology
social constructionist ontology
subjectivist epistemology
understanding
explanation
"genuine-because" motives
"in-order-to" motives
grounded theory

Discussion Questions

1. What has each of the founding perspectives discussed in this chapter (hermeneutics, phenomenology, and symbolic interactionism) contributed to interpretive theory as it is practiced today? How do these founding perspectives overlap?
2. What are the implications of the epistemology of interpretive theory for the methodology that might be used to develop interpretive theories? How does a researcher look for emergent understanding from an insider's perspective?
3. How should interpretive theory be judged? Are criteria for judging interpretive theories different for general interpretive theories than for grounded interpretive theories? Why or why not?
4. Think about an activity you participate in on a regular basis. Then think about how you might go about developing a grounded theory about behavior and communication in that activity. What methods would you use to develop the theory? What kinds of concepts do you think you might include in the theory?

5 Critical Perspectives on Theory Development

In Chapters 3 and 4 we discussed perspectives on theory building that are distinct from each other in many fundamental respects. Post-positivist and interpretive theorists differ in their ontological and epistemological foundations. That is, these approaches to theory see the social world in vitally different ways and look to gain knowledge about that social world in ways that differ both in fundamental assumptions and in methodological practices. Indeed, after reading Chapters 3 and 4, you might conclude that post-positivist theorists and interpretive theorists of communication have little or nothing in common. However, as we will see in this chapter, which introduces a third perspective on theory development, post-positivists and interpretivists do share some basic ideas about the role of theory in scholarly endeavors.

Interpretivists and post-positivists see the social world in different lights, and they seek different kinds of knowledge about that social world. They agree, however, that the goal of theory is to gain understanding (from the interpretive perspective) or explanation (from the post-positivist perspective) of communication and society. That is, the goal of theory is a *representational* one, though the representations developed in these two schools of thought have different ontological and epistemological foundations. The representations in post-positivist theory are constructed as generalizable and

causal explanations of communication phenomena. The representations in interpretive theory are local understandings of meaning developed through the interactions of social actors and the interpretations of the researcher regarding these interactive contexts. For both groups, the mirror metaphor is an apt one because the theorist strives to represent the nature of communication in the social world.

Many people question this scholarly goal of representation. Some of these questioners are current thinkers, postmodern scholars (e.g., Rorty, 1979) who see social reality as ultimately fragmented. In such a world, all representations are ultimately illusory ones. For these theorists, "postmodern connotes a world in which there is nothing—no things at all in the traditional sense of a universe of objects separate and distinct from their representation" (Holstein & Gubrium, 2000). But questions about the representational function of theory did not begin recently. Indeed, since the late 1800s, some scholars have advocated theory as an activist force in society. Theorists in the **critical theory** tradition feel a responsibility not to simply represent the social world (though they would see representation as an important first step in the theoretical process) but to work as active agents of reform and radical change. It is this perspective on theory that we consider in this chapter. We begin by looking at the work of Karl

Marx, who many see as the starting point for most critical perspectives on theory. We then outline a strand of critical theory that has had a substantial impact on social research, and the field of communication in particular, the Frankfurt School. After this historical overview, we consider aspects of critical theory as it has developed in communication studies and related fields of social research. In explicating this critical perspective, our discussion of the ontological, epistemological, and axiological commitments of critical theorists is illustrated with particular attention to the work of Jurgen Habermas and Anthony Giddens. Finally, we discuss two contemporary strands of scholarship in communication that fall under the general umbrella of critical theory—cultural studies and feminist studies.

■ HISTORICAL ROOTS OF CRITICAL THEORY

In Chapter 4, we discussed German idealism and the influence it has had on social research. This tradition, founded by Immanuel Kant, argues that humans engage in interpretive processes that are central to our understanding of the social world. Kantian philosophy was developed by theorists such as Husserl, Dilthey, Weber, and others and has served as the philosophical framework for the interpretive perspectives on theory development that we discussed in Chapter 4.

Another of Kant's followers, Georg Wilhelm Hegel (1770–1831), developed these idealist philosophies in another direction. Hegel emphasized both the dialectical relationship between individual subjective experience and the outside world and the tension inherent in that relationship. According to Burrell and Morgan (1979), "Hegel presents human beings as living in a world characterised by a constant interplay between individual consciousness and its objectification in the external world" (p. 280). For Hegel, this relationship between the individual and the external world was historically situated and depended on the epoch in which an individual lived. Morrow (1994) explains, "For all his wisdom Aristotle could not criticize Athenian slavery because he was a prisoner of the 'spirit' of his time (his *Zeitgeist,* as Hegel would say); only later, with the development of the universal 'right of man,' did this criticism become possible" (p. 94). Hegel's line of thinking influenced many students of the day. Many of these, known as Right Hegelians, wed Hegel's philosophy to a very conservative political position. Other followers, known as Left Hegelians or Young Hegelians, went in a more idealistic direction—sometimes known as radical humanism—and led to currents of thought still prominent in critical approaches to theory. The most noteworthy of these Young Hegelians was Karl Marx.

The Influence of Marxism

Karl Marx (1818–1883) had a wide-ranging intellectual life and has been, of course, extremely influential in a variety of political and academic arenas. Writings in both his early and his later careers have had a strong influence on critical theory, and we deal briefly with both of these periods. In our discussion, we consider a vast simplification of Marx's ideas and highlight only the concepts that have particular relevance for the development of critical theory in communication.

The "early" Marx was influenced by Hegel's ideas about the tension between internal subjective experience and the external world and by the historical nature of that tension. Marx believed that the external world was one that was humanly created and then reified and made to seem objective and external to the subjective individual. This process of objectification and reification, according to Marx, sometimes served as a fundamental source of **alienation.** As Burrell and Morgan (1979) argue, "Marx, in particular, started from the premise of the alienation of man. He saw the society of his day as dominating human experience; objectified social creations reflected back upon man as an alienating force, dominating his essential being and nature" (pp. 281–282). This general notion of alienation suggests that individuals become alienated when "the institutional order is assumed to have taken on a life of its own independently of human intentions and needs; society is perceived as controlling human behavior" (Seidman, 1994, p. 130).

The "later" Marx specified further the nature of alienation in the historical epoch in which he lived—during the growing prevalence of capitalism and industrialization. Specifically, in later years, Marx moved away from an idealist position that emphasized the role of humans in the creation and reification of their social world and the dialectic tension and alienation that emerged from this process. Instead, after his epistemological break, Marx expounded on a more realist or materialist interpretation of the social world. The heart of this work was the distinction between the substructure of society and the superstructure of society. The **substructure** consisted of the economic and production base of society and included both the **modes of production** (i.e., the economic conditions that undergird the production process, such as capitalism or communism) and the **means of production** (i.e., the processes through which products are made and services rendered, including technology and labor). Marx posited that the economic conditions of capitalist society were marked by the class distinctions between the bourgeoisie (i.e., those who controlled the modes and means of production) and the proletariat (i.e., those who were engaged in production for wages). These basic economic and class distinctions are the substructure of society in Marxist theory. In contrast, the **superstructure** of society was seen as noneconomic factors such as religion, politics, art, and literature.

Two factors regarding the substructure and superstructure are important to consider. First, in conceptualizing these social structure factors, Marx was moving to a realist position regarding ontology and epistemology. That is, the "late" Marx saw the substructure and superstructure of society as material factors that could exist in agreement or contradiction with each other and

could be causally connected. Further, in this realist framework, these structures and the relations between them could be studied in scientific ways. Second, Marx believed there to be a specific relationship between substructure and superstructure, such that factors in the substructure (i.e., modes and means of production) were seen as creating an "unnatural condition whereby all humans are prevented from realizing their fullest nature" (Huspek, 1997, p. 267). As Deetz and Mumby (1990) summarize, "In Marx's view, industrialization brought with it dehumanization and alienation from work and work products. . . . [T]he division of labor, the treatment of labor as a commodity, and the separation of the individual from his or her product produced a fragmented, lost person, estranged from his or her own production activities" (p. 20). Marx saw industrialization and technology as alienating as part of a capitalist system in which the surplus labor of the proletariat serves as profit for the bourgeoisie. As Surber (1998) explains, "Anyone who has worked for an hourly wage at some repetitive and mechanical task will realize not only how one's own physical activity can come to appear alien but also how easily she or he can be replaced by another person willing to do the same work" (p. 77).

Thus, both the early and the late Marx developed views of the relationship between the individual and society. For the early Marx, this relationship was a socially constructed one fraught with dialectic tension. For the late Marx, the relationship was a real and material one in which economic conditions of the substructure influenced superstructure factors, and both substructure and superstructure elements caused alienation and estrangement. For both the early and the late Marx, however, this imbalance between the individual and the external world was untenable and required **critique** in order to reveal fundamental truths about the human condition. As Marx (1967) noted, "What we have to accomplish at this time is all the more clear: relentless criticism of all existing conditions, relentless in the sense that the criticism is not afraid of its findings, and just as little afraid of the conflict with the powers that be" (p. 212). The necessity of critique, and the nature of critique, was further developed by a group of intellectuals that have come to be known as the **Frankfurt School.** The work of these scholars is considered next.

The Frankfurt School

In 1923, the Institute for Social Research was founded in Frankfurt, Germany. A number of scholars were associated with the Institute, including Max Horkheimer (who became director of the Institute in 1930), Herbert Marcuse, Theodor W. Adorno, Erich Fromm, and Walter Benjamin. This collection of scholars soon became known as the Frankfurt School and their intellectual commitments known as Critical Theory (in its capitalized form). In summarizing the focus of the Frankfurt School, Huspek (1997) notes, "The school itself is best thought of as a loose collection of scholars, often in disagreement with one another, but all committed nevertheless to the critical analysis of society's current state as well as to the development of normative alternatives which might enable humans to transcend their unhappy situation through critical thought and action" (p. 266).

The Frankfurt School clearly grew out of Marxist ideology in its emphasis on critique. However, the Critical Theory of the Frankfurt School departed in several ways from orthodox Marxism of that time period. Most important, Frankfurt School scholars did not embrace the materialist theorizing characteristic of Marx in his later years. Thus, the Frankfurt School did not follow the school of scientific Marxism, which attempted to use positivistic research methods to determine the laws through which the economic substructure was related to the cultural and psychological superstructure (Morrow, 1994). Neither did Frankfurt School scholars advocate political revolution as the primary means for achieving emancipation. At this time, "Marxism had become a closed system in which adherents, rather than reflecting upon the historical origins and application of discourse with-

in the social world, signaled and tested their affiliation through the recitation of dogma" (Farrell & Aune, 1979, p. 95). Scholars in the Frankfurt School eschewed these dogmatic tendencies and instead returned to the early Hegelian Marx in advocating a "revolution of consciousness" (Burrell & Morgan, 1979, p. 291).

Critical theorists, then, were embarking on a journey of "revolutionary praxis," which would first involve "the critical self-consciousness of historical subjects in a struggle . . . fought in the realm of culture and consciousness" (Pollock & Cox, 1991, p. 174). From the base of this critique, it was then hoped that scholars could work toward liberation through discourse by creating "a linguistic space free and protected from the contaminations of commercial culture" (Pollock & Cox, 1991, p. 174). That is, the Frankfurt School sought to make political theory itself a moral force working toward human emancipation (Seidman, 1994). Some of the central concepts that guided the critical project of the Frankfurt School—including **totality, consciousness,** alienation, and **critique**—are summarized in Table 5.1.

History intervened on the critical project of the Frankfurt School, however, with Hitler's rise to power in Germany and the rise of Stalinism in the Soviet Union. Many Frankfurt School intellectuals, including Horkheimer, Adorno, and Marcuse, left Germany for the United States. During this period, the work of these Critical Theory scholars "was marked by an attitude of pessimism and the apparent need for practical retrenchment" (Farrell & Aune, 1979, p. 100). Indeed, Morrow argues that the disillusionment of this period led many intellectuals away from Critical Theory and eclipsed its influence as a research program.

In more recent decades, however, the work of Frankfurt School scholars has been rediscovered and sometimes reinvented. The enduring tenets of the Frankfurt School—that a wide range of social structures and practices can be subject to critique—has served as the base for critical theorists operating in many social disciplines,

Table 5.1	Key Concepts from Critical Theory

Critical Theory of the Frankfurt School: Central Concepts and Orientations

Totality

The notion that any understanding of society must embrace in their entirety the objective and subjective worlds which characterize a given epoch. Totality embraces everything; it has no boundary. An understanding of this totality must precede an understanding of its elements, since the whole dominates the parts in an all-embracing sense.

Consciousness

The force which ultimately creates and sustains the social world. Consciousness is internally generated but influenced by the forms which it assumes through the process of objectification and the dialectic between subjective and objective worlds.

Alienation

The state in which, in certain totalities, a cognitive wedge is driven between man's consciousness and the objectified social world, so that man sees what are essentially the creations of his own consciousness in the form of a hard, dominating, external reality. This wedge is the wedge of alienation, which divorces man from his true self and hinders the fulfillment of his potentialities as a human being.

Critique

In their critique of contemporary society, critical theorists focus upon the form and sources of alienation, which they see as inhibiting the possibilities of true human fulfillment. The various exponents of this perspective approach it in somewhat different ways, at varying levels of generality.

Source: From Burrell & Morgan (1979).

including communication. In the next section, we consider the ontological, epistemological, and axiological frameworks for the critical approach to communication theorizing today.

■ CONTEMPORARY CRITICAL THEORY

In Chapters 3 and 4, we argued that understanding a particular approach to social theorizing requires an understanding of the metatheoretical commitments that guide theorists working from that perspective. In this chapter, we again consider the role of metatheory—the theorist's underlying beliefs about reality, knowledge, and values that structure and guide scholarship. As with the post-positivist and interpretive approaches, commitments to these metatheoretical positions are not unanimous among theorists working in the critical tradition. However,

we will try to sketch the broad strokes of the framework in which most critical communication theorists work.

In discussing the metatheoretical positions of critical theorists, this section draws especially on two key contemporary scholars, Jurgen Habermas and Anthony Giddens. Habermas is the most forceful and influential spokesperson today for the Frankfurt School tradition. Some of his most important works include *Knowledge and Human Interests* (1971), *Communication and the Evolution of Society* (1979), and *The Theory of Communicative Action* (1984). Giddens and his structuration theory have emerged since the mid 1970s as a central ontological position informing theorists from a variety of perspectives but especially critical theory. Giddens's key works include *New Rules of Sociological Method* (1976), *Critical Problems in Social Theory* (1979), and *The Constitution of Society* (1984). The specific ideas of both Habermas and Giddens are used here to explain the more general metatheoretical commitments of contemporary critical theorists.

Ontological Commitments

Issues of ontology refer to questions of reality. For social researchers and theorists, ontological commitments involve discussions of the nature of the social world or, as Outhwaite and Bottomore (1993) put it, "the entities posited or presupposed by some particular substantive scientific theory" (p. 429). As we discussed in previous chapters, ontological views can range from the realist to the nominalist, with post-positivists generally taking a tempered realist stance and interpretivists taking a more subjective stance informed by nominalism and work on the social construction of reality.

As our historical discussion of Marx and the Frankfurt School suggests, critical approaches can, and have, taken a variety of ontological positions. For example, the late Marx and his followers who take a scientific Marxist position clearly favor more objective views of reality in which the world is seen in material terms that distinguish between substructure and superstructure factors. This ontological view is realist, in that it sees these societal structures as relatively fixed and with clear causal force on other societal processes. That is, the economic conditions of the modes and means of production have force on superstructure conditions such as culture and politics. In contrast, scholars following the early Marx would take a much more subjective view informed by the German idealist emphasis on the centrality of the individual spirit. Most critical theorists today would probably place themselves on this more subjective side of the ontological scale, but their position is usually a complex one informed by ideas about the importance of reification and objectification in the social world. The work of Anthony Giddens exemplifies many of these ideas.

It has been argued that Giddens's structuration theory should be viewed as a system of ontology (Banks & Riley, 1993), and we explore the ontological implications of this complex theory here (we return to other aspects and implications of structuration theory in Chapters 12 and 13). Giddens first distinguishes between the ontological status of the natural world and of the social world, arguing for the **double hermeneutic** of social life. This concept "refers to the way the structures of the social world were constructed originally by human agents, whereas those of nature were not" (Morrow, 1994, p. 156). Thus, theorists and researchers must recognize the ontological distinction between nature and society. Structuration theory, then, describes the ontological complexities of social life.

According to Giddens, social life must be considered in terms of both structure and agency. Structures are the rules, norms, and beliefs that characterize the social world. Agency is the behavior and interaction of humans within that world. A central tenet of structuration theory is that the relationship between structure and agency should be defined in terms of a **duality of structure.** This concept argues that structures are produced by human agents but that these structures at the same time are the medium in which agency operates. According to Giddens (1976), "It is this dual aspect of structure, as both inferred from observation of human doings, yet as also operating as a medium whereby those doings are made possible, that has to be grasped through the notions of structuration and reproduction" (p. 122).

An example can serve to illustrate (though rather simplistically) this notion of duality of structure. As you sit in a college classroom, certain structures guide your interaction. You know you should not talk while the professor is lecturing. You know you should raise your hand to secure an opportunity to talk in class. You know that once you have the floor, certain topics of talk are encouraged (e.g., questions about the lecture, comments on its applicability to specific life issues) and certain topics are discouraged (e.g., irrelevant comments on the weather, or the query "Will this be on the test?"). These rules and structures serve as the medium in which your interaction occurs.

However, the concept of the duality of structure reminds us that these rules were created by interaction. Over the years, rules were developed through repetitive interaction in college classrooms. This notion that our interaction has socially constructed the structures we interact has several implications. First, the duality of structure suggests that a variety of structures can be produced—and reproduced—in human interaction. That is, we can create different sets of rules for interacting in a large freshman lecture hall and in a small graduate seminar. Second, the duality of structure suggests that these structures can be changed by human interaction. Professors and students can use their agency, with perhaps varying levels of consciousness, to produce new structures in which classroom interaction takes place. For example, a professor could purposefully change the rules by calling on students who are not raising their hands. Students could change the culture of the classroom by continually delving into topics not explicitly considered on the course syllabus. Thus, though structures guide our interaction and are often reproduced by that interaction, we can also produce new structures that will have varying levels of influence on subsequent interaction.

The ontological position outlined by Giddens's structuration theory is representative of the position taken by many critical theorists, in that it emphasizes the complex and dialectical relationship between structure and action. In some ways, it recalls the early roots of critical theorizing, Marx's interpretation of Hegel's "historicized" individual who is conditioned by the era in which he or she lives, in unavoidable—and often unnoticed—ways. Indeed, Giddens (1984) emphasizes this point in his comment that structuration theory is "an extended reflection upon a celebrated and oft-quoted phrase to be found in Marx. . . . 'Men make history, but not in circumstances of their own choosing'" (p. xxi).

It has been argued, though, that Giddens's ontology privileges agency over structure. Huspek (1993) makes this point in two respects.

First, Giddens emphasizes that structures do not just constrain action but also enable it. As Giddens (1979) states, "Structure . . . is not to be conceptualized as a barrier to action, but as essentially involved in its production" (p. 70). Second, as noted earlier, Giddens emphasizes the ability of agents to purposefully and knowledgeably influence the structures in which they interact. As we will see, his ontological privileging of the agent over the structure has important implications for the axiological commitments of critical theorists.

Epistemological Commitments

Epistemology refers to the nature of knowledge and how knowledge is to be gathered and used in the social world. Jurgen Habermas has delved most specifically into the epistemological commitments of critical theory in his continuing development of the line of thought instituted by Frankfurt School theorists. Habermas was interested in showing the links between power and knowledge by laying out a "politics of epistemology" (see Mumby, 2000, p. 71). Habermas's most direct contribution to this epistemological position is his distinction among three so-called knowledge constitutive interests in society: the empirical-analytical interest, the hermeneutic-historical interest, and the critical-emancipatory interest (Habermas, 1971). In defining these knowledge constitutive interests, Habermas wants to "make us wary of the claim that knowledge is identified by a single interest" (Morrow, 1994, p. 146). That is, he emphasizes that scientific knowledge is not the only kind of knowledge that should count in the world.

The **empirical-analytical cognitive interest** is rooted in the technical desire to exert control over the physical and social world. This cognitive interest is associated with the post-positivist approach to research and theory discussed in Chapter 3. It argues that knowledge should consist of deterministic and general laws of nature and society that can be used to gain technical control over both physical and social processes. The **hermeneutic-historical cognitive interest** is rooted in the desire to understand the uniqueness of human activities. This interest, associated with interpretive approaches to theory discussed in Chapter 4, sees positivist approaches as reductionistic and believes that knowledge should be based on emergent and local texts that are historically situated. The interest here is a practical one in that it is rooted in the daily practices necessary for human survival.

Finally, the **critical-emancipatory cognitive interest** sees knowledge as a process of self-reflection through which historical constraints and exigencies can be revealed. As Mumby (2000) states, this interest reflects "the human proclivity for self-reflection leading to autonomy and empowerment" (p. 71). Morrow (1994) argues that, in an epistemological sense, the critical-emancipatory interest is related to the hermeneutic-historical interest in that both see knowledge and meaning as socially and historically situated. However, critical theorists introduce a political dynamic into this historical-hermeneutic representation through the concepts of ideology and power.

Ideology refers to "the taken-for-granted assumptions about reality that influence perceptions of situations and events" (Deetz & Kersten, 1983, p. 162). This definition has several important facets. First, ideology refers to more than a set of attitudes and beliefs. Rather, ideology shapes our understanding of what exists, what is good, and what is possible (Therborn, 1980, p. 18). Second, ideology involves assumptions that are rarely questioned or scrutinized. For example, we rarely question the hierarchical structuring of the teacher-student relationship. Third, by shaping our view of the world, ideologies can also influence our behaviors.

For critical theorists, though, ideology is not a neutral concept but is intimately tied to systems of power and domination (Mumby, 1989). This leads us to the concept of **hegemony,** developed by Gramsci (1971). Hegemony refers to a process in which a dominant group leads another group to accept subordination as the norm (Hall, 1985). It is "manufactured consent" (Habermas, 1971) in which individuals in socie-ty willingly adopt and reinforce the dominant power structure. This notion of hegemonic control is central to the stance of scholars within critical social research today. As Mumby (2000) points out, Marx described relationships between the social classes "primarily in coercive terms with the emphasis on capitalism as an intrinsically exploitative political and economic system," while "subsequent generations of critical scholars have attempted to explain the exercise of power as a dynamic process of consent" (p. 70).

Thus, scholars working within the critical-emancipatory interest see the emergent historical subject as one shaped by the power of ideology and hegemony. By introducing these concepts, the critical theorist transforms the role of knowledge into one that requires realization and change of these ideological and hegemonic structures. Morrow (1994) argues that the difference between the critical-emancipatory interest and the hermeneutic-historical interest "involves a different attitude toward meanings: Rather than merely describe and understand them, the objective is to criticize and transform them" (p. 148). Thus, the epistemological position of critical theory, as explained by Habermas (1971), sees knowledge as serving the interests of change and emancipation: "In self-reflection, knowledge for the sake of knowledge comes to coincide with the interest in autonomy and responsibility" (p. 197). This epistemological position is related directly to axiology, the metatheoretical area we examine next.

Axiological Commitments

In its axiological commitments, critical theory most clearly breaks from post-positivist and interpretive theorists. As discussed at the beginning of this chapter, these approaches to scholarship see theory as taking a representational role, though the representations provided by post-positivist and interpretive theories differ in many respects. In representational modes of scholarship, values in the research process should be excised or controlled (i.e., the post-positivist position) or acknowledged and explored (i.e., the interpretive position) but never really acted upon. Critical theorists turn sharply from these axiological positions: "Critical theory springs from an assumption that we live amid a world of pain, that much can be done to alleviate that pain, and that theory has a crucial role to play in that process" (Poster, 1989, p. 3). Thus, for critical theorists, values are not to be excised and controlled or even acknowledged and explored. Rather, values should guide scholarship, and theorists should work as change agents in supporting those values.

Once again, the works of Giddens and Habermas are instructive in understanding the axiological position of critical theorists. In our discussion of ontology, we considered Giddens's duality of structure and the privilege he gives to agency within this dialectic (Huspek, 1993). In this dialectic, agents can exercise the power to change social structure, instantiating the transformative value that is so central to the axiology of critical theorists. Power is seen as "the capability of the actor to intervene in a series of events so as to alter their course; as such it is the 'can' that mediates between intentions or wants and the actual realization of the outcome sought after" (Giddens, 1976, p. 111). Thus, the ontology of critical theory (i.e., the duality of structure) serves as the basis for the axiology of critical theory (i.e., the transformative and emancipatory potential of social actors and, more specifically, theorists).

Habermas is even more expansive on the emancipatory role of critical theory. It is instructive to consider a metaphor that Habermas uses to represent the relationship between the critical theorist and society. Following Frankfurt School scholars who have incorporated ideas from Freud into their theorizing (see Farrell & Aune, 1979), Habermas compares the emancipation process to the process of psychotherapy. In this analogy, the critical theorist is the analyst and society is the patient. A psychoanalyst's job is to help a patient break down resistance and gain a deep level of self-understanding. Bern-

stein (1976) notes, "The success of therapy ultimately depends not on the analyst's understanding of the patient, but on the extent to which the patient by his own self-reflection can appropriate this analytic understanding and dissolve his own resistances" (p. 201). Similarly, according to Habermas, the role of the critical theorist is to reveal the social structures and processes that have led to ideological hegemony. When alienated people are able to consider their condition critically, emancipation will be possible. The process of psychoanalysis also has implications for the analyst (i.e., the critical theorist). As Surber (1998) argues, "In the process [of this kind of change], the would-be social analyst should also gain self-reflexive knowledge of her or his own propensities for being trapped in . . . distorted discourse, hence initiating the process of her or his own emancipation from them" (p. 151).

Habermas goes beyond this psychoanalytic metaphor, however, in considering how emancipation is possible within the critical project (see Habermas, 1979, for this development in his work). Habermas has proposed the concept of universal pragmatics in which emancipation will be achieved when interaction occurs within an **ideal speech situation.** Habermas, relying to some extent on speech act theory (see Chapter 9), proposes that the **communicative competence** of interactants will determine the extent to which an ideal speech situation is realized. The concept of an ideal speech situation argues that the human interest in emancipation is not mere fancy or whimsy. Rather, Habermas believes that the emancipatory interest is apprehended a priori through a process of logical reflection. In Habermas's theory of communicative competence, he argues that every act of symbolic communication prefigures and presupposes the values of truth, freedom, and justice. Thus, because these values are not arbitrary, they can serve as a foundation for critique.

This critique is not always put into play in everyday action, of course. As Huspek (1991) argues, "Competence is an ideal which is rarely if ever fully realized in practice, but which is immanently present among all speakers, in all speech communities" (p. 227). Thus, in order to fully realize the values of critique, speakers must communicate in competent ways that draw on those values of truth, freedom, and justice. Communicative competence consists of claims regarding the comprehensibility of the utterance, the truth of the utterance's content, the legitimacy of the content, and the veracity of the speaker. When these claims are realized, it is possible to approach an ideal speech situation in which emancipation is possible. As Bernstein (1976) summarizes,

> Ideal speech is that form of discourse in which there is no other compulsion but the compulsion of argumentation itself; where there is a genuine symmetry among the participants involved, allowing a universal interchangeability of dialogue roles; where no form of domination exists. (p. 212)

Summary

Critical theorists work from a metatheoretical framework that is not always unitary but that is very different from the foundational commitments of post-positivist and interpretive theorists. Though ontological commitments vary, most critical theorists today subscribe to a social constructionist ontology: The ontology of Giddens's structuration theory with its duality of structure is a prime example of this position. Epistemologically, critical theorists are involved in the critical-emancipatory cognitive interest described by Habermas. This epistemology emphasizes that knowledge structures are ideologically formed and may involve hegemonic processes of power, control, and alienation. Finally, axiologically, critical theorists emphasize their role in uncovering alienating power structures and emancipating individuals from those forces.

▪ CRITICAL APPROACHES IN COMMUNICATION

In 1983, a leading journal in the field of communication, *Journal of Communication* (Vol. 33, No. 3, 1983), published a special issue entitled "Fer-

ment in the Field." In this special issue, six U.S. researchers wrote essays that served as a focal point of the discussion. In the first 52 pages of the issue, only two comments considered critical theory (Real, 1984). What was incredible, though, were the commentaries that followed these "keynote articles." As Real (1984) notes, "The most striking characteristic of the remaining 310 pages—more than 86 percent of the issue—is the dominance of the debate about critical communication research and theory" (p. 73). Thus, in the early 1980s, post-positivist research still reigned as the establishment paradigm in communication. However, there was a strong insurgent movement for critical theory, and that insurgency has continued unabated since then.

Today, as we will see in the rest of this book, a variety of specific theories of communication have been informed by the critical approach to theorizing. For example, coordinated management of meaning theory (Chapter 9), dialectical theory (Chapter 11), concertive control theory (Chapter 12), adaptive structuration theory (Chapter 13), standpoint theory (Chapter 16), and muted group theory (Chapter 16) have been influenced—to a greater or lesser extent—by the metatheoretical framework developed in critical theory. In the remainder of this chapter, however, we consider two more general areas of scholarship that have emerged as important influences in communication studies and that are squarely situated within the critical traditions described in this chapter. These two areas of scholarship are **cultural studies** and **feminist studies.** We present these two areas to highlight major areas of scholarship within communication studies that have clear critical commitments. However, we are presenting orienting looks, not detailed presentations, of these complex and multifaceted scholarly perspectives.

Cultural Studies

Cultural studies is a multifaceted intellectual area that explores the ideological interconnections among media, politics, economy, and practices of individuals in a cultural system. A variety of work has served as a foundation for current cultural studies scholars. For example, Hardt (1989) and Corcoran (1989) point to the influence of American pragmatist philosophers such as William James (1842–1910), Charles Peirce (1839–1914), and John Dewey (1859–1952). A pragmatist philosophy emphasizes the connection of philosophy and research to humane and practical problems of society (Tice & Slavens, 1983) and is certainly in line with the action-oriented axiology of critical theorists. The major influence on cultural studies, however, has been work in the British cultural studies tradition, associated with the Centre for Contemporary Cultural Studies at the University of Birmingham. The origins of this work are typically traced to the writings of Richard Hoggart, Raymond Williams, and E. P. Thompson in the 1950s. The leader of this movement since the 1970s has been Stuart Hall (see Morley & Chen, 1996, for critical essays by Hall and other cultural studies theorists).

Scholars in the cultural studies tradition emphasize the complex ways in which a variety of cultural factors are interwoven. As Carey (1983) states,

> Cultural studies attempts to think about the mass media not in relation to this or that isolated problem (violence, pornography, children) or institution (politics, economy, family) or practice (film production, conversation, advertising), but as elements, in Raymond Williams's phrase, "in a whole way of life." Societies, in this view, are complex, differentiated, contradictory, interacting wholes. They are threaded throughout, held in this complex unity, by culture: by the production and reproduction of systems of symbols and messages. (p. 313)

Within this tradition, culture is not a simple or unitary thing. Culture is the weaving of values and beliefs that undergird a particular society or group. Culture is also the practices or ways of life of the group. Most important, culture is the ways in which these values, beliefs, and practices are linked together and interwoven. Following theorists such as Giddens, culture is seen as the

ways in which ideology and values are produced and reproduced through cultural practices.

Following the principles of critical theory outlined earlier in this chapter, this interconnection between cultural structures (e.g., the media, political parties) and cultural practices is not a neutral one. Rather, cultural studies theorists argue that a dominant minority can shape cultural practices through economic and political control of the media and that this shaping of cultural practices is largely hidden from the public. As Corcoran (1989) explains, "A certain social order is maintained through the ability of a dominant minority to fashion public meanings that are then 'naturalized' throughout the whole of mass consciousness" (p. 604). That is, an ideology exists that is produced and reproduced through cultural structures and practices. That ideology is largely one that serves dominant political forces. However, this ideological control is typically hegemonic and consensual. That is, people who are being controlled by the ideology are active participants in the control process. Indeed, cultural theorists argue that the influence of ideological structures involves a "saturation of the whole process of living—to such a depth that the pressures and limits of what can ultimately be seen as a specific economic, political, and cultural system seem to most of us the pressures of simple experience and common sense" (R. Williams, 1977, p. 110).

Consider, for example, the culture of fast food. We are confronted repeatedly with fast-food images—through the plethora of restaurants on our streets and highways, through advertising on television, and through sponsorships of sporting and other cultural events. This fast-food culture is interpenetrated with other cultural experiences, as restaurants offer icons from each new motion picture or current collecting craze as bonuses with meals for children. Fast food is so much a part of modern American culture that we don't think about it much. Indeed, when we do think about it we might appreciate the convenience of the food and the entertainment value for the kids. A cultural studies approach to this phenomenon, however, would consider the ideology of fast-food culture and the ways in which this ideology has been naturalized in American life. This ideology is one of efficiency, of "busy-ness," and of disposability. This ideology supports dominant capitalist interests (e.g., profits for fast-food restaurants, promotion of the movie and television industries), but it has become so engrained in American practices that we don't see the ideological overtones as we appreciate the convenience and perhaps curse the quality of the food.

Even within cultural studies a wide diversity is found in the specific approaches taken by researchers. For example, Grossberg (1984) identifies 10 different positions in cultural studies, divided into three broader categories. Classical approaches in cultural theory focus on the relationship between cultural texts and producers and largely assume the influence of these texts on the audience. These approaches could be seen as subscribing to the late Marxist deterministic distinction between the substructure and superstructure. Hermeneutic approaches consider the complex ways in which cultural texts shape and transform everyday cultural practices. This approach to cultural studies draws more from early Marxist ideas regarding the situated nature of the individual. Finally, discursive approaches concentrate on the overdetermined and contextualized nature of cultural texts. That is, scholars in this framework explore the ways in which cultural texts are inserted into networks of other texts and cultural practices.

Feminist Studies

Like cultural studies, feminist studies encompasses a wide range of viewpoints. Interestingly, some of these viewpoints stand in stark opposition to strands of critical theory in that they see such theory as representing the world in a male way that emphasizes class and power. However, scholars working within the tradition of feminist studies generally share many of the metatheoretical commitments of critical approaches discussed earlier—a social constructionist view of the social world, a belief in the connection between the knower and the known in epistemological systems, and a commitment to social change and emancipation. Given these metatheoretical commitments, feminist studies is included here as an example of critical theorizing in contemporary communication studies.

Feminist scholars begin with the claim that gender is among the most important defining features of social life. Gender influences the way we behave, the way we think, and the way we feel in a manner that is often invisible to us. Further, feminists claim that society has been socially constructed in patriarchal (i.e., male-dominated) ways. This patriarchal nature of society can be seen in all areas of life. Men dominate in the political sphere, they hold most major business posts, they are paid more than women for the same work, they dominate the sporting world, and so on. These are some of the obvious ways in which society is patriarchal. For feminist scholars in communication, however, some of the less obvious ways are important. For example, feminist scholars argue that the very structure of language is patriarchal and oppressive (Penelope, 1990), that the discourse of science on which we base most of our contemporary knowledge claims is patriarchal (Harding, 1987), and that the voices of women in all spheres of life have been systematically silenced or muted (Foss & Foss, 1991). We deal much more completely with this position when we consider muted group theory in Chapter 16. Scholars in this tradition advocate the value of understanding and listening to a feminine voice that is distinct from the masculine and that privileges feminine values of intimacy, nurturing, and relationship over masculine values of rationality, hierarchy, and control (Gilligan, 1982). However, these scholars also recognize that feminist voices do not speak in unison, and feminists often emphasize the importance of appreciating a variety of women's viewpoints that might vary depending on economic, class, and experiential factors.

Beginning with these basic commitments about the nature of society, a variety of schools of thought have developed within the feminist movement. Table 5.2 outlines a wide range of specific approaches to feminism in terms of the roots of female subordination, society's policy toward women, and the corrective action that the feminist theory would require for emancipation. Several more general trends with regard to feminist theorizing can be inferred from this table and from other work. Specifically, four distinct and important strands of feminism are discussed here. These four strands of thought agree with the general tenets of feminism outlined earlier. However, they differ substantially in terms of what action should be taken by feminists, once sources of alienation have been identified and analyzed.

Liberal feminists (sometimes called reform feminists) believe that remedies for gender-based inequities should come from within the current social structure and that women should work to gain their fair share of control in institutions currently run by men. This is a "work within the system" approach to emancipation that many other feminists balk at, arguing that it serves only to support and reinscribe the patriarchal nature of society. **Radical feminists,** in contrast, believe that emancipation for women can occur only through the destruction of male-dominated institutions or through the total separation of women from those institutions. This separatist strategy argues that the current system is clearly broken and cannot be fixed using the rules now in place. Both liberal and radical feminists urge political and action-based responses, though very different ones. For example, after noting that a glass ceiling often exists in organizations, keeping women from promotions to the upper echelons of corporations, radical and liberal feminists might have very different reactions. A liberal feminist would work to change legal opportunities, workplace support, and corporate culture to enhance opportunities for women in today's organizations. In contrast, a radical feminist might advocate the creation of organizations run for and by women, in which the glass ceilings of patriarchal corporations would not exist.

Two other strands of feminism argue for more symbolic courses of action. **Standpoint feminists** emphasize the position that not all women speak with a single voice. We deal much more extensively with standpoint theory in Chapter 16. This theory highlights the fact that, by virtue of very distinct material and experiential existences, women view the world from a different standpoint than men. Further, not all women will have identical standpoints. For example, a middle-class homemaker with a husband and four children, a female executive of a Fortune 500 company, and a young single immigrant mother struggling to get by on government assistance are all women and thus share some common experiences. However, standpoint feminists emphasize that, because of their different social situations, these women all have very different concerns, and all these voices—especially the marginalized ones—need to be heard in academic, social, and political discourse. That is, we should not "essentialize" or "universalize" the experiences of women in claiming that a single and all-encompassing woman's point of view exists. Rather, the experiential and material factors that create specific standpoints should be understood. **Postmodern feminists** also concentrate on symbolic societal themes. However, rather than emphasizing the need to hear women's voices, feminists in this school look at the current discourse in society and attempt to deconstruct those male-dominated meaning systems in order to highlight women's perspectives that are currently hidden.

■ SUMMARY

Critical perspectives on theorizing within communication represent a diverse set of viewpoints. Some perspectives look for sources of alienation and oppression within specific societal structures. For example, theorists from the Frankfurt School look consistently to economic and class explanations, and feminists look consistently to the patriarchal nature of society. These theorists take largely structuralist approaches in their theorizing. Other theorists

Table 5.2	Major Feminist Approaches		
Perspective	Root of female subordination	Society's policy toward women	Feminist demands
Liberal feminism	Exclusion from legal constraints; society's belief in women's inferiority; structural inequalities	Make rules in public sphere; reify oppressive social roles for women	Legal remedies to ensure that women and minorities are not systematically disadvantaged
Marxist feminism	Class structure; ownership of production systems; relationships dominated by power, exchange systems	Devalue women's work; coerce through argument of economic necessity	A world in which women experience themselves as whole; re-education in common goals and interests
Radical feminism	Patriarchy as the root of oppression; importance of female biology; exploitation	Promote sexual aggression and violence through pornography; encourage submissive roles	The affirmation of values men have devalued
Psychoanalytic feminism	Female psyche; socialization	Socialize into beliefs of biological inferiority; project social problems on women's unconscious desires	The understanding that sexuality is socially constructed and that feminist experience begins with women, not fathers
Contemporary socialist feminism	Systemic power relations; domestic labor, need to be wage-earners, class, ideology	Devalue women's work	An appreciation for how women's experiences fit within systems of class and economy
Existential feminism	Society that classifies women as the other	Treat women as outsiders, the other	The encouragement of women to take the risk to develop self
Postmodern feminism	Unified truth promoted by patriarchy	Treat women as the other; unify explanations in dominant ideology	Enhanced diversity through deconstruction and philosophical debate
Cultural feminism	Oppression by male and female values and stereotypes	Maintain stereotypes that constrain human growth	A society in which women's values and forms are revalued

Source: Adapted from Buzzanell (1994).

in the critical school (deriving more from the post-structuralist school) look for more complex and interwoven systems of meaning that can alienate individuals in society. Cultural theorists are examples of this scholarly direction.

Similarly, critical theorists are not united in their preferred response to power differentials

and alienation in society. Some theorists advocate direct political action of either a progressive (e.g., liberal feminist) or a radical (e.g., radical feminist) nature. Others prefer a symbolic course of action in which the surfacing of oppressed voices (e.g., standpoint feminists) or the development of communicative competence and civil discourse (e.g., the work of Habermas) will open avenues for change. Still others prefer a more intellectual approach, in which emancipation and change can come as academic dialogue sets the stage for societal action.

Critical theorists are largely united, however, in the metatheoretical bedrock that supports their scholarship. Today, at least, critical theorists see the world largely as socially constructed and consistently reified. Critical theorists see these reified structures as ideological constructions fraught with power for the dominant and alienation for the oppressed. Critical theorists acknowledge the hegemonic nature of these structures in that the oppressed often play active roles in their own alienation. And critical theorists argue that social scholars and researchers cannot stand by and take a representational role by observing, understanding, and explaining the social world. Rather, critical theorists are united in the need for theories that are normative in their statement of preferred values and that are activist in their commitment to social change. These foundational values—social construction and reification, the power of ideology and hegemony, and the normative role of theory in the process of social change—unite the wide range of academics who take a critical approach to theory.

Key Terms

critical theory
alienation
substructure
modes of production
means of production
superstructure
Frankfurt School
totality
consciousness
critique
double hermeneutic

duality of structure
empirical-analytical cognitive interest
hermeneutic-historical cognitive interest
critical-emancipatory cognitive interest
ideology
hegemony
ideal speech situation
communicative competence
cultural studies
feminist studies
liberal feminists
radical feminists
standpoint feminists
postmodern feminists

Discussion Questions

1. How has Marxism influenced the metatheoretical tenets of the critical perspective on theory in communication? What aspects of Marxism are most relevant (and least relevant) for critical theorists today?
2. Which metatheoretical assumptions separate critical theorists most clearly from post-positivist and interpretivist theorists? In what ways does convergence exist among the three perspectives on metatheoretical assumptions?
3. How are the concepts of ideology, hegemony, alienation, and emancipation linked in a critical perspective on theory? What is the role of the critical theorist with regard to these concepts?
4. In what ways are cultural studies and feminist studies representative of the critical movement in communication scholarship? What aspects of critical theory are most important in these two areas of scholarship?
5. How should one judge a critical theory? Are the standards from post-positivist or interpretivist theory appropriate? If not, what standards should be applied?

PART TWO

Theories of Communication Processes

Some things are easy to sort. Animals and plants can be sorted by their genus and species. Foods can be sorted by their ingredients or the meal at which they are typically eaten. Cars can be sorted by their manufacturer, their size, or even their number of doors. Of course, even these straightforward classification systems can break down. A stew might include a multitude of ingredients, and some people revel in eating waffles for dinner.

The sorting process is especially difficult when it comes to communication theories. As we have seen in the first section of this book, communication is an incredibly complex process, and the communication discipline is a many-faceted enterprise. Thus, sorting communication theories into neat little piles is a task fraught with challenges. However, it is also important to look for connections among various theories, for they are clearly not an undifferentiated mass.

In Part Two we look at the first major category of theories, those that consider various *processes* of communication. Six processes will be considered: processes of symbolic organization (Chapter 6), processes of message production (Chapter 7), processes of message reception (Chapter 8), processes of discourse and interaction (Chapter 9), processes of relational development (Chapter 10), and processes of communication in ongoing relationships (Chapter 11). Though these processes of communication cut across various contexts (that is, message production can be seen as important in interpersonal communication, as well as in group, organizational, and mass communication), they all deal with the basic ways in which communication works in our everyday lives.

6 Theories of Symbolic Organization

All of us have been in unfamiliar situations. Perhaps you have traveled abroad to an area of the world in which customs were strange to you. Perhaps you set off for college after spending very little time away from your hometown. Perhaps you found yourself at a formal wedding reception and had no idea what to do with all the cutlery that made up the place setting. In these situations, we are placed in contexts that we need to make sense of. If we are to behave and communicate in comfortable ways, we need to have a way of understanding what is happening around us. Unfamiliar situations of this type are particularly difficult for us, because in most other situations we know what is going on without questioning. We understand how to order food at a drive-through window. We recognize typical storylines on television dramas or the nightly news. We feel comfortable explaining why our parents, friends, or children behave in certain ways. In other words, as social beings, we have well-organized ideas about how the world works and how we should communicate and behave in that symbolic world.

In this chapter, we consider the ways in which social theorists believe we organize our ideas about the social world. These theories set the stage for the theories we examine in subsequent chapters, for these theories deal with the perceptual lens through which we understand what is going on around us rather than dealing with actual interaction processes. We discuss here two distinct sets of theoretical positions regarding the organization of symbolic reality. The first set of theories springs from the social scientific side of the communication discipline and has roots in both cognitive psychology and social psychology. The theories we consider in the first section—schema theory and attribution theory—provide but a taste of approaches used in psychology to explain processes of cognitive organization, but they are representative theories that have been widely used (and further developed) by theorists in the communication discipline. The second set of theories have their roots in the humanist side of the communication discipline and have had wide influence on both rhetorical and interpretive theorizing. These theories—narrative theory and dramatism—consider the literary and performative lenses through which we understand the social world.

■ SOCIAL SCIENTIFIC APPROACHES TO SYMBOLIC ORGANIZATION

S. E. Taylor (1981) argues that social and cognitive psychologists have been guided by three important metaphors in considering how individuals make sense of their social lives. These metaphors help theorists understand the ways in which people find cognitive and emotional comfort in the world and can get on with the activities of daily living. One of these metaphors—that of the *consistency seeker*—considers the desire people have to feel comfortable about how their belief structures fit together. If inconsistency is present, individuals feel discomfort and work to restore consistency. We deal a bit more with this metaphor when we talk about dissonance theory in Chapter 8. The other two metaphors are more germane to our discussion in this chapter because they consider the processes through which individuals make sense of daily activities in the social world. One of these metaphors, the model of the individual as the *naive scientist*, suggests that people in everyday life—like scientists in the laboratory—want to have explanations for what is happening. This model of individuals is the metaphor that guides the attributional approach we talk about later in this chapter. The final model of the individual is that of the *cognitive miser*. This metaphor suggests that when we try to make sense of the world, we are motivated to do so in an efficient way. As suggested in the opening to this chapter, it would be exhausting to have to deal with every situation as a fresh and new encounter. Thus, theories have been developed to explain the efficiencies we adopt in understanding the social world.

Schema Theory

The concept of efficiency is at the heart of the cognitive miser model of human information processing. Thus, it is helpful to think about this concept of efficiency in other settings. Consider, for example, the admissions process at a university. Imagine what the process would be like if every individual who wanted to attend the university was treated as a totally new situation. University officials would gather around, perhaps, to talk to the prospective candidate, find out more about his or her background, ruminate about what kind of person might be successful in the college environment, and so on. In some ways, we might like this system—there is certainly a lot of personal and individual attention

here, and it might lead to excellent admissions decisions. However, such a system clearly is not an efficient manner of handling the admissions process. In most college admissions offices around the country, efficiency has been ensured by developing application forms, performance standards, appeal protocols, and so on. In short, introducing efficiency into the admissions process has involved the development of behavioral templates that allow for the quick and standardized processing of information.

Theories of individuals as cognitive misers transport these ideas to our understanding of individual information processing. That is, theorists in this tradition look at the forms and structures that help individuals process a wide variety of information about the social world in an efficient way. As Wicks (1992, p. 119) states, "Schema theory suggests that people are active processors of information and that schematic thinking derives from the need to organize thinking for the purpose of cognitive economy." Though a variety of theories have been developed to explain this process (e.g., theories of plans, scripts, episodes), we use **schema theory** as one representative way of looking at these concepts (but see Mandler, 1984, for a much more specific interpretation of schema theory concepts). In other words, as cognitive misers, we use schema theory as a template for understanding this entire family of cognitive theories. There are two important issues to consider in understanding schema theory. The first issue is a question of *what* and the second is a question of *how* or, in Arbib, Conklin, and Hill's (1987) words, the distinction between the representation and process aspects of schemas. That is, theorists have considered both the content of cognitive schemas and the way those schemas are activated as we attempt to understand and behave in the social world.

The "What" of Schema Theory   The social world is highly complex. Thus, we need to use a variety of templates or **schemas** in our sense-making processes. These schemas provide ways of organizing information about the social world

Table 6.1	Social Schemata Typology	
Schemata type	Definition	Examples
Person schemata	An understanding of the psychology of typical or specific individuals	▪ People are generally honest. ▪ Fred hates to get dressed up.
Self schemata	An understanding of one's own psychological and behavioral tendencies	▪ I'm a real pessimist about things. ▪ I tend to take over in group projects.
Role schemata	An understanding of the appropriate norms and behaviors for social categories (e.g., age, race, sex, occupation)	▪ Young children should be seen and not heard. ▪ Clerks in retail stores should be friendly and helpful.
Event schemata	An understanding of the typical sequences of events in standard social occasions	▪ It's nice to bring a gift when invited to a dinner party. ▪ When you first meet someone, you shouldn't talk about highly personal issues.

Source: Adapted from Fiske & Taylor (1984).

and provide guides for understanding and interaction. Fiske and Taylor (1984) have suggested one organizing framework for social schemas. Their framework is presented in Table 6.1.

As Table 6.1 illustrates, a variety of frames can be drawn on to help us understand different situations. For example, at a wedding, we might draw on person schemas (e.g., "Fred and Ginger are such a romantic couple"), self schemas (e.g., "I always cry at these things"), role schemas (e.g., how members of the wedding party should act), and event schemas (e.g., what behavior is proper in the receiving line) both to make sense of what we observe and to behave and communicate during the experience. Several aspects of the content of schemas should be emphasized. First, these various types of schemas are not independent. For example, our schemas for the roles of bride and groom are contingent on our schemas for wedding behavior, and our schemas for Fred and Ginger intersect with our schemas for bride and groom in this instance.

Second, these schemas exist at varying levels of abstraction. That is, our schema for receiving-line behavior is at a very low level of abstraction. However, that particular schema might be embedded within more abstract event schemas for weddings and for formal events. Similarly, our specific bride and groom schemas are probably embedded within more abstract schemas involving romantic couples and men and women. Kellermann, Broetzmann, Lim, and Kitao (1989), following the work of Schank (1982), have talked about this embedding of schemas in terms of **memory organization packets (MOPs)** that organize sequences of interaction. A MOP might involve a variety of scenes (e.g., a MOP for a wedding would involve scenes for receiving line, ceremony, reception, and the like) and might be part of larger meta-MOPs (e.g., for ceremonies, formal events, celebrations, and the like).

The "How" of Schema Theory A number of processes are involved in understanding schema theory. We detail many of these processes regarding the communication context when we talk about action assembly theory in Chapter 7, but a brief discussion is in order here, as well. The first question of process involves the mechanisms through which a particular schema is developed and activated. In terms of development, a schema begins whenever a person comes in contact with a new situation or idea. That is, when you attend your first fraternity party, you begin to develop a schema for what such parties are like. In terms of the activation of existing schemas, it is likely that a schema will be activated if it is a close match to the current situation, if you have a well-developed schema for a particular situation, and if that schema has been recently activated. For example, when you attend a funeral, you might activate schemas involving how to comfort or how to behave in a formal setting, depending on how well-developed those schemas are and how recently they have been used (for discussion of schema activation processes, see Higgins & King, 1981; Wyer & Srull, 1981). People who have well-developed schema systems in a particular area will be able to apply more specific schemas to the situations they encounter (e.g., distinguishing among various religious denominations with regard to appropriate funeral behavior).

The second process involves the dynamic change and development of schemas. That is, schemas are not set in stone, and they change with new information and new experiences. Wicks (1992, p. 122) outlines three models of how new information might change existing schemas:

- the *bookkeeping model,* in which changes are gradually made to schemas to account for discrepant information and encounters
- the *conversion model,* in which a meaningful encounter with discrepant information can totally change a schema
- the *subtyping model,* in which subcategories of the overall schema are formed to deal with new and discrepant information

The subtyping model has received the most empirical support (Weber & Crocker, 1983) and is in line with the model of schema structure presented earlier. That is, if you attended a pagan wedding that took place in the woods and at which all attendees sang and danced, you would be unlikely to totally change your model of what a wedding is like. Instead, you would develop a more complex schema system in which the subtype of "pagan wedding" is included under the general rubric of wedding schemas.

Schema Theory in the Communication Discipline   The concepts of schema theory are implicated in all our communicative behavior, for if we are to proceed in a variety of communication situations we must either draw on existing schemas for understanding or, perhaps, develop new schemas that will be used in subsequent interaction. Thus, it is not surprising that a variety of scholars have been attracted to the concepts of schema theory in developing an understanding of communicative behavior. We briefly consider three lines of research within the communication discipline that have drawn on the concepts of schema theory to a greater or lesser extent.

First, as noted earlier, Kathy Kellermann and others have looked at the concepts of a MOP for understanding how we make sense of interaction in interpersonal conversation (see, e.g., Kellermann et al., 1989; Turner & Cullingford, 1989). These scholars have taken the concept of a MOP developed by Schank (1982) and applied it to the specific process of conversation. Schank sees a MOP as a "schematic structure used to organize long-term, conceptual, episodic memory" (Turner & Cullingford, 1989). MOPs consist of smaller units (or scenes), are organized into larger units (or meta-MOPs), and are associated with goal-related behavior. For example, you might have the goal of getting your clothes clean. To accomplish this goal, you might have to instantiate a variety of scenes including buying detergent, going to the laundromat, getting change, sorting clothes, operating the washer, operating the dryer, and folding clothes. Because these scenes are hierarchically related to the more general MOP, they could be readjusted as goal-related needs change. For example, if you buy a washer and a dryer, you still need to include some scenes to accomplish the clean clothes goal (e.g., sorting clothes, folding clothes, getting detergent), but other scenes might drop out of the picture (e.g., getting change).

This idea of a MOP has been applied in communication by developing the concept of a *conversational MOP*, or the way in which various scenes are put together to accomplish particular conversational goals. For example, Kellermann et al. (1989) discuss research into the typical goal-related scenes in initial interaction. These scenes include accomplishing initiation-phase goals—through greeting and discussion of the present situation or the weather—and maintenance-phase goals—through discussion of hometown, common acquaintances, or educational major. Though these researchers noted variance across conversations, they also concluded that "the possibility of a universal conversational scene suggested by our data is believed to be provocative and powerful for understanding discourse structure and comprehension" (Kellermann et al., 1989, p. 51).

A second area of research within interpersonal communication also draws on the general concept of schemas. This research, conducted by James Honeycutt and his colleagues (e.g., Edwards, Honeycutt, & Zagacki, 1988; Honeycutt, 1990; Honeycutt & Cantrill, 1991; Honeycutt, Cantrill, & Greene, 1989; Honeycutt, Zagacki, & Edwards, 1990; Zagacki, Edwards, & Honeycutt, 1992) deals not with schemas for the exchange of information in initial interactions but with the conversations that mark our ongoing and intimate relationships. Honeycutt and his colleagues begin with the straightforward notion that people develop expectations about how friends and relational partners will behave in interaction (we explore these ideas more in our discussion of relational communication in Chapters 10 and 11). They take this idea one step further, however, in proposing that people have cognitive knowledge structures (schemas or MOPs) that help to organize how a relationship should develop. For example, a person with a detailed schema structure about relational development might have clear ideas about what should happen on a first or second

date, how you should behave when meeting parents, what behaviors will serve to escalate the relationship, and so on. This research is interesting because it extends the concept of schemas beyond a particular event and into the trajectory of continuing relationships.

Honeycutt and his colleagues add another interesting twist to the concept of schemas, though. In addition to talking about mental structures that define how particular interactions and relationships should work, they add a process notion by arguing that an important form of cognition is the imagined interactions or internal dialogues we engage in when we anticipate or recall interaction with another individual. Honeycutt et al. (1990) have found that these imagined interactions serve several functions: They allow *rehearsal* for anticipated interaction, they provide *catharsis* after interaction, and they *enhance understanding* of self and other in the interaction. Honeycutt and his colleagues see imagined interactions as an important form of symbolic understanding and as a process that relies on other cognitive structures such as schemas, scripts, and MOPs.

Finally, research in mass communication has also relied on the concept of schemas for understanding communication processes. As Wicks (1992) argues, we have schemas not only for social interaction with others but also for various media channels and programmings. That is, you have some idea of what to expect from a legal thriller showing in the movie theater. Your schema for a show on The Food Network is very different from your schema for an ESPN offering. And you know that the spin of *The Washington Post* will be very different from that of *The National Enquirer*. Altheide and Snow (1988) believe that the very format of mediated communication helps to structure our expectations. They note that "a strange event can become meaningful when it is made available to us through a familiar medium" (Altheide & Snow, 1988, p. 219). Further, our schemas about social life are used as we encounter depictions in the media. For example, Hitchon and Chang (1995) report that schemas about the politician role and about gender roles are used in evaluating male and female political candidates. Specifically, they found that male politicians were categorized first as candidates whereas female politicians were categorized first as women. Further, these schemas about candidates and women (e.g., that candidates might be dishonest or that women are best in nurturing roles) influenced ways in which individuals interpreted media advertising.

Attribution Theory

In the preceding section, we talked about how schema theory answers questions about what happens in social interaction. However, as actors in the social world, we often go beyond these questions of what happens to consider the issue of why something happens or why people behave the way they do. In other words, as we noted earlier, we look for explanations in social life, much in the manner of a naive scientist. Understanding of the ways in which these explanations for social life are sought and applied forms the basis of **attribution theory.** As Jaspars, Hewstone, and Fincham (1983) summarize, "Attribution theory, in the widest sense of the term, . . . deals with the . . . common sense way of answering 'why' questions" (p. 4). Consider, for example, the following situations:

- You flunk a test.
- Your girlfriend or boyfriend is very quiet and withdrawn throughout an evening together.
- Your parents fail to phone at their prearranged weekend time.

These events call out for answers to the "why" question. What is the explanation for your poor test performance? What is causing your girlfriend or boyfriend to be quiet and withdrawn? What are the reasons for your parents' failure to phone? The processes through which we answer these and similar "why" questions have had the attention of attribution researchers since the 1960s. In this section we first consider some basic concepts of attribution theory and then look at research in communication that has drawn on attributional concepts.

Basic Concepts in Attribution Theory Attribution theory began in the discipline of social psychology with theorists such as Fritz Heider (e.g., Heider, 1958), Harold Kelley (e.g., Kelley, 1967), and Edward Jones (e.g., Jones, 1976). These theorists took the view of "human-as-scientist" and proposed that individuals looked for the causal reasons that could be used to explain observed behavior. Classic attribution theory sees this as a purposeful and logical process. For example, Manusov (1990) states that two basic assumptions about information processing in attribution theory are that "people are active interpreters of the events occurring in their social sphere" and that "attributions use consistent and logical bases upon which to make their causal claims" (p. 105). Scholars have backed away from this rational and logical stance to some extent, noting that we are not always mindful of our behavior and accounts (e.g., Langer, 1978) and that individuals do not always take the strict logic of scientific explanation into common-sense understandings of social life (e.g., Jaspars et al., 1983). However, attribution theory and research make it clear that individuals do look for an understanding of social life (even if that understanding might not involve *causes* in the strictest sense of the word) and that attributions attributed to social behavior have widespread effects on "our feelings about past events and our expectations about future ones, our attitudes toward other persons and our reactions to their behaviour and our conceptions of ourselves and our efforts to improve our fortunes" (Kelley & Michela, 1980, p. 489).

The most basic distinction made in attribution theory is between an **internal attribution** for behavior and an **external attribution** for behavior (e.g., Weiner, 1986). An internal attribution locates the cause of a particular behavior within the social actor, and an external attribution locates the cause of the behavior in the situation. For example, if your date is quiet and withdrawn, you might attribute it to her experience of an exhausting day at work (i.e., an

Table 6.2	Attributional Judgments Regarding Interpersonal Events	
Attribution dimension	Definitions	Examples
Locus	**Internal:** The cause of the event rests with the actor. **External:** The cause of the event rests with the situation.	My spouse is yelling at me because of a nasty disposition. My spouse is yelling at me because of a bad day at the office.
Stability	**Stable:** The cause of the event is always present. **Unstable:** The cause of the event varies over time and context.	My spouse's personality (or bad work situation) will never go away. You can never tell how my spouse is going to feel (or how work is going to go).
Controllability	**Controllable:** The actor can affect the cause that influences an event. **Uncontrollable:** The cause of an event is beyond the actor's influence.	My spouse could get feelings under control (or deal with problems at work) with a little effort. My spouse has no control over feelings (or work situation).

Source: Developed from Weiner (1986).

external attribution) or to her depression over the state of your relationship (i.e., an internal attribution). If a classmate is late to a meeting, you might attribute it to inherent laziness (i.e., an internal attribution) or to car trouble (i.e., an external attribution).

Early work in attribution theory identified a fundamental attribution error in this regard (see Nisbett & Ross, 1980) such that observers trying to explain someone's behavior will tend to overestimate the importance of internal factors and underestimate the importance of external factors. That is, you will be more likely to think that your classmate is lazy than that car trouble was the cause of his or her tardiness. Interestingly, though, this tendency shifts with the situation. For example, this error doesn't seem to hold when we explain our own behavior. As Jones and Nisbett (1972) explain, "There is a pervasive tendency for actors to attribute their [own] actions to situational requirements, whereas observers tend to attribute the same actions to stable personal dispositions" (p. 2). However, other aspects of the situation might lead to results counter to this *fundamental attri-*

bution error (see Ajzen & Fishbein, 1983, for review). Given mixed findings regarding the tendency to make internal and external attributions (Monson & Snyder, 1977), a more nuanced approach to attributions seems to make sense.

Weiner (1986) proposed one such approach. Weiner argues that the causes of behavior are not seen simply along the dimension of internal versus external but along two additional dimensions of **stability** and **controllability.** Table 6.2 summarizes these three dimensions.

The conceptualization of attributions presented in Table 6.2 shows the variety of judgments that are used to explain social behavior. It also indicates that these dimensions are independent of one another. That is, an internal attribution could be seen as stable or unstable and as controllable or uncontrollable. However, Weiner argues that attributions along these dimensions can influence outcomes such as motivation (e.g., "If I don't think my spouse is ever going to change, why should I even talk to him about it?") and emotional states (e.g., "I don't feel too bad about this because I know it's something I can't control and something that won't last.").

Attribution Theory in the Communication Discipline Attributional processes are implicated in communication processes in a number of ways. In a very basic sense, we tend to talk about our attributional understandings of behavior; hence, causal inference often makes up a part of our day-to-day conversations (see, e.g., Burleson, 1986). We also make attributions about communication behavior (e.g., "Why did she say that?"), and the nature of these attributions is likely to be closely linked with the nature of our relationships, with how those relationships progress, with behavioral outcomes, and with our feelings about interaction and relationships. Finally, our contact with various communication sources, be they interpersonal, group, or mediated, tend to influence the attributions we make about a variety of social situations.

Research investigating attributions about interpersonal behavior has been conducted primarily in the subdiscipline of interpersonal communication. Scholars in this area have looked at how attributions are influenced by the relationship and other factors and how attributions, in turn, influence subsequent communicative behavior. In considering the impact of the relationship on attributions, research by Vangelisti (1992) is illustrative. Her work considered the attributions made about communication problems in satisfied and unsatisfied relationships. She found that satisfied couples tended to attribute problems to external rather than internal causes, whereas the opposite was true for unsatisfied couples. Thus, the quality of relationship influenced the types of attributions made about communicative behavior. Similarly, Manusov (1990) found that nonverbal behaviors (e.g., avoiding eye contact, turning away, facial unpleasantness) were attributed as more intentional, stable, and internal among couples with low levels of relational satisfaction than among couples who were more satisfied with their relationship. In short, it appears that the nature of the relationship can have important effects on the reasons we provide for another's communicative behavior.

Scholars have also considered the effect of attributions on subsequent interaction. One illustrative study was conducted by S. R. Wilson, Cruz, Marshall, and Rao (1993) with regard to compliance-gaining interaction. These investigators found that research participants were more persistent and used persuasive strategies such as guilt or appeals to altruism when confronted with resistance based on a controllable and internal attribution. Thus, explanations for why people behaved in the way they did had an impact on subsequent communicative behavior.

Studies of mediated communication have also drawn on attribution theory. For example, Hindeman (1999) examined the attributions made by media sources about why there was "poor, even unethical" coverage in the pretrial stage of the O. J. Simpson case (p. 499). Hindeman notes how media sources shifted responsibility for this coverage to external sources or defended their coverage as part of their watchdog journalistic role. Griffin and Sen (1995) have illustrated how exposure to the media can influence more general social attributions. Their study found that people who had watched specific movies about the Vietnam War were more likely to attribute Vietnam veterans' problems to external causes. Finally, scholars have identified a basic attribution error called the third-person effect with regard to explanations for media effects (Davison, 1983; Gunther, 1991). Specifically, these scholars argue that individuals tend to think that other people are more strongly influenced by the media than they, themselves, are.

Summary of Social Scientific Approaches

Both schema theory and attribution theory present models of symbolic organizing that emphasize the cognitive structures and processes of individuals. These approaches, as post-positivist theories, propose causal explanations regarding the ways in which our cognitions about the social and symbolic world are organized, with these explanations centered on procedures through which we organize and respond to social stimuli in ways that are efficient, logical, and comfortable. Whether the theoretical model of the individual is that of a cognitive miser (i.e., schema theory) or a naive scientist (i.e., attribution theory), a rationality sustains both the predictions of these theories and the way the theories have been tested in scientific experiments. We now turn to two theories that move us in a different direction in understanding our encounters with the symbolic and social world.

■ HUMANISTIC APPROACHES TO SYMBOLIC ORGANIZATION

A humanistic approach to understanding the social world tends to eschew many watchwords of social scientific explanation. There is not a search for cognitive structures, as in schema theory, or for causal analysis, as in attribution theory. Furthermore, an understanding of how we perceive and understand the social world is not analyzed through laboratory studies that evaluate the impact of social cognitive organization. Instead, humanists turn to the human experience as a whole and try to understand the ways in which we have encountered and made sense of the world throughout history. The values of interpretive theory described in Chapter 4—an embracing of subjective and intersubjective ontologies, an allegiance to emergent and insider epistemologies, and an appreciation for the values inherent in both human interaction and scholarship—all mark humanistic approaches to understanding symbolic reality. In the next two sections, we consider two humanistic approaches to understanding the ways in which people encounter the social worlds around them. In keeping with interpretive traditions of often relating communication phenomena to the concepts of texts (e.g., as in the hermeneutic tradition described in Chapter 4), these theories both draw on textual and dramatic metaphors. We will first consider narrative theory as developed by Walter Fisher and then consider dramatism as developed by Kenneth Burke.

Narrative Theory

In our discussion of social scientific theories of symbolic organization, we noted several metaphors that guide thinking about what humans are like. In schema theory, humans are depicted as cognitive misers who try to efficiently process experiences in the social world through the filters of schemas and MOPs. In attribution theory, we encounter the metaphor of people as naive scientists—everyday individuals who create and use causal explanations for their own and others' behaviors. With Walter Fisher's narrative theory, we introduce yet another metaphor, that of people as "homo narrans" or as the "storytelling animal" (MacIntyre, 1981, p. 201). In developing his **narrative paradigm** for human communication, Fisher (1984, 1985, 1987) sees storytelling as the most basic and universal of all human activities. Throughout history, across cultures, and throughout the world, people have told and continue to tell stories. Thus, individuals approach their social world in a narrative mode and make decisions and act within this narrative framework. We consider several important aspects of narrative theory in the following sections: narrative as an organizing framework for human communication, analysis in narrative theory, and applications of narrative analysis in the communication discipline.

A Narrative World View   The concept of narrative has certainly been around for a long time, and scholars in a variety of disciplines (e.g., English, literature, history) have long recognized the power of narrative in human experience (see, e.g., Martin, 1986). Fisher takes this concept a large step further in proposing that narrative is an overarching and universal paradigm (Fisher, 1987). Though there are a variety of ways to understand the word *paradigm* (see, e.g., our brief discussions of Thomas Kuhn in Chapters 2 and 3), Fisher sees a paradigm as a humanistic conceptual framework that can be used to understand universal processes of human communication. Several quotes from Fisher illustrate the breadth of the narrative paradigm as he views it:

✳ SPOTLIGHT ON THE THEORIST

Walter Fisher

Since Walter Fisher received his Ph.D. from the University of Iowa in 1960, he has taught and lectured at colleges and universities throughout the United States and beyond. He has been a professor at the University of Southern California for many years and has won important national awards for his scholarship, teaching, and service. Fisher has also edited several journals in the communication discipline and held offices in a number of professional associations. He is perhaps best known, however, for his work in formulating the narrative approach to rhetoric and communication theory. Indeed, the article that launched this theory won a Golden Anniversary Monograph Award from the Speech Communication Association in 1979, and his book describing the theory won the Herbert A. Wichelns Award for Distinguished Scholarship in Rhetoric and Public Address.

Fisher acknowledges that the entire field of communication has not embraced the ideas in his narrative paradigm. As he notes in a straightforward way—"some liked it, some didn't." But he also believes that the wide citation of his work and the fact that scholars have used narrative as a basis for their own research speaks to the resonance of the ideas in narrative theory. And he does not see the present state of narrative theory as the endpoint of its development. Indeed, he notes that he is now working on a new book that explores the ethical dimensions of the narrative paradigm. The tentative title of this book is *Practical Wisdom Reconfigured: The Other Side of the Narrative Paradigm.*

When asked about his advice for students encountering communication theory for the first time, Fisher points to the importance of such theory at multiple levels and for many aspects of everyday life. He recommends that students of communication theory "try to understand it, and appreciate what it has to offer in explaining how people symbolically transact who they are, how they construct and deconstruct human relationships, both interpersonally and in public." Thus, he believes that communication theory can help us answer very basic questions regarding human conduct and relationships.

For scholars embarking on careers in the communication discipline, Fisher suggests an open and inquisitive approach to inquiry. He knows that it is easy to get sidetracked in an academic career, and he advises that young scholars "be the best *you* can be and don't get distracted by what others may achieve. Discover your own talents and gifts; nurture them and apply them well in every assignment or challenge you may face in classrooms and in professional organizations." Though Fisher directed these comments to students embarking on academic careers, it is certainly good advice for all of us.

- "I think that when any form of human communication is taken seriously . . . it should be viewed as a story" (Fisher, 1988, p. 50).

- "In short, the narrative paradigm is a philosophical statement that is meant to offer an approach to interpretation and assessment of human communication—assuming that all forms of human communication can be seen fundamentally as stories, as interpretations of aspects of the world occurring in time and shaped by history, culture, and character" (Fisher, 1989, p. 57).

- Humans "experience and comprehend life as a series of ongoing narratives, as conflicts, characters, beginnings, middles, and ends" (Fisher, 1987, p. 24).

Thus, Fisher sees the narrative paradigm as a very general way of understanding the ways in which humans encounter and behave within their social world. Our individual encounters

Table 6.3	Comparison of the Rational World and Narrative Paradigms
The rational world paradigm	**The narrative paradigm**
People are essentially rational.	People are essentially storytellers.
People make decisions based on arguments.	People make decisions based on good reasons.
The communicative situation determines the course of our argument.	History, biography, culture, and character determine what we consider to be good reasons.
Rationality is determined by how much we know and how well we argue.	Narrative rationality is determined by the coherence and fidelity of our stories.
The world is a set of logical puzzles that we can solve through rational analysis.	The world is a set of stories from which we choose, and constantly re-create, our lives.

Source: Adapted from Fisher (1987).

with friends and family members can be understood as stories. The trajectory our lives take through careers, relationships, and personal developments can be understood as stories. The events of public and political life can also be understood as stories.

These examples illustrate ways in which Fisher might see that narrative paradigm as an organizing framework as we encounter the social world. But what are the characteristics of this narrative paradigm? What does it mean to analyze communication through a storytelling lens? Fisher (1987) describes important features of the narrative paradigm through a contrast with what he labels as the **rational world paradigm.** As Fisher sees it, a rational world paradigm has characterized thinking for many years within the realms of both science (e.g., with adherence to cause and effect and the scientific method) and rhetoric (e.g., with adherence to the value of logic and argument). Distinctions between the rational world paradigm and the narrative paradigm are presented in Table 6.3.

As Table 6.3 illustrates, Fisher sees differences between the rational world paradigm and the narrative paradigm in terms of who we are, what our world is like, and how we make decisions as a part of that social world. Further, because Fisher sees the narrative paradigm as universal, he would argue that we can understand all of human discourse and texts through reference to the narrative concept. He does not believe that all discourse and texts take the classic literary form of narration (see Fisher, 1988, pp. 50–51). However, he believes that "all forms of discourse can be considered stories, that is, interpretations of some aspect of the world occurring in time and shaped by history, culture, and character" (Fisher, 1995, p. 170). Thus, whether considering something in the classic narrative genre (e.g., a story told by a grandfather), a scientific treatise (e.g., a book about the effect of automobile emissions on the ozone layer), a political communique (e.g., a politician's speech or campaign advertisement), or an interpersonal encounter (e.g., a couple's argument over where to go for vacation), Fisher believes there are good reasons that inform the discourse and that narrative rationality can be used to analyze the text.

The Analysis of Narrative Rationality How then are we to decide whether a good or a bad (or most reasonable and humane) story has been told? How will narratives guide our subsequent decision making and behavior? Fisher proposes that we judge narratives in terms of their **narrative coherence** (sometimes called narrative probability) and in regard to their **narrative fidelity.** Narrative coherence deals with the integrity of the story's structure, whether the audience thinks that it hangs together as a story should. Narrative coherence considers issues such as the extent to which the plotline is consistent, the extent to which there is enough detail to understand the story, the extent to which characters behave in a reliable manner, and the extent to which there are no unrealistic surprises or other plausible interpretations left out by the narrator. We can judge narrative coherence because we have encountered many other stories and hence have developed standards for what makes sense in a story and for judging the merits of the story before us. We could evaluate narratives from many levels of society in terms of their coherence: the government's explanation for military action, a business leader's speech about why stock prices are down, or a child's recounting of events on the playground. Within these communicative interactions, stories are told that can be evaluated in regard to whether they make sense as stories, that is, whether they are coherent.

Stories can also be judged in terms of narrative fidelity. Narrative fidelity deals less with the structure of the story—its plotline, characters, timing, and presentation—and more with the underlying truthfulness of the story. A narrative has high fidelity if it rings true with the beliefs of the listener, or when it satisfies the considerations of fidelity (Fisher, 1978, 1987). Fisher (1987) details five dimensions of fidelity that encompass varying levels of abstraction:

- questions of *fact* that examine the values embedded in the story, either explicitly or implicitly

- questions of *relevance* that consider the connection between the story that is told and the values being espoused

- questions of *consequences* that consider the possible outcomes that would accrue to people adhering to the espoused values

- questions of *consistency* between the values of the narrative and the held values of the audience

- questions of *transcendence* that consider the extent to which the story's values represent the highest values possible in human experience

Fisher believes that the best stories are those that fulfill these five requirements. Such stories communicate to us about what is most truthful and humane in our everyday lives and in the world at large. They tell us in compelling ways about issues of real consequence to the social world. Clearly, not all individuals share the same values; hence, judgments of fidelity (like judgments of coherence) are incumbent on who is doing the judging. However, Fisher (1987) believes that our most revealing look at a story's fidelity comes from imagining an audience "that believes in the values of truth, the good, beauty, health, wisdom, courage, temperance, justice, harmony, order, communion, friendship, and oneness with the Cosmos" (pp. 187–188). A story appealing to the values of such an audience would indeed be a story of high merit, worthy of belief and the basis of action.

Narrative Theory in Communication Research The concept of narrative has certainly captured the attention of many scholars in the communication discipline. Narrative forms of symbolic organization have been examined in the organizational setting (e.g., Mumby, 1987), in family interaction (e.g., Langellier & Peterson, 1993), and in the communication of racism (e.g., Nakagawa, 1990). Much of this work, however, has dealt with narrative and stories in a general sense and not with specific aspects of Fisher's narrative theory. The breadth of this body of research points, however, to the importance of the narrative form as a way of perceiving, organizing, and responding to the social world.

A number of studies have looked specifically at communication through the lens of narrative theory. For example, Hollihan and Riley (1987) examined interaction during a Toughlove parental support group and analyzed the story created (and re-created) by parents attending these groups. They found that the Toughlove story had high narrative coherence and struck a chord of fidelity with parents attending the group. As they note, "The story met the test of narrative fidelity because it resonated with their own feelings that they were essentially good people whose only failing had been that they were too permissive and not as tough as their own parents had been" (Hollihan & Riley, 1987, p. 23). However, the truth of the Toughlove story can also be criticized because it encouraged possibly risky action (e.g., kicking a kid out if he or she did not respond to the bottom line set by the parents) and allowed for no alternative storyline. Another interesting study in Fisher's narrative tradition examined the fidelity and coherence of the "stories" presented in Republican and Democrat Party platforms in 1984 (L. D. Smith, 1989). Smith found that although the platforms were markedly different, they both passed the tests of coherence and fidelity by adhering to standards of internal consistency and remaining consistent with the transcendent values represented in party tradition.

These studies point to the wide range of situations in which a narrative approach can provide insights into the symbolic organization of our social world. Neither of these texts (interaction in a support group or a party platform statement) would be construed as a narrative in the classic sense. In spite of the use of narrative theory in nontraditional settings like these, however, scholars have engaged in heated debate over Fisher's claim that the narrative paradigm is universal. For example, Fisher (1988) responds to critics such as Bruce Gronbeck, Michael McGee, and Allan Megill, who propose that the narrative paradigm is not applicable to the analysis of historical texts because history is written as an argument rather than as a narrative. Rowland (1989) argues that the narrative paradigm should be limited to texts of clearly narrative form, and he attempts analyses of other forms (i.e., a science fiction novel, a political book, and a propaganda film) to argue for the inapplicability of narrative analysis in many cases. Rowland (1989) notes problems in both the breadth and the content of the narrative paradigm, stating that "the narrative paradigm both defines narrative so loosely that the importance of story-telling may be obscured and fails to provide an adequate method for evaluating the epistemic quality of stories" (p. 52). Fisher (1989) and others (e.g., Haynes, 1989) disagree with placing limits on the narrative paradigm, contending that all forms of reasoned human communication can be seen fundamentally as stories. However, it should be clear that— whether universal or not—assessing the coherence and the truth of the stories we encounter is a fundamental process in the social world.

Dramatism

The final theoretical tradition we consider in this chapter springs from the work of a man who has had far-reaching impact both on the field of communication and on other disciplines such as philosophy, anthropology, linguistics, religion, history, and economics. Kenneth Burke (1897–1993) had a long and productive intellectual career spanning activities such as literary critic, social critic, poet, fiction author, translator, composer, and social theorist. Though Burke never graduated from college, he taught at a number of institutions of higher education and had contacts that spanned a wide range of intellectual thought. He is now recognized as a crucial contributor to both social and literary theoretical traditions.

Burke was "introduced" to the field of communication by Marie Hochmuth Nichols in 1952 in her contrast between the old rhetoric (e.g., the rhetorical traditions of Aristotle and neo-Aristotelians) and the new rhetoric (e.g., the ideas of Burke) (Nichols, 1952). In the years since,

Burke's work has been enthusiastically embraced by communication scholars—particularly rhetoricians. There is now a Kenneth Burke Society, there have been many conference tributes to Burke and his work, and numerous volumes have been published celebrating both the man and his legacy (e.g., Brock, 1999; Brummett, 1993; Simons & Melia, 1989). It is not surprising that Burke's influence has been strongest and most enduring in rhetorical studies—Burke's literary and social criticism has deep and direct connections with this kind of scholarship. However, Burke has also had more diffuse and wide-ranging effects on the field of communication. Burkean theory has shaped the way many scholars think about language, about our motives for using language, and about the way we encounter and live in a social and symbolic world. We turn to these more general concerns in this section. In organizing this work, we draw on an essay written about Burke's connections with another general field of social inquiry, sociology. Gusfield (1989, p. 30) writes that four aspects of Burke's thought have been particularly influential in shaping views of the social world:

- an understanding of language as a form of action
- an understanding of human action as dramatic in form and, consequently, as amenable to analysis in the same framework as literary work
- an understanding of human actions as rhetorical, as strategies developed to cope with situations involving a performer and an audience
- a pluralistic and dialectical program for analysis of human behavior

The fourth of these issues is inherent in all multidisciplinary applications of Burke's ideas (including this one). The first three issues are used to organize the following discussion of Burke's views of how we encounter the social and symbolic world.

Language as a Form of Action   In understanding humans and the social world, Burke makes a critical distinction between motion (i.e., behavior that is controlled by external stimuli) and action (i.e., behavior that is motivated by the needs and desires of the social actor). Burke, in line with symbolic interactionists such as George Herbert Mead and Alfred Schutz (see our discussion of these and related theorists in Chapter 4), believed that the distinction between action and motion is what makes humans distinct from other animals and that the use of symbols—especially the most important form of symbols, language—moves humans from the realm of motion into the realm of action (Burke, 1945). Burke's (1966) poetic and oft-quoted "definition of man" (with *man* used in the general sense to include both men and women) illustrates his position:

> Man is
>
> the symbol-using inventor of the negative
>
> separated from his natural condition by instruments
>
> of his own making
>
> goaded by the spirit of hierarchy
>
> and rotten with perfection. (p. 16)

A complete analysis of this poem is clearly beyond the scope of this chapter. However, this "definition of man" points to several important nuances regarding the ability of humans to engage in symbolic action. First, in this poem Burke reflects on some of the social complexities that are introduced with the use of language. With language, we become separated from the natural state of the world (e.g., the world of motion) but we can still be reflexive and comment on that world. Though we are symbol using, we are also still animals, and Brummett (1993) observes that Burke "teeters between the realizations that some of what we do is motivated by animality and some of it by symbolicity" (p. xii). With language we introduce the concept of the negative. Burke (1968) notes that "there are no negatives in nature, where everything simply is what it is and as it is" (p. 9). This introduction of the negative makes our perception of the world and our behavior in the world much more complex. With language we also introduce the explicit notion of hierarchy, that is, the symbolic and social structuring of the world into various forms of order. Finally, with language we introduce ideals and concepts of perfection that humans can never actually attain. Burke (1968, p. 484) believes that there are "compelling principles of perfection implicit in the nature of language" and that such principles are central to our motivations in the symbolic world.

In the most basic sense, though, the move from motion to action—through the use of symbolism, and especially language—marks humans as agents rather than reactors in the social world. Conrad and Macom (1995) see the problem of agency as a crux for understanding a Burkean view of the world. Specifically, for Burke, the concept of agency introduces a vital tension into the social world—a tension between the free will of symbol-using humans and the constraints on action placed by history and situation. As Abrams (1982) describes, "The problem of agency is the problem of finding a way of accounting for human experience which recognises simultaneously and in equal measure that history and society are made by constant and more or less purposeful individual action and that individual action, however purposeful, is made by history and society" (p. xiii). Understanding the full implications of symbolism and language in human interaction, then, requires a way to approach the problem of agency. Burkean analysis deals with this in the view of the symbolic and social world as drama.

Action as Dramatic Burke believed not just that life is like a drama but that life *is* a drama. His dramatistic approach to understanding social and symbolic life is a central and defining aspect of his philosophy and analysis. Life as drama can be considered in several ways within Burke's work. We first look at the grand sweep of life and how it is often played out in the dramatic tension of guilt and redemption cycles. We then look at how smaller dramatic scenes are

constituted and can be analyzed in Burke's approach to the symbolic world.

The Process of Guilt and Redemption Burke (1935) believed that the drama of life is motivated by guilt. Burke does not use *guilt* in a narrow judicial sense or even in the sense of being guilty or responsible for particular social actions. Rather, Burke conceived of *guilt* as a way to refer to a variety of negative processes—anxiety, embarrassment, shame, disgust—that permeate the human condition. Guilt comes when we are estranged from the natural world or when we are estranged from others in the social world. Guilt serves as a motivating factor that drives the human drama.

To purge our guilt, Burke argued that we engage in a process called victimage. *Victimage* suggests that someone must be sacrificed (i.e., serve as a victim) in the human drama, and there are two ways that victimage might be played out. First, we often turn and blame ourselves for the guilt we experience. This self-victimage is referred to as *mortification*. In the mortification process, we admit wrongdoing, we accept responsibility, and we apologize for our actions. The second option is *scapegoating*, in which blame is placed on some other sacrificial vessel. The scapegoat in this process might take many forms. For example, we could blame another individual, a disliked social group, a dysfunctional family, even the system as a whole. Whatever form it takes, scapegoating finds an external source for our experience of guilt. Through either mortification or scapegoating, the cycle is complete with the sense of *redemption*, a return to a new order after guilt has been purged. Burke noted, however, that redemption is often short lived because the social world inherently involves guilt that will begin a new cycle.

The process of victimage through either scapegoating or mortification can be seen in a wide range of both grand and small human dramas. When the *Exxon Valdez* ran aground and spilled oil off the coast of Alaska, Exxon officials took actions involving both scapegoating (i.e., blaming the captain of the ship) and mortification (i.e., accepting responsibility for the cleanup and for reviewing systems regarding alcohol abuse in the organization). When a college student performs poorly on a test, she might enact a human drama that blames the difficulty of the test and the tough curve instituted by the instructor (i.e., scapegoating), or she might admit that she had rarely attended class and hadn't studied and that her test performance might have been influenced by those factors (i.e., mortification). When a child is caught drawing with crayons on the wall, he might cry in shame because of his mother's unhappiness (i.e., mortification) or blithely scapegoat an imaginary playmate for instigating the art session.

The Dramatistic Pentad In addition to these large cycles of guilt and redemption that mark the human symbolic experience, Burke proposed an analytical mode for approaching individual events in human life. His proposal of the **dramatistic pentad** (Burke, 1945, 1968) considers five aspects of social life that should be considered in order to understand how we behave, and talk about our behavior, in the symbolic world:

- The *act*, or what is done by a person.
- The *scene*, or context surrounding the act. The scene includes both immediate context and the historical and social situation in which the act is situated.
- The *agent*, or person or people who perform the act.
- The *purpose*, or the explicit or implicit goal of the act.
- *Agency*, or the means or methods used to perform the act.

Burke believed that the pentad provides a way of viewing the world that can be quite revealing, in terms of looking at both the social situation (e.g., what happened during the *Exxon Valdez* oil spill) and, perhaps more important, the communication about the event (e.g., statements by company officials, Alaskan residents, and environmental advocates about the spill). Analysis via the dramatistic pentad goes beyond a simplistic labeling of the various portions of the dramatic

event and involves a consideration of what aspects of the event were put in the foreground and which were relegated to the background. This analysis can be accomplished through Burke's method of the *pentadic ratio*. For example, a statement about the *Exxon Valdez* accident that emphasizes the agent might be used to highlight the captain's role in the event. In contrast, a statement emphasizing aspects of the scene might downplay his control and instead point to the harm to the environment that was caused and to the role of Exxon's rules, regulations, and procedures in the event. By emphasizing various aspects of social life, then, language works as a **terministic screen** (Burke, 1935), shaping and filtering our perceptions of reality.

Action as Rhetorical Finally, Burke's theorizing points to the inherently rhetorical nature of symbolic action. Burke (1976) saw rhetoric as a process of persuasion, symbolic action designed "to produce effects 'beyond' the act, as when exhorting the audience to favor this cause rather than that" (p. 67). But for Burke, rhetoric was not merely a logical process of persuasion through the presentation of reasons and evidence. Rather, Burke saw rhetoric as a process of creating, re-creating, and drawing on *identification*. An understanding of identification requires a consideration of Burke's conception of *substance*. We all have ways of characterizing ourselves. For example, I am an American woman, a baby boomer, a college professor, a mother to a daughter, a wife, a Democrat, an accomplished cook, a reader of contemporary fiction, an avid sports fan, and a believer in progressive social causes. These are all ways of characterizing my substance or my identity, though they are all partial statements of that identity. Burke argued that there are times when we feel our substance is very different from those around us—when we are divided from individuals and the community. There are other times when we feel that our substance is joined to others or overlaps with others, and this overlap comes through symbolic action. Burke (1950) called this joining or overlap *consubstantiation* and stated that "substance, in the old philosophies, was an *act*; and a way of life is an *acting-together*; and in acting together, men have common sensations, concepts, images, ideas, attitudes that make them *consubstantial*" (p. 21). Through consubstantiation, we establish a sense of identification with others in the social world.

The concept of identification is implicated in communication in several ways. First, social actors draw on their areas of consubstantiation to identify with their audiences or with others in the interaction situation. We feel more connected in interaction with those who are like us; thus, speakers often try to establish a sense of identification with audiences. Of course, this is a huge challenge in social life. As Heath (1986) notes, "Identification acknowledges that communication is difficult because humans have different experiences and because ambiguity allows each of us to hold different meanings of terms" (p. 209). Effective communicators recognize this, and their actions reveal the extent to which identification is a tool we use in our interaction with others. But identification is also a goal in symbolic action. As social beings, we are drawn into communion and community with others. This community is accomplished (if imperfectly) through symbolic processes. Indeed, Heath (1986) argues that "Burke's rhetoric is founded on the goal of achieving social harmony, even though he demonstrates how words frustrate efforts to achieve perfect harmony" (p. 210).

Burkean Analysis in Communication Research
As noted in the preceding section, the most prevalent applications of Burke's ideas have been in the area of rhetorical analysis, and a review of these investigations is well beyond the scope of this chapter. Suffice it to say that reviews of Burke's influence point to both the explicit use of Burkean concepts (e.g., analyses of the guilt and redemption cycle and use of the dramatistic pentad) in enhancing understanding of rhetorical texts and the implicit influence of his ideas across a wide body of rhetorical theory and research. For example, Klumpp (1995), in an analysis of work published in the seminal rhetoric journal *Quarterly Journal of Speech,* concludes that "assumptions such as the motivating power of discursive form, the ritualistic nature of common discursive action, and the centrality of naming and attitudinal functions within symbolic action characterize essays without comment about their roots. This maturing in which Burke's assumptions attain a sort of taken-for-granted status is a profound indicator of the power of the ideas in his age" (p. 3).

Also notable is the use of Burkean concepts in areas apart from rhetorical analysis. Simons (1989) has noted the ways in which many ideas have become so much a part of our lexicon for both criticism and communication that, in the words of Ben Yagoda (1980), many new ideas "seem to have one thing in common: Kenneth Burke thought them up nearly fifty years ago" (p. 67). It does seem almost commonplace to think about the symbol-using capacity of humans as what divides them from motion-driven animals. And the metaphor of life as drama is one we draw on in our conversations and use to analyze the social world. Indeed, we see specific reference to Burke's ideas about identification and consubstantiation used as a basis for specific theories of organizational communication (see Chapter 12). In short, Burke's influence has been widespread across disciplines and within the communication discipline and can be seen both in the purposeful use of his concepts and methods and in the way his views of the symbolic and social world have shaped theory and research in much more subtle ways.

■ COMPARISON AND COMMENTARY

In some ways, the theoretical frameworks discussed in this chapter could not be more different. The first two theories—schema theory and attribution theory—were developed in cognitive psychology and social psychology and hence are firmly established in the post-positivist tradition of theory construction. Researchers working from these theories look for causal explanations of phenomena through carefully crafted research investigations. Using the criteria of post-positivist theorists, both schema theory and attribution theory can be seen as highly successful theories. Each has fruitfully contributed to knowledge both in social psychology and in other disciplines such as communication. Each proposes a coherent mechanism (e.g., humans as cognitive misers or as naive scientists) that leads to specific theoretical and empirical predictions. And each is consistent, both internally and with other contemporary ideas about social cognition and interaction.

In contrast, the second two theories—narrative theory and dramatism—have their roots in the humanistic traditions of rhetoric and criticism. Scholars working from these theories look for insight regarding the formal and informal texts we produce in the social world. Thus, in terms of ontology, epistemology, axiology, and methodology, these theories occupy very different portions of the intellectual spectrum. As theories more in line with the interpretive traditions discussed in Chapter 4, narrative theory and dramatism provide compelling accounts of how humans organize experience as they subjectively encounter the social world. These theories are not explanatory in the causal sense of a post-positivist theory but instead enhance our understanding of symbolic organization by elaborating the ways we enact and encounter the social world as text.

Thus, the four theories we have looked at in this chapter provide divergent conceptualizations of the social world. However, these theories are amazingly similar in terms of the understanding they provide about how we, as humans, come to understand the social and symbolic world in which we live. This can be seen both in a general way and in specific understandings about symbolic organization. On a general level, for example, schema theory and dramatism both talk about the scenes and actors in social interaction. Similarly, attribution theory and narrative theory both show the ways in which humans look for reasonable explanations of the social world, either by assessing narrative coherence and fidelity or by developing causal expla-

nations. On a more specific level, a comparison could be drawn between attribution theory's concepts of internal and external attributions and Burkean concepts of mortification and scapegoating. And in those theories, these concepts of blaming self and blaming others for events are seen as having critical implications for our ongoing interactions.

Highlighting these points of similarity and convergence is not meant to deny the critical independent contributions made by each of these theories. Obviously, an understanding based on Burke's guilt and redemption cycle is very different from an explanation stemming from a view of conversational MOPs. An interaction analyzed through the narrative fidelity of stories told will lead to different insights than an interaction analyzed by considering the effects of causal attributions. However, these theories show the need humans have to make sense of their social worlds in ways that hang together comfortably and coherently. Without such maps of the social world, communication would indeed be a difficult undertaking.

Key Terms

schema theory
schemas
memory organization packets
attribution theory
internal attribution
external attribution
stability
controllability
narrative paradigm
rational world paradigm
narrative coherence
narrative fidelity
dramatistic pentad
terministic screen

Discussion Questions

1. Using the scenario of registering for classes, develop a memory organization packet

(MOP) or schema that guides behavior and interaction. How are the scenes and goals in this MOP readjusted when lines get long and classes get filled?

2. How do schema theory and attribution theory differ in their conceptualization of cognition, behavior, and communication? Are these theories compatible, or would their predictions conflict in some situations?

3. How could the concepts from the narrative paradigm help us understand the stories of women in situations of domestic violence? How could we judge the coherence and fidelity of these stories?

4. Using Burke's dramatistic pentad and the presidential election of 2000, analyze the rhetoric surrounding political and legal challenges in Florida. What happens when various portions of the pentad are emphasized in your analysis?

7 Theories of Message Production

There is little doubt that the processes involved in producing messages are central to communicative interaction. Early definitions of communication typically emphasized the encoding process, and areas of research within the discipline such as persuasion and interpersonal communication have continued to stress the importance of message choice and message behavior in the study of communication. However, S. R. Wilson (1997) notes that not until 1982 was the term *message production* used as an organizing framework for understanding this area of communication scholarship (O'Keefe & Delia, 1982). Since then, edited books (e.g., Cody & Mc-Laughlin, 1990; Dillard, 1990a; Greene, 1997b) and special issues of journals (e.g., *Human Communication Research*, Vol. 16, No. 1, 1989; *Communication Theory*, Vol. 10, No. 2, 2000) have given increasing attention to the processes through which messages are produced in communicative interactions.

Work in the 1960s and much of the 1970s on message production topics was marked by attention to specific variables that are important in the message production process. For example, a great deal of research in this era investigated personality and individual-difference variables such as communication apprehension (see McCroskey, 1984, for review) or rhetorical sensitivity (see Hart & Burks, 1972). These lines of research considered the extent to which the

traits and states of individuals might influence message behavior. For example, research in the communication apprehension tradition proposed that individuals who were high in communication apprehension would have difficulty producing effective messages in many communicative situations and would even avoid interaction.

Another influential line of research during this era was work on compliance gaining. This work began with Marwell and Schmitt's (1967) publication of a typology of strategies that could be used to gain compliance in interpersonal influence situations. Among Marwell and Schmitt's 16 strategies were *promising* (promising a reward for compliance), *positive altercasting* (saying that a person of good qualities will comply with the request), and *negative esteem* (saying that the target will be liked less if he or she does not comply). This typology served as an impetus for a great deal of work in communication, beginning with G. R. Miller, Boster, Roloff, and Seibold's (1977) seminal work. Compliance-gaining research has considered alternative ways of conceptualizing compliance gaining and the influence of individual and situational variables on the selection of compliance-gaining message tactics (see Seibold, Cantrill, & Meyers, 1985, for review).

These lines of research have been extremely productive ones. For example, work in compliance gaining has been prolific. Boster (1995) notes that more than 100 papers on the topic were published or presented in the 15 years following the Miller et al. (1977) work. However, this work has also been critiqued as being largely variable analytic—that is, research in which variables associated with the major constructs of interest (e.g., compliance gaining) are selected on a relatively ad hoc basis. For example, Boster (1995, p. 92) argues that "there is no theory, or set of competing theories, to explain the existing data" on compliance gaining. Kellermann and Cole (1994) leveled more biting critiques of this literature in arguing that the classification schemes used in compliance-gaining research have been inadequate, incomplete, unclear, and possibly invalid. In short, though individual studies during the 1960s and 1970s yielded important insights about message production behavior, they were rarely guided by a coherent theoretical focus.

In the late 1970s, several areas of scholarship were developed with the goal of providing theoretical coherence to explanations of message production. These theories have attempted both to codify a great deal of what we already know about message production behavior and to suggest theoretically consistent areas for continuing research. We discuss three of these theoretical developments in this chapter: (a) constructivism, and the related theory of message design logics, (b) action assembly theory, and (c) theories of planning and goals. These theoretical positions have in common the notion of connecting cognitive processes in individuals to message production behavior. However, the theories are quite different in terms of the nature of cognitive structures examined, the type of message production considered, and the manner in which cognitive structures are linked to message production behavior.

■ CONSTRUCTIVIST THEORY

Constructivist theory, or constructivism, is a theoretical approach to communication developed in the 1970s by Jesse Delia and his col-

leagues. Constructivism has represented perhaps the most coherent research program in interpersonal communication since the 1970s as scholars have systematically mapped out theoretical terms and relationships, elaborated on underlying assumptions, and tested predictions of the theory in a wide range of message production situations. Our examination of the theory begins with metatheoretical and theoretical foundations; sketches out the important propositions of the theory; discusses theoretical mechanisms and tests of the theory; and discusses the newest development in the constructivist project, Barbara O'Keefe's model of message design logics.

Metatheoretical Foundations of Constructivism

The philosophical foundations of constructivism are discussed in great detail by Delia, O'Keefe, and O'Keefe (1982), who consider the metatheoretical commitments of constructivism in terms of *philosophy of anthropology* and *philosophy of science*. In the terms we've used to discuss various approaches to theory, these roughly correspond, respectively, with ontology and epistemology.

The philosophy of anthropology laid out by Delia et al. (1982) describes an ontological position that is largely interpretive and social constructionist in nature. They quote Delia and Grossberg (1977) in explaining this position, noting that constructivist theorists recognize the "creative emergent process of the social reconstruction of reality as involving an interplay of individual interpretive processes and socially and historically constituted processes and contexts" (p. 36). In other words, constructivism's ontology recognizes that social reality is created through the ongoing interaction of individuals but also holds that such interaction is constrained by previously constructed social structures and contexts.

Constructivists also articulate an epistemological position in their philosophy of science. Delia and colleagues (1982) use Suppe's (1977) term *Wentanschauungen* to summarize their position. As embodied through constructivism, this epistemology emphasizes the theory-laden nature of observation and hence the importance of an articulated theoretical position in the development of research methods. For the constructivist research program, this has led to an emphasis on open-ended responses in research and theoretically based coding systems for interpreting those responses.

The Construct System

The constructivist approach to understanding message production begins with the cognitive systems of individuals. Several theoretical frameworks within social research have provided the bedrock on which constructivist views of individual cognition rest. The first of these is Kelly's (1955) theory of personal constructs. Kelly argues that people make sense of the world through constructs, or groupings of events based on similarities and differences (e.g., smart or stupid, short or tall, interesting or dull). Constructs are the basic building blocks of cognitive organization and can be joined in interpretive schemes. For example, an individual might build an interpretive scheme in which constructs about educational achievement, intelligence, and verbal ability are linked. Constructivists further rely on H. Werner's (1957) orthogenetic principle that proposes that cognitive systems follow a developmental trajectory in which they become more organized, more complex, and more abstract over time. For example, a child might have a relatively simple set of constructs for understanding television programming (e.g., cartoon or not cartoon, loud or soft, colorful or drab) whereas an adult might develop a much more elaborate interpretive scheme.

Thus, constructivist theory argues that human cognitive systems can be understood as **construct systems** that can be described in various ways (see Burleson, 1987; Burleson & Caplan, 1997, for review). The most fundamental way in which constructivists describe construct systems is in terms of their differentiation. Individuals whose construct systems include a great many constructs are said to be characterized by high

levels of **construct differentiation.** Construct systems can also be described in terms of their organization (e.g., what constructs are linked to other constructs) and their level of abstraction. These descriptors of construct systems, taken together, index an individual's level of **cognitive complexity.** As Burleson and Caplan (1997) summarize, "A cognitive system composed of a comparatively large number of finely articulated, abstract, and well integrated elements is regarded as relatively complex" (p. 23).

Construct systems can also be considered in terms of various domains. Consider a chef who has a highly differentiated construct system for dealing with cooking terms, equipment, and procedures but who is less cognitively complex with regard to constructs relevant to automobile repair. Burleson and Caplan (1997) emphasize that "individual differences in cognitive complexity, like various forms of expertise, are domain specific" (p. 239). For constructivists, the most critical domain has been constructs about other people, or the **interpersonal construct system.**

In the constructivist tradition, cognitive complexity within the domain of the interpersonal construct system has typically been measured through the use of the **role category question (RCQ).** The RCQ was developed by Crockett (1965) and involves the coding of open-ended responses. Specifically, respondents to the RCQ are asked to articulate (either in writing or orally) their impressions of a liked and a disliked peer. These descriptions are then coded by researchers who identify and count separate constructs and who may also rate those constructs in terms of abstractness and organization (see D. J. O'Keefe & Sypher, 1981). These assessments are then used to represent social cognitive structures and social perception processes such as role-taking ability (see Burleson, 1987, p. 310).

Person-Centered Communication

The other major component of constructivist theory involves the messages that are produced. Again, several theoretical foundations inform constructivist propositions about features of communication. The first of these is Bernstein's (1975) sociolinguistic theory that posits that individuals can take either a person-centered orientation to the world or a position-centered orientation. Bernstein proposes that person-centered individuals will use an elaborated code that recognizes the intentions, feelings, and perspectives of others. In contrast, position-centered individuals will use a restricted code that follows the rules and norms of the culturally defined situation. Constructivists combine Bernstein's theoretical insights with Piaget's (1926) model of communicative development and the symbolic interactionist (e.g., Mead, 1934) description of communication as "strategic, contextual, and multifunctional" (Burleson, 1987, p. 314). These theoretical roots converge in the constructivist concept of **person-centered communication.**

According to constructivist theory, "person-centered messages reflect an awareness of and an adaptation to the subjective, affective, and relational aspects of communicative contexts" (Burleson & Caplan, 1997, p. 249). Constructivists have studied person-centered communication in a variety of contexts, including persuasion, comforting, informing, conflict management, and discipline. In any of these contexts, a person-centered message is one that adapts to the needs of the listener, accounts for situational contingencies, and attends to multiple goals. Consider, for example, a child who wants to convince his mother to take him to the park. A message low in person-centeredness might be, "Please, Mommy, you never take me to the park." In contrast, a person-centered message might be, "Mommy, going to the park would give us both some fresh air, and I know you could use a break from your work."

As in their assessment of construct differentiation, constructivists typically assess the extent to which messages are person centered through the coding of open-ended responses. For this message analysis, study participants are typically asked to produce a message based on a specific situation (e.g., comforting a friend who just broke up with a boyfriend or girlfriend, talking a parent into a sleepover). These messages are then coded using hierarchically ordered coding systems developed for the specific message situation. The coding schemes look for specific features of the messages that embody various levels of person-centeredness. Person-centeredness is seen as arrayed on a continuum, and a research participant's score on the coding scheme is generally seen as reflecting his or her competence for producing person-centered messages in the relevant message domain.

Linking Constructs and Communication

We have sketched out the constructivist view of the cognitive construct system and the constructivist view of person-centered message production. How are these two ideas linked? According to constructivists, the link is a clear one: Individuals with more differentiated construct systems (i.e., individuals who are more cognitively complex) will produce more person-centered messages. As Burleson (1987) argues, "The basic theoretical notion underlying these studies has been that the use of person-centered message strategies . . . is dependent on the ability to infer and internally represent relevant psychological characteristics of the listener" (p. 320). Since the beginning of the constructivist research program, studies testing this relationship have used remarkably similar procedures. Indeed, Burleson (1989) argues that the "original" constructivist research study (Clark & Delia, 1977) has served as a research exemplar that has guided the paradigm. In most constructivist studies, construct system development is assessed through the RCQ. The person-centered nature of communication is assessed through the hierarchical coding of messages produced in response to hypothetical interactive situations. Then, the relationship between these two measures is assessed, typically through correlational techniques.

After many studies of this relationship (see Burleson, 1987; Burleson & Caplan, 1997, for reviews), the results are quite clear. As Burleson

(1987) summarizes, there is "little doubt that measures of interpersonal construct system development are moderately associated with measures tapping the person-centered quality of communication" (p. 327). Furthermore, this relationship holds across diverse populations of research participants; for different communicative goals, regardless of the specific assessments used within the coding schemes; and across both oral and written communication. In short, ample empirical evidence supports the major claim of the constructivist research program that construct differentiation is associated with the production of person-centered messages.

However, even with this relationship well-established, an important question remains: Why do cognitively complex people produce more person-centered messages? What is the underlying theoretical mechanism that drives this relationship? Burleson (1987) explores several explanations proposed to elaborate on the causal force underlying the relationship. He first considers the possibility that only a spurious relationship exists between cognitive complexity and person-centered messages. That is, some additional factor might cause both cognitive complexity and person-centered messages. However, after exploring a number of possibilities for this so-called third variable (e.g., rhetorical sensitivity, communication apprehension, empathic disposition), Burleson largely rejects this explanation. The second explanation Burleson considers is that the relationship is driven by a person's role-taking ability. He notes that "from this perspective . . . the acquisition and elaboration of the ability to 'take' (i.e., infer and internally represent) the perspective of another is regarded as the crucial cognitive development underlying the production of socialized or adapted speech" (Burleson, 1987, p. 330). Burleson also criticizes this explanation as being conceptually simplistic and unsupported by empirical data.

Burleson finds the most promise in the third explanatory mechanism, originally developed by B. J. O'Keefe and Delia (1982). A central component of this explanation is the concept of goals. Specifically, this account posits that individuals in interaction are attempting to manage goals that are both instrumental (e.g., persuading someone or informing someone) and relational (e.g., supporting the face of the other, presenting yourself in a favorable light). Some communicative situations are relatively simple with respect to goals, and others are more complex. For example, a supervisor providing a negative performance appraisal to a liked subordinate would face a complex situation that includes simultaneous goals of informing the subordinate of poor performance, providing motivation and instruction for changing that poor performance, and protecting the friendship.

B. J. O'Keefe and Delia (1982) use the term *behavioral complexity* to refer to the extent to which these complex needs are managed in interaction and suggest that person-centered messages are more behaviorally complex because they manage multiple goals. The production of these behaviorally complex messages can then be linked to cognitive complexity. Specifically, individuals with differentiated construct systems will generate complex definitions of interpersonal situations and will, as a result, produce messages that are more behaviorally complex and more person centered.

In 1987, Burleson saw this explanation as intriguing and theoretically sophisticated but also noted that it needed elaboration and further testing. By 1997, Burleson and Caplan argued that "the goal complexity account represents an important step in developing more comprehensive accounts of the message production process and the role cognitive complexity may play in that process" (p. 253). In the decade between these two assessments, important progress was made, much of it by Barbara O'Keefe in the development of her theory of message design logics. This theoretical extension of constructivism began with the goal complexity explanation discussed in this section and is discussed further in the next section.

Message Design Logics

O'Keefe's model of **message design logics** is based on the same metatheoretical ground as constructivism, and many of the theoretical

Table 7.1	The Three Message Design Logics		
	Expressive design logic	**Conventional design logic**	**Rhetorical design logic**
Fundamental premise	Language is a medium for expressing thoughts and feelings.	Communication is a game played cooperatively by social rules.	Communication is the creation and negotiation of social selves and situations.
Key message function	Self-expression	Secure desired response	Negotiate social consensus
Message/context relationship	Little attention to context	Action and meaning determined by context	Communication process creates context
Method of managing face	Editing	Politeness forms	Context redefinition
Evaluation of communication	Expressive clarity, openness and honesty, unimpeded signaling	Appropriateness, control of resources, cooperativeness	Flexibility, symbolic sophistication, depth of interpretation

Source: Adapted from O'Keefe (1988).

influences discussed in the preceding section (e.g., symbolic interactionism, Kelly's theory of personal constructs, the developmental theories of Werner and Piaget) are still relevant. However, message design logics also draws on an additional theoretical framework, Brown and Levinson's politeness theory (1978) (see our discussion of this framework in Chapter 16). As O'Keefe (1997) explains,

> Brown and Levinson argued that the various forms of politeness within a language could be understood as rational resolutions of goal conflicts that naturally arise when a speaker undertakes a face-threatening action: to achieve his/her goal, the speaker needs to be clear, but being clear will mean being more face-threatening; and conversely, to save face, the speaker must sacrifice getting the point across. (p. 96)

Thus, interactive situations are often characterized by multiple and conflicting goals. These conflicts are often between instrumental needs and face needs. The message design logics model argues that individuals have different logics that

are used for dealing with these conflicting goals. As O'Keefe (1988) summarizes, "Observed variation in goal management strategies could result from variation in the systems of principles used in reasoning from ends to communicative means, differences in the very definitions of communication that individuals construct and employ" (p. 84).

In the initial study that led to the message design logics model (O'Keefe & Shepherd, 1987), these contrasting logics were described as (a) *selection,* in which individuals choose between competing goals; (b) *separation,* in which competing goals are dealt with in different parts of a particular message; and (c) *integration,* in which the individual attempts to reconcile competing goals and remove obstacles within the message. Since then, O'Keefe has elaborated on these ideas and has proposed three message design logics: expressive, conventional, and rhetorical. Key elements of these design logics are defined in Table 7.1.

Messages representative of the three logics are defined in the points that follow and are illustrated with research participants' responses to a scenario in which a group member in a class assignment (Ron) has been perpetually late or absent from meetings and has not prepared work on time. His irresponsibility now threatens the grade of the entire group.

- An **expressive design logic** reflects the view that communication is a straightforward process of encoding thoughts and feelings. Expressive logic messages are literal and direct. For example: "Ron, I can't believe you haven't finished your research. You have been inconsiderate to the group all along. Several members even suggested that you be taken out of the group but we decided to give you a chance. Now what are we supposed to do? It was your responsibility and you backed out. I'm afraid that I'm going to tell the T.A. that you haven't done your share. I will be so mad at you if we get a bad grade on this—I need an A in this course" (O'Keefe, 1990, p. 95).

- A **conventional design logic** reflects the view that interaction is a cooperative game that is played according to rules, conventions, and procedures. Conflicting goals in the situation are sometimes dealt with in conventional logics but typically through add-ons in the interaction or through trivial politeness forms such as "please." For example: "Well, Ron, I'm sorry you don't have your part of the project done. We have given you several breaks thus far, and I don't see how we can give you any more. The whole group is depending on you, so I would suggest to you to get it done or at the most bring in what you have gotten done" (O'Keefe, 1990, p. 96).

- A **rhetorical design logic** reflects the view that communication serves to structure and create reality. Thus, rhetorical interactants use communication to define the situation in a way that will facilitate the meeting of multiple instrumental and face goals. For example: "Well, Ron, it's due

next week, and we have to get it all to the typist. OK, if it's not done it's not. Tell you what. Why don't you jot down your main ideas so that we can include them in the introduction and conclusion. Also, tell me when you think your section should come in the whole project. Then get it to my apartment by 10:00 tomorrow because I have to get it to the typist by 2:00. Is this okay? I'll just explain to the group that you'll have it done but not by meeting time. We all want a good grade, so if you need the time to make your part better, go ahead. But if I can't get it to the typist in time, you'll have to type it. All right, take it easy" (O'Keefe, 1990, p. 97).

Though empirical work using the message design logics framework is just beginning to develop (see O'Keefe, 1997), several initial studies suggest that it holds some promise (Lambert & Gillespie, 1994; O'Keefe & McCornack, 1987; O'Keefe & Shepherd, 1987; Saeki & O'Keefe, 1994). Perhaps the largest contributions of the framework are its explication of multiple and conflicting goals as an explanatory mechanism within the constructivist framework and its specification of particular communicative logics—architectures that link message functions to message forms (O'Keefe, 1997, p. 111). Furthermore, by arguing that message design logics come into play as communicators manage specific goals, the framework highlights the ongoing control of message production in interaction. O'Keefe and Lambert (1995) describe this as an approach that emphasizes "the local management of the flow of thought—both the management of thoughts by the producer and the management of the other's thoughts in the service of communicative goals" (p. 55).

ACTION ASSEMBLY THEORY

Action assembly theory was developed by John Greene (1984) and has been elaborated and tested since then by Greene and his colleagues.

SPOTLIGHT ON THE THEORIST

John Greene

John Greene considers himself "very fortunate" in his work as a professor of communication—particularly in terms of his theoretical and research work with action assembly theory. He had some of his initial ideas for the theory as early as his undergraduate work at Purdue University and continued developing these ideas while working on his master's degree at Pennsylvania State University and his Ph.D. at the University of Wisconsin. As Greene notes, "Virtually everything I'd learned in nine years of coursework (plus two additional years devoted to explicating the theory in my dissertation) exerted some sort of influence on my thinking." Greene doubts that his interest in the concepts of action assembly theory will wane. Indeed, he says that "I fully anticipate that I'll continue to pursue the various paths suggested by [action assembly theory] for the duration of my career." He has worked for almost all of his career on the faculty at Purdue.

Greene traces the development of action assembly theory to four fundamental observations about human behavior that he believes are "beautiful in their simplicity and intuitive appeal": (a) that we tend to produce behaviors appropriate to our goals and the situation; (b) that our abstract ideas about what we're doing influence our physical movements; (c) that we often behave automatically, with little thought or effort; and (d) that our behavior reflects both repetitive patterns and novelty and creativity. These basic observations have led to a theory of message production that crosses a variety of boundaries.

As Greene notes, a key attribute of action assembly theory is "that it is a theory about the processes underlying the production of *all* behavior—verbal and nonverbal, controlled and automatic, motoric and symbolic."

Greene has been gratified by the impact of his theory on the communication discipline. His theory is typically cited in theory textbooks (like this one), and the original article describing action assembly theory was awarded the prestigious Charles Woolbert Award from the National Communication Association in 1994. This award is given to scholarship that has "stood the test of time" and had a major impact on subsequent theory and research in communication. Greene says, though, that he is most pleased that action assembly theory has influenced the way we conceptualize communication. As he says, "The very notion that messages are 'assembled' has emerged as a part of our collective understanding of communication processes." This influence indicates that assembly is "a resonant metaphor that has influenced the way scholars think and write that extends far beyond the theory itself."

Greene is clearly a scholar who is excited about his research and about his part in the theory development process. He says that "most people wake up on Monday morning and think 'I've got to go to work'—I am very fortunate to feel each day that 'I *get* to go to work." He hopes that students in the communication field will share his excitement about the research endeavor. To that end, he advises that neophyte scholars read widely in many fields. He suggests that students should "go where your interests lead you, regardless of how many disciplinary boundaries you have to cross." Greene believes that such a journey will be both fascinating and rewarding.

Proponents of action assembly theory have a goal very similar to that of constructivists: "to provide a theoretical account of verbal and nonverbal behavior by specifying the cognitive structures and processes that underlie the pro-

duction of those behaviors" (Greene & Geddes, 1993, p. 30). However, action assembly theory differs significantly from constructivism in a host of respects: metatheoretical commitments, description of cognitive structures, description of message behavior, and explanatory links between cognitive structures and message behaviors. Recently, Greene (1997a, 2000) has described a second-generation action assembly theory. Because most of the empirical testing of Greene's ideas has been based on his original explication of action assembly theory, the description provided here concentrates on those ideas. However, as we work through major components of the theory, concepts from the second-generation theory are discussed to consider the current development of the theory and areas for future empirical testing.

Metatheoretical Commitments

Action assembly theory is based in the social scientific—even positivistic—study of communication. Greene (1989) places action assembly theory squarely within the traditions of cognitive science in which the goal of theory is to explain some set of phenomena in terms of the so-called black box of the mental system. Theory building becomes a process of making inferences about cognitive structures and processes after observing regularities associated with input to and output from the mental system.

In a further elaboration of action assembly theory's metatheoretical position, Greene discusses the school of *generative realism* (Greene, 1990, 1995). A generative realist takes an ontological stance in which human action is seen as an amalgam of real social, physiological, and psychological components. A generative realist can emphasize any one of these components. For example, action assembly theory emphasizes the psychological system, though it also acknowledges the importance of physiological and social influences on human action. In terms of epistemology, generative realism adheres to an objectivist emphasis on scientific explanation. Specifically, within generative realism, "human action is seen to be the result of the complex interplay of numerous causal mechanisms; explanation is held to be given by specifying the nature of the

causal structures and processes that give rise to the phenomena of interest" (Greene, 1995, p. 52). Thus, an adequate explanatory account within the cognitive paradigm must specify both the structures and processes that operate in the cognitive system.

Structures in Action Assembly Theory

At the center of action assembly theory is the concept of a **procedural record.** A procedural record is part of an individual's memory system in which information about how to execute various behaviors is stored. A procedural record consists of three types of information (nodes) and links between the nodes. Specifically, procedural records contain information about *action* (what a person might do), *outcomes* (what might happen as a result of the action), and *situations*. As Greene and Geddes (1993) explain, "Procedural records preserve action-outcome-in-situation contingencies" (p. 30). For example, a procedural record might state that "traveling at excessive speed (action) in a zone that specifies a low speed limit (situation) can result in the issuance of a ticket (outcome)." Particularly important to Greene's theory are procedural records related to communication behavior. One such procedural record might be "using polite terms (action) when meeting my girlfriend's father (situation) will convey an attitude of respect (outcome)."

In second-generation action assembly theory, Greene (1997a) emphasizes the ways in which these nodes (action, outcome, situation) become linked in procedural records. Specifically, this linking of nodes can occur in an associative way, through the repeated concurrent linking of nodes in a record. Greene (1997a) uses the example of depressing the clutch before shifting when driving a standard transmission car, to illustrate an associative link. In contrast, nodes can be linked in a symbolic way in which the meaning of the link is taken into account. For example, if the procedural record includes the notion of pushing in the clutch in order to avoid stripping the gears when shifting, the

Table 7.2	Output Representation Levels in Action Assembly Theory
Level of output representation	**Example in "asking for a date" situation**
Interactional representation	"I would like to ask this person for a date in a manner that will be effective and not embarrassing."
Ideational representation	"I will mention a new movie that has come out and see if there is any interest in a date."
Utterance representation	**Chris:** "Hey, I hear *Gladiator* is just great. Have you seen it yet?" **Pat:** "No, I've been meaning to, though." **Chris:** "Do you want to go out on Friday night and catch it with me?"
Sensorimotor representation	Actual production of these messages in a clear and friendly tone with adequate eye contact

symbolic relationship in the procedural record is emphasized.

Several aspects of these procedural records (either associative or symbolic) are important in action assembly theory. First, procedural records exist at many levels of abstraction. For example, "some procedural records are employed in controlling muscle movements while others are responsible for abstract planning" (Greene, 1989, p. 120). Second, procedural records vary in terms of strength. A strong record is one that has been used frequently or recently. Thus, procedural records for routine behavior such as driving or greeting others are probably relatively strong. Third, procedural records are generally conceived of as being independent of each other. However, records that are used together frequently can form "unitized assemblies." For example, procedural records for restaurant behavior (e.g., ordering, chatting with the waiter, asking for the check) might be joined in a unitized assembly.

The second kind of structure specified in action assembly theory is the **output representa-tion,** or the actual behavior produced from procedural records. Greene (1984) proposes that output representations exist at a variety of levels and that these levels are hierarchically ordered from the most abstract to the least abstract. The most abstract level is the *interactional representation,* in which plans for reaching interactional goals are held. The second level, *ideational representation,* consists of specific ideas about the moves that will get an individual to a particular goal. Next, the *utterance representation* consists of the words in a message and the way those words are put together. Finally, the *sensorimotor representation* consists of the sensing and motor skills involved in behavior. These levels are illustrated in Table 7.2.

Activation and Assembly Processes

Thus, there are two kinds of structures in action assembly theory: procedural records and behavioral representations. As you might imagine, there are an incredible number of procedural records in any individual's memory, and only a small subset of these will be used for any particular behavioral production. A central aspect of action assembly theory, then, is to specify the processes that link procedural records to behavioral representations. These processes fall into two categories: **activation processes** and **assembly processes.**

Activation is the process by which particular procedural records are selected. Activation is seen to be a function of (a) the match between an individual's goals and the outcome portion of the procedural record and (b) the match between the current situation and the situation on the procedural record. That is, if you were in a situation in which you needed to effectively discipline your child for swearing, all procedural records relevant to this goal and situation would be activated. The speed at which procedural records are activated is posited to be a function of the strength of the procedural record. Remember that record strength is a function of the recency and frequency of activation. Thus, if your common disciplinary tactic is to put your child in time out, a procedural record specifying this action would likely be activated most quickly. Records specifying the action of yelling or ignoring the problem would be activated more slowly.

However, activation is only part of the process linking procedural records to action. Because many procedural records can be activated simultaneously, it is important to consider also the process of assembly. The assembly process organizes a set of activated records into a coherent behavioral representation. In early formulations of action assembly theory, assembly was seen as a serial process that proceeds from more abstract specifications to more concrete specifications. That is, assembly was conceptualized as a serial and largely top-down process that begins at the interactional level, then proceeds through related records at the ideational, utterance, and sensorimotor levels. In the second-generation theory, however, the assembly process is seen as proceeding through the formation of coalitions, or "momentary assemblages of activated behavioral features that could be said to

'fit' together" (Greene, 1997a, p. 159). Greene (1997a, 2000) argues that this coalition formation is not necessarily a serial or hierarchical process but rather one in which "a great many action features, relevant to a variety of goals and functional requirements, will be activated above their resting levels at any given moment" (Greene, 2000, p. 149).

An important implication of the assembly process (either the hierarchical process of action assembly theory or the coalition formation process of the second-generation theory) is that it makes demands on a person's information processing capacity. That is, though the action assembly process may not always be conscious, it does take time. However, these processing demands can be lessened in two situations. First, as noted earlier, when procedural records are often activated together, they can form a unitized assembly that would lessen required assembly time. Second, when individuals have a chance to assemble in advance of production—that is, to plan what they are going to say and do—assembly time during interaction should be reduced.

Action Assembly Theory: Evidence and Extensions

The proposition that "assembly takes time" forms the bedrock of empirical tests of action assembly theory. That is, most tests of the theory have evaluated the dependent variables of speech onset latency (e.g., pausing before speaking) and hesitations during speaking. Such latencies and hesitations are assumed to be indicators of the cognitive processing involved in activating and assembling procedural records. The tests of action assembly theory have then proposed that certain factors should influence required assembly time and hence influence latencies and hesitations. Two lines of research are particularly noteworthy: studies of the effects of planning and studies regarding multiple goals (see reviews of research in Greene, 1989, 1995).

In terms of planning, Greene (1995) notes that ample evidence indicates that people who are given an opportunity to plan will produce messages more rapidly and more fluently than those not given the opportunity to do so. This observation supports action assembly theory. However, more compelling support is provided by an early study in the action assembly theory program. In this study, Greene (1984) gave some participants the opportunity to plan the structure of their message, but they had no information about the message topic and content. Even when just considering structural planning, individuals who had a chance to plan produced messages with fewer latencies and hesitations than those not given the chance to plan. Greene (1995) also discusses relevant research in the areas of online planning and deception and concludes that "taken together, these results are generally supportive of the notion that planning . . . reduces cognitive load at the time of message production" (p. 74).

A second important line of support for action assembly theory comes from studies of multiple-goal messages. When an interaction situation involves multiple goals, the theory posits increased demands on an individual's information processing capacity. That is, assembly may be difficult because aspects of behaviors associated with one goal may be incompatible with behaviors associated with the other goal. Thus, multiple-goal situations should be characterized by more speech latencies and hesitations, though the opportunity to plan or the existence of unitized assemblies might mitigate this effect. Greene (1995) reviews a series of studies that largely supports this line of reasoning.

Finally, it is important to note some additional ways in which action assembly theory has been extended in recent years. One important extension is really a theoretical application of action assembly theory. Greene and Geddes (1993) use the propositions of the theory to understand a variety of research on social skills. They begin by noting that it is "an unavoidable and frustrating fact of our social lives that on many occasions we produce messages only, on further reflection, to succeed in formulating a response that would

have been more skilled or effective than the message we actually gave" (p. 26). Greene and Geddes go on to use action assembly theory as a way of explaining those situations in which adequate social skills and motivation fail to produce the desired social behavior.

Second, as we have noted throughout this discussion, Greene (1997a, 2000) has proposed a second-generation theory that extends many of his original ideas. We have dealt with some of these extensions already as they relate to the concepts of procedural records and the activation and assembly of those records. Greene has also added other ideas to action assembly theory that revolve around the neurophysiological components of message production. The specific details of this portion of the second-generation revision are beyond the scope of this chapter, but the next decade may reveal that this second-generation theory provides progressive developments to the original action assembly theory.

◼ PLANNING AND GOALS

The third and final area of theoretical development in message production that we consider here involves the notions of plans and goals. Like the theories discussed so far in this chapter, this theoretical framework provides an understanding of cognitive structures and how those structures influence verbal and nonverbal behavior. As Chuck Berger (1995) notes, "The constructs of *goal* and *plan* have frequently been invoked to explain how persons understand the actions of others and symbolic representations of these actions in narrative texts" (p. 143). A great deal of recent research in communication has centered on these constructs, though the research is not as theoretically coherent as that found in the constructivist or action assembly traditions. In this section, we first consider the concepts of goals and plans and then discuss the way the concepts have been linked by Berger in a recent theory of planning and strategic communication.

Explicating Relevant Constructs

The Goal Construct Dillard (1997) states that "in the past decade, we have witnessed a landslide of work attesting to the importance of the goal construct in theories of communication" (p. 47). This is not surprising, as we often think of communication as goal directed. Thus, a consideration of the types and nature of goals is often seen as central to theories linking cognition to message production. However, theorists often deal with the concept of *goal* in very different ways. Dillard (1997) lists a variety of issues that should be considered in explicating the goal construct. For example, he considers questions such as "Must goals be conscious?," "Is commitment a necessary feature of goals?," and "Do goals have subcompartments?" as issues that theorists must grapple with as they theorize about the impact of goals in interpersonal interaction.

Three aspects of the goal construct have been particularly relevant to theoretical work in this area. First, individuals will have multiple goals within any interaction. Dillard and his colleagues (Dillard 1990b; Dillard, Segrin, & Hardin, 1989) have provided a useful consideration of these multiple goals by differentiating between primary goals and secondary goals. **Primary goals** define a particular communicative situation: They constitute what a person is trying to accomplish in the interaction. For example, a person might have the primary goal of changing an attitude, of informing, of comforting, or of gaining compliance. These primary goals provide the push in the interaction. In contrast, **secondary goals** often provide a counterforce to the primary goals and are typically concerned with relational issues. Specifically, Dillard et al. (1989) consider five types of secondary goals:

- *Identity goals* involve preservation of the self-concept.
- *Interaction goals* are concerned with being socially appropriate.
- *Relational resource goals* are concerned with increasing or maintaining relational assets such as support, attention, or stimulation.

- *Personal resource goals* are concerned with increasing or maintaining an individual's personal assets.
- *Arousal management goals* are concerned with maintaining arousal within an acceptable range.

A second and related issue to be considered with regard to goals involves the notion of overall *meta-goals* that influence interaction. Kellermann (1992) proposes that meta-goals regulate and constrain behaviors in a variety of social contexts. The meta-goal of **efficiency** suggests that interactants often want to achieve their primary goals without wasting time and resources. However, the meta-goal of **appropriateness** typically places a brake on efficiency and is related to the goals of politeness theory discussed earlier in this chapter. The meta-goals of efficiency and appropriateness thus shape and constrain behavior as interactants attempt to achieve social objectives in ways that protect the face of both the source and the receiver. For example, if you were trying to convince a friend to loan you some money, a meta-goal of efficiency might suggest a very direct approach. However, the meta-goal of appropriateness would curb this direct approach and perhaps lead you to compliance-gaining strategies that involve complimenting and promising instead of making a direct request.

Finally, S. R. Wilson (1990, 1995) has considered the ways in which goals are formed and activated within the cognitive system. His **cognitive rules model of goals,** in some ways similar to Greene's action assembly theory, assumes that goals are connected to situational features within long-term memory via cognitive rules. Goals will be triggered from memory when there is a fit between the current situation and the situation in memory (e.g., when there is a relevant cognitive rule), when the rule linking goal and situation is strong, and when the rule has been recently activated. Consider, for instance, a situation in which you want to ask someone out on a date. Your choice of strategy might depend on strategies you have used (successfully or unsuccessfully) when asking out similar people in similar situations.

Explicating the Plan Process Goals provide the destination for communicative interaction. That is, goals tell us where we want to go, both instrumentally and relationally. However clear the destination is, though, the goal does not specify directions. Instead, the road map for achieving our interactive goals is provided by **interaction plans.** Berger (1997) reviewed a number of definitions of plans and concluded that they converged on several issues. Berger conceptualizes plans as hierarchical and mental representations of goal-directed action sequences. In noting that plans are mental representations, Berger emphasizes that the plans are not the actions themselves, and hence there can be gaps between a plan and its enactment. In noting that plans are hierarchical, Berger highlights that there are more and less concrete ways to represent an action sequence. For example, the plan of "providing a good argument to convince my spouse to go on a diet" is more abstract than the plan of "providing relevant statistics that link weight gain with serious health problems." Finally, Berger emphasizes that plans often contain alternative action sequences for reaching goals. For example, in talking to a professor about the impact of poor performance on an examination, a student could either argue for getting more points on the test or ask for opportunities for extra credit. Because plans contain a variety of contingency action sequences, social actors must often make decisions "online" in the interaction about what route to take (see Waldron, 1997, for additional explication of the **online planning** process).

Berger's Theory of Planning

Berger and his colleagues have embarked on a research program that takes this planning concept and investigates its implications for interpersonal interaction. That research program has been summarized in a book titled *Planning Social Interaction* (Berger, 1997). In his theory of planning, Berger proposes explanations for how plans are created and formulated, for how plans vary in terms of complexity and contingencies, for how social actors react to the thwarting of plans, and for the impact of plan success or failure on affect and plan fluidity. The specific propositions of Berger's planning theory are presented in Table 7.3.

Space does not permit a full discussion of the research that supports Berger's various propositions. However, substantial work has supported his ideas about the antecedents and consequences of plans (see Berger, 1997, chapter 3) and about the role of affect in the planning process (see Berger, 1988). For example, Berger and his colleagues have noted that particular individual traits (e.g., self-monitoring, cognitive complexity) predict the extent to which individuals are likely to construct complex plans for interaction. Furthermore, the complexity of plans formulated is likely to influence the fluidity with which plans are put into action and the reactions individuals have when their plans are thwarted.

Some of the most interesting recent work in planning theory has involved the **hierarchy principle** instantiated in Proposition 6 of Berger's theory (see Table 7.3). This principle considers what happens when plans are thwarted and suggests that individuals will first change plans at the lowest level of abstraction. That is, communicators will change concrete aspects of the message (e.g., word choice and delivery) before changing more abstract aspects of message content. As the title of one article investigating this phenomenon states, "If at first you don't succeed, say it louder and slower" (Berger & diBattista, 1993). In a series of studies (summarized in Berger, 1997, chapter 4), Berger and his colleagues found support for this proposition as well as for the notion that changes in abstract aspects of plans were more cognitively demanding than lower-level changes.

A great deal of research on the planning process has involved the use of relatively contrived experimental situations (see Berger, 1997, for review). This is not surprising, given the need for control in testing the specific hypotheses proposed in planning theory. However, recent calls for increased attention to context in message planning and production (Dillard & Solomon, 2000) and for additional attention to online plan-

Table 7.3	Propositions of Berger's Planning Theory

Proposition 1: When persons derive plans to meet goals, their first priority is to access long-term memory to determine whether an already-formulated or canned plan is available for use.

Proposition 2: As the desire to reach a social goal increases, the complexity with which plans are formulated also tends to increase.

Proposition 3: Increases in strategic domain knowledge and specific domain knowledge tend to produce increases in the complexity of plans within that domain.

Proposition 4: Strength of desire and levels of strategic and specific domain knowledge interact to produce differences in plan complexity. High levels of desire and high levels of knowledge produce more complex plans. Low and high desire levels coupled with low knowledge levels should produce less complex plans.

Proposition 5: Increased concerns for the meta-goals of efficiency and social appropriateness tend to reduce the complexity of plans to reach social goals.

Proposition 6: When people experience thwarting internal to the interaction, their first response is likely to involve low-level plan hierarchy alterations. Continued thwarting will tend to produce more abstract alterations to plan hierarchies.

Proposition 7: Attainment of a superordinate goal will produce positive affect. Interruption of a plan will result in the induction of negative affect.

Proposition 8: Repeated thwarting of plans will lead to the instantiation and enactment of progressively less socially appropriate plans.

Proposition 9: With repeated thwarting over time, resulting in the induction of higher levels of negative affect, plans will become increasingly less complex.

Proposition 10: Under conditions of goal failure, individuals whose plans contain no alternative actions and those whose plans contain numerous action alternatives at the point of thwarting will manifest lower levels of action fluidity than those whose plans contain a small number of contingent actions.

Proposition 11: Increased access to planned actions will generally increase action fluidity levels in such a way that the curvilinear relationship between the number of alternatives and action fluidity will be maintained but displaced upward relative to the same function obtained under conditions of reduced action access.

ning during interaction (Waldron, 1997) suggest that a wider range of research situations can and should be considered. S. R. Wilson (2000), for instance, has looked at the plans parents use when disciplining their children, arguing that "abusive parents are less skilled than nonabusive parents at coordinating their own goals and plans with those of their children" (p. 218). Thus, research on planning and goals can be extended to everyday—and problematic—situations marked by complexity in both the goals of interactants and the contexts in which they are behaving.

■ COMPARISON AND COMMENTARY

The theories we examined in this chapter share an overarching aim—to shed light on the processes that contribute to the production of messages in a variety of interpersonal communication contexts. The theories also choose some similar routes in understanding these issues: All consider cognitive structures and the ways in which those structures influence the messages that are produced. However, the theories also differ in many ways. Each theory focuses on a different type of cognitive structure: construct systems in constructivism, procedural records in action assembly theory, and goals and plans in Berger's theory of planning. The theories also differ in terms of the types of message behavior explained and in the processes that link cognitive structures with message production.

If we were to apply some of the criteria for theory discussed earlier in this book, each of these theories would fare quite well. For example, consider Kuhn's criteria for theory discussed in Chapter 3. Kuhn (1977) proposed that theories should be chosen based on the criteria of accuracy, scope, fruitfulness, simplicity, and consistency. In terms of accuracy, the theories we discussed in this chapter have met with widespread empirical support. Although not all aspects of all three theories have been tested, empirical observations have largely been consistent with predictions of the theory. The theories also include a relatively wide scope of message production behaviors. Indeed, Greene (1997) states that the explanatory scope of action assembly theory is "human behavior, broadly construed, but with particular emphasis on the sorts of verbal and nonverbal behaviors that people produce in interactions with others" (p. 152). Third, the theories we discussed have been quite fruitful. All three research traditions (especially constructivism) have generated substantial research, extensions to new scholarly areas, and even some practical application. The fourth criterion, simplicity, is a difficult one to judge. This standard essentially deals with the elegance of the theory, suggesting that a theory should be streamlined and parsimonious to the extent possible without sacrificing explanatory power. The theories considered here, like most theories of cognition, are highly complex, but some would argue that this complexity is necessary given the conceptual domain being described and explained.

There could also be a bit of debate about the final criterion, consistency. There is little doubt that these theories are internally consistent. The propositions and processes set forth in each theory do not contradict each other, and they form coherent packages of explanation. However, the theories may not meet the criterion of external consistency quite as convincingly. This criterion states that a theory should not contradict other widely held theories in a relevant domain. Though the theorists considered here have worked to embed their theories within wider theoretical frameworks (e.g., politeness theory for message design logics, cognitive theory for action assembly theory), these scholars have rarely addressed the issue of consistency with each other. Berger (1997) provides one exception to this pattern in a chapter that compares his theory of planning to other theories of message production. But, in general, theorists in each of these traditions remain insulated from each other. Workers in the action assembly theory tradition do not consider cognitive complexity or planning. Workers in constructivism deal only with their own view of the cognitive and message production systems. And though this pattern has been useful in creating a system of "normal science" within each of these traditions, it also runs the risk of blinding scholars to the potential contribution of other theorists working in the same discipline.

In a similar vein, researchers in each of these theoretical traditions have tended to rely on standard research tools and procedures in their work. For example, scholars investigating action assembly theory almost always consider the dependent variables of response latencies and hesitations as indicators of cognitive activity and load. Though convincing arguments are made for these measures, researchers do not know what cognitive activity is occurring during pauses and latencies. In planning theory, Berger and his colleagues have relied extensively on several research procedures. For example, studies of the hierarchy principle have largely been based on plans for providing directions for getting from one familiar landmark to another. Though research in this area has been compelling, reliance on this single experimental procedure limits the extent to which a broad scope can be claimed for this theoretical proposition.

The reliance on standard instruments and procedures has been particularly pronounced within the constructivist tradition. As noted earlier, Burleson (1989) saw early constructivist studies as providing a research paradigm that was followed closely in subsequent work. In this paradigm, construct differentiation is measured with the role category questionnaire, or RCQ, and relevant message behavior is measured by applying a relevant hierarchical coding system to an open-ended message response. Gastil (1995), following Lakatos's concept of scientific research programs (Lakatos, 1978), has called this the protective belt of constructivism; that is, it protects the basic assumptions of the theoretical tradition. Two issues are important in considering this protective belt. First, questions have been raised periodically about precisely what the RCQ and the hierarchical coding systems measure (see Gastil, 1995, for review of critiques and Burleson & Caplan, 1997, for argument supporting the use of the RCQ). These questions have been raised at both the conceptual and the operational levels. Second, strong reliance on specific conceptualizations and measurement tools can be extremely limiting. As Gastil (1995) argues, "If the theoretical scope of Constructivism is as broad as it appears, then empirical research must begin to spread itself out within this scope" (p. 96).

Finally, though these theories were all developed within the traditions of post-positivism or interpretivism, it is useful to briefly shine an ethical light on them. These theories deal with message production and the processes that affect message production. Thus, these theories deal either directly or indirectly with the issues of competence and effectiveness. As a result, issues of good and bad are woven into the theoretical fabric. For example, are individuals with the ability to produce more complex plans better communicators? Are individuals whose assembly processes allow them to deal effectively with multiple goals more advanced in their message production capabilities?

These issues of good and bad are particularly important in the constructivist research tradition, in which theorists and researchers clearly argue that messages that are more person-centered or that embody a rhetorical design logic are more developmentally advanced and more effective. Indeed, research participants have largely rated these kinds of messages as more effective. However, most of the research in the constructivist tradition has involved college students in North America. Perhaps in other contexts or with other populations, messages using expressive or conventional logics might be seen as equally or more effective. Gastil (1995) asks the question this way:

> Should society view a high level of cognitive complexity as a valuable resource? If so, it is important to know who has it and who does not because a democratic society relies upon a broad distribution of both material and social resources, including cognitive and communication competencies. . . . If cognitive complexity is not evenly distributed, researchers need to learn how it is acquired. How does it develop during childhood, and does it solidify in adulthood? What social conditions or public education programs are conducive to its development in children and adults? (p. 98)

As Gastil notes, though, many of these issues are empirical ones. As such, these questions—and others like them that could be generated about action assembly theory and planning theory—should provide important new directions for these and other theories in the area of message production.

Key Terms

constructivist theory
construct systems
construct differentiation
cognitive complexity
interpersonal construct system
role category questionnaire
person-centered communication
message design logics
expressive design logic
conventional design logic
rhetorical design logic

action assembly theory
procedural record
output representation
activation processes
assembly processes
primary goals
secondary goals
efficiency
appropriateness
cognitive rules model of goals
interaction plans
online planning
hierarchy principle of plans

Discussion Questions

1. The theories discussed in this chapter are cognitive theories of communication. What specific kinds and processes of cognition are important in each theory?

2. What are the difficulties of testing cognitive theories of communication? How does the research associated with each theory deal with these difficulties?

3. How would each theory discussed in this chapter consider a situation in which you are attending a highly formal wedding for the first time and you find yourself next in the receiving line?

4. Which theories of symbolic organization (discussed in Chapter 6) are the best fit with the theories of message production discussed in this chapter? What other types of message production theories might be appropriate when using different models of symbolic organization?

8 Theories of Message Processing

At the beginning of Chapter 7, we noted that most definitions of communication include the concept of encoding. This basic observation led us to our consideration of message production theories such as action assembly theory, constructivism, and theories of message goals and planning. In this chapter, we explore the other side of the coin, for, not surprisingly, most definitions of communication also include the concept of decoding, or the process of receiving and processing incoming messages. As the theories in this chapter illustrate, this is definitely not a simple and straightforward undertaking because people are not blank slates receiving messages or simple machines processing the information they receive. Instead, as the theories of symbolic organization considered in Chapter 6 illustrate, humans are beings in which cognition and emotion play integral roles in the complex enterprise of message reception and message processing.

Traditionally, theories of message processing have tried to explain the reception of a particular type of message. These messages have been designed by their sources to change or reinforce the behaviors and attitudes of others. Thus, theories describing the reception and processing of these messages are often described as theories of persuasion. However, the processes proposed in these theories are often relevant to

message processing in a more general sense, and the final theory we will consider in this chapter, problematic integration theory, purposefully takes on a much wider range of message processing issues than those considered in typical persuasion theories.

Theories of message processing are of interest to a variety of behavioral science disciplines, and many of the theories most widely used over the years were generated in the fields of psychology and social psychology. In this chapter, however, we concentrate on theories of message processing that have strong and current connections to the communication discipline. Two of these theories (the elaboration likelihood model and inoculation theory) were developed by social psychologists but continue to generate both research and theory development by communication scholars. The third, problematic integration theory, is an emerging theory from within the communication discipline. Before we move to our detailed consideration of these theories, however, it is worthwhile to take a brief look at some classic models of persuasion. By considering these theories, we can see how they have shaped contemporary models of message processing. More detailed consideration of these theories from the perspective of communication scholars can be found in D. J. O'Keefe (1990) and Stiff (1994).

THREE CLASSIC MODELS OF PERSUASION

Models of persuasion are a mainstay of social psychological research. These theories propose explanations of the processes through which social influence occurs in a variety of contexts (e.g., in interpersonal settings, in group settings, or through contact with the media). G. R. Miller (1980) has pointed to the range of communicative activities and situations that are potentially persuasive, defining *persuasive communication* as "any message that is intended to shape, reinforce, or change the responses of another, or others." By pointing to these three functions of persuasive communication (i.e., shaping attitudes and behaviors, reinforcing attitudes and behaviors, and changing attitudes and behaviors), Miller emphasizes the wide range of settings in which persuasion occurs and the wide range of messages that can be seen as persuasive communication.

Myriad theories have been proposed to describe and explain the persuasion process. In psychology, the period from the late 1950s through the mid 1970s gave birth to a number of theories that had a strong influence on our thinking about how attitudes are shaped, reinforced, and changed. In this section, we look briefly at three classic theories of persuasion and attitude change that emerged during this time period: cognitive dissonance theory, the theory of reasoned action, and social judgment theory. We consider only thumbnail sketches of these theories and do not review the huge range of research that has sprung from them. These brief sketches, though, should illuminate traditional views of persuasion that have influenced the theories we consider in more detail later in the chapter.

Cognitive Dissonance Theory

Cognitive dissonance theory, developed by Leon Festinger (1957), is one of the most well-known and influential theories of persuasion ever developed. Cognitive dissonance theory examines the relationship between attitude and behavior—the link between what you think

about an issue and how you behave regarding that issue. Our common sense about this process would suggest that attitudes cause behavior. For example, you might vote for a particular candidate (behavior) because you feel positively about that candidate (attitude). Or your attitude about a particular social cause might lead you to participate in rallies or contribute money for that cause. In cognitive dissonance theory, however, the tables are turned, and the emphasis is on the ways in which behavior influence attitude.

The initial test of cognitive dissonance theory was conducted by Festinger and Carlsmith (1959). In this study, research participants were asked to perform a very boring experimental task (sorting spools and turning pegs). After completing this activity, the participants were asked to interact with the next research "participant" (actually an experimental confederate) and describe the task as interesting and fun. Research participants were promised either $1 or $20 to do this. (Keep in mind that $20 in 1959 would be more than $60 today!) The researchers then measured the extent to which attitudes about the boring task changed (or didn't) following this behavior. Festinger and Carlsmith found that attitudes about the task did not change in the $20 condition but did change in the $1 condition. That is, people who were paid $1 to say that they liked the task reported actually liking the task more as a result. In the $1 condition, but not in the $20 condition, behavior influenced attitude.

What can explain these results? Cognitive dissonance theory says that the key concept for understanding this process is the need individuals have for consistency between their attitudes and behaviors. That is, if we behave in a way that is inconsistent with our attitudes, we feel an uncomfortable sense of dissonance that must be relieved in some way. We often maintain consistency in our attitudes by exposing ourselves only to messages that are consistent with our attitudes. For example, an advocate of gun control would be unlikely to read the literature of the National Rifle Association because it might produce uncomfortable dissonance. However, when we behave in a way that seems inconsistent with our beliefs (like the participants in Festinger and Carlsmith's study), we need to change our attitude to match our behavior. Interestingly, though, the participants paid $20 did not change their attitude. According to cognitive dissonance theory, this is because the $20 provided a justification for expressing a positive opinion about the task (e.g., "I said that the task was fun because I was being paid so much to do so"). Because those being paid $1 did not have such a justification, they relieved their dissonance (i.e., the uncomfortable contrast between attitude and behavior) by shifting their attitude to match their behavior.

Dissonance theory led to a great deal of research during the 1960s and 1970s, and there has been consistent support for its general predictions (see, e.g., Cooper & Fazio, 1984, for review). However, cognitive dissonance theory has also been criticized because it is difficult to falsify (e.g., if the attitude didn't change, a scholar could simply conclude that there must not have been any dissonance), and it has been revised to add new theoretical concepts such as the level of commitment and free choice involved in the behavior (Brehm & Cohen, 1962). Perhaps the most important critique of cognitive dissonance theory has been the proposal of an alternative theoretical mechanism to explain the results seen in research. Specifically, Bem (1967, 1972) has suggested that dissonance results can be explained through the process of self-perception. That is, the attitude is not changed in order to reduce psychological discomfort but simply because an individual observes himself or herself behaving in a certain way and infers that he or she must hold an attitude in line with that behavior.

Theory of Reasoned Action

The **theory of reasoned action,** developed by Martin Fishbein and Icek Ajzen (Ajzen & Fishbein, 1980; Fishbein, 1967), again looks at the link between attitudes and behaviors, in this case by considering the ways in which attitudes toward a particular issue might influence behaviors relevant to the issue. This theory has a number of

components and is perhaps best explained through an extended example. Let's say, for instance, that we want to predict whether you will embark on a new exercise program. The theory first proposes the somewhat obvious idea that the best prediction of your exercising (the behavior) is your intention to exercise (**behavioral intention**). Thus, the theory takes as its major dependent variable (i.e., the concept the theory tries to explain) the prediction of behavioral intention.

According to the theory of reasoned action, two major factor sets will predict your behavioral intention to exercise. The first of these is your attitudes about exercising. Attitudes are defined as the sum of beliefs about a particular behavior weighted by evaluations of those beliefs. For example, you might have the beliefs that exercise is good for your health, that exercise makes you look good, that exercise takes too much time, and that exercise is uncomfortable. Each of these beliefs can be weighted (e.g., health issues might be more important to you than issues of time and comfort). According to the theory, when you add these weighted beliefs, you have your attitude about exercise.

The second factor set that influences behavioral intention in the theory of reasoned action is the subjective norms about the behavior. This concept looks at the influence of people in your social environment on your behavioral intentions. For example, you might have some friends who are avid exercisers and constantly encourage you to join them. However, your spouse might prefer a more sedentary lifestyle and scoff at those who work out. The theory contends that the beliefs of these people, weighted by the importance you attribute to each of their opinions, will influence your behavioral intention.

Putting these factors together, the theory of reasoned action proposes that behavioral intention is a function of both attitudes toward a behavior and **subjective norms** toward that behavior. It is not likely, though, that attitudes and norms will be weighted equally in predicting behavior. Indeed, depending on the individual and the situation, these factors might have very different effects on behavioral intention; thus, a weight is associated with each of these factors in the predictive formula of the theory. For example, you might be the kind of person who cares little for what others think. If this is the case, the subjective norms would carry little weight in predicting your behavior.

These factors, then, are combined in the following equation:

$$BI = f(W_1A + W_2SN)$$

This equation states that behavioral intention (BI) is a function (f) of attitudes (A) and social norms (SN) each weighted by a measure of how important the factor is in predicting behavioral intention (W_1 and W_2).

Research investigating the theory of reasoned action has found relatively strong support for its predictions. Both attitudes and subjective norms have been found to predict behavioral intention (though the attitude factor has been found to have a stronger impact), and behavioral intention has been found to predict actual behavior (see Sheppard, Hartwick, & Warshaw, 1988, for review). However, to gain even more predictive ability, Ajzen (1985) extended the theory of reasoned action into what he calls the **theory of planned behavior.** This extension involves the addition of one major predictor, perceived behavioral control, to the model. This addition was made to account for times when people have the intention of carrying out a behavior, but the actual behavior is thwarted because they lack confidence or control over the behavior. For example, your intention to exercise might be discouraged because you don't know good exercise techniques or don't have the proper equipment to carry out exercise plans. The theory of planned behavior is illustrated in Figure 8.1. The figure shows that three factors—attitude, subjective norms, and behavioral control—will have important (though differently weighted) effects on a person's intention to behave in a particular way.

Social Judgment Theory

The third classic theory of persuasion we consider was developed by Muzafer Sherif, Carolyn Sherif, and their colleagues (see Sherif & Hov-

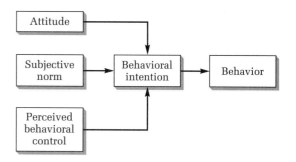

Figure 8.1   The Theory of Planned Behavior
Source: Adapted from Madden, Ellen, & Ajzen (1992).

land, 1961; Sherif, Sherif, & Nebergall, 1965). **Social judgment theory** proposes that attitude change will be influenced by cognitive judgment processes in which a proposed position is compared with a person's existing system of attitudes and beliefs. An understanding of social judgment theory begins with the idea that, on any topic, a wide range of position statements could be made. Think, for example, about all the statements that could be made (and are often made) about abortion. These statements might include some of the following:

- "All life is sacred."
- "A woman should have control over her own body."
- "Tax dollars should not fund abortion."
- "Cases of rape and incest are different from other pregnancies."
- "Life begins at conception."
- "The right to privacy is absolute."
- "Legal restrictions on abortion lead to dangerous 'back-alley' operations."

These statements are just a few that represent various positions on abortion, and the statements could be arrayed on a continuum ranging from pro-life views to pro-choice views. You probably agree with some of these statements, disagree with others, and perhaps feel indifferent about still others. According to social judgment theory, the statements you agree with constitute your **latitude of acceptance,** the statements you disagree with constitute your **latitude of rejection,** and the statements you are indifferent to constitute your **latitude of noncommitment.** These latitudes can be of varying sizes (e.g., you might have a very large latitude of rejection on this issue) and can be arrayed in various ways on the continuum (e.g., a latitude of acceptance might be on either end of the continuum or perhaps in the middle of the continuum). These latitudes essentially represent your attitude structure on a particular topic.

When you receive a message about an issue, your reaction to the message will be influenced by the anchor of your existing structure of attitudes (the anchor is the center of your latitude of acceptance). Specifically, if you receive a message that is within your latitude of acceptance (e.g., close to your attitudinal anchor), you will judge the message to be closer to your own opinion than it actually is. This process is known as **assimilation.** When you receive a message that is within your latitude of rejection, you will judge the message as more discrepant from your own position than it actually is. This process is known as **contrast.** These processes of assimilation and contrast are heightened when the issue at hand is an important one to you, that is, if you are ego-involved in the topic.

So what do these judgment processes have to do with persuasion? Social judgment theory predicts that attitude change will depend on these processes of assimilation and contrast in specific ways. First, if a message received is within an individual's latitude of rejection, there will be little or no attitude change: The contrast effect will simply be too strong. Obviously, a message that is totally in line with an individual's anchor (i.e., in the middle of the latitude of acceptance) will not lead to change, though it might serve to reinforce the existing attitude. Attitude change, instead, will occur when the message received is in an individual's latitude of noncommitment or at the edges of the latitude of acceptance, that is, when a message is somewhat discrepant, but not too discrepant, with a person's opinion on the issue. Stiff (1994) reports that considerable research supports this so-called discrepancy curve, in which a moderate difference between the message and an individual's position results in larger attitude change than that caused by either small or large differences.

Summary

These three classic theories of persuasion have been discussed with great brevity, and the presentations only scratch the surface of work on attitude change that was prevalent in social psychology and communication during the 1960s and 1970s. However, even these cursory sketches of cognitive dissonance theory, the theory of reasoned action, and social judgment theory point to the importance of several key factors in understanding processes of message reception and processing. First, these theories highlight the importance of individual attitudinal structures, whether in the form of attitude-behavior relationships, beliefs about attitude objects and subjective norms, or latitudes of attitudes. Second, these theories indicate that a variety of kinds of messages might serve to change behavior (e.g., messages of different discrepancy, messages that change norms or beliefs). Third, these theories point to processes of comparison (e.g., between attitude and behavior) and combination (e.g., of attitudes and subjective norms) in predicting behavioral intention and behavior.

The three theories we consider in the remainder of this chapter continue to highlight some of these processes. These theories have more current and substantial connections to the field of communication, however. The first theory we consider, the elaboration likelihood model, was developed in social psychology but has received a great deal of testing and critique by other scholars, especially those in communication. The second, inoculation theory, was again developed in psychology but has been used to enhance our understanding of many applied communication issues. The final theory we consider, problematic integration theory, is an approach that has been proposed from within the communication discipline to address more broadly based issues of message reception and processing.

■ ELABORATION LIKELIHOOD MODEL

The elaboration likelihood model was developed by two social psychologists, Richard Petty and John Cacioppo (1981, 1986). The model begins with the assumption that individuals are motivated (for social reasons) to hold "correct" attitudes. However, the model further assumes that individuals will not always be willing and able to process messages in a way most appropriate to reach this goal. Hence, the elaboration likelihood model attempts to explain different ways of processing messages, why different processing modes will be used, and the results of those processing modes on attitude change.

Central and Peripheral Routes to Persuasion

The elaboration likelihood model posits that there are two major routes to persuasion: the central route and the peripheral route. When embarking on the **central route to persuasion,** an individual will carefully scrutinize the content of the message, looking at the strength of the arguments proposed. In the language of the model, the central route involves message elaboration, in which a great many cognitions (thoughts) about the message's arguments are generated by the individual receiving the message during the evaluation process. If the thoughts generated in the elaboration process are favorable, acceptance of the message content is likely. Conversely, if unfavorable thoughts are generated, the individual will not accept the message. For instance, you might receive a mailing about the importance of donating blood in an upcoming campus blood drive. If you use the central route in evaluating this message, you will read the message carefully and consider the logical quality of the arguments presented for donating blood. If you evaluate those arguments favorably, the model predicts that you are likely to donate blood during the drive.

In contrast, the receiver of a persuasive message might embark on the **peripheral route to persuasion.** On this route, the receiver does not elaborate on the message through extensive cognitive processing of arguments. Instead, the receiver will rely on cues in the persuasion environment to guide decisions about message acceptance. These cues are generally unrelated to the logical quality of the message and might involve factors such as the credibility or attractiveness of the source of the message, the production quality of the message, or a jingle or slogan associated with the message. In our example about blood donations, a person processing the message along the peripheral route might choose to donate blood because a popular television star "asked" for the donation or because the bright colors on the slick brochure were attention getting. As Petty, Cacioppo, and Schumann (1983) summarize about the peripheral route, "Rather than diligently considering the issue-relevant arguments, a person may accept an advocacy simply because it was presented during a pleasant lunch or because the source is an expert" (p. 135).

Which Route Do You Take?

The elaboration likelihood model suggests that several factors will predict which route an individual will take in any persuasive situation. The two most consistently noted factors are motivation and ability. First, the model predicts that some individuals will have a particularly strong motivation to process the message at hand and will thus tend to take the central route. Motivation to elaborate on message content is most strongly influenced by the personal relevance of the topic for the receiver (i.e., their involvement in the issue). For example, if you are now of typical undergraduate or graduate student age, the issue of social security funding might not be highly involving for you. You might reason that retirement is a long way off for you and that the social security program may not even exist by the time you reach retirement age. The model would predict that this low level of involvement would lead you to peripheral processing of messages regarding social security. In contrast, your parents or grandparents might be highly involved in the topic and thus highly motivated to process messages about social security using the central route. Motivation to elaborate on message content is also predicted by a person's need for cognition (Cacioppo & Petty, 1982, 1984). That is, individuals who enjoy thinking logically and evaluating arguments will be more likely to take the central route.

In addition to motivation, a second necessary factor for central processing is ability. This factor seems obvious, but it is important. If a person is unable to critically evaluate arguments, he or she will not take the central route to persuasion. Ability to elaborate on message arguments will be influenced by individual variables (e.g., a person's intelligence, education, or knowledge about a particular topic), by message variables (e.g., the difficulty or complexity of the arguments presented in the persuasive appeal), and by situational variables (e.g., the extent to which the environment provides an opportunity to process the message with minimal distractions). Clearly, then, ability to process via the central route will vary a great deal, even for a particular individual. For instance, though you may have the ability to process a blood donation message that makes straightforward arguments about public health, a more complex message about the value of various blood products in specific medical procedures might tax your abilities and lead to processing via the peripheral route.

And Where Does It Get You?

Thus, your motivation to elaborate on message content (predicted by your personal involvement with the topic and your need for cognition) and your ability to elaborate on message content (predicted by individual, message, and situational factors) will lead you down either the central or the peripheral route to persuasion. If you take the central route, you will cognitively elaborate on message arguments and evaluate the message based on those cognitions. If you take the peripheral route, you will draw conclusions based on cues such as source credibility and message production values. The question at this point becomes, Will the route taken change the outcomes of the persuasion process? If either

route can result in attitude change, does it matter what road you take?

As in the Robert Frost poem, the road taken does make a difference. Specifically, the elaboration likelihood model proposes that attitude change developed through the central route will be "relatively enduring, resistant, and predictive of behavior" whereas attitude change developed through the peripheral route will be "relatively temporary, susceptible, and unpredictive of behavior" (Petty, Cacioppo, & Kasmer, 1988, p. 121). Consider, again, our blood donation example. The model predicts that if you evaluate the persuasive message regarding blood donation using the peripheral route, you might indeed emerge with an attitude toward blood donation that is more positive than your attitude before reading the message. However, when the attitude change is through the peripheral route, you will be less likely to act on the attitude (i.e., give blood), the attitude is unlikely to last very long, and the attitude will be easy to change with subsequent messages. That is, if you were convinced to give blood simply because a television star asked you to, you might never make it to the bloodmobile or you might be easily convinced by a friend that giving blood isn't such a great idea. In contrast, if you have cognitively elaborated on the message arguments (i.e., taken the central route), the elaboration likelihood model would predict that you would soon be visiting the bloodmobile and that your positive attitude about blood donation would last a long time and be resistant to change attempts.

These factors of the model—the central and peripheral routes to persuasion, the role of ability and motivation in predicting message elaboration, and the attitudinal and behavioral outcomes of central and peripheral processing—are summarized in Figure 8.2.

Critiques of the Elaboration Likelihood Model

An incredible amount of research has tested propositions of the elaboration likelihood model and garnered support for various portions of the model (see, e.g., O'Keefe, 1990; Petty et al.,

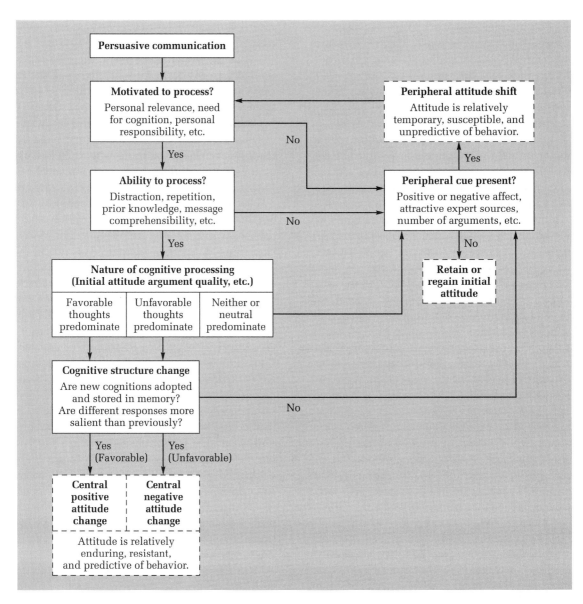

Figure 8.2 The Elaboration Likelihood Model *Source:* From *Communication and Persuasion: Central and Peripheral Routes to Attitude Change* by Richard E. Petty and John T. Cacioppo. © 1986 by Springer-Verlag. Reprinted by permission of the publisher.

1988; Stiff, 1994). Of particular interest is the extent to which the model has been applied to a variety of settings, including school psychology (Petty, Heesacker, & Hughes, 1997), attitudes about gender roles (Brooks-Harris, Heesacker, & Mejia-Millan, 1996), employment interviewing (Forret & Turban, 1996), and advertising (Park & Hastak, 1995; Petty & Cacioppo, 1983). In short, the processes proposed in the model have a great deal of intuitive appeal and have been incredibly productive in generating both basic and applied research.

However, the elaboration likelihood model has also generated substantial discussion and debate, particularly within the communication discipline. This debate began with Jim Stiff's (1986) critique of the model and has been continued by others (e.g., Allen & Reynolds, 1993; Hamilton, Hunter, & Boster, 1993; Mongeau & Stiff, 1993), labeled by Petty and his associates as the Michigan State critics (Petty et al., 1993). Though a number of specific issues have been raised in these critiques, two deserve highlighting.

Consider, first, the scarecrow in *The Wizard of Oz*. When Dorothy and Toto first encounter the scarecrow, he stands at a fork in the road. The scarecrow notes that "some people go this way, and some people go that way," then adds, to Dorothy's confusion, that "some people, of course, go both ways." It is this conundrum, of which way people go and whether they can go both ways, that was the central point in Stiff's (1986) critique of the elaboration likelihood model. Specifically, Stiff argued, based on both verbal and graphic presentations from the original theorists (see, e.g., Figure 8.2), that the model proposes that individuals take either the central or the peripheral route to persuasion but not take both routes. Stiff posited, instead, that people are capable of parallel processing of both central and peripheral cues and that, given various levels of involvement, individuals might process various combinations of central and peripheral information. Though elaboration likelihood model theorists have taken issue with this critique (Petty, Kasmir, Haugtvedt, & Cacioppo, 1987), Stiff and Boster (1987) emphasize that both the original presentation and continued discussions of the model emphasize this either-or process and argue against this idea on both conceptual and empirical grounds. For example, Stiff found that at moderate levels of involvement, the processing of both message content and source credibility judgments had an influence on subsequent attitudes.

Second, critics of the model (Mongeau & Stiff, 1993; Stiff, 1994; Stiff & Boster, 1987)

argue that it does not clearly specify relevant concepts and causal relationships and hence detracts from the falsifiability of the theory. These critics raise, especially, the role of various message cues in the model. Petty and Cacioppo (1986) argue that a particular cue can serve multiple persuasive roles, depending on the situation. They use the example of a model with beautiful hair in a television commercial. In an automobile commercial, the authors argue, this hair serves as a peripheral cue (i.e., something that makes the message source more attractive), but in a shampoo commercial, the same hair could serve as a central cue (i.e., an argument for the shampoo). This might seem a reasonable position. However, as Stiff (1994) points out,

> The problem with this conceptual flexibility is that it "allows the [elaboration likelihood model (ELM)] to explain all possible outcomes of an experimental study" making it practically impossible to falsify (Stiff & Boster, 1987, p. 251). For example, under conditions of high involvement, if the quality of a model's hair is positively related to attitudes, then ELM proponents can argue that this stimulus must have been processed centrally. However, if the same conditions produce a nonsignificant effect for this stimulus, then ELM proponents could argue that this stimulus served as a peripheral cue. (pp. 187–188)

Finally, an alternative theory of cognitive information processing has been proposed that shares some factors with the elaboration likelihood model but makes some distinct predictions about the persuasion process. This model, the **Heuristic Model of Persuasion,** was proposed by Shelley Chaiken (1987). Like the elaboration likelihood model, this model posits two different processes of persuasion. In the heuristic model of persuasion, **systematic processing** is very similar to central processing in the elaboration likelihood model and involves the careful consideration of message content. The second mode of processing in the heuristic model, **heuristic processing,** is somewhat different than the peripheral route. Specifically, heuristic processing involves the use of "simple decision rules that allow people to evaluate message content without effortful scrutiny of message content" (Stiff, 1994, p. 192). For example, people might hold the heuristic that "politicians always lie" or that "the majority rules." According to Chaikin, people use heuristics because they often don't want to make the effort to engage in highly active and conscious processing. In the heuristic model of persuasion, unlike the elaboration likelihood model, systematic and heuristic processing are seen as parallel processes, rather than mutually exclusive processes. Furthermore, it is predicted that individuals will typically engage in heuristic processing (especially if the heuristics are ones that have been used frequently and recently) and will turn to systematic processing only when they have the ability and motivation to do so (similar to the elaboration likelihood model). Thus, the key distinctions between the elaboration likelihood model and the heuristic model of persuasion are (a) the distinction in the conceptualization of peripheral and heuristic cues and (b) the explicit recognition of parallel processing in the heuristic model.

■ INOCULATION THEORY

At the beginning of this chapter, we talked about the complexity of the message reception process and how even the concept of persuasion involves processes of attitude maintenance, development, and change. The next theory we consider in this chapter illustrates the breadth of theorizing in the message reception area. **Inoculation theory** deals not with attitude change per se but with the processes through which we resist attitude change attempts that we might receive in interpersonal interaction or through the mass media. These attitude change attempts come on a daily basis. Consider just a few possibilities:

- A teenager must deal with friends who want him to try smoking marijuana "just for fun."
- A direct mail piece in a political campaign attempts to get you to shift loyalties by attacking your candidate of choice.

- A television advertising campaign tries to get you to change ketchup brands by illustrating how thin and drippy the brand you normally use is.

These examples vary in a number of ways: the seriousness of the issue at hand and the medium through which the messages are sent, for instance. All three examples, however, involve the same process: trying to get you to change your opinion (i.e., about drug use, about a political candidate, or about ketchup brand) through the process of persuasion. Scholars in the inoculation theory tradition look at situations like this and ask how individuals react to these messages and how they might be able to resist these and similar persuasion attempts in their everyday lives.

Inoculation theory was developed by the psychologist William McGuire in the early 1960s (McGuire, 1961, 1964). McGuire was interested in the ways in which individuals resist persuasion and used a biological metaphor to describe the process he proposed. Many of you, when you were young children, probably suffered through a bout of chicken pox. However, probably very few of you had whooping cough, polio, or even the mumps. Why this difference? The answer is straightforward. When you were a child, you were probably inoculated (or immunized) against whooping cough, polio, and the mumps, but when you were growing up, an inoculation against chicken pox was not available (though it is now). In essence, an inoculation enhances your resistance to a particular disease and thus has kept that disease from affecting you in subsequent years.

How does the inoculation process work? Biologically, inoculation works when an individual receives a vaccine that contains a weak dosage of the virus (e.g., mumps or polio). The inoculation then causes the body's immune system to create antibodies to fight the virus. These antibodies will kill the weak virus included in the vaccine and leave a reserve to fight subsequent attacks of the virus in the future. In the communication context, McGuire posited that if you are presented with weak arguments against one of your beliefs, you will be able to fight off that attack and subsequent attacks. In essence, if your beliefs are attacked, you will develop a defense system, that is, arguments and strategies to counter the attacks on your attitudes in the future.

In initial tests of the inoculation concept, McGuire and his colleagues found support for their position (see, e.g., Anderson & McGuire, 1965; McGuire, 1962, 1964; McGuire & Papageorgis, 1961). Resistance to persuasion was created more effectively through an inoculation procedure than through a bolstering procedure, in which the original position is supported without reference to possible attacks and counterarguments. The concept of inoculation, and the general process of resistance to persuasion, was taken up by communication scholar Michael Burgoon and his associates in the 1970s (see, e.g., Burgoon & Chase, 1973; Burgoon, Cohen, Miller, & Montgomery, 1978; Miller & Burgoon, 1973). Since the late 1980s, theory and research in the inoculation tradition has been led by Michael Pfau and his colleagues (see, e.g., Pfau, 1992, 1995, 1996; Pfau & Burgoon, 1988; Pfau, Kenski, Nitz, & Sorenson, 1990; Pfau et al., 1997; Pfau, Van Bockern, & Kang, 1992).

These developments within the communication discipline have represented several major movements away from McGuire's original work. First, McGuire proposed his theory to explain resistance to persuasion regarding cultural truisms (e.g., "you should brush your teeth after every meal"). In contrast, Pfau and other researchers in communication have extended the focus of inoculation theory to a wide variety of contexts including adolescents and smoking, political advertising, and corporate advocacy. Second, communication scholars have worked to carefully delineate the components of inoculation theory and to test the effect of these components in applied persuasion settings.

Components of the Inoculation Process

The inoculation process has two major features: threat and refutational preemption. According to inoculation theorists, both features are necessary to provide resistance to subsequent persuasive messages. The first feature, **threat,** involves a forewarning that a challenge to existing attitudes is possible or likely. The following messages would constitute a threat component in an inoculation against the beliefs discussed earlier in this section:

- "Now that you're in high school, there are a lot of kids who might try to get you to change your mind about smoking pot."
- "The campaign season is starting in earnest. So unless you live in a cave, you're going to hear a lot of bad things about our candidate."
- "When you use the #1 selling ketchup, everyone is always trying to convince you to switch."

These messages constitute the threat portion of inoculation in that they warn the listener that attacks on their existing attitudes are likely. This concept of threat should not be confused with a threatening message that might appear in a persuasive fear appeal (e.g., extolling the dangers of using drugs). Instead, the threat component of an inoculation message will "trigger the receiver's motivation to bolster attitudes and gives inoculation its distinctive power" (Pfau, 1995, p. 101).

The second portion of the inoculation process is the **refutational preemption.** In this part of the message, specific challenges to existing attitudes are raised and then refuted. Consider the following three statements, again related to our problems of marijuana use, voter preference, and ketchup use:

- "They'll tell you that using marijuana is harmless, but studies show that using pot can be harmful to your health and can lead to the use of even more dangerous drugs."
- "The opposition might argue that our candidate is weak on educational issues, but her record during 12 years in the state legislature is consistently supportive of educational initiatives."

✳ SPOTLIGHT ON THE THEORIST

Michael Pfau

Michael Pfau taught for many years at Augustana College in Sioux Falls, South Dakota. He received his Ph.D. from the University of Arizona and was a professor at the University of Wisconsin-Madison from 1993 to 2001. He recently began a new position at the University of Oklahoma. In summing up his scholarship, Pfau simply notes, "I was, and am, a student of persuasion." His long-time fascination with a wide variety of persuasive processes has led to his interest in theories such as inoculation theory and in the application of those theories to a variety of contexts, including health and politics.

Pfau notes that when he first encountered William McGuire's inoculation theory, initially published in 1961, he was "impressed by how truly novel the theory was." Typically, theories of persuasion talk about how the process of persuasion works, and Pfau believes that "it is surprising that there has been so little attention paid to how to protect people against persuasion." But, because McGuire's work on inoculation theory was discontinued after a decade, Pfau believed that there was a great deal more work to be done, both in terms of developing unresolved theoretical issues and in terms of applying the theory to politics, to "protect potential voters against the influence of attack advertising," and health prevention, to "safeguard children against the inevitable temptations that accompany adolescence." Pfau argues that "the early research on inoculation, and on resistance in general, largely ignored potential applications."

Pfau looks to the many research reports on inoculation in leading communication journals as evidence of the enthusiasm with which the theory has been received. For example, Pfau's own work has been published in outlets including *Human Communication Research*, *Communication Monographs*, *Communication Research*, and *Journal of Communication*. However, he notes that debate about the theory has been limited, "in large part because the theory encompasses a narrow domain, and the methodological rigor (some might say tedium) required to conduct inoculation research is considerable." A number of Pfau's graduate students at the University of Wisconsin have been drawn to inoculation theory and its implications, though, and he believes that their work will spark enhanced dialogue about the theoretical and applied possibilities for inoculation theory.

In considering directions for future work in persuasion—and communication in general—Pfau advises students to concentrate on a particular functional theoretical issue about which they have a genuine passion. By considering functions of communication that focus on end states of the communication process (e.g., informing, shaping perceptions, persuading, resisting persuasion), he believes that scholars will cross communication contexts and address "a broad audience of communication scholars and practitioners." He has found in his own work on inoculation and other communication processes that "it is more rewarding to address theories that explain a broader range of human communication behavior."

- "Don't believe it when they say their ketchup is yummier—our taste tests prove otherwise."

Thus, an inoculating message consists of a threat that an attack on existing attitudes is likely, followed by a presentation and refutation of one or more possible attacks. The inoculation process is proposed to work in several ways. First, behaviorally, the refutational preemption provides individuals with specific material to defend the attitude against attacks that might be forthcoming. For example, you could draw specifically on your candidate's voting record to counter arguments about her stands on education. More generally, though, the inoculation process serves a motivational role. By warning an individual that the attitude might be attacked and then providing examples and refutations, an inoculating message is proposed to provide general protection against a wide range of attacks, whether those attacks are the same ones received in the inoculation treatment or novel ones. As Pfau (1995) argues,

> By first motivating receivers and only then preemptively refuting one or more potential counterarguments, inoculation spreads a broad umbrella of protection, safeguarding against both those counterarguments addressed by refutational preemption and those not addressed. (p. 101)

These are the basic components of the inoculation process. However, other factors have also been raised in looking at this process. First, scholars have examined the concept of **booster messages,** the provision of additional messages after the initial inoculation message (like booster shots for a vaccine). Though original inoculation messages rarely have long-lived effects, booster messages can help to some degree (see Pfau, 1995). Second, drawing on theoretical traditions such as the elaboration likelihood model and the heuristic model of persuasion (discussed earlier in this chapter), Pfau et al. (1997) have considered the extent to which involvement in the message topic influences the inoculation process. Specifically, this theoretical extension suggests that the inoculation effect should be the most pronounced for involved receivers.

Tests of Inoculation Theory

Tests of inoculation theory have demonstrated consistent, but modest, support for the inoculation process. In most studies of inoculation, an effect is found, but it is relatively weak, short lived, or limited to a particular subset of respondents (e.g., those that are highly involved or those with low self-esteem). These tests seem to suggest that the inoculation process is a viable

explanation of attitude resistance but only in a limited set of circumstances. Recall that the inoculation concept was originally applied to attitudes about cultural truisms that have never been attacked. That is, these attitudes had lived in a "germ-free" environment, and the inoculation process was particularly effective in protecting subsequent attacks against these cultural truisms. It is not surprising, perhaps, that an extension of inoculation theory to real-world situations will lead to weaker explanations of how people respond in resisting persuasive attempts.

The clearest case in point here is the extensive research of Pfau and his colleagues on adolescent smoking behavior (Pfau, 1995; Pfau & Van Bockern, 1994; Pfau et al., 1992). This research on inducing resistance to persuasion among young people has had clear, but limited, effects. Specifically, it appears that inoculation messages must be introduced during the critical period of transition between elementary school and secondary school (e.g., middle school or junior high). During elementary school, children have widespread negative views about smoking. Past this point, however, it appears that the attitudes are far from germ free, and inoculation has very limited influence. As Pfau and Van Bockern (1994) conclude, "Beyond this pivotal juncture, adolescents' attitudes opposing smoking quickly deteriorate, therefore rendering the resistance paradigm inappropriate" (p. 413).

■ PROBLEMATIC INTEGRATION THEORY

The final theory we discuss in this chapter is one of rather recent origin. Austin Babrow proposed **problematic integration theory** in 1992 as a way to integrate ideas from communication and related disciplines about how individuals receive, process, and make sense of specific messages and situations in their lives. Problematic integration theory is, then, a very general theory of message reception and processing, and given its recent development, it has received only limited empirical testing. However, it is an important theory to consider in this chapter, because it was developed within the communication discipline and because it attempts to take various strands of theorizing in other areas and pull them into a coherent understanding of how we make sense of interaction in our daily lives. In this section, we examine central issues in problematic integration theory and look at some limited but very interesting research that has been done to assess communicative examples of problematic integration.

What Is Being Integrated in Problematic Integration?

Problematic integration theory (Babrow, 1992) begins with the proposal that we make two kinds of judgments about events and issues in our lives: probabilistic judgments and evaluative judgments. **Probabilistic judgments** involve an assessment of how likely something is to occur. For example, the following are judgments regarding probability:

- "I'm sure I won't have any problem getting into the graduate school of my choice."
- "As a woman over 40, I'm more likely to experience an airplane highjack situation than to find a suitable husband."
- "I have no idea how my parents will react when I tell them I'm thinking about moving out of state."

These statements reflect beliefs about probabilities, that is, how likely it is that something will happen. Note that these expressions of probability run the gamut from an event being very likely (the first statement), to an event being very unlikely (the second statement), to a statement of being unclear about the relevant probabilities (the third statement).

The second kind of judgment we make about events in our lives is **evaluative judgments.** These judgments assess the relevant goodness of a particular state of affairs. The following evaluative statements correspond with the statements of probability listed previously:

- "Going to graduate school will be great! It will be challenging and give me a lot of career opportunities."
- "Being alone for the rest of my life is the worst thing I can imagine—all that matters in life is a relationship with a significant mate."
- "It doesn't really matter *how* my parents react—I'm so excited about my new job, I'm sure they'll adapt eventually."

Again, note the range in these evaluative statements. The first statement reflects a positive evaluation about graduate school, the second a negative evaluation of a solitary lifestyle. The third statement reflects a neutral evaluation (e.g., "it doesn't really matter how my parents react") but also includes an interesting twist. The neutral evaluation is buttressed with an additional statement about probability ("I'm sure they'll adapt eventually"). It is natural to combine evaluative and probability assessments in this way, and it is the nature of these combinations, and how we process the combinations in our lives, that form the central themes of problematic integration theory.

When Is Integration Problematic?

There are many times when integrating an assessment of probability with an assessment of evaluation is not problematic. Consider the sample statements regarding graduate school. The statement regarding probability ("I'm sure I won't have any problem getting into the graduate school of my choice.") is easily integrated with the statement regarding evaluation ("Going to graduate school will be great! It will be challenging and give me a lot of career opportunities."). Babrow (1992) argues that integration will not be problematic in cases like these when probability is high and evaluation is positive (e.g., a good thing is likely to happen) or

Austin Babrow

Austin Babrow received his Ph.D. from the University of Illinois in 1986, and he has taught at Purdue University in West Lafayette, Indiana, ever since. He teaches courses in persuasion, health communication, and research methods, and his work has been published in outlets including *Journal of Communication, Health Communication, Communication Monographs, Human Communication Research,* and *Social Science and Medicine.*

Babrow published the first statement of his problematic integration theory in 1992. He was inspired to develop this theory after reading a great deal of current research in persuasion, especially theories that saw human action as "determined by a cold, machine-like aggregation of expectancies," such as the theory of reasoned action. Though Babrow appreciated the influence of this theory, he was concerned that persuasion was not always a dispassionate process. His belief that "people's expectations and their desires are foundational to human experience" served as an inspiration for his development of problematic integration theory.

Babrow had high initial hopes for his theory. Indeed, he says (clearly tongue in cheek) that he "was convinced that it would revolutionize the field." His high hopes were founded on his contention that the theory "spoke to issues that crossed the vast expanse of the discipline" and that it "said or very clearly implied some novel, sometimes counterintuitive, and generally very useful things about issues that had long interested communication scholars." Problemat-

ic integration theory did not, however, have the "revolutionary" impact that Babrow hoped for. Instead, he notes that "the theory has developed very slowly, for reasons I can only guess." He notes, though, that progress with the theory seems to be tied to the linking of problematic integration with concrete problems, especially those related to health and illness. Babrow has been very heartened by other scholars' reactions to the theory—he says that "no matter who I tell about the theory, no matter their interest area, they invariably tell me about connections triggered in their mind by [problematic integration]-related ideas." Thus, he is very hopeful that the theory will develop further as he, and others, are able to make specific and concrete applications of the theory to everyday life. He also hopes that the theory can serve as a model of what communication theory should be like—that is, he says, "We should be constructing theories that grapple with the complex interrelationships among the multiplicity of linguistic, psychological, social, cultural, historical, and even biological processes that comprise 'communication.'"

Babrow has a great deal of excitement for the future of the discipline of communication and for students studying communication processes. As he says, "I try to tell students to remember that life is far more complex than any idea we will ever have about it" and that though theories are important, they are always incomplete and often inconsistent with each other. He hopes, though, that students will be excited by this complexity and embrace it both intellectually and emotionally. As he says, "The best work that I have read is always very clearly the product of both head and heart." And this, clearly, is one of the major lessons of problematic integration theory.

when probability is low and evaluation is negative (e.g., a bad thing is unlikely to happen). As Babrow (1992) summarizes, "Integrating one's probabilistic and evaluative orientations is a routine matter when probabilities are clear,

evaluations are consistent, *and* when probabilities and evaluations converge" (p. 97).

Babrow then lays out four basic forms of integration that are problematic: divergence, ambiguity, ambivalence, and impossibility. *Divergence* occurs when a discrepancy exists between what we want (i.e., an evaluation) and what is likely (e.g., a probabilistic judgment). *Ambiguity* occurs when the probabilities associated with a particular event are unknown or uncertain. *Ambivalence* occurs when two mutually exclusive alternatives are valued in similar ways or when the same alternative evokes contradictory responses. Finally, *impossibility* occurs when there is certainty that something cannot happen. Examples of these forms of problematic integration are given in Table 8.1.

As Table 8.1 illustrates, situations of problematic integration involve issues of probability assessments, evaluative assessments, and the combination of these two. For example, both ambiguity and impossibility deal with problematic situations arising from probability assessments, ambivalence deals with problematic situations arising from evaluative assessments, and divergence deals with problematic combinations of probability and evaluation. Note that situations of problematic integration are not independent of each other. Rather, Babrow (1992, 1995) argues that problematic integration often "chains out" in that various forms of problematic integration are interrelated, various foci (i.e., topics) of problematic integration are interrelated, and problematic integration becomes interrelated at various layers of experience (see Babrow, 1995, p. 287).

Communicative Implications of Problematic Integration

To this point, we have talked about problematic integration as a largely internal process based on people's assessments of probability and evaluation. However, problematic integration theory is proposed as a theory of communication for a number of reasons. Babrow (1995) explains that communication is implicated as a source, medium, and resource in the process of problematic integration. Seeing communication as a source of problematic integration deals with the constitutive role of communication in our social world

(see, e.g., our discussion of ontology in interpretive theory in Chapter 4). That is, through communication we create and re-create relationships and our understandings of the world and hence often come face to face with problematic integration. As Babrow (1995) explains,

> To the extent that we can know the world only through communication, and to the extent that the meanings of symbolic representations are ambiguous and fraught with evaluative connotations (and hence with the potential for ambivalence), communicative constructions weave problematic integration into the fabric of experience. (p. 286)

Communication also serves as the medium through which our understandings of probabilities and evaluations flow. For example, a doctor facing the task of giving bad news to a cancer patient must deal explicitly with the framing of both probabilistic orientations (e.g., how to talk about the likelihood of survival) and evaluative orientations (e.g., how to talk about quality of life during treatment and beyond). Similarly, we learn about what is good and bad, and about what is likely and unlikely, through messages of the mass media, through educational and religious institutions, and through interpersonal contact with family and friends. Thus, communication serves as the channel through which perceptions and beliefs about problematic integration flow.

Perhaps most interesting, though, is the notion that communication serves as a resource in the problematic integration process. Here we get to the point of asking how individuals resolve problematic integration and hence make it less problematic. Babrow (1992) talks about a wide range of ways that problematic integration can be resolved, and they are too numerous to detail here. For example, Babrow distinguishes among hot, cold, and warm ways of resolving problematic integration. Harkening back to some classic persuasion theories, Babrow sees a "cold" solution as a mechanistic way of combining various probabilities and evaluations. For example, in the theory of reasoned action discussed earlier in

Table 8.1	Forms of Problematic Integration	
Form of problematic integration	Definition	Examples
Divergence	A discrepancy exists between a probability judgment and an evaluative judgment.	A woman believes that a diagnosis of breast cancer is very likely and is afraid of such a diagnosis. Or, a child wants to go to Disneyland but knows that family finances make this a very unlikely possibility.
Ambiguity	The probability of an event is unknown or uncertain.	A job candidate is unable to predict the likelihood of being selected for a second interview.
Ambivalence	(a) Two mutually exclusive alternatives are evaluated in similar ways, or (b) an event evokes contradictory evaluative responses.	(a) A high school girl receives two invitations to the senior prom and she likes both boys a great deal. (b) An anticipated move is looked forward to as a great opportunity but mourned in terms of the loss of familiar friends.
Impossibility	There is certainty that an event will not happen (e.g., a zero probability).	A teenager yearns to be an Olympic athlete but knows with certainty that he doesn't have the talent to reach that goal.

this chapter, it is assumed that people can just add up the various beliefs about the attitude object and their beliefs about subjective norms to come to a rational behavioral intention. A "hotter" notion of integration would involve the development and shifting of emotions with regard to problematic situations. "Warm" solutions combine concepts of cognition and emotion and highlight the tension that arises in the integration of probabilities (a rational and cognitive judgment) and evaluations (a more emotional or affective judgment).

To date, there have been only a few applications of problematic integration theory (Babrow, 1995; Ford, Babrow, & Stohl, 1996; Hines, Babrow, Badzek, & Moss, 1997) and certainly no tests of all the theory's tenets. However, these applications point to the potential of the theory to deal with some interesting aspects of message reception and processing. For example, Ford et al. (1996) examine the process of providing so-

cial support messages for patients with breast cancer. Some social support literature suggests that support works primarily to reduce uncertainty and thus help the support recipient cope more effectively with problematic life situations (Albrecht & Adelman, 1987). However, from the perspective of problematic integration theory, the challenge faced by support providers is much more complicated than simply reducing uncertainty. Rather, there might be times when you would want less certainty about an outcome (e.g., if that outcome were evaluated negatively). Or, there might be times when supportive communication should work not to manage probability assessments (i.e., uncertainty) but to frame evaluative assessments (e.g., construct a likely outcome in a more positive light or an unlikely outcome in a more negative light). By looking at the perceptions of cancer patients with regard to social support messages, Ford et al. (1996) demonstrate how a nuanced look at message processing based on problematic integration theory could demonstrate the interplay of emotion and cognition in the comforting process (see also Babrow & Kline, 2000, for a consideration of the distinction between reducing and managing uncertainty).

■ COMPARISON AND COMMENTARY

The theories we examined in this chapter are quite different in terms of their ontological and epistemological roots. The elaboration likelihood model and inoculation theory were developed in a social psychological tradition that is clearly post-positivist in its metatheoretical assumptions. Though both of these theories deal largely with cognitive structures that are inside people's heads, they also assume that these structures are real and that explanations regarding these structures can be tested through experimental research in the scientific tradition. Thus, it is possible to judge these theories using the classic criteria we developed in Chapter 3: accuracy (and hence testability), consistency, broad scope, simplicity, and fruitfulness.

The elaboration likelihood model certainly passes with flying colors on several of these criteria. It has been fruitful, spurring both basic and applied research in a wide range of social science disciplines. Perhaps it has been so fruitful because of its strong balance between simplicity and scope. That is, the model explains a wide range of persuasive and information processing situations, yet the concepts used to explain these situations are quite simple and elegant. In short, the model has great appeal in terms of its heuristic value and its elegant presentation of issues regarding information processing and attitude change.

The elaboration likelihood model's major problems come in terms of its accuracy (especially testability) and its consistency. Specifically, the model has been criticized as being unfalsifiable because any outcome can be justified through theoretical mechanisms. Consider a few

examples. If attitude change was short lived, then the peripheral route must have been used. If people don't process the message's arguments, then they must not have been involved in the message topic. If a cue leads to message elaboration, it must have served as a central cue. In short, the model's very elegance and attractiveness as a theoretical approach to a wide range of persuasive situations provides ways to explain (or explain away) many varied outcomes in research and practice.

Inoculation theory also has a great many strengths when viewed in terms of the criteria for post-positivist theory. Like the elaboration likelihood model, inoculation theory has proved fruitful in terms of generating both theoretical and applied work, though this work has not been nearly as widespread as research on the elaboration likelihood model. And, like the elaboration likelihood model, inoculation theory provides an elegant and pleasing explanation of resistance to attitude change attempts. However, inoculation theory can be falsified; that is, research can clearly indicate when an inoculation explanation does not explain the data observed in research. Indeed, this ability to test the tenets of inoculation theory demonstrates its two most obvious weaknesses. First, though an inoculation explanation seems accurate in some cases, it rarely provides a complete explanation of observed behavior. In the parlance of scientific explanation, a great deal of variance is left unexplained. Relatedly, inoculation explanations seem to hold in a relatively narrow range of instances (e.g., relatively unchallenged attitudes similar to the cultural truisms considered in McGuire's original formulation of the theory). Thus, inoculation theory's scope is quite narrow.

In contrast to the elaboration likelihood model's and inoculation theory's roots in the post-positivist tradition, problematic integration theory has been drawn from more eclectic sources. Indeed, one of Babrow's original explications of the workings of the theory involved its application to a fictional work, Milan Kundera's *The Book of Laughter and Forgetting* (Babrow, 1995). Thus, it is difficult to apply some of the criteria of post-positivist theory to problematic integration theory, though quantitative empirical work has also been used to explore some of its predictions (Ford et al., 1996; Hines et al., 1997). At this stage of its development, problematic integration theory's strong suit—its broad-stroked attempt to deal with a wide range of communicative and interpretive phenomena—can also be seen as its biggest challenge. It will be important for researchers who adopt such a framework to carefully delineate relevant limits and predictions, lest problematic integration develop into a theory that attempts to understand a great deal and explains very little as a result. However, problematic integration theory is noteworthy in its attempt to draw on diverse traditions and pull together multiple processes of communication (Babrow, 1993) into a coherent understanding of message reception and processing in human interaction.

Key Terms

cognitive dissonance theory
theory of reasoned action
behavioral intention
subjective norms
theory of planned behavior
social judgment theory
latitude of acceptance
latitude of rejection
latitude of noncommitment
assimilation
contrast
elaboration likelihood model
central route to persuasion
peripheral route to persuasion
heuristic model of persuasion
systematic processing
heuristic processing
inoculation theory
threat
refutational preemption
booster messages
problematic integration theory
probabilistic judgments
evaluative judgments

Discussion Questions

1. After buying a car, you see another car you like better. What will happen next, according to cognitive dissonance theory? What reasons might you give to justify your purchase?
2. How do the psychological theories presented in the early part of this chapter differ from the communication theories presented? How do they serve as foundations for the communication theories?
3. Several theories considered in this chapter look at the notion of involvement as an important concept. How is involvement implicated in persuasion processes and in other processes of communication?
4. Problematic integration theory is proposed at a much more general level than some of the other theories of persuasion presented in this chapter. In what ways could this theory serve as an umbrella theory that could integrate the other perspectives we have looked at here?

9 Theories of Discourse and Interaction

In Chapters 7 and 8, we considered theories of communication that take the perspective of either the source or the receiver in interaction. In Chapter 7, we examined theories of message production that proposed explanations for the ways sources construct messages that will serve them in interaction. In Chapter 8, we looked at theories of how those messages influence receivers in communicative interaction through processes of persuasion and message integration. However, as our discussion of conceptualizations of communication in Chapter 1 emphasized, an understanding of communication cannot rest solely on either the source or the receiver. Rather, communication is a transactional process in which the actions of one individual have wide-ranging influences on the actions of others. Thus, in this chapter we consider four theories that look at ways in which people have mutual impact on each other in the course of interaction.

A great deal of scholarship in communication stems from the tradition known as *conversation analysis* (see McLaughlin, 1984; Psathas, 1995). This research, based on the tradition of ethnomethodology in sociology (Garfinkel, 1967), investigates ways in which conversations occur in stable and orderly ways, in particular, the manner in which conversations are sequenced and seen as coherent by participants. We draw on work by conversation analysts as we discuss several theories in this chapter. However, be-

cause conversation analysis is a method more than a codified theory, it is not dealt with in a separate section of the chapter.

The specific theories we examine in this chapter vary a great deal in terms of metatheoretical commitments, the extent to which they consider the mutual influence of interactants, and the underlying theoretical mechanisms seen as driving interaction and discourse processes. All, however, take as a preliminary supposition the idea that communication is best conceptualized as an interactive process in which communicators have ongoing and mutual influence on each other. We first consider the most foundational of these theories and the only one developed to a large extent outside the discipline of communication: speech act theory. We then discuss three theories that have had enormous influence on the field of communication: coordinated management of meaning theory, communication accommodation theory, and expectancy violation theory.

■ SPEECH ACT THEORY

A consideration of **speech act theory** must be grounded in an understanding of the ways philosophers and linguists have conceptualized and studied language processes during the 20th century. A guiding typology of these linguistic conceptualizations was presented by Charles Morris in the 1930s (Morris, 1938). Morris divided linguistic investigations into studies of semantics, syntactics, and pragmatics (see Cushman & Kunimoto, 1981, for a useful summary for communication scholars). The study of **semantics** concentrates on the link between signs (e.g., words) and referents (e.g., the things those words stand for). In simple terms, the study of semantics involves investigating the meaning or the truth value of various types of linguistic propositions. The study of **syntactics,** in contrast, deals with the rules that govern the way utterances are constructed in terms of sequence and order. These rules are typically called grammars, and they can be studied either by describing grammars in use in a particular language or by looking for an explanatory mechanism that generates instances of a particular language. Finally, the study of **pragmatics** looks at language in use. That is, pragmatic inquiry considers the ways in which the communicative situation and a communicator's intent might lead to particular types of linguistic utterances.

A second, and related, foundation important for understanding speech act theory involves developments in the field of philosophy. In the early 20th century, scholarship in linguistics and philosophy was largely centered on formal systems. In linguistics, this meant primary attention to the study of syntactics and semantics. In the philosophy of science, this meant a concentration on the logic of verification (as discussed in Chapter 3's consideration of logical positivism). Scholarship in this era rarely concentrated on actual behavior and action, attempting instead to lay out decontextualized and formal systems of logic. This changed in the middle of the century, however, with the ordinary language movement in philosophy. This philosophical approach emphasized the consideration of language in use, not language as a formal and sterile system. The most well-known proponent of this movement was Ludwig Wittgenstein, who proposed that we should study so-called language games (Wittgenstein, 1953) that are defined by rules, constraints,

skill, context, and change. For example, you might think of asking for a monetary loan as a language game that is constituted by particular rules and might be accomplished with more or less skill by different players. As Jacobs and Jackson (1983) note, "From this viewpoint the question of how people construct and recognize coherent discourse is equivalent to asking how the game is played" (p. 52).

Speech act theory sprung in large part from these developments in linguistics and philosophy. It is clearly a pragmatic theory of language in use that attempts to codify the rules of various language games that people use in interaction. However, speech act theory is not totally disconnected from semantics, syntactics, and more formal systems of linguistics and philosophy in that the theory still attempts to codify a system of how interactants can use language to accomplish communicative goals.

Original Formulations of Speech Act Theory

The concept of a speech act was proposed by J. L. Austin (1962), and what we now think of as speech act theory was most fully developed by his protégé, John Searle (see Searle, 1969, for original statement; see Searle, 1979, 1992, for further developments). The concept of a speech act rests on the foundations of a pragmatic and ordinary language approach to linguistics. In short, speech act theory proposes that when we say something we are not just stringing together words (i.e., syntactic level) or even representing some meaning (i.e., semantic level). Rather, we are performing an action with the words. This centrality of action is implicit in the very labeling of the concept (speech *act*) and in the title of Austin's original work, *How to Do Things with Words* (Austin, 1962).

To sort out this central tenet of speech act theory, it is useful to look at the levels on which we can examine a particular utterance, for example, the statement "It's cold in here." The first level on which we can examine this statement is as an *utterance act*, or the mere stringing together of words. On the second level, this statement can be viewed as a *propositional act* in which you are saying something that you believe to be true. A propositional act deals with the connection between the utterance and the world to which it refers. Together, the concepts of utterance and proposition form the notion of a *locutionary act*. The next level for considering a statement is the most critical one for speech act theory—the **illocutionary act.** This level conveys the force of the utterance, or "how it . . . is to be taken" (Austin, 1962, p. 98). Some illocutionary acts are quite straightforward. For example, the statement "Please pass the salt" can in most situations be taken as a request. What, however, is the illocutionary force of the statement "It's cold in here"? This illocutionary act could be a statement of sensory experience. Or it could be a request for a sweater or a thermostat adjustment. Thus, the assessment of illocutionary force is not always straightforward, but it always involves the notion of what the source wants to do by making a particular statement. Finally, a statement can also be seen as a **perlocutionary act** that has a particular effect on a receiver. The statement "It's cold in here" could have the perlocutionary force of engendering sympathy in a companion or causing that companion to put another log on the fire. In either case, perlocutionary force deals with the impact on the feelings, thoughts, and behaviors of the other interactant.

Speech act theory deals primarily with the illocutionary (especially) and perlocutionary levels of utterances. Thus, speech act theory is not concerned as much with the syntactical form of utterances or even the semantic meaning of utterances. Rather, Speech Act Theory considers the actions performed by speech acts and to some extent their effect on others. One of the primary goals of speech act theory has been one of classification: to sort out the various types of illocutionary force inherent in speech acts. Austin (1962) based his ideas on the concept of *performative verbs*. In the English language, "these verbs are typically issued in the first person present indicative (e.g., 'I promise . . . ,' 'I

order . . . ,' 'I state . . . ,' etc.), and act as a 'bracket,' or 'container' for the locution to follow" (D'Andrade & Wish, 1985, p. 231). By looking at these performative verbs, Austin (1962) estimated that there could be as many as 10,000 illocutionary forces, and hence speech acts, in the English language. Thus, the developers of speech act theory attempted to classify speech acts into major groups.

A variety of category systems have been suggested for speech acts. These include Austin's (1962) original category system of five types of performative verbs, Vendler's (1972) development of seven speech act types, and Searle's (1975) six-category system. In the category scheme presented here, there are five types of speech acts:

- *assertives* that advocate the truth value of a proposition (e.g., to state, deduce, claim, declare, hypothesize)
- *directives* that attempt to get the listener to do something (e.g., to order, request, beg, invite, permit, advise, ask)
- *commissives* that commit the speaker to a future act (e.g., to promise, vow, commit)
- *expressives* that communicate about the speaker's psychological state (e.g., to apologize, commend, condemn, congratulate, welcome)
- *declaratives* that, by their very assertion, make something so (e.g., to quit, nominate, appoint, christen, define, name)

After laying out the various types of speech acts, the next step is to consider the ways in which interactants make sense of a particular utterance in a conversation. At the level of the speech act, this is accomplished by applying criteria known as **felicity conditions.** These conditions are used to evaluate what action is being performed by a particular speech act. For example, a felicity condition for accepting the declarative of "I now pronounce you husband and wife" is that the speaker has the legal authority to perform a marriage. Beyond the notion of felicity conditions, however, speech act theorists contend that we make sense of ongoing interaction through the application of rules. As Searle (1969) states, "Speaking a language is engaging in a rule-governed form of behavior" (p. 22). Speech act theorists look specifically to rules that help to define what meaning is communicated in a particular utterance (i.e., constitutive rules) and how the utterance should be used in the course of interaction (i.e., regulative rules). The concepts of constitutive and regulative rules are developed more fully in our discussion of coordinated management of meaning theory later in this chapter, but they originated in speech act theory's notion that certain utterances can count as different things, depending on the conditions under which they occur.

Applications and Challenges

Applications Speech act theory was developed by linguists and philosophers of language, but it has had far-reaching impacts on a variety of areas within the social sciences and humanities. Flowerdew (1990) lists some of these areas of application, including anthropology, ethnography, literary criticism, education, cultural studies, and language acquisition. These applications all point to the importance of the speech act classificatory system for understanding both the development of language skills and the use of linguistic systems in a variety of interactive contexts. Within the communication discipline, speech act theory has been used to describe the sequencing of utterances in conversation, most often in conjunction with the methodological tenets of conversation analysis. For example, Jacobs and Jackson (1983) use speech act theory as a springboard for proposing a rational model explaining how a variety of utterances can be seen as coherent within a given interaction. For example, Jacobs and Jackson (1983, p. 50) note that the question "What time is it?" could be answered with utterances including the following:

- "It's 11:00."
- "There's a clock in the hall."
- "It was 10:45 when we left for class."

- "Quit worrying."
- "I don't have a watch."
- "Class starts in three minutes."

All these responses could be seen as coherent depending on the conditions of the interaction and the rules that the interactants are following in a particular language game. The felicity conditions surrounding the utterance will define the illocutionary force of the comment within interaction. Thus, speech act theory serves as a base for understanding those rules of rational and coherent interaction.

Challenges Speech act theory has also met with a number of challenges since the 1970s. The most vociferous of these challenges have been levied by conversation analysts—scholars who study the structure and sequencing of actual conversations, typically in naturally occurring contexts. The primary critics in this camp are Levinson (1979, 1981, 1983) and Schegloff (1980, 1984, 1988). Also of note is Geis (1995), who proposed a version of speech act theory designed to deal with the ongoing dynamics of conversation. van Rees (1992, p. 32) has summarized the critiques of these theorists as falling into three major categories. The first of these, the issue of *feasibility*, considers whether "it is actually possible to relate utterances in a systematic fashion to . . . speech acts." That is, can utterances be categorized in a meaningful typology? The second category of criticism, the issue of *empirical validity*, examines whether speech act theory accounts for "an accurate description of conversationalists' actual understanding of utterances." That is, does the typology represent the way people interpret utterances? Finally, the third category of criticism, the issue of *explanatory potential*, questions "whether a speech act theoretical account can actually deal with the indefinitely wide variety of ordinary conversational usage." That is, is speech act theory a useful tool for understanding talk?

These categories of criticism deal to some extent with the ability of speech act theory to deal with language in use. Such an account must deal with the context of a given situation and with the indirect ways in which language is often used. As a pragmatic theory of language, speech act theory should consider these issues. However, as Geis (1995) argues, "Though anyone who works in pragmatics must take at least the ritual stance that context plays a critical role in utterance interpretation, it is remarkable the degree to which pragmatic analyses either ignore or, at least, fail to fully exploit context" (p. 21). In downplaying the role of context in conversation, speech act theory has been criticized for not dealing effectively with times when a request is made indirectly (e.g., asking someone out by saying "Are you doing anything Friday night?"), for not recognizing that accomplishing a specific speech act often requires many conversational turns, and for not recognizing the diffuse and indeterminate use of much language behavior (see Flowerdew, 1990, for discussion of these critiques).

Some scholars have suggested that the discipline of communication is particularly well suited to deal with some of these critiques. For example, Lyne (1981) suggests that traditions within speech communication, including the study of speech topics, audience analysis, and the study of discourse traditions, could help speech act theory move beyond sterile conceptualizations of communication. Similarly, Hopper (1981) suggests that communication scholars could use frame analysis (Goffman, 1974) to understand aspects of language in use that are typically taken for granted in conversations. Further, as noted earlier, scholars such as Sally Jackson and Scott Jacobs (e.g., Jackson & Jacobs, 1983) have already moved in this direction in their adaptation of speech act theory with the methods of conversation analysis.

■ COORDINATED MANAGEMENT OF MEANING THEORY

Whereas speech act theory has its roots in linguistics and philosophy, **coordinated management of meaning theory** (CMM) has its roots

firmly within the communication discipline, though it draws from a number of sources. CMM was developed by Vernon Cronen and Barnett Pearce in the 1970s and was codified in their book *Communication, Action and Meaning: The Creation of Social Realities* (Pearce & Cronen, 1980). The theory has undergone substantial development in subsequent years (see Pearce & Pearce, 2000, for the most recent steps in its evolution). At its heart, CMM attempts to provide some understanding of how meanings are created, coordinated, and managed in the social world. When CMM was developed, it was seen as quite different from the typically scientific accounts of interpersonal communication in vogue in the 1970s. As Pearce (1976) put it in an early presentation of the theory,

> The coordinated management of meaning differs from other treatments of interpersonal communication largely because it is avowedly general, unabashedly theoretical, deliberately based on a set of assumptions differing from recent orthodoxy, and self-consciously two levels of abstraction away from observable exchanges of messages. (p. 18)

In subsequent years, though, as interpretive and critical theory have gained ascendency, it is no longer on the edge of theoretical thought. As Pearce and Pearce (2000) argue, "The constellation of ideas on which CMM was based has moved from the periphery toward the center of scholarly thought" (p. 405).

Metatheoretical Foundations

Though the assumptive base of CMM might not be seen as unusual by today's theoretical standards, in the 1970s it was a radical departure. CMM's ontology, as noted in the title of Pearce and Cronen's foundational book, is clearly one of social constructionism (see Pearce, 1995). That is, CMM ascribes to the notion that "conversation is to be thought of as creating a social world" (Harré, 1983, p. 65) and that the social world we often think of as solid and fixed is actually the product of human actions. As Cronen, Chen, and Pearce (1988) explain,

The apparently stable social world—dinners and dates, commodity exchanges and capital creation, emotion and thought—is deceptive. It does not consist of "found things" but rather is created, maintained, and transformed in the process of communication. It sometimes seems that individuals communicate to express their emotions and to refer to the world around them. But whence come these "individuals," "emotions," and "events/objects"? They are constructed in the process of communication.

The epistemology of CMM follows from the ontological base. Specifically, the theory can be viewed as a rules theory in which knowledge does not take the form of universal and context-free laws. Instead, the goal of a rules theory account is the understanding of the ways in which human action is guided by rules within particular contexts and interactions. A rules understanding will involve a consideration of the practical force of a person's behavior (e.g., in order to get mom to do something, a child must say "please") rather than behavior that is governed by a law. As Pearce (1976) describes the knowledge that emerges from a rules perspective, "The picture is of persons who have learned a set of rules which describe how they and others should behave in conversation and who make strategic choices about which rules to follow and which persons to converse with in order to achieve a satisfactory mode of sociation" (p. 20).

Finally, the axiology of CMM has undergone some change since the theory's development (see discussion of Phillipsen, 1995, pp. 40–41). Originally, the theorists took no clear axiological position or assumed one in which the goal of theorizing was to understand coordination in order to enhance harmonious interaction. In what Phillipsen (1995) sees as middle stages of theoretical development, there is "an explicit acknowledgment that 'coordination' may be a code word for repression and that many patterns of human interaction that do not fit neatly under some version of coordination should be acknowledged as morally legitimate and practically defensible" (p. 40). In recent writings

(Pearce & Pearce, 2000), CMM is presented as a practical theory that helps people to "discover openings for effective action" (p. 420).

Central Concepts of Coordinated Management of Meaning Theory

It is somewhat difficult to break down CMM into discrete components because the various portions of the theory are largely interdependent. However, in this section we look at these interwoven theoretical concepts by considering the constituent terms in the theory's name: *management, meaning,* and *coordination.*

Management: Rules in Interaction We noted earlier that theorists in the CMM tradition are interested in understanding how meaning is created, coordinated, and managed in human interaction. This is no easy task because human interaction can take on innumerable forms that we are required to make sense of. How, for example, do we know that when a friend says, "Get out of here," that she is not really asking you to leave? Or that a stern look from a parent means that you've violated a family rule? Or what should be said when meeting someone for the first time? These situations are examples of interaction that must be managed, and CMM invokes the concepts of rules to explain this management process.

We briefly introduced the concepts of constitutive rules and regulative rules in our discussion of speech act theory, but these notions have been more fully developed in CMM. **Constitutive rules** specify what particular behaviors count for in interaction. In the earlier examples, you might invoke the constitutive rule that the phrase "Get out of here" counts as an expression of mild disbelief and that a particular look from a parent constitutes a nonverbal rebuke. **Regulative rules,** in contrast, specify a particular sequence of behaviors that should be called upon in certain situations. In the earlier examples, there are regulative rules for meeting people that specify appropriate greeting behavior, appropriate forms of address, and appropriate patterns of interaction. How do we know that a particular set of behavior is rule governed? Pearce (1976, pp. 26–27) has suggested criteria for making this assessment, including the following:

- Rule-governed behavior will exhibit a recurring pattern.
- Communicators are able to generate sequences of rule-governed behavior.
- Communicators can perceive alternative sequences of behavior that would be seen as inappropriate.
- Positive or negative sanctions are applied to deviations from rule-governed behavior.

In summary, rules help to regulate and define (i.e., manage) our interaction. It is important to emphasize, though, that rules are not the same as laws. That is, they do not work by necessary force. Rather, rules work by forces that can be seen as *practical* (i.e., in order to gain y, I must do x) or *prefigurative* (i.e., in situation y, I should do x). A rule of practical force might be one that states, "I better be nice to a person if I'm going to ask her for a loan." A rule of prefigurative force could be, "I should compliment the bride when going through the receiving line at a wedding." Rules, then, help us to structure and interpret communicative behavior, but they do not absolutely dictate that behavior.

Meaning: Systems of Social Reality Of course, not all rules hold in all situations and for all people. Whereas joking is sometimes called for, at other times it is virtually forbidden. Whereas some people are comfortable with social kissing of acquaintances, others recoil at the practice. These examples suggest that for different people and in different situations, the same behavior can have very different meanings. This echoes the critique of speech act theory discussed earlier—that the meaning of an utterance will depend to a large extent on the context in which the utterance is offered.

CMM deals with this issue by proposing a **hierarchy of meaning** through which social reality is defined. That is, different constitutive and regulative rules will hold in different contexts. Though this hierarchical model of meaning changes a bit in various writings of CMM theorists (e.g., Cronen et al., 1988; Pearce, 1976; Pearce & Cronen, 1980; Pearce, Cronen, & Conklin, 1979), all the presentations in this area agree on two key points. First, the hierarchy of meaning defines the contexts in which regulative and constitutive rules are to be understood. Second, these contexts are arranged in a hierarchy of abstractness, such that higher levels of the hierarchy help to define—and may subsume—lower levels.

Figure 9.1 provides one version of this hierarchy of meaning. As the figure indicates, meanings can be interpreted at levels ranging from the content level through the level of cultural patterns. An example of how a constitutive rule might work at each of these levels will help illustrate their distinctions.

Consider the comment "You can count on me." At the *content level*, this statement can be considered in terms of the dictionary definitions of each term. Obviously, though, this does little to help sort out the meaning of the utterance. At the *speech act level*, this comment seems to count as a promise, though, again, there may not be enough information at this level to make much constitutive sense out of the utterance. At the *episode level*, we can begin to see how context can influence constitutive meaning. For example, if the episode is a work meeting in which various tasks are being divvied up, this comment might well count as a contractual promise to accomplish a particular piece of work. In the context of two friends discussing boyfriend trouble, the comment could be seen as a much more global statement of support. When we move to the *relationship level*, we can again see some of the complexities of constitutive rules. That is, the comment "You can count on me" might mean very different things in a long-standing intimate relationship than in a conversation between two people who have just met. At the *life script level*, every individual's history of relation-

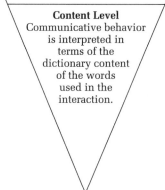

Figure 9.1 The Hierarchy of Meaning in Coordinated Management of Meaning Theory

ships and interactions will influence their rules and interaction patterns. That is, "You can count on me" might not mean much to a child who has been repeatedly abandoned. Finally, *cultural patterns* also serve to define rules and meaning. In some cultures, "You can count on me" is a solemn oath, whereas in others it might be a mere conversational nicety.

These levels are seen as hierarchically ordered (e.g., the cultural level is at a higher level than the other levels), but this ordering does not always take precedence in interpreting communicative behavior. Furthermore, two interactants might not be interpreting meaning using the same level of analysis. For example, imagine a situation in which a husband shows his affection for his wife during a long sermon. He is relying on relational definitions of the behavior and believes his wife will appreciate a discreet kiss (e.g., the constitutive rule of "a kiss counts as a sign of affection"). His wife, however, rebukes him with the whispered comment, "Not in church!" She is obviously relying on the episode level and sees his behavior as a violation of regulative rules guiding appropriate behavior.

Coordination: Interaction Processes The example just presented leads us to the final aspect of CMM—the notion of *coordination* in interaction processes. Clearly, interactants are not on their own in communicative behavior, and individuals bring different meaning systems and rules to any conversation. What then is meant by coordinated interaction? According to Phillipsen (1995), coordination refers to "the degree to which persons perceive that their actions have fitted together into some mutually intelligible sequence or pattern of actions" (p. 18). That is, if people can recognize what has occurred as a conversation or an argument or a stranger asking for directions, then we can say that the interaction was coordinated.

Several comments about coordination are important. First, coordination refers to the meshing of action (because it is from action that meaning arises), not the perfect sharing of interpretations. That is, two people could agree that they were having an argument but have very different interpretations about who came out on top. Similarly, a stranger asking for directions might not receive help in getting to a desired destination. Second, there are certainly many cases in which coordination is not achieved or when coordination is only partially achieved, and these cases should be seen as "humanly important, and morally defensible, patterns of interaction" (Phillipsen, 1995, p. 19). Indeed, some of the most interesting cases for analysis by communication scholars are interaction patterns that are not well coordinated, such as paradoxes and double binds (e.g., Cronen, Johnson, & Lannamann, 1982).

Consider, for example, the classic paradox of Person A saying to Person B, "Be spontaneous" (we will revisit this paradox again in Chapter 11 when we discuss relational communication). The paradox comes from the impossibility of following this dictum because to be spontaneous is to be obedient (to this particular request).

CMM can help to unravel this paradox through the consideration of various levels of meaning. That is, if this comment is interpreted not at the episodic level (e.g., "Be spontaneous in this particular situation") but at the relational level (e.g., "I'd like us to have more spontaneity in our relationship"), then it is possible for enhanced coordination of action and meaning.

Evidence for and Critiques of Coordinated Management of Meaning Theory

As we noted earlier, the developers of CMM see their theory as an expansive theory of human communication. Cronen (1991) has asserted, in fact, that the aim of the theory is to shed light on the overall human condition, not on particular aspects of human behavior. As the description of CMM presented in the preceding sections indicates, the theory does not have specific and testable hypotheses on which we can evaluate its quality. Indeed, Phillipsen (1995) has argued that CMM is a theory that "proceeds not so much by the development of a system of lawlike propositions as it does by the application of its descriptive-interpretive apparatus to a series of themes and contexts, with the aim of refining the stance it takes toward the social world" (p. 25). In this sense, CMM has fared well, as it has been applied across a wide range of contexts, including investigations of a variety of conversational patterns, functional and dysfunctional relationships, intercultural interaction, and even organizational communication (see Phillipsen, 1995, for review). In these areas, the use of CMM concepts has added richness and insight to our understanding of communication processes.

However, CMM has been confronted with criticism when evaluated in more conventional terms. These critiques have included the highly abstract nature of the theory and the shifting definitions of many terms and concepts (e.g., the various levels defined in the hierarchy of meaning). The theory is also criticized as being too broad. As Poole (1983a) notes, "It is difficult . . . to paint with broad strokes and at the same time give difficult areas the attention they deserve" (p. 224). This argument is developed even further by Brenders (1987), who contends that in its broad-stroked approach to human interaction, CMM has missed many of the linguistic, interactional, and theoretical nuances necessary for an understanding of communicative meaning.

■ COMMUNICATION ACCOMMODATION THEORY

When you think about your interaction with others, you can undoubtedly think of many instances when you change your style of talk or the words you use based on the person with whom you are conversing. A kindergarten teacher, for instance, will adjust his vocabulary to the level of his students. A Minnesota native might begin to speak with a drawl on a trip to the Deep South. A teenager might use a great deal of slang just to irritate her mother during a conversation. These situations are instances of accommodating communicative behavior during the course of interaction. Processes such as these have been the interest of Howard Giles and his colleagues since the 1970s.

In 1973, Giles published the first article in this tradition, noting the phenomenon of accent convergence in an interview situation (Giles, 1973). In subsequent investigations, researchers have explored the concepts of convergence and divergence during interaction, developing what was first known as speech accommodation theory and is now known as **communication accommodation theory** (for reviews of the theory at various stages of development, see Giles, Mulac, Bradac, & Johnson, 1987; Giles, Coupland, & Coupland, 1991b; Coupland, Coupland, Giles, & Henwood, 1991; and Gallois & Giles, 1998). In this section we explore the development of this theory, by considering the key concepts of accommodation, convergence, and divergence; examining antecedents and consequences of

these processes; and finally looking at evidence for and critiques of the theory.

Central Concepts—What Happens in Interaction?

The central goal of accommodation theory is to explain the ways in which interactants influence each other in the course of interaction. Communication accommodation theory focuses on the way social psychological processes (e.g., the way we perceive ourselves and others in social situations) influence the behavioral dynamics observed in interaction. *Accommodation,* then, refers to the ways in which individuals in interaction monitor and perhaps adjust their behavior during interaction. In recent theoretical developments, it has been suggested that *attuning* might be a better term than *accommodating* for describing this process because it suggests a more broadly based process. For example, Coupland and Giles (1988) argue that "communicative accommodation can usefully be construed as the full range of interpersonal addressee-oriented strategies in discourse whereby speakers 'attune' their talk to some characteristics of the hearer" (p. 178).

Accommodating and *attuning* are both very broad terms, however, and they say little about what happens in interaction. To describe these interaction processes more precisely, communication accommodation theory concentrates on the specific concepts of convergence, divergence, and maintenance.

Convergence, Divergence, and Maintenance
The most frequently studied concept in the theory is **convergence.** In early presentations of communication accommodation theory, convergence was defined as occurring when "individuals adapt to each other's speech by means of a wide range of linguistic features, including speech rates, pauses and utterance length, pronunciations and so on" (Giles et al., 1987, p. 14). In later versions of the theory, convergence was expanded beyond just patterns of speech to include a wide range of communicative behavior. Examples of convergence, then, would

include a student dressing in a professional way in order to be like an interviewer, or an individual talking in a softer manner than usual with a quiet conversational partner.

The second key process in the theory is **divergence.** Divergence occurs when interactants try to accentuate communicative differences between themselves and others in the interaction. For example, someone from England might accentuate his or her accent in order to make a point about national allegiance. Finally, **maintenance** occurs when an individual's communicative patterns remain stable throughout the interaction.

Theorists in this area have spent a great deal of time developing ideas about these concepts, emphasizing that they are not simple processes. This work has developed a number of distinctions about convergence and divergence processes. In the following list, we examine these distinctions with regard to convergence, but note that many of them apply to the process of divergence, as well.

- Convergence can be either *upward* (i.e., toward a socially sanctioned form of communication or speech) or *downward* (i.e., away from a socially sanctioned form of communication).

- Convergence can occur to varying extents. It can be *full* (i.e., the individual actually matches the communicative behavior of the other), *partial* (i.e., the individual approaches but does not match the communicative behavior of the other), or even *hyper* or *cross-over* (i.e., the individual goes beyond the behavior of another on a particular dimension).

- Convergence can be *unimodal* (e.g., converging on the dimension of vocabulary but not on the dimensions of accent or speech rate) or *multimodal* (e.g., converging on several dimensions of communicative behavior).

- Convergence can be *symmetrical* (i.e., both parties in the interaction attempt to converge toward each other) or *asymmetrical*

(i.e., only one party in the interaction attempts to converge).

- Convergence can be based on *objective* communicative behavior (e.g., the actual speech rate, accent, or vocabulary of the other), it can be *perceptual* (e.g., the perceived speech rate, accent, or vocabulary of the other), or it can be *psychological* (e.g., the believed speech rate, accent, or vocabulary of the other).

Given all these dimensions, an incredibly wide range of accommodative behaviors could be observed. Figure 9.2 illustrates just a few of these possibilities with regard to symmetry of convergence. Even more complex situations are possible, however. For example, scholars studying communication with the elderly have noted that caregivers often use baby talk with their clients, even when the client exhibits no cognitive impairment. This is an example of psychological and asymmetrical convergence that is likely to be multimodal and cross-over. These dimensions of convergence and divergence have implications for the conduct and outcomes of communicative interaction.

Antecedents to Accommodation

What factors lead interactants to accommodate in conversation, through either convergence or divergence? Giles and Powesland (1975) argue that both convergence and divergence can be seen as motivated by the processes of conformity and identification—that is, processes through which we define our connections to others in an interaction situation. However, the specific ways in which these processes manifest themselves in interaction have been explained somewhat differently for the processes of convergence and divergence. As Giles et al. (1991b) note, "Convergence is a strategy of identification with the communication patterns of an individual internal to the interaction, whereas divergence is a strategy of identification with . . . some reference group external to the immediate situation" (p. 27). Thus, these two categories of explanation, for convergence and divergence, are considered separately here.

Explanation	Speaker and Partner
1. Symmetrical convergence	A ——→ ←—— B
2. Asymmetrical convergence	A ——→ ←— B
3. Convergence in the face of maintenance	A ——→ B
4. Convergence in the face of divergence	A —→ B ——→
5. Symmetrical divergence	←—— A B ——→
6. Asymmetrical divergence	←—— A B —→
7. Divergence in the face of maintenance	←—— A B
8. Symmetrical maintenance	A B

Note: Lines indicate direction and amount of change over time (long or short term). The table takes the perspective of Speaker A and should be reversed for B's perspective. Accommodation may be intergroup or interpersonal, may be behavioral or perceived, and may or may not be in accord with optimal levels. The extent of accommodation may be great or small and, in the case of convergence, may result in a cross-over in behavior.

Figure 9.2   Examples of Symmetry in Communication Accommodation
Source: Adapted from Gallois & Giles (1998).

Explanations for Convergence   Early explanations for convergence in interaction were based on the psychological work of Byrne (1971) in the area of similarity attraction. This foundational work suggests that we are attracted to people who we are similar to and that, concurrently, we want to be similar to those we like. As an explanation for accommodation processes, "interpersonal convergence through speech is one of many strategies that may be adopted in order to become more similar to each other" (Giles et al., 1987, p. 16). Thus, if one interactant identifies with another and wants to be integrated with that other, the first interactant will converge toward the communicative behaviors of the other. For example, you might adapt your rate of speech—probably unconsciously—to a friend's speed during conversation.

This need for social approval, and hence convergence, in interaction is not a universal process. Instead, communication accommodation theory proposes a number of factors that might moderate the extent to which convergence occurs. For example, need for social approval might have a particularly strong impact if there is likely to be future interaction with an individual or for individuals with particular personalities (see Natale, 1975). By far the most studied moderator factor, however, is the social status or power of the other interactant.

Giles et al. (1991b) conclude that "the power variable is one that often emerges in the accommodation literature and in ways that support the model's central predictions" (p. 19). Specifically, accommodation theorists predict that the tendency to converge in interaction will be strongest when the other interactant is of high status or has power over the first interactant. For example, Wolfram (1973) has noted that Puerto Ricans in New York City converge toward the dialect of blacks, who are generally seen as having more power and prestige than Puerto Ricans in that locale. Or perhaps you can imagine trying to sound smart when communicating with a professor whom you particularly admire. These processes are examples of how power and status can influence the level of convergence during interaction.

Theorists in this area do not think that convergence will always occur in such situations.

✳ SPOTLIGHT ON THE THEORIST

Howard Giles

Howard Giles has been a professor of communication, with affiliated appointments in the departments of psychology and linguistics, at the University of California, Santa Barbara since 1989. For many years before that, he was on the faculty of the University of Bristol in England. Giles's influence in the discipline of communication has been substantial. Indeed, he was the first recipient of the International Communication Association's Career Achievement Award in 2000. Though his career has encompassed a wide range of teaching and research interests, a great deal of his influence has involved the development of communication accommodation theory.

Giles first became interested in processes of accommodation in the 1960s. He notes that he "was fascinated originally with how many individuals would modify their communication styles depending on whom they were talking [to]," but he felt that the theoretical explanations available for these processes at that time were inadequate. Communication accommodation theory was designed to answer the generic questions of "Who accommodates to whom, how, when, why, and with what effects." Giles has been pleased that the theory "was well-received across a range of disciplines and has been applied in a plethora of different fields," but he also notes that there have been a number of critiques and debate regarding the theory. He sees such debate as healthy, however, and argues that communication accommodation theory "has been continually refined to itself accommodate criticisms and limitations."

Giles feels strongly that students of communication—at both the undergraduate and graduate levels—should appreciate the importance of theories of communication and can play an important role in the development of those theories. He sees theory development as an active and ongoing process. Indeed, he suggests that you could even develop a theory about your reactions to this book and the course you are taking. As he notes, "Individual differences, book structure and layout, commitment to the discipline, time available are a few of the factors impacting what you get from this book. Map out your working model here explicitly and see how it operates." Giles believes that we create these "implicit lay theories" all the time and that we need to make these theories more explicit in order to "enhance our communicative ideals and missions."

In formulating these theories, Professor Giles suggests that budding scholars begin with questions that are important for practice and compelling for the individual. As he states, "If we're not asking cogent questions, we can't expect to find good answers or solutions to problems that are ever-changing." Then, in seeking out answers to these questions, Giles instructs us to range widely across literatures and experiences: "Remember that advances are usually made by transporting and transforming ideas from one area into quite another. Hence, in asking your questions, mine *all* areas you have studied, as some of what you might consider to be the remotest from the current questions can oftentimes be emancipatory to understanding it."

Giles et al. (1991b) point out several important caveats for this effect, including the idea that sometimes the costs of convergence will outweigh the benefits and that some situational norms will override the desire to converge. Consider, for example, an interview situation in which you are eager to make a good impression. In most of these situations, the interviewer would be seen as having more status. This power balance, along with your desire to make a good impression, might lead you to converge on communicative behaviors such as vocabulary, speech rate, and mode of dress. However, you might realize during the interview that the company is looking for independent thinkers, and this situation might lead you to converge less. Or you might realize during the interview that this is not your kind of company, and hence you might want to emphasize this distinction by maintaining your own typical pattern of interaction.

In short, though some factors tend to predict convergence during interaction, these factors can be attenuated or overridden by other situational or personal characteristics. Given this, theorists in this area conclude that "further complexities abound and, as such, underscore the need for research on the relationships between the management of social identities and the dilemmas of appropriately sequencing interpersonal accommodations in context" (Giles et al., 1991b, p. 22).

Explanations for Divergence Explanations for divergence during communicative interaction have tended to look directly at the notion of identity, specifically at Tajfel's theory of intergroup relationships and social identity (Tajfel, 1978; Tajfel & Turner, 1979). In this approach, divergence is explained as a means by which an interactant can establish and emphasize his or her association with a particular social group that is not represented by the other interactant. For example, a speaker in Quebec might use French when talking with tourists to emphasize a connection with his French Canadian social group. As Giles et al. (1991b) explain, intergroup comparisons will

> lead individuals to search for, or even create, dimensions on which they may be seen to be positively distinct from a relevant outgroup. The perception of such a positive distinctiveness contributes to individuals' feelings of an adequate social identity, which enhances their feelings of self-worth. (p. 27)

Like predictions regarding convergence, again, variables can accentuate or attenuate the influence of intergroup identity on the divergence process. These variables include the salience of intergroup allegiances, the vitality or status of the groups involved, the existence of multiple group memberships, and the hardness or permeability of group boundaries. Putman and Street (1984) have also suggested that divergence

might simply indicate disdain for the other interactant rather than allegiance to a particular social group.

As an example of explanations of divergence, consider interaction between a mother and her teenage daughter. Because the daughter feels a great deal of allegiance toward her social group (e.g., teenage girls), she might make particular efforts to differentiate her communication behavior from that of her mother. This divergence might involve different ways of dressing, different vocabulary, or different styles of speaking. However, this divergence might not be as strong if the tie to the reference group weakens (e.g., as the daughter approaches adulthood), if family allegiances outweigh group allegiances, or if the situational pressures toward convergence outweigh the intergroup pressures toward divergence (e.g., the daughter needs to curry favor with her mother in a particular instance). In short, as with convergence, there can be "a plethora of complexities and situational caveats" (Giles et al., 1991b, p. 32) when discussing the process of divergence in interaction.

Consequences of Accommodation

Communication accommodation theory has also considered a variety of consequences of attunement in interaction. These have included the effects on the individual, on the other interactant, and on observers of the interaction process. Though the research on these outcomes is widespread, several principles regarding the consequences of accommodation can be drawn.

First, consequences of accommodation will depend on the perceived motives of the interactant. This conclusion has its roots in research on interpersonal attributions (e.g., Heider, 1958) that suggests that we often evaluate behavior in light of the motives we assume are driving the behavior (see our discussion of attribution theory in Chapter 6). For example, the attribution that someone is converging in order to curry favor in a particular situation might lead to more negative opinions than the attribution that someone is converging in order to break down intergroup barriers. Similarly, lack of convergence attributed to situational constraints might not be negatively sanctioned, whereas lack of convergence attributed to lack of effort could engender negative attitudes (see, e.g., Giles, 1980).

Second, research indicates that there may be optimal levels of accommodation in interaction. This can be seen in several ways. For example, studies of multimodal accommodation (Giles & Smith, 1979) have found that convergence on single variables in communication (e.g., pronunciation, speech rate, and message content) were more positively evaluated than convergence on all three variables. Giles and Williams (1992) have also explored the area of *hypercorrection*, when accommodation goes beyond the behavior of the other interactant. Though hypercorrection could be viewed positively, it could also be seen as an effort to upstage or dissociate from another and hence have negative consequences.

Third, consequences of accommodation will depend on the perceiver. For example, patterns of divergence or maintenance could be seen as insulting by some interactants. Similarly, reactions toward convergence could also depend on who is involved in the interaction. As mentioned earlier, studies of communication with the elderly, for instance, have found that the use of baby talk is viewed negatively by older people who have few functional impairments but is viewed as comforting by some elderly interactants with more problems in daily living activities (see, e.g., Coupland et al., 1988; Ryan, Giles, Bartolucci, & Henwood, 1986; Williams, Giles, Coupland, Dalby, & Manasse, 1990).

Evidence for and Critiques of Communication Accommodation Theory

The impact of communication accommodation theory has been incredibly widespread. As the reviews already cited here attest, scholars from many academic disciplines have applied the theory to a variety of interaction situations. For example, the edited volume *Contexts of Accommodation: Developments in Applied Sociolinguistics*

(Giles, Coupland, & Coupland, 1991a) included applications of accommodation theory to the mass media, to legal trials, to medical consultations, to therapy, to mental disability, to organizational communication, to interethnic communication, and to native-nonnative interactions. The theory has even been used to explain the ways in which telephone callers respond to the structure and content of messages on answering machines (Buzzanell, Burrell, Stafford, & Berkowitz, 1996). By applying the theory to this wide range of communication contexts, its scope has been enlarged, and specific concepts of the theory have been refined.

This breadth of application serves as a means for critiquing the theory as well. Although communication accommodation theory has incredible heuristic power and has been applied in a variety of contexts, it also suffers from weaknesses in terms of the central theoretical criterion of falsifiability. This weakness can be seen in our earlier discussion about the antecedents of convergence and divergence. The theory proposes several variables that could influence convergence or divergence in a particular communicative situation. Thus, some predictions can be made about when convergence or divergence will occur. If convergence or divergence does not occur, however, it is possible to point to mediating or moderating conditions that could be at work in that particular interaction and thus explain why there wasn't convergence or divergence. Thus, the very scope and complexity of the theory detracts from its ability to make specific and testable predictions about communication behavior and the relationship of that behavior to social psychological processes.

■ EXPECTANCY VIOLATION AND INTERACTION ADAPTATION THEORIES

The final pair of theories we discuss in this chapter are similar to communication accommodation theory in that they look at the ways interactants adapt behavior during interaction. In particular, these theories consider the notion that we develop ideas about how communication should proceed in a particular interaction and will behave in particular ways depending on whether those predictions are confirmed or violated during communication. The first approach we consider, **expectancy violation theory,** was developed by Judee Burgoon in the mid 1970s and has been further developed in subsequent years. The final theory we examine is the most recent statement of Burgoon and her colleagues, interaction adaption theory, which attempts to refine the predictions of expectancy violation theory and combine them with insights from other theories of verbal and nonverbal adaptation during interaction.

Original Statement—Expectancy Violation Theory

Expectancy violation theory was first presented by Burgoon and Jones (1976) as a theory of nonverbal behavior. The most complete statement of early development of the theory is found in Burgoon and Hale (1988). In more recent years, the theory has been expanded to consider behaviors other than nonverbal ones and to refine its explanatory mechanisms and empirical predictions. The next few sections trace key concepts in early versions of the theory and discuss tests and development of the theory since these foundational statements.

Expectancies A central tenet of expectancy violation theory is that we all have expectations—or **expectancies**—about what interaction should and will be like. These expectations include behaviors such as distance during interaction, speech rate, volume, eye gaze, touching, and a host of others. To a large extent, we are not aware of these expectancies, and they do not have much impact on us. However, we become aware of our expectancies when they are violated. When someone stands too close (or too far), stares at us (or averts his gaze), or touches us (or keeps her distance), we become aware that our

expectations about how interaction should go have been violated. It is this notion of expectancies that forms the heart of the theory.

In early statements of the theory, Burgoon and her colleagues made several key points about the concept of expectancies. First, expectancies deal with actual behavior within the interaction. Second, expectancies are a function of both societal norms and idiosyncratic differences. That is, society has specific standards for maintaining eye contact during interaction. However, a particular married couple may develop behavioral patterns in which they engage in much more direct and enduring eye contact. Thus, as Burgoon and Hale (1988) note, "Idiosyncratic differences based on prior knowledge of the other, relational history, or observation may be factored in to yield person-specific expectations" (p. 60). Finally, expectancies are not defined in an absolute sense but instead operate within a range. That is, there is not one specific physical distance that is seen as appropriate in conversation but a range of distances that can be tolerated.

Violations of Expectations This final aspect of expectancies sets the stage for the next crucial concept in expectancy violation theory. Only when behavior deviates from a threshold level is the behavior recognized as violating an expectation (Burgoon & Jones, 1976). If the violation is within a range of tolerability, it will simply be "perceptually assimilated as part of the expected behavior pattern" (Burgoon & Hale, 1988, p. 60). When a violation occurs, the theory predicts a specific result—**arousal.** Some models of arousal highlight its physiological characteristics, but the theory emphasizes the role of arousal in attentional processes. Specifically, expectancy violation theory suggests that arousal will "cause an alertness or orienting response that diverts attention away from the ostensive purpose of the interaction and focuses it toward the source of the arousal—the initiator of the violation" (Burgoon & Hale, 1988, p. 62). For example, imagine that you are discussing a class assignment with a fellow student. The conversation seems to be proceeding normally, and

☀ SPOTLIGHT ON THE THEORIST

Judee Burgoon

Judee Burgoon received her doctorate from West Virginia University and has held faculty positions at the University of Florida and Michigan State University. She is currently professor of communication and family studies at the University of Arizona. Burgoon has received many honors for her scholarship, including serving as editor of *Communication Monographs* and being elected as a fellow of the International Communication Association. Her scholarship has been published in a wide range of highly regarded journals in fields including communication and psychology, in numerous book chapters, and in scholarly books. In short, Burgoon is highly regarded as a theorist and as an incredibly productive researcher in the area of interpersonal communication.

Scholars are often told that their teaching and research should be intimately connected, and Burgoon illustrates this principle in noting that expectancy violation theory "originated as a graduate course assignment to make sense out of the literature on proximity." In the more than 20 years since, she has seen the theory "garner a fair amount of attention in communication" though she would not characterize much of this attention as debate. Burgoon has been less happy with the fact that expectancy violation theory has not been taken up as much by theorists in other areas because she believes such interdisciplinary connections would be fruitful. As she argues,

"The theory's propositions transcend culture and context, making [expectancy violation theory] more comprehensive than many theories." However, she knows that sometimes theorists in other disciplines see things differently than scholars in communication. She recounts that "perhaps the most critical response to [expectancy violation theory] came from a psychologist, who disagreed that communicators have valences associated with them. Within our discipline, this is probably one of the least controversial and most accepted precepts of the theory."

Burgoon believes that the study of theory can yield benefits both for our understanding of communication processes and the world around us and for our understanding of ourselves. As she states eloquently, "To articulate one's theories and hunches is to be forced to confront one's own private assumptions and beliefs and to see if they withstand closer scrutiny. So studying theory, apart from the substantive knowledge one may gain, is an extremely important analytical exercise." Burgoon also has advice for scholars beginning research careers. She believes that there are great rewards to be garnered in academic life that involve "the stimulation that comes from living the 'life of the mind' and the satisfaction associated with generating and/or disseminating meaningful knowledge." However, she argues that such satisfactions can come only through intense engagement with the subject matter at hand and that engagement can be maintained only through "tackling real problems and large puzzles" of communicative life by studying them "deeply, persistently, and at close range."

then your interaction partner reaches out and touches you on the arm. You don't really notice this at first, but the touches continue. At this point, the touching has moved beyond the threshold of expected touching behavior, and your attention is aroused and diverted to your conversational partner. You start to wonder what the touches mean and how you should react to them. According to expectancy violation theory,

the answers to these questions—the impact of the violation—will depend on two factors.

Impact of Violation   The impact of a violation will depend on two factors: (a) the evaluation of the violation itself and (b) your assessment of the person who committed the violation. With regard to the first of these factors, Burgoon and her colleagues note that some violations are widely viewed as either positive or negative. For example, Burgoon, LePoire, and Rosenthal (1995) note that behaviors of increasing behavioral involvement are widely viewed as positive. However, other violations might not be seen in such a straightforward manner. In this case, the assessment of the other interactant comes into play. Expectancy violation theory proposes that we evaluate the other person in the conversation in terms of his or her **communicator reward valence.** This reward valence is based on a host of factors (e.g., personality, physical attractiveness, likelihood of future interaction, status or power) and indicates a net balance of rewards and costs for communicating with a particular individual. The theory posits that communicator reward valence will influence assessment of violations in two ways. First, when there is ambiguity about how a particular violation is to be interpreted, positive communicator reward valence will lead to assigning a socially desirable attribution to the behavior. Second, even when there is little ambiguity about the meaning of the violation, it will be evaluated more positively if it comes from a person with high reward valence.

Consider again the classmate who has begun to touch you repeatedly on the arm during a discussion about a class assignment. If this person is someone you find attractive, you will interpret this behavior as a show of affiliation and affection and respond favorably to it. If, in contrast, you are uninterested or even repelled by this person, you might interpret the behavior as a clear invasion of privacy and react negatively to the violation.

Tests and Development of the Theory

Since the development of expectancy violation theory, there have been numerous empirical tests of the theory and elaborations of concepts and mechanisms within the theory. Several areas of theoretical development and testing are highlighted here.

- Many tests of the theory have concentrated on outcomes of expectancy violations and have provided moderate support for the theory. Outcomes considered include variables such as satisfaction, attraction, and ratings of credibility (see Burgoon & Hale, 1988; Burgoon, Stern, & Dillman, 1995, for reviews). In general, empirical tests of the theory's predictions have found support for some predictions of the model but not others, and support that has been weak to moderate in terms of effect size.

- Efforts have been made to more thoroughly explore the nature and development of particular expectancies. For example, Burgoon and Walther (1990) examined expectations for the nonverbal behaviors of touch, conversational distance, and posture and found that attractiveness influenced the evaluation of these expectancies (see Afifi and Burgoon, 2000, for current development of the expectancy concept).

- Burgoon and her colleagues have worked to further understand the nature of arousal in interaction, particularly by investigating the ways in which arousal serves as an orienting tendency (as opposed to arousal as a fight-or-flight tendency). LePoire and Burgoon (1996), for instance, tested this distinction through an investigation of the physiological correlates of arousal during expectancy violation.

- A number of scholars have applied the concept of expectancy violation (rather than the actual theoretical content of the theory) to other interpersonal contexts such as cross-cultural communication (Manusov, Winchatz, & Manning, 1997), date initiation (Mongeau & Carey, 1996), and relational development (Afifi & Metts, 1998).

Interestingly, though, the most recent work of Burgoon and her colleagues has dealt not with testing or refining expectancy violation theory but with reconstituting the theory as a more comprehensive explanation of adaptation in interpersonal interaction. The theory that has developed from this work, **interaction adaptation**

theory, focuses attention on the process through which interactants adapt their behavior. Though work on this new theory is just beginning, we sketch out in the next section the outline of the theory as an illustration of how theories can be developed, and even changed to new theories, through the continuing efforts of a community of scholars.

Interaction Adaptation Theory

In developing interaction adaptation theory, Burgoon and her colleagues (Burgoon, Dillman, & Stern, 1993; Burgoon, Stern, et al., 1995) first reviewed the large array of theories in psychology, linguistics, social psychology, and communication that had been developed to account for adaptation in interpersonal behavior. These theories include, among others, discrepancy-arousal theory (Cappella & Greene, 1984), arousal-valence theory (Andersen, 1985), sequential-functional theory (Patterson, 1982), their own expectancy violation theory, and communication accommodation theory (discussed earlier in this chapter). After reviewing these theories, Burgoon and her colleagues concluded that the default condition in interaction is one in which interactants match (or reciprocate or converge with) each other. However, this tendency is far from universal. As LePoire and Yoshimura (1999) argue,

> This is not to say that the reciprocal and compensatory patterns are immutable over the course of any one interaction. Indeed, the patterns may change over time in an interaction on the basis of the degree of satisfaction of one's needs and desires. (p. 3)

The question of when matching patterns will prevail or when other patterns might come into play, then, defines the major explanatory goal of IAT.

Burgoon and her colleagues propose interaction adaptation theory in relatively straightforward terms. Indeed, in their explication of the theory (Burgoon, Stern, et al., 1995, pp. 265–279) they "recognize the hazards of such simplification and invite the reader to join us

in fleshing out this skeletal model in the future" (p. 265). The theory begins with the distinction among **required** (R) factors governing behavior, **expected** (E) socially based factors governing behavior, and **desired** (D) individually based factors governing behavior. These three factors (RED) combine to create an **interaction position** (IP) that defines a predisposition for behavior and an anticipation for the partner's behavior (i.e., an expectancy). In interaction, this IP can be compared to **actual behavior** (A), and this positioning of A with regard to the IP will predict whether communicators will diverge (or compensate or maintain) communicative behavior, or converge (or reciprocate or match) the other's behavior. The theory predicts that divergence will occur when A is less positively valenced than the IP and that convergence will occur when A is more positively valenced than the IP. Definitions for the various terms in this model are presented in Table 9.1.

Of course, the theory goes beyond these initial predictions to discuss ways in which the RED factors can combine to create a particular IP, how the IP might shift during a particular interaction, and how these interaction patterns might be linked to outcomes. Given the embryonic status of interaction adaptation theory, many of these ideas remain to be tested (but see Afifi & Burgoon, 1999, Floyd & Burgoon, 1999, and LePoire & Yoshimura, 1999, for recent tests of the theory). It is important to emphasize, however, that the theory illustrates the ways in which explanations of communicative behavior can develop and even transform themselves through empirical testing and subsequent theoretical refinement.

■ COMPARISON AND COMMENTARY

After considering the theories of discourse and interaction presented in this chapter, there is little doubt that what we think of in everyday life as the simple process of having a conversation is indeed complex. Taken as a whole, the theories considered here provide a comprehensive look at the microscopic processes that make up discourse

Table 9.1	Key Elements of Interaction Adaptation Theory
Concept	**Definition**
Required (R)	Biologically based factors governing behavior that incorporate basic human needs and drives, that operate primarily below conscious awareness, and that often take precedence over other components.
Expected (E)	Socially based factors governing behavior that are determined by knowledge of the context, communication functions operative within the context, and knowledge of how a particular partner behaves within that context; *E* components include both predictive (typical, normative) and prescriptive (appropriate) expectations and are strongly influenced by social factors.
Desired (D)	Individually based factors governing behavior that incorporate personality, preferences, moods, and other individual difference variables.
Interaction position (IP)	A derivative term combining *R*, *E*, and *D* factors and serving as a valenced behavioral predisposition for one's own interaction behavior or for what is anticipated (required, expected, and/or desired) from a partner.
Actual behavior (A)	Partner's enacted behavior(s), also valenced, and placed on a behavioral continuum relative to self *IP* or partner *IP*.

Source: From Burgoon, Stern, & Dillman (1995).

and the social psychological and behavioral influences that come into play during interaction.

Speech act theory and coordinated management of meaning theory concentrate primarily on the discourse itself—the things that are said during conversation—and see conversation as a rule-governed activity. Speech act theory takes a more formal view of interaction, whereas coordinated management of meaning theory considers the complexities of the context that influence the use of particular utterances, that is, factors such as the episodic, relational, life history, and cultural influences on the production and interpretation of any utterance or series of utterances. In short, these theories look at the meat of conversation and help us understand how people do a wide variety of things with words.

Communication accommodation theory, expectancy violation theory, and interaction adaptation theory all move to a less linguistic level in looking at the influence of a variety of factors on patterns of communicative behavior. Instead of looking at what particular utterances do in conversation, these theories look at general tendencies to converge and diverge with conversational partners and at the situational, psychological, and behavioral factors that will lead to these attunements in interaction. These theories are more interested in considering how dyadic processes influence interaction, and explanation within these theories depends on the behavioral and social psychological relationship between two interactants.

The complexity of the phenomena modeled in these theories, however, creates a quandary for the theorist. If the theorist attempts to provide an elegant view of the discourse process, he or she can be accused of being too general, too abstract, and not cognizant enough of individual factors that might mediate and moderate the process of interaction. These have been some of the critiques levied against speech act theory and coordinated management of meaning theory. In contrast, if an attempt is made to account for all the complexities of interaction within a given theory, the theorist can be accused of having so many contingency conditions within the theory that predictions within a particular situation are virtually impossible. Critiques of this nature have been raised against communication accommodation theory and expectancy violation theory.

Perhaps these quandaries come with the territory when grasping for an understanding of interaction and discourse processes. And perhaps the lesson to be gained from these critiques is that no single theory will suffice in an understanding of these complex communicative processes. Instead, we need the elegant orientation of coordinated management of meaning theory, the microscopic analysis of speech act theory, and the comprehensive looks at social psychology and behavior provided by communication accommodation theory and expectancy violation theory. It is likely that a comprehensive picture of discourse and interaction processes will come into focus only when the diverse viewpoints of these theories are taken together.

Key Terms

speech act theory
semantics
syntactics
pragmatics
illocutionary act
perlocutionary act
felicity conditions
coordinated management of meaning theory
constitutive rules
regulative rules
hierarchy of meaning
communication accommodation theory
convergence
divergence
maintenance
expectancy violation theory
expectancies
arousal
communicator reward valence
interaction adaptation theory
required/expected/desired factors
interaction position
actual behavior

Discussion Questions

1. Pearce and Cronen claim that coordinated management of meaning theory is liberating and hence should be categorized as a critical theory. The argument can also be made that this is an interpretive theory. What aspects of the theory are best seen as interpretive and which are best seen as critical?

2. To what extent does context play a role in speech act theory?

3. Using expectancy violation theory, explain why seeing your professor out at the local undergraduate bar may be noteworthy. How might his or her behavior at the bar influence your interpretations?

4. Provide and discuss examples of accommodating communication in your everyday life. When do you converge, diverge, or maintain particular aspects of your interaction? Why do you believe you behave in these ways?

10 Theories of Communication in Developing Relationships

The concepts of communication and relationships are inextricably enmeshed. It is through communication that our relationships are forged, and it is within the context of relationships that the conversations of our lives—both mundane and profound—are played out. It is little surprise, then, that the study of interaction in developing relationships is a topic that has interested communication scholars for many years. This interest began to flourish in the late 1960s and during the 1970s, when the social culture in the United States (and in many other parts of the world) was moving toward a philosophy of openness and relational freedom. The 1960s were known as a time of sexual revolution, and a great deal of value was placed on "rapping" and "letting it all hang out." Formality and adherence to rationality were often being usurped by casual attitudes and a value for emotion. These social movements served as the societal backdrop for the genesis of the theories we discuss in this chapter.

In this chapter, we consider two general theoretical approaches to the study of developing relationships: social penetration theory and uncertainty reduction theory. We begin with social penetration theory because it is the more general and wide-ranging of theoretical statements about relational development. This theory tracks the development and dissolution of relationships through a series of interconnected stages. The second theory we examine—uncertainty reduction theory—periscopes our attention on relational development in two ways. First, uncertainty reduction theory calls our attention to the very early stages of relational development, the period of initial interaction. Second, this theory concentrates on one specific process within relational development, that of reducing uncertainty about the individuals with whom we interact.

■ SOCIAL PENETRATION THEORY

As each new semester starts, you begin a new set of classes with new professors and classmates. You might already know students in some of your classes. Perhaps you have had them in other courses, or perhaps you have decided with friends to take classes together. There are probably many others in the class whom you have never met. Some of these students will remain relative strangers, others will become acquaintances you chat with during class or when you see them on campus, and still others may become long-time friends. Thus, in this small microcosm of a new class, you can see the variety of relationships that can exist—strangers, acquaintances, friends, enduring friends—and the idea that these relationships will ebb and change over time. But how does this happen? Why does one person remain a stranger and another become a close friend? Why do some relationships click and progress quickly, whereas others move more slowly toward increasing levels of intimacy? Questions such as these motivated Irwin Altman and Dalmas Taylor to propose their **social penetration theory** in the early 1970s.

Altman and Taylor developed their theory in the field of social psychology. Thus, many of the processes seen as central to relational development are psychological in nature. However, Altman and Taylor also laid out a number of communication processes in their theory. Not surprisingly, social penetration theory has been embraced (and adapted) by many theorists in communication studies and has played a prominent role in our ideas about communication as a central process in the development of relationships.

Original Statement of Social Penetration Theory

Social penetration theory has gone through a fair amount of theoretical development over the years, though much of this development has taken place in a rather patchwork fashion. Thus, in understanding the theory, it is useful to consider some of the original concepts at its core, as developed by Altman and Taylor in the early 1970s. We then look at adaptations of the theory, both by the original theorists and by scholars in the field of communication.

The Process of Relational Development Altman and Taylor's original statement of social penetration theory was laid out in their book *Social Penetration: The Development of Interpersonal Relationships* (Altman & Taylor 1973). Their theory was a processual one that highlighted the development, maintenance, and deterioration of social relationships. The most central aspect of the theory is the conceptualization of relational development as a process. More specifically, Altman and Taylor specified that relationships go through sequential stages as they devel-

op. In the original explication of social penetration theory, four stages were defined:

- In the earliest stage, **orientation,** individuals are cautious and tentative in their interaction, and these interactions are ruled by social conventions and formulas. Little information is shared during the orientation stage.

- In the second stage, **exploratory affective exchange,** the individuals begin to relax their guard a bit and share some information beyond the socially approved small talk of the orientation stage. In this stage, interactants are more relaxed and friendly with each other.

- In the third stage, **affective exchange,** many barriers have been broken down, and a great deal of open exchange occurs. Altman and Taylor see this stage as the one that would often characterize close friendships and romantic relationships.

- Finally, the **stable exchange** stage is characterized by continued openness and richness in interaction. Interactants understand each other very well, and communication can often occur at the nonverbal level.

Several aspects of these stages are worth noting. First, though Altman and Taylor (1973) acknowledge that the social penetration process is complex and may involve "ebbs and flows" (p. 135), these theorists see movement through the stages as primarily linear and sequential. That is, interactants begin at the orientation stage and then move through subsequent stages as the relationship develops. As Altman, Vinsel, and Brown (1981) summarize,

> This aspect of the theory assumes a directional and cumulative quality of the social penetration process. It is directional in stating that relationship growth proceeds toward greater mutual openness. It is cumulative in presupposing that exchange at more superficial levels of personality occurs before interaction takes place at more intimate levels. (p. 109)

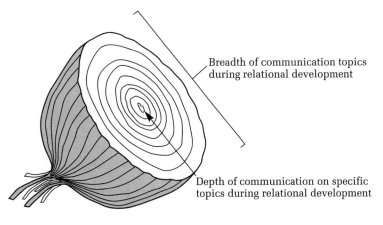

Breadth of communication topics
during relational development

Depth of communication on specific
topics during relational development

Figure 10.1   The Onion Model of Social Penetration

Second, Altman and Taylor see relationship dissolution as following the same stages, though in reverse. That is, "once set in motion, the exchange processes that occur in the dissolution of an interpersonal relationship are . . . systematic and proceed gradually, this time from inner (intimate) to outer (nonintimate) levels of exchange" (D. A. Taylor & Altman, 1987, p. 260). Thus, both relational development and relational disintegration occur as interactants move in a linear fashion through these varying stages of intimacy.

Breadth and Depth of Communication The preceding discussion of stages alludes several times to the notion of exchange between interactants. But what is being exchanged as people move into more or less intimate relationships? What is the medium through which interpersonal relationships develop? According to social penetration theory, relationships develop as overt interpersonal behaviors move from the superficial to the intimate, and the most central of these behaviors is communication.

Altman and Taylor propose an "onion" model to describe the ways in which communication shifts as relationships move through varying stages of intimacy. The onion is an apt metaphor in social penetration theory, because it includes both clear layers through which communication in relationships can travel and a round surface

that suggests varying points of entry for moving to the center of the onion. This metaphor highlights the notion that as relationships develop, they are characterized by increasing depth of communication (e.g., moving toward inner areas of the onion) and increasing breadth of communication topics (e.g., as more surface area of the onion is explored). This onion metaphor is represented in Figure 10.1.

According to social penetration theory, relationships develop as communication—and hence knowledge and understanding of the relational partner—increases in both depth and breadth. For example, during the orientation stage, communication is characterized by low levels of depth and breadth. That is, you talk about only a few topics (e.g., academic major, hometown) and don't go into much detail on even these. In contrast, a relationship that has progressed all the way to the stable exchange stage would be characterized by high levels of both breadth and depth. For example, with a spouse or a very close friend, you feel comfortable talking about a wide range of topics and feel comfortable revealing a great deal about these issues. The intervening stages of exploratory affective exchange and affective exchange would be marked by varying levels of breadth and depth as the relationship develops. For example, in exploratory affective exchange, you may have talked about a fair number of topics (e.g., school, sports, music, television) but not about others (e.g., politics, religion). Thus, there would be moderate breadth in this relationship. It is also possible that you've talked in depth about a few topics (e.g., school and sports). As the relationship moves from exploratory to affective exchange, more topics are considered and greater depth is explored in each topic, leading to a more developed relationship.

Self-Disclosure and Reciprocity   The behavioral process through which this breadth and depth of interaction is achieved is **self-disclosure.** Self-disclosure involves, quite simply, communication about self and can include both intimate and nonintimate topics. That is, statements such as "I was born in Michigan," "I used to dream of being an actress," "When it comes to politics, I guess you'd call me a liberal," and "It is difficult for me to establish close friendships" are examples of self-disclosure, though they represent varying levels of intimacy. According to social penetration theory, the communicative process of self-disclosure enhances both the breadth and depth of relational sharing and hence moves the relationship through various stages of the theory's trajectory. Though there have been many studies of the self-disclosure process (see, e.g., Dindia, 1994, for review), several overall patterns are particularly important to an understanding of social penetration theory:

- There is a general norm of **reciprocity** in self-disclosure processes. That is, when one person reveals something about himself or herself (e.g., academic major), the other person will tend to reply with similar information. Reciprocity is a norm, though, not a universal law. As Derlega, Metts, Petronio, and Margulis (1993) point out, reciprocity "is a common and expected occurrence but is not invariant or automatic." Further, self-disclosure is not always reciprocated on a tit-for-tat basis but might involve the acknowledgment of disclosure at one point in time and reciprocation at a later point in time (Dindia, 1994).

- Information that is public or peripheral will tend to be exchanged before private information (see, e.g,. Berger, Gardner, Clatterbuck, & Schulman, 1976). That is, in initial stages of the relationship, individuals will talk about issues such as demographics, background, and hobbies. Later, interactants will move on to more personal information such as attitudes, beliefs, hopes, and fears.

- The rate of exchange changes as individuals move through relational stages. That is, during early stages of the relationship there is a great deal of disclosure on largely public topics. However, as interactants push through the layers of the onion, social norms and individual reluctance will slow down the extent of self-disclosure. Indeed, in social penetration theory, this reluctance helps explain why many relationships never move past the orientation or affective exploratory stages.

Motivational Force: Social Exchange   Social penetration theory proposes that individuals move through relational stages of varying breadth and depth as information is exchanged through processes of self-disclosure. However, it is clear from our experiences that very few relationships reach the stable stage or even the stage of affective exchange. Furthermore, we clearly have preferences with regard to these relationships. There are a few relationships that we value highly and want to keep at an intimate level. At other times, our desire is to keep a relationship at a superficial level. We also have preferences for movement among relational stages, as we talk about our desire to move a relationship to a new level or get some distance in a friendship. What is the motivational force that drives these desires and that pushes and pulls relationships from one stage to another? According to social penetration theory, it is the important process of social exchange.

Social exchange is not a singular theory but a family of theories that proposes that individuals place varying values on aspects of relationships

Social Exchange Situations

Situation A	Situation B	Situation C	Situation D
outcomes	CL_{ALT}	CL_{ALT}	CL
CL	CL	outcomes	outcomes
CL_{ALT}	outcomes	CL	CL_{ALT}

Figure 10.2   Four Social Exchange Situations

and make decisions about relationships based on those values. The particular approach to social exchange that is most compatible with social penetration theory is the **social exchange theory** proposed by John Thibaut and Harold Kelley (e.g., Thibaut & Kelley, 1959). According to social exchange theory, individuals evaluate relationships in a relatively rational manner akin to an economic analysis. This analysis involves an assessment of the rewards derived from a relationship, the costs of a relationship, and the rewards and costs that are perceived from past relationships and possible future relationships. These concepts come together in defining relational outcomes, comparison levels, and comparison levels of alternatives.

An assessment of the **outcomes** of a particular relationship involves a consideration of both the rewards derived from the relationship and the costs of the relationship. For example, in evaluating a long-distance romance, you might be rewarded by the ability to share thoughts and feelings, enjoyment in being together, shared interest in the theater, and similarity in background. However, you might also see costs in the relationship such as travel and phone expenses in maintaining the relationship, inability to share everyday activities, and dissimilarity in life and career goals. These costs and rewards are often highly complex and dynamic. A social exchange perspective, however, argues that these costs and rewards can be assessed in assigning an overall rating of the outcomes of a particular relationship. A relationship with many rewards and few costs would have high outcomes; one with few rewards and many costs would have low outcomes.

On the face of it, it would seem that we would always stay in relationships with high outcomes and get out of relationships with low outcomes. However, social exchange theory argues that it's not so simple. Instead, we compare our outcomes in current relationships to past relationships and to possible future relationships. These comparisons help determine our satisfaction with the current relationship and our motivation to change the status of relationships. Our assessment of past relationships is known as our **comparison level** (CL). If we have had many fine and satisfying friendships in the past (and present), we would have a high CL for this kind of relationship. Our assessment of possible future relationships is known as our **comparison level of alternatives** (CL_{ALT}). That is, if we believe there are lots of fish in the sea, or if we've had a first date that is highly promising, we might have a high CL_{ALT}.

These concepts serve as a framework for understanding why individuals are motivated to either escalate or deescalate relationships in the social penetration framework. As Taylor and Altman (1987) argue, "In social penetration theory the concept of reward/cost assessment is viewed as the motivational basis for relationship growth through the various stages of development" (p. 265). In essence, individuals make psychological assessments of their current relationship and compare that assessment to past relationships and potential future relationships. Consider, for example, the four scenarios laid out in Figure 10.2.

In situation A, outcomes are higher than both the CL and the CL_{ALT}. That is, an assessment of rewards and costs led to the conclusion that this relationship was more rewarding than both past relationships and potential future relationships. An individual in this situation will likely want to maintain the relationship and perhaps move the relationship to more intimate levels. In contrast, situation B portrays a case where outcomes are lower than both CL and CL_{ALT}. In this case, it is likely that the relationship will deescalate and potential alternative relationships will be explored. The situations portrayed in C and D are not so straightforward. In situation C, outcomes are higher than those in past relationships (leading to relative satisfaction with the relationship) but not as high as potential alternatives. In situation D, current outcomes are lower than those in past relationships (leading to relative dissatisfaction with the relationship), but there are no viable alternatives on the horizon. In these cases, decisions about movement among the social penetration stages is not so straightforward and may depend on other situational and psychological factors.

Meanwhile, in the Field of Communication . . .

As noted in the preceding discussion, social penetration theory was developed in the field of social psychology. Indeed, a recent retrospective review (Derlega, 1997) highlights the critical role the theory has played in advancing the social psychological study of personal relationships. However, it is clear from our discussion that the process of communication is central to social penetration theory. Indeed, Derlega (1997) points out that before the theory came along, most psychologists looked at relationships in terms of psychological variables such as liking and attraction and that "a major contribution of social penetration theory is to focus attention on the nature of social exchanges between individuals as personal relationships develop, including the role of self-disclosure in intimate relationships" (p. 102). Given the theory's communicative focus, it is instructive to go back to the time period in which the theory was introduced in order to explore how the concepts of social penetration—and similar ideas—were adapted or independently developed in the field of communication. Here we consider two books written by professors in the communication discipline during the same time period as Altman and Taylor's seminal work.

Knapp's *Social Intercourse* Five years after Altman and Taylor's book was published, Mark Knapp published a book entitled *Social Intercourse: From Greeting to Goodbye* (Knapp, 1978). The relationship of this book to Altman and Taylor's work is apparent in several ways. First, the concept of social intercourse is obviously similar to the metaphor of social penetration, though the former highlights the communication exchange process that is central to relational development. Second, Knapp acknowledges in the first chapter of his book that he is taking an approach that owes some degree of intellectual debt to social penetration theory.

However, Knapp also adapted Altman and Taylor's work in important ways. First, Knapp redefines the stages of the relational development process. One set of stages incorporates the processes of developing relationships and includes initiating (when people first come together), experimenting (when people begin to try to discover the unknown through processes such as small talk), intensifying (when intimacy increases through mutual self-disclosure and enmeshed behavior), integrating (when the relationship takes on a quality of fusion or being "a couple"), and bonding (when public rituals make relational commitments formal and institutionalized). A second set of stages characterizes the relational dissolution process. These include differentiating (becoming distinct and increasing interpersonal distance), circumscribing (decreasing the breadth and depth of information in a relationship), stagnating (marking time in the relationship), avoiding (increasing physical separation from the other), and terminating (ending the relationship). Like Altman and Taylor, Knapp conceptualizes these stages as being generally sequential, but he also highlights that not all relationships advance to the

---

☀ SPOTLIGHT ON THE THEORIST

Mark Knapp

Theory is not a purely academic endeavor. Indeed, theory often springs from the life experiences of theorists, as they try to understand and explain things that happen in everyday life. Such is the case for Mark Knapp, the Jesse H. Jones Centennial Professor in Communication at the University of Texas, and his work in the area of relational development. When asked about the impetus for his book *Social Intercourse: From Greeting to Goodbye,* Knapp states, "I went through a divorce in 1974 and had all kinds of questions for myself about why my relationship went the way it did so I started reading as much as I could on intimacy and close relationships." He found that much of the literature in the communication discipline at the time had more to do with message production (e.g., the study of credibility, comprehension, and persuasion) than with the development of relationships. However, in social psychology, Knapp found that he "resonated particularly well with [sociologist] Murray Davis' *Intimate Relations* and Altman and Taylor's *Social Penetration.*" Thus, Knapp used these ideas as a jumping-off point for his own theoretical work.

Knapp argues that his work on relational development is "like a multi-layered chess game in which the different levels are represented by a given conversation, a time in a relationship, and a specific time in one's lifespan." Though he regrets that some of these layers (e.g., the emphasis on specific conversations and lifespan development) were deemphasized in

subsequent editions of his book, he is "very pleased" with the way in which his ideas about relational stages have been taken up by others in communication and related fields. As he notes about scholars in communication, "Whether they like what I did or not, the field of interpersonal communication has almost become the study of relationships. I'm not suggesting that I'm responsible for that—only that with that much attention to a subject, we certainly have learned a lot about it . . . and that's what I was seeking in the first place."

Knapp acknowledges that there has been a great deal of criticism of his theoretical ideas, particularly the notion of relationships as a series of stages. However, he states, "I never intended for my stages to be viewed as static or inflexible. As a person who has lived communication in relationships, I know all too well it is not a simple, linear process." However, he welcomes developments of his and other theories regarding relational development. As he says, "That's how knowledge grows." Knapp is particularly happy that his ideas about relational development seem to have some resonance with students of communication even a quarter century after they were formulated. As he recounts, "From the messages I get, a lot of students have eureka experiences as they read about communication and relationship change. Nothing could be more satisfying to me because the process seems to have come full circle. I started out wanting to get some answers about how relationships work and now students are telling me my ideas help them understand what is happening to them. I feel good that a lot of students from around the country have found my ideas useful to them in their daily relationship life."

---

same degree (e.g., a relationship might get to the intensifying stage and then begin decaying with the circumscribing stage without advancing to more intimate relationship levels) and that steps can be skipped or "approached from differing initial conditions and through a variety of paths" (Knapp, 1978, p. 33).

In addition to Knapp's reconfiguration of the relational development stages, his work was important in emphasizing communicative aspects of the social penetration process. His book highlights interaction patterns, such as small talk, forms of address, communicative norms, self-disclosure, and nonverbal behavior, that mark the movement among various relational stages. In short, Knapp (1978) argues for the centrality of communication in relational development, stating that "relationships are created, sustained, moved, and killed by messages" (p. 51).

Miller and Steinberg's *Between People* A second relevant book published in this same time period does not have a direct connection to social penetration theory (indeed, Altman and Taylor's book is not even cited), but the parallels between them are notable. *Between People,* by Gerald Miller and Mark Steinberg (1975), also advocated a processual approach to relational development. Indeed, Miller and Steinberg argue that a relationship should not even be defined as interpersonal until it is well along the relational development continuum. Their conceptual framework, then, highlights the ways in which communicative relationships may or may not move along the developmental continuum to become interpersonal in nature.

One of the crucial distinctions made by Miller and Steinberg is in the nature of information people have about each other. Some of this information is *cultural* in nature, or based on the dominant norms, beliefs, values, and behaviors of a cultural group. An example of this kind of information is the statement "Of course Angela likes pasta, she's Italian, isn't she?" Some information is *sociological,* or based on a person's membership in groups (e.g., college student, mother, republican). For example, "Fred wouldn't want to go to the ballet—you know how men are." Finally, some information we have about each other is *psychological,* or what you know about a person as a unique individual. For example, "A lot of girls like Barbies, but Janie would much rather play with trucks."

Several points related to these three levels of information are important in Miller and Steinberg's developmental theory. First, Miller and Steinberg believe that our communication is enhanced by our ability to make predictions about another person and that we will be able to make much better predictions if we are using psychological rather than cultural or sociological information. In essence, when making predictions

from cultural or sociological data, we are engaged in *stimulus generalization* (i.e., how this person is similar to others in the group), whereas when using psychological data, we are engaged in *stimulus discrimination* (i.e., how this person is different from others in the group). Second, Miller and Steinberg argue that self-disclosure serves as a way of moving from a reliance on cultural and sociological information to a reliance on psychological information. They also note the importance of empathic communication in the process of developing relationships. Finally, Miller and Steinberg make the concept of trust central to their conceptualization of developing relationships, arguing that only when trust is person specific rather than generalized can a relationship be clearly labeled as *interpersonal.*

Developments and Tests of Social Penetration Theory

Social penetration theory presents a view of relationships that is processual and multifaceted. By the early 1980s, the development of the theory could be summarized as follows: Relationships develop as individuals provide increasing breadth and depth of information through the self-disclosure process. Motivation for movement from stage to stage is predicated on current relational outcomes, past relational experiences, and future relational possibilities. As relationships become more developed, factors such as trust, intimacy, and ability to predict the other's behavior will be enhanced. Relationships can also fall apart and move backward through the stages of social penetration.

Like relationships, however, theories grow and develop (and sometimes disintegrate). So it has been with social penetration theory. In this section, we highlight some of the key areas of support for the theory and review critiques and revisions of the theory.

Empirical Support for the Theory Because social penetration theory is a theory of long-term relational development, few studies have tested the whole of the theory. The rigors of the research process and ethical concerns about following intimate relationships as they develop and dissolve make such tests difficult if not impossible. Instead, tests have considered a truncated model of the theory, in which shorter spans of relational development are examined. For example, D. A. Taylor (1968) conducted an early study that was a precursor to social penetration theory, in which he studied college roommates for 13 weeks. As Taylor and Altman (1987) note, "His findings confirmed several hypotheses derived from social penetration theory: progressive development in exchanges over time, with less rapid development in intimate than nonintimate ones, and a general slowing down of the process at later time periods" (p. 261). Other studies that have confirmed these basic properties of relational development are reviewed by Taylor and Altman (1987).

Other empirical investigations have examined specific processes that are central to social penetration theory. Foremost among these is the process of self-disclosure (see, e.g., Derlega et al., 1993, and Dindia, 1994, for reviews). Though this work is complex and multifaceted, it has generally found that self-disclosure tends to be reciprocated, enhances attraction, and plays a role in the development of interpersonal relationships. These conclusions certainly support the theory's claims regarding self-disclosure. Other investigations have looked at the social exchange process as a motivator for relational change. Taylor and Altman (1987) review research indicating that individuals do, indeed, assess rewards and costs in making relational decisions and the importance of considering both context and alternatives in a social exchange framework. However, it can be difficult to falsify predictions made in a social exchange framework (e.g., if an individual chooses a particular relational alternative, we can simply revise our theoretical assessment of his or her costs and rewards).

Critiques of the Theory   In spite of this general support for both the social penetration process and some of the underlying mechanisms in social penetration theory, there have been many critiques of the theory since its inception. Some of these critiques have been on philosophical grounds and have taken several directions. For example, some scholars question the value of an economic model in the realm of relational development because such models make relational development and choice a purely rational decision. For example, Wood (1997) argues that "relationships are not governed by and cannot be explained by economic principles or cost-benefit considerations" (p. 234; see also Wood & Duck, 1995). Other scholars question the ideological basis of the theory. Recall that social penetration theory was developed in a period when openness and candor in relationships was a highly valued standard. The ideology of total openness, and the related value for self-disclosure and relational intimacy, have been questioned in the years since the theory's development. For example, Parks (1982) and Bochner (1984) have argued that there are many times when we should value nonintimate relationships and downplay the importance of self-disclosure in interaction. Bochner argues this position in strong terms:

> Self-disclosure appears to be a highly overrated activity. Perhaps the time has come to lift the fog of ideology surrounding the concept. The fact that there has been only mild, if any, opposition to the thesis that openness leads to better and more satisfying relationships suggests that some investigators have been lulled into an uncritical acceptance of an untenable proposition. (p. 608)

Social penetration theory has also been criticized on empirical and evidentiary grounds. These critiques have largely questioned Altman and Taylor's description of the social penetration process. In particular, critics have questioned the linear structure proposed in the theory. To many, it seems intuitively clear that relationships are not on a direct march toward intimacy. Rather, our personal experiences tell us that relational development can move backward and forward, can stall at certain stages, and can skip stages. As noted earlier, Altman and Taylor (1973) recognized this possibility in their early theorizing, stating that "the process ebbs and flows, does not follow a linear course, cycles and recycles through levels of exchange" (pp. 135–136). However, in spite of this cautionary note, most initial testing of social penetration theory conceptualized relational development as a linear process. Indeed, Knapp's elaboration of the theory in communication argued that a sequential process should be expected because (a) each stage contains presuppositions for the next stage, (b) following a linear sequence allows interactants to forecast the future of the relationship, and (c) skipping stages is risky for individuals. However, when put to the test, the linear pattern of relational development did not always hold up. Thus, in recent years social penetration theory has been revised to include nonlinear processes of relational development.

Dialectical Revisions of the Theory In response to concerns about the overly linear nature of social penetration theory, both the original theorists and scholars in communication have suggested revisions to the social penetration model. Most of these adaptations have been based on the idea that relational development is influenced by so-called **dialectical tensions** that emerge through communication. We talk much more about dialectics in Chapter 11 when we discuss communication in ongoing relationships. In the context of social penetration theory, however, a dialectical approach suggests that relational development is not an inevitably linear one but is, instead, a process marked by tensions in relational development. These tensions include the contrasting desire for openness and closedness and the tension between dependency and autonomy. Further, a dialectical approach suggests that these tensions will lead to cyclical patterns in relational development.

The dialectical revision of the theory was proposed by the original theorists in the early 1980s (Altman et al., 1981). Dealing primarily with the openness dialectic, Altman et al. responded to scholars who had criticized both the theory's philosophical underpinnings (e.g., open relationships are always good) and its empirical viability (e.g., relationships always proceed in a linear fashion):

> There are psychological dangers in an unlimited openness of people to one another, including mutual intrusion, increased vulnerability and exposure, and the potential loss of individuality and dignity. We will hypothesize later that, while some relationships may generally proceed toward greater openness, they also probably have cycles or phases of closedness between participants. People not only make themselves accessible to one another; they also shut themselves off to one degree or another, break off contact, engage in more distant styles of interaction, and exhibit an ebb and flow of exchange. (p. 112)

In the field of communication, the investigation of social penetration as a dialectical process has been most thoroughly investigated by Arthur Van Lear (e.g., Van Lear, 1987, 1991). Van Lear used sophisticated statistical techniques to assess the cycles of openness and closedness that could be observed in developing interpersonal relationships. His research has demonstrated that patterns of openness and self-disclosure do exhibit cycles, both within conversations and across the trajectory of the relationship. Furthermore, his research indicates that relational partners generally match each other in these cycles, supporting the contention that "the dialectical tension between openness and closedness, revelation and restraint, is *relational*" (Van Lear, 1991, p. 356).

Summary and Evaluation of Social Penetration Theory

Since its inception, social penetration theory has had a great deal of influence both in social psychology and in communication. This influence has been largely heuristic in nature. The social penetration model provides a compelling way to describe the development of interpersonal relationships, and to a large extent it resonates with our individual experiences as processes of self-disclosure propel our relationships forward or as we close up when relationships are ending. Thus, the theory has been widely used as a model in teaching about interpersonal relationships and as an overarching framework for considering relational development.

Social penetration theory does not fare quite so well when we consider other criteria for theory in the post-positivist tradition. It certainly fares well in terms of scope: Modeling the entire relational development process encompasses a great deal of territory in interpersonal behavior. However, in part because of this large scope, the theory does not meet the criterion of accuracy nearly so well. These weaknesses in accuracy stem from three areas. First, the linear development of relationships posited by the theory does not seem to hold true in empirical tests. Second, it is difficult to even assess the theory's accuracy because of the ethical and procedural dilemmas in conducting research on relational development. Most researchers do not have the time or resources to follow a large number of relationships, and many would question whether doing so would violate the privacy of those being studied. Third, some of the processes in the theory suffer from problems with falsifiability. For example, the social exchange component posits that relationships move forward because of assessments of relational costs and rewards and the comparison of those outcomes to past and potential relationships. These assessments can lead to problems in falsifying the theory. For example, if a relationship doesn't move forward, we could simply reason that the individual evaluated rewards and costs in an idiosyncratic way or that he or she saw alternatives that we didn't know were available. In short, because social penetration theory is both a complex model and one that is not minutely specified and defined (e.g., what actually constitutes rewards and costs in a relationship?), it is difficult to find occasions when the theory is clearly wrong in its predictions.

■ UNCERTAINTY REDUCTION THEORY

Uncertainty reduction theory has perhaps had more influence in the field of communication than any other theory in the post-positivist tradition. Although proposed as a narrow theory of interpersonal communication, it has been adopted in many other fields and changed substantially to meet the theoretical needs of a variety of scholars. Thus, it is not surprising that the theory has also generated a great deal of controversy. In our discussion we consider the original statement of the theory and the extensions made by the original theorists; and we examine ways in which the theory has been critiqued, revised, and adapted by others in the communication discipline.

Original Statement of Uncertainty Reduction Theory

Scope and Goals of the Theory   Uncertainty reduction theory was proposed by Charles Berger and Richard Calabrese (1975) as a first effort to model the process of interaction during the initial stage of relational development. In considering only the entry stage of relational development, Berger and Calabrese are clearly narrowing the longitudinal focus from the overtime trajectory considered in social penetration theory. Berger and Calabrese also narrow the theoretical focus from the wide path cut by social penetration theory. Specifically, the theory begins with the guiding assumption that, in the initial stage of interaction between strangers, people are driven by their desire to reduce uncertainty about each other. This uncertainty can be both cognitive and behavioral in nature. With cognitive uncertainty, we are unsure about the beliefs and attitudes of the other. With behavioral uncertainty, we are unsure about how the other will behave in interaction. Even with strangers, we often have some level of behavioral certainty because there are scripts that guide interaction in various situations (see our discussion of schema theory in Chapter 6). That is, we might not have ever met the clerk at a supermarket, but we can still predict his or her behavior with a high degree of accuracy. Thus, uncertainty reduction theory generally concentrates on the reduction of the high level of cognitive uncertainty present in initial interaction. Berger and Calabrese also distinguish between a *predictive component* (e.g., we're uncertain about what a person will do) and an *explanatory component* (e.g., we're uncertain about why a person did something). Both of these types of uncertainty are relevant to the theory. Thus, in formulating uncertainty reduction theory, Berger and Calabrese were attempting to model the processes through which communication is used to reduce uncertainty in initial interaction between strangers.

Axioms and Theorems   Uncertainty reduction theory was formulated as an axiomatic theory in the tradition of positivist and post-positivist theory development. Berger and Calabrese followed the theory construction processes recommended by Hubert Blalock in his book *Theory Construction* and thus formulated **axioms** and then used those axioms to derive theorems. A few points about this form of theory development are relevant, and they are often misrepresented in presentations of uncertainty reduction theory and similar theories. First, axioms are conceptualized by Blalock—and used by Berger and Calabrese—as basic causal statements that incorporate relevant theoretical concepts. In presentations of uncertainty reduction theory, this notion of an axiom is often misrepresented. For example, Griffin (2000) refers to these axioms as "self-evident truths that require no additional proof" (p. 137). Similarly, Wood (1997) states that "an axiom is a statement that is presumed to be true on its face value and, therefore, does not require proof or explanation" (p. 219). However, this notion of unquestioned and unprovable truth was not the meaning of axiom presented by Blalock or adopted by Berger and Calabrese. Rather, Blalock (1969) argues,

> It is of course rare in the social sciences to find very many unquestioned assumptions, and therefore we need to recognize that the term "axiom" is used in the sense of an untested (or untestable) assumption, rather than as an assumption the truth of which is taken for granted. . . . For a considerable period of time, social scientists will have to settle for highly tentative theories based on axioms that are really nothing more than rather plausible assumptions. (p. 11)

Thus, the theory's axioms are not self-evident truths but rather the basic building blocks of the theory. These axioms can be used to derive the-orems that can be tested. Then, as Blalock (1969) notes, "If the theorems prove false the theory must be modified or the axioms of the theory even abandoned" (p. 11). Blalock suggested that axioms should be formulated as causal statements. These causal statements can then be used to derive theorems of covariation that can be tested. To use a rather whimsical example, two axioms regarding precipitation might be that "rain causes umbrella use" and "rain causes worms to emerge from underground." A theorem derived from these two axioms, then, would state that "umbrella use will be positively related to worm emergence."

With that background in mind, what are the axioms and theorems of uncertainty reduction theory? Berger and Calabrese proposed seven axioms in their original presentation of the theory (Table 10.1). An examination of this table shows that these axioms consider the causal relationships between uncertainty and seven other key theoretical variables (verbal communication, nonverbal affiliative behavior, information seeking, intimacy level, reciprocity, similarity, and liking). These relationships are linear and causal in nature. For example, Axiom 3 proposes a positive (direct) relationship between uncertainty and information seeking and Axiom 7 proposes a negative (inverse) relationship between uncertainty and liking. In presenting the axioms, Berger and Calabrese (1975) also reviewed research and theory in the fields of communication and psychology that provided at least basic support for the proposed relationships.

Theorems were then derived from these axioms by Berger and Calabrese. For example, Axiom 4 proposes a negative relationship between uncertainty and intimacy, whereas Axiom 7 proposes a negative relationship between uncertainty and liking. The logical conclusion of these two axioms is that there is a positive relationship between intimacy and liking, which is stated in Theorem 14: "The intimacy level of communication content and liking are positively related." By logically relating all axioms to each other, 21 theorems are derived. These are also presented in Table 10.1. An examination of these theorems reveals that some

Table 10.1	Axioms and Theorems of Uncertainty Reduction Theory
Axiom 1	Given the high level of uncertainty present at the onset of the entry stage, as the amount of verbal communication between strangers increases, the level of uncertainty for each interactant in the relationship will decrease. As uncertainty is further reduced, the amount of verbal communication will increase.
Axiom 2	As nonverbal affiliative expressiveness increases, uncertainty levels will decrease in initial interaction situations. In addition, decreases in uncertainty level will cause increases in nonverbal affiliative expressiveness.
Axiom 3	High levels of uncertainty cause increases in information seeking. As uncertainty levels decline, information seeking decreases.
Axiom 4	High levels of uncertainty cause decreases in the intimacy level of communication content. Low levels of uncertainty produce high levels of intimacy.
Axiom 5	High levels of uncertainty produce high reciprocity rates. Low levels of uncertainty produce low reciprocity rates.
Axiom 6	Similarities between persons reduce uncertainties, whereas dissimilarities increase uncertainty.
Axiom 7	Increases in uncertainty produce decreases in liking; decreases in uncertainty produce increases in liking.
Theorem 1	The amounts of verbal communication and nonverbal affiliative expressiveness are positively related.
Theorem 2	The amount of communication and the intimacy level of communication are positively related.
Theorem 3	The amount of communication and information seeking are negatively related.
Theorem 4	The amount of communication and the reciprocity rate are negatively related.
Theorem 5	The amount of communication and liking are positively related.
Theorem 6	The amount of communication and similarity are positively related.
Theorem 7	Nonverbal affiliative expressiveness and the intimacy level of communication are positively related.
Theorem 8	Nonverbal affiliative expressiveness and information seeking are negatively related.
Theorem 9	Nonverbal affiliative expressiveness and the reciprocity rate are negatively related.
Theorem 10	Nonverbal affiliative expressiveness and liking are negatively related.
Theorem 11	Nonverbal affiliative expressiveness and similarity are positively related.
Theorem 12	The intimacy level of communication and information seeking are negatively related.
Theorem 13	The intimacy level of communication and the reciprocity rate are negatively related.

(continued)

Table 10.1	*(continued)*
Theorem 14	The intimacy level of communication content and liking are positively related.
Theorem 15	The intimacy level of communication content and similarity are positively related.
Theorem 16	Information seeking and the reciprocity rate are positively related.
Theorem 17	Information seeking and liking are negatively related.
Theorem 18	Information seeking and similarity are negatively related.
Theorem 19	The reciprocity rate and liking are negatively related.
Theorem 20	The reciprocity rate and similarity are negatively related.
Theorem 21	Similarity and liking are positively related.

of them make sense to us (e.g., Theorem 10, which states that "nonverbal affiliative expressiveness and liking are positively related"), whereas others are not as intuitively obvious (e.g., Theorem 18, which states that "information seeking and similarity are negatively related"). Berger and Calabrese (1975) note that "some of the theorems generated by the model have already received strong empirical support while others have not been subjected to direct test" (p. 110). Following the post-positivist tradition, they call for additional research to either provide support for the theory or suggest paths for the reformulation of uncertainty reduction theory.

Berger's Extensions to Uncertainty Reduction Theory

Before many tests of uncertainty reduction theory were undertaken by researchers in communication, however, Berger wrote several articles that can be seen as extensions of the theory's original formulation. Some of these extensions were related to specific critiques leveled against the initial presentation of the theory, whereas others can be seen as natural parts of the theory development process. Two areas of extension are considered here: strategies for seeking information in the reduction of uncertainty and motivations for reducing uncertainty in initial interaction.

Strategies for Seeking Information   The theory's original formulation dealt with rather global constructs such as liking, similarity, and, of course, uncertainty. These vague and global concepts can be troubling for the process of testing theory because various operationalizations of the constructs could lead to radically different outcomes. One vague area of the theory that was particularly troubling was **information-seeking strategies** because Berger and Calabrese did little in their original formulation to specify the processes through which uncertainty is reduced in initial interaction. Because these processes are central to a communicative understanding of uncertainty reduction, Berger clarified his ideas about the processes of information seeking in subsequent writing (Berger, 1979, 1987; Berger & Bradac, 1982; Berger & Kellermann, 1994).

Three categories of information-seeking strategies were proposed. The first of these, *passive strategies*, involves observation of the other in a variety of social situations. A passive information-seeking strategy might involve watching the way an individual reacts to stimuli in the environment (called a reactivity search) or watching the ways in which an individual acts in situations that involve few social norms and rules (called a disinhibition search). These passive strategies allow for information to be gathered without interaction. Berger (1979; Berger & Bradac, 1982) also considers the use of *active strategies,* in which an individual might ask other people questions about the target individual or might structure the environment in ways that information can be gathered. Finally, information can be gathered through *interactive strategies,* in which the target person is asked direct questions or in which self-disclosure is used with the hope that reciprocation will lead to more information about the target. These strategies can be further explained by considering a situation in which you want to learn more about a new acquaintance's (Glenda's) attitudes toward alcohol consumption. The following strategies could be used:

- You could watch how Glenda acts during parties (reactivity search) especially those at which she is particularly comfortable (disinhibition search).
- You could talk with Glenda's friends about her drinking behavior (asking others) or invite her to a gathering where you know alcohol will be served (environmental structuring).
- You could ask Glenda direct questions about drinking alcohol (interrogation) or share your own views on drinking with the hopes that she will reciprocate (self-disclosure).

Motivations for Reducing Uncertainty Berger (1979) also extended his theory by expanding on the driving force in the theory, that is, the need to reduce uncertainty. In this extension, Berger attempts to both explain why we want more certainty in initial interaction and lay out situations in which the need to reduce uncertainty will be either enhanced or reduced. Berger considers three factors that influence the need to reduce uncertainty. The first of these is *incentives*. This factor suggests that we will be more likely to want to reduce uncertainty about an individual if we perceive that the individual can be rewarding to us. That is, your desire to reduce uncertainty about an interviewer at a job placement center will be higher if he or she represents a firm you really want to work for than if the job in question is not particularly desirable.

The second factor Berger discusses is *deviation*. That is, if people act in ways that are unexpected or that violate rules and norms of interactions, it piques our desire to know what is going on with that individual. There are probably limits to this effect. For example, we don't want to investigate someone who is acting in an extremely crazy or dangerous way, but if someone we've just met behaves in a somewhat unusual manner (e.g., perhaps kisses your hand upon introduction), we are motivated to reduce uncertainty both out of curiosity and out of a need to increase our ability to predict future behavior from this individual. Finally, Berger proposes that the need to reduce uncertainty will be enhanced by the prospect of *future interaction*. That is, if we know we will be talking with someone in the future (regardless of whether we want to—that is an issue of incentive), we will want to reduce uncertainty about that individual. However, if we know we will never speak to someone again, there is little motivation to learn more about the individual.

Tests and Critiques of Uncertainty Reduction Theory

Empirical Support for the Theory Uncertainty reduction theory was developed based on existing research in interpersonal behavior, initial interaction, and social psychology. Thus, there was some support for the theory before its formulation. Since then, a great deal of research has been conducted looking at theorems of uncertainty reduction theory and at its extensions. Some of this research is reviewed in Berger and Gudykunst (1991), and although the evidence is too voluminous to review in detail here, some of the key areas of support for the theory are as follows:

- Considerable evidence supports the proposition that uncertainty is reduced over time through both verbal and nonverbal

✹ SPOTLIGHT ON THE THEORIST

Charles R. Berger

Charles R. Berger, who received his Ph.D. from Michigan State University in 1968 and has been a member of the faculty at Northwestern University and now at University of California, Davis, has appeared twice in this book—back in Chapter 7 with his planning theory and here in Chapter 10 with uncertainty reduction theory. He sees these as very different lines of research but notes that "someone pointed out that planning is another facet of uncertainty reduction." Both of these areas of scholarship, though, point to Berger's influence in the discipline of communication, both as a scholar of interpersonal communication processes and as a commentator on theory and the future of the discipline.

Berger recounts formulating uncertainty reduction theory in part as a response to students who questioned the possibility of predicting and explaining human communication through social scientific approaches. He then began to "look for everyday communication situations that are highly patterned and very predictable," and his observation of interaction between strangers was the beginning of the theory's explanation of "a highly predictable interaction ritual." He also believes that this theory was important in emphasizing the role of communication in relational development, an avenue largely ignored by the social psychological

theories of relationships that were in vogue in the late 1960s and early 1970s.

Berger expresses some surprise in the "long half-life" of uncertainty reduction theory. He notes that "after the 1975 paper was published, not much happened in the way of interest" but that others have "carried it forward" in work in the 1980s and since. Thus, in looking at his work on message planning, he comments that "so far, there doesn't seem to be very much interest in moving it ahead, but I have learned it is still early in the game."

As a long-time scholar and active participant in the communication discipline, Berger has a great deal of insight into the future of the field. He argues that "we are coming to a time when the relative 'youth' of the field cannot be invoked to defend the field's fragmentation." Furthermore, "justifying the field by claiming that communication is 'ubiquitous' is not particularly telling." Thus, he believes that the communication discipline needs to specify goals that show practitioners and scholars outside of the field who we are and what we are about. According to Berger, this is "a top priority for the field's long-term survival." He believes that "many fields are organized around efforts to find cures for various problems or to produce things. While we cannot set out to 'cure communication,' we need some set of discernable goals for the field." Berger argues that it is only through attacking such problems—and developing theoretical ways of approaching the problems—that the communication discipline can survive and take a leadership role in the 21st century.

interaction (see Berger & Gudykunst, 1991; Clatterbuck, 1979).

- Evidence supports the links between uncertainty and liking as posited by the theory, though Berger and Gudykunst (1991) cite evidence that the relationship is not a simple causal one in which reduced uncertainty leads to liking. Rather, it is also possible that "when persons become attracted to others they expend the effort

necessary to reduce their uncertainty about them" (p. 36).

- There is some support for the role of anticipated future interaction, incentive value, and deviance in motivating individuals to reduce uncertainty. These factors do not necessarily increase uncertainty per se (see Kellermann, 1986), but they seem to increase motivation to reduce uncertainty.

- Research suggests that individuals use a variety of passive, active, and interactive strategies to reduce uncertainty (see Berger, 1997), though these strategies may vary in use and in terms of effectiveness and social appropriateness.

Critiquing the Motivational Force in the Theory Perhaps the most important critiques of uncertainty reduction theory leveled since its inception involve the question of the basic underlying force that drives communication in initial interaction. The two most important of these critiques were presented by Michael Sunnafrank (1986) and Kathy Kellermann and Rodney Reynolds (1990). Sunnafrank (1986) put forth the first major critique and revision of the theory, arguing that uncertainty was not the driving force in directing behavior in initial interaction but was subordinate to the more dominant concern of increasing positive relational outcomes. In his reformulated **predicted outcome value theory,** Sunnafrank argues that the most central force in initial interaction is the prediction of positive and negative relational outcomes. This proposition mirrors social penetration theory's predictions regarding social exchange as a motivating force in relational development and argues that interactional attempts to reduce uncertainty stem from a more general drive both to learn about possible rewards and costs and to derive direct rewards from the interaction.

Recall that Berger may have anticipated this critique in his 1979 arguments about why people want to reduce uncertainty. One of his proposals was that the incentive value of the relationship would enhance uncertainty reduction efforts. Clearly, this is similar to Sunnafrank's arguments regarding predicted outcome values. The distinction is in which of the two processes (uncertainty reduction or maximization of relational outcomes) is more central. Sunnafrank argues that individuals may use some uncertainty reduction strategies in order to assess possible relational outcomes; that is, uncertainty reduction serves the larger goal of outcome maximization.

In contrast, Berger argues that individuals may assess possible outcomes in deciding whether to reduce uncertainty; that is, predicting relational outcomes serves the larger goal of uncertainty reduction. One study attempted to pit these two explanations against each other in predicting initial interaction patterns with able-bodied and visibly disabled strangers (Grove & Werkman, 1991). Their study provided some support for predicted outcome value theory in that students' apprehension influenced interaction patterns more than their curiosity.

A second major critique of the theory was undertaken by Kellermann and Reynolds (1990). These scholars, like Sunnafrank, were concerned with the motivational force in uncertainty reduction theory. However, instead of positing a contrasting explanation (e.g., predicted outcome value), Kellermann and Reynolds argue that we should make the conceptual distinction between level of uncertainty and motivation to reduce uncertainty. That is, there are cases when we have a high level of uncertainty but little desire to reduce it. In contrast, there may be times when uncertainty is relatively low, but a strong desire to reduce uncertainty exists. Kellermann and Reynolds (1990) argue,

> Presently, the axioms of uncertainty reduction theory state relationships only in terms of one's uncertainty level, though any predictions made by the theory would somehow have to incorporate both one's uncertainty level and one's concern about reducing that uncertainty. Leaving concern for uncertainty outside the axiomatic framework makes uncertainty reduction theory difficult to falsify. (p. 8)

Kellermann and Reynolds then worked to reformulate the theory by incorporating motivation to reduce uncertainty, as well as the concepts of deviance, incentive value, and anticipation of future interaction as proposed by Berger (1979). Though their predictions and research were complex, their findings indicated that level of uncertainty and desire to reduce uncertainty were far from isomorphic and, indeed, were predicted by different variables. Specifically, incentive value and deviance were related to level of uncertainty but not desire to reduce uncertainty, whereas anticipation of future interaction was related to desire to reduce uncertainty but not level of uncertainty. They concluded by offering a variety of axiomatic revisions to the theory that can take into account these distinctions and the variables that predict both level of uncertainty and desire to reduce uncertainty.

Expanding the Scope of Uncertainty Reduction Theory

Beyond these extensions of the basic structure and predictions of uncertainty reduction theory, a vast array of research and theory has pushed the original boundaries of the theory. Recall that Berger and Calabrese (1975) formulated the theory to explain communicative behavior during initial interaction between strangers. They acknowledge that this focus is quite narrow and close their explication of the theory with these words: "Hopefully, subsequent research and reformulation will result in a more general theory of the developmental aspects of interpersonal communication" (Berger & Calabrese, 1975, p. 111). That hope has certainly been rewarded, in that the boundaries of uncertainty reduction theory have been stretched and expanded in a variety of domains. Some of these extensions have added specific axioms and theorems that expand the theory's scope. Others have reformulated the theory in ways that shift its domain and boundaries. Still others have used the theory not as a theoretical statement but as an orienting principle in domains far removed from initial interaction between strangers. These expansions are discussed in the sections that follow.

Uncertainty in Continuing Relationships
Probably the major expansion envisioned by the original theorists was moving the concepts of uncertainty reduction theory beyond the period of initial interaction and into a "full blown theory of interaction development" (Berger & Calabrese, 1975, p. 111). Not surprisingly, several

scholars have taken up this call in examining the role of uncertainty in continuing relationships, though the result would certainly not be seen as a "full blown theory." For example, Planalp and Honeycutt (1985) investigated relational events that increase uncertainty in established relationships, and Afifi and Burgoon (1998) investigated relationships in which uncertainty is tolerated, or even desired, because the expected information is seen as undesirable.

The work most explicitly addressed to uncertainty reduction theory as a theory is that of Parks and Adelman (1983). These scholars looked at romantic relationships and found that relational stability and breakups were predicted, in part, by uncertainty in the relationships. In addition to this expansion of the theory to developed relationships, however, Parks and Adelman also expanded the theory to include the social context in which relationships develop and dissolve. Specifically, they found that communication with the partner's family and friends reduced uncertainty to the same or greater extent as variables from the theory's original formulation, such as similarity and direct communication.

Uncertainty in Intercultural Relationships
Probably the most wide-ranging adaptation of uncertainty reduction theory has been in the area of intercultural relationships. These efforts have been spearheaded by Bill Gudykunst, who has developed a reformulation of the theory that he calls anxiety uncertainty management theory (see Gudykunst, 1985, 1989, 1993, 1995). This reformulation is a wide-ranging theory. A version of the theory summarized in Gudykunst (1995) included 47 central axioms that covered categories of self and self-concept; motivation; reactions to strangers; social categorization; situational processes; connection with strangers; and anxiety, uncertainty, mindfulness, and effective communication.

Anxiety uncertainty management theory expands on uncertainty reduction theory in several important ways. First, anxiety uncertainty management theory moves beyond the interpersonal and cognitive levels of explanation to include intergroup factors. Gudykunst argues that a complete theory of interaction among individuals must include concepts such as social identity and cultural identity that can be considered only through the inclusion of group-level variables. Second, the theory includes anxiety—an affective variable—as well as uncertainty—a cognitive variable—as a key motivational component. Gudykunst believes that anxiety is always present in communicative interactions but can be particularly pronounced in intergroup or intercultural encounters. Thus, "to understand either interpersonal or intergroup encounters, anxiety must be incorporated" (Gudykunst, 1995, p. 81). Finally, anxiety uncertainty management theory augments uncertainty reduction theory by specifying intercultural adaptation as a critical outcome variable. That is, when anxiety and uncertainty are managed effectively, the result will be communication that aids individuals in their adaptation to intercultural and intergroup situations. Gudykunst's research program has provided a great deal of empirical support for, and contributed to the development of, his theory. For example, Gudykunst and Hammer (1988) found that perceptions of social identity had an impact on the uncertainty reduction process, and Gudykunst and Nishida (1984) found that both individual-level and cultural variables influenced uncertainty reduction. However, given the range and size of anxiety uncertainty management theory, it is difficult to reach conclusions about support for the general theory at this point.

Other Applications of the Theory Uncertainty reduction theory has also been applied in more limited ways in other contexts. For example, in the area of organizational communication, scholars have applied uncertainty reduction concepts to the organizational socialization process. Michael Kramer uses the theory extensively in his studies of how job transferees make sense of changes in their work environment (e.g., Kramer, 1993). Kramer acknowledges that

this use of theory moves far beyond its original focus, but he argues that "the theory has implications for exploring communication as a means for resolving incompatibilities between cognitive structures, experiences, and behaviors in various settings" (Kramer, 1993, p. 179). Similarly, V. D. Miller and Jablin's (1991) model of information seeking during organizational socialization draws heavily on uncertainty reduction principles, especially Berger's (1979) ideas about the processes through which uncertainty is reduced. The concept of uncertainty was also mobilized by Albrecht and Adelman (1987) in their work on social support. Indeed, they define social support as an uncertainty reduction process, stating that social support is "verbal and nonverbal communication between recipients and providers that reduces uncertainty about the situation, the self, or the relationship, and functions to enhance a perception of personal control in one's life experience" (p. 19). Clearly, this use of the theory encompasses the global concept of uncertainty but does not specify or test hypotheses that stem from a detailed application of the theory's axioms or theorems.

Summary and Evaluation of Uncertainty Reduction Theory

Uncertainty reduction theory has generated a great deal of empirical research and additional theorizing in communication. This generative value of the theory can be seen both in terms of its narrow scope of information seeking in initial interaction and as a general metaphor for communication processes in a variety of contexts. The concept of uncertainty—and the theory in its more narrow and axiomatic form—has a great deal of heuristic power and has been extremely fruitful.

The major critiques of uncertainty reduction theory have revolved around its accuracy as an account of relational development. Some of these criticisms have been issues of scope. That is, scholars argue that uncertainty reduction is not a driving force during many aspects of relational development but downplay the fact that the theory was developed as a narrow-scope theory of initial interaction with strangers. However, other criticisms have cut to the heart of the theory, arguing that even in initial interaction, uncertainty reduction is not the driving force of interaction. These critiques would seem to be more damning of the theory on the turf it has established: explaining patterns and motivations of communication in early relational stages.

It is interesting to note, though, that these critiques have been largely based on empirical investigations of the original theorems. Also, these critiques have generally taken the form of proposed alternatives or extensions to the theory. These alternative formulations have often led to further testing and even to adversarial tests that pit versions against each other (e.g., Grove & Werkman, 1991). Thus, scholarship in uncertainty reduction theory has taken the trajectory proposed by Karl Popper and other philosophers of science who argue that the value of science comes in the community effort at conjecture and refutation. In other words, these critiques have not been stinging indictments and have not caused the theory to be dismissed by scholars. Instead, these developments have largely fulfilled Berger and Calabrese's initial wish that their presentation of uncertainty reduction theory serve as a springboard for additional research on communication processes during initial interaction.

■ COMPARISON AND COMMENTARY

Our discussion of the critiques of social penetration theory and uncertainty reduction theory individually indicates much that they share in terms of theoretical strengths and weaknesses. Both theories stem from the post-positivist tradition and have been quite successful based on standards for this type of theory. Though empirical support has sometimes been weak (e.g., with regard to uncertainty reduction theory) and though it has sometimes been difficult to test the full trajectory of predictions (e.g., with regard to social penetration theory), both theories

have been notable in terms of their generation of research and theoretical elaboration and their impact on a wide range of scholarship within the discipline of communication.

The strength of these theories as post-positivistic theories that provide clean causal explanations of communication phenomena has also led to the most widespread criticisms of both theories. Social penetration theory and uncertainty reduction theory have been critiqued as being overly rational, both in terms of the logic of the theory (e.g., the linear nature of social penetration theory or the mechanical way of moving from axiom to theorem in uncertainty reduction theory) and in terms of the logic of the people being theorized. That is, it is sometimes difficult to conceive that people actually weigh costs and outcomes in the manner suggested by social penetration theory or make decisions about future interaction with the dry logic suggested by uncertainty reduction theory. Related to this critique of rationality is a criticism regarding the complexity of both theories. The elegance of these theories—with one or two causal mechanisms driving the process of relational development—may downplay the complicated way relationships play out in social life. Finally, these theories have been criticized as being removed from the real life of continuing relationships. Because the predictions of these theories have been tested largely in laboratory settings and with young adults, it is likely that additional theoretical perspectives could help us in considering the processes through which relationships develop across a spectrum of contexts and over the lifespan. We turn to some of these additional theories in Chapter 11.

Key Terms

social penetration theory
orientation
exploratory affective exchange
affective exchange
stable exchange
self-disclosure
reciprocity

social exchange theory
outcomes
comparison level
comparison level of alternatives
dialectical tensions
uncertainty reduction theory
axioms
information-seeking strategies
predicted outcome value theory
anxiety uncertainty management theory

Discussion Questions

1. Altman and Taylor state that relationships grow during periods of compatibility and deteriorate in response to crises. How does this happen, according to social penetration theory? How is communication implicated in this process?

2. Social penetration theory, and the related social exchange theory, assume that people make rational choices about relationships. Is this a reasonable assumption? Can these theories help explain why an individual might choose to stay in an abusive relationship?

3. Discuss the difference between trying to reduce uncertainty and attempting to predict the valence of relationship outcomes. How are these mechanisms used as the driving force in different theories of initial interaction? Would you approach initial interaction differently based on the extent to which you held these different goals?

11 Theories of Communication in Ongoing Relationships

Exploring the beginnings and trajectories of relationships is an exciting enterprise, as the theories discussed in Chapter 10 illustrate. Through communication, we learn more about each other, make decisions about relational continuity, and explore areas of each other's lives. Many of the most valuable relationships in our lives, however, are not the new and developing ones. Rather, the fabric of our everyday existence is often woven with communication and relationships that we have had for many years—or even for a lifetime. Spouses, parents, siblings, long-term friends, and colleagues—communication within these relationships shapes our lifeworlds and meanings far beyond their early stages of social penetration or uncertainty reduction. This is not to suggest, though, that these relationships are static and predictable. Indeed, long-term relationships are often marked by tension, development, conflict, and growth: processes mediated by communicative interaction within ongoing relationships.

These communicative processes are the focus of this chapter. The two theories we consider, however, are not tightly developed causal theories of how communication works in ongoing relationships. Rather, we look at two approaches to the study of communication in relationships that explore some of the tensions, contradictions, conflicts, rules, and rewards that permeate our everyday communicative lives. The first of these, the Palo Alto group's relational system approach, was an early and influential statement about communication in family and close relationships that had its genesis in psychiatry but has had a long-term effect on communication theory and research. The second theoretical approach we consider, relational dialectics, has its roots in philosophical theories of dialectics and dialogue and has only since the 1980s been used to enhance our understanding of friendship, romantic, and family relationships.

■ RELATIONAL SYSTEMS THEORY: THE PALO ALTO GROUP

The Players: Gregory Bateson and Colleagues

During the 1950s, Gregory Bateson (1904–1980) served as an ethnologist for the Veteran's Administration Hospital in Palo Alto, California. Bateson, an internationally noted anthropologist, had turned away from the fieldwork that marked cultural anthropology in the middle of the 20th century and had become interested instead in theoretical issues of meaning in human interaction. As Wilder (1979) describes, Bateson and his research group were concerned with understanding the general nature of communication and how communication could be understood by considering various levels of interaction. In the 1950s, however, the **Palo Alto group** at the Mental Research Institute was awarded a grant to study the role of communication in psychiatric pathologies, particularly schizophrenia. Throughout the remainder of the 1950s and 1960s, Bateson and his research group, including scholars such as Paul Watzlawick, Don Jackson, and Janet Beavin Bavelas, developed a new view of interaction in relationships that had a wide-ranging impact on fields including psychiatry, family therapy, philosophy, and communication.

The Concept: Shifting the Focus from Individual to System

Before the work of the Palo Alto group, schizophrenia and other related psychiatric dysfunctions were seen as individual-level phenomena. Thus, in therapy, the focus would also be on the patient and his or her mental state and physiology. Mental illness treatments—whether chemical, behavioral, or therapeutic—were also designed with this individual-level focus in mind. The Palo Alto group shifted this focus by redirecting the view of both theorists and therapists toward the system that surrounded the patient. The most typical system considered was the nuclear family, though other systems (e.g., extended family, friends, schools, medical institutions) could be implicated as well.

In this systems view, mental illness cannot be understood as the disease of an individual. Instead, a systems view traces responsibility back to the communicative systems in which the individual is embedded, and understanding dysfunctional communication requires an appreciation for the interdependent interactions of multiple people over time. Several concepts are particularly important for an appreciation of the Palo Alto systems view, including concepts from classical systems theory, concepts from the philosophical theory of logical types, and concepts from rules approaches to communication.

Systems Concepts In 1942, Bateson attended a Macy Foundation conference on cybernetics. At this conference and in subsequent years, Bateson met theorists who were central in the newly developing systems approach to physical, biological, and social sciences, including Norbert Wiener, John von Neumann, Ross Ashby, and Warren McCulloch. Bateson applied these developing systems concepts to the context of functional and dysfunctional human interaction. Some of the systems concepts that were particularly critical to the Palo Alto group were the concepts of feedback, homeostasis, and equifinality.

The concept of feedback suggests that behaviors of individuals in a system are interdependent with, and are often the response to, the behaviors of others. The interdependence of individual behavior is instantiated in communication through processes of feedback, which can be negative or positive. **Positive feedback** is deviation amplifying and leads to change or loss of stability in the system. **Negative feedback** is deviation counteracting; that is, it preserves the status quo of the system. Negative feedback thus keeps the family on a steady state, or what D. D. Jackson (1957) referred to in early work as "family homeostasis." Clearly, this maintenance of a steady state in the system could be either a good thing or a bad thing, depending on the functionality of the system under investigation. For example, in an abusive family, a wife might be beaten every time she strays from her subordinate role by offering an opinion. These beatings (i.e., the negative feedback) keep the family on its steady—and violent—course.

The concepts of feedback and interdependence of members also suggest that family systems will be characterized by **equifinality.** This concept proposes that the same final state can be achieved through many different developmental pathways. The idea of equifinality was important to the Palo Alto group both for understanding the genesis of dysfunctional family sytems (e.g., the family could have become dysfunctional through a number of different routes; there isn't a single causal factor) and for the concentration on present behavior in treating family systems. As Wilder (1979) explains, "If the same behavior can spring from quite different causes, the argument goes, then it is both more economical and more effective to focus upon present process" (p. 173).

The Theory of Logical Types A second key influence on Bateson and his research group was the philosophical work of Bertrand Russell, particularly his **theory of logical types.** This work considers the concept of hierarchy in logic and argues that varying levels of abstraction can be considered when looking at systems. This hierarchical distinction, put most simply, is between classes and members of classes and notes that a class cannot be a member of itself nor can a member of the class be itself the class. Consider, for example, the concepts of fruit (i.e., the class) and apple (i.e., member of the class). The theory of logical types posits that statements about fruits and apples must distinguish between these levels of abstraction.

These concepts seem straightforward (and even a bit silly, perhaps) when talking about fruit. However, Bateson and his colleagues believed that making a clear distinction between levels of abstraction in communication was critical for understanding functional and dysfunctional interaction within family systems. For example, clear misunderstandings could arise if one spouse is talking about a specific behavior (e.g., taking out the garbage) and the other spouse is talking about the meaning of that behavior for the relationship. In essence, one person is talking about a class (i.e., behaviors that say something about our relationship) and one is talking about a member of that class (i.e., taking out the garbage). If the interactants don't recognize and appreciate this distinction, misunderstandings and relational difficulties are likely to emerge.

A Rules Orientation Finally, a key shift in Bateson's approach to communication was the proposal that rules are central to an understanding of communication in relationships and families. Rules are relational agreements that prescribe how communication is supposed to work in a particular family system. For example, one family might have a rule that daily experiences should be shared in conversation at the dinner table. Another family might have a rule that children always say "ma'am" and "sir" when addressing an adult. Several points about rules are important. First, harkening back to our discussion of coordinated management of meaning theory in Chapter 9, rules can be either constitutive (e.g., defining what particular communication acts stand for) or regulative (e.g., defining preferred sequences of communication behavior). Second, communication rules are sometimes explicit (e.g., "You know you're supposed to say please and thank you, Johnny") but are often implicit. For example, a family with an alcoholic parent might have an implicit rule that "we never talk about mom's drinking." Finally, taking a rules orientation again moves the focus of explanation away from the individual and to the system. That is, a person doesn't communicate in a particular way because of his or her needs, drives, or personality but because systemic rules prescribe certain kinds of behavior.

The Book: *Pragmatics of Human Communication*

Many of these ideas were presented in a book that has now become a classic in the field of communication, *The Pragmatics of Human Communication*, authored by Paul Watzlawick, Janet Beavin, and Don Jackson (1967). Wilder (1979) has suggested that some of the original researchers from Bateson's group were not happy that *Pragmatics* was published when it was because it could be received as a premature codification of systems principles that were still being worked out. However, the book was warmly received by much of the academic community at the time and has had a strong influence on subsequent work by scholars who study communication in interpersonal and family relationships. In this section we review some of the major issues covered in *Pragmatics*. We consider the five axioms that make up the central argument of the book and look at some of the tentacles that developed from these axioms. Note that the original theorists proposed these as tentative axioms rather than as underlying and unquestioned truths.

Axiom 1: "One Cannot Not Communicate"
We encountered this first axiom in Chapter 1, when we considered ways that communication has been defined in our discipline. In the more narrow arena of relational communication being considered in *Pragmatics*, this axiom points to the ubiquity of communication and meaning in our interaction. Watzlawick et al. saw communication and behavior as virtually synonymous concepts. When viewed this way, it is easy to see how the axiom arose, as "activity or inactivity, words or silence all have message value: they influence others and these others, in turn, cannot *not* respond to these communications and are thus themselves communicating" (Watzlawick et al., 1967, p. 49). To illustrate this, the authors point to how a person at a crowded lunch counter who looks straight ahead and an airplane passenger who sits with closed eyes are clearly communicating something to others, though they may not *say* anything. Communication thus occurs regardless of whether it is intentional, conscious, or successful; that is, communication occurs whenever meaning is received.

Janet Beavin Bavelas (1992) has revisited this axiom and now argues that a distinction should be made between nonverbal behavior and nonverbal communication. She notes that "an act that is nonverbal behaviour occurs for noncommunicative reasons. An observer may make inferences from such behaviour but there is (1) no sender-receiver relationship and (2) no encoding and decoding by means of a shared code" (p. 16). Thus, Beavin Bavelas now sees that the original axiom had a receiver bias in imputing communicative intent to all actions that a receiver might wish to call communication. Regardless of this revision, however, the original point of the axiom—that meaning can be inferred in relational systems through a wide variety of behaviors and messages—is a central one to the Palo Alto approach.

Axioms 2 and 4: Distinctions in Communication Types Axioms 2 and 4 in *Pragmatics* are related in that they both talk about levels and types of communication. Axiom 2 states that "every communication has a content and a rela-

tional aspect such that the latter classifies the former and is therefore a metacommunication" (Watzlawick et al., 1967, p. 54). The ideas relevant to this axiom were first developed by Bateson and suggest that communication works at various levels in relationships. For example, when I say to my daughter, "Why don't you go upstairs and clean up your room?" the message has a **content function** (e.g., I think her room should be cleaned up) and a **relational function** (e.g., as her mother, I have the right to request room cleaning). These levels are interrelated and, of course, subject to interpretation. The content and relational functions of the message are not necessarily related to the literal form of the message. For example, the message about room cleaning is phrased as a question, but if my daughter answered the question in some ways (e.g., "Because I have better things to do with my time"), she would be violating the message's content and relational functions.

Axiom 4 states that human beings communicate both digitally and analogically. **Digital communication** has a powerful and well-defined syntax (e.g., the English language) that can be agreed upon. **Analogic communication** does not have a clear and agreed-upon syntax but can communicate powerful meanings about relationships (e.g., body language used to express affiliation or emotion).

In use, these two axioms have often been joined together with the concepts of verbal and nonverbal communication in sometimes unfortunate ways. The equalities have been set up like this:

- content communication = digital communication = verbal communication
- relational communication = analogic communication = nonverbal communication

These equations do not express the complexities of human communication in relationships because, for example, relational messages can often be sent through verbal channels (e.g., in the example about room cleaning), and some nonverbal messages have clear and unambiguous content associated with them (e.g., a thumbs-up sign). However, the basic concepts within each of these axioms are important: first, that individual messages contain information about both content and relationship and, second, that various code systems in human communication have differing levels of syntactical and semantic power.

Axiom 3: Punctuating Communication Sequences   The third axiom proposed by Watzlawick et al. looks at the ongoing stream of interaction in a relationship and how participants in that relationship make sense of it. They note that outside observers may see communication as an uninterrupted sequence of interchanges but that individuals within the relational system organize the stream of interaction in order to make sense of the relationship and behaviors represented in the interaction. The classic example noted by Watzlawick et al. is the nag-withdrawal pattern seen in some close relationships. A look at punctuation reveals two very different interpretations of communication in the relationship: The "nagging wife" says, "I only nag because he won't listen to me," while the "withdrawing husband" says, "I only withdraw because she nags all the time." The punctuation of communication can occur within a given conversation, or two individuals might punctuate entire relationships in very different ways.

Axiom 5: Symmetry and Complementarity in Interaction   The final tentative axiom proposed in *Pragmatics* involves, again, the way interaction is patterned in relational systems. Watzlawick et al. (1967) state that "all communicational interchanges are either symmetrical or complementary, depending on whether they are based on equality or difference" (p. 70). A **symmetrical interaction** is based on equality or mirroring; that is, statements of a certain type are matched by other statements of the same type. Bateson (1958) uses the example of boasting in some cultural groups as an illustration. Consider, for instance, a conversation in which two individuals are trying to lay claim to having the more difficult childhood, which might include a statement such as "Well, I had to walk

uphill both to and from school in the snow with no shoes." These interactions will be characterized by escalation through deviation-amplifying (i.e., positive) feedback. In a **complementary interaction,** communication is characterized by maximizing difference. For example, in some relationships one member might be domineering and the other passive. Or one partner might be forceful about opinions and the other deferential toward those opinion statements. This kind of interaction involves stabilizing (i.e., negative) feedback.

Dysfunctional Communication: Paradoxes and Double Binds   These axioms describing human communication in general can point to areas in which interactional systems can become dysfunctional. For example, if someone interprets a different relational message than what was intended, interactional problems could develop. If individuals punctuate interactions differently, relational problems could escalate. Or if an individual gets stuck in an uncomfortable complementary pattern, the definition of the relationship could be disrupted.

One of the important dysfunctions discussed by Watzlawick et al. is the notion of paradoxes and **double binds** in interaction. There are five ingredients to a double bind:

- two or more persons in an important relationship
- repeated experience
- a primary negative injunction
- a secondary injunction conflicting with the first at a more abstract level
- a tertiary negative injunction prohibiting the victim from escaping the field

For example, Watzlawick et al. note that statements such as "You ought to love me," "Don't be so obedient," "I want you to dominate me," or "Be spontaneous" all present double binds. In these statements, if a person responds to the primary injunction (e.g., by being less obedient, spontaneous, or dominating), he or she is by necessity not responding to the secondary injunction. That is, if a person tries to be less obedient, he or she is being obedient to the command. As Bochner and Eisenberg (1987) summarize, the concept of the double bind can be

> interpreted as describing an interpersonal situation in which the victim is "damned if he does and damned if he doesn't" but a careful reading shows clearly that a double-binding context is one in which the victim cannot choose one without choosing the other. His bind is that "if he obeys, he is disobeying, and if he disobeys, he is obeying" (Haley, 1976). (p. 548)

Theorists in the Palo Alto group suggest that situations such as double binds can have devastating effects on individuals and family systems, especially when "exposure to double binds is long-lasting and gradually becomes a habitual expectation" (Watzlawick et al., 1967, p. 213). These predictions regarding the effects of double binds are difficult to test either scientifically or even in a therapeutic sense (see Bochner & Eisenberg, 1987). As Bateson (1966) notes, the concept of the double bind is "slippery—so slippery that perhaps no set of empirical facts could contradict it" (p. 415). However, the notion of a double bind illustrates how looking at issues such as levels of communication, content and relational messages, and symmetry and complementarity can lend insight to the processes of communication in relational systems.

Systemic Change: The Process of Reframing
Some of the basic concepts that defined the Palo Alto approach to communication systems also suggest the ways in which change can occur in relationships. For example, the move from an individual focus to a systems focus suggests that change cannot be instituted by a single member of the system and must involve the larger interaction patterns and rules that have been instantiated in the family. Furthermore, the movement from intrapsychic to interactional variables suggests that systems can change through purposive adjustments to behavioral and communication patterns.

One of the most basic concepts of change within this approach stems from the original concept of different logical types drawn from Bertrand Russell's philosophical writings. Recall that this concept refers to the distinction between a class and members of that class. In applying this idea to the concept of change, Palo Alto theorists make the distinction between **first-order change** and **second-order change.** First-order change is change *within* a system and is often ineffective when dysfunctional interaction patterns are present. In contrast, second-order change involves change *of* the system. That is, in second-order change, we move to a higher level in the interaction. Second-order change often involves intervention from an outsider (e.g., a family therapist), in which relational members are encouraged to consider a more abstract level of analysis and reframe the problem at that level.

Consider, for example, the system discussed earlier, in which a couple has developed a pattern of nagging and withdrawing. Trying to change either of these behaviors directly would constitute first-order change and might not be effective because the system of interaction would continue to perpetuate itself. However, if the couple in this system could step back and look at the whole system over time, it is possible to reframe the situation not as one of reacting to specific behavior but as a pattern that has established itself over time as part of the relationship.

Developments from the Palo Alto Group in Communication

Since Watzlawick et al. published their book, it has had wide influence on communication scholarship. As noted earlier, some of this influence, particularly with regard to the first axiom, has been in defining the concept of communication. However, *Pragmatics* has had influence beyond this debate. In this section, we discuss three strands of research that have been directly influenced by the work of the Palo Alto theorists, though in fundamentally different ways.

Extending the Core Axioms First, Bavelas and her research group in Victoria, British Columbia, have worked to extend and develop some of the core ideas from *Pragmatics* into a more

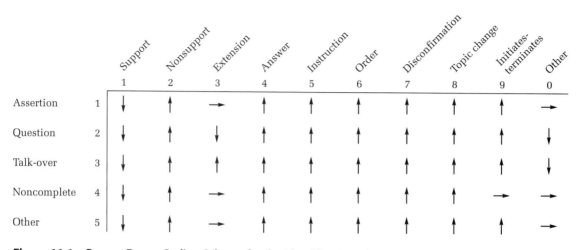

Figure 11.1   Rogers-Farace Coding Scheme for the Identification of Complementary and Symmetrical Interaction Patterns

comprehensive understanding of relational communication processes. Bavelas and her colleagues see this work as basic research in communication processes (rather than applied or clinical), and much of their research has been experimental in nature. The basics of this work are summarized in Bavelas (1992), and an extended look at the experimental work on equivocal communication is included in Bavelas, Black, Chovil, and Mullett (1990). Though this work has helped in sorting out some of the nuts and bolts with regard to concepts in the Palo Alto group's view of relational communication, the work has also been criticized because, in its attempt to scientifically investigate these processes in controlled settings, it has removed them from the complex family and relational contexts in which they are embedded. Hence, these experimental investigations may not say a great deal about the complexity of family and relational interaction originally theorized by the Palo Alto group. As Eisenberg (1991) summarizes, "As words are spoken between people, meaning emerges, changes, gets qualified and revised, and is in general co-constructed in dialogue . . . [thus] whatever 'measurement' of meaning is done must capture more of the situated sense-making processes of the interactants" (p. 354).

Coding Interaction Sequences   Second, Bavelas, Edna Rogers, Vince Farace, Frank Millar, and others have concentrated on one particular aspect of the Palo Alto group theorizing: the notion of complementarity and symmetry in interaction sequences. Specifically, these researchers have proposed, tested, and applied a coding scheme for analyzing ongoing interaction in dyadic communication (see Millar, Rogers, & Bavelas, 1984; L. E. Rogers & Farace, 1976; L. E. Rogers, Millar, & Bavelas, 1985). This coding scheme categorizes each utterance in interaction as a **"one-up"** (i.e., an utterance that takes control), a **"one-down"** (i.e., an utterance that gives control), or a **"one-across"** (i.e., an utterance that neither gives nor takes control). The coding of the utterances is based on the form of what is said (e.g., is it a question, a reply, a command?) and how the utterance functions in the interaction. The coding scheme developed by L. E. Rogers and Farace (1975) is illustrated in Figure 11.1.

In using this coding scheme, however, researchers are not encouraged to look simply at the distribution of individual codes in an interaction by noting, perhaps, that a particular person tended to have more one-up moves and another tended to have more one-down moves. As Rogers et al. (1985) note, "It seems a particular-

---

✳ SPOTLIGHT ON THE THEORIST

Janet Beavin Bavelas

Janet Beavin Bavelas is an interdisciplinary scholar who is passionately interested in communication. She states, "I am fascinated by what we all share (even as strangers) about how to do communication. My research focus is on face-to-face dialogue as a ubiquitous, unique, and little understood form of language use. I want to know its principles and processes." This passion for understanding the basic processes through which communication works began with (or even before) her early association with the Palo Alto group in the work that led to *Pragmatics of Human Communication.* And her passion continues today in her experimental work on interaction and discourse as a professor of psychology at the University of Victoria in British Columbia. Clearly, her passions have led to important insights and scholarship. She has been elected as a fellow of the Canadian Psychological Association, the International Communication Association, and the Royal Society of Canada (the highest academic honor bestowed in Canada).

Bavelas believes that her research has often gone against the grain of established scholarship. She notes that the early work of the Palo Alto group was "very much a reaction to the way the established literature was dealing with certain problems in terms of isolated individuals." And she believes she is still well out of mainstream social psychology today, in her at-

tempt to "develop a truly social, communicative approach to social processes" and to investigate those processes through both experimental research and close observation. But she is happy when her work stimulates some degree of controversy. Indeed, though she is pleased that *Pragmatics* has achieved the status of a classic, she also worries that it is often misinterpreted in an attempt to assimilate it into existing paradigms. She notes, "I would have been happier with less adulation and more debate. We were and still are proposing some pretty big changes in how we should think about people."

Perhaps because of her experience with the reception of *Pragmatics*, Bavelas advises that we must always look at theory development as a dynamic and changing enterprise. She believes that "too many theories are like museum pieces, which we take students on tours through. At best, our theories tend to be opinions that never change, that never evolve with data and debate. At worst, theories become 'camps' or sects, defended or attacked only for personal or political reasons, not as scientific discourse." Thus, she advises that students shouldn't "take theory alone too seriously" and that it should always be considered in concert with empirical research. As she notes, "Yes, you need a guiding framework and some hypotheses, but you don't necessarily need Big Theory right now." Though Bavelas clearly is ambitious in her goals for understanding communication processes, her advice is to look initially to "clearer and empirically supported models." It is through such work that she continues on the trajectory she started many years ago.

---

ly wasteful strategy to gather the family or marital dyad together for interaction, only to devote the analysis to dissecting their interaction" (p. 179). Instead, scholars are encouraged to use the coding system to identify patterns of complementarity and symmetry in interaction by looking at **interacts** (i.e., a sequence of two utterances) and **double interacts** (i.e., a sequence of three utterances). That is, scholars using the

coding scheme are looking at the symmetrical and complementary processes inherent in relational communication by considering the sequencing of interactional behaviors. The coding scheme developed by Rogers and Farace (1975) has been used to analyze interaction in a variety of relational dyads including relational partners (e.g., Courtright, Millar, Rogers, & Bagarozzi, 1990), doctor-patient interaction (e.g., Cecil,

1998; Escudero, Rogers, & Gutierrez, 1997), and supervisor-subordinate interaction (e.g., Fairhurst, Rogers, & Sarr, 1987).

Applications to Family Communication   The application of the Palo Alto group theorizing that has perhaps been most true to the spirit of Bateson and his research group is the work on family communication that has been developed by Art Bochner and his colleagues. Bochner draws heavily on Palo Alto group ideas in his theoretical discussions of family interaction (Bochner, 1976; Bochner & Eisenberg, 1987; see also Yerby, 1995) and has used these ideas in empirical research into dilemmas of family interaction. For example, Cissna, Cox, and Bochner (1990) used both dialectics (discussed in the next section of this chapter) and concepts from the Palo Alto group to look at the communicative dilemmas of stepfamilies in establishing the primacy of the marital dyad and in establishing disciplinary patterns with children.

Summary

The Palo Alto theorists have gone a long way in "revisioning" communication within family and relational systems. They argue that interaction within these systems is complex and open to multiple interpretations. And they note that often the only way to fully understand the communication of an individual or a dyad is to look at the ways in which that interaction is embedded within larger systems of meaning and relationship. The next theory we discuss is also explicit in recognizing the complex and messy nature of relationships through a consideration of the tensions that characterize relationships and the practices relational participants use in working with those tensions on a daily basis.

■ THEORIES OF RELATIONAL DIALECTICS

The theories of relational development discussed in Chapter 10 painted a picture of relationships that could be described as neat and

tidy. Relationships developed as individuals desired more rewarding interactions and as they wanted to reduce uncertainty about relationships and those around them. The relationships developed in a patterned and often linear way, as relational partners self-disclosed and learned more about the personalities, intellects, and behaviors of the other. This increased knowledge enhanced the intimacy of the relationship, and often satisfaction with the relationship as well. And if the relationship was not going well, the process could be reversed and the relationship dissolved as neatly as it came together.

Of course, even scholars in the relational development tradition had trouble with this picture of relationships as neat and tidy, and this view certainly is in contrast with much of our interpersonal experience. Indeed, our daily lives and interactions tell us that relationships are inherently complex—even messy—and cannot be predicted or even described with simple and linear models. Such critiques of social penetration theory and uncertainty reduction theory set the stage for dialectical approaches to emerge in communication during the 1980s and 1990s.

A dialectical approach to relationships proposes that relationships are comprised of inherent contradictions. These contradictions are conceptualized not as dualisms—either-or concepts in which a particular option in the pair must be chosen—but as **dialectics** in which the tension inherent in the contradiction is not something to be resolved through choice but something that defines the nature of the relationship and sustains the life of the relationship. For instance, consider the concepts of autonomy and dependence in a relationship. A dualistic approach to these concepts would suggest that a relationship is defined by either dependence or autonomy and that as a relationship develops it might move through various stages of dependence. In contrast, a dialectical approach proposes that individuals in a relationship could want both autonomy and dependence and that coping with the tension of this dialectic is what gives a relationship life, sustenance, and movement. Dialectical approaches to relationships attempt to describe the nature of dialectical tension in relationships, discover the content of the contradictions that define varying types of relationships, and understand the processes through which dialectical tension is dealt with in relationships at all stages of the relational continuum. In discussing theories of relational dialectics, we first consider the philosophical roots of dialectical approaches. We then look at some of the defining features of dialectics, including the concepts of contradiction, totality, process, and praxis. Finally, we examine ways in which dialectical approaches to relationship have been used to understand friendship, intimate relationships and marriage, and family dynamics. In our review, we draw heavily on several communication theorists who have been instrumental in the development of dialectical approaches to relationships, particularly Leslie Baxter, Barbara Montgomery, and William Rawlins.

Philosophical Roots

Though dialectical theories of relational development were proposed in communication just since the 1970s, the roots of a dialectical approach, in general, go back much further. Indeed, the basis of relational dialectics can be traced back to ancient societies in both Western and Eastern cultures. Baxter and Montgomery (1996) look to the East in describing the concepts of yin and yang in which "the dark yin and the light yang of the universe are in constant interplay and motion. . . . [W]hen either the yin force or the yang force reaches an extreme, it contains the seed of its opposite" (p. 20). Baxter and Montgomery also consider Greek philosophers such as Heraclitus, who believed that "the deepest reality was change that comes from opposing forces; reality was like the simultaneously destructive and creative power of fire" (p. 21). Thus, the ancient seeds of dialectical approaches can be seen in both Eastern and Western philosophy.

Since the mid 19th century, several philosophers and social theorists have been central in the development of dialectical theory and in its application to relational and communication processes. Perhaps the theorists most closely associated with dialectics in the social world are Georg Hegel and his student, Karl Marx. Recall from our discussion of critical theory in Chapter 5 that these theorists were instrumental in developing an understanding of the social world as controlled by fundamental distinctions in power. For example, Marx outlined the importance of understanding control over modes and means production in the substructure of society and control over cultural processes in the superstructure of society. In discussing the goal of emancipation from these fundamental structures of oppression, Hegel and Marx outlined a philosophical approach that has come to be known as *material dialectics*. In this dialectical approach, the **thesis** is seen as the current structure. The **antithesis** is the overthrow or reversal of this structure. **Synthesis** is the resolution of structural inequalities.

Several aspects of this approach to dialectics are noteworthy. First, Hegel and Marx see the source of contradictions as lying primarily in material structures in the social world (e.g., control over production and economic processes). Second, this approach to dialectics emphasizes the eventual resolution of dialectical tension through the thesis-antithesis-synthesis process. Baxter and Montgomery (1996) summarize that "the struggle between thesis and antithesis eventually will get resolved [through some] kind of transcendent change" (p. 12). As we will see, current approaches to relational dialectics differ from material dialectics in both of these respects. That is, relational dialectical scholars rarely look to the material basis of relationships and rarely see transcendent change evidenced in relational development.

A final social theorist who has been particularly influential in Baxter and Montgomery's interpretation of dialectics is Mikhail Bakhtin, a Russian intellectual who wrote primarily in the 1920s and 1930s. His work was wide ranging, and much of it centered on the interpretation and criticism of literary works. However, since his rediscovery in the 1970s and 1980s, scholars

✳ SPOTLIGHT ON THE THEORIST

Leslie Baxter

Leslie Baxter received her Ph.D. from the University of Oregon in 1975 and has taught at the University of Montana, Lewis and Clark College, and the University of California, Davis. Baxter has been a professor of communication at the University of Iowa since 1994. Throughout her career, her work has centered on issues of interpersonal communication and relationships, but only since 1988 has she been publishing work specifically relevant to a dialectical approach to interpersonal relationships.

Baxter says that she became interested in dialectics during research projects in which she interviewed people about their relational experiences. As she puts it, she kept "bumping up against the opposites of what the research literature was focusing on." For example, scholarship in communication emphasized the importance of uncertainty reduction (see Chapter 10), but Baxter "never saw any theoretical attention on how people offset boredom to create or sustain novelty" in relationships. Scholarship in communication emphasized openness, "yet people experience and value discretion." Research considered how people connected with others but showed "no recognition that independence and autonomy are as important in connecting as interdependence." A dialectical approach to relationships provided Baxter with a means of grappling with these opposites that she kept bumping into.

Baxter notes that as she (and others) have published more on dialectics, there have been more and more opportunities for scholars who encounter the theory to "use it, reject it, critique it, embrace it." She is happy that others are looking at relationships through a dialectical lens, but she is disturbed when researchers use a cookie-cutter approach to dialectics, by "taking the 'basic 6' contradictions I have pointed to as if they were the only contradictions." Instead, Baxter emphasizes that "contradictions need to be studied in their unique situations, and this of course will lead to a multitude of different contradictions that are identified." She also stresses that "dialectics is not a theory of prediction, explanation, and control. It is a theory designed to help us render intelligible the ongoing tensions and dilemmas that face communicators as they 'do' relating."

With Baxter's dislike of a cookie-cutter approach to dialectics work, it is not surprising that she advocates a clear understanding of specific theories and what they lend to both scholarship and application. She notes that students and scholars should "appreciate that not all theories are designed to do the same kind of work. Theories are tools—for some problems and tasks, a given theory will be more or less helpful than another theory." Baxter does not believe that theory and research can ever be separated, though. "Research should always be sensitive to theory (whether inductive or deductive), and research should always inform theory. I can't imagine good research that isn't theoretical in both of these senses." Not surprisingly, her own work in dialectics is a clear illustration of these general principles.

from a variety of social research fields have been drawn to his work, primarily because of his explication of dialogue as central to all phases of life.

Bakhtin's work on dialogue is far too complicated to do it justice here, but a few points will illustrate some of the nuances of his position (see Bakhtin, 1981, for original source). He was centrally interested in reconceptualizing social life from an intellectual position that emphasized closed monologues of certainty and ratio-

nality to one that emphasized the open-ended "dialogic" nature of experience. For social researchers, several aspects of this dialogue concept are important. First, Bakhtin saw dialogue as consisting of at least two different voices that had distinct tendencies: centripetal forces (i.e., forces of unity) and centrifugal forces (i.e., forces of difference). This tension between unity and difference is at play in all aspects of social life: in the construction of self, in our relationship to societal structures, and in our interplay with others in the social world. As Baxter and Montgomery (1996) explain,

> Social life is an ongoing dynamic tension between forces of unity and difference, order and disorder. This interplay cannot be reduced to a single, static binary opposition; centripetal and centrifugal forces are multiple, varied, and ever-changing in the immediate context of the moment. The tension between centripetal and centrifugal themes, beliefs, ideologies, and values takes concrete form in the everyday interaction practices of social life. (p. 26)

A second aspect of Bakhtin's concept of dialogue is also important. This is the notion of time and space for dialogue. According to Bakhtin, every dialogue occurs within a concrete temporal and spatial context and is influenced by that context. That is, not only are there different voices within dialogue, and competing forces of unity and tension within dialogue, but dialogues are also embedded within a larger time-space continuum, in which the immediate context, the past, and anticipated contexts influence the nature of the interaction. Thus, when you ask a professor for an extension on a class project, that interaction is influenced by past interactions you have had with each other, past relationships and interactions with others, and the space and situation in which the current interaction is occurring.

Central Concepts in Dialectics

Theorists in communication have used these philosophical foundations to provide an understanding of the ways in which relationships are sustained and challenged by inherent tensions. In this section we consider several key concepts in a dialectical approach. In the next section we see how these concepts have been used to understand relational dynamics.

Contradiction Perhaps the most central and defining feature of a dialectical approach is the concept of **contradiction.** A dialectical contra-

diction is "the coexistence and conflict of interpenetrated opposites" (Rawlins, 1989, p. 159). Contradictions in dialectical theory are not just conflicts or differences; instead, they are tensions that are dependent on each other for their very definition.

Many theorists have explained the nature of contradiction in this theory by contrasting the concepts of a *dualism* and a *dialectic*. A dualism is an opposition in which the two polar points cannot exist together. For example, it is impossible for a substance to be hot and cold at the same time; thus, these concepts form a dualistic relationship. In contrast, a dialectical opposition is one in which both forces can—and do—exist simultaneously. For example, in a relationship you can simultaneously desire intimacy and distance. You may want a close and intimate relationship with a romantic partner but also seek to be your own person. Indeed, to a large extent your desire for each of these is defined by your experience of the other. You appreciate and desire intimacy because of loneliness and disconnection you have experienced in the past, and you want to maintain a separateness because in the past you may have experienced a smothering kind of closeness. Rawlins talks about this as the mutually conditioning nature of dialectical contradictions. That is, we define and experience each portion of the dialectic through our encounters with the other portion of the contradiction.

Totality and Process These dialectical contradictions must be understood through the use of two additional terms important to dialectical theory: totality and process. **Totality** refers to the notion that the contradictions in a relationship are part of a unified whole and cannot be understood in isolation. There are two implications of the totality of dialectics. First, as argued earlier, the terms of each dialectic (e.g., dependence and independence; openness and privacy) cannot be separated from each other. They exist together and mutually define each other. The concept of totality goes beyond this, however, in suggesting that not only are the oppositional terms of each dialectical tension intrinsically related to each other, but they are also intrinsically related to other dialectical oppositions in a relationship. As C. M. Werner and Baxter (1994) state, "Contradictions cannot be understood in isolation but are embedded in a total knot of interrelated contradictions" (p. 355). That is, the tension between dependence and independence cannot be separated from the tension between openness and privacy because each works to condition and define the other.

Dialectical contradictions must also be understood as parts of social **processes** that exist on a variety of levels. These could include processes of conversation, processes of relationship, processes of lifespan. As Rawlins (1989) explains, "Movement, activity and change are fundamental properties of social life in a dialectical perspective" (p. 160). Thus, in understanding the dialectic of privacy and openness, we must look at how this tension plays out within individual interactions (e.g., an individual may fluctuate between disclosure and secretiveness within a single conversation), within relationships (e.g., a couple may move through shifting periods of honest and open communication), and across relationships over time (e.g., your experiences with being extremely open in one relationship might either encourage or discourage you from similar openness in a subsequent relationship).

Praxis A final concept important to a dialectical perspective is that of **praxis.** The notion of praxis is based on the argument that life and interaction go on in the midst of these dialectical contradictions. Indeed, following a social constructionist point of view, the dialectical tensions that define relationships are created and re-created through the active participation and interaction (i.e., the practices) of social actors. An analysis of praxis, then, considers the choices social actors make in the midst of dialectical tensions and the ways in which these choices and actions create, re-create, and change the nature of dialectical contradictions.

Relational Dialectics: Contradictions

In the context of interpersonal relationships, theorists and researchers have identified a variety of dialectical tensions. Though these dialectics are not independent of each other (according to the concept of totality), and there is probably an infinite number of tensions that could be defined in even a single relationship, several relational contradictions have stood out in dialectical theory and research.

Major Relational Contradictions Early work by Baxter (1988, 1990) defined three major dialectical tensions. The use of these three contradictions has been continued in her subsequent theoretical work (e.g., Baxter and Montgomery, 1996) and by other researchers. The first of these central relational contradictions is the *connection-autonomy dialectic*. This dialectic has been noted as the most central to relationships (Rawlins, 1983), perhaps because the existence of a relationship is predicated on the connection between two people. However, the tension between connection and autonomy should be familiar to anyone who has sustained family and friendship relationships. Indeed, think about your relationships with a parent, romantic partner, or close friend, as you read the following explanation of the dialectical relationship between autonomy and connection (Baxter, 1990):

> No relationship can exist unless the parties forsake individual autonomy. However, too much connection paradoxically destroys the relationship because the individual entities become lost. Simultaneously, autonomy can be conceptualized only in terms of separation from others. But too much autonomy paradoxically destroys the individual's identity, because connections with others are necessary to identity formation and maintenance. (p. 70)

The second key dialectic identified by relational theorists is the *certainty-uncertainty dialectic*, sometimes labeled as the *predictability-novelty dialectic*. This dialectic takes us back to one of the theories we discussed in Chapter 10, uncertainty reduction theory, which proposed that a central goal of relational development (at least in early stages) is the reduction of uncertainty in order to enhance predictability about the relationship. A dialectical approach to relationships, though, argues that healthy relationships are sustained not only by the reduction of uncertainty but also by the novelty and uncertainty in a relationship. This view suggests that a relationship that is totally predictable and certain would also be boring and could not be sustained. However, total uncertainty is equally untenable, and dialectical theorists argue that managing the tension between certainty and uncertainty is a central part of relational communication.

The third contradiction consistently noted by dialectical theorists is the *openness-closedness dialectic*. This dialectic has clear relevance for the certainty-uncertainty dialectic because uncertainty is reduced through open communication. However, the openness-closedness dialectic is distinct in that it deals with the process through which both public and private information is exchanged and the vulnerability that can accompany both open exchange and discretion. As Baxter and Simon (1993) state, "This dialectic captures the tension experienced between the two partners in what to say and what not to say to one another. Relationship well-being requires the parties to display both candor and discretion in the information that they disclose to one another" (p. 228).

Baxter has proposed these three central dialectics as important in all relationships. Rawlins has identified additional dialectics that are particularly relevant to friendships. One of these is the *affection-instrumentality dialectic*, in which a tension exists between the functionality of friendship for instrumental reasons (e.g., accomplishing something through the friendship) and functionality for reasons of affection or liking. This contrast between friendship as an end in itself and friendship as a means to an end points out the complexity of this relationship (see Rawlins, 1989, pp. 171–174). Rawlins also considers the tension between judgment and acceptance that is inherent in many friendships. As Rawlins (1992) describes the dialectical relationship, "people value a

friend's acceptance, especially when they know the other takes their ideas, thoughts, and actions seriously. They also appreciate judgment and criticism from a person who primarily accepts and cares about them" (pp. 21–22).

Internal and External Dialectics In discussing contradictions, dialectical theorists propose that tensions in relationships exist not only within the relationship. Rather, following the importance of context discussed in our consideration of dialectical totality, these scholars highlight the tensions between the relational partners and others in the social world (see, e.g., Baxter, 1993). That is, just as some tensions define your relationship with your romantic partner, other tensions occur in managing how that relationship fits in with other relationships you have and how you present that relationship to others in your social world. These dialectical tensions are called **external dialectics** as compared with the **internal dialectics** that exist in interaction within the relationship. Some of the internal dialectics discussed earlier can be transformed into external dialectics:

- The external form of the connection-autonomy dialectic is an *inclusion-seclusion dialectic*. In this dialectic, partners in a relationship must negotiate the tension between doing things as a couple and doing things within a larger group.

- The external form of the certainty-uncertainty dialectic is a *conventional-unique dialectic*. This suggests that relationships are marked by a struggle about how they conform to the expectations and beliefs of others in the social world.

- The external form of the openness-closedness dialectic is a *revelation-concealment dialectic*. There are some relationships (or some periods within a relationship) when you want to keep the nature or even the existence of the relationship hidden from others. At other times, the nature of the relationship is made very public, perhaps even through ceremonies of relational commitment such as a wedding.

Furthermore, some external dialectics are distinct from the internal ones. For example, Rawlins identifies the *ideal-real dialectic,* in which relational partners struggle with the nature of their relationship in light of idealized versions of relationships that have been socially defined and constructed by society. As Rawlins (1992) states with regard to friendship, "Friends may attempt to communicate in ways that conform with the ideals of their era, but in doing so, they create and encounter real constraints and contradictions. The manner in which they handle these exigencies may revise or ratify the original ideals" (pp. 14–15).

Relational Dialectics: Praxis

The contradictions discussed in the preceding section serve as a typology of sorts for understanding the nature of relationships, but they do little to illuminate the communicative nature of those dialectical tensions. That is, defining these dialectics says little about how individuals deal with the tensions as they develop, live within, and dissolve relationships. Moving beyond defining the dialectics to a consideration of interaction within the dialectics requires an understanding of praxis. As Baxter and Montgomery argue, "From the perspective of relational dialectics, social actors give life through the communicative practices to the contradictions that organize their relationships" (p. 59).

Dialectical theorists discuss several ways in which tensions can be approached in social life. Baxter and Montgomery (1996) highlight eight different **praxis patterns,** which are presented and defined in Table 11.1. They argue that two of these patterns—denial and disorientation—are largely dysfunctional ways of approaching contradiction in relationships, though they may be used frequently in relational life. The other praxis patterns illustrated in Table 11.1 show varying ways of coping with, or even embracing, the dialectical tensions in relationships.

To illustrate a few of these praxis patterns, consider the central autonomy-connection dialectic. We experience this dialectic in relationships with family members, for example, when a child grows through adolescence and the strength of connection between parent and child must be negotiated. We also experience this dialectic in romantic relationships, when we want closeness but also want independence. This tension, though, can be handled in various ways. Consider four of the patterns defined in Table 11.1.

- The use of a *denial* pattern would involve the claim that this tension did not exist. For example, if a couple stated that they were "inseparable" and "always wanted to be together," they would be denying the existence of any need for autonomy. This praxis pattern is likely to be dysfunctional in the long run because needs for independence would eventually surface and have to be dealt with.

- The use of a *segmentation* pattern would involve defining particular spheres of the relationship in which connection would be honored and other spheres of the relationship in which autonomy would be honored. For example, a couple might decide that they will be independent and autonomous in career and work-related matters but connected in social situations.

- The use of a *balance* pattern would involve a compromise between connection and autonomy. That is, the couple might decide that they should be connected to each other but not smother each other.

- The use of a *reaffirmation* pattern would acknowledge that the couple have competing needs for autonomy and connection and would allow them to tolerate—or even enjoy—the tension created by these competing needs and desires. Baxter and Montgomery (1996) quote one illustration of a couple using a reaffirmation pattern: "We just think this is the way any relationship is like, if it's a long-term and commit-

Table 11.1	Patterns of Relational Praxis
Praxis Pattern	**Definition**
Denial	An effort is made to subvert, obscure, and deny the contradiction by legitimating only one pole of the contradiction.
Disorientation	A fatalistic attitude is adopted in which contradictions are regarded as inevitable, negative, and unchangeable.
Spiraling inversion	Each pole of the contradiction is dominant at various points over time. There is an ebb and flow between the two poles of the dialectic.
Segmentation	Each pole of the contradiction is dominant, depending on the nature of the topic or activity domain.
Balance	All poles are legimated at once in a compromise. This serves to dilute each pole of the contradiction.
Integration	Relational parties are able to respond fully to all opposing forces at the same time without compromise or dilution.
Recalibration	The poles of the dialectic are transformed in a particular situation so that they are no longer regarded as oppositional.
Reaffirmation	The contradictory poles of the dialectic are accepted and celebrated as enhancing the richness of the relationship.

Source: Identified by Baxter & Montgomery (1996, pp. 59–68).

ted one. When we're having a particular problem with issues like 'me' versus 'we,' we just tell ourselves that the relationship is for real, or we wouldn't be facing these things" (p. 66).

Thus, relational participants act within the tensions of relational dialectics in a variety of ways. Some of these patterns are more functional than others. A functional pattern is "one that celebrates the richness and diversity afforded by the oppositions of a contradiction and that tolerates the tensions posed by their unity" (Baxter & Montgomery, 1996, p. 60). A dialectic approach, though, would propose that the use of these patterns is not simple or straightforward. Relational partners might deal with a particular dialectic in their relationship in different ways over time, and they might deal with different dialectics in different ways. Furthermore, relational partners might have very different perceptions of the di-

alectical tensions and want to deal with them in different ways. Thus, dealing with multiple dialectical tensions over time in different ways is an inherently messy, fuzzy, and slippery process. As Baxter and Montgomery (1996) summarize,

> Relationship parties are forever improvising their relationship, forever coordinating the multiple centripetal and centrifugal voices of the historical past and the anticipated future into a praxical action of the moment that functions to keep the conversation of their relationship alive. (p. 77)

Research on Dialectics

There has been burgeoning interest in dialectics as an approach to communication in interpersonal relationships, and it has spawned a great deal of research. Much of this research has been descriptive in nature, as scholars have interviewed people to try to enhance our understanding of what dialectics are prevalent in different kinds of interpersonal relationships and what praxis patterns are used as people live and communicate in these relationships. In this section, we consider a few areas of representative research that have taken a dialectical approach in investigating different types of interpersonal relationships.

Dialectics in Friendships One important and wide-ranging research program has been Rawlins's work on dialectics in friendships. Rawlins's work is summarized in his book *Friendship Matters: Communication, Dialectics, and the Life Course* (Rawlins, 1992). He takes a lifespan perspective by considering the differences in friendship dialectics among childhood friendships, adolescent friendships, adult friendships, and friendships in later stages of life. His work, based primarily on the analysis of interviews, has been insightful in identifying both the varying nature of dialectics within friendship processes and the complex ways in which friends deal with these tensions both externally and internally.

Rawlins's work in the areas of adolescent and young adult friendships has been particularly revealing. For example, Rawlins (1989) examines the dialectical tensions inherent in young adult friendships and the way those tensions are managed in light of the challenges posed by gender, marriage, and work. A study by Rawlins and Holl (1988) looks at adolescent relationships by considering the dialectics inherent in both parent-child interaction and peer interaction. These scholars highlight the ways in which various dialectics and various relationships are interpenetrated as adolescents negotiate the complex dialectics of judgment versus acceptance and historical perspective versus contemporary experience.

Dialectics in Romantic Relationships A great deal of the research in dialectics has considered romantic relationships, both dating relationships and marriages. For example, in early work, Baxter directly confronted stage approaches to relational development in examining the dialectical contradictions in romantic relationships (see, e.g., Baxter, 1988, 1990). She found that

dialectical contradictions were present in the majority of relationships and at most stages of relational development. These findings contradicted the belief of relational development theorists who proposed that developing relationships are characterized by steadily increasing levels of connection, openness, and predictability. Interestingly, though, the presence or absence of contradictions did not influence relational satisfaction. Rather, the ways in which the contradictions were managed (e.g., the praxis patterns discussed earlier) were predictive of individuals' happiness in their relationships. Baxter's continuing examination of interviews with individuals discussing relationships has further defined the complexities of dialectical tensions in romantic relationships (see Baxter & Montgomery, 1996; Baxter & Simon, 1993; Baxter et al., 1997).

Other researchers have looked at romantic relationships at later stages such as marriage and divorce. For example, Braithwaite and Baxter (1995) examined the ways in which the renewal of marriage vows helps couples manage a number of dialectical tensions (private-public, stability-change, conventionality-uniqueness) through a public ritual. Masheter and Harris (1986) analyzed the relational trajectory of one couple through marriage, divorce, and subsequent close friendship, illustrating the ways in which the dialectical management of relational tensions can lead to outcomes other than the linear progression of relational development, maintenance, and dissolution.

Family Dialectics Finally, some scholars have used dialectical approaches to enhance our understanding of relationships in the family context, sometimes in combination with insights from the Palo Alto approach discussed earlier in this chapter. For example, Yerby (1995) argues for a dialectical approach to the study of family systems that recognizes the tensions between stability and change, the individual and the system, and the family and the culture in which it is embedded. The Cissna et al. (1990) study of relationships within the stepfamily, mentioned

✴ SPOTLIGHT ON THE THEORIST

William K. Rawlins

William K. Rawlins found early on in his academic career that, for many academics, friendship didn't seem to matter. He recounts that "most work addressing friendship at all did so in the context of social attraction studies" and that "friendship often appeared as a residual form of participation in demographic and sociometric studies, contrasting friendships (often implied by the questionnaire choice, 'other') with family and work relationships." Thus, when Rawlins, who has a Ph.D. from Temple University and is a professor of communication at Purdue University, wrote his book *Friendship Matters: Communication, Dialectics, and the Life Course* in 1992, he was truly breaking new ground. With this book and his other early research in dialectics, he opened up an important exchange about the value of a dialectical perspective for inquiry about human relationships. As Rawlins notes, "The wide engagement with these ideas by numerous students, researchers and textbook authors has been both confirming and stimulating."

Rawlins remains fascinated with the nature of friendship. As he says, "What's so intriguing to me about communication in friendships is that you cannot make people be friends. People remain friends to the degree that they are able to live up to their mutu-

ally established expectations and standards for edifying treatment of each other, and to the extent that their social circumstances allow it." In studying these processes, Rawlins has found that he needs to explore new theories and methodologies, and he needs to forge a close connection between scholarship and lived experience. He is very skeptical about highly formalized theories that are not grounded in relational experiences. He argues, "My work has made a strong statement that our theorizing about communication needs to stay close to the persons' lives as they are lived. We need to be careful in our zeal for abstraction not to miss the point of what we are studying."

Given these commitments to a connection between lived experience and scholarly work, the advice Rawlins provides for students and beginning researchers is not surprising. He worries that scholars often "fold up and even cave in to get their degrees, secure tenure, and/or advance their careers." He hopes, instead, that we can resist this and "live, study, teach, and write with courage" and that we do this by making a connection between lived experience and scholarship. Rawlins implores us to "connect your work with the life you are leading or are seeking to lead" and to "allow your work to speak with immediacy to your everyday cares and convictions." This can be difficult, of course. But he believes that "life is too short to waste merely acting out somebody else's research agenda." Indeed, we can see in Rawlins's own work on dialectics and friendship the importance of pursuing important questions in a vital and engaged way.

earlier, is an example of this kind of research. Their study identified dialectical tensions within the development and maintenance of stepfamily relationships—the tension of who has the authority to discipline children and the tension regarding the primacy of the spousal relationship and the parent-child relationship. Following the precepts of dialectical theory outlined in this chapter, Cissna et al. conclude that satisfaction will not depend on the existence of

these tensions, for they will inevitably exist. Rather, "the quality of life in the stepfamily may depend on *how* tension . . . is managed" (p. 56).

■ COMPARISON AND COMMENTARY

In this chapter, we considered two theories of relational communication that are complementary with each other but largely distinct in their theoretical and content focus. Both theories can be seen as having roots in interpretive approaches to theorizing. Their ontology relies heavily on social constructionist approaches in emphasizing the primacy of interaction and relationship in defining the social realities of relational members. Epistemologically, the views of members of the relational system (e.g., an insider perspective) are given primacy over the views of the researcher (e.g., an outsider perspective). That is, Palo Alto theorists look for ways in which family members interpret their rules and relationships and use those interpretations to understand the workings of the system. Similarly, researchers in the dialectical tradition elicit accounts about relationships and interaction within those relationships to develop an understanding of what tensions exist in relationships and how those tensions are created and managed through communicative praxis.

This largely interpretive focus on relationships differentiates the theories discussed in this chapter from the more positivistic theories highlighted in Chapter 10. For example, uncertainty reduction theory looks for causal relationships and predictability in relational development during initial interaction and beyond. In contrast, both the Palo Alto school and dialectical theory emphasize the possibility of multiple causes (e.g., the Palo Alto concept of equifinality and the cyclical and spiraling nature of causes and effects in dialectical praxis).

Both dialectics and the Palo Alto school provide theoretical positions with strong heuristic value and appealing aesthetics. These theories present frameworks that ring true with us as we consider our own relationships. We can recognize some of the paradoxes that we faced growing up within a family system, and we nod knowingly at considerations of the tension experienced by couples as they negotiate ways of feeling both connected and independent. These theories also seem consonant with existing research on relationships and have, as a result, generated a substantial and continuing body of research.

Both dialectics and the Palo Alto school can be questioned, though, on several grounds. Clearly, scholars in the post-positivist camp would question the standing of either of these approaches as a theory. Consider dialectical theory. Many of the concepts and processes described in a dialectic approach are slippery. For example, think about the praxis options presented in Table 11.1. These praxis possibilities are not as well defined as a post-positivist theorist would probably like, and there are no clear predictions either of when a particular praxis pattern might be used or of what the impact of a praxis pattern might be in a relational situation. Dialectical theorists would claim that this slipperiness is desirable and even necessary because relationships are messy entities. However, this slipperiness and messiness makes dialectics difficult to pin down in terms of specific areas of understanding and explanation and perhaps makes the theory difficult to falsify in the classic sense of theory construction. Indeed, Baxter and Montgomery (1996) acknowledge that dialectics is not a theory in the post-positivist sense. As Baxter articulates, "Relational dialectics is not a formal theory of prediction and causal explanation. But it is a theory in the sense of a coherent vocabulary and a set of questions to bring to the understanding of communication" (pp. 235–236).

Finally, research stemming from both of these theories has been largely descriptive in nature. Research in the Palo Alto tradition has worked to illustrate various kinds of paradoxes and interaction patterns that characterize relationships and family systems. Similarly, scholars working within a dialectical approach have attempted to develop an understanding of the contradictions inherent in interpersonal relationships and the ways that relational participants use praxis patterns to cope with those contradictions. Perhaps the next step for dialectical theory and work within the Palo Alto tradition is further investigation into the "why" questions raised by these descriptions. For instance, within the dialectical tradition, these questions might include "Why are some patterns of praxis chosen over others?" and "Why are some more functional than others in sustaining relationships?" Consideration of questions like these would continue to contribute both to the way we see relationships and to our understanding of how and why they work.

Key Terms

Palo Alto group
positive feedback
negative feedback
equifinality
theory of logical types
content function
relational function
digital communication
analogic communication
symmetrical interaction
complementary interaction
double binds
first-order change
second-order change
one-up/one-down/one-across statements
interacts
double interacts
dialectics
thesis
antithesis
synthesis
contradiction
totality
processes
praxis
external dialectics
internal dialectics
relational dialectics
praxis patterns

Discussion Questions

1. The Palo Alto group provides a vocabulary for helping us understand functional and dysfunctional communication in family settings. Think about your own family, and identify situations in which ideas of the Palo Alto group could help you shed light on communication patterns and processes.
2. What is the difference between a dualism and a dialectic? Give examples of each of these.
3. Could ideas from social penetration theory or uncertainty reduction theory (Chapter 10) be used in conjunction with ideas from the Palo Alto group or dialectics? How could the different metatheoretical bases of these theories be dealt with?
4. The theories presented in this chapter highlight the messy nature of relationships. In your experience, are relationships really that messy? Or is a simpler theory of relational dynamics a more helpful way to model typical relational situations?

Theories of Communication Contexts

As we have seen in Part Two, the processes through which we perceive the symbolic world, produce and receive messages, manage our interaction, and develop and maintain relationships are extremely complex. These communication processes occur in a wide range of life situations. Thus, understanding these processes takes us a long way in our journey toward appreciating communication in our lives.

However, communication theorists are often interested in the ways in which these processes are embedded in the social fabric of our lives. That is, many communication scholars want to look at how communication processes work in specific situations and contexts. These contexts are often conceptualized as levels of communication that involve increasing numbers of people in communication processes.

In Part Three, then, we consider one final "sorting" of communication theories by looking at five different contexts in which communication theory has been developed. These contextual areas of scholarship are theories of organizational communication (Chapter 12), theories of small group communication (Chapter 13), theories of media processing and effects (Chapter 14), theories of media and society (Chapter 15), and theories of culture and communication (Chapter 16).

12 Theories of Organizational Communication

The study of organizational communication is highly interdisciplinary, both in its roots and in the resources drawn on in current research. Connections can be drawn from organizational communication to fields such as management, sociology, social and industrial psychology, as well as to other subdisciplines within communication. As a result, the theories we consider in this chapter also have connections to other disciplines, though all have been developed extensively by scholars within communication. To understand the specific contemporary theories we discuss here, however, it is useful to take a brief look at the development of the field of organizational communication in a more general sense. This can be accomplished by examining some of the metaphors that were used to understand organizations and organizational communication during the 20th century.

Gareth Morgan, in his seminal book *Images of Organization* (1986, 1997), argues that organizational metaphors guide both organizational practice and organizational research. As he notes, "The use of metaphor implies *a way of thinking* and *a way of seeing* that pervades how we understand our world" (1986, p. 12). A number of metaphors have characterized the way organizational scholars have viewed their particular slice of the world over the years.

In the early part of the 20th century, the predominant metaphor guiding organizational theory and practice was that of a machine. A machine metaphor, as exemplified in work such as Frederick Taylor's theory of scientific management, Henri Fayol's theory of classical management, and Max Weber's theory of bureaucracy, highlights the perspective that organizations (and communication within organizations) are ruled by standardization, by specialization, and by predictability (K. I. Miller, 1999). A machine metaphor views organizations—and the individuals who inhabit them—as rational decision-makers concerned with the functionality and goals of the organization as a whole.

Though the machine metaphor can certainly be seen in theory and practice today, it has been joined and sometimes supplanted by other metaphoric ways of viewing organizations. In organizational communication, the systems metaphor gained ascendency in the 1960s and 1970s (see, e.g., Farace, Monge, & Russell, 1977). This view sees organizations as complex systems of interconnected and interdependent parts. Systems are hierarchically ordered in nested subsystems and supersystems and are open to their environment. Understanding organizational communication from within the systems perspective thus requires the researcher to investigate the connections and causal relationships among systems components, often by using complex statistical techniques. Systems research in organizational communication thus highlights concepts such as feedback, communication networks, and information flow.

Several other metaphors for understanding organizational communication have become particularly prevalent since the 1980s. Scholars frustrated with the rationality and objectivity of the machine and systems approaches turned to an interpretive metaphor—the organization as culture—in the early 1980s, and that metaphor remains central to much organizational communication research today. The cultural metaphor, taken from anthropology, looks to organizational stories, values, rites and rituals, and everyday behaviors as the best way to understand organizations and their members. This approach relies on concepts from interpretive theory (see Chapter 4) including social constructivism and the importance of meaning grounded in the local interactions of organizational participants. Another area of theorizing that has gained importance since the 1980s is what Morgan labels the "organization as instruments of domination" metaphor. Critical theorists (see Chapter 5) in this area have investigated ways in which dominant modes of thinking, talking, and acting within the organization might shape ideologies and oppress workers.

These are the most dominant metaphors that have guided thinking in organizational communication in recent years, but they are far from the only ones. Research has flourished within all these metaphoric traditions. The systems tradition has spawned studies of communication networks, of supervisor-subordinate feedback, and of interorganizational relationships (see, e.g., Monge & Contractor, 2001, for review of representative organizational systems research). Within the cultural tradition, organizational communication researchers have studied organizational narrative, the role of metaphor in conflict, and the creation of communication rules within cultural systems (see, e.g., Eisenberg & Riley, 2001). Critical studies (see, e.g., Mumby, 2001) have investigated gender roles in organizational settings, the role of stories in maintaining the status quo, and the possibility of enhancing democratic organizations through participative

structures and processes. To a large extent, though, the research in these areas has relied on the metaphorical framework and on specific concepts of interest but not on well-developed theories of organizational communication.

The four theories we consider in this chapter are exceptions to this general rule. These theories have distinct histories, but all have been influential in shaping thinking and research in organizational communication. Two of the theories (Weick's theory of organizing and Giddens's structuration theory) were developed outside the field of communication but have been enthusiastically embraced by organizational communication scholars. The other two theories (Taylor's text and conversation theory and Barker and Cheney's concertive control theory) have emerged from within the field of organizational communication since the mid 1980s.

■ WEICK'S THEORY OF ORGANIZING

Karl Weick is an organizational theorist whose work has had a profound impact on scholars in organizational communication. His book *The Social Psychology of Organizing* was published in 1969, and through this book, its second edition (1979), and his later book, *Sensemaking in Organizations* (1995), Weick has worked to articulate key concepts about the intertwining of organizing and communicating. Weick has been writing about the organizing process for over 30 years, and many of his core ideas have remained consistent, though he has elaborated them over time. In describing the coherent nature of his theoretical program, Weick himself said that "the safest prediction about the nature of my version of organizing theory in 1999 is that it will sound much like my version in 1969" (Weick, 1989, p. 242), and he described his theoretical ideas as discussions "about a loosely coupled, enacted world held together by good conversation" (p. 242). Indeed, it was Weick's explicit acknowledgment of the centrality of communication in organizing that caught the attention and imagination of organizational communication theorists when his initial work was released.

Over 30 years ago, the title of Weick's first book signaled the important move he was making in theorizing about organizational processes. A comprehensive and influential book had recently been published entitled *The Social Psychology of Organizations* (D. Katz & Kahn, 1966). Weick altered a single word in this title—changing *organizations* into *organizing*—and in this change from noun to verb transformed the way that many theorists thought about interaction in organizational contexts. The simple change of moving from a noun (*organization*) to a verb (*organizing*) suggests an approach in which we switch from thinking about organizations as containers in which communication happens to thinking about organizing and communicating as intertwined processes that continually and mutually influence each other. This move has had particular resonance for communication scholars (see R. C. Smith, 1992) because it highlights the role of interaction and symbolism in the ongoing process of organizing. In the next section, we outline the core ideas of Weick's theory by examining the processes introduced in his 1969 book: enactment, selection, and retention.

The Process of Organizing

Weick's ideas about the process of organizing were influenced by thinking in a wide range of academic fields including information theory, evolutionary theory, and general systems theory (see Kreps, 1990, for discussion of these roots). In his highly complex model, Weick (1969) defines the process of organizing as "the resolving of equivocality in an enacted environment by means of interlocked behaviors embedded in conditionally related processes" (p. 91). This rather dense definition can be "unpacked" by considering the interrelated processes of enactment, selection, and retention.

Enactment Processes   Following from concepts developed in general systems theory and open systems theory, Weick believes that organizations are embedded in an environment. However, Weick's concept of the environment does not refer to the physical environment or even to the environment of other organizations and institutions in which organizations must struggle to survive. Rather, Weick's theory considers the importance of an information environment in which activities and experiences are imbued with meaning by organizational participants.

Weick posits that the environment encountered by organizational members is not "out there" in an objective and premade sense. Rather, Weick argues that during the **enactment** process, organizational members *bracket* some event in the ongoing stream of activity or act in such a manner that the environment becomes constituted in a particular way. For example, when you enter a meeting, others sitting around the table might be laughing. Depending on how you behave in this event, the environment could be enacted in a variety of ways. Perhaps you try to stop the laughter because it is unproductive. Perhaps you worry that the people are laughing at you. Perhaps you stop the conversation to ask what the joke is. Perhaps you join in, hoping to catch up with the conversation in time. The point is that what you notice (or bracket) from the ongoing stream of experience and how you behave in that stream will affect the organizational environment you encounter. As Weick (1995) explains,

> There is *not* some kind of monolithic, singular, fixed environment that exists detached from and external to . . . people. Instead, . . . people are very much a part of their own environments. They act, and in doing so create the materials that become the constraints and opportunities they face. There is not some "they" who puts these environments in front of passive people. Instead the "they" is people who are more active. (p. 31)

Selection Processes   What happens as individuals in organizations enact these environments? Weick argues that a primary function of

Table 12.1	Properties of Sensemaking
Sensemaking is . . .	Explanation
Grounded in identity construction	The nature of our sensemaking is driven by who we are, and, reciprocally, these definitions of self are influenced by the ways we make sense of enacted environments.
Retrospective	We make sense of enacted environments by looking back and imbuing experiences with meaning. As Mead (1956, p. 136) explains, "We are conscious always of what we have done, never of doing it."
Enactive of sensible environments	Through sensemaking processes, we produce (or enact) the social environments we face. Sensemaking is "a process that creates objects for sensing" (Weick, 1995, p. 36).
Social	Sensemaking depends on interaction with others in the creation of intersubjective sense. Even cognitive sensemaking is "never solitary because what a person does internally is contingent on others" (Weick, 1995, p. 40).
Ongoing	Any instance of sensemaking depends on what has come before and will influence future sensemaking opportunities. As Weick (1995, p. 43) states, "People are always in the middle of things."
Focused on and by extracted cues	In order to make sense of the enacted environment, we must rely on "familiar structures that are seeds from which people develop a larger sense of what may be occurring" (Weick, 1995, p. 50).
Driven by plausibility rather than accuracy	In making sense of the enacted environment, "people will believe what can account for sensory experience, but what is also interesting, attractive, emotionally appealing, and goal relevant" (S. Fiske, 1992, p. 879).

Source: Based on Weick (1995, Chapter 2).

organizing is to make sense of the information environment, and much of this **sensemaking** occurs during what Weick calls **selection** processes. As Weick (1979) notes, "Selection involves the imposition of various structures on enacted equivocal displays in an attempt to reduce their equivocality" (p. 131). In other words, selection processes are opportunities for sensemaking: processes that involve the "placement of items into frameworks, comprehending, redressing surprise, constructing meaning, interacting in pursuit of mutual understanding, and patterning" (Weick, 1995, p. 6). Some of Weick's recent ideas about characteristics of the sensemaking process are presented in Table 12.1.

Of central importance to sensemaking processes is the concept of **equivocality.** Weick argues that aspects of the enacted environment will vary in terms of their equivocality and that the level of equivocality will influence the ways in which sense can be made. Weick uses the term *equivocality* in a very specific way, though scholars drawing on Weick often use the term more loosely. For Weick, equivocality refers to the existence of multiple interpretations of the same event. Equivocality does not refer to uncertainty or ambiguity about the meaning of an event. Consider the meeting laughter described earlier. This environment could be described as equivocal if an individual could put forth multiple viable explanations for the laughter (e.g., "they're laughing about that funny e-mail message that was circulating this morning" or "they're laughing because everyone is punchy from working so many long hours"). If you don't have any ideas about what is causing the laughter, the situation would not be construed as equivocal. As Weick (1995) explains, "The problem is that there are too many meanings, not too few. The problem faced by the sensemaker is one of equivocality, not one of uncertainty. The problem is confusion, not ignorance" (p. 27).

How does an individual make sense of equivocal (or even unequivocal) environments? Weick proposes a number of processes. Initially, drawing on Alfred Schutz (1964), Weick talked about the importance of **recipes** in the organizing process. A recipe provides both a way to interpret the environment and a guide to action. For example, in the culinary sense, a recipe can help you identify what you have eaten and help you create a desired dish. In the organizational sense, a recipe can help you make retrospective sense out of observed behavior, or in a more active sense, a recipe "tells how to handle people and situations so that satisfactory results are obtained and so that undesirable consequences are minimized" (Weick, 1979, p. 46). The use of recipes for sensemaking is particularly appropriate in situations of low equivocality, for in these situations it is easy to know which recipe to apply. In cases of higher equivocality, organizational members may not have a recipe to help them choose between the alternative interpretations presented in the enacted environment. In these cases, communication with others in the situation will be required in the sensemaking process because only through interlocked behaviors can the meaning of particular environmental events and displays be negotiated. As Weick explains,

> Equivocality removal is essentially an interpersonal process and involves at least two members interlocking some behaviors to accomplish this removal. . . . Once members can reach some agreement as to what is consequential and what is trivial in their elapsed experience, and once they

can get some kind of agreement as to the nature and direction of the connections among these consequential elements, then the elapsed experience becomes more sensible. (p. 142)

In more recent work, Weick (1995) has expanded on these concepts of sensemaking in positing a variety of belief-driven and action-driven routes to sensemaking. Though there is not room to present the details of these ideas here, note that this concept expands on earlier notions of sensemaking as driven by both recipes and communication cycles. That is, sensemaking is both an individual psychological process (belief-driven by recipes) and an interactive social process (action-driven through communication cycles).

Retention Processes   The existence of recipes for sensemaking points to the final process in Weick's model, that of **retention.** When particular interpretive schemas are used to make sense of an equivocal (or unequivocal) information environment, they can be stored for future use. This storage might be as formal rules and procedures in the organization (e.g., "we always review a prospective employee's resume with the hiring committee before extending an interview invitation") or might simply be in the minds of organizational members (e.g., "never knock on the supervisor's door if it is closed"). These interpretations are often stored in the form of **causal maps** that link particular behaviors with their likely outcome (e.g., "if I knock on the supervisor's closed door, he's likely to chew me out for interrupting him"). These causal maps serve as ways to interpret subsequent encounters with the environment and to drive subsequent action. Retained causal maps are not necessarily consistent with each other and do not necessarily represent effective ways of dealing with various situations. For example, a fear of getting chewed out might keep an employee from developing a good relationship with his or her supervisor or from accomplishing important organizational tasks. However, the retention process provides a link to the beginning of Weick's model, as retained recipes and causal maps shape the ways in which subsequent information environments will be enacted.

Tests and Applications of Weick's Model

This presentation of Weick's model of organizing is a cursory one that merely highlights some of the key processes that link interaction and organizing in a model of sensemaking. In subsequent work on organizing, Weick has addressed a variety of questions that stem from this basic model, including expanding on the nature of sensemaking opportunities and processes (Weick, 1995), considerations of how the strength of links or coupling in organizational systems can influence sensemaking (e.g., Weick, 1985), the role of sensemaking in crisis situations (e.g., Weick, 1988, 1990), and the problem of what happens when individuals have no recipes or opportunities for communication cycles—the failure of sensemaking (Weick, 1993). In this work, Weick has pointed to the complexity of organizational systems and to the interplay between cognitive and communicative processes in organizing.

Researchers in communication have been strongly influenced by Weick's work. In many instances, this influence has been at a rather abstract level, as the concept of sensemaking has resonated with organizational communication scholars. For example, a great deal of work in organizational socialization has been influenced by Weick in that an individual's encounter with an organization is seen as an opportunity to make sense of environments both equivocal and unequivocal (see, e.g., Jablin & Kramer, 1998; Louis, 1980; V. D. Miller & Jablin, 1991). Others have looked at how employees make sense of ongoing processes in organizations such as differential treatment by supervisors (Sias, 1996) or ambiguously defined organizational roles (K. I. Miller, Joseph, & Apker, 2000). These projects have relied heavily on the concepts of belief-driven and action-driven sensemaking as ways of explaining communication processes in an organizational context.

There have also been several attempts by communication scholars to explore or test Weick's organizing model more explicitly. Three examples are particularly noteworthy. Gary Kreps (1980) considered the role of equivocality in the sensemaking process and found that the equivocality of the enacted environment did drive communication cycles for sensemaking. Linda Putnam (1989) explored ways in which individuals make sense of interaction during labor negotiations and the ways in which sensemaking within bargaining contributes to beliefs and actions in the larger organizational environment. Finally, Charles Bantz applied Weick's model to the media industry, exploring both the ways in which the environment is enacted and made sensible within a newsroom (Bantz, 1980) and the ways in which the media industry is enacted through relationships among news organizations (Bantz, 1989). Although none of these projects have confirmed the totality of Weick's model, they have provided support for his contentions about the nature of sensemaking in organizational environments and the centrality of communication processes within sensemaking activities.

■ STRUCTURATION THEORY

We encountered Anthony Giddens's **structuration theory** in Chapter 5, when we discussed Giddens's work in terms of its influence on the ontology, epistemology, and axiology of communication theory, particularly among theorists taking a critical point of view. We consider structuration theory again in Chapter 13, when we discuss theories of small group interaction. As these multiple encounters suggest, structuration theory, developed by Giddens, a British sociologist, has had an enormous impact on communication theory. Nowhere has this impact been felt more than in the subdiscipline of organizational communication, where aspects of the theory have been adopted (and many would say unreasonably adapted) with great enthusiasm.

In this section we consider structuration theory as it has influenced the thinking and work of scholars in organizational communication. This presentation does not attempt to consider the totality of Giddens's work or even many of the details of structuration theory. For more comprehensive discussions of the theory, it is useful to turn to both Giddens's original work (e.g., Giddens, 1976, 1979, 1984) and to thorough presentations in secondary sources (e.g., I. J. Cohen, 1989; Gregory & Urry, 1985; Held & Thompson, 1989). In this section we concentrate on aspects of Giddens's writings that have been particularly influential in the theory and research of organizational communication scholars.

The Duality of Structure

Although scholars in other fields have concentrated on various aspects of structuration theory in their work (see Banks & Riley, 1993), most organizational communication theorists have embraced the concept of the **duality of structure** as the centerpiece for theory and investigations in the structurational mode. This concept attempts to break down the typical dualism that is posited between agency and constraint and between action and structure by proposing that these concepts work not as part of a dualism (e.g., in a competitive or either-or sense—a situation is characterized by agency *or* constraint) but as a duality in which "the structural properties of social systems are both medium and outcome of the practices they recursively organize" (Giddens, 1984, p. 25). As Banks and Riley (1993) explain,

> The duality of structure embraces the notion that action relies for its achievement on tacit knowledge of histories of social and cultural practices and agents' own personal biographies, and it simultaneously reproduces and further reinscribes into knowledge those histories and biographies as consequences and concomitants of its accomplishments. (p. 173)

In other words, actions serve to both produce and reproduce social structures, and those structures simultaneously enable and constrain action. For example, the interactions of individuals create rules for behavior in interactions during performance appraisals. These rules, then, constrain our communication as we partic-

ipate in the appraisal process. In order to better understand this central notion of the duality of structure, it is useful to take apart the duality and consider some of the key components of structuration theory. Of course, we need to remember that this dismemberment is artificial, as Giddens argues that these concepts exist in reciprocal and ongoing relationships with each other.

Key Concepts

Agency and Reflexivity   At the core of structuration theory is the concept of active agents interacting in the social world. Indeed, what we think of as the social world is generated through the behaviors of active agents. It is through this **agency** that we all manage to get on in the world, as we encounter both the routine and taken-for-granted activities of daily life and the more unusual situations that sometimes confront us. When we act in this social world, we draw on many resources we have developed in our society and culture. We use shared language, rules for interaction, and knowledge of the setting and people to shape our interaction. However, we are not dictated by these social resources or "inherited social system" (Banks & Riley, 1993, p. 171). Indeed, as Layder (1994) points out,

> We act "creatively" . . . by bringing to bear our unique characteristics upon socially shared knowledge. We interpret "rules" about how to act in the presence of others . . . just as we all have our own unique ways of dealing with situations. (pp. 133–134)

The ability of agents to act in both constrained and creative ways is indicative of the reflexive conceptualization of agency in structuration theory. That is, agents can observe or look back on what they are doing in order to apply knowledge from past situations, to give accounts of behavior, and to act creatively in a situation. For example, our knowledge of how performance appraisals are supposed to work allows us to respond during appraisals in ways that conform with and challenge the rules in a particular appraisal episode. As Banks and Riley (1993) explain, *reflexivity* "means being immersed in the continuous flow of action and deriving from experience a logic of action that enables agents to go on" (p. 172). Layder (1994) argues that this reflexivity allows active agents to be flexible in the face of expected situations and unforeseen circumstances.

The combined concepts of agency and reflexivity also point to another core concept of structuration theory, the *dialectic of control*. This concept argues that reflexive agents always have the capacity to make a difference. According to Giddens (1979), "All social actors, no matter how lowly, have some degree of penetration of the social forms which oppress them" (p. 145). Thus, through the concepts of reflexive agency and the dialectic of control, Giddens emphasizes that individuals are not puppets controlled by social forces but have the power to change the structures that guide many of their behaviors.

Structures and Systems The concept of agency accounts for half of the dualism of structure discussed earlier in this section. Recall that this dualism proposes that agency is both enabled and constrained by structure and that action produces and reproduces structure. Thus, the other key component for understanding the dualism of structure is understanding the concept of **structure** itself. An appreciation of the *structure* in structuration theory is made more difficult because Giddens does not use the term *structure* in the way we do in everyday interaction. That is, structures are not the physical—or even the social—edifices we create. Rather, structures are the rules and resources that constrain and enable action.

Rules act as recipes for social life, in that they are generalizable procedures about how to get things done. For example, in knowing how to order food at a take-out window, we are relying on rules. Rules might be very explicit, even written down in statements of procedure. But very often, rules are unstated and drawn on in social interaction in a routine way. **Resources** are the capabilities that social agents draw on to get things done. They are of two types. *Allocative resources* are material objects such as land, raw materials, or money, whereas *authoritative re-* *sources* are "non-material factors (such as status or hierarchical position) which enable command over other human beings" (Layder, 1994, p. 138). Together, these rules and resources constitute the structures that are created by, that enable, and that constrain action. As Harrison (1994) summarizes,

> Actors draw upon structure for knowledge about how to act and for the power that enables action. Thus structure may be conceived as the stocks of knowledge and abilities that actors draw upon to shape conduct, making interaction possible, meaningful, and legitimate. (p. 254)

It should be highlighted, again, that these structures—rules and resources—are not hard and concrete things. Indeed, Giddens argues that structures exist only as memory traces for social actors and that if these structures are not mobilized in practice, they will no longer exist. For example, in some organizations Robert's Rules of Order are used to run meetings. If an organization turns to more casual ways, however, and doesn't rely on Robert's Rules, those rules can no longer be said to be structures that constrain and enable behavior (though they may still exist as memory traces for some organizational actors). However, if structures are drawn on routinely in action they begin to have a more durable and discernable existence. Giddens calls structures that have continually been reproduced in behavior to the point that they are a routine feature of society *social systems* and *institutions*. "Social systems refer to reproduced practices while institutions refer to reproduced rules and resources" (Layder, 1994, p. 140). Thus, if an organization routinely holds "electronic meetings" using a computer listserv, structures (i.e., rules and resources) will develop that enable and constrain such meeting behavior and may eventually be concretized as social systems and institutional practices. Banks and Riley (1993) summarize this process of institutionalization:

> Those relationships that are patterned across time and space are the virtual structural properties of social systems, and therefore "are constituted of situated practices" (Giddens, 1981, p. 26). . . . As practices "stretch out" across time and space,

orders of institutional relationships are formed, codified, memorialized, and concretized as contextual features in the structuration of social life. (p. 176)

Structuration Theory in Organizational Communication

It should be clear from our discussion thus far that structuration theory was developed as a theory of social relations writ large—a theory of *The Constitution of Society* (Giddens, 1984) rather than a theory of organizational communication. It should also be clear that structuration theory is a highly complex and abstract theory. As Banks and Riley (1993) note, "Structuration lacks certain characteristics that communication researchers and other social scientists often find appealing: It is not quickly read, immediately intuitive, or parsimonious" (p. 178). Thus, it is important to consider the ways in which structuration theory has influenced theorists interested specifically in organizational communication.

Structuration theory has been applied in the understanding of some classic concepts in organizational studies: organizational structure and organizational climate. Bob McPhee (1985, 1989) has argued that "formal structure is a set of rules and resources drawn upon by organizational actors to coordinate their interactions" (Bastien, McPhee, & Bolton, 1995, p. 88). Understanding the gaps between the rules and resources that individuals draw on in interaction and the formal organizational chart helps to explain problems in coordination in organizational settings.

In a related program of research, Scott Poole, McPhee, and colleagues (e.g., Bastien et al., 1995; Poole, 1985; Poole & McPhee, 1983) have proposed that the climate of an organization can best be understood within a structurational framework. Following a meteorological metaphor, organizational climate describes what it feels like to work in a particular organization (i.e., what the "weather" is like at a particular company). For example, an organization's climate might be described as "friendly," "competitive," or "innovative." A structurational approach to this concept sees climate as "one sort of structure, produced and reproduced in communication and social interaction" (Bastien et al., 1995, p. 89). Climate is seen as an intersubjective concept created through discourse but perhaps enacted and interpreted in different ways by different organizational members. Poole (1985) talks about "kernel climates" that might be labeled in the same way but interpreted differently across organizational levels or work groups. For example, an organization might have a kernel climate of innovativeness. This climate will be instantiated differently in different parts of the organization (e.g., regular meetings to brainstorm, flexible work schedules to enhance creativity, reward systems for new ideas that benefit the company). By taking a structurational approach to climate, it is possible to see how climates develop and change as various structures (i.e., rules and resources) are drawn on and enacted in organizational communication.

Beyond these programmatic considerations of structure and climate, the 1990s witnessed a large amount of organizational communication scholarship influenced by structuration theory. One interesting area of research has looked at genres of communication and the ways that these genres are structured and restructured over time (Kuhn, 1997; Yates, 1989; Yates & Orlikowski, 1992). The concept of *genre*, drawn from scholars in English and rhetoric, proposes that there are families of discourse "that share situational requirements, substantive and stylistic characteristics, and an organizing principle" (Kuhn, 1997). For example, Yates and Orlikowski (1992) look at the memo genre and how it has developed over time. A structurational approach to genres is useful because it highlights the recursive nature of genre development. That is, when writing a memo, a manager is constrained by the rules for memo construction (e.g., the structure). However, as organizational contingencies change, active agents can change their practices and hence reconstitute the rules. Genre structures influence—but do not dictate—practice, and the genre structures can be reconstituted through the ongoing practices of organizational actors.

Other noteworthy works in organizational communication have drawn on structuration theory. In an essay relevant to our consideration of identification and control in the final section of this chapter, Scott, Corman, and Cheney (1998) explicate a model in which identification with an organization (or with other collectives such as teams or professions) is conceptualized as a structurational process. Howard and Geist (1995), in a study influenced by Giddens's concept of the dialectic of control, explore the reactions of organizational members to the contradictions emerging in an organizational merger. They note that ideological structures constrained discourse to some extent but also enabled empowerment and change in the face of organizational uncertainty. Witmer (1997) analyzes discourse from an Alcoholics Anonymous group within a structurational framework and concludes that "the alcoholic self is both agent and outcome as it evolves through recursive group practices and individual actions" (p. 324). Finally, Corman and Scott (1994) use structurational concepts to explore a methodological quandary in organizational communication: the gap between actual communication practices and the perceptions of interaction by organizational members. In short, the dualism of agency and structure described in structuration theory has helped organizational communication scholars understand a wide range of basic and applied communication processes.

■ THE TEXT AND CONVERSATION OF ORGANIZING

The theories we have talked about so far in this chapter have been developed primarily outside the field of communication, though both Weick's theory of organizing and Giddens's structuration theory have been enthusiastically embraced by organizational communication scholars. The third theoretical position we consider in this chapter was proposed by a communication scholar, James R. Taylor, and has been developed by Taylor and his colleagues at the University of Montreal and elsewhere. Taylor, unlike Weick (a social psychologist and management scholar) and Giddens (a sociologist) has his home within the communication discipline, and though he cites work from an eclectic array of scholars in the development of his ideas, he remains first and foremost a communication theorist.

Because Taylor draws on scholarship with a high level of cultural, disciplinary, and chronological diversity, it is hard to pin down a starting point for his theory. However, one clear and often-discussed inspiration for Taylor's recent ideas is in the very label for his field: *organizational communication*. Taylor, inspired by Ruth Smith's (1992) work on the root metaphors that guide this area of study, problematizes the concept of organizational communication by asking what such a term really means and what scholars in such an area should study. Smith (1992) and Taylor (1993, 1995; Taylor, Cooren, Giroux, Robichaud, 1996) are both troubled by the container metaphor implied in the term *organizational communication*. That is, the term suggests that organizational communication is simply any communication that happens inside an organization. This container metaphor, as Cooren and Taylor (1997) point out, has explanatory implications in that the organization is seen as having a causal influence on the communication that occurs within it. Thus, these scholars have explored other ways of interpreting the term *organizational communication*, including the notions that organizations are produced through communication and that organization and communication produce each other. In either case, the organization is no longer seen as a physical entity that holds communication. As Taylor et al. (1996) explain,

> We are not saying there is no organization, just that it is not an objective "thing." That it must be born and recreated in the equivocal interpretations that are intrinsic to communication does not make it less real—just not "real" in the material sense. (p. 5)

Taylor and his colleagues then take on the task of making sense of this reciprocal relationship

---

✦ SPOTLIGHT ON THE THEORIST

James R. Taylor

James R. Taylor received his Ph.D. from the University of Pennsylvania and is professor emeritus of communication at the University of Montreal. He has had a lifetime of experiences informing his theorizing about organizational communication. In addition to his academic positions, for instance, he has worked as a policy advisor for the Canadian government and as a television producer. These experiences, along with his study of a wide range of literature outside the traditional boundaries of the communication discipline, led Taylor to a rich and complex understanding of organizational communication processes. He states that "organizations are neither completely crystallized, nor are they chaotic, formless interaction. But how do we capture such a tension in theory? That has been the question that drove me to explore the paths that I have."

Taylor—who recounts theoretical influences including cybernetics, formal logic, urbanism and city planning, and semionarrative theory—notes that he "found it very hard to make connections with the mainstream preoccupations of organizational communication scholars." Indeed, he says that many of the ideas for his work were developed in the 1980s, though these ideas weren't published until the 1990s. Since then, though, the work of Taylor and his graduate students has been seen frequently in both books and communication journals. When he had two books published in 1993, he says that "neither book drew much reaction" but that he was not sur-

prised by this, "since I knew the themes and modes of expression of my writing were not those of most people in my field."

Taylor notes that his ideas have garnered more awareness recently, particularly as his work with doctoral students has been published in mainstream communication journals. Indeed, he believes that his collaborative work has been a "terrifically stimulating experience" and that it is in interaction with students in seminars (not at academic conventions) where the important debates surrounding his theory took place. Those seminars, Taylor says, are "where I was challenged to defend my ideas." He is hopeful, though, that his theory is now receiving more recognition with a wider audience, and he is particularly gratified with the connections made between his work and the work of Karl Weick and Anthony Giddens.

Taylor confesses to "being very leery about giving advice to anyone, least of all students." He does comment, however, that students of communication would be well served to explore areas well beyond the confines of the communication discipline. In particular, Taylor thinks that the rigor of the communication discipline will be increased if students consider work in fields including cybernetics, formal logic, linguistics, and game theory. Whether in these fields or others, though, Taylor exhorts scholars to seek out variety and to remain curious about a wide variety of issues. And for those who criticize the practice of "borrowing" ideas from others, he concludes that "there's nothing wrong with borrowing—I have done it all my life—but there comes a time when we have to give something back!"

---

between organization and communication in terms that draw from communication sources and thus make concepts such as meaning and interaction central in our understanding of organizational communication. To do this, Taylor and his colleagues begin with the basic concepts of text and conversation and then embellish and

embed these concepts for a fuller understanding of organizational communication processes. In the following discussion, we consider some of these basic concepts, with the understanding that we are not covering the full range of Taylor's ideas or the complexity of the sources he draws on in their development.

The Core Concepts: Text and Conversation

The basic building blocks in Taylor's theory of organizational communication are the concepts of text and conversation. Taylor et al. (1996) define **text** as the content of interaction, or what is said in interaction. Text (or meaning) can be made available to other individuals through face-to-face interaction or an alternative communicative system such as phone, electronic mail, a blackboard, and the like. **Conversation** is the communicative interaction itself, that is, what is happening behaviorally between two or more interactants. Thus, text is the meaning and conversation is the activity, and as Taylor et al. point out,

> One tempting way to think of a conversation. . . would be to see it as a string of texts, collaboratively produced by people who have positioned themselves to interactively generate and collect a sequence of texts that, by common agreement, are supposed to cohere together, reasonably well, by a quasi-logical principle of ordering where each succeeding text is supposed to link to the ones that preceded it—a kind of text-string. From this perspective, texts are the *matter* of conversation—the basic material out of which it is composed. (p. 8)

However, Taylor and his colleagues see the relationship between text and conversation as more complex than this. Indeed, they suggest that understanding the relationship requires a consideration of two translation processes: the translation of text into conversation and the translation of conversation into text.

Translation One: From Text to Conversation

The first translation process (and the order is really arbitrary, given that both translation processes occur simultaneously and recursively influence each other) is from text (i.e., meaning) to conversation (i.e., interaction). In understanding this translation, Taylor and his colleagues rely heavily on speech act theory (see Chapter 9). As you recall, speech act theory, developed by Austin (1962) and Searle (1969),

is concerned with the ways in which speech serves not as a description of some reality but as action. Through this notion of the illocutionary force of a speech act (i.e., what a person is trying to do with a particular statement), the translation of text to conversation becomes apparent. Text (or meaning) can be a very bare-bones kind of concept. However, this bare-bones meaning takes on life in conversation when the illocutionary force of a speech act is realized. In order to understand the illocutionary force of a speech act, it is important to consider the intent of the speaker, the context in which he or she is speaking, and the relationship between the speaker and the hearer. Through these concepts of intent, context, and relationship, text is transformed into conversation.

Consider, for instance, an organizational situation in which a worker calls his boss and tells her that he will not be in for work because of family problems. In looking at this as text, the meaning is relatively simple. However, the transformation of this text into conversation must take into account the relationship between the supervisor and subordinate (perhaps strained, perhaps friendly and supportive), the context in which the interaction takes place (perhaps in the midst of a drawn-out family illness, perhaps in the midst of many unexcused absences), and the intent of the speaker (perhaps to garner ongoing understanding and support, perhaps to maintain employment in a tenuous situation). Thus, the bare-bones meaning of an utterance (i.e., the text) is transformed into conversation through the background assumptions and context in which the utterance is produced.

Translation Two: From Conversation to Text

Taylor and his colleagues posit that the relationship between conversation and text is a reciprocal and recursive one. Thus, to fully understand these concepts, a second (ongoing and simultaneous) translation process is necessary. Taylor et al. (1996) call this the "textualization of the conversation," or the translation from conversation to text. To explain this translation, Taylor again harkens back to classic theory in communication, this time to the notion of framing and bracketing that we considered in our discussion of the Palo Alto school of theorizing on relational development (see Chapter 11). That is, in order to make sense of the flow of interaction in a conversation, the hearer must bracket or frame what is heard in a way that makes sense. Taylor and his colleagues believe that hearers largely interpret conversations in narrative fashion, that is, in a manner that gives the conversational content a beginning, a development, and an end (Taylor et al., 1996, p. 15). As Taylor et al. argue, "This is not the conversation any more, but a summary of it, [a text], recalled in retrospect" (p. 16). For example, in our consideration of the worker who calls his boss, both boss and worker will bracket this conversation to make sense of it as an event or a text. This bracketing might occur only in a psychological sense, but it might also be textualized in a more formal manner, perhaps as a memo or note in the worker's performance file.

From Text and Conversation to Organizational Communication As you are reading this description of Taylor's ideas, you might be wondering why these concepts are being included in a chapter on organizational communication rather than in a chapter on message production, discourse and conversation, or even relational development. These musings are natural given the basis of Taylor's theory in foundational theories of language and communication. Taylor is explicit and purposeful in these choices. He is interested in the so-called micro-practices of conversation (e.g., specific verbal and nonverbal behavior), and he believes that these "cells of talk" are the building blocks of organization (Taylor, 1995, p. 5) and that an understanding of organizational communication must begin with these building blocks. However, it is possible—indeed, imperative—to connect these ideas to the larger concept of organizational communication. Taylor and his colleagues do this in several ways.

First, recall that the transformation of text to conversation requires the understanding of intent, context, and relationship. Taylor et al. (1996) argue that these concepts that distinguish a speech act (i.e., conversation) from mere locution (i.e., text) "are precisely what we usually mean by *organization*" (p. 12). That is, when we try to understand *organization*, we talk about goals, plans, activities, relationships, structures, situations, and so on. These concepts can be put under the rubric of the context, relationship, and intention that serve to transform text into conversation. Thus, organizational communication can be construed as the process through which texts are transformed into conversation. "Organizational communication is not just information; it is action in context" (p. 12).

Second, this notion can be elaborated even further in understanding the ways in which text and conversation relate to organization by considering Taylor's concepts of distanciation (drawn from Ricoeur, 1981, 1986) and degrees of separation. These concepts are concerned primarily with the second translation, the transformation of conversation into text. **Distanciation** refers to the distance between the intended meaning of the speaker (e.g., the text) and what is created and retained in interaction. Taylor elaborates on this notion of distanciation by arguing that several **degrees of separation** should be considered in an understanding of organizational communication.

The first degree of separation is the distance between the intended meaning and what is created in interaction. This degree of separation deals with the first translation, between text and conversation. The remaining degrees of separation consider levels of the second translation, from conversation to text. These degrees of separation are summarized in Table 12.2.

As Table 12.2 illustrates, these degrees of separation move from the meaning of an individual source through the expression of that meaning in conversation, and then to the layered objectification of that conversation in narrative form, specialized language, formalized procedures and structures, and dissemination to a wider public.

Table 12.2	Degrees of Separation in Taylor's Theory of Organizational Communication
First degree of separation	Intent of the speaker is translated into action and embedded in conversation.
Second degree of separation	Events of the conversation are translated into a narrative representation, making it possible to understand the meaning of the exchange.
Third degree of separation	The text is transcribed (objectified) on some permanent or semi-permanent medium (e.g., the minutes of a meeting are taken down in writing).
Fourth degree of separation	A specialized language is developed to encourage and channel subsequent texts and conversations (e.g., lawyers develop specific ways of talking in court, with each other, and in documents).
Fifth degree of separation	The texts and conversations are transformed into material and physical frames (e.g., laboratories, conference rooms, organizational charts, procedural manuals).
Sixth degree of separation	The standardized form is disseminated and diffused to a broader public (e.g., media reports and representations of organizational forms and practices).

Source: Based on Taylor et al. (1996, pp. 24–25).

These degrees of separation illustrate the role of communication and interaction in building and creating what we know of as organizations. However, these degrees of separation also point to the reciprocal nature of organization and communication and of text and conversation. Each conversation, each instantiation of text, is embedded within these more abstract degrees of separation, and this embedding of conversation constrains and enables particular kinds of interaction. That is, what we say in conversations is conditioned by issues such as past narratives, professional language, organizational rules and structures, and media and societal portrayals of organization. Furthermore, how we interpret any conversation is conditioned by these same factors. Thus, the concepts of conversation and text are reciprocal, as are the concepts of organization and communication. Taylor et al. (1996) summarize this position, referring to their frustration with the container metaphor that has ruled organizational communication studies:

We believe that communication does occur *in* organization. If communication is the interaction that makes the conversation, then the organization is its setting, pointing to its persons, its circumstances, its objects, and its procedures, but never defining them. That organization, however, is a *product* of communication, arrived at by a complex process of textualization and conversational embedding, as a result of which the characteristics of organizational structure, although still interpretable, are more or less fixed, identities (including that of the organization) more or less established and the objects of organization more or less reified through their textualization. (p. 29)

Thus, Taylor and his colleagues have proposed a theoretical framework for understanding organizational communication that is in some ways similar to structuration theory (e.g., it highlights the recursive relationship between interaction and structure and emphasizes the tension between enablement and constraint that is inherent in that relationship). However, Taylor's perspective is important because of its base in communication theory and concepts. Taylor and his colleagues are continuing to develop these ideas in relation to reference frames such as semiotics (e.g., Cooren, 1999; Cooren & Taylor, 1997) and theories of organizational and individual cognition (e.g., Taylor, 1999). Though there have not been extensive empirical tests of the interrelated concepts of text and conversation, the work of Taylor and his colleagues points to an important way to connect organizational research to basic ideas in communication theory.

■ UNOBTRUSIVE AND CONCERTIVE CONTROL THEORY

The three theories we have considered thus far have looked quite broadly at processes of organizational communication. That is, Weick's theory of organizing, Giddens's structuration theory, and Taylor's notion of the text and conversation of organizational communication can be used to understand a variety of situations and contexts in organizational communication. Each theory could be applied, for instance, as an understanding of supervisor-subordinate interactions, organizational culture and climate, or group interaction. The final theory we discuss in this chapter breaks from this mold in considering more specific aspects of organizational communication: the influence of communication and identification on processes of decision making and team functioning in organizations.

The theoretical position we talk about here has come to be known as **concertive control theory** (see Barker, 1999, for the most thorough explication). However, these ideas have developed over time through the work of a group of scholars—most notably Jim Barker, George Cheney, and Phil Tompkins—who have been interested in the ways an individual's sense of connection to the organization (i.e., organizational identification) can influence interaction and behavior in decision making and team-based organizational settings. We discuss the

theory here by exploring the interrelated notions of control, identification, and discipline.

Control

Barker, Cheney, and Tompkins begin with the straightforward premise that much of organizational life is premised on the concept of control. Organizations are typically formed as goal-directed entities, and in order to coordinate behaviors in the pursuit of these goals, some kind of control is necessary. In the simplest terms, an organization needs control to get things done. But how is control exerted and exercised in organizational settings? Barker and Cheney (1994) rely on the work of Edwards (1981) to describe control processes within organizations. They note that these control processes have to a large extent developed historically as organizations have changed over time in response to trends in society at large. However, the development of new forms of control does not necessarily supplant the old forms: The forms of control described here all can (and do) exist in today's organizations.

Edwards (1981) enumerates three basic kinds of control in the organizational setting. The first of these, **simple control,** involves the direct and authoritarian exertion of power in the workplace. For example, if a supervisor exerts control by ordering a subordinate to do something or by threatening punishment if a task is not completed, this is the exercise of simple control. Barker (1999) notes that simple control is exemplified in 19th-century factories and even in many small family-owned companies today. The second kind of control, **technological control,** is premised on the physical technology used in an organization. The classic example of technological control is the assembly line, in which the continual movement of the line controls the behaviors of workers. Similarly, a great deal of computer technology today constrains the behaviors of workers by allowing only particular functions to be performed.

The third kind of control is **bureaucratic control.** The concept of bureaucracy was first articulated by Max Weber, a German sociologist. Weber proposed the bureaucracy as a type of or-

---

✴ SPOTLIGHT ON THE THEORIST

James R. Barker

James R. Barker received his Ph.D. from the University of Colorado and is now the director of research and associate professor of organizational theory and strategy at the U.S. Air Force Academy. He has also held faculty positions in communication departments at Marquette University and the University of New Mexico and is a former Army officer. Barker's work has been published in a number of journals in the communication and management disciplines, and the article published in *Administrative Science Quarterly* that served as the beginning of concertive control theory won an award as outstanding publication in organizational behavior.

Barker traces his interest in concertive control processes in organizations to his own work experience. He recounts, "Prior to beginning my doctoral studies, I had worked in a business that had converted from hierarchical management to teams. I knew that 'something' happened when organizations became more participative—any change in an organization's communication system will have consequences, and I wanted to find out what that 'something' was." His work on concertive control that sprung from this initial interest took the literature beyond earlier concerns with the economic benefits of changing to a consideration of the social consequences of teamwork that are engendered by the change to new organizational forms.

Barker has been very pleased with the reception of his work and with the worldwide attention garnered by the processes of concertive control. He is particularly happy that other researchers have taken up the project and that theorists from both the United States and Europe have debated the theory's merits. Beyond this response from academics, though, Barker notes that "accounts of teamwork in practitioner publications will often mention several of the consequences I described in my 1993 article when they discuss the success and failures of team endeavors." This impact on the practical world of organizations is especially gratifying.

Not surprisingly, Barker argues that students of communication theory should look for the connections between abstract theorizing and applications in everyday life. He says, "We all know that communication is a very practical discipline. Thus, a 'good' theory should be clearly evident in day-to-day communicative activity; students should be able to 'see' the theory happening when they study people communicating." Similarly, Barker advises graduate students embarking on careers as communication scholars to look, especially, at the practical consequences of communication activities. In his own work, Barker discusses the organizational imperative of both "doing well" (i.e., succeeding in an organization) and "doing good" (i.e., acting, as an organization, in an ethical manner). He believes that "by focusing our scholarly attention on the consequences of communication, what communication does to us, we can better teach our students and our organizations how to do well and do good."

---

ganization characterized by clearly defined hierarchy, division of labor, centralization, and separation from the environment. Most important for our consideration of control, however, is the notion of how authority is exercised in the bureaucratic form. In bureaucratic control, power is based on a system of rational-legal rules and the connection of these rules to rewards and punishments. In bureaucratic power, control is not wielded by the individual but by the system of rules itself. As Weber (1968) notes, "Every single bearer of powers of command is legitimated by the system of rational norms, and his power is legitimate insofar as it corresponds with the norm. Obedience is thus given to the norms rather than to the person" (p. 954).

Edwards (1981) argues that these three kinds of control—simple, technological, and bureaucratic—provide a thorough characterization of control processes within an organizational setting. However, Barker, Cheney, and Tompkins believe that changes in organizations in the last part of the 20th century have led to an additional kind of control that has come to be labeled as *concertive control*. These scholars looked at organizational forms that were emerging at the end of the 20th century—team-based organizations and organizations premised on concepts such as participation and empowerment—and argued that control in these kinds of organizations could not be understood as simple, technological, or bureaucratic. Rather, control in these organizations must be understood by considering the connections that individuals have with organizations and workgroups and the influence of these connections on organizational interaction and behaviors.

Identification

Central to an understanding of concertive control is an examination of the concept of **identification.** Identification refers to "the perception of oneness with or belongingness to [a collective], where the individual *defines* him- or herself in terms of the [collective] in which he or she is a member" (Mael & Ashforth, 1992, p. 104). For example, a nurse might feel a sense of identification with the nursing profession, with the hospital he or she works for, with a specific unit, or with a care team. The key point is that identification is a process that, in the words of Barker (1999), bonds an individual to some social group or community. Barker, Cheney, and Tompkins rely heavily on the work of Kenneth Burke in their consideration of identification. Recall from our discussion of dramatism in Chapter 6 that Burke is a literary and social scholar who sees identification (or consubstantiation) as a profound process through which individuals transcend their divisions in social interaction (e.g., Burke, 1950). Thus, through identification individuals form the sense

of "we" that is central to much of organizational and group life. As Barker (1999) argues, "Identification represents . . . the point at which the individual and the collective merge . . . the point of transcendence for the natural differences between individual identity and collective identity" (p. 128).

Discipline

The question then is, What does identification have to do with control? The answer to this question is really the heart of concertive control theory and rests on the concept of **discipline.** Barker and Cheney (1994) rely on the work of Foucault (1976) in fleshing out how identification, discipline, and control are connected. These scholars see discipline as embedded within the communicative practices or *discursive formations* of a social group. Barker (1999) talks about these discursive formations as a generative discipline in which the culture of the organization and identification with the organization join to direct the behavior of organizational members. As Barker (1999) summarizes,

> When team members act in accordance with their concertively developed norms and values for doing good work, they are being disciplined. Generative discipline, then, refers to the mechanisms we use to act as good people in the organization. (p. 42)

Thus, discipline in an organization comes into play when people identify with an organization and use the norms and values established by the organization as a guide to behavior. This can happen in several ways. First, as Tompkins and Cheney (1985) argued in early work on this theory, there are processes of **unobtrusive control** in which the decisions of organizational members are premised on the values established by the organization. These values are used as decision premises when individuals hold a strong sense of organizational identification. That is, when deciding about whether to work late on a project, a worker with a strong sense of identification might use the organization's value for customer service as a premise for deciding that working late is a good choice.

The link between identification and control can be seen in more obtrusive ways, as well, in the setting of the work group. These can be seen as processes of **concertive control.** For example, Barker (1993, 1999) describes ways in which work groups in team-based organizations develop techniques to reward and punish behavior that conforms with or deviates from the values identified as critical to the success of the organization and team (i.e., the generative discipline). Barker (1999) demonstrates how team members discipline each other by directing, monitoring, rewarding, and punishing others in the work group. In illustrating this process, Barker (1993) quotes one worker in a team-based organization whose work group had to deal with problems of team member punctuality:

> Well we had some disciplinary thing, you know. We had a few certain people who didn't show up on time and made a habit of coming in late. So the team got together and kinda set some guidelines and we told them, you know, "If you come in late the third time and you don't wanna do anything to correct it, you're gone." That was a team decision that this was a guideline that we were gonna follow. (p. 426)

These processes of unobtrusive and concertive control can be seen in a variety of organizational systems in which members feel a strong sense of identification with the collective and then use the values of the collective to guide decisions and behaviors. For example, you might see these processes at work in your lives as college students. At Texas A&M University, for instance, students identify strongly with the values associated with being an Aggie. These values are inculcated during socialization processes (e.g., fish camp) and through the many rituals that mark campus life in College Station, Texas (e.g., silver taps, elephant walk, bonfire, muster). In talking with my students and with A&M alumni, it is clear that this strong sense of identification influences decisions they make (e.g., regarding careers, financial support of A&M).

This influence of organizational identification over individual decisions could be characterized as unobtrusive control. Beyond this, however, students discipline each other (e.g., exercise concertive control) to fall in line with the values of Aggieland. For example, if a student does not take off his hat when entering the Memorial Student Center on campus, others will instruct him to do so or even remove it for him. If a student doesn't participate by "humping it" during "yells" at football games, others will mete out verbal discipline to bring her into line. In short, because of their strong identification with Texas A&M, students are controlled by the values of the university, even without the institution of simple, technological, or bureaucratic authority.

Research Applications of Concertive Control Theory

The most extensive illustration of concertive control processes was developed by Barker and his colleagues (Barker, 1993, 1999) in a study of an organization that had recently moved from a hierarchical model (marked by technological and bureaucratic control) to a team-based model (marked by concertive control). Barker describes how organizational members came to identify with the values of the organization, creating a culture and a generative discipline. This identification created decision premises for group members and often led to overt disciplinary behaviors and the creation of team-based disciplinary systems. However, the system became so normalized, so much a part of the natural order of the organization, that team members did not recognize the powerful forces of control at work. As Barker (1999) argues,

> When we engage in participative work, we enter the eye of the norm. We are confronted by a powerful system of control, but we cannot readily or easily see our constrained condition, much less analyze it. The eye of the norm represents a near-totalizing experience. We create the concertive community. We identify with it. We live by its

methodology. Concertive control is us. It is how we do participative work. (p. 174)

Other researchers have also explored the power of unobtrusive and concertive control. Connie Bullis (Bullis, 1991; Bullis & Tompkins, 1989) explored identification processes within the U.S. Forest Service, examining how identification influenced key decision premises in the workplace. Scott (1997) investigated the extent to which identification with various targets (e.g., the work group, the organization) might influence organizational communication processes. And in a fascinating study of the Grameen Bank Cooperative in Bangladesh, Papa, Auwal, and Singhal (1997) looked at ways in which field workers and loan recipients at the bank responded to control processes of "value consensus, rational rules, identification, and peer pressure" (Barker, 1999, p. 175). For example, in describing the behavior of field workers at the bank, Papa et al. (1997) note that they "do not receive pressure from upper management if their loan recovery rate falls below 99% but they place incredible pressure on each other" (p. 209). These studies, in various ways, consider the links among the key concepts of identification, control, and discipline in organizational communication.

■ COMPARISON AND COMMENTARY

One of the most notable aspects of the four theories we discussed in this chapter is that none of them have strong links to the post-positivist approach to theorizing. Instead, they draw on the ontological and epistemological assumptions of both interpretive and critical schools of thought. Weick's model of organizing and Taylor's theory of text and conversation are largely rooted in interpretive views of the world. These theories look both at the importance of the actual talk and interaction occurring in organizational settings and at how these conversations are interconnected and the ways individuals make sense of the conversations through cognitive and communicative means. Structuration theory and concertive control theory have roots in critical ontology and epistemology, emphasizing the tension between agency and constraint and the ways in which discourse can shift control processes in organizational settings.

What is particularly interesting about these theoretical roots is that, though interpretive and critical research areas are flourishing in organizational communication, a great deal of research in organizational communication (historically and currently) follows post-positivist tenets, in terms of both epistemology and methodology (see Corman & Poole, 2000, for consideration of all three areas of theory and research in organizational communication scholarship). What is to explain the existence of post-positivist research when the theories we have reviewed here are so clearly rooted in interpretive and critical schools of thought? Several factors are important. First, a great deal of research in organizational communication is descriptive and problem solving in nature. This is perhaps not surprising in a clearly applied area such as organizational communication. Indeed, research in organizational communication has been criticized as being overly functional and having a managerial bias (e.g., Putnam, 1983). Second, organizational communication scholars have often relied on post-positivist theories from other fields (e.g., management or sociology) and other subfields of the discipline (e.g., uncertainty reduction theory).

However, the subfield of organizational communication is becoming increasingly theoretical, through both the adaptation of theories from other fields (e.g., Weick's theory of organizing and Giddens's structuration theory) and the development of home-grown theories of organizational communication (e.g., Taylor's text and conversation and concertive control theory). As is evident in our discussion, these theories are abstract and complex, and they don't lend themselves to clear and straightforward empirical tests. It is clear, though, that these theories are powerful in terms of providing wide and compelling understandings of organizational communication processes. Thus, these theories have a great deal of aesthetic and heuristic value and will undoubtedly continue to be used and adapted by organizational communication scholars.

Key Terms

enactment
sensemaking
selection
equivocality
recipes
retention
causal maps
structuration theory
duality of structure
agency
structure
rules
resources
text
conversation
distanciation
degrees of separation
concertive control theory
simple control

technological control
bureaucratic control
identification
discipline
unobtrusive control
concertive control

Discussion Questions

1. Weick's theory of sensemaking emphasizes the equivocality of the information environments that are enacted in organizations. What is meant by equivocality in Weick's theory? How does equivocality influence the communication that goes on during sensemaking processes?

2. Compare and contrast Giddens's structuration theory with Taylor's theory of text and conversation. How might each theory help you explain and understand the employment interview process?

3. What differentiates unobtrusive control from concertive control? What is the role of identification in each process? What is the role of discipline in each process?

13 Theories of Small Group Communication

One sure way to evoke a groan in a college class-room is to announce that a portion of the students' grades will be based on a group project. Though working in student groups is clearly not reflective of our experience in all groups, these groans reflect a cultural truism—that working with groups can be a difficult and time-consuming task and it may come with few rewards. Indeed, groups are often derided as making lower-quality decisions than individuals while wasting the valuable time of group members. Sayings coined by the prolific author "anonymous" opine that "a camel is a horse designed by a committee" and "a committee is a cul-de-sac down which promising young ideas are lured and then quietly strangled." In short, group work is a much-maligned part of social life.

However, communication in groups can also be highly rewarding. Many of us have been lucky enough to be members of groups where everything clicks. In such groups, the time flies by, high-quality decisions are made, and relationships are formed that extend beyond the spatial and temporal boundaries of the group. What is the difference between these rewarding groups and those that make students groan? How can we differentiate times when two heads will be better than one from those when too many cooks will spoil the broth? The theories presented in this chapter try to answer these questions by proposing explanations of how

communication in groups works and how communication influences group outcomes such as decision quality and attitudes of group members. In this chapter, we first develop a context for understanding small group communication theories by considering some of the research conducted in this area in the 1960s and 1970s and look briefly at critiques of that research. We then examine three theories developed to answer questions regarding the "how" and "why" of small group communication: functional theory, structurational approaches, and symbolic convergence theory.

■ FORMATIVE RESEARCH IN GROUP INTERACTION

The study of group process has a long history (see Frey, 1996; Gouran, 1999, for reviews). This history began in the early 20th century and flourished between 1945 and 1970 (what Frey calls the grand old days) as scholars in psychology, sociology, and communication attempted to describe the processes through which groups developed relationships and made decisions. Gouran (1999) sees the 1950s as the time when research on group communication was emerging and the 1960s as a period when the focus on group interaction flourished through consideration of both functional task and developmental processes.

Much of the work conducted during this time period was highly descriptive and mechanistic, modeling either the phases through which groups progressed or the input factors and process factors that would lead to valued output factors. For example, B. A. Fisher's (1970) model of **group development** identified four phases of group development in decision-making groups: orientation (in which group members become acquainted with each other and with the problem at hand), conflict (in which possible solutions are presented and debated), emergence (in which the group arrives at some level of consensus), and reinforcement (in which the decision is supported by group members). Fisher's model is typical of the so-called phase models rampant from the 1950s to the early 1970s. A representative model of the input-output variety is Collins and Guetzkow's (1964) model that distinguishes among problem sources (in both the task and interpersonal environment), group behaviors (in both the task and interpersonal system), outputs (at the individual and group levels), and rewards. Models such as these present lists of factors proposed to influence group performance.

Phase and factor models have a great deal of heuristic value in helping us look at decision-making groups, track their progress, and recognize issues that might be affecting outcomes. However, these models of the grand old age of group study were also criticized as early as 1970 (Gouran, 1970) and into the 1980s and 1990s (e.g., Cragan & Wright, 1990; Poole, 1990; Hirokawa, Salazar, Erbert, & Ice, 1996). The critiques of these models were wide ranging, but two factors are particularly important. First, these models were criticized as being overly simplistic in suggesting simple and sequential phases and a limited number of descriptive factors. Second, these models were criticized as being overly descriptive and not providing theoretical explanation of why groups developed the way they did and why particular factors influenced outcomes in particular ways.

The first of these critiques (i.e., regarding the simplicity of phase models) has been answered to a large extent by work that has rejected models of simple and unitary group development. The most comprehensive of this work has been undertaken by Scott Poole and his colleagues (Poole, 1983b; Poole & Doelger, 1986; Poole & Roth, 1989a, 1989b) in developing a **multiple sequence model** of group development in decision-making groups. This work, based on the coding of continuous interaction of actual groups, has resulted in a typology of *decision paths* that might be followed in group interactions. These decision paths (from Poole & Roth, 1989a) include the following:

- *Unitary sequence path.* Group interaction generally follows the traditional sequence of orientation, problem analysis, solution, and reinforcement (noted in 23% of groups studied).
- *Complex cyclic path.* Group interaction consists of multiple problem-solution cycles (noted in 47% of groups studied).
- *Solution-oriented path.* Group interaction centers on solutions and involves no activity related to problem definition or analysis (noted in 30% of groups studied).

For example, a group reaching a decision about what kind of computer system to buy for a small business might use a careful and rational model of analysis (i.e., unitary sequence path). However, the group would be more likely to decide quickly on a purchase choice solution and then justify that decision through interaction (i.e., solution-oriented path) or to work around the problem in multiple interactions that deal with various parts of the decision such as software applications, price, networking capabilities, and the like (i.e., complex cyclic path). In sophisticated developments such as this, Poole and his associates have worked to respond to the first major criticism of early group communication scholarship. That is, they have found that groups engage in complicated sequences of cycles and that no simple and straightforward group process model should be accepted.

The majority of this chapter, however, looks at responses to the second critique of early group communication work—the criticism that descriptive models of phases and inputs and outputs do little to answer the question of why groups develop and make decisions as they do. As Gouran (1999) notes, the later decades of the 20th century were marked by the exploration and advancement of theories that have worked to codify answers to these "why" questions of group functioning, particularly group decision-making.

In this chapter, we consider three theories that provide different kinds of explanations for the group decision-making process. Though these theories all draw inspiration from earlier theoretical work in fields such as psychology and sociology, their major development occurred within the field of communication, particularly during the 1980s and 1990s. The three theories we will examine are functional theory (developed primarily by Randy Hirokawa and Dennis Gouran), adaptive structuration theory (developed primarily by Scott Poole, David Seibold, and Bob McPhee), and symbolic convergence theory (developed primarily by Ernest Bormann and his colleagues). In the commentary section of this chapter, we discuss the bona fide group perspective, which has already begun to have a large impact on group communication research as we enter the 21st century.

▮ FUNCTIONAL THEORY

Our social history is peppered with group decisions that in retrospect can be seen as either good decisions or bad decisions. When a group decision was made to launch the space shuttle *Challenger*, in spite of problems that had been raised in group discussion, it is clear that a bad decision was made by the group. When Richard Nixon and his colleagues decided to cover up the Watergate break-in, the nature of interaction in the group may have been influential (see Cline, 1994). In contrast, decisions made by the Kennedy administration during the Cuban missile crisis have "been heralded by many people as an example par excellence of effective collective judgment" (Gouran, Hirokawa, Julian, & Leatham, 1993, p. 578). In

your own life, you can probably think of many times when a group you were a part of came through with effective outcomes and others where results were subpar.

What distinguishes these effective and ineffective groups? This question of why some groups make good decisions and others make bad decisions is at the heart of **functional theory** as developed by Hirokawa, Gouran, and their colleagues. For these scholars, the basis of any answer to this question must center on communication. Functional theory proposes that "group communication processes play a vital role in determining whether a group will arrive at a low- or high-quality decision" (Hirokawa, 1988, p. 488). In expanding on this concept, functional theory attempts to answer the key questions of how and why communication makes the difference in decision-making groups.

Formative Influences of Functional Theory

Scholars developing functional theory drew on a number of sources in developing their ideas. Two of the most important influences came from group researchers in social psychology (Gouran et al., 1993). The first major influence was the work of Robert F. Bales in his classic book, *Interaction Process Analysis* (1950). In this work, Bales argued that a small group is faced with four functional problems: adaptation (i.e., adjustment to the social environment outside of the group), instrumental control (i.e., removing or managing barriers to goal attainment), expression (i.e., the management of intragroup tensions and emotions), and integration (i.e., the formation of a unified group). Bales then proposed ways of assessing the extent to which a group was successful in dealing with these problems by observing and coding their interaction. This formative work provides the basis for functional theory in two ways. First, it highlights the notion of functions that groups must manage if they are to be successful in their tasks. Second, it points to the critical role of interaction in dealing with these functional goals. These two basic

✴ SPOTLIGHT ON THE THEORIST

Dennis Gouran and Randy Hirokawa

Dennis Gouran received his Ph.D. from the University of Iowa and is now professor of communication at Pennsylvania State University. Randy Hirokawa received his Ph.D. from the University of Washington and is now professor of communication at the University of Iowa. Professors Gouran and Hirokawa met at a communication convention in 1981, and they have worked together on ideas related to the functional theory of group decision-making ever since. Both theorists trace their interest in functional theory to the need to understand how communication processes contribute to decision making and problem solving in groups. As Hirokawa says, "The key question that led to the development of the functional perspective is the deceptively simple question: Why do some groups make good decisions while others make bad ones?" Beginning with this question, their work has continued on a progressive trajectory exploring, as Gouran summarizes, "how communication influences the performance of decision-making and problem-solving groups."

Hirokawa and Gouran are pleased with the reception functional theory has received from academics. Gouran notes that though there have certainly been critiques of functional theory, those critiques "have been constructive in pointing to weaknesses and limitations of the various versions of the perspective." They also believe that functional theory is compatible with many other theories of group communication, especially in serving as a means for critiquing the effectiveness of group processes. Both theorists think, however, that one of the most important areas of influence for the theory has been on practitioners. Hirokowa, for instance, believes that functional theory "has been received most enthusiastically by those who have to teach and train decision-making and problem-solving groups," and he jokes that "there are more organizational consultants who have made money using the functional perspective than I can count."

Gouran and Hirokawa believe that students of communication need to approach the broad range of theory when confronting any phenomenon. As Hirokawa argues, "Communication is such a complex phenomenon that it is unlikely for any single theory to explain it fully." However, they acknowledge that the study of theory can be difficult. Gouran believes that "students too often are confronted with material cast in the form of theories without a very good understanding of what theories are," and as a result he advises that students obtain rudimentary knowledge about theory building and development. Hirokawa suggests that the search for theory can be enhanced through connections with real-world phenomena. As he says, "I think it is essential to look for evidence of a theory in everyday life which either confirms or supports theoretical propositions about how communication works." According to Hirokawa, by following this type of advice when confronting theories, it is likely that students and scholars of communication will be able to "ask interesting questions, investigate questions in creative ways, and persevere." When we do that, we will reap the benefits of "a way of life that is intrinsically and highly rewarding," according to Gouran.

ideas form the framework for the more detailed theory of Hirokawa and Gouran.

A second major influence on functional theory was work on **groupthink** developed by Irving Janis (1972, 1982). This concept, developed through the analysis of historical decision examples and experimental decision-making groups, refers to "a mode of thinking that people engage in when they are deeply involved in a cohesive in-group, when the members' striving for unanimity overrides their motivation to realistically appraise alternative courses of action" (Janis, 1982, p. 9). In a group characterized by groupthink, group members have a strong desire to get along with each other and maintain good feelings about the group. Because of this strong desire for a cohesive group, individual group members will be reluctant to raise contrary points of view, will try to keep others in agreement with the group as a whole, and will maintain a belief (usually illusory) that the group is in complete agreement and is invulnerable to errors. The scholars who developed functional theory looked at the concept of groupthink and wanted to better understand the communication processes through which groupthink occurred and through which groupthink could be avoided. That is, the dysfunctional process of groupthink led these scholars to propose specific communication processes through which effective decision making was likely to occur.

Assumptions and Predictions of Functional Theory

Functional theory has undergone some revision in its development as the theorists have refined their thinking and conducted empirical tests of the theory's predictions. The most complete and current statement of the theory is found in Gouran et al. (1993; see also Gouran and Hirokawa, 1996; Hirokawa & Salazar, 1999). This presentation of the theory starts with several assumptions that undergird the theory. Stohl and Holmes (1993) have suggested that these assumptions should be more accurately referred to as *boundary conditions* because they describe the group situations in which the predictions of functional theory should hold. These boundary conditions are presented in Table 13.1.

These assumptions set the limits for situations in which functional theory should predict the quality of decisions made by groups. As Table 13.1 illustrates, functional theory limits its predictions to decision-making and problem-

solving groups that are attempting to work in a rational way, have the resources and capabilities to solve the problem, and are motivated to make a good decision.

Within these parameters, functional theory attempts to identify the key things that must happen in a decision-making or problem-solving group in order to make an effective decision. These functions that must occur are the ones that you might think of when you recall effective (and ineffective) groups of which you have been a member. Think, perhaps, of a family meeting in which you were trying to decide on priorities for scheduling or travel plans. Or consider a group project in a class in which you needed to deal with the problems in an assigned case. Or perhaps you have worked in an organizational setting with a team of employees trying to deal with a production problem or make a crucial hiring decision. In these instances, according to functional theory, there are processes (i.e., functions) that must be dealt with in order for a good outcome to arise from group interaction. These functions, in a general sense, deal with understanding the problem at hand, understanding the possible solutions to the problem, and having a system in place to evaluate the appropriateness of particular solutions for the specific problem. As outlined by Gouran et al. (1993, p. 580), these functions are as follows:

- The group should show correct understanding of the issues to be resolved.

- The group should determine the minimal characteristics any alternative must possess in order to be acceptable.

- The group should identify a relevant and realistic set of alternatives.

- The group should carefully examine the alternatives in relationship to each previously agreed-upon characteristic of an acceptable choice.

- The group should select the alternative that analysis reveals to be the most likely to have desired characteristics.

Given these functions, the question that researchers in the functional theory tradition

Table 13.1	Boundary Conditions of Functional Theory

The propositions of functional theory should hold when:

1. The members of a decision-making or problem-solving group are motivated to make an appropriate choice.

2. The choice confronted is nonobvious.

3. The collective resources of the group, with respect to the particular task, exceed those of individual members.

4. The requisites of the task are specifiable.

5. Relevant information is available to the members or can be acquired.

6. The task is within the intellectual capabilities of the members to perform.

7. Communication is instrumental.

Source: From Gouran et al. (1993).

want to answer is how communication within the group can contribute to meeting these functions and hence contribute to making a high-quality decision. Functional theory researchers have generally looked for several communication factors that they believe will contribute to effective decisions. The first communication factor deals with analysis of the problem situation. As Gouran et al. (1993) note, "It is vital for a group to understand fully the matters with which it is confronted if the members are to proceed through subsequent phases of the decision-making or problem-solving process and ultimately make an appropriate choice" (p. 584). Related to the analysis of the problem, functional theory proposes that communication in effective groups will include a consideration of criteria for an effective decision. This establishment of criteria involves understanding both the specific objectives that need to be achieved and the standards by which various options for reaching those objectives will be evaluated (Hirokawa, 1988, p. 489).

Third, communication in effective decision-making groups will be marked by attention to the attributes of specific solutions that are proposed to solve the problem. This analysis will in-clude analysis of both positive and negative aspects of proposed solutions. In other words, "the evaluation process followed by 'effective' groups will be far more thorough and rigorous than the evaluation procedures employed by 'ineffective' groups" (Hirokawa & Pace, 1983, p. 370). Finally, functional theory proposes that effective problem-solving groups will establish general norms or operating procedures that will guide interaction throughout the group process. Hirokawa (1983) suggests that such communicative behaviors will help the group decide (a) what needs to be done, (b) how members should approach the task, and (c) how members should structure group discussion.

Studies in the functional theory tradition, then, assess whether these communication processes are present in interaction and hypothesize that the existence of these communicative activities will lead to higher-quality decisions or more effective problem solving. Poole (1999) summarizes the predictive direction of functional theory, stating that "if group activities are in the service of adequate problem analysis, clear and realistic goal setting, and critical and realistic evaluation of information and options, a group should be more likely to make an effective

Table 13.2	Typical Predictions of Functional Theory
Hypothesis 1	Groups characterized by higher frequencies of communication *analyzing the problem/task* will arrive at decisions of greater utility than groups characterized by lower frequencies.
Hypothesis 2	Groups characterized by higher frequencies of communication *serving to orient/establish procedures* will arrive at decisions of greater utility than groups characterized by lower frequencies.
Hypothesis 3	Groups characterized by higher frequencies of communication *serving to establish criteria for an acceptable choice* will arrive at decisions of greater utility than groups characterized by lower frequencies.
Hypothesis 4	Groups characterized by higher frequencies of communication *evaluating the positive consequences of considered choices* will arrive at decisions of greater utility than groups characterized by lower frequencies.
Hypothesis 5	Groups characterized by higher frequencies of communication *evaluating the negative consequences of considered choices* will arrive at decisions of greater utility than groups characterized by lower frequencies.

Source: From Propp & Nelson (1996).

decision" (pp. 43–44). An exemplary set of hypotheses illustrating the predictions typical within functional theory is presented in Table 13.2.

Empirical Tests, Critiques, and Revisions of Functional Theory

A number of studies have been conducted to test the propositions of functional theory. In order to test the propositions, researchers have (a) assessed the extent to which groups exhibit the communicative behaviors that will lead to the satisfaction of important group functions and (b) assessed the extent to which the decisions reached can be judged as effective or high-quality decisions. Typically, group process is assessed through coding videotapes of group interaction, often using multiple coders and a specific coding scheme such as the function oriented interaction coding system (Hirokawa, 1985, 1987). The output variable, decision quality, is judged with the use of some objective standard or through the assessments of expert judges. Functional theory would then predict that

groups making higher-quality decisions will be marked by higher levels of functional communication behavior.

Results of these studies have been somewhat mixed (see reviews by Gouran & Hirokawa, 1996; Gouran et al., 1993; Hirokawa & Salazar, 1999). In almost all studies guided by functional theory, one or more of the communication functions has been related to effective decision making. However, studies often point to different functions as being particularly important. As Hirokawa and Salazar (1999) summarize,

> Of all the criticisms leveled against research conducted from the Functional Perspective, the most irrefutable concerns its inconsistency. That is, although group decision performance has been found to be correlated with the enactment of a variety of functional communicative behaviors, the specific functions that correlate with group performance tend to vary from study to study. (p. 182)

For example, Hirokawa (1983) found that communicative behaviors related to establishing operating procedures and analyzing the problem were particularly important in reaching high-quality decisions. In contrast, Graham, Papa, and McPherson (1997) found that communication related to establishing evaluative criteria and evaluating positive aspects of alternative solutions was most important in predicting group outcomes. In short, communication regarding important group functions does matter in influencing the quality of decisions made in groups. However, the research in this tradition has yet to develop a detailed and nuanced picture of which functions are most important under various decision-making conditions.

One response to these inconsistent results has been to call for more careful research in terms of definition, measurement, and experimental control (see Gouran et al., 1993). Indeed, Hirokawa and Salazar (1999) argue that "the crux of the problem lies in the insensitivity to task differences in current explanations of the perspective" (p. 182). However, other commentators have suggested that shortcomings of functional theory reside not in research design and execution but in the heart of the framework itself. Specifically, two important critiques of functional theory have been put forth.

First, critics have charged that functional theory is very narrowly defined and applies only to zero-history and ad hoc groups—typically groups of college students making decisions about fabricated problem situations. To some extent, this criticism is one of research design, and several studies have been conducted to assess the extent to which the tenets of functional theory will hold in nonlaboratory settings, that is, in real organizations with real employees making real decisions (see, e.g., Graham et al., 1997; Hirokawa & Keyton, 1995; Propp & Nelson, 1996). These studies have demonstrated that the propositions of functional theory can be applied to some extent to actual organizational settings. However, Stohl and Holmes (1993) have taken this critique one step further in proposing that the very boundary conditions built into the assumptions of functional theory (see Table 13.1) limit it to ad hoc and zero-history groups. That is, these scholars argue that the assumptions that the

group is motivated and able to solve the problem, that resources are adequate, that the choice is nonobvious, and that tasks are specifiable can be accomplished only in zero-history groups. In groups that are embedded in organizations, other factors such as politics, shifting group boundaries, information deficits, lack of training, and the like will always preclude the group from satisfying these basic conditions.

Second, there is the related concern that functional theory is relevant only for task-related groups and task-related functions within groups, with tasks defined in relatively narrow ways (see Poole, 1999, for a summary). However, groups are often more complex than this. Effectiveness can be judged on an individual level or a group level (e.g., one member might gain a great deal of insight and experience even from a group that doesn't make the "right" decision). Effectiveness can be judged on a long-term and short-term basis. And, perhaps most important, groups do a lot more than just attend to tasks. They socialize, they exercise power, and they work on side projects. As Billingsley (1993) summarizes,

> Our understanding of groups is based on many factors, task being only one. The functional perspective places task accomplishment as key to understanding the process and effectiveness of group communication. However, process itself rests upon more than task, and framing it simply through task leaves out much of what makes group communication unique, such as its developmental patterns, its idiosyncrasies, and its influence on members' behaviors, both in the group and outside of it. (p. 617)

The authors of functional theory have begun to respond to these critiques. For example, Gouran and Hirokawa (1996), based on work by Janis (1989) on the constraints that hamper the effectiveness of groups, have proposed that effective group communication will respond to a wide range of possible negative factors, including cognitive constraints (e.g., a task when time or information is limited), affiliative constraints (e.g., relational concerns hamper the quality of a group's performance), or egocentric constraints (e.g., when one member of a group has a high need for control). Moves such as these could take functional theory past the bounds that have been criticized as too narrow. However, at this point these ideas are templates for future work that have yet to be realized in either theoretical elaboration or empirical research.

■ STRUCTURATIONAL APPROACHES

For our second major theoretical approach to communication in small groups, we once again return to Anthony Giddens and **structuration theory.** Recall that structuration theory was discussed in Chapter 5 as an influence on the general ontological and axiological positions held in the development of critical theory. The theory was raised again in Chapter 12 as an important theoretical position in organizational communication. In this chapter, we look at how ideas from structuration theory have been used to inform theory in the area of group interaction and decision making. We first review some of the key concepts of structuration theory, particularly those that have most strongly influenced small group theorists. Then we consider two ways in which structurational ideas have been used in understanding small groups—first by examining the argumentative discourse that typically characterizes small group interaction and then by looking at how technology can influence the process and outcomes of group decision making.

Structuration Theory Revisited

Because the key ideas of structuration theory (Giddens, 1976, 1979, 1984) have been developed in earlier parts of this book (see Chapters 5 and 12), the presentation here will be brief. For a more thorough consideration of structuration theory as adapted within communication studies, see Banks and Riley (1993). For a discussion of structuration theory as applied to small group communication research, see Poole, Seibold,

and McPhee (1986, 1996). A number of concepts are worth reiterating here, though, with special attention to their relevance for small group communication.

At the heart of structuration theory is the concept of the **duality of structure.** This concept suggests that action and structure are intrinsically intertwined such that "action relies for its achievement on tacit knowledge of histories of social and cultural practices and agents' own personal biographies, and it simultaneously reproduces and further reinscribes into knowledge those histories and biographies as consequences and concomitants of its accomplishment" (Banks & Riley, 1993, p. 173). In other words, our practices of social life depend on the rules and resources (i.e., the structures) through which we can get things done. However, these structures are created, maintained, and changed through our action.

Consider an example of small group interaction. Imagine that you are a member of a jury in the civil trial of a corporation being accused of firing an individual because of the individual's age or race. When you enter the jury room you have a set of rules and resources that you can use to guide your interaction. These rules and resources are the structures of jury deliberation (see Sunwolf and Seibold, 1998). Several points about these structures are important. First, these structures exist only in each juror's mind. Until they are drawn upon in interaction during the jury deliberation process, they are simply memory traces. Second, these structures will vary in specificity and content. There might be structures that guide group interaction in general (e.g., "don't interrupt when someone else has the floor"), structures that guide jury interaction in particular (e.g., "take a vote first to see where everyone stands, and then begin discussion"), and structures that guide decisions about wrongful termination in employment situations (e.g., "the only reason you can be fired from your job is if you have been derelict in your duties"). Third, these structures will be held differently by various jurors. Some in the group might have well-codified ideas about how juries behave,

Table 13.3	Modalities in Structuration Theory		
	Modalities of meaning	Modalities of control	Modalities of morality
Action and practice level	Communication	Power	Sanction
Structures level	Interpretive schemes	Facilities	Norms
Institutional level	Signification	Domination	Legitimation

Source: Adapted from Poole et al. (1986) and Banks & Riley (1993).

whereas others might have only vague ideas of the rules for jury deliberation. Finally, these structures have been created from a variety of sources: from prior jury service, from media accounts of juries, from workplace experiences with discrimination and proper or improper firing, from discussions with friends, and from experience in other small groups.

During jury deliberations, these structures are drawn on and serve to influence action. And, in action, jurors can look at their behavior (because people act as **reflexive agents**) and note the extent to which structures are being used in interaction. That is, jurors can monitor their behavior and give accounts for what has happened and why. This might lead to a juror noting that a few people are dominating discussion and suggesting that more people be encouraged to speak. Finally, through interaction, structures can be reinforced, changed, or even created. For example, the interactions of this jury might reinforce a rule in the minds of jurors that workers cannot be dismissed from their job because of age or race. There might also be new structures that emerge from this interaction about how individuals should be compensated for wrongful termination in the workplace or how arguments can be formulated to convince others of your position in group discussion. These structures will then be taken by the jurors (as memory traces) into subsequent interactions with other groups.

Several other concepts from structuration theory are important in the application to small group interaction. The concept of a **system** in structuration theory, for example, points to the notion that when structures are consistently enacted across space and time, the pattern of social relationships and structures becomes institutionalized. Structuration theory also highlights several **modalities,** or forms of knowledgeability, that operate at the levels of action, structure, and institution. These modalities consider "interpretive schemes in communication processes, . . . norms that guide behavior and undergird judgments about others, . . . and facilities in power and influence processes" (Poole et al., 1996, p. 122). These modalities can be seen at the level of action, structures, and institutions, as illustrated in Table 13.3. Finally, various structures do not work independently in action, which points to the importance of considering the relationship—or interpenetration—among structures (Poole et al., 1996). Poole et al. point out, for instance, that structures can mediate each other (e.g., when a structural rule for democracy mediates a structural rule for taking turns in talk) or they can contradict each other (e.g., when a structural rule for relying on expertise in the group contradicts a structural rule for letting everyone participate).

These concepts—the duality of structure, the reflexivity of action, the institutionalization of systems, the modalities of structure, and the interpenetration of structures—have been instrumental in crafting structurational understandings of small group interaction and decision making. In the next two sections, we consider two lines of theory and research that have drawn on concepts from structuration theory in proposing specific explanations of small group communication. Specifically, we look at the structuration of group arguments and the adaptive structuration understanding of technology in small group communication.

The Structuration of Group Arguments

David Seibold, Renee Meyers, and their colleagues have undertaken a line of research that uses structuration theory as a foundation for understanding the argumentative discourse that is the basis of many small group discussions (see Meyers & Brashers, 1999, for general review and discussion of the role of argument and influence processes in group interaction). Meyers & Seibold (1990) begin by critiquing two dominant perspectives for understanding argument in small groups. One of these, the **cognitive-informational tradition** (exemplified by Hample, 1981, or Burnstein, 1982), focuses on argument as a thought (i.e., cognition) within the individual and the process of group interaction as simply one way of presenting these arguments so that they can be considered by others in the group. The consideration of arguments by the individual is critical in this perspective. As Meyers and Seibold (1990) explain, "Interaction may evoke or stimulate cognitive processing (e.g., self-argumentation), thereby indirectly affecting argument generation and opinion change, but interaction is not considered a direct cause of influence or opinion change" (p. 270).

A second approach to argument in interaction is the **social-interactional tradition** (exemplified by Jacobs & Jackson, 1982), which sees argument not as something that happens within an individual but as a language game that is organized and guided by social rules and institutions. Jackson and Jacobs (1983) position their ideas in opposition to the cognitive-informational tradition, stating that "conversational argument and influence are collaborative activities; influence is not something that a speaker does to an addressee, nor is a line of argument developed from the plan of a single speaker" (p. 274). In-

stead, the social-interactional tradition sees arguments as collaboratively produced messages that emerge in interaction and that are a process of mutual interactive influence (Meyers & Seibold, 1990, p. 274).

Clearly, the cognitive-informational and social-interactional positions on argument stand in sharp contrast to each other. Is argument something that is in a person's head or something that emerges during conversation? Meyers & Seibold (1987, 1990) propose that a structurational approach to group argument can transcend these two entrenched positions. Specifically, they propose that argument should be conceived as a social practice that is produced and reproduced in interaction by drawing on the rules and resources (i.e., the structures) for arguing. "Arguments are produced in use, but reproduced through use; they are both medium and outcome of interaction" (Meyers & Seibold, 1990, p. 285). The structures of group argument can be idiosyncratic or shared, and they can deal with the content or the form of the argument. These structures, in essence,

> constitute the generative mechanism by which statements relating to the reasons for supporting or opposing given alternatives and the peculiar manner in which they are expressed become manifest. The social practices of which arguments are composed, in turn, affect individual and collective rules and resources. (Gouran, 1990, p. 318)

A structurational approach to group argument, then, links the cognitive-informational and social-interactional perspectives in the literature. Arguments do exist in the heads of individuals, in the form of rules and resources regarding both the content and the form of argument. But these structures become manifest only in interaction, and that interaction can in turn transform the individual and collective structures regarding the argument at hand or regarding the process of argument in general. To date, limited research has investigated these ideas (see Canary, Brossman, & Seibold, 1987; Meyers, 1989), but this approach points to the role structuration theory can play in transcending disparate positions and in stimulating further integrative research.

Adaptive Structuration Theory

A second use of structuration theory in the group context has been undertaken by Scott Poole and Gerardine DeSanctis and has generated a number of studies by other researchers as well. **Adaptive structuration theory** uses basic concepts from Giddens's structuration theory but adapts them to a particular context and a particular level of analysis, resulting in a situated theory of structuration (Poole, 1999, p. 50). Specifically, the theory uses structurational ideas to explore micro-level processes (e.g., processes of interaction) in group situations that involve the use of information and communication technology. As DeSanctis and Poole (1994) summarize, the theory "provides a model that describes the interplay between advanced information technologies, social structures, and human interaction" (p. 125).

One technology that has been of particular interest in the development of adaptive structuration theory is the **group decision support system** (GDSS). A GDSS is a system designed to assist problem-solving teams through the use of computer, communication, and decision technologies (for complete descriptions, see Poole & DeSanctis, 1992; Scott, Quinn, Timmerman, & Garrett, 1998). GDSSs have several qualities that contribute to the decision-making process, including the facilitation of anonymous communication, the potential for equalizing participation, and the potential for removing undue influence of particular group members (Scott et al., 1998). These qualities are made possible through technical features of the GDSS, including agenda setting, decision modeling methods, structured group methods, rules for group interaction, private and public messaging, and vote tabulation (Poole & DeSanctis, 1992).

Adaptive structuration theory attempts to explain the ways users of GDSSs and other technological systems "appropriate structures and adapt them to their own purposes, [resulting in] a configuration of structures-in-use specific to

the system" (Poole & DeSanctis, 1992, p. 10). Though a complete description of the theory's explanations is beyond the scope of this chapter, several key ideas are worth highlighting. These involve the nature of structures in technological group situations and the process through which these structures are appropriated within group interaction.

The theory makes an interesting distinction in discussing the structures (i.e., the rules and resources) at play in technologically mediated groups. Specifically, it distinguishes between the *spirit* of the structure, or the general value that is promoted by the technology, and the specific *structural features* of the technology that are designed to enable that spirit to be realized in group interaction. For example, a GDSS includes features such as anonymous input of ideas and voting tools. The spirit of these structural features—as intended by the designers of the GDSS—is to enhance democratic decision making. However, as Poole et al. (1996) point out, "Features are functionally independent of spirit and may be used in ways inconsistent with it" (p. 132). This leads us to the concept of **appropriation,** which is central to the theory.

Adaptive structuration theory sees appropriation as a process "by which structural features are adapted to specific groups and circumstances, and which may lead to structural innovation and change" (Poole, 1999, p. 49). Appropriation is proposed to occur through "a series of *structuring moves*" (Poole et al., 1996, p. 132). These moves are micro-level actions (e.g., the behavior of group members) through which the structural features of the technology (or presumably other rules and resources of interaction) can be adopted or adapted. Poole and DeSanctis (1992) identified 37 "moves," or ways in which appropriation can occur. These moves were then divided into nine categories, summarized in Table 13.4. As this table indicates, appropriation can be relatively straightforward, it can involve the change of structures, and it can involve more than one structure in the appropriation process. For example, *direct appropriation* is a simple and straightforward move, whereas

SPOTLIGHT ON THE THEORIST

M. Scott Poole

M. Scott Poole received his Ph.D. from the University of Wisconsin in 1980. He has taught at the University of Illinois and the University of Minnesota and is now a professor at Texas A&M University. Poole is well known for his research in small group communication and organizational communication as well as for his expertise in research methodology and theory development. Indeed, his interest in these areas began early in his academic life. He recounts that "from my undergraduate years, I have been fascinated by the way in which social life seems to be determined by deeper layers of power, motivation, and symbolism." He believes that he has been fortunate to have been surrounded by other academics who have helped him grapple with these ideas. At the University of Illinois, he and colleagues Bob McPhee and Dave Seibold worked on the basic application of structuration theory to group communication, and he moved this interest into the area of group decision technology when he met Gerry DeSanctis at the University of Minnesota. Poole clearly recognizes the value of collaboration in both theory-building and research, commenting, "I have been exceptionally lucky to have been blessed with wonderful, stimulating colleagues."

Poole makes the distinction between the development of "Theory with a capital 'T' "—the development of an overarching theory of structuration in group interaction, and "theory with a small 't'," in which theories are developed to explain specific phenomena such as group development and the influence of group decision support systems. In Poole's mind, these two kinds of theorizing inform each other. As he notes, "Most of the individual studies I have done seem to me to contribute most to the development of theory [with a small t]; but each contributes an insight or piece to the development of Theory [with a capital T] as well." He also emphasizes the importance of testing theories with methods appropriate to the theory and phenomenon at hand. Structuration theory, for instance, "calls for the development of novel methods, since it asks researchers to study unobservable structures that are potentially dynamic over time."

Given Poole's emphasis on theory (and Theory), it is not surprising that he advises new scholars to guide their work in theoretical ways. He observes that "problem-driven research is interesting and useful" but believes that the most impact comes from research with a strong theoretical base. Poole also provides advice for students learning about and evaluating theory. He cautions that students shouldn't look for "truth" in theorizing but should instead evaluate theory in terms of the story it tells about human communication and behavior. Harkening back to our discussions in Chapter 6, Poole advises that students should "look for a convincing narrative, because that is what a theory really is." It is clear from Poole's impact on the field of group communication that the narratives told by his theoretical accounts have a great deal of value for both practitioners and researchers.

---

combination might involve a complex—and perhaps even paradoxical—use of technological features.

Adaptive structuration theory has also made the simpler distinction between a *faithful appropriation*, in which the structures are appropriated in a way consistent with the spirit of the technology, and an *ironic appropriation*, in which structures are appropriated in ways contrary to the intended use of the technology. For example, Scott et al.

(1998) point to a number of ways in which the anonymity feature of GDSSs can be adapted. A faithful appropriation of the technology would involve the facilitation of democratic votes in which all felt comfortable expressing their conscience. An ironic appropriation might involve using the anonymity feature to surreptitiously identify the source of some comments without the knowledge of the source. This appropriation would undermine the intended use of a GDSS.

Table 13.4	Categories of Appropriation Moves in Adaptive Structuration Theory
Move category	**Description**
Direct appropriation	Actively using the structure in a manner that is either explicit or implicit
Substitution	Using another structure in place of one that is being proposed for direct use
Combination	Incorporating two structures together in a way that is either consistent (composition) or inconsistent (paradox)
Enlargement	Relating two structures through allusion or metaphor to gain an understanding of structures in use
Constraint	Narrowing a structure to gain a better understanding of it or to use it more effectively
Contrast	Understanding one structure in light of another structure
Affirmation	Indicating that the group endorses the appropriation or interpretation of a structure
Negation	Indicating that the group disagrees with the appropriation or interpretation of a structure
Ambiguity/neutrality	Indicating uncertainty or confusion or neither agreeing nor disagreeing with the appropriation or interpretation of a structure

Source: From Poole & DeSanctis (1992, pp. 18–20).

This review has covered only some of the ideas and research proposed by adaptive structuration theory (see Poole et al., 1996, for more complete review). The theory clearly has both promise and shortcomings. It is a promising approach in that it has taken the relatively abstract ideas of structuration theory and put them to use in explaining group interactions that are of great importance in contemporary society. This micro-level explanation has generated careful research that has illuminated much about the ways actors in groups use the structures of technology, and the structures of groups in general, in their interaction (see, e.g., Contractor & Seibold, 1993; Contractor, Seibold, & Heller, 1996; Poole & DeSanctis, 1992; Poole, Holmes, & DeSanctis, 1991; Scott et al., 1998). However, adaptive structuration theory takes but a small portion of structuration theory into account, and some might argue that this appropriation of structuration theory is not faithful to

the original work of Giddens (see Banks & Riley, 1993, p. 179). Indeed, Poole and his colleagues have acknowledged that the theory is, indeed, an adaptation and that the complexity of the concepts in structuration theory requires complex research designs that allow the scholar to consider "a duality that continuously and instantaneously produces and reproduces itself and, in the bargain, involves both macrolevel social institutions and microlevel behavior" (Poole, 1999, p. 51).

■ SYMBOLIC CONVERGENCE THEORY

As we turn now to the final major theory we consider in this chapter, we need to switch gears a bit. To do this, think about a group in your present or your past that you feel particularly connected to—a group you enjoyed being a member of, a group whose get-togethers felt less like meeting and more like communing. This group might be a social group (e.g., a fraternity or sorority, a book club, simply a group of friends), or it might be a task-related group (e.g., a class project group, a work team, a committee at church). Then think about the communication that was (or is) typical of interaction in that group. Chances are, that communication is marked by many shared stories, by a common way of referring to things, by inside jokes that may be funny only to people in the group. Chances are, also, that this group didn't start out as such a community. Instead, the sense of shared group consciousness probably developed over time, through frequent gatherings and a great deal of interaction.

Understanding the processes through which some groups develop this sense of community and group consciousness—and others don't—is the goal of **symbolic convergence theory.** Symbolic convergence theory is a wide-ranging theory of communication (Bormann [1980] refers to it as a general theory of communication), and its attendant methodology, fantasy theme analysis, has been used in many rhetorical studies of public and mass-mediated communication. However, the theory had its genesis in the analysis of small group communication, and its theoretical explanatory mechanisms (as opposed to its methodology) are still most applicable to the small group context. Thus, the following discussion deals primarily with symbolic convergence within group settings. We first consider the precursors to the development of symbolic convergence theory. Then we look at the theory's major components and how they fit together and discuss some explanations of when and why symbolic convergence will occur in small groups.

Theoretical Precursors and Original Development

Symbolic convergence theory was developed by a group of scholars at the University of Minnesota in the 1960s and 1970s. These scholars, led by Ernest Bormann, were interested in the processes through which group discussions developed

and through which decisions were made in groups. The researchers used a case study form of analysis, in which the transcripts of group meetings were analyzed and the natural language of the groups was considered in rhetorical terms.

In analyzing these case studies, the Minnesota group noticed many instances in which the group would take off on a given topic. There might be a lull in the conversation, someone would jump in with a joke or a story, others would laugh or add pieces to the story, and soon the group would be rolling again on the original or a new topic. In trying to understand this group phenomenon, the Minnesota researchers were drawn to ongoing work in social psychology that we considered briefly earlier in this chapter—Bales's work in interaction process analysis (Bales, 1950). Recall that Bales was concerned with how groups satisfied the various functions they must perform, and he developed a coding scheme for analyzing the interaction of task-related groups. One of his categories was "shows tension release." This category (later relabeled as "dramatizes" [Bales, 1970]) served as an impetus for the Minnesota researchers. But rather than looking at the psychological processes through which tension is released in group situations, these scholars turned to a consideration of the symbolic and rhetorical nature of this communicative process in small group interaction. To summarize, symbolic convergence theory seeks to explain "the way in which two or more private symbolic worlds incline toward each other, come more closely together, or even overlap during certain processes of communication" (Bormann, 1983, p. 102).

The Symbolic Convergence Framework

Like many theories, symbolic convergence theory consists of technical terms that are not used in the same way in the theory as they are used in natural conversation. Some scholars have criticized this use of familiar terms in unfamiliar ways (e.g., Farrell, 1980; Gronbeck, 1980; Mohrmann, 1980), but proponents of the theory defend its terminology as technical language that must be understood within the theory's analytical framework (e.g., Bormann,

Cragan, & Shields, 1994). Indeed, we have encountered several theories in which common terms are used in ways that belie their common usage, for example, the term *structure* in structuration theory. Thus, in symbolic convergence theory, as in all theories, it is important to lay out relevant terms and consider how these concepts fit together within the theoretical framework.

Concepts in Symbolic Convergence Theory
The theory's central concept is the **fantasy theme.** A fantasy theme is a dramatizing message—perhaps a pun, story, analogy, figure of speech, or double entendre—that ignites group interaction. The dramatizing message is never in the here and now. The fantasy theme, instead, always refers to something outside of the immediate time and space of group experience. For example, a fight that breaks out in the midst of a group meeting might be seen as dramatic, but it is not a dramatizing message or a fantasy theme because it is not outside of the here and now. In contrast, a story about a fight, or a reference to a fight seen on television the night before, would each have the potential to be a fantasy theme.

Very often in groups, dramatizing messages such as puns, jokes, or stories seem to fall on deaf ears. They have no effect on subsequent interaction. However, sometimes the group picks up on the message. People in the group embellish the story, join in on the punchline, or perhaps share in the sorrow of the dramatizing message with their own related narratives. In symbolic convergence theory, this participation is known as a **fantasy chain,** and when this so-called chaining-out happens, the individuals have shared in a **group fantasy.** The sharing of group fantasies is the most critical aspect of the theory, for it is in the sharing of group fantasies that groups develop a sense of community and shared identity. As Bormann et al. (1994) explain,

> When people share a fantasy they make sense out of what before may well have been a confusing state of affairs and do so in common with the others who share the fantasy with them. They have created a group consciousness and have come to share some symbolic common ground. They can

then talk with one another about that shared interpretation with code words or brief allusions like the inside joke in a small group. (p. 281)

These fantasy themes often become linked with each other in group interaction. When this happens, what develops is called a **fantasy type,** or "a general scenario that covers several of the more concrete fantasy themes" (Bormann et al., 1994, p. 281). For example, an organizational group might have a number of fantasy themes related to the ineptitude of a particular supervisor in the company. Themes within this fantasy type would be related in the consciousness of the group, and they would all be accessed in interaction through similar symbolic cues. At an even more abstract level, these fantasy types can be linked in a **rhetorical vision.** These rhetorical visions are often referenced in slogans or labels (e.g., referring to a particular group as a "cutting-edge committee" or as "just like a family").

Symbolic convergence theorists have done a great deal to identify ways of analyzing these fantasies and visions. Rhetorical scholars have identified the dramatic structure of rhetorical visions, including a consideration of the dramatic personae, plotlines, and themes of rhetorical visions (see Cragan & Shields, 1994, for discussion). For example, a fantasy theme might have an identifiable hero and villain and a moral that is relevant to group functioning. Scholars (e.g., Bormann, 1982) have also considered the types of rhetorical visions that dominate social interaction such as a *righteous master analogue* (stressing concepts of right and wrong, moral and immoral, just and unjust), a *social master analogue* (stressing concepts of humanity, community, and caring), and a *pragmatic master analogue* (stressing concepts of effectiveness, efficiency, and utility). These issues of the specific content of symbolic convergence have been important in considerations of public rhetoric that have used fantasy theme analysis. However, in the area of small group communication, these specific plotlines and story themes are not as important as the function that symbolic convergence serves in the small group context.

The Impact of Symbolic Convergence Scholars in the symbolic convergence tradition believe that the sharing of group fantasies and the process of symbolic convergence can serve a number of specific functions in the group context. One of the most basic functions is creating a common identity and identifying who is "in" and "out" of the group. In essence, this function points to the importance of fantasy themes in creating a sense of community. As Bormann (1996) explains, "Fantasies that clearly divide the sympathetic or good people (we) from the unsympathetic or evil people (they) aid the group's self-awareness and are crucial to the emergence of its consciousness" (p. 105).

Two examples in very different types of groups serve to illustrate this role of symbolic convergence in forging group identity. Lesch (1994) studied storytelling in a witches' coven from a symbolic convergence framework in order to consider the ways in which group consciousness was sustained over time. She found that "dramatistic rhetorical acts mark group members' efforts to preserve the coven while adapting to the inevitable antagonistic forces of time and change" (p. 81). In a very different type of group, L. L. Putnam, Van Hoeven, and Bullis (1991) analyzed interaction in a collective bargaining context and found that each group in the negotiation developed a distinct group identity through the sharing of group fantasies. These fantasies also served to establish connections between the groups, however, and, as a result, facilitated the negotiation process. As the authors note, "Opposition to outsiders, unification through common enemies, and references to the turbulent past united the two sides and deterred them from overt expression of their differences and hostilities" (p. 99).

Beyond this notion of group identity and community, however, symbolic convergence scholars believe that fantasies about group process can aid in group decision-making, group motivation, and group creativity (Bormann, 1996). For example, a group might return frequently to stories of its tendency to make decisions on the spur of the moment or

might joke about the group's intuitive nature. Fantasy themes like these could influence the extent to which systematic problem solving is valued (and used) in group interaction. However, these outcomes occur through the more basic processes of establishing group identity. As Poole (1999) states, "Symbolic Convergence Theory does not posit deterministic relationships concerning the . . . effects of symbolic convergence on other group processes and outcomes. Instead, it indicates how the grounds for group identity and collective action are constituted" (p. 47).

Explanations for Convergence in Small Group Communication

Thus, symbolic convergence theorists have considered the processes through which fantasies are shared in group settings and the possible consequences of the introduction and sharing of group fantasies. But when will the sharing of fantasies occur? Are some groups more likely to reach symbolic convergence than others? What individual in the group will introduce fantasy themes to the interaction? Why will some groups chain-out and others not? Bormann (1996) notes that these questions regarding the antecedents of symbolic convergence (in essence, the "why" questions of the theory) are the most difficult to answer and that much work remains to be done in this area. However, theorists identify three factors that have been considered as precursors to the symbolic convergence process.

First, following Bales (1970), symbolic convergence theorists suggest that the individual needs and the psychodynamic characteristics of group members might influence the sharing and chaining of fantasy themes. Second, it is possible that the common concerns developed during group interaction might provide particularly fertile ground for the sharing of fantasies. Finally, it is likely that the rhetorical skill of group members might influence the extent to which fantasy themes are developed. For example, a particularly talented joker or storyteller might be more likely to introduce fantasy themes and spur the chaining of those themes in group interaction than a shy and retiring member of the group.

■ COMPARISON AND COMMENTARY

The three theories we considered in this chapter provide very different kinds of understanding about group interaction. Functional theory is the most post-positivist of the theories in that it clearly identifies communicative concepts proposed to predict the extent to which a group will make effective and productive decisions. Functional theory has clearly delineated boundaries, variables that can be conceptually and operationally specified, and a methodological tradition for coding both the interaction within the group and the effectiveness of the decisions the group makes. In contrast, symbolic convergence theory springs from interpretive and rhetorical roots, considering the ways that narrative, symbolism, and ritual can influence the sense of identity and community within small group settings. Structurational approaches have social constructionist and critical precursors and provide a focus for considering how a variety of group phenomena are enacted in interaction and how they enable and constrain future interaction. Structurational approaches try to bridge the chasm of microscopic and macroscopic approaches and serve as a connection between approaches that emphasize action and those that emphasize constraint.

In spite of their diverse philosophical underpinnings, these theories have been instrumental in spurring a wide range of research in small group communication. In 1980, many commentators were bemoaning the death of the small group communication tradition and blaming its demise on the lack of interesting and insightful theory. A great deal of empirical research was being conducted during the 1960s and 1970s—often with the help of elaborate and clever laboratory research designs and extensive interactional coding schemes—but there was little theory-building to accompany the research. The 1980s, however, were marked by the develop-

ment of the theories we reviewed in this chapter, theories that go beyond the simple input-output models of group interaction and begin to answer questions of why groups communicate in the ways they do and how that communication influences the identity, behaviors, decisions, and outcomes of individuals and the group as a whole.

However, to a large extent, these theories have dealt only with specific kinds of groups and with specific kinds of interaction within those groups. For example, as we noted earlier, functional theory has been criticized because research stemming from its framework has relied primarily on zero-history and ad hoc groups (e.g., groups formed for the purpose of the research) in laboratory situations. Recent work has taken functional theory into the field, but the research continues to concentrate on clearly defined groups with clearly defined goals and process orientations. Structurational approaches and symbolic convergence theory have not always relied on laboratory studies, but they can be critiqued for considering largely intact groups with well-defined boundaries and tasks. As a result, the most movement in small group communication research has been to look to contextual factors that influence group process and to look at how groups are constituted and how they interact in natural settings. Indeed, an influential volume (Frey, 1994) concentrated exclusively on research emphasizing these notions of context and natural groups.

This move to the consideration of context and natural groups has also begun to influence theorizing in small group communication. One theory that is now emerging in the discipline has been particularly effective in responding to these issues. The **bona fide group perspective** was proposed by Linda Putnam and Cynthia Stohl (1990) and has been developed in subsequent work by these scholars and others (Stohl & Holmes, 1993; Stohl & Putnam, 1994; Putnam & Stohl, 1996). A bona fide group perspective acknowledges that in today's society and organizations, groups are rarely well-defined in terms of membership, context, or task. Instead, a "bona fide group approach is a theoretical perspective that treats a group as a social system linked to its context, shaped by fluid boundaries, and altering its environment. . . . Departing from traditional models, the bona fide group perspective casts decision making as a process that shapes and is shaped by dynamic group boundaries and multiple contexts" (Putnam & Stohl, 1996, p. 148). Though the bona fide group perspective is still developing, theorists using this framework highlight several aspects of the lived experience of groups that is often missing from traditional research and even from the theories we considered in this chapter:

- Bona fide groups are marked by shifting membership and permeable boundaries; individuals enter and leave groups as the needs of the group (and the individuals) shift. For instance, organizations often form task forces and committees in which membership is not fixed and changes from meeting to meeting.

- These permeable and shifting boundaries suggest that individuals within groups have multiple memberships and may need to deal with role conflict as a result. Individuals hold membership in many groups simultaneously, and this can both enrich and challenge interaction. These multiple memberships mean a huge range of resources are brought to each conversation, but also a wide range of goals and commitments must be considered. For example, the needs of a church's education committee might conflict with the same church's outreach committee. When there are individuals who are members of both groups, group interaction—and the reactions of individuals—become highly complex.

- Bona fide groups are highly interdependent with their contexts. Bona fide groups are clearly not zero-history or ad hoc groups. Instead, they are embedded within larger organizational and institutional systems that must be considered in understanding the interaction of the group. For example, church committees must respond to the needs of the full congregation and of the community as a whole.

These insights provide a sampling of some of the ideas from the bona fide group perspective. The perspective has been used in research on interdisciplinary health care teams (Bertiotti & Seibold, 1994), surgical teams (Lammers & Krikorian, 1997), and even gangs (Conquergood, 1991). The theory highlights the complexity associated with studying real groups, which is often absent from studies that have emanated from theoretical perspectives such as functional theory, adaptive structuration theory, and symbolic convergence theory. This is not to suggest, however, that these theoretical perspectives should be rejected. Indeed, the bona fide group perspective can be seen as a sensitizing concept for these theories. This move has already been made with regard to considering a functional perspective for bona fide groups (Stohl & Holmes, 1993). A similar move could also be made with symbolic convergence theory and structuration theory by examining how notions of embeddedness, interdependence, and shifting membership might influence the explanations of each of these frameworks.

Key Terms

group development
multiple sequence model
functional theory
groupthink
structuration theory
duality of structure
reflexive agents
system
modalities
cognitive-informational tradition
social-interactional tradition
group decision support system
appropriation
symbolic convergence theory
fantasy theme
rhetorical vision
fantasy chain

group fantasy
fantasy type
bona fide group perspective

Discussion Questions

1. How does functional theory try to support the notion that communication matters in group decision-making processes? Are particular types of communication helpful (or not helpful), according to the functional perspective?

2. Think about your communication theory class. Have any fantasy themes developed over the course of the class? How are these themes started and chained-out during interaction? How have these fantasy processes influenced groups in the class?

3. How do the uses of structuration theory presented in this chapter (i.e., with regard to group decision-making technology and group arguments) differ from the uses discussed in Chapter 12, on organizational communication?

4. In both organizational and small group communication studies, the container metaphor has been critiqued. How does the bona fide group perspective respond to that critique? What new metaphor does this perspective provide?

14 Theories of Media Processing and Effects

At the turn of the last century (i.e., from the 19th to the 20th), a discussion of communication media would have been a short one indeed. The only media of communication with any widespread use at that time were face-to-face interaction and print sources such as books and newspapers. Since then, however, the number of media types and sources has exploded. In a typical day, you likely access multiple media including newspapers, radio, network and cable television, the Internet and World Wide Web, telephone, electronic mail, video and audiotape, and the list goes on. Oh yes, and we *still* talk to each other in face-to-face conversations! In short, the volume of communication we are involved in has increased substantially, as has the variety of channels through which we send and receive messages. It is not surprising, then, that social scientists have been extremely interested in how contact with these media affects our beliefs, attitudes, interaction, and other behaviors.

In this chapter, we consider theories that deal primarily with the ways individuals access and process media content and the ways contact with mass media sources influences those individuals. We discuss four major theoretical approaches: social cognitive theory, uses and gratifications theory, media systems dependency theory, and theories of emotion and the media. Before we move on to these theoretical frameworks, however, it is important to put them in historical context.

Thus, we first take a brief historical trip through the study of media effects, concentrating on some important developments that occurred during the middle of the 20th century.

■ THE DEVELOPMENT OF MEDIA EFFECTS RESEARCH

Basic textbooks on mass communication (e.g., DeFleur & Ball-Rokeach, 1989; McQuail, 1994) point to a number of important developments in the history of mass communication. DeFleur and Ball-Rokeach (1989) chart the movement from "the age of signs and signals" to "the age of speech and language" to "the age of writing" to "the age of print." These ages, not surprisingly, span thousands of years of human development. However, not until "the age of mass communication" was ushered in by widespread distribution of newspapers (in the 19th century), by the development and popularization of motion pictures (at the turn of the 20th century), by the invention of radio and its adoption in many households (1920s through 1940s), and by the invention and diffusion of television (1950s and 1960s) could commentators really see the reach of communication media to mass audiences.

The history of mass communication research began in earnest in the 1920s and 1930s. During this time period, newspaper circulation increased and hence reached a widespread audience, motion pictures and other media were used extensively for national and social propaganda (e.g., during World War I) , and radio use was reaching a peak in the everyday lives of Americans. Thus, it is not surprising that social scientists wanted to understand the effects of these media on the way people thought and behaved. A recounting of the explanations of the time will undoubtedly oversimplify those views (see Lang & Lang, 1993); however, it is important to consider the development of ideas about how the mass media influence us in order to put current theories into proper focus.

The Bullet and the Needle

In the 1920s and 1930s, scholars were concerned with making sense of the influence of both wartime propaganda and what were seen as widespread effects of radio and newspapers on the attitudes of individual citizens. The words of Harold Lasswell, a prominent mass communication researcher during this time, reflect the thinking then. In *Propaganda Techniques in the World War*, Lasswell (1927) wrote,

> But when all allowances have been made and all extravagant estimates pared to the bone, the fact remains that propaganda is one of the most powerful instrumentalities in the modern world. . . . In the Great Society it is no longer possible to fuse the waywardness of individuals in the furnace of the war dance; a newer and subtler instrument must weld thousands and even millions of human beings into one amalgamated mass of hate and will and hope. A new flame must burn out the canker of dissent and temper the steel of bellicose enthusiasm. The name of this new hammer and anvil of social solidarity is propaganda. (pp. 220–221)

Thus, the view of media effects that developed during the 1920s and 1930s was one of very strong effects, for only a very powerful influence could "meld thousands and even millions of human beings into one amalgamated mass." This view has been labeled, in retrospect, by the memorable monikers of the **magic bullet effect** and the **hypodermic needle effect.** In short, these views see the mass media as capable of shaping public opinion and swaying behavior in whatever direction is preferred by the communicator. The media are seen to work as a magic bullet or a hypodermic needle, shooting the desires of the source directly into the thoughts, attitudes, and subsequent behaviors of the receivers.

The magic bullet theory seems quite simple and straightforward, but several points about this view of the media bear mentioning. Specifically, this view brings with it not only assumptions about the media but also assumptions about the audience. The audience in this formulation is seen as a mass society. DeFleur and Ball-Rokeach (1989) chart the development of this view of society, primarily through the work of sociologists in the 19th and early 20th centuries. These scholars (e.g., Auguste Comte, Herbert Spencer, and Emile Durkheim) looked at the increasing complexity of society through industrialization, urbanization, and other factors and concluded that individuals were becoming isolated and thus unable to form meaningful connections of community with each other. This view of the mass society emphasized the following characteristics (DeFleur & Ball-Rokeach, 1989, p. 159):

- Individuals are presumed to be in a situation of psychological isolation.
- Impersonality prevails in individuals' interactions with each other.
- Individuals are relatively free from the demands of binding informal social obligations.

Individuals in this conception of society were seen as easy targets of the magic bullets from the media. Individuals in a mass society were disconnected, or atomized; hence, the powerful media could affect them directly and strongly. As DeFleur and Ball-Rokeach (1989) summarize, "The media messages are received in a uniform way by every member of the audience and . . . immediate and direct responses are triggered by such stimuli" (p. 164).

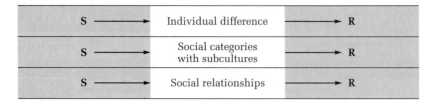

Figure 14.1   **Selective Influence Theories of Mass Media Effects** *Source:* From DeFleur & Ball-Rokeach (1989, p. 196).

Alternatives to Strong Effects

The magic bullet and hypodermic needle theories proposing strong effects of the mass media did not hold sway for long. Several factors served as an impetus to change thinking in this regard. First, on philosophical grounds, the picture of the individual as the unthinking and easy dupe of the media was untenable for many commentators. This model of humanity did not fit with beliefs of the time. Second, theoretical developments in psychology and sociology discredited the view of the individual inherent in theories of mass society. These developments emphasized both cognitive and social factors that needed to be considered. Finally, empirical research into the effects of the mass media on individuals provided data that were contrary to the **strong effects model.** Because of these philosophical, theoretical, and empirical developments, scholars began to look for factors that reduced the effects of the media, and the era of the **limited effects model** was ushered in.

The initial concept that media had limited effects was based not as much on a model of media content but on shifting views of the audience. In the parlance of basic psychological theory, a strong effects paradigm can be viewed as a simple stimulus-response (S-R) model. That is, the stimulus (i.e., the media) instigates a direct response in the individual (i.e., in the form of an attitude, belief, or behavior). In this model, no intervening process comes between the stimulus and the response. However, in the middle of the

20th century, a variety of alternatives to the basic S-R model were developed in psychology, and related ideas in mass communication research followed suit. In the most basic sense, these are labeled S-O-R models, in which some factor of the organism (O) is seen as coming between the stimulus and the response. In considering the mass media, these S-O-R models look at the ways media have selective influence on the responses of individuals. DeFleur and Ball-Rokeach (1989) have outlined three types of processes that replaced the magic bullet theory in the middle of the 20th century (Figure 14.1).

Figure 14.1 highlights several factors that might come between the magic bullet of the media and the responses of individuals. For example, the media might influence people with different personalities or at different stages of development in different ways. This type of explanation could elucidate, for instance, the differential effects of cartoon violence on children of different age groups. Second, the media could influence various groups of people in different ways. For example, cable television programming might be developed for specific social strata or interest groups and affect the attitudes and behaviors of only those subsets of individuals. Third, social relationships and interpersonal connections could influence the effects that media have on individuals. For example, Elihu Katz (1957) provided an early alternative to the strong effects paradigm in his conclusion that there is a two-step flow of influence for the mass media, in which the media influence opinion leaders with direct media contact and those opinion leaders in turn influence friends and family members.

Thus, as Figure 14.1 illustrates, mass communication scholars began to explore how the power of the media was limited by a variety of factors. Much of this research was scattered and haphazard, however, as scholars listed and investigated the factors that might limit strong effects. However, in the 1960s, ideas about the interplay between audience and media began to coalesce into several specific theoretical traditions. The first theory we consider here, social cognitive theory, takes the most specific look at the psychological processes that influence the relationship between mass media content and behavioral reactions of audience members.

◼ SOCIAL COGNITIVE THEORY

As media theorists moved away from the strong effects models of the magic bullet injecting its content into the undifferentiated mass audience and toward limited effects models, many scholars relied on psychological theories that distinguished between S-R models and S-O-R models. In other words, theorists began to ask about what human qualities—in particular, what psychological qualities—came between the stimulus of the media message and the audience's response. One of the most obvious conceptualizations for this role of the organism (i.e., the "O") is to see people as learners whose cognitions could make a difference in the acquisition of new attitudes and behaviors. Thus, turning to learning theories made a great deal of sense in the middle of the 20th century.

Early psychologists in the behaviorist mode (e.g., John B. Watson and B. F. Skinner) were concerned with the extent to which human action is a conditioned response to external stimuli. This behaviorist point of view— represented by processes labeled as *operant conditioning*—is an S-R model that suggests that humans learn by being rewarded (e.g., receiving positive reinforcement) or punished (e.g., re-

ceiving negative reinforcement) when they respond to a particular stimulus. For example, imagine that a child bites her nails. Her parents might paint her nails with bitter nail polish so that she will receive negative reinforcement every time she tries to bite them. Or a parent might promise a reward like a new toy if the nails are grown to a particular length. By directly rewarding and punishing behavior, the parents are hoping the child will learn the preferred behavior.

However, operant conditioning is an inefficient way to learn things. Imagine, for instance, that we had to learn about the dangers of encountering fire only through direct reward and punishment when confronted with this stimulus: The hospitals would be full of burn victims! It simply doesn't make sense to presume that everyone has to learn everything through direct experience. Thus, it seems obvious that humans learn in other ways, and one of the most important alternative routes to learning is through watching others who are demonstrating behaviors (and perhaps being rewarded or punished for those behaviors) and imitating those behaviors. As Bandura (1977b) argues,

> Observational learning is vital for both development and survival. Because mistakes can produce costly, or even fatal, consequences, the prospects for survival would be slim indeed if one could learn only by suffering the consequences of trial and error. For this reason, one does not teach children to swim, adolescents to drive automobiles, and novice medical students to perform surgery by having them discover the appropriate behavior through the consequences of their successes and failures. The more costly and hazardous the possible mistakes, the heavier is the reliance on observational learning from competent examples. (p. 237)

The concept of learning through observation and imitation was first proposed in the psychological literature by N. E. Miller and Dollard (1941). These researchers posited that if humans were motivated to learn a particular behavior, they would be able to learn by observing models and then being positively reinforced by imitating those models. These ideas were the first version of **social learning theory.**

Since these early ideas were proposed about the role of imitation in the acquisition of behavior, theoretical thinking about social learning has developed. The leader in the development of social learning theory (relabeled in the 1970s and 1980s as **social cognitive theory**) has been Albert Bandura. Bandura's first key ideas in the area (Bandura, 1962) further developed Miller and Dollard's earlier ideas about imitative learning. In more recent publications, Bandura has elaborated on the process of social learning and on cognitive and behavioral factors that influence the learning process (see, e.g., Bandura, 1969, 1977a, 1977b, 1986, 1994, 1995). In the next few sections, we outline some of the key components of social cognitive theory and then discuss how it has been instrumental in studying the effects of mass media presentations on individuals in the audience.

Key Concepts in Social Cognitive Theory

As should already be clear, the key concept in social cognitive theory is the notion of **observational learning.** When there are models in an individual's environment—perhaps friends or family members in the interpersonal environment, people from public life, or figures in the news or entertainment media—then learning can occur through the observation of these models. Sometimes the behavior can be acquired simply through the modeling process. Modeling, or imitation, is "the direct, mechanical reproduction of behavior" (Baran & Davis, 2000, p. 184). As Baranowski, Perry, and Parcel (1997) point out, "This process accounts for family members' often having common behavioral patterns" (p. 160). Modeling processes can also be seen with regard to media sources. That is, you might learn a new trick for rolling out pie dough simply by watching a cooking show on television. But there are times when simple modeling is not enough to influence or change behavior. In these cases, social cognitive theo-

rists turn to the basic operant conditioning concepts of rewards and punishments but place those concepts in a social learning context.

Baranowski et al. (1997) state that *"reinforcement* is the primary construct in the operant form of learning" (p. 161). Reinforcement processes are also central to social learning processes. In social cognitive theory, reinforcement works through the processes of inhibitory effects and disinhibitory effects. An **inhibitory effect** occurs when an individual sees a model being punished for a particular behavior. Observing this punishment will decrease the likelihood of the observer performing that same behavior. For example, social cognitive theory would predict that when we observe criminals on television being incarcerated for their misdeeds, we will be less likely to engage in crime. In contrast, a **disinhibitory effect** occurs when an individual sees a model being rewarded for a particular behavior. In this situation, the observer will be more likely to perform the behavior. For example, if a character on a situation comedy is rewarded for deceptive behavior, social cognitive theory would predict that the observer will be more likely to engage in similar behavior.

The effects posited here depend not on actual rewards and punishments but instead on vicarious reinforcement. According to Bandura (1986), vicarious reinforcement works because of the concepts of outcome expectations and outcome expectancies. **Outcome expectations** suggest that when we see models being rewarded and punished, we come to expect the same outcomes if we perform the same behavior. As Baranowski et al. (1997) state, "People develop expectations about a situation and expectations for outcomes of their behavior before they actually encounter the situation" (p. 162). Furthermore, individuals attach value to these expectations in the form of **outcome expectancies.** These expectancies consider the extent to which any particular reinforcement observed is seen as a reward or a punishment. This highlights the notion that different things are rewarding to different people and that the value of the reward to the particular individual will influence the extent to which social learning will occur.

This is the basic process of learning posited in social cognitive theory. However, several other concepts posited in the theory will influence the extent to which social learning takes place. For example, if an individual feels a strong psychological connection to a model (i.e., if he or she feels a sense of identification with the model), social learning is more likely to occur. According to White (1972), identification "springs from wanting to be and trying to be like the model with respect to some broader quality" (p. 252). That is, if a child wants to be like a favorite sports hero, he might imitate that sports hero in terms of clothing and food choices.

Social cognitive theory also considers the importance of an observer's ability to perform a particular behavior and the confidence the individual has in performing the behavior. This confidence is known as **self-efficacy** (Bandura, 1977a), and it is seen as a critical prerequisite to behavioral change. Think back again to our example of learning a new way to roll out pie dough from a cooking show on television. Social cognitive theory would argue that learning from the model would not occur if an individual had always bought preformed pie crusts and had always believed that making and rolling out pie dough was an incredibly difficult task best left to professional pastry chefs. It is likely that this individual would not have the necessary level of self-efficacy regarding pie dough to effectively learn from the model in the cooking demonstration.

Social Cognitive Theory and the Communication Media

To this point, we have sketched out some of the basic ideas proposed in social cognitive theory. From these ideas (and from some of the examples we have presented), the applications of social cognitive theory to research in the mass media should be clear. That is, in today's society, many of the models that we learn from are those we see, hear, or read about in the mass media.

These models might be people who we observe on news and documentary shows. They might be characters we see in dramatic presentations on the big or small screen or read about in books. Or they might be singers or dancers who we hear on the radio and CDs or who we see in music videos. In short, there are a plethora of models in the media who are consistently being rewarded or punished by their behavior, and many media theorists believe that children and adults change their behaviors based on the observation of these models.

One area in which social cognitive theory has had a strong impact is in the study of media violence. Gunter (1994) reviews the research on the impact of media violence on children and adults and concludes that there is a great mix of evidence regarding the effects of violent media depictions on the behaviors, attitudes, and cognitions of viewers. Social cognitive theory, most concerned with behavioral effects, would suggest that depictions of violence could lead to either increases or decreases in violent behavior, depending on whether the behavior of the model was rewarded or punished. Indeed, early research by Bandura (1962) and Berkowitz (1964) supported this contention. However, recent research has added complexity to this equation, arguing that issues such as preexisting aggressive tendencies, cognitive processing of the media, realism of the media depictions, and even diet can affect the extent to which individuals "learn" violence from the media (see Potter, 1997, for review).

A second area in which social cognitive theory has had a strong impact is in considerations of health communication (see Baranowski et al., 1997; Slater, 1999). The application of the theory in this area moves us from a consideration of the often unintended consequences of media depictions to the purposeful development of media campaigns to change health-related behavior. For example, a media campaign planner interested in changing behaviors regarding the use of sunblock might use social cognitive theory in designing a campaign. That campaign might emphasize an attractive and recognizable model (encouraging identification) who is rewarded with healthy skin and compliments when using sunblock (i.e., positive reinforcement). This campaign would be expected to encourage the use of sunblock, particularly when accompanied by messages about people's efficacy regarding the use of sunblock on a regular basis.

Summary

Social cognitive theory provides an explanation of how behavior can be shaped through the observation of models in mass media presentations. The effect of modeling is enhanced through the observation of rewards and punishments meted out to the model, by the identification of audience members with the model, and by the extent to which audience members have self-efficacy about the behaviors being modeled. This theory, though based in the field of social psychology, has had strong effects both on our understanding of the effects of media violence on adults and children and on the planning of purposeful campaigns for behavior change launched through media sources. In the next section, we turn our attention to a model of media effects that highlights the concept of an active audience, which is critical in many limited effects models.

■ USES AND GRATIFICATIONS THEORY

As I write this section, the most popular television show in the United States, by far, is *Who Wants to Be a Millionaire* on ABC. The program generally airs three or four times a week and is watched by a broad spectrum of the American public (especially older Americans). It is the only television show my 7-year-old daughter watches (apart from sporting events and cooking demonstrations), and it has become a cultural icon, as "Is that your final answer?" is now a familiar catch-phrase. The popularity of the show serves as an appropriate test case for understanding the impact of the media on individuals in the audience and on larger societal groups.

Interestingly, the study seen as the first piece of research on the uses and gratifications approach was spurred by a similar media phenomenon. In the late 1930s and early 1940s, quiz shows were popular with radio audiences, and Herza Herzog asked the simple question of why this kind of show appealed to a wide variety of people. In asking this question, Herzog countered the assumption of mass society and strong effects on audiences and considered the notion that audience members might listen to a radio show for different reasons. In summarizing Herzog's (and other) research, McQuail, Blumler and Brown (1972) concluded that individuals listen to (or watch) quiz shows for reasons including (a) self-rating, (b) social interaction, (c) excitement, and (d) educational appeal. It is likely that these same categories could be used to describe the appeal of *Millionaire* today, as individuals watch the show to share in the thrills experienced by the contestant, to test and gain knowledge, or to interact with family members during the broadcast.

Thus, in the 1940s, researchers were beginning to ask questions about how the needs and desires of the audience might influence the effect of mass media programming. Swanson (1992) has labeled early research efforts such as Herzog's (1941, 1944) as the first phase in the development of the uses and gratifications approach and has noted three attributes of this research that were important in leading to the theoretical framework developed later. First, this research introduces the idea of an active audience, in which individuals have their own reasons for accessing the media. Second, this research began to conceive of these audience motives as *gratifications* that were obtained by individuals from the media (though that specific term was not used at the time). Third, research in this tradition highlighted the ability of audience members to provide useful information about their motives and desires with regard to the media.

Not until the mid 1960s and early 1970s was the uses and gratifications approach codified into a coherent theoretical framework. The first formal statement of the **uses and gratifications** theory came from Katz, Blumler, and Gurevitch (1974), who enumerated basic points of the framework in the oft-quoted statement that uses and gratifications studies address:

> (1) the social and psychological origins of (2) needs, which generate (3) expectations of (4) the mass media or other sources, which lead to (5) differential patterns of media exposure (or engagement in other activities), resulting in (6) need gratifications and (7) other consequences, perhaps mostly unintended ones. (p. 20)

Palmgreen (1984), in a review of uses and gratifications theory, has noted that scholars have tended to concentrate on the middle portion of this statement, with little research attention directed toward the origin of mass media needs (1) or the unintended consequences of need gratification (7). However, there has been a great deal of theoretical and research development with regard to items (2) through (6), as scholars have considered the ways in which an active audience selectively engages and reacts to the media. The uses and gratifications approach is explained in more detail in the next two sections, in which we first examine the question of what gratifications are sought and obtained from the media and then look at the question of how the media are used in this gratification process.

What Gratifications Are Sought and Obtained from Media?

The bulk of studies in the uses and gratifications tradition have attempted to answer the question regarding the gratifications sought and obtained from the media by developing typologies of those gratifications. These studies attempt to codify ideas about why individuals choose certain media at various times and what they get out of their connection with the media. Most of these studies have relied on self-reports of audience members (Palmgreen, 1984), though observational and experimental techniques for assessing audience gratifications have also been used. A variety of typologies of gratifications have been proposed, one of which is presented in Table 14.1.

As Table 14.1 indicates, research has identified a large number of ways in which an active media audience uses the media in order to gratify various needs. For example, my daughter watches *Millionaire* because she finds it is exciting (e.g., intrinsic aesthetic enjoyment), because she picks up new trivial facts (e.g., learning, self-education), and because she likes to feel smart when she can answer the lower-level questions (e.g., gaining a sense of security through knowledge). She watches cooking shows for very different reasons (e.g., connecting with my interests in cooking, satisfying curiosity and general interest) and sporting events for still other reasons (e.g., relaxation, learning, and conversational content). Thus, even within one medium (i.e., television) and for one person, a variety of gratifications are being served. Of course, if we looked at different people and at different media, we would find a still larger variety of gratifications being sought and satisfied through media content.

Uses and gratifications theory goes beyond lists, however, in considering the concept of what uses are served by the media. Two theoretical developments are particularly noteworthy. First, some scholars have suggested that these lists of needs can be divided into fundamentally different types of gratifications. These distinctions have included content versus process gratifications (Cutler & Danowski, 1980), cognitive versus affective/imaginative gratifications (McQuail, 1984), and instrumental versus ritual gratifications (Rubin, 1984). According to Swanson (1992), these distinctions all point to the difference between "gratifications that result from the pleasurable experience of media content and are realized during consumption . . . and gratifications that result from learning information from media content and subsequently putting it to use in practical affairs" (p. 310). Thus, a person might access the World Wide Web in a search for specific information required for a class project or simply to

Table 14.1	Typology of Gratifications Sought and Obtained from the Media
Gratification category	Examples
Information	▪ Finding out about relevant events and conditions in immediate surroundings, society, and the world ▪ Seeking advice on practical matters or opinions and decision choices ▪ Satisfying curiosity and general interest ▪ Learning, self-education ▪ Gaining a sense of security through knowledge
Personal identity	▪ Finding reinforcement for personal values ▪ Finding models of behavior ▪ Identifying with valued others (in the media) ▪ Gaining insight into one's self
Integration and social interaction	▪ Gaining insight into circumstances of others: social empathy ▪ Identifying with others and gaining a sense of belonging ▪ Finding a basis for conversation and social interaction ▪ Having a substitute for real-life companionship ▪ Helping to carry out social roles ▪ Enabling one to connect with family, friends, and society
Entertainment	▪ Escaping or being diverted from problems ▪ Relaxing ▪ Getting intrinsic cultural or aesthetic enjoyment ▪ Filling time ▪ Gaining emotional release ▪ Experiencing sexual arousal

Source: From McQuail (1983, pp. 82–83).

enjoy interacting with virtual friends in a chat room.

A second important theoretical development with regard to gratification typologies is the distinction between **gratifications sought** and **gratifications obtained.** This distinction makes the point that what an individual wants from the media is not always what an individual gets from the media. Mick Jagger would argue that "you can't always get what you want," and this has certainly been found to be true in uses and gratifications studies, as gratifications sought are often distinct from gratifications obtained. However, these two concepts are related to each other (see Palmgreen, 1984, for review), though not in a deterministic manner.

How Are Media Used in the Gratification Process?

Thus, a variety of gratifications are sought and obtained from the media, and these gratifications can be described using content categories and at various levels of abstraction. The theoretical question remaining for the uses and gratifications approach, then, is the process through which these gratifications relate to the behaviors and attitudes of audience members. Once typologies of gratifications were established, these questions of process captured the attention of media researchers.

One basic line of research has investigated the processes through which audience gratifications influence behavior and outcomes. Kim and Rubin (1997) summarize much of this research, noting three ways in which audience activity facilitates media contact and effects. The first of these is *selectivity*, in which individuals who seek particular gratifications will selectively expose themselves to particular media. For example, a person wanting to escape after a long day at work might choose to watch music videos rather than a news program on television. The second process is *attention*, in which individuals will allocate cognitive effort to media consumption, depending on gratifications sought. For example, a person seeking detailed information will pay more attention to the content in a home improvement magazine than a person merely leafing through the magazine to pass the time. Finally, the third process is *involvement* with the media, in which an audience member is often caught up in the message and may even develop a "relationship" with media characters. This type of involvement is sometimes called **parasocial interaction** (Horton & Wohl, 1956). To go back to our *Millionaire* example, many viewers feel a very real and personal connection with the host, Regis Philbin, and hence have a high level of involvement with the show.

In addition to considering these different processes through which gratifications are connected to audience activity with the media, other scholars have worked to understand the underlying theoretical mechanism through which gratifications influence behavior. Much of this work has taken an expectancy-value approach based on basic social psychological processes (see, e.g., Fishbein & Ajzen, 1975, and our discussions of the theory of reasoned action and problematic integration theory in Chapter 8). An expectancy-value explanation suggests that an individual's behavior will be guided by two assessments: an assessment of the value of a particular outcome and an assessment of the probability of that outcome occurring. In the framework of uses and gratifications theory, an expectancy-value approach would suggest that we value particular things (e.g., escape, information, companionship) and that we have expectations about the probability that these things can be obtained from various media sources. These estimates of value and probability combine to predict gratifications we seek from the media, which then predict media consumption and gratifications obtained. As a result of those gratifications obtained, we may revise our assessments of both what we want and the probability of obtaining it from various media sources (see Babrow & Swanson, 1988; Rayburn & Palmgreen, 1984; Swanson & Babrow, 1989, for discussion).

For example, if you participate in a fantasy football league, you might have a strong value for current information about what players have scored in Sunday National Football League games. If you expect that such information can be gleaned from watching the halftime shows on network television, you might seek to satisfy that need through exposure to those shows. However, upon tuning in, you might find that you get very little information about who has scored in the current games and, instead, just hear ex-jocks bantering and demonstrating plays in the studio. As a result, you would likely adjust your assessment of your need for current information being satisfied through halftime shows and, instead, turn to alternative media that might better gratify your desires (e.g., logging on to the World Wide Web or listening to a radio show that continually updates scoring for current games).

Extensions and Critiques of the Uses and Gratifications Approach

The two questions discussed in the preceding sections (i.e., about what gratifications are sought and how media are used in the gratification process) make up the bulk of uses and gratifications research. However, Swanson (1992) points to some work that has looked at the precursors of the uses and gratifications approach by considering psychological and social influences on gratification seeking. This work has considered how disparate factors such as personality attributes (Conway & Rubin, 1991), psychological needs (Finn & Gorr, 1988), and social situation (Rubin & Rubin, 1982) might influence the development of particular gratifications sought through the media. In contrast, other researchers have tried to connect various uses and gratification patterns with the effects of exposure to the media (e.g., Rubin & Perse, 1987).

These research efforts, though productive and interesting, point to one of the critiques that has been leveled against the uses and gratifications framework: that uses and gratifications research has been quite fragmented and has not led to a statement of a coherent theory. As De-Fleur (1998) argues about mass communication theory in general, studies in uses and gratifications have often answered questions about individual pieces of the model, without taking the big picture into account: "Mass communication research seldom follows a programmatic approach, holding back the pace of theoretical development" (p. 92). Thus, we know a lot about parts of the uses and gratifications framework (e.g., typologies of gratifications, mechanisms connecting gratifications and exposure) but little about how well the overarching framework fits together as an understanding of individual media behavior.

The uses and gratifications model has also been critiqued as being overly narrow in two senses. First, Swanson (1992) notes that little attention has been paid to the processes through which audience members interpret the texts presented by the media. It is assumed that individuals have "latitude to interpret or decode messages in ways that serve their desires to experience particular gratifications" (p. 320). However, the specific interpretive processes at work are never specified, and uses and gratifications becomes a narrow cause-and-effect theory rather than a richer theory that encompasses processes of interpretation. Second, uses and gratifications research has been critiqued as being an overly individualistic theory. That is, in moving from the strong effects paradigm of the 1930s to a belief in the active audience, it can be argued that uses and gratifications theorists have swung the pendulum too far and ig-

nored cases in which the media do have strong impacts on audiences. Uses and gratifications researchers often ignore the larger context of media consumption (e.g., economic relationships and production processes) in favor of an individualistic explanation of media exposure and effects.

This final critique is addressed to some extent by the next theory we address: media systems dependency theory. As we will see, this theory continues to look at the ways in which individuals use the media to satisfy needs, but it also considers relationships among media and societal organizations that are not included in the uses and gratifications framework.

■ MEDIA SYSTEMS DEPENDENCY THEORY

Media systems dependency theory (MSD) and uses and gratifications are often compared (or seen as nearly identical) in presentations of media theories. Indeed, there has been an attempt to combine these two theories into a "uses and dependency model of mass communication" (Rubin & Windahl, 1986). However, the developers of MSD, Sandra Ball-Rokeach and Melvin DeFleur, see their framework as distinct from uses and gratifications; hence, it is treated here as an independent theory. As we work our way through MSD, we highlight areas of comparison with uses and gratifications, but it is important to remember, as Ball-Rokeach emphasizes in the title of an article comparing the two approaches, that these frameworks represent "different stories, questions, and ways of thinking" (Ball-Rokeach, 1998, p. 5). These different stories, questions, and ways of thinking often move MSD into a more macroscopic arena than other theories considered in this chapter. Thus, MSD could easily fit into our discussion of theories of media and society in Chapter 15. However, because of the ties MSD has with uses and gratifications, we discuss it here.

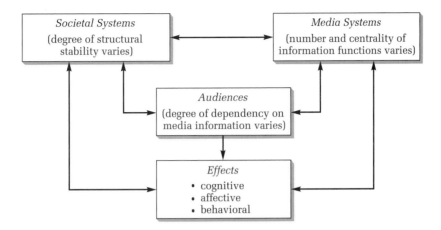

Figure 14.2   The Tripartite Media Dependency Relationship *Source:* From Merskin, 1999.

Media Systems Dependency Theory: The Basic Framework

MSD, first proposed by Ball-Rokeach and De-Fleur (1976), has at its heart a tripartite system in which **media, audience,** and **society** are seen to have **dependency relationships** with each other. This tripartite system is illustrated in Figure 14.2.

Each of these system components (i.e., media, audience, and society) is seen as depending on the other components in the system by drawing on resources in order to satisfy goals. In the words of Ball-Rokeach and DeFleur (1976), dependency is "a relationship in which the satisfaction of needs or the attainment of goals by one party is contingent upon the resources of another party" (p. 6). For example, a media organization might be dependent on a political structure (i.e., a society system) for permission to broadcast. Or a manufacturing organization might depend on media systems to advertise its products and enhance sales. Or an individual might rely on the newspaper to provide information about what apartments are available for rent. These are examples of dependency relationships, in that one portion of society relies on the resources of another portion to reach goals.

In MSD, particular attention is given to the resources of media systems in modern society. MSD theorists see media systems as taking on an increasingly important role as industrialization and urbanization have decreased the influence of interpersonal social networks. As Merskin (1999) explains, "As society has become more urbanized and industrialized, life has become less organized around traditional social groups, such as the family and the church" (p. 78). In such a social setting, the media control many informational resources through their capacity to create, process, and disseminate information to audiences on a national or even global scale. Because the media control these critical informational resources, individuals develop dependency relationships around the need for understanding (of self and others), orientation (regarding action and interaction), and play (in both solitary and social settings). As Loges and Ball-Rokeach (1993) describe this relationship, "As individuals develop expectations that the media system can provide assistance toward the attainment of their goals, individuals should develop dependency relations with the media or medium they perceive to be the most helpful in pursuit of their goals" (p. 603).

This particular relationship (e.g., the dependency of the individual on media) might sound

Sandra Ball-Rokeach

 Sandra Ball-Rokeach received her Ph.D. in sociology from the University of Washington in 1968. She is currently a professor at the University of Southern California, with a dual appointment in sociology and at the Annenberg School for Communication. Ball-Rokeach's work has been published in a wide range of books and journal outlets, and her influence on the discipline can also be seen in her recent editorship of *Communication Research* and in her receipt of numerous research grants and contracts.

Ball-Rokeach traces the beginning of media systems dependency theory to her education as an undergraduate and graduate student. She notes, "I was thoroughly trained to believe that the media had weak, if any, effects due to selective processes and to interpersonal influences, both of which were supposed to operate as barriers or buffers against media influences." However, when Ball-Rokeach looked around at the tumultuous events of the late 1960s, it was hard to believe in these limited effects. Her subsequent work set out to answer the question "Under what conditions will the media have important effects and why, and under what conditions will they not have important effects and why?" She suspected that answering this question would involve a consideration of both institutional- and organizational-level processes as well as interpersonal processes. She also suspected that a key to this problem would be exploring the specific relationships individuals have with media. The subsequent development of media dependency theory extended these initial hunches through a theory that has "sensitized theorists and researchers to the need to conceive of media power or influence at multiple levels of analysis." To a large extent, Ball-Rokeach has been pleased with the reception of her theory, though she acknowledges that it is often difficult for scholars to break away from concentrating on either the micro- or macro-level of analysis. As she says about some readings of her theory, "They think they can understand the theory in the old way of talking about dependency as a personal characteristic, not as a relationship that varies in structure, intensity, and scope."

Ball-Rokeach believes that "each of us is a theorist" and that a key for understanding theory is "to look not only for how one theory is different from another, but also look for how they are alike." By making these comparisons and by examining our own assumptions, Ball-Rokeach believes that we can develop "the all-important willingness to ask questions that open us up to the experience of ambiguity." She also argues that scholars of communication must be passionate about their work if they are to be successful. She stresses that "if you are not genuinely curious about what you are studying, don't do it. This is a life where you have to put yourself on the line in so many ways—to your students, your critics, and your colleagues. If you do not have a basic love of the journey, the stress and experience of rejections will not be worth it." Thus, scholars should "hang in there" and not "defeat yourself by giving up on your curiosity," for this curiosity is the sustenance of academic life.

quite a bit like a uses and gratifications explanation. Indeed, when taken in isolation, clear similarities exist between the two approaches. However, MSD goes beyond this individual-media relationship to provide a more complex picture of the dependency relationship between individual needs and media use that includes both microscopic and macroscopic influences on dependencies (Ball-Rokeach, 1985). The major way this is done is through the consideration of other dependencies in the tripartite relationship of media, audience, and society. That is, MSD proposes that individuals are not always powerful actors in the satisfaction of their needs because the dependencies of other organizational and societal entities may come into play.

Consider, for the last time, our example of *Who Wants to Be a Millionaire.* In May 2000, the show was extremely popular. To satisfy a variety of gratifications, individuals would undoubtedly seek out the show, view it, and vault ABC into a first-place showing in the television sweeps competition. At that time, however, a corporate feud was going on between Time-Warner (controller of many cable networks) and Disney (controller of ABC and hence *Millionaire*). To punish Disney, Time-Warner decided to black out ABC stations from the cable offerings in many major television markets. Thus, when viewers tuned in to see Regis Philbin, they were instead confronted with a screen from the cable system (Time-Warner) announcing, "Disney has taken ABC away from you" (www.cnn.com, May 2, 2000). Clearly, the audience was not powerful in this case. Unless audience members went out to buy rabbit ear antennae or a satellite dish, their dependency on a television show was being thwarted by the dependencies between two huge media organizations. This illustrates Ball-Rokeach's (1998) argument that MSD is a theory of media power rather than a theory of media use. She explains how media power is implicated in the dependency relationship between individuals and the media:

> For individuals, the most proximate condition for media power is intense and broad-scoped implication of media system resources in individuals' goal attainment. This condition, however, cannot be fully understood without reference to the ecology of macro dependency relations between the media and other organizations and systems. (p. 15)

MSD also expands on the concept of individual-media dependency by specifying antecedent conditions and consequences related to dependency relationships. First, the theory proposes that dependency on the media will increase during times of conflict and change within society. DeFleur and Ball-Rokeach (1982) believe that, during such times, there will be an enhanced need for information and orientation and that established social relationships will be insufficient to provide such information. For example, Kellow and Steeves (1998) argue that during the social and political upheaval that marked Rwandan society in 1994, the citizenry of that country came to depend on the radio coverage of a single influential station. As a result, the messages of this station may have had a particularly marked effect on the ensuing genocide in Rwanda.

MSD theorists believe that this theoretical distinction regarding contexts of dependency is critical because it helps to deal with the debate between strong effects and limited effects media traditions. That is, in times of social upheaval, individuals may depend a great deal on the media and be affected by the media. During these times, a strong effects model would be supported. During more stable historical periods, limited effects would likely be observed (McQuail, 1994).

MSD also considers some of the consequences of dependency relationships. For example, a dependency relationship might lead individuals to frame particular issues as important ones to consider. This process of agenda setting is covered in much more detail in Chapter 15. With regard to MSD, it is crucial to point out that this process, again, involves relationships among a variety of societal organizations (e.g., media, government, commercial) and hence serves as a bridge between micro-level media consumption and macro-level power relationships among societal institutions and organizations. MSD also emphasizes that dependency relationships go both ways and that media sources may adjust their content based on audience dependency relationships.

Tests and Extensions of Media Systems Dependency Theory

Applications of MSD have looked primarily at audience-media dependencies. These applications have included explanations for newspaper readership (Loges & Ball-Rokeach, 1993), for access to relational advice in men's and women's magazines (Duran & Prusank, 1997), for parasocial interaction and dependencies on television shopping networks (Grant, Guthrie, & Ball-Rokeach, 1991; Skumanich & Kintsfather, 1998), and for the development of personal advertisements by U.S. daily newspapers (Merskin

& Huberlie, 1996). Though these investigations of micro-level dependencies are similar to studies of uses and gratifications, most studies in a dependency tradition also take macro-level relationships into account. For example, Grant et al. (1991) examine the dependencies among merchandisers, program producers, television networks, and local stations in explaining the dependencies that develop between audience members and television shopping programs. Similarly, Merskin and Huberlie (1996), in explaining dependencies regarding personal ads, look at both the readers' relational needs and the newspapers' desires to enhance revenue, readership, and customer service.

Theoretical developments in MSD have also revolved around the relationship between micro-level issues (e.g., individual use of the media) and macro-level issues (e.g., relationships among media organizations and other societal institutions). For instance, DeFleur and Dennis (1996) have tried to draw out these distinctions by splitting the theory into two parts: media systems dependency theory (macro) and media information dependency theory (micro). Ball-Rokeach (1985) has taken on the task of laying out the sociological (i.e., macro) origins of media systems dependency in order to bolster our understanding of how structural factors play into the development of dependency relationships. However, some critics (e.g., Tuchman, 1988) believe that MSD could go even further in considering how hegemonic power relationships of ownership and control are implicated in the dependencies that develop among media organizations, institutions, and individual audience members.

■ THEORIES OF THE MEDIA AND EMOTION

When we looked at social cognitive theory at the beginning of this chapter, we were largely talking about the impact of media sources on behavior. And when we consider the dependencies that exist among media players or discuss the

uses made of the media, we are often talking about cognitive and informational issues. This is not entirely true, of course, because typologies of media gratifications (see, e.g., Table 14.1) typically include some entertainment functions. However, reactions such as enjoyment, disgust, fear, and excitement often seem to take a backseat to issues such as attitude change, issue framing, and learning. This is not true of the final theoretical framework we examine in this chapter. Here we find a set of explanatory statements that put processes of arousal, emotion, and affect at center stage. Though the work we discuss here does not constitute a single coherent theory, it is being considered in this chapter for two important reasons. First, this work is clearly theoretical in that it proposes ways of explaining the emotional and affective reactions of individuals to media presentations. Second, this work represents the cumulative and coherent efforts of a set of related scholars within the communication discipline. Much of this work began with Dolf Zillmann and his basic work on emotion and the media. The work has been continued by Zillmann and his colleagues (e.g., Jennings Bryant, Joanne Cantor, Ron Tamborini, Jim Weaver) for more than 30 years and has investigated a wide-ranging set of questions regarding emotional and affective reactions to the media.

In considering the emotional impact of the media, it is helpful to start out with two commonplace ideas about our everyday lives. First, we often talk about watching television (or listening to music, reading a book, or surfing the Web) as a way to unwind after the stress of a hard day. In contrast, we are drawn to many media events (e.g., a television drama, a movie, a big sporting event) because of the excitement we anticipate experiencing. Thus, our common sense suggests that presentations in the mass media have the ability to both excite and calm our emotions. Research bears out this basic observation, as Zillmann's (1991a) review of the literature concludes that media can serve both as the "great unwinder" and as a source of excitement, depending on the individual, the media presentation chosen, and the context.

Thus, the basic premise that contact with the media influences emotions is undoubtedly true. However, the theorizing of Zillmann and his colleagues goes well beyond this simple cause-and-effect relationship in specifying a variety of mechanisms through which media content and exposure can influence the audience's affective and emotional reactions. Though the research is voluminous (see, e.g., the edited volume by Bryant & Zillmann, 1991), we consider three important strands that these theorists have embarked on: the role of excitation transfer, the role of empathy, and the impact of social and developmental factors.

Excitation Transfer Theory

The process of excitation transfer was one of the first areas of explanation identified by Zillmann and his colleagues in understanding emotional reactions to the media (see Zillmann, 1971, 1983, for complete discussion of the theory). **Excitation transfer theory** begins with the basic concept of arousal. **Arousal** is generally defined as a unitary force that serves to intensify or energize behavior (Schachter, 1964; Zillmann, 1983). Arousal is not necessarily positive or negative, and it does not define any particular direction for subsequent behavior. According to Hebb (1955), arousal "is an energizer, but not a guide; an engine but not a steering gear" (p. 249). Thus, you might be aroused by a variety of media stimuli, for example, by a goal scored in the Stanley Cup playoffs, by a poignant scene between father and son in a family movie, by a brutal "kill" in a game on the Internet, or by the sexual content of a pornographic magazine. These stimuli are obviously very different in terms of medium and, especially, content, but they all have the capacity to arouse.

Because arousal has this nonspecific character, Zillmann proposes that the arousal (or excitation) from one stimulus can be transferred to affect or behavior related to another stimulus. As Zillmann (1991a) explains, "A person who is still aroused from something that happened a while ago, whatever it may have been, and who is now confronted with a situation that causes

him or her to respond emotionally, should experience this emotion more intensely and also behave more intensely than he or she would without the presence of residual arousal from the earlier arousing experience" (pp. 116–117). For example, your arousal from a music video might be transferred to aggression toward a roommate. Or sexual arousal might enhance your enjoyment of music or appreciation of humor (see Zillmann, 1991a, p. 117, for review of basic research results).

With regard to exposure to mediated communication, excitation transfer properties have been demonstrated both after and during exposure. For example, Zillmann (1971) found that aggressive behaviors followed exposure to either an aggressive or an erotic film and that the most aggressive behaviors were associated with exposure to the erotic film (which was more arousing). This suggests that the aggression was a function of the arousal in a general sense rather than of the specific aggressive content. Excitation transfer processes have also been observed during exposure. For example, sexual scenes during horror films were found to intensify the fright and enjoyment of later horror scenes and of the movie as a whole (Oliver, 1994), and suspenseful scenes have been found to intensify the enjoyment of a just resolution at the end of the movie (Zillmann, 1980). In a different genre, Perry, Jenzowsky, Hester, King, and Yi (1997) found that humorous television commercials enhanced the enjoyment of the television programs in which they were embedded.

In summary, excitation transfer theory proposes that an instance of arousal from the media has residual effects that are transferred to subsequent experiences, and this explanation has received a great deal of empirical support in a variety of settings. Two important aspects of the theory should be emphasized. First, as should be clear from the examples provided, there is no need for a match to exist between the emotionally arousing experiences. Though arousing content might enhance feelings of aggression in some situations, that content could just as easily enhance feelings of joy and euphoria. Second,

✳ SPOTLIGHT ON THE THEORIST

Dolf Zillmann

After receiving his Ph.D. from the University of Pennsylvania, Dolf Zillmann taught for a number of years at Indiana University. He is currently professor of communication and psychology (as well as associate dean for graduate studies and research) at the University of Alabama. Zillmann's impact has been great in both the communication and psychology disciplines (he has been honored as a Fellow of the American Psychological Association), and he has served as a visiting professor at various European universities. Zillmann's theoretical work, throughout his career, has centered on the intersection between media and emotion and has included considerations of domains including comedy, erotica, suspense, mystery, horror, tragedy, sports, and music.

Zillmann traces the genesis of his theoretical idea to his fascination "with Stanley Schacter's daring assertion that acute emotions are not associated with specific, unique arousal patterns." This notion that "emotions are intensified by an undifferentiated, general sort of physical arousal" was a major challenge to conventional wisdom, and Zillmann has used this as a key element in his theorizing about excitation transfer and emotional reactions to the mass media. Once Zillmann elaborated these ideas in his own work, he was gratified to see the concepts "adopted and creatively used by fellow scholars." Interestingly, Zillmann notes that this interest was strongest in the psychology discipline and that, within communication studies, "only scholars with a strong psychological orientation incorporated it in their theorizing and research." He is particularly pleased with these incorporations because this kind of theorizing "brings a balance to media research that has far too long confined itself to working with models of unflappable rationality."

Zillmann has provocative suggestions for scholars embarking on theory development projects. He speaks disparagingly of broad theories that try to explain everything, seeing them as "necessarily vague, postdicting much but predicting little, if anything." He says, "If you are faint of heart, this is your kind of theory, as nobody will be able to prove you wrong." However, Zillmann sees more value in specific and predictive theories, noting that "science progresses" through theories of these types. He explains, "If you are the daring type, be specific to the highest degree possible. In case you have a sound basis for predictions and a contradiction-free rationale, you and others will determine the merits of the system by systematic experimentation. If predictive hits outnumber the misses, you can celebrate true contribution to the field. If you fail, try again." Only by formulating these kinds of theories, by having "a few good ideas about important issues," and by knowing "the methodology that defines your field" can theorists break new ground in understanding communication and media processes.

the effects of excitation transfer are not long lived. Indeed, Zillmann (1991a) concludes that "residual arousal is likely to dissipate within several minutes after exposure" (p. 118).

Empathic Reactions to Media Content

Excitation transfer theory deals with the general and nonspecific emotions aroused by media contact. It is also important to consider the emotional responses that are more content specific: our affective reactions to what we are seeing on the screen or reading on the page. Thus, a second area that has captured the attention of Zillmann and his colleagues involves the emotional connection between members of the media audience and the content they encounter. This connection has been examined with reference to the concept of empathy. **Empathy** is a widely studied psychological concept that considers the responses of one individual to the observed experiences of another (Davis, 1983). A plethora of definitions and models of empathy have been proposed (see, e.g., Zillmann, 1991b). One useful categorization (Tamborini, 1996) is a distinction between cognitive dimensions of empathy (e.g., the ability to take the perspective of another) and affective dimensions of empathy (e.g., emotional concern for another or the adoption of emotions parallel to the observed person). With regard to mediated communication, audience members might experience cognitive or affective empathy (or both) as they try to work through problems with the character on the screen or feel the sadness of a wronged protagonist in a novel.

What effect, then, do these empathic feelings have on reactions to the mass media? Though this area of research is not as well codified as excitation transfer theory, Zillmann and his colleagues have investigated several theoretical issues. For example, Tamborini (1996) has proposed a theoretical model of empathy and emotional reactions to horror films that considers both the immediate emotional experiences of anxiety, relief, or amusement and longer-term cognitive, affective, and behavioral outcomes. These outcomes are seen as depending on both the content of the film and the degree and type of connection (i.e., empathy) felt by the audience member.

A more general approach is proposed by Zillmann and his colleagues in recent work on dramatic structure and media as theater (e.g., Zillmann, 1994, 1996; Zillmann, Taylor, and Lewis, 1998). This work makes the straightforward observation that we empathically identify with characters in the media (i.e., the fictional ones in movies and books and the real ones on the news) as either protagonists (good guys), antagonists (bad guys), or bit players in the drama. Not everyone will have identical reactions to these media players. Indeed, our connection to real and fictional characters might vary substantially based on such factors as personality or politics. For example, it has been widely noted that viewers had varying perceptions of the "characters" in the O.J. Simpson murder trial depending on their

background and experiences. These empathic connections, though, will determine our reaction to the media. Specifically, when outcomes are positive for protagonists, our reaction will be positive, and when outcomes are positive for antagonists, our reaction will be negative. The inverse would be true for negative outcomes. As Zillmann et al. (1998) explain with regard to news coverage, "Put bluntly, empathy theory predicts that bad news that reveals mishaps, setbacks, endangerments, victimizations, or tragic losses for specific agents or groups will prompt distress and genuine sadness in some, amusement and outright delight in others, and leave yet others untouched emotionally" (p. 155).

These processes of empathic reactivity have been supported in a wide range of studies (see Zillmann, 1991b; Zillmann et al., 1998). In particular, these processes have been observed in both fictional and dramatic presentations (e.g., Zillmann, 1994, 1996; Zillmann & Cantor, 1976) and in reactions to news programming (Zillmann et al., 1998). That is, the processes of witnessing the event and feeling empathic connections to players in that event are similar regardless of our knowledge of the reality of what we are observing. According to Zillmann et al. (1998),

> Whether in fiction, the news, or immediate interaction, then, witnessing personas or persons doing agreeable, good things will foster liking and friend-like treatment, witnessing them doing disagreeable, bad things, in contrast, will foster disliking and enemy-like treatment. (p. 156)

Social and Developmental Factors

A final area that has received attention in theorizing about emotion and the media is the consideration of developmental and social factors that might influence affective reactions. A great deal of research has been conducted in these areas, so we look at just a few ideas that relate to the notions of excitation and empathy discussed earlier.

In terms of development, Joanne Cantor and her colleagues have devoted a lot of work to children's emotional reactions to media, especially frightful presentations in the media (see, e.g., Cantor & Omdahl, 1991; Cantor & Sparks, 1984; Cantor & Wilson, 1988; Hoffner & Cantor, 1991). For example, emotional responses to the media change as children develop the ability to distinguish between fantasy and reality and as they begin to process information cognitively rather than perceptually (see Cantor, 1991). Furthermore, research suggests that excitation transfer processes influence the ways in which children process arousing media content (Hoffner & Cantor, 1991). With regard to empathy, work in this area suggests that a connection between viewer and character develops early, but judgments regarding morally equitable and just outcomes for those characters are not always as well developed (see Wilson, Cantor, Gordon, & Zillmann, 1986). In short, research investigating the reactions of children and adolescents to media depictions has delineated specific details about the role of empathy and excitation in media reactions.

Similar refinements have been made with regard to the role of social relationships. Most of the theory and research we discussed in this section has involved individual reactions to media. However, we often are in the company of others when we watch television or go to a movie. Thus, some scholars have investigated the role of a companion—in particular, a male versus a female companion—in emotional reactions to the media. The first investigation in this line was conducted by Zillmann, Weaver, Mundorf, and Aust (1986), and research in this area is summarized by Zillmann and Weaver (1996). Essentially, these theorists argue that boys are socialized to be fearless and protective and girls are socialized to be dependent and fearful. Then, when encountering the content of horror or suspense, both men and women will want to behave in gender-appropriate ways. Their enjoyment of the media will be enhanced if they behave appropriately, and this enjoyment will be magnified if peers (e.g., a date or friends) are there to witness (and participate in) the appropriate emotional response. That is, when a teenage boy goes to a horror film, he wants to "protect" his fearful date. If his date is not afraid

(or he is not able to protect), his enjoyment will be diminished. The inverse is true of adolescent girls. Though these ideas are of limited scope, they have received consistent empirical support and point to the general conclusion that emotional experiences with the media are not totally individual-level phenomena. Instead, processes of social comparison and social interaction can greatly influence affective reactions to the media.

■ COMPARISON AND COMMENTARY

The four theories we looked at in this chapter consider the relationship between the individual and the media in terms of exposure and effects. These theories largely adhere to the postpositivist paradigm in proposing general and causal explanations of communication phenomena and in testing theories through the accumulation of social scientific evidence. Beyond these general comments, though, the theories differ substantially.

Social cognitive theory provides a very basic look at processes through which social learning can occur in media contexts. The theory highlights the importance of imitative processes in conjunction with the observation of rewards, identification with media models, and the development of self-efficacy with regard to modeled behavior. The theory has been used both to explain the effect of media presentations on audiences (e.g., the effect of violence) and to plan media campaigns for behavioral change (e.g., in health promotion campaigns).

Uses and gratifications research has played a pivotal role in the investigation of the media, in that it provided an important explanatory framework to enhance the limited effects research that replaced the magic bullet approach of the 1930s and 1940s. Specifically, this framework shifted the question from "Why don't the media have effects?" to "What do individuals do with the media?" (Ball-Rokeach, 1998, p. 8). This question opened the floodgates for a huge amount of research that served both to catalogue relevant uses and gratifications and to explain the process through which gratifications are obtained through media exposure. However, research in the uses and gratifications tradition was often fragmented and sometimes criticized as consisting of too many lists and not enough understanding. Uses and gratifications theorists also emphasized the active audience to such an extent that little attention was paid to the constraints put on those audience members by larger societal structures and processes.

In a sense, media systems dependency theory was a response to some of these issues, though it was certainly not proposed as a replacement. Loges and Ball-Rokeach (1993) explain that uses and gratifications theory and media systems dependency theory are similar in terms of metatheoretical commitments and in terms of the object of explanation (e.g., "both emphasize the link between individual purposes and the large social apparatus of mass media" [Loges & Ball-Rokeach, 1993, p. 602]). However, they also differ in substantial ways. Loges and Ball-Rokeach highlight three of these differences:

- Media systems dependency theory provides a more coherent system of theoretical concepts suitable for testing.
- Media systems dependency theory weakens the power of the active audience by proposing "the audience member's relation to the media as one of inherent subordination" (Loges & Ball-Rokeach, 1993, p. 603).
- Media systems dependency theory can be applied to dependency relationships at a variety of levels (e.g., group, organizational, and societal), whereas uses and gratifications deals almost exclusively with the individual-media relationship.

Thus, media systems dependency theory enlarges, codifies, and complicates some ideas that have been explored in uses and gratifications research. As such, it is a theory of much wider scope and (possibly) much greater explanatory

power. However, this still is just a possibility, because scholars have tested only small portions of the theory. Indeed, many of the tests have dealt with the same individual-media relationships examined in uses and gratifications research. Though some scholars have begun to investigate the ways in which other dependency relationships play into the process (e.g., Grant et al., 1991; Kellow & Steeves, 1998; Merskin & Huberlie, 1996), much more research is necessary before media systems dependency theory can be evaluated in terms of general explanatory power regarding both micro-level media use and macro-level relationships among media and societal institutions.

The fourth theoretical framework we considered—explanations of emotion and the media—is more diffuse than the other theories in this chapter. The ideas regarding emotion and media are not gathered into a specific theory of emotion and the media, but the explanations have been generated by a related group of researchers and deal with similar issues of how arousal works during and after media exposure, how people relate to what they see or hear in the media, and how patterns develop and are influenced by others in the social environment. What marks this theoretical approach is the extreme care researchers have taken in experimentally testing explanations for reactions to the media and in building on the research of others in this tradition. This cumulative gathering of evidence is a cornerstone of scholarship in the post-positivist tradition. The challenge for these scholars, perhaps, is to step back from the research and explanations of individual phenomena to search for overarching understandings of emotion and the media.

Thus, the theories we considered in this chapter provide insightful understanding of how and why individuals use the media and are affected by the media. Challenges remain for them in codifying theoretical explanations and in understanding the impact of larger social and institutional processes on individual behavior. Perhaps the largest challenge for these theories, however, is to consider newer communication media that now dominate many hours of our everyday lives. Consider this: When the first studies of uses and gratifications were being undertaken, the family gathered around the radio every night to listen to favorite programs. In the years since, we have added the media of television, cable television, theater multiplexes, and videotape. Without a doubt, though, the largest change in media behavior is now being wrought by computer technology and by widespread home access to the Internet and the World Wide Web. Will patterns of use and effects regarding the Web follow the same pattern as with television? Or is the Internet a whole new ball of wax that must be considered with unique theories of media use and effects? Undoubtedly the answers to these questions will be complex because "the entry of the Internet is not tabula rasa; rather, it occurs in context of the established media system" (Ball-Rokeach, 1998, p. 31). It is clear, though, that the changing face of media access possibilities will lead to important developments in our understanding of media exposure patterns and media effects.

Key Terms

magic bullet effect
hypodermic needle effect
strong effects model
limited effects model
social learning theory
social cognitive theory
observational learning
inhibitory effect
disinhibitory effect
outcome expectations
outcome expectancies
self-efficacy
uses and gratifications theory
gratifications sought
gratifications obtained
parasocial interaction
media systems dependency theory
media/audience/society dependency relationships
excitation transfer theory
arousal
empathy

Discussion Questions

1. How did the way theorists think about the audience change when mass communication scholars moved from a magic bullet model to the theories presented in this chapter? Do you think models of strong or limited effects are more accurate descriptors of the influence of the mass media today?

2. Explain the popularity of soap operas, using concepts from uses and gratifications theory. What gratifications are sought and obtained from this type of show? What are the effects of obtaining these gratifications?

3. Robert Putnam's book *Bowling Alone* (2000) argues that television is a prime cause of the decreasing level of societal involvement in clubs and organizations. As television has gained in popularity, the number of persons joining groups has fallen. How would media systems dependency theory account for this observation?

4. How are the theories of emotion and communication considered in this chapter similar to, and different from, social cognitive theory? Are emotional and cognitive reactions to the media distinct, or do they follow similar patterns?

15 Theories of Media and Society

In recent decades, we have heard more and more about the powerful mass media and their ubiquitous effects on public opinion. Politicians track polling data with great interest, hoping to shape campaign promises and policy practices in ways that will meet with large-scale approval. Commentators lament that there has been a moral decline and blame the media for creating a culture very different from American ideals remembered from earlier times. Everywhere we turn, the media tout the newest craze, and we follow what is in and out with unflagging devotion. In short, the mass media—television, newspapers, magazines, radio, and the Internet—are increasingly seen as shapers of our societal viewpoints and practices. The theories examined in this chapter consider the processes through which media sources can and do have these long-lasting and widespread effects.

Of course, an examination of the effects of media on society cannot be separated from the effects that media sources have on individuals (the substantive focus of the theories covered in Chapter 14). Indeed, the theories discussed in this chapter deal with individual-level processes such as cognition, attribution, and emotion both implicitly and explicitly as the building blocks through which societal effects are forged. However, these theories share a concentration on explaining public opinion and the processes through which the media shape our view of the

world: what the world is like, what is important enough to pay attention to, and how to deal with societal issues. Thus, these theories have a different focus than the ones considered in Chapter 14.

We examine in this chapter three major approaches to media and society. Agenda setting theory considers the ways in which media sources influence perceptions about what are the important issues of the day. Spiral of silence theory attempts to explain how mediated and interpersonal communication work together to silence some voices in public debate and influence the ebb and flow of public opinion. Finally, cultivation theory looks at how television shapes our views of what the social world is like.

■ AGENDA SETTING THEORY

Few theoretical traditions within communication have as clear—or as well charted—intellectual histories as **agenda setting theory.** Rogers and Dearing (1988) have traced this history and found that the power of public opinion has been noted for many centuries. The modern concept of agenda setting, however, is often attributed to Walter Lippmann (1922) who, in his book *Public Opinion*, argued that the mass media create images of events in our minds and that policy-makers should be cognizant of those "pictures in people's heads." In the middle of the 20th century, however, the attention of media scholars turned away from this rather diffuse effect and looked instead for ways in which the media have strong and direct effects on individuals and societies. As we described in Chapter 14, theorists in this tradition—often known as the magic bullet or hypodermic needle paradigm—were influenced by the effect of propaganda in wartime (especially World War I) and the role of the media in Hitler's rise to power in Europe. These mass communication scholars hoped to explain how media sources could have pervasive influences over individuals and society.

As we noted in Chapter 14, empirical studies rarely found such strong magic bullet effects, and many researchers became dissatisfied with this search for strong and direct effects (see, e.g., our discussion of uses and gratifications in Chapter 14). In this dissatisfaction, theorists were looking for alternative conceptualizations, and many began exploring ways in which the media might have less direct, but still important, influences on society. In the late 1950s and early 1960s these alternatives were explored. The following oft-cited quote in the development of the agenda-setting literature is attributed to Bernard Cohen. In his study of foreign policy, Cohen (1963) noted that the press

> may not be successful much of the time in telling people what to think, but it is stunningly successful in telling its readers *what to think about.* And it follows from this that the world looks different to different people, depending not only on their personal interests, but also on the map that is drawn for them by the writers, editors and publishers of the papers they read. (p. 13, emphasis added)

Thus, Cohen's work started to stimulate research that investigated how the media shaped not direct opinions about a topic but instead the very topics that were seen as important enough to have opinions about. For example, research following this hypothesis would predict that individuals watching the news on television or reading newspapers would agree that abortion, taxes, and national defense are important issues of the day. However, the media would not influence specific opinions about these topics.

It was almost a decade later before this work was codified and given a theoretical label. This occurred when Max McCombs and Donald Shaw (1972) conducted a study of the media's role in the 1968 presidential campaign in Chapel Hill, North Carolina. In this study, McCombs and Shaw found that the media were highly influential in telling readers and viewers what to think about, and they coined the term *agenda setting* to describe this process. In the years since, the concept of agenda setting has served as a theoretical touchstone for many mass communication theorists and researchers.

Defining Agenda Setting

The literature on agenda setting is voluminous and wide ranging. Rogers, Dearing, and Bregman (1993) note over 200 articles on the topic in their bibliographic review, and many more have been published since. This review, however, points out that there are a number of ways to define the boundaries of the agenda-setting tradition. These could be referred to as broad-scope definitions of the theory or narrow-scope approaches.

The broad-scope definition of agenda setting involves the consideration of three related agendas: the media agenda, the public agenda, and the policy agenda. The **media agenda** is the set of topics addressed by media sources (e.g., newspapers, television, radio). The **public agenda** is the set of topics that members of the public believe is important. Finally, the **policy agenda** represents issues that decision-makers (e.g., legislators and those who influence the legislative process) believe are particularly salient. Each agenda can be seen as a dependent variable in a causal equation. That is, we can ask, "What variables and processes influence the media agenda?" or "What variables and processes influence the public agenda?" or "What variables and processes influence the policy agen-

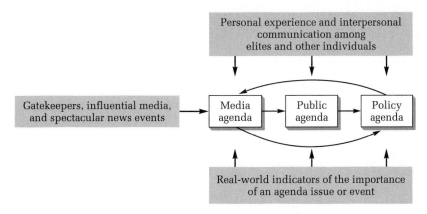

Figure 15.1   A Broad-Scope View of the Agenda-Setting Process *Source:* From
Rogers & Dearing (1988).

da?" as separate but interrelated questions. These
questions are illustrated in Figure 15.1.

The consideration of these three processes
(i.e., public agenda-setting, media agenda-
setting, and policy agenda-setting) defines agenda setting theory and research in a broad scope.
Traditionally, these three areas have been the
purview of different academic disciplines. For
example, investigation of the public agenda-
setting process has been undertaken by mass
communication researchers, policy agenda-
setting has been considered by political scientists, and media agenda-setting has been largely
the purview of sociologists (Kosicki, 1993).
However, there is little doubt that these three
agendas are interrelated and a broad-scope view
of agenda setting recognizes and attempts to delineate these connections.

A more narrow-scope view of agenda-setting
research concentrates on work stemming in a
relatively direct way from McCombs and Shaw's
(1972) study. This work has been conducted primarily by scholars within the communication
discipline and concentrates on the link between
the media agenda and the public agenda. The
following review of agenda setting theory concentrates on this narrow-scope definition of
agenda setting theory, though references will be
made to relevant work in the other traditions as
appropriate.

Agenda Setting: The Core Proposition

What, then, is agenda setting? As laid out by Mc-
Combs and Shaw, the agenda-setting hypothesis
is a relatively straightforward one. Specifically,
"agenda-setting is the process whereby the news
media lead the public in assigning relative importance to various public issues" (Zhu & Blood,
1997). The media agenda influences the public
agenda not by saying "this issue is important" in
an overt way but by giving more space and time
to that issue and by giving it more prominent
space and time. That is, if headlines of newspapers and lead stories of television newscasts all
highlight a study touting the role of cholesterol in
increasing heart disease, this issue is likely to be
seen as an important item on the public agenda.

McCombs and Shaw's (1972) original investigation of this phenomenon was quite straightforward. These researchers first conducted a
content analysis of newspaper and television
coverage of the 1968 presidential election. This
content analysis considered the time and space
accorded to various issues (e.g., foreign policy,
law and order, public welfare, civil rights, and
fiscal policy) and served as a representation of
the media agenda. McCombs and Shaw then interviewed 100 undecided voters in the Chapel
Hill, North Carolina, area and asked them what
issues they believed were most important. This

SPOTLIGHT ON THE THEORIST

Maxwell E. McCombs

Max McCombs was involved in graduate work at Stanford University in the early 1960s. He notes that before this, "there had been two decades of sustained empirical research on the effects of mass communication" and that there "initially had been an expectation of strong effects." However, by the early 1960s, scholars were concluding that the media had minimal consequences, and "some scholars even wrote obituaries for the field of mass communication research." McCombs, though, remembers that "many of us with a background in journalism thought that the heavy emphasis in the early years on research on attitude and opinion change was misdirected. These were not the kinds of effects central to journalism and we turned our attention to cognitive effects." Then, "in the late 1960s these ideas gained new salience and during the 1968 presidential election Donald Shaw and I conducted the original agenda-setting study in Chapel Hill, North Carolina." This study, described in the text, launched the agenda-setting tradition in media studies.

McCombs now holds the Jesse H. Jones Centennial Chair in Communication and is professor of government at the University of Texas, Austin. He is also associated with the University of Navarra in Pamplona, Spain, and the Catholic University of Chile in Santiago. Throughout his career, McCombs has been a leading figure in mass communication and political communication and has received awards from the American Political Science Association, the Association for Education in Journalism and Mass Communication, and the International Communication Association. These awards are not surprising, for his work in the agenda-setting tradition has met with substantial interest. McCombs notes that "more than 350 empirical studies on agenda setting have been conducted on diverse public issues and other topics," and he finds himself "awed by the sustained, widespread interest in this theory." He believes that the theory has "continued to evolve for more than three decades because it complements and is compatible with a variety of other ideas in the social sciences."

When asked about his advice for communication students and researchers, McCombs admits to a fondness for metaphor and highlights a distinction between explorers and surveyors. "During graduate school days," McCombs suggests, "you should be an explorer. Look around and become at least passingly familiar with a wide variety of scholarship in our field." After this, you can become a surveyor and work to "identify the portion of the scholarly terrain in our discipline that you wish to map, theoretically and empirically, in great detail." And, though exploration is both necessary and important, McCombs concludes that "success for an individual—and significant advancement for the field—ultimately comes from the work of surveyors, those scholars who undertake the sustained mapping of some portion of the communication landscape."

public opinion polling served as a representation of the public agenda. In looking at the relationships between these two variables (i.e., media agenda and public agenda), McCombs and Shaw found an incredibly strong correlation. The public agenda was a virtual reflection of the media agenda. Subsequent investigations have confirmed this relationship between the media agenda and the public agenda (for reviews, see Rogers & Dearing, 1988; Zhu & Blood, 1997).

However, is this relationship between the media agenda and the public agenda sufficient for inferring that the media agenda causes the public agenda? That is, are the media influential in telling the public what to think about? Recall from our discussion of causality in Chapter 3 that three factors are necessary for claiming causality: Covariation must exist between the cause and effect, the cause must come before the effect in time, and alternative explanations for covariation must be ruled out. Thus, a simple correlation is not sufficient for claiming that the media agenda causes the public agenda. Indeed, it could be argued that the media agenda is caused by the public agenda (e.g., a "tell the public what it wants to hear" type of explanation) or that both the media agenda and the public agenda are caused by a third variable (e.g., the policy agenda or events in real life).

Since McCombs and Shaw's early work, subsequent investigations have attempted to establish this causal relationship between the media agenda and the public agenda through more sophisticated methodologies. For example, McCombs and Shaw used a panel design with *cross-lagged correlations* in their next study as a way to consider the direction of causality between the media and public agendas. In this research design, the correlation between the media agenda at time one and the public agenda at time two is compared with the correlation between the public agenda at time one and the media agenda at time two. This methodological design again supported the agenda-setting hypothesis (Shaw & McCombs, 1977) and has been replicated in a number of studies. In subsequent studies, other researchers have used additional methodological variations to investigate the causal ordering between the media agenda and the public agenda, including laboratory experiments (Iyengar & Kinder, 1987), field experiments (Protess et al., 1991), structural equation modeling (Hugel, Degenhardt, & Weiss, 1989), and time series analysis (e.g., Zhu, Watt, Snyder, Yan, & Jiang, 1993). Though there have been some mixed results and some indication that the public agenda can influence the media agenda or that there can be reciprocal influence, there is, overall, strong evidence for the causal impact of the media agenda on the public agenda. Indeed, Zhu and Blood (1997) conclude that "these multiple methods have demonstrated a clear causal influence of the media agenda upon the public agenda. It is likely that no other theoretical hypothesis in human communication research has received as much empirical attention by so

many scholars and with such diverse methods as has agenda-setting" (pp. 98–99).

Theoretical Developments in Agenda Setting

Thus, there is substantial empirical support for the core relationship between the media agenda and the public agenda. But many scholars have wanted to go beyond this correlation to explore more specific issues about why the relationship exists, how it works, and in what situations agenda setting might be particularly prevalent. These theoretical developments in the agenda-setting program of research are considered in the next few sections.

Contingency Factors   Though there has been strong support for the existence of a general agenda-setting process, the relationship is far from perfect. Thus, scholars have searched for factors that might predict when the influence of the media agenda on the public agenda is particularly pronounced. Research attention has focused on characteristics of the audience, the issue, and the media that might predict variations in the agenda-setting effect.

The most prominent characteristic of the audience suggested as a contingency factor is an individual's **need for orientation,** proposed by Weaver (1977). Need for orientation is a combination of high interest in an issue and high uncertainty about that issue. Thus, an individual might believe that economic policy is interesting but might know little about the topic. Such an individual will be led to active use of the media and would thus be more likely to be influenced by the specific agenda items highlighted in the press and on television. Other extensions of the theory in this area have included the notion that educational level and political interest might moderate the extent to which the media set the agenda for particular individuals.

Other scholars have considered the ways in which some issues might be more prone to the agenda-setting effect than others. The most important extension in this regard has considered the concept of **issue obtrusiveness** (Zucker, 1978). According to Zucker, an issue is obtrusive if most members of the public have had direct contact with it and less obtrusive if audience members have not had such direct experience. Thus, on a general level, foreign policy issues are less obtrusive than domestic policy issues. Or if we consider domestic issues alone, income tax relief is a more obtrusive issue than environmental policy. Zucker argues that agenda-setting results should be strongest for unobtrusive issues because audience members must rely on the media for information on these topics. A number of studies have found support for this proposition (see Zhu & Blood, 1997, for review).

There have also been debates about how various types of media influence the public agenda. Do newspapers have a stronger impact than magazines on the public agenda? Do the effects of television news outweigh the effects of print media? Some studies have considered these questions, but clear results have not emerged, and many studies still rely on single-media definitions of the media agenda. However, some comparative research (e.g., Hugel et al., 1989) and recent work considering how various media set the agenda for each other through *intermedia agenda setting* (e.g., Roberts & McCombs, 1994; Lopez-Escobar, Llamas, McCombs, & Lennon, 1998) suggest that the process is probably a complex one. Indeed, one review (Wanta, 1997) proposed that, though broadcast media have a quicker impact on the public agenda, the agenda-setting function is more long lived for print media. Differences among these media in the agenda-setting process might be made even more complex through the rise of cable news programming and the availability of news information on the Internet.

Second-Level Agenda Setting   In addition to considering contingency factors that might influence agenda setting, other theorists have extended the theory to consider different levels of agenda setting. For example, McCombs, Shaw, and Weaver (1997) make the distinction between first- and second-level agenda setting.

First-level agenda setting deals with the objects on the media and public agendas. This is the traditional domain of agenda-setting research in which the media are seen as influencing what issues are included on the public agenda. In contrast, **second-level agenda setting** considers attributes of these objects. At this level, the media not only suggest what the public should think about but also influence how people should think about the issue. For example, an examination of first-level agenda setting might conclude that media coverage of welfare reform has set the topic as an agenda item for the public. Second-level agenda setting would argue that the media also present this issue in particular ways that might be pro–welfare reform or anti–welfare reform. This move to second-level agenda setting contradicts Cohen's classic agenda-setting quote. That is, second-level agenda setting suggests that the media are, indeed, influential in telling the public what to think.

The concept of **framing** is central to a consideration of second-level agenda setting (see reviews of conceptual development and empirical investigations presented in Ghanem [1997] and Takeshita [1997]). In the context of agenda setting, framing is a process through which the media emphasize some aspects of reality and downplay other aspects. Framing can be accomplished through the consideration of particular subtopics, through the size and placement of a news item, through the narrative form and tone of the presentation, and through particular details included in the media coverage.

Consider, for example, the issue of school violence that became particularly important in the late 1990s. When Columbine High School in Littleton, Colorado, became the site of school violence in April 1999, the media had a variety of options for framing the issue. A story could concentrate on causes of school violence, perhaps highlighting issues of gun control, parental supervision, violence in the media, or religion in school settings. A journalist could take a sociological bent or could concentrate on the personal stories of individual victims. The presentation could use highly sensational pictures and quotes or could attempt to present a more low-key examination of issues. Proponents of second-level agenda setting would suggest that these choices made by media professionals could have profound impacts on how the public thinks about school violence and a host of other issues.

Explication of the Dependent Variable   The concept of second-level framing is also related to theoretical development calling for more explicit consideration of the dependent variable in agenda-setting scholarship. Edelstein (1993) argues that the notion of an agenda is a vague concept and that we need more clarity about the dependent variable in agenda-setting research than the simple notion of what the public is thinking about. Others (e.g., Zhu, 1992) argue that the concept of an agenda is flawed because issues are always competing on the agenda; thus, independent tests of correlation will not reflect the complexity of the agenda-setting process. In dealing with the first of these concerns, Edelstein proposes the more complex dependent variable of the *problematic situation,* in which the media influence not just the vaguely defined notion of "thinking about" an issue but also specific problematic areas and ways of thinking about them. In dealing with the second concern about the criterion variable in agenda setting, Zhu (1992) and others advocate looking at agenda setting as a zero-sum process in which the rise of one issue on the agenda necessarily pushes other items off the agenda. For example, in November 2000, when the media were concentrating on the Florida recount in the presidential election contest between George W. Bush and Al Gore, other issues (e.g., violence in the Middle East, President Clinton's historic trip to Vietnam) were not covered nearly as much in the media and as a result were pushed off the public agenda.

Explication of the Psychological Mechanism   Finally, although agenda setting theory was proposed as an aggregate-level theory (i.e., one that predicts the distribution of public opinion based on the distribution of news coverage), some scholars have moved to a more microscopic

level to explore the mechanisms through which the media agenda might influence an individual's assessment of what is important. Of particular note in this area is the issue of **priming,** an area of social and cognitive psychology that has been wed to investigations of agenda setting by scholars such as Iyengar and Kinder (1987), McCombs, Einsiedel, and Weaver (1991), and Willnat (1997).

Priming can be defined as the effects of a particular prior context on the retrieval and interpretation of information (Fiske & Taylor, 1991). In essence, this cognitive process suggests that if a specific stimulus is frequently accessed or prominent in an individual's cognitive structure, it will serve as a way of interpreting ambiguous stimuli. Willnat (1997) provides an example of this priming effect:

> If, for example, a person reads a newspaper article about a new computer virus that destroyed data stored on a government computer and an ambiguous conversational reference to "virus" occurs a few minutes later, the person is likely to think of "virus" as a destructive computer program rather than as a microscopic organism. (p. 53)

Priming provides one explanation for the psychological processes that undergird the agenda-setting effect. That is, when the media accord a great deal of space and time to certain issues, these issues become particularly accessible and prominent in an individual's cognitive structure. These primed topics will then be considered especially important for individuals (first-level agenda setting). Furthermore, because humans have limited information-processing capabilities, these primed topics will serve as a way of analyzing other—particularly ambiguous—information (second-level agenda setting).

Critiques of Agenda Setting Theory

In evaluating any theory, qualities that are appealing to one critic are damning to another. That is, one person's steak tartare is another person's raw hamburger. This is particularly true of agenda setting theory, perhaps because it has engendered such wide-ranging research. Indeed, some scholars do not even believe that agenda setting is a theory, preferring to call it a *model*, a term more modest than *theory* (Kosicki, 1993).

Given its emphasis on general explanation and causal relationships, agenda setting is most appropriately categorized as a post-positivist theory, and it is reasonable to evaluate agenda setting theory on the criteria of accuracy (and the related criterion of testability), consistency, simplicity, scope, and fruitfulness. Some scholars have argued that agenda setting is a success on all these counts (e.g., Zhu & Blood, 1997), but agenda setting theory excels in some areas more than in others. For example, agenda setting theory has clearly been fruitful. This heuristic value is evidenced by the huge amount of research that has sprung from the initial study by McCombs and Shaw. Indeed, agenda setting theory has been used to explain mass communication phenomena as diverse as public opinion about the Health Security Act of 1993 (Huebner, Fan, & Finnegan, 1997) and the coverage of the American Revolution in the German press from 1773 to 1783 (Wilke, 1995). The fruitfulness of the theory can perhaps be attributed to its simplicity, in that the original agenda setting model hypothesis that the media agenda will cause the public agenda is indeed a straightforward one. This initial simplicity has also led to the theory's most typical critiques, as scholars have noted that ambiguity exists about the level of effect, the nature of effect, and the mechanism through which the effect occurs (e.g., Kosicki, 1993). The extensions of agenda setting discussed in this chapter, however, have attempted to address many of these problems. Though these extensions have certainly detracted from the elegant simplicity of the theory, they have also added to its accuracy and ability to predict a variety of societal media effects.

■ SPIRAL OF SILENCE THEORY

During the summer and fall of 1965, Elisabeth Noelle-Neumann, the head of a prominent public opinion research institute in Germany, ob-

served an interesting phenomenon. The two major parties in the German election, the Christian Democrats and the Social Democrats, had been involved in a very close race. While this close race ensued, however, there were dramatic shifts in public opinion polling regarding predictions about who would win the election. As Noelle-Neumann (1991) notes, "In midwinter, when the first estimates were recorded, expectations were about even for both parties, but six months later, about two months before the election, they favored the Christian Democrats four to one" (p. 258). Then, as the election drew near, the close race was resolved as voting intentions shifted to the Christian Democrats, who won the national election by a sizable margin.

This phenomenon, in which predictions about the outcome seemed to sway the attitudes and behaviors of voters, led Noelle-Neumann to formulate the theory that has come to be known as the **spiral of silence theory** (Noelle-Neumann, 1984, 1991, 1993). Noelle-Neumann sees the spiral of silence theory as an all-encompassing theory of public opinion that connects disparate processes of social psychology, interpersonal communication, and mass media.

Major Components of Spiral of Silence Theory

Noelle-Neumann invokes a number of major concepts and processes in describing her theory. Some of these are psychological processes, some social psychological and interpersonal, and some clearly sociological. In this section, we consider the components of spiral of silence theory as Noelle-Neumann describes it. These specific theoretical assumptions are summarized in Table 15.1. Then we discuss tests of the theory and extensions that have been developed as a result of those empirical investigations.

Fear of Isolation   Noelle-Neumann begins by positing that individuals have a strong need to be connected to a social collective and that cohesiveness within that collective must be

Table 15.1	Assumptions of Spiral of Silence Theory

Testable assumptions of spiral of silence theory

Society threatens deviant individuals with isolation.

Individuals experience fear of isolation continuously.

This fear of isolation causes individuals to try to assess the climate of opinion at all times.

The results of this assessment affect behavior in public, especially the open expression or concealment of opinions.

Taken together, the preceding four assumptions are considered responsible for the formation, defense, and alteration of public opinion.

Source: From Noelle-Neumann (1991).

constantly ensured. She bases some of this reasoning on the experiments of Solomon Asch (1951) and Stanley Milgram (1961), social psychologists who demonstrated that individuals will express opinions and behave in ways that they know are wrong in order to avoid social censure and criticism and to remain part of the crowd. Noelle-Neumann notes that this force is one driven by fear of ostracism and **fear of isolation,** not by the desire to be part of the winning team or on the bandwagon. Furthermore, Noelle-Neumann (1984) argues that the threats associated with isolation from the mainstream of public opinion can be very real: "Slashed tires, defaced or torn posters, help refused to a lost stranger—questions of this kind demonstrate that people can be on uncomfortable or even dangerous ground when the climate of public opinion runs counter to their views" (p. 56). In her emphasis on the fear of isolation and public abandonment, E. Griffin (1997, p. 389) argues that Noelle-Neumann would agree with Mother Teresa's assessment that "the worst sickness is not leprosy or tuberculosis, but the feeling of being respected by no one, of being unloved, deserted by everyone."

Assessing Public Opinion   Given this fear of isolation, it is important for individuals to be able to gauge public opinion, for in order to fit in on a particular issue, you need to know what

others think about that issue. Noelle-Neumann develops several ideas relevant to an individual's assessment of public opinion. First, she proposes that individuals have an innate ability to judge the climate of public opinion. She calls this the **quasi-statistical sense** and finds evidence for this ability in both the willingness of individuals to make predictions about public opinions and the uncanny accuracy of many of those predictions. However, Noelle-Neumann acknowledges that assessments of opinion climate are not always accurate. She blames much of this "pluralistic ignorance" (E. Katz, 1983) on the mass media. Noelle-Neumann argues that media presentations influence individual assessments of public opinion because the media are ubiquitous and continuous (i.e., they are everywhere in terms of both time and space and cannot be avoided by the individual), and positions presented by the media are consonant (i.e., various media sources present essentially the same image of a given topic). These media images also influence an individual's sense of prevailing public opinion and sometimes lead to an inaccurate reading of the public climate.

Willingness to Speak   Combining the first two factors (fear of isolation and the assessment of public opinion) leads to the key prediction of spiral of silence theory. Specifically, Noelle-Neumann argues that because individuals fear isolation, when they believe prevailing opinion is opposed to their own opinion or is moving in a direction away from their opinion, those individuals will not be willing to speak out. That is, if you believe most people are opposed to the right to burn the flag, you will tend to keep quiet about your own belief that flag-burning is a right protected by the Constitution's freedom of speech clause.

Noelle-Neumann's classic test of this prediction is the train test (or, in more contemporary presentations, the plane test). In this survey question, individuals are asked to imagine that they are in a train compartment for a long ride with an individual who expresses a particular opinion on a subject (e.g., abortion). The individual is then asked if he or she would be willing to express a contrary opinion in that situation. Other operationalizations of willingness to speak have included willingness to wear a campaign button, willingness to participate in a media interview, or willingness to attend a protest. Spiral of silence theory proposes that individuals will be unwilling to express an opinion if they believe current opinion is contrary to their own or if they believe the tide is turning toward an opinion contrary to their own. Noelle-Neumann believes that this effect will be particularly pronounced with regard to the dynamic prediction of public opinion on an issue and will depend on the future assessment of opinion when current and future assessments do not agree.

The Spiral of Silence Noelle-Neumann sees the spiral of silence as a dynamic process, though cross-sectional research designs are often used to test its propositions. That is, Noelle-Neumann believes that the unwillingness to speak out on a particular issue will further enhance media portrayals and personal assessments that prevailing opinion is against a certain opinion. As these portrayals and assessments become even more codified, some individuals will defect to the opinion that seems to be prevailing or will at least fail to recruit new people to the less-dominant position. As a result, actual opinion will follow predictions of

opinion and spiral down. As Noelle-Neumann (1991) describes it,

> The visibility of one side encourage[s] its other supporters to make a public commitment, thus increasing the impression of numerical superiority. Conversely, supporters of the side with less public visibility [are] discouraged by being underestimated. They [are] increasingly reduced to silence, causing their other supporters to conceal their convictions, to the point where this camp [begins] to lose its public presence. (p. 258)

Contingency Factors Noelle-Neumann does not propose that the spiral of silence is a universal process, however. She points to three caveats that limit the applicability of the theory to specific issues and people. First, the theory will operate only when the issue at hand is a moral issue of good and bad, not a factual issue that can be argued and settled through rational and logical interaction. That is, the spiral of silence should occur with regard to public opinion about capital punishment or abortion but not with regard to public opinion about inflation rates. Second, Noelle-Neumann notes that the unwillingness to speak out will be less pronounced in highly educated and more affluent portions of the population. Third, Noelle-Neumann contends that, for any topic, a hard core of proponents will always be willing to speak out on an issue, regardless of perceptions that prevailing opinion is in the opposite direction.

Evidence for and Extensions of Spiral of Silence Theory

Evidence On the face of it, spiral of silence theory is a relatively straightforward model of public opinion formation and change. However, in some ways it is quite complex, for it involves phenomena at a variety of levels of analysis (i.e., psychological, interpersonal, and media) and posits complicated over-time changes. Thus, complete tests of the theory are difficult to undertake (though see C. Katz & Baldassare, 1994, for one example of a dynamic test of the spiral of silence process). Instead, scholars have tended to test subportions of the theory (e.g., the testable assumptions presented in Table 15.1), assessing whether individuals really do make assessments about prevailing public opinion, whether the media are indeed inaccurate in many portrayals, and, especially, whether perceptions about prevailing and future public opinion influence an individual's willingness to express an opinion on a particular topic.

Evidence indicates that individuals do indeed make assessments and express opinions about prevailing public opinion, as public opinion polling rarely uncovers a large number of people who are unwilling to say, for instance, what they believe the outcome of an election will be—though the close 2000 presidential election was an exception to this general rule. There is also evidence that the mass media influence these perceptions of public opinion. For example, a study of public opinion during the Persian Gulf War (Eveland, McLeod, & Signorielli, 1995) found that individuals' perceptions of widespread public support for the war were influenced by mainstream media portrayals that reported, perhaps inaccurately, overwhelming support for the military operation.

The majority of research efforts on spiral of silence theory, however, have looked at the central thesis of the theory: the effect of perceptions of public support on willingness to express an opinion. In general, these studies have revealed consistent—but quite weak—effects. For example, a meta-analysis of a number of these studies (Glynn, Hayes, & Shanahan, 1997) cumulated quantitative estimates of the relationship between perceptions of both current and future support and willingness to speak out. This meta-analysis found an overall correlation between perceived current support and willingness to speak out of $r = .048$ and an overall correlation between perceived future support and willingness to speak out of $r = .050$. Though these correlations are statistically significant, they are also very small. To illustrate, these correlations indicate that less than one quarter of one percent of "willingness to speak out" can be predict-

ed from perceptions of current and future public opinion. As a result of these small effect sizes for a key component of the theory, scholars have attempted to extend and refine the theory, looking for moderator variables and descriptions of the process that could lead to the prediction of more robust effects.

Extensions Extensions of spiral of silence theory have been developed in two major areas. First, some scholars have developed theoretical predictions regarding the group that people consider when assessing prevailing opinion. Specifically, it has been suggested that individuals do not look so much to overall societal opinions as to the opinions of relevant reference groups (Krassa, 1988). Krassa argues that some opinions are valued more than others and that the spiral of silence will depend on predictions about the opinions of these valued others. For example, this theoretical extension would predict that your willingness to speak out would be influenced by your perception of what your friends think but not by public opinion in general. Research on this extension of the theory has been mixed. For example, in a laboratory experiment, Oshagan (1996) found that perceived reference group opinions had a larger effect on opinion expression than perceived societal opinions. In contrast, Glynn and Park (1997) found that individuals were more comfortable expressing dissenting opinions within a valued reference group. These results suggest that the spiral of silence effect does depend on the reference group but that this relationship might be a complex one.

A second area of development for the theory has involved further explication of the characteristics of those who are silenced—and those who still speak out—in the face of contrary public and reference group opinion. Recall that Noelle-Neumann originally posited that the spiral of silence effect would not be as strong for highly educated and affluent portions of the population and that a hard core of individuals would always be willing to speak out. The scholars developing the theory in this direction, then, are essentially working to further define the nature of that hard-core group. Several additional variables have been identified as factors that predict willingness to speak out in the face of contrary public sentiment. These include strength and certainty of opinion (Lasorsa, 1991; Oshagan, 1996), political interest and extremity (Baldassare & Katz, 1996; Shamir, 1997), the obtrusiveness of the issue (Lasorsa, 1991), and an individual's level of self-efficacy (Lasorsa, 1991).

Critiques of Spiral of Silence Theory

The spiral of silence theory has generated a great deal of attention, both empirically and critically. Kennamer (1990, p. 393) has called Noelle-Neumann's theory "one of the most influential recent theories of public opinion formation," and as a result it has been the subject of intense scrutiny. Indeed, Salmon and Moh (1992) note that there are as many critiques of the theory as there are empirical tests. Many scholarly commentators have dealt with the lack of empirical support for key tenets of the theory, especially the relationship between perceived public opinion and willingness to speak. Other scholars have criticized the theory for its lack of clarity and falsifiability (see, e.g., Price & Allen, 1990).

Perhaps most interesting, however, has been a body of writing that has dealt with the ideological base of spiral of silence theory. Though we can't give full treatment to this debate here, some critics have explored the links that connect Noelle-Neumann's early work in the 1930s and 1940s and her ties to the Nazi Party and its journalistic arm to her current and continuing theoretical work (see, especially, Bogart, 1991; Salmon & Moh, 1992; and Simpson, 1996). These critics make two key points. First, they note that spiral of silence theory was foreshadowed in Noelle-Neumann's early academic and journalistic work, in terms of both theoretical content and methodological choices. In terms of theoretical foreshadowing, Simpson

(1996) summarizes one argument from Noelle-Neumann's dissertation (Noelle, 1940):

> She argued, in part, that a majority of Americans held positive attitudes towards Germany and Germans, and hostile attitudes toward Jews, Italians, and others, because of their personal experiences with various ethnic groups. . . . The popular goodwill toward Germany had been eclipsed, however, by hostile news reports and anti-German propaganda that left most Americans unwilling to speak frankly about their pro-German views—A clear precursor of the argument she was to elaborate later in the *Spiral of Silence*. (p. 153)

From this foreshadowing, and from Noelle-Neumann's journalistic work during World War II, these critics then argue that the spiral of silence theory has a clear ideological bias. There are several aspects to the theory's ideological direction. First, Noelle-Neumann takes a conservative position and argues that the media have a consonant left-wing bias. Second, Noelle-Neumann sees the people who might be immune to the spiral of silence effect as the educated and affluent—society's upper class. From this, Noelle-Neumann argues, in a manner consistent with the views of mass society presented in Chapter 14, that the vast majority of the population is relatively powerless in the face of public opinion and the liberal press that shapes that opinion. As Salmon and Moh (1992) conclude,

> Implicit in her thinking is that the individual is largely impotent, certainly not powerful enough to effect changes in public policy. The individual is viewed as malleable and manipulable, the object rather than the source of political influence. Further, the basis of opinion expression is seen as emotion or fear rather than detached rationality. (p. 152)

As we noted in Chapters 2 and 5, many theories (some would claim all) have ideological biases; hence, the ideology that undergirds spiral of silence theory is not surprising. However, two notes about the theory's ideology are important.

First, Noelle-Neumann claims that all her statements are scientifically based and she often ignores contrary evidence (see Simpson, 1996). That is, she situates her theory as having no ideological underpinnings. Second, Noelle-Neumann's starting point of a liberal press has interesting implications, ones that lead to the conclusion that individuals are relatively powerless and that ascribe little faith to the democratic process. If, instead, you begin with an assumption of a conservative and status-preserving media, as many mass communication scholars do (e.g., Gitlin, 1980), the spiral of silence becomes a theory more closely aligned with leftist critical theorists who claim that individuals are oppressed by the hegemonic influence of the state and big business and that participative democracy (Deetz, 1992) and competent civil discourse (Habermas, 1984) are the necessary palliatives for this situation.

CULTIVATION THEORY

The two theories we have looked at so far in this chapter have considered the effects of a variety of media sources (e.g., television, newspapers, magazines) on public opinion about the news of the day. The last theory we examine, **cultivation theory,** differs from agenda setting theory and spiral of silence theory in two important respects. First, cultivation theory concentrates on one specific medium: television. Second, cultivation theory predicts not direct impacts on our thinking about specific issues or the attributes of those issues but impacts on the very way we view the world. Thus, cultivation theory presents a picture of the media that is both more narrow (in concentrating on just television) and more broad (in concentrating on social construction effects) than the theories we have considered thus far.

Historical Background

It is important to begin a discussion of cultivation theory with the reminder that life in the United States changed substantially in the 1950s with the introduction of television into most homes. At first, television was a novelty, but in the ensuing decades it became a way of life. As Gerbner, Gross, Morgan, and Signorielli (1986) describe in the opening of their summary of cultivation theory,

> The longer we live with television, the more invisible it becomes. As the number of people who have never lived without television continues to grow, the medium is increasingly taken for granted as an appliance, a piece of furniture, a storyteller, a member of the family. Ever fewer parents and even grandparents can explain to children what it was like to grow up before television. (p. 17)

Thus, at the beginning of the 21st century, television is a ubiquitous part of American life. The widespread influence of television was noted more than 30 years ago and was a concern for many scholars and policy-makers. In the late 1960s, civil unrest, the assassinations of Bobby Kennedy and Martin Luther King, Jr., and other events convinced many that we had to know more about how television affects us. As a result, several large-scale research projects were launched. These included the National Commission on the Causes and Prevention of Violence in 1967 and 1968 and the Surgeon General's Scientific Advisory Committee on Television and Social Behavior in 1972. These applied projects were concerned with the effects of television programming (particularly violent programming) on the attitudes and behaviors of the American public.

George Gerbner and a team of communication researchers from the Annenberg School at the University of Pennsylvania became major players in these research projects. In gathering data for these research investigations—and a host of others throughout the years—Gerbner and his colleagues have developed a theory that posits that television should not be studied in terms of targeted and specific effects (e.g., that watching *Superman* will lead children to attempt to fly by jumping out the window) but in terms

Table 15.2	Assumptions of the Cultivation Approach

Generalizations from cultivation analysis

Television is a unique medium requiring a special approach to study.

Television messages form a coherent system, the mainstream of our culture.

Those message systems (i.e., content) provide clues to cultivation.

Cultivation analysis focuses on television's contributions over time to the thinking and actions of large and otherwise heterogenous social aggregates.

New technologies extend rather than deflect the reach of television's messages.

Cultivation analysis focuses on pervasive stabilizing and homogenizing consequences.

Source: From Gerbner (1990).

of the cumulative and overarching impact it has on the way we see the world in which we live. Thus, cultivation theory moves us away from the specific impact of the media described in social cognitive theory (see Chapter 14) to a more broadly conceived consideration of the social construction of public perceptions.

Assumptive Base of Cultivation Theory

Cultivation theory is based on several assumptions about television and the way we view it. These assumptions did not precede the research program but have developed as theorists in this research tradition accumulate more and more evidence about how we watch television and the effects of television on our daily lives and views of the world. These assumptions were summarized by Gerbner (1990) and are presented in Table 15.2.

The Nature of Television Of central importance to cultivation analysis is the notion that television is a unique medium. Several characteristics contribute to the power of television. First, television is *pervasive*. By the beginning of the 1990s, almost all American households owned a television, and most had more than one set. And those television sets are not idle, as cul-

tivation scholars report that the television is on for an average of seven hours per day in American households and that individual family members watch for an average of three hours per day (Morgan & Signorielli, 1990, p. 13). Television is also highly *accessible*, regardless of literacy or other skills. But perhaps the most important point cultivation theorists make about television is that it is *coherent*, presenting the same basic messages about society across programming and across time. As Gerbner et al. (1986) summarize,

> Television has obviously changed on many levels . . . , but these changes are superficial. The underlying values, demography, ideology, and power relationships have manifested only minor fluctuations with virtually no significant deviations over time, despite the actual social changes which have occurred. (pp. 26–27)

The Nature of Viewing Cultivation theorists have also developed ideas about how we view television. Specifically, they argue that "viewers watch by the clock" (Gerbner, 1990, p. 254). That is, according to cultivation theorists, most people do not choose to watch particular shows or even a particular genre of shows. Rather, there are certain times of the day (or week, or year) when they watch, and whatever is on at that time will be watched. In this case, television viewing is seen as highly nonselective and even ritual in nature (Gerbner, Gross, Signorielli, Morgan, & Jackson-Beeck, 1979). When combined with the assumptions made about the nature of television (e.g., that it provides a coherent view of the world across program types and time), an important implication emerges. Specifically, as Potter (1993) summarizes,

> If one is able to accept the postulated position that all television programs are the same in terms of the narratives and credibility of their messages *and* that viewers watch nonselectively, then the only important difference among viewers is how much time they spend watching. (p. 572)

The Cultivation Effect Given the unique nature of television and the centrality of television viewing in our lives, Gerbner and his colleagues then propose that television will serve to cultivate our views of the world. The notion of **cultivation** describes a long-term and cumulative impact of television on our views of reality. Cultivation theorists believe that television can create and maintain very basic sets of beliefs about the world and that these influences are cumulative and long-lived ones. Indeed, cultivation theorists are adamant in arguing that cultivation is not a simple stimulus-response model, a model of unidirectional change, or a model of reinforcement (Morgan & Signorielli, 1990). Rather, cultivation

> implies long-term, cumulative consequences of exposure to an essentially repetitive and stable system of messages. . . . It is concerned with continuity, stabilization, and gradual shifts rather than outright change. A slight but pervasive shift in the cultivation of common perspectives may not change much in individual outlooks and behavior but may later change the meaning of those perspectives and actions profoundly. (p. 18)

Testing Cultivation Theory

Cultivation theory has most often been tested through a comparison of the content of television and the beliefs people hold about the na-

ture of the world. In the early and defining work of Gerbner and his colleagues, these two pieces of the puzzle were referred to as content analysis and cultural indicators analysis.

Content Analysis: The Television World The first step for testing cultivation theory in these early (and many subsequent) studies was the determination of television content through **content analysis**. Gerbner and his colleagues began in 1969 to chart the content of prime-time and weekend children's television programming, and Gerbner et al. (1986, p. 25) noted that 2,105 programs, 6,055 major characters, and 19,116 minor characters had been analyzed by 1984. Specifically, Gerbner et al. (pp. 25–26) noted the following patterns:

- Men outnumber women three to one on television.
- Older people and younger people are under-represented on television.
- Blacks and Hispanics are under-represented on television.
- Seventy percent of television characters are "middle middle class."
- Crime is ten times as rampant in the "television world" as it is in the real world.

In short, content analyses reveal a television world that is "far from reality" (p. 25) in terms of the people who populate the world and the things that happen in the world.

Cultural Indicators: Perceptions of the World The second part of testing the cultivation process involves assessing individuals' beliefs about what the world is like. This portion of the research endeavor was accomplished through what Gerbner and his colleagues call the **cultural indicators** project. This analysis involved surveys of individuals who were asked factual questions about the world. For example, an analysis of perceptions about violence might ask respondents about the likelihood of being a victim of violent crime. The forced-choice answers to these questions would include both a "television response" (e.g., a one out of ten chance of being a victim) and a "non-television response" (e.g., a much smaller chance closer to the actual likelihood of being a victim). These questions would not be at all connected to television viewing for the respondent, though a separate measure (often at a different point in time) would assess the overall viewing habits of the individual. Cultural indicators could be taken on a wide range of topics, including demographic distributions, crime and violence, stereotypes of women and the aged, politics, and economics.

Putting it Together: Cultivation Analysis

The test of the cultivation hypothesis would then consist of a comparison between light television viewers and heavy television viewers. If heavy television viewers tended to provide answers that were more in line with the television response, researchers would have support for the cultivation hypothesis. For example, early work by Gerbner and his colleagues indicated that heavy viewers were more likely to see the world as a violent and mean place than were light viewers (e.g., Gerbner & Gross, 1976; Gerbner, Signorielli, Morgan, & Jackson-Beeck, 1979). This link between the amount of television viewing and views of the world that are consonant with television reality, but at odds with the real world, thus form the heart of cultivation theory.

Critiques and Extensions of Cultivation Theory

There have been widespread critiques of cultivation theory, and "lively debate" (to use a friendly term) has ensued between Gerbner and his colleagues and various commentators. Early critics of cultivation theory (e.g., Hirsch, 1980, 1981; Hughes, 1980; Newcomb, 1978) tended to attack the empirical and philosophical base of cultivation theory and argue for a total rejection of cultivation effects. These critiques were met with strong opposition from Gerbner and his colleagues (e.g., Gerbner, Gross, Morgan, & Signorielli, 1981). In more recent years, the discus-

sions regarding cultivation theory have been somewhat more measured and more concerned with extending the theory in useful ways (e.g., Hawkins & Pingree, 1980; Potter, 1993).

Weak and Limited Effects of Cultivation
Some of the earliest (and continuing) critiques of cultivation theory noted the relatively small effects that were found for cultivation processes and the fact that these effects were further diminished when controlling for a number of relevant demographic variables (e.g., age, gender, education). For example, in an essay that reanalyzed some of the original cultivation data, Hirsch (1980) concluded that "across most of the attitude items reported by the Annenberg group, as well as for others they chose not to report, the effect of television-viewing is clearly minimal when the responses of nonviewers and extreme viewers are analyzed separately. When two or more controls were applied simultaneously, we found the 'separate and independent' effect of television viewing to be nonexistent" (p. 449). A more recent meta-analysis of cultivation research (Morgan & Shanahan, 1997) found an average effect size for cultivation effects to be only .01.

Cultivation theorists have had several responses to these critiques of weak and limited effects. First, in a general sense, they have argued that any effect would have been difficult to detect and that even minute effects can be extremely important. According to Morgan and Signorielli (1990),

> If we argue that the messages are stable, that the medium is virtually ubiquitous, and that it is accumulated exposure that counts, then almost everyone should be affected, regardless of how much they watch. . . . It is clear, then, that the cards are stacked against finding evidence of cultivation. Therefore, the discovery of a systematic pattern of even small but pervasive differences between light and heavy viewers may indicate far-reaching consequences. (p. 20)

More important than these global responses, however, are two ways in which cultivation theorists have extended their theory to account for small effects and differences in effects among subgroups. The two concepts added to the theory in this regard are mainstreaming and resonance.

Mainstreaming refers to the tendency of television to homogenize viewers or bring them into the mainstream views of society. This effect occurs when a category of individuals who have widely varied views as light television viewers have homogeneous views as heavy television viewers. For example, a mainstreaming effect would occur if light-viewing women expressed a variety of beliefs about the prevalance of women in politics but heavy-viewing women tended to center on the mainstream television view of under-represented women in political life. As Gerbner et al. (1986) summarize, "Mainstreaming means that television viewing may absorb or override differences in perspective and behavior that stem from other social, cultural, and demographic influences. It represents a homogenization of divergent views and a convergence of disparate viewers" (p. 31).

Resonance is another concept proposed to explain differential cultivation effects across groups of viewers. This concept suggests that the effects of television viewing will be particularly pronounced for individuals who have had related experience in real life. That is, for a recent mugging victim or someone who lives in a high crime neighborhood, the portrayal of violence on television will resonate and be particularly influential. As Morgan and Signorielli (1990) explain, in such cases "everyday reality and television provides a double dose of messages that . . . amplify cultivation" (p. 21).

Assumptions about the Nature of Television and Viewing Recall that cultivation theory assumes that television provides a uniform message and that television viewing is nonselective and primarily "by the clock." Several critics have questioned these basic assumptions and suggested that changes in these assumptions might lead to better predictions about the cultivation effect. For example, Potter (1993) and Tamborini and Choi (1990) question the concept of uniform content, especially in recent years when technological advances have led to increased diversity in programming. As Potter (1993) argues,

> During prime time, the range of messages still includes sitcoms and action/adventure shows, but it is also composed of music videos, sports, home shopping, headline news, in-depth documentaries, stand-up comedy, school board meetings, cartoons, low-budget science fiction, and fundamentalist preaching. What is the "uniformity" across these messages? (p. 573)

Critics have also questioned the assumption of a nonselective audience. Again, a good part of this critique rests on the notion that television viewing has changed substantially since the late 1960s and early 1970s and that, with cable television, satellite, pay-per-view, remote controls, and VCRs, there is a great deal more opportunity for viewing selectively. For example, a relatively heavy viewer might well concentrate his viewing on the offerings of The Health Network and House and Garden Television—hardly the places to find the violent programming highlighted by cultivation researchers.

The questioning of these assumptions has led some critics to call for more finely-tuned theorizing and research designs. For example, Tamborini and Choi (1990) called for a consideration of cross-cultural differences in viewing patterns and content differentiation. Others have called for further attention to various genres of television viewing (e.g., Potter, 1993). Indeed, some investigations that considered genres in addition to overall viewing time found that there were differential effects for the viewing of different types of television programming (Carlson, 1983; Hawkins & Pingree, 1980; Hoover, 1990).

The Cultivation Effect Finally, several critiques have been levied against the link between viewing patterns and resultant views of the world. First, some scholars have suggested making a distinction between first-order cultivation effects and second-order cultivation effects (Hawkins & Pingree, 1982; Potter, 1991b). **First-order cultivation effects** refer to the effects of television on statistical descriptions about the world, whereas **second-order cultivation effects** refer to effects on beliefs about the general nature of the world. For example, with regard to violence, a first-order effect would suggest that heavy viewers would overestimate the likelihood of being the victim of a crime. A second-order effect would suggest that heavy viewers would be more likely to view the world as a mean or scary place. Potter (1991b) notes that cultivation theorists have appreciated this distinction on an operational level but never developed the implications of the distinction on a theoretical level. In contrast, some critics (Hawkins & Pingree, 1982, 1990; Hawkins, Pingree, & Adler, 1987; Potter, 1991b) have elaborated this distinction and suggest that the processes of *learning* first-order effects are very different from the processes of *constructing* second-order effects.

Finally, Potter (1991a, 1993) has argued that the relationship between television viewing and views of the world might not be the linear and symmetrical one presumed by cultivation theory. If the relationship between viewing and beliefs takes on a different form (e.g., curvilinear or exponential), then alternative methodological and analytical choices must be made to tease out the nature of the cultivation relationship.

■ COMPARISON AND COMMENTARY

In our introductory comments regarding agenda setting theory, we harkened back to a comment made by Walter Lippmann in 1922. He noted that the media have the power to create "pictures in people's heads." This metaphor has been a guiding one for theorists of media and society in the years since, and the theories we considered in this chapter have looked at this foundational effect of mediated messages. Of couse, the three theories take different approaches to this connection between media and perception. Agenda setting theory concentrates on issues of news and politics. Spiral of silence theory considers the creation, change, and maintenance of public opinion on moral issues of the day. And

cultivation theory concentrates on the pervasive role of television in creating our views of what the world is like. Interestingly, though, theorists and researchers working in each tradition rarely cite each other and work along parallel rather than intersecting paths. This is unfortunate because the ideas within these theories overlap to a great extent and could usefully inform each other in the processes of theory development and testing.

In theorizing the links between media and society, the original formulations of all three theories considered here were amazingly simple. For agenda setting theory and cultivation theory, these underlying logics are nearly identical. That is, both theories posit that the content of the media (news agendas for agenda setting theory and entertainment television content for cultivation theory) will influence public perceptions and constructions of reality. Spiral of silence theory adds the social psychological components of perceptions of prevailing opinion and willingness to express opinion, but this theory, too, is quite straightforward in its predictions. It is undoubtedly the elegance of these theories that has led to their widespread testing and application.

However, this theoretical parsimony can also be a downfall, and in the years since these theories were conceived, all three have gone through substantial development, both by the original theorists (e.g., cultivation theorists' development of mainstreaming and resonance, or agenda setting's consideration of need for orientation and second-level agenda setting) and by other scholars (e.g., reference groups in spiral of silence theory or genres in cultivation theory). Though these extensions have taken a variety of specific directions, most have used two primary modes of extension. The first of these is a more intense look at the processes that underlie the connection between media content and public opinion, and the second is the disaggregation of the public into more well-defined groups. Both of these kinds of extensions have proved useful for the theories: They have enhanced the explanatory power of the theory and added needed theoretical specificity. They also point to the impossibility of separating processes of mass communication from processes of interpersonal and group communication.

Finally, it is useful to examine these theories in terms of their metatheoretical commitments. Explicit and implicit references to social constructionism are shot through all three theories. Indeed, it could be argued that these theories center on the concept of social constructionism. However, in spite of this ontological focus, these theories can still be placed solidly in the post-positivist camp, especially in terms of their epistemology and methodology. That is, all three theories posit that there are regularities in the world that should be accounted for, that these regularities take the form of causal relationships (especially between media and perception), and that these regularities can best be tested using social scientific methods (e.g., survey methods and public opinion polling, content analysis of media sources).

Useful developments of these theories might come, however, from the interpretive and critical schools of theory-building. For example, all three theories are built on an ontological base that embraces (or at least hints at) social constructionist processes. This ontological base could be further explored using the qualitative and emergent research methods typical of the interpretive school of theory development. Further, all three theories have ideological underpinnings regarding the nature of the media and the role of theorists in understanding the connections between media and society. Though these ideological bases are rarely acknowledged, they could provide fertile ground for both theoretical development and pragmatic action. For instance, Kielwasser and Wolf (1992) have used ideas from cultivation theory and spiral of silence theory in a critical exploration of the silencing of gay and lesbian adolescents. Developments like this suggest that the acknowledgment of ideological processes could enhance both theoretical development and the application of those theories to real-world problems created and sustained by the pervasive connections between the media and society.

Key Terms

agenda setting theory
media agenda
public agenda
policy agenda
need for orientation
issue obtrusiveness
first-level agenda setting
second-level agenda setting
framing
priming
spiral of silence theory
fear of isolation
quasi-statistical sense
cultivation theory
cultivation
content analysis
cultural indicators
mainstreaming
resonance
first-order cultivation effects
second-order cultivation effects

Discussion Questions

1. How might agenda setting theory be changing with the development and prevalence of new media forms? For example, would you expect the agenda-setting process to be the same for the World Wide Web as it is for television and newspapers?

2. In what ways does the spiral of silence theory work in your own everyday interactions? In what situations are you most likely to be silenced? How does the media play into these interpersonal interactions?

3. In what ways could cultivation theory be used to help us understand the social construction of our views of relationships and romance? What are the implications of media depictions of relationships for interpersonal communication?

16 Theories of Culture and Communication

The term *culture* is bandied about a great deal. For example, we are told that the United States is a "cultural melting pot," that we should honor aspects of our "cultural heritage," that we should develop a "corporate culture" that will allow our organization to be productive and profitable, and that we need to keep our children away from the destructive values held by members of the "drug culture." These phrases all invoke the notion of culture, though in somewhat different ways. A culture can be seen as a group of people bonded by national or ethnic background, as a set of common experiences and behaviors, or as values and norms that guide behaviors. These invocations of culture are relevant to the theories of culture and communication that we discuss in this chapter. Before we examine these specific theories, though, it is worth considering some general ideas about the concept of culture and how it can be theorized.

The notion of culture can be conceptualized in terms of both form and function. In terms of form, Philipsen (1987) points to several ways in which scholars have approached the general question of what culture is (see Hall, 1992, for discussion). First, some scholars see **culture as a community** or a named group of people that share a common cultural identity and common cultural memories. This approach to culture puts a border around a group of people (e.g., Italian Americans or Valley Girls) and looks for the

characteristics and processes that are shared by that group of people. Following this tradition, for example, Samovar, Porter, and Jain (1981) define culture as "the deposit of knowledge, experiences, beliefs, values, attitudes, meaning, hierarchies, religion, timing, roles, spatial relations, concepts of the universe, and material objects and possessions acquired by a large group of people in the course of generations through individual and group striving" (p. 24). A second approach to the form of culture sees **culture as conversation** that patterns people's lived experiences. This approach to culture centers the concept in the interactions of individuals and sees culture as constantly emerging through the discourse of cultural members. This approach to culture is exemplified by coordinated management of meaning theory (see Chapter 9), in which culture is described as "an ongoing creation of the everyday activities of its members and, though generally shared, contains diverse, but harmonious, expressions of lived experience" (B. J. Hall, 1992, p. 53). Finally, a third approach to cultural form sees **culture as a code** of values, meanings, and behavioral norms that constrains, but does not dictate, the behavior of cultural members.

Culture can also be considered in terms of its functions, or what culture does. Theorists have proposed a variety of functions of culture, which are drawn upon to varying extents in the theo-

Table 16.1	Emic and Etic Approaches to the Study of Culture and Communication
Emic approach	**Etic approach**
Studies behavior from within the system.	Studies behavior from a position outside the system.
Examines only one culture.	Examines many cultures, comparing them.
Structure discovered by the analyst.	Structure created by the analyst.
Criteria are relative to internal characteristics.	Criteria are considered absolute or universal.

Source: From Gudykunst and Ting-Toomey (1996).

ries we consider in this chapter. For example, culture can serve as

- a performance script or schema for life. For example, the cultural norm of "respect for elders" provides specific guidelines for behavior in particular conversation as well as for larger choices in life.

- a way of organizing and interpreting experience. For example, a child talking in an animated way at a formal dinner can be seen either as a disrespectful example of speaking at an inappropriate time or as delightful and precocious. How this behavior will be interpreted will depend on the cultural lens brought to the situation.

- a means through which individuals can participate in the world of the community and a means for integrating cultural members separated by time and space. For example, the rituals associated with some Native American cultures serve to reaffirm an individual's membership in the cultural group and to emphasize cultural values across generational groups and among geographically dispersed individuals.

In addition to considering these conceptualizations of culture, it is also important to look at how culture is typically studied by scholars interested in culture and communication. Though a variety of methodological approaches are evident in this research, one of the most common distinctions made in this area of work is between the emic and etic approaches to culture. These approaches can be contrasted as "inside" and "outside" views of culture and correspond to some extent with the interpretive and post-positive views of theory presented in Chapters 3 and 4. Details of the distinction between etic and emic approaches are presented in Table 16.1. As this table illustrates, an **emic approach** follows many of the ontological and epistemological guidelines we discussed in our consideration of the interpretive approach in Chapter 4. That is, an emic approach seeks to understand the local view of cultural insiders by describing emergent aspects of observed culture. A scholar in the emic tradition would often use qualitative research methods like those associated with the development of grounded theory. In contrast, an **etic approach** holds with many of the ontological and epistemological views of the post-positivist approach to theory discussed in Chapter 3. This approach seeks a universal understanding of culture through the objective observation and comparison of many cultures. A scholar in this tradition would most likely use the scientific method to conduct cultural research.

In this chapter, we consider three theoretical frameworks that provide very different lenses for the explanation and understanding of communication and culture. As we will see, these frameworks—speech codes theory, theories of face and culture, and theories of co-cultural groups (i.e., standpoint theory and muted group theory)—draw variously from the concepts of cultural form, function, and research stance discussed earlier. However, some theories we examined earlier in this book also have been highly relevant to the study of communication and culture. One example of this can be seen in our discussion of cultural studies (see Chapter 5) as a general movement within critical theory. With regard to specific theories, three of the theories we discussed in Chapter 9 (coordinated management of meaning theory, expectancy violation theory, and communication accommodation theory) deal with issues of culture and communication in their consideration of how values and norms shape, and are shaped by, the interaction process. Other theories discussed in this book have been extended to deal explicitly with intercultural communication. The most prevalent of these extensions is the anxiety uncertainty management theory extension of uncertainty reduction theory discussed in Chapter 10. In short, because of the centrality of the culture concept to our ideas about communication, it is not surprising that many theories are relevant to our understanding of communication and culture. In the remainder of this chapter, we examine three theoretical frameworks developed explicitly to look at these important connections.

■ SPEECH CODES THEORY

The theory we consider in this section has a rich history in the fields of anthropology, linguistics, and communication and is variously known as **speech codes theory** and as ethnography of speaking. In this chapter, we concentrate on the aspects of this framework developed and adapted within the communication discipline by Gerry Philipsen and his colleagues (e.g., Tamar Katriel, Chuck Braithwaite, Bradford 'J' Hall, George Ray, and, especially, Donal Carbaugh). In considering some of the basic aspects of communication and culture outlined in the introduction to this chapter, the speech codes frame-

work conceptualizes the form of culture as a code system that lays out meanings and ideals. Philipsen (1992, pp. 7–8), drawing on Clifford Geertz (1973), defines culture as "a socially constructed and historically transmitted pattern of symbols, meanings, premises, and rules." As such, a culture functions to guide and constrain behavior, to coordinate behavior in a recognizable way, and to integrate and bind cultural members. As Philipsen (1992) states,

> A culture transcends any individual or any individual's social network, such that two people who meet for the first time can partake of a common culture and use it in making sense with each other. Likewise two people might never meet and yet partake of a common culture, a culture that is available to all who hear its terms spoken in public life. (p. 8)

The speech codes framework is typically categorized as an emic approach (see, e.g., Gudykunst & Ting-Toomey, 1996) because it attempts to identify the speech codes that enable and constrain communicative interaction within a particular speech community. Thus, a strong value is placed on local and emergent understandings developed through observation of and interaction with cultural members. However, the speech codes approach is not a purely emic one. For example, Carbaugh (1995) points out that this approach holds to both an "axiom of particularity" and an "axiom of generality." That is, there is a strong value for the emic tradition of "attending to local systems of practices" (p. 271). This is the *axiom of particularity*. However, scholars within the speech codes tradition also "want to know what this local way, and other local ways, suggest generally about human communication" (p. 271). Thus, the speech codes tradition also embraces the etic value of understanding similarities and differences across the cultures of various speech communities.

Formative Influences

Philipsen (1997) points to several lines of research in the 1960s that had an influence on the speech codes tradition as it was developed within communication. These two traditions were very distinct,

---

Gerry Philipsen

Gerry Philipsen received his Ph.D. from Northwestern University in 1972 and since then has served on the faculties of the University of California, Santa Barbara (from 1972 to 1978) and the University of Washington (since 1978). Philipsen believes that his research career "has followed a pretty straightforward path." As described in the text, he "set out initially to describe and compare two (or more) culturally distinctive ways of communication and to use my own descriptive studies and those of others who pursue work of a similar nature with other cultures to develop theories about the nature of communication." Thus, Philipsen sees himself and his work "as contributing to a larger move within the discipline, that 'move' being characterized as 'cultural communication.'" Philipsen believes this movement is important because it encompasses a wide array of scholars who are proposing arguments about "ways that culture shapes communication and ways that, in turn, people use communication to shape culture."

Although Philipsen's research career began several decades ago in the "Teamsterville" field research described in the text, only since 1997 has the research been codified into a theory. So far, Philipsen is pleased with attention the theory has received, seeing both positive and negative responses as evidence that scholars are focusing their attention on cultural communication. He anticipates that as more responses to his theory are published, he will be assisted even further in his work of "crystallizing issues in cultural communication."

Philipsen believes that the best way to advance theory and research in communication is to understand the wider context in which communication theory and research are situated. This context, according to Philipsen, can be seen in terms of both historical time and disciplinary space. In terms of time, he suggests that theorists should "consider theory in the context of 2500 years of theorizing about communication," while still considering the "very detailed evidence (material, data) pertaining to the communication process." Furthermore, Philipsen believes that communication theory will be advanced only if students and scholars look beyond the narrow parochial boundaries of the discipline. He advises that we should "become as broadly educated as possible, reading history, literature, philosophy, social science, as well as become narrowly educated in some particular thing."

---

but each provided theoretical and methodological inspiration for Philipsen and his colleagues.

One formative influence was the work of British sociologist Basil Bernstein (1971, 1973). Bernstein introduced the notion of **speech codes** to sociology, arguing that "a coding principle is a rule governing what to say and how to say it in a particular context" (Philipsen, 1997, p. 122). Bernstein, in his studies of speech codes in Great Britain, made a distinction between an *elaborated* coding principle, in which the speaker uses a great deal of novelty, complexity, and diversity in interaction, and a *restricted* coding principle, in which the speaker relies less on what is said and more on the context shared by interactants (e.g.,

social status, gender, occupation). Bernstein found that working-class groups in contemporary England were more likely to converse using a restricted code, whereas middle-class groups were more likely to communicate using an elaborated code. Though Bernstein's work has been criticized on a number of grounds (see, e.g., Rickford, 1986), it was important in introducing the concept of speech codes to our understanding of interaction and in connecting these codes with the cultural contingencies of social life.

A second important influence on speech codes theory was the work of anthropologist and linguist Del Hymes (e.g., Hymes, 1962, 1972). Hymes (1962) formulated the concept of the ethnography of speaking, arguing that scholars of communication should devote themselves to the study of local practices of speech in a variety of cultural and societal groups. Hymes married the content of sociolinguistics (i.e., an understanding of how speech functions in social situations) with the methodology of anthropology (i.e., the in situ understanding of local cultures through ethnographic methods) in proposing that we should seek to understand the discursive practices of social groups that could be identified as distinct speech communities. The formative influence of both Bernstein and Hymes provided a new way of looking at the intersection of culture and communication. As Philipsen (1997) explains,

> The work of Bernstein and Hymes, taken together, suggested to me the possibility that communicative conduct is an activity that is radically cultural—something practiced and formulated distinctively across speech communities and cultures. (p. 124)

A Seminal Study: "Talking Like a Man in Teamsterville"

These formative influences first came to fruition in the communication discipline in an important study conducted by Philipsen in the late 1960s and early 1970s in a neighborhood on the south side of Chicago. Philipsen labeled this neighborhood Teamsterville because the modal occupation among adult men was truck-driving. After many months of interaction, Philipsen came to a variety of understandings about how conversation worked among Teamsterville men. That is, he could now describe the speech code that guided interaction for members of this particular speech community.

A full consideration of Philipsen's understanding of the Teamsterville code is beyond the scope of this chapter (see Philipsen, 1975, 1976, 1992). However, a few key points about this speech community will provide a flavor of his research. First, Philipsen found that the concept of place was very important to the men of Teamsterville. *Place* was conceived of both in a physical sense (e.g., where do you live and what is your nationality?) and in a social sense (e.g.,

what is your occupation and your place in the social hierarchy?), and references to both types of place permeated Teamsterville conversations. The most important place in the Teamsterville lexicon was the neighborhood, a location that could be described in terms of specific streets and in terms of the people who lived there and their ways of doing things.

Second, this sense of place (both physical and social) was intimately connected to ways of speaking in Teamsterville. References to place were liberally sprinkled in Teamsterville conversation, and ways of speaking could be easily identified as from the neighborhood or from outside. Philipsen, for example, recounts that his ways of speaking did not mesh with Teamsterville talk. Beyond this, though, physical and social place helped to define the rules for conversation in Teamsterville. For example, the men and boys of Teamsterville would speak extensively but only with each other and only in the proper place (e.g., on "their corner" or in "their bar"). When a Teamsterville man was interacting with people who occupied other places in the social hierarchy, talk was discouraged. For example, disciplining children was accomplished through threat or physical force, not through talking it out. Thus, the social structure itself provided rules for when talk was appropriate and rules for what kind of talk was appropriate. Philipsen (1997) describes the breach of one of these speech codes in his own conduct:

> Where I valued, and used, speaking as a means to assert influence and secure cooperation, my neighborhood interlocutors heard my acts of speech—in the particular contexts in which they were performed—as a sign of weakness and incompetence in dealing with the adolescent boys and girls who were under my supervision. To the Teamstervillers, a man who merely talked with these young people, instead of using his power to discipline and punish them, was not a proper man. (p. 127)

In more recent work, Philipsen and Katriel (see Katriel & Philipsen, 1981; Philipsen, 1992) have contrasted Teamsterville talk with the talk of mainstream American (labeled *Nacirema*, or

American spelled backwards). In contrast to Teamsterville, Nacirema speakers place a high value on communication and differentiate between *communication* (as open, real, and supportive) and *mere talk* (also labeled as small talk or normal chitchat). The value for communication in Nacirema speech leads to very different patterns in interaction and different ways of talking about talk than those found in Teamsterville.

The Speech Codes Framework: Current Commitments

Based on the investigations of Teamsterville and Nacirema cultures—as well as on studies of a variety of speech communities that we review later in this chapter—Philipsen has formulated several theoretical statements that outline current commitments of scholars working within the speech codes tradition. These propositions (presented in Philipsen, 1992, 1997) answer a variety of questions about speech codes (e.g., their existence, substance, sites, observation, and force) and "form the core of speech codes theory" (Philipsen 1997, p. 122).

The Distinctiveness of Speech Codes The first proposition of speech codes theory states that "wherever there is a distinctive culture, there is to be found a distinctive speech code" (Philipsen, 1997, p. 135). For example, the Teamsterville and Nacirema cultures discussed in the preceding section had distinctive codes for speech behavior. Further, speech code theorists have found that over a very large number of studies in the ethnography of speaking tradition (see Philipsen & Carbaugh, 1986), cultural communities exhibit distinctive rules, premises, definitions, and metaphors for speaking in the culture. For example, the speech code of the cultural community of Mexican-American teenage boys living in the Rio Grande valley in Texas will be distinct from the speech code of the cultural community of Puerto Rican teenage boys living in New York City. Each cultural community will encompass different rules for talk, different ways of understanding interaction, and different ways of talking about talk. In short, this proposition

deals with the very existence of speech codes, proposing that distinct speech codes can be recognized in various cultural communities.

The Substance of Speech Codes The second proposition of speech codes theory states that "a speech code implicates a culturally distinctive psychology, sociology, and rhetoric" (Philipsen, 1997, p. 138). This proposition goes beyond the mere existence of speech codes to consider how these codes function in a speech community—as "a medium of self expression, embodiment of common values, and discovery of truth" (p. 137). Consider examples of these three functions of speech codes in the Teamsterville culture:

- First, the speech code of Teamsterville helped to define a distinctive *psychology* by establishing identity and personhood through speech (see also Carbaugh, 1994). By following—or not following—particular codes of interaction, a person's identity was defined and reinforced. The speech code served to define what it means to "be a man" in the Teamsterville cultural community.

- Second, the speech code of Teamsterville articulated a particular social structure and an individual's place within that structure. The speech code affirmed individuals as members of the neighborhood and placed those individuals within or outside of the social structure (e.g., a man, a kid, a wife, a boss, an outsider). This is the *sociology* implicated through the use of a particular speech code.

- Third, a speech code functions to define what is true and important in a particular speech community (i.e., the *rhetoric* of the speech code). For example, the Teamsterville speech code emphasized the centrality of the concept of honor among the men of Teamsterville, and those who did not speak within the constraints of the speech code dishonored members of the speech community.

The Meaning of Speech Codes The third proposition of speech codes theory states that "the significance of speaking is contingent upon the speech codes used by interlocutors to constitute the meanings of communicative acts" (Philipsen, 1997, p. 140). This proposition moves beyond the notions of the existence of speech codes (Proposition 1) or the substance of speech codes (Proposition 2) to the consideration of the role that speech codes play in the interaction process. Scholars in this tradition believe that speech codes are critical to the interpretation brought to bear on any communicative act. That is, following the ideas of speech act theorists (see Chapter 9), the speech code of a given cultural community gives **constitutive meaning** to particular practices. In other words, a speech code defines what a particular utterance should count as in interaction. In one speech community, a derogatory comment might count as playful teasing, whereas in another speech community the same comment might count as "dissing" that is taken very seriously. In this way, the speech code serves as an interpretive lens that guides how understandings are developed in communicative interaction. As Philipsen summarizes,

> The question, What happens when people talk?, is thus reconfigured here as, What do interlocutors interpret—or experience— themselves to be doing in speaking? And the answer is: it depends upon the speech code they use to constitute—to construct, to define, to interpret—their communicative acts. To the extent that this claim is true, . . . then the meaning of speaking is always, at least in part, a function of culture. (p. 141)

The Site of Speech Codes   The fourth proposition of speech codes theory states that "the terms, rules, and premises of a speech code are inexplicably woven into speaking itself " (Philipsen, 1997, p. 142). This proposition has important implications for research methodology in that it points to where one should look in the search for the speech code of a particular speech community. Philipsen suggests several ways in which speech codes can be discovered:

- First, speech codes can become apparent in the analysis of the interaction of cultural members. In considering these patterns of

speaking, however, it is critical to consider the speech as it is embedded in the cultural life of the community. Hymes summarizes this in his SPEAKING mnemonic (see Carbaugh, 1995), in which a complete understanding must include a consideration of situation, *participants*, *ends*, *acts*, *key*, *instrumentalities*, *norms*, and *genre*. This SPEAKING model is summarized in Table 16.2.

- Second, speech codes are woven into speaking in the use of a particular *metacommunicative vocabulary*, or a way of talking about talk. For example, in the Nacirema cultural community a value is placed on relational discussion (e.g., "can we just talk about this?"). This **metacommunication** reveals definitions within the speech code (e.g., what does *communication* mean to a Nacirema speaker?) and highlights the importance of that kind of speech within the cultural community.

- Third, speech codes are woven into the cultural community through culturally distinct rhetorical forms. Philipsen (1987, 1992, 1997) suggests that three specific cultural forms might be particularly important in understanding the speech code of a particular community. The first of these, a *totemizing ritual*, is a routine and structured sequence for a particular kind of interaction. For example, greeting rituals might be very different in the speech communities of Teamsterville, a college dormitory, or a corner in an inner-city neighborhood. Second, *cultural myths* (i.e., narratives that hold particular value in a speech community) can be examined in developing an understanding of the speech codes in a culture. Finally, *social dramas*, in which the moral behavior of another is criticized, can be used to understand the speech codes that guide and constrain interaction in cultural communities.

The Discursive Force of Speech Codes   The fifth proposition of speech codes theory states that "the artful use of a shared speech code is a

Table 16.2	Methodological Commitments Described by the SPEAKING mnemonic
Term	**Explanation**
Situation	An analysis of the setting or scene in which the speaking takes place
Participants	An analysis of the personalities, social positions, and relationships of those involved in the speaking situation
Ends	An analysis of the goals and outcomes desired and obtained in the speaking situation
Acts	An analysis of the message content, form, sequences, and force inherent in acts within the speaking situation
Key	An analysis of the tone or mode of interaction observed in the speaking situation
Instrumentalities	An analysis of the communication channels or modalities used in the speaking situation
Norms	An analysis of the frameworks used to produce and interpret interaction in the speaking situation
Genre	An analysis of the type of interaction (e.g., native or formal) apparent in the speaking situation

Source: Developed from Carbaugh (1995).

sufficient condition for predicting, explaining, and controlling the form of discourse about the intelligibility, prudence, and morality of communicative conduct" (Philipsen, 1997, p. 147). As Philipsen explains, this proposition deals with the power or force that speech codes exert in social life. The proposition does not suggest that speech codes have a deterministic force. Though speech codes clearly shape interaction, members of a culture sometimes communicate in a way that is contrary to behavior outlined in the speech code. For example, men in Teamsterville might, on occasion, hold an animated conversation with someone from outside the neighborhood or might have an emotional talk with a teenage boy. Or a

Nacirema speaker might decide that she doesn't want to share her feelings, even with a close friend. In short, the speech code does not determine or cause the behavior of members within a speech community.

However, Proposition 5 suggests that the speech code does exercise discursive force. This can be seen in several ways. First, people in a speech community tend to behave in a way consistent with the code. According to Philipsen (1997), there is "a great deal of anecdotal and systematic evidence to support the idea that people experience a kind of social pressure to make their behavior conform to social norms" (p. 146). Second, the discursive force of a speech code can be seen in the metacommunication of members of the speech community. We noted earlier that members of a culture sometimes behave in a way contrary to the speech code. This breach of the code, however, is likely to generate comment (i.e., metacommunication). For example, the Teamsterville man who talks to an outsider or the Nacirema woman who doesn't want to share with a close friend will be seen as behaving in a way deserving of comment, and the Teamsterville man or Nacirema woman might have to repair the breach or defend his or her violation of the speech code.

Research in the Speech Codes Tradition

A great deal of research has been conducted on the ethnography of speaking since Hymes originally called for such work (see Philipsen & Carbaugh, 1986). In this section, we briefly highlight some of this research from the communication discipline. This research illustrates the contention that work on speech codes encompasses a variety of research and theoretical goals.

First, a number of studies have taken the traditional emic perspective on speech codes by describing the speech codes of particular speech communities. Clearly, the descriptions of Teamsterville and Nacirema cultures are prime examples of this kind of research. Other researchers have described aspects of speech communities in Israeli culture (e.g., Katriel, 1986), among the Blackfeet people (Carbaugh, 1999), in rural Kansas counties (Procter, 1995), and among Vietnam veterans (Braithwaite, 1997). These studies have typically highlighted one or several noteworthy aspects of the cultural community's speech code. For example, Carbaugh (1999) considers the role of listening in the Blackfeet culture, and Braithwaite (1997) discusses the way in which a variety of thematic topics (e.g., "the 'Nam," "coming home," and "the wall") and ritual processes legitimate a speaker's membership in the community of Vietnam veterans.

Second, taking a more etic approach, ethnography of speaking scholars have compared the speech codes of diverse cultural communities.

The most noteworthy of these comparisons is Philipsen's (1992) juxtaposition of Teamsterville and Nacirema cultures. Other scholars have considered metacommunication across speech communities (Carbaugh, 1989) or considered the way gossip functions across cultures (Goldsmith, 1989/1990). One interesting comparative study looked at the clash of speech codes within a single interaction. Carbaugh (1993) examined an interaction on the *Donahue* talk show to compare Soviet and American speech codes for talking about self. His analysis revealed that the dichotomy between public and private life was much more important in the code of the Soviet speech community than in American culture.

Finally, some work in the speech codes tradition has used an understanding of particular speech codes to argue about universal principles in speaking. Fitch (1991), for example, used an examination of "Madre" terms in Colombian speech to draw conclusions about universal principles governing forms of address and the constitution of a social system. Carbaugh (1994) used a variety of research from the ethnography of speaking tradition to propose theoretical connections between social interaction and an individual's identity or personhood. Efforts such as these highlight the potential for this approach to bridge the emic and etic traditions. As Carbaugh (1995) argues about speech code scholarship, "This dual attention to local practices and cross-local principles creates a kind of balanced view of communication, an exploration into its particulars of practice and abstractions of the general principles exhibited in those particular practices" (p. 271).

◼ THEORIES OF FACE AND CULTURE

The next approach to communication and culture we consider here is not an individual theory but is instead a framework that links a specific perspective on culture with the concepts of face and facework. Scholars working within this framework (e.g., William Gudykunst and Stella Ting-

Toomey) largely adhere to the assumptions of post-postivist theory and propose causal frameworks that link various levels of analysis. For example, the macro level of culture is linked with micro-level cognition and affect as well as with concepts relevant to relationships and interaction.

Scholars in this tradition tend to view culture from the community perspective discussed at the beginning of this chapter. That is, a culture is conceptualized as a social grouping that provides a sense of social identity and shared social practices based on the experiences of group members. This perspective does not assume that every member of a culture will have identical values, but culture can be seen as "a kind of abstract average based on the knowledge, experience, and so on, of all members of a group" (Hall, 1992, p. 52). As a result of this conceptualization, culture is usually measured in terms of membership in a particular identifiable group (typically a racial, ethnic, or national group), and culture functions as a schema that guides thoughts, feelings, and behaviors. Individual cultural members may enact this script in idiosyncratic ways, but culture still serves as "a general guide for what the individual should do, think, and feel in various social situations" (pp. 54–55).

In this section, we discuss how the concepts of culture, face, and facework have been linked. We first look at the concept of culture and the ways cultures are seen as varying by theorists in this tradition. Because theorists of face and facework often take an etic perspective on culture (see Gudykunst & Ting-Toomey, 1996), the concept of cultural variability is particularly critical. We then look at the concepts of face and facework that consider, respectively, issues of individual identity (i.e., face) and how that identity is created and maintained in communicative interaction (i.e., facework). As we consider each of these concepts, we link them to concepts of culture and cultural variability.

Dimensions of Cultural Variability

An etic approach to intercultural theorizing involves the comparison of various cultures on concepts of interest to the researcher. For a communication researcher, then, questions such as "Do members of different cultures deal with conflict differently?" or "Do members of different cultures interact differently when first meeting?" would be reasonable to ask. However, theorists want to go beyond a mere sorting of how cultures communicate to propose reasons why members of various cultures might interact in different ways. That is, an attempt has been made to find the underlying dimensions of cultural perception and understanding that might cause particular kinds of communication behavior. A wide array of typologies have been proposed in the literature (see Gudykunst & Kim, 1997, for review). We consider a few of the most often used dimensions of cultural variability in this section.

In 1980, Geert Hofstede analyzed organizational behavior in 40 different national cultures and identified four dimensions on which the cultures varied. For example, Hofstede (1980, 1991) found that cultures differed in terms of *uncertainty avoidance* (e.g., whether cultural members have tolerance for ambiguity), *power distance* (e.g., "the extent to which the less powerful members of institutions and organizations accept that power is distributed unequally" [Hofstede & Bond, 1984, p. 419]), and *masculinity-femininity* (e.g., an emphasis on "things, power, and asssertiveness" versus an emphasis on "people, quality of life, and nurturance" [Gudykunst, 1997, p. 334]). The fourth dimension proposed by Hofstede, however, has been the most often used in both scholarly and popular treatments of intercultural variability. This is the distinction between individualistic and collectivistic cultures (see also Hui & Triandis, 1986).

An **individualistic culture** is a social grouping in which "the needs, values, and goals of the individual take precedence over the needs, values, and goals of the ingroup" (Gudykunst, 1997, p. 331). In an individualistic culture, the primary focus is the "I" identity and the individual's rights and desires in interaction, and a premium is placed on autonomy and personal choice (Ting-Toomey, 1988). Examples of individualistic cultures (in alphabetical order) are Australia, Belgium, Canada, Denmark, France, Germany, Great Britain, Ireland, Israel, Italy, Netherlands, New Zealand, Norway, Sweden, Switzerland, and the United States (p. 332).

In contrast, a **collectivistic culture** is a social grouping in which "the needs, values, and goals of the ingroup take precedence over the needs, values, and goals of the individual" (Gudykunst, 1997, p. 331). In a collectivistic culture, the primary focus is the "we" identity and adaptability to group norms and goals in interaction, with a premium placed on interdependence and reciprocal obligations (Ting-Toomey, 1988). Examples of collectivistic cultures (in alphabetical order) are Brazil, China, Colombia, Egypt, Greece, India, Japan, Kenya, Mexico, Nigeria, Pakistan, Panama, Peru, Saudi Arabia, Thailand, Venezuela, and Vietnam (Gudykunst, 1997, p. 332).

One additional dimension of cultural variability is important to note because it, like the individualistic-collectivistic dimension, has clear implications for communicative interaction. This is the distinction made by Edward Hall (1976, 1983) between high-context and low-context cultures. The labels applied to these cultures stem from the notion that in interaction, members of a **low-context culture** will derive meaning primarily from the verbal content of a message (i.e., what is said) and not from the situation and social relationships among speakers (i.e., the context). In contrast, the actual message is often but a small part of meaning within a **high-context culture.** Instead, interaction in these cultures requires an understanding of the social situation, the social standings of and relationships among interactional participants, and the cultural norms in play.

In summary, etic cultural scholars argue that cultural groups vary in terms of a number of important dimensions. Two of the most critical of these dimensions are individualistic/collectivistic and high-context/low-context cultures. In the next two sections, we consider the concepts of face and facework and relate these

concepts to these critical dimensions of cultural variability.

The Concept of Face

The notion of face is used as a metaphor in a variety of contexts. We have often heard about people "losing face" in a social situation that is embarassing or uncomfortable, or we think about "putting on a good face" in a particular situation or interaction. In these examples, we are not talking about just the eyes, nose, mouth, and cheeks that make up the physical face. Instead, we are talking about a more holistic sense of the face we present to the world. This metaphor of face has been considered for many years in a wide range of academic and philosophical realms (see Ting-Toomey & Cocroft, 1994, for review). In this section, we briefly consider four prominent positions that chart, over time, the development of the face concept as relevant to communication theory. We then examine these conceptualizations of face in light of the dimensions of cultural variability discussed in the preceding section.

Hu (1944) traces the concept of face to two Chinese concepts: *lien* and *mien-tzu*. *Lien* is the sense of worth ascribed to all moral members of a society and can be lost only through reprehensible conduct. For example, an individual could lose *lien* if he or she was convicted of a serious crime but would not lose *lien* through a lapse of social judgment in interaction. In contrast, *mien-tzu* is a more dynamic form of face that responds to the social expectations enacted by individuals in interaction. One could lose the *mien-tzu* form of face by not using a correct form of address, perhaps, or by speaking in a too-familiar way with an elder or a stranger. As Ho (1976) points out, this form of face is "inherently social because it is dependent upon the perceptions of other people" (Ting-Toomey & Cocroft, 1994, p. 309).

These concepts of face from Chinese culture were adapted by Erving Goffman (1959) in his book *The Presentation of Self in Everyday Life.* Goffman talks about individuals as having *lines,* or patterns of verbal and nonverbal interaction in which evaluations are made of self and other social participants. Goffman defines face as "the positive social value a person effectively claims for himself [or herself] by the line others assume he [or she] has taken up during a particular contact" (p. 213). In other words, face is the self-presentation of identity in interaction, and it depends on the self, the situation, and others involved in the interaction. As such, face is something that can be lost, maintained, or enhanced during interaction. Imagine, for example, a job interview in which you are conversing with the head of human resources at a large company. You clearly have a sense of "who you want to be" with this individual, perhaps defined in terms such as *confident, intelligent, dependable,* and *hard-working*. Through your interaction, you and the personnel director negotiate the extent to which you can claim that sense of face.

A third seminal development regarding the concept of face is the work of Penelope Brown and Stephen Levinson in their development of politeness theory. Brown and Levinson (1987) conceptualize face as the public image that all interactants want to claim and distinguish between two types of face, labeled (some say unfortunately) as positive face and negative face. **Positive face** refers to an individual's need for social approval, connection, and inclusion. That is, we all, to some extent, want to be validated and regarded positively by others. **Negative face** refers to an individual's need for autonomy and independence. This points to our need to be free from impediments in social interaction. These two types of face are not necessarily antithetical to each other. That is, we may simultaneously desire autonomy *and* social approval and connection (see, e.g., ideas from dialectical theory as discussed in Chapter 11).

Finally, within the communication discipline, Tae-Sop Lim and John Bowers (Lim, 1994; Lim & Bowers, 1991) have expanded on Brown and Levinson's concept of face to propose three dimensions of face that need to be considered. Like other face theorists, Lim and Bowers believe that face is the "public image that a person claims for him/herself" (Lim, 1994, p. 210). They further suggest, though, that face includes the three dimensions of **autonomy face,** a desire to appear independent, in control, and responsible; **fellowship face,** a desire to be seen as cooperative, accepted, and loved; and **competence face,** a desire to appear intelligent, accomplished, and capable. The first two of these are similar to negative and positive face as defined by Brown and Levinson. However, Lim and Bower's conceptualization is important because it labels these aspects of face in a more value-neutral and descriptive way and because it adds the notion of competence, which is not included in other conceptualizations of face.

Culture and Face Thus, a large body of research and theory identifies face as a crucial concept regarding the public image we present and negotiate in social interaction. As Tracy (1990) summarizes, face refers to the "socially situated identities people claim or attribute to others" (p. 210). How, then, does the concept of face intersect with the concept of culture? The first intersection is a simple one. This is the claim that face is a "universal social phenomenon" (Ting-Toomey, 1994, p. 3) that cuts across all cultures and social situations. As Ho (1976) argues, "It is virtually impossible to think of a facet of social life to which the question of face is irrelevant" (p. 883).

However, scholars of culture and communication have proposed that the concept of face has different implications for different cultures. For example, Ting-Toomey (1988) argues that within individualistic cultures, there will be a desire to maintain consistency between private self-image and public self-image (i.e., face). Because the notion of a core identity is critical in these cultures, there is a desire to be "real" and be yourself in social interaction. In contrast, collectivistic cultures see the self as situationally and relationally defined (e.g., the group defines the individual). Thus, the concept of presenting a pure and real self-image makes little sense to members of these cultures. Instead, the self "is bounded by mutual role obligations and duties and it is structured by a patterned process of give-and-take" (p. 216). Similarly, Ting-Toomey (1988; see also Ting-Toomey & Cocroft, 1994) argues that members of individualistic cultures will be concerned primarily with issues of autonomy (i.e., negative face) whereas members of collectivist cultures will attend to both autonomy and connection concerns (i.e., both negative and positive face).

The Concept of Facework

The ideas discussed in the preceding section see face as a relatively static entity. However, most theorists of face do not see it as an unchanging attribute. Rather, face is something that is negotiated among individuals in interaction. This negotiation is often a smooth one because we want to be considerate of others and respect their needs for presenting themselves in a certain light. As Cupach and Metts (1994) state, "Under normal circumstances . . . individuals reciprocate face support and cooperate to ensure that each other's face is protected. . . . This mutual cooperation in the maintenance of face is so ordinary and pervasive that it is considered a taken-for-granted principle of interaction" (p. 4). However, there are times when this natural cooperation breaks down, and face is threatened.

Face threats occur when an individual's desired identity in an interaction is challenged. Perhaps someone belittles an achievement that you are particularly proud of. This is a threat to your positive face or sense of value and respect. Or perhaps you feel constrained and smothered in interaction with a new friend. This is a threat to your negative face or sense of autonomy. In both cases, the identity you wish to present to the world is compromised in some way.

The ways in which these threats to face are managed in interaction is known as **facework.** Facework can be **preventive.** In other words, interaction that threatens face can be avoided or minimized before it occurs. Cupach and Metts note that two prevalent types of preventive facework are *disclaimers* and *politeness strategies.* For

example, if someone begins a statement with "I may be way off base on this, but . . ." or "As your friend I think I should tell you . . . ," he is using a disclaiming strategy. If a friend apologizes in advance of asking to borrow money, she is using a politeness strategy. In short, preventive facework tries to head off the threat to face before it occurs.

Facework can also be **corrective** in an attempt to repair face damage that has already occurred. Corrective facework could be offered by the person who was responsible for the transgression or by others who have observed the loss of face. Corrective facework includes strategies such as apologies, accounts, excuses, justifications, avoidance, and humor and involves ongoing interaction. As Cupach and Metts (1994) argue, "The facts that facework can be performed by observers and participants, that it can be accepted or rejected, and that its effectiveness depends on the features of a particular situation underscores how challenging problematic events can be. The restoration of lost face and the smooth realignment of a disrupted episode are truly cooperative accomplishments" (pp. 8–9).

Culture and Facework   Like the general concept of face, the practices of facework have also been linked to cultural variability. That is, following an etic framework, it is believed that culture will influence the extent to which various interaction strategies are used to protect against and correct face-threatening acts in discourse. On a general level, for instance, individuals in collectivistic cultures will be more likely to protect face and people in individualistic cultures will be more likely to simply restore face after it has been threatened (Ting-Toomey, 1988). However, more specific predictions are also made. With regard to interactive facework strategies, Cupach and Imahori (1993) found that Americans were more likely than the Japanese to use responses such as humor, accounts, and aggression, and the Japanese were more likely than Americans to use apology and remediation. With regard to conflict resolution,

Ting-Toomey and her colleagues (1991) found that interactants from collectivistic and high-context cultures were most likely to use strategies such as accommodating, bargaining, and avoiding, whereas those in individualistic cultures were more likely to be competitive or work in active problem-solving modes.

■ THEORIES OF CO-CULTURAL GROUPS

The approach to communication and culture we consider in this section is very different from the two we discussed so far. Specifically, we look at the ways in which feminist theorists—and others advocating the emancipation of marginalized groups through listening to and valuing voices on the edge—conceptualize the intersection of concepts such as culture, power, gender, sex, and communication. We examine two theoretical frameworks that have been influential in the work of communication scholars: standpoint theory and muted group theory. Though these theories are rarely linked in a specific way in the literature, they provide intersecting arguments about the ways in which the positioning of women and others within society influence perspective, knowledge, power, and communication.

These theories have been most thoroughly developed by feminist scholars. However, as we discuss in more detail later, theorists in both the standpoint and muted group traditions argue that the processes inherent in standpoint theory and muted group theory could well be used to enhance understanding of other groups in society that have been historically kept from the center of power (e.g., people of color, people of varying ethnicities, people of varying social classes, people of varying sexual orientations, children, the elderly). Orbe (1995, 1996, 1998) has used the term co-culture to highlight the multiplicity of cultural groups, particularly in U.S. society, and to highlight the power differentials inherent in this multiplicity. As Orbe (1998) argues,

Because an assortment of co-cultures simultaneously exists in our society, co-cultural communication theory also is grounded in the notion that over time one co-culture (that of European-American heterosexual middle- or upper-class males) has acquired dominant group status in the major social institutions (i.e., political, corporate, religious, and legal institutions) across the land. This central position of one dominant co-cultural group has rendered other co-cultural groups as marginalized with the predominant societal structures. (p. 2)

The two theories we consider here, then, explore the ways in which the position of **co-cultural groups** in society and the experiences associated with those positions influence perception, power, and communication.

Standpoint Theory

Background   Though **standpoint theory** as expressed today in feminist scholarship is of relatively recent origin, it has its roots in philosophical ideas from several hundred years ago. Georg Wilhelm Friedrich Hegel, a German philosopher, wrote about the influence of social position on views of the world and society. The example he used was of the master and the slave. Though the master and the slave may occupy the same chronological and geographical positions and may live in a common society, the radically different social positions of the master and the slave lead to very different views of the world. Karl Marx later used this central idea as a foundation in his critique of class structure and capitalist society. Specifically, Marx argued that the capitalist economic system creates an ownership class and a worker class and that the historical conditions of these classes shape views of the world and knowledge of class members. At the heart of Marxist theory is the idea that owners expropriate surplus labor from workers and thus place owners and workers in very different positions within economic and class structure (see Chapter 5).

Feminist scholars looking at Marxist theory appreciate the recognition that an individual's position in society has important consequences for what can be perceived, known, and understood. In other words, there is a material and experiential base that underlies knowledge and power. However, feminist theorists argue that the Marxist conception of history and society is woefully ignorant of the role of women in the economic system. As Nancy Hartsock (1997) states about Marx:

> Despite the fact that he recognized that the situation of women was less than satisfactory, that bourgeois marriage was a form of prostitution, that widows were part of the lowest layer of the reserve army of the unemployed, he lost track of women's labor in reproducing the working class. And so at the heart of his theory—the theory of how surplus value is produced and extracted— women are not present. (p. 99)

Thus, standpoint theory was conceived to provide an alternative and feminist understanding of power and of the relationship of lived experience to knowledge and power. Hartsock (1983), in her original explication of standpoint theory, argued that women in Western industrial societies occupy a position that is shaped by history, by material influences, and by their experiences. Because a sexual division of labor exists—that is, men do the "productive" work in the factories and women do the "nurturing" work in the home—men and women have very different views of the world. According to Welton (1997), "If we accept the argument that the work we do shapes our material existence and epistemological perspective, then the substantive difference of women's work, in its very concreteness and grounded nature, grants women a uniquely privileged standpoint position from which to view the world" (p. 11).

Current Commitments   From these foundations, standpoint theory has developed as a project that looks critically at the ways in which social structure and experience shape both ontology (i.e., ways of being) and epistemology (i.e., ways of knowing). There were early concerns with standpoint theory as a perspective that might serve to *universalize* or *essentialize* women. That is, critics charged that standpoint

theory could lead some to believe that all women are the same (i.e., a concern with universalizing) and that a **feminist standpoint** is always marked by concerns with the nurturing and emotional roles of women (i.e., a concern with essentializing). However, more recent writing has made it clear that standpoint theory should be seen as a methodological and epistemological position rather than as a specific content. As Hirschmann (1997) argues,

> The central notion of a standpoint approach . . . is that material experiences shape epistemology. Hence, to the degree that people share a particular set of experiences, for instance, if large numbers of women have exclusive responsibility for raising children or perform uncompensated household labor for men, then they may share a standpoint. But by the same token, to the degree that experience differs, as childrearing practices do from culture to culture, then standpoints will differ as well. [Standpoint theory] provides the means for women within various groups to resist their oppression by drawing on the epistemological power their particular shared experiences affords to rename those experiences. (p. 76)

Thus, though issues regarding standpoint theory have been widely debated (see, e.g., Kenney & Kinsella, 1997), the framework is now an influential theory for enhancing the understanding of women and other disenfranchised groups. Hartsock (1998, p. 229) has stated that the "most important aspects of standpoint theory" include the following points:

- *Material life (class position in Marxism) structures and sets limits on understandings of social relationships.* The experiences of a woman working in the home, in essence, provide a very different point of view for understanding the social world and interactions within that world than the experiences of a man working in a hierarchical corporation.

- *If material life is structured in fundamentally opposing ways for two groups, the understanding of one will represent an inversion of the other.* This principle extends on the first by arguing not only that the standpoints of individuals in different social positions contrast but also that, as Hartsock believes, the standpoint of the ruling class will be "partial" and "perverse" and is likely to harm those occupying the marginalized standpoint.

- *The vision of the ruling group structures the material relations in which all persons are forced to participate.* In other words, those who hold positions of power within the social world also set the rules and create the standards in that world. Hence, a woman in the home is derided as a mere housewife and certain jobs are seen as scut work.

- *In consequence, the vision available to an oppressed group must be struggled for and represents an achievement.* Hartsock believes that it is this point of standpoint theory that "seems to be the most consistently missed" (p. 237), for it argues that one does not represent a standpoint simply from being in a particular spot in the social structure but through political struggle to gain an understanding of the implications of that position.

- *As an engaged vision, the potential understanding of the oppressed, the adoption of a standpoint, makes visible the inhumanity of relations among human beings and increases the opportunities for liberation of oppressed groups.* Standpoint theory, then, serves not just as a vehicle for understanding the implications of social position and experience, but also in service of our "yearning for a better and more just world" (p. 229).

Within communication theory and research, standpoint theory has been called on to enhance our understanding, and increase liberatory potential, in several areas. For example, Brenda Allen (1996, 2000) has used the standpoint notion of an "outsider within" to write about her experiences as a black woman in academia. In her work, Allen talks both about her experiences in being socialized in an organizational context that is a nontraditional occupational role for black women and about how she has used acts of resistance to "actively shape a new identity of [her]self, rather than allowing other forces to shape [her]" (Allen, 2000, p. 202). Bullis and Stout (2000) have also proposed a feminist standpoint theory of organizational socialization, and Burrell, Buzzanell, and McMillan (1992) used feminist standpoint theory to explore varying approaches to conflict, arguing that "women do not share the same life experiences and social realities, and, therefore, one woman cannot speak for all women" (p. 117).

Muted Group Theory

Background For many years, anthropologists have attempted to understand cultures different from their own through field research and the writing of ethnography. Through the work of these cultural anthropologists, it has been assumed that we have gained a detailed, complete, and accurate description of the people in a culture, their ways of life, their rituals, and their stories. However, in the mid 1970s, two cultural anthropologists, Edwin Ardener and Shirley Ardener, pointed out an interesting thing about the work of cultural anthropologists (E. Ardener, 1975; S. Ardener, 1978). Specifically, they noticed that cultural anthropologists typically talked to the adult men in a culture and then wrote in their ethnographies about the culture as a whole. Thus, entire portions of a culture (i.e., women, children, others in powerless positions) were not being represented as their cultural stories were written.

The Ardeners argued that this phenomenon had two facets. First, the anthropological researchers (who were usually white men) didn't hear the voices of the powerless. Because the researchers were accustomed to listening to men, and hearing the language of men, they didn't seek out or understand women's voices in the research process. Women were seen as inarticulate by researchers, and Edwin Ardener (1975) posited that "if the men appear 'articulate' compared with the women, it is a case of like speaking like" (p. 2). Second, beyond this deafness on the part of males, women were "muted" during the research. Shirley Ardener (1978) saw this process as occurring over time: "Words which continually fall upon deaf ears may, of course, in the end become unspoken" (p. 20). This cycle of deafness and mutedness serves as the basis for **muted group theory.**

Current Commitments Muted group theory has been developed most completely by Cheris Kramarae and her colleagues (Houston & Kramarae, 1991; Kramarae, 1978, 1981). Like standpoint theory, muted group theory has been articulated primarily as a feminist theory (i.e., with women as the muted group) but has been applied to other marginalized cultural groups as well (see Orbe, 1994, 1998). As Orbe (1998) explains, "Within any society in which asymmetrical power relationships are maintained, a muted-group framework exists" (p. 21).

Kramarae (1981) lays out three assumptions that are central to her feminist presentation of muted group theory:

- Women perceive the world differently than men because women and men have had very different experiences. These differential experiences are rooted in societal division of labor.
- Because men are the dominant group in society, their system of perception is also dominant. This dominance impedes the free expression of women's alternative models of the world.
- Thus, in order to participate in society, women must transform their own models in terms of the dominant (i.e., male) system of expression.

The first of these assumptions is similar to the basis of feminist standpoint theory. That is, because women experience the world differently, they will perceive the world differently. Furthermore, those differences of experience are often found in the distinction between the public world of work, commerce, and competition and the private world of home, family, and nurtu-

rance. For both standpoint theorists and muted group theorists, these differences in experience shape differences in perception.

Muted group theory goes beyond this concept of perception, however, and brings communication processes to the forefront. Specifically, muted group theory proposes that because the dominant group (typically white European males) controls public means of expression (e.g., the dictionaries, the media, the law, the government), their styles of expression will be privileged. This favoring of white male communication will include everything from the dominance of rationality in public and organizational talk to the use of sports metaphors to derogatory comments and jokes about women.

Women's "other" ways of talking (e.g., emotional discourse, metaphors relevant to home life) will not have a place in this man's world, and men will claim that they can't understand women or their modes of expression. Through processes including ridicule, ritual, gatekeeping, and harrassment (Houston & Kramarae, 1991), women will be rendered silent or inarticulate in public discourse forums. Specifically, women will often feel uncomfortable speaking in the mainstream of society, will have to translate ideas into the parlance of public communication, will simply not speak, or will use "underground" forms of interaction such as diaries, journals, coffee klatsches, or women-only chatrooms. Table 16.3 summarizes Kramarae's (1981) ideas about the impact of being muted.

Co-Cultural Communication

Both standpoint theory and muted group theory have been developed as feminist theories of social position and social interaction. However, theorists in these areas are always clear in noting that the processes inherent in the theories could be used to understand the experiences of other groups. Like women, people of color, people with gay or lesbian sexual orientations, and the elderly (to name a few groups) are often constrained by the perceptions and experiences of a dominant societal group.

Table 16.3	Hypotheses Regarding Muted Group Theory

- Females are more likely to have difficulty expressing themselves fluently within dominant public modes of expression.

- Males have more difficulty than females in understanding what members of the other gender mean.

- Females are likely to find ways to express themselves outside the dominant public modes of expression used by males in both their verbal conventions and their nonverbal behavior.

- Females are more likely to state dissatisfaction with the dominant public modes of expression.

- Women refusing to live by the ideas of social organization held by the dominant group will change dominant public modes of expression as they consciously and verbally reject those ideas.

- Females are not as likely as males to coin the words that become widely recognized and used by both men and women.

- Females' sense of humor will differ from males' sense of humor.

Source: Developed from Kramarae (1981, p. 4).

Mark Orbe is a communication theorist who has taken these ideas very seriously in applying the ideas of muted group theory and standpoint theory first to black American males (Orbe, 1994, 1995) and then to co-cultural groups in general (Orbe, 1998). Orbe's work on co-cultural groups has made two important extensions to these theories. The first of these extensions is in arguing that the processes of marginalization and muting described in standpoint and muted group theories can be usefully applied to a variety of cultural groups. Perhaps more important, though, Orbe (1998) has taken these theories more directly into the realm of interaction by examining the ways in which members of co-cultural groups deal with the structures and messages of dominant society. Orbe (1998) identified 26 different practices and argued that choice among these practices will depend on factors such as an individual's abilities, perceived cost and rewards, past experiences, and preferred outcomes as well as the situational context. A few of the practices identified by Orbe are presented and

defined in Table 16.4. These practices illustrate that there is not a single or monolithic way that members of co-cultural groups can confront discourse that has been shaped by powerful others.

■ COMPARISON AND COMMENTARY

Unlike the theories discussed in some other chapters of this book, the three frameworks we considered here have run the gamut of approaches to communication theory. From the post-positivist approach apparent in theories of face and culture to the interpretive commitments of speech code theory to the critical and feminist commitments of standpoint theory and muted group theory, these theories of culture and communication speak of the importance of diversity not just in our social world but also in our theorizing.

Martin, Nakayama, and Flores (1998) highlight the complexity of the area of culture and communication and argue that it is essential

---

✳ SPOTLIGHT ON THE THEORIST

Cheris Kramarae

Cheris Kramarae received her Ph.D. from the University of Illinois and taught at that institution for many years. She is truly an interdisciplinary scholar, with ties to the fields of communication, sociology, women's studies, and linguistics. In addition to her connection to the University of Illinois, Kramarae holds a visiting appointment with the Center for the Study of Women in Society at the University of Oregon and is a research-scholar-in-residence for the Education Foundation of the American Association of University Women.

Kramarae traces the roots of her theoretical ideas about muted groups to a course she taught in the early 1970s, entitled "Sex-Related Differences in Language." She began to look, in her own research, at stereotypes about women's talk and writing (as she notes, "There was no problem in finding the stereotypes!"), and within a decade she was joined by other researchers interested in the issue of how men's and women's talk could be differentiated and understood. In looking for theoretical approaches to understanding these issues, she was drawn to the work of Edwin and Shirley Ardener and developed their ideas further in her 1981 book on gender and language.

Kramarae has been pleased with the continued interest scholars have had in muted group theory. As she notes, "Many, perhaps most, theories do not stick

around for decades." Kramarae believes that this staying power is probably a function of both the ease with which the ideas of muted group theory can be explained and "the fact that it seems to many people to be a telling way to describe many women's experiences." Interestingly, Kramarae believes that muted group theory is a bit of a misnomer and an "unfortunate name" for the theory. As she argues, "the proposal is not that women—or other subordinate groups—are actually muted but that they do not control language and speech in the same way that men as a group do."

Though muted group theory has been around for several decades, Kramarae's work on women and language has been extended in several ways. One extension is the consideration of these issues in cultures other than modern Western ones. As Kramarae recounts, "Working with feminists in many cultures during the past three decades has taught me that what questions are asked and what methodologies and theories are utilized is highly dependent upon one's culture and training." These questions of women and language in multiple cultures, then, provide fertile ground for future research. Kramarae has also joined her interest in women and language with a consideration of new communication technologies. At the University of Illinois, she co-started a program called "Women, Information, Technology, and Scholarship," which has helped to facilitate the voice of women in determining technology priorities for the university.

---

that we consider social scientific, interpretive, and critical scholarship in our search for understanding. With regard to these three approaches, they argue,

> Each represents one angle or one view of a very complicated topic, the intersections of culture and communication. Actually it's more a matter of what each considers important. Most scholars would agree on the components of intercultural

communication: culture, communication, context, power. But they would disagree on the relative importance of each, how they are interrelated, and the best methods for understanding intercultural communication. (p. 13)

Martin et al. go on to argue that social scientific researchers emphasize cultural differences, interpretive researchers emphasize context, and critical researchers emphasize power. These distinctions

Table 16.4	Examples of Co-Cultural Communicative Practices
Practice	Description
Emphasizing commonalities	Focusing on human similarities while downplaying or ignoring co-cultural differences
Censoring self	Remaining silent when comments from dominant group members are inappropriate, indirectly insulting, or highly offensive
Manipulating stereotypes	Conforming to commonly accepted beliefs about group members as a strategic means to exploit them for personal gain
Strategic distancing	Avoiding any association with other co-cultural members in attempts to be perceived as a distinct individual
Communicating self	Interacting with dominant group members in an authentic, open, and genuine manner; used by those with strong self-concepts
Educating others	Taking the role of teacher in co-cultural interactions; enlightening dominant group members of co-cultural norms, values, and so forth
Avoiding	Maintaining a distance from dominant group members; refraining from activities or locations where interaction is likely
Exemplifying strengths	Promoting the recognition of co-cultural group strengths, past accomplishments, and contributions to society
Using liaisons	Identifying specific dominant group members who can be trusted for support, guidance, and assistance
Increasing visibility	Covertly, yet strategically, maintaining a co-cultural presence within dominant structures
Intragroup networking	Identifying and working with other co-cultural group members who share common philosophies, convictions, and goals

Source: Identified by Orbe (1998).

can be seen in the theories considered here, as our consideration of face and culture emphasizes the ways in which face is perceived and maintained differently among different cultural groups. Speech code theory focuses on context in looking at how local cultural communities develop recognizable speech codes that function to enact and preserve cultural values, and muted group theory and standpoint theory emphasize the role of power in the position and communication of co-cultural groups.

Because the theoretical and research commitments of these three frameworks differ so substantially, it is difficult to compare them in a critical way. Indeed, the work conducted by scholars within a single framework presented in this chapter will rarely intersect with work conducted by scholars in the other frameworks. However, all three frameworks have been highly influential within their own areas of the communication discipline. Each framework has resulted in scholarship conducted beyond the confines of the original theoretical traditions, and each has led to important insights about the intersections between communication and culture.

Key Terms

culture as a community
culture as conversation
culture as a code
emic approach
etic approach
speech codes theory
speech codes
constitutive meaning
metacommunication
individualistic culture
collectivistic culture
low-context culture
high-context culture
positive face
negative face
autonomy face
fellowship face
competence face
face threats
facework
preventive facework
corrective facework
co-cultural groups
standpoint theory
feminist standpoint
muted group theory

Discussion Questions

1. Are there ever times when a particular gender or ethnic group is restricted from or discouraged from using certain speech codes? Consider, for example, whether women are able to use vulgar language in particular settings. Who determines these speech codes and what gives them power?

2. Does a relationship exist between individualistic/collectivistic cultures and high-context/low-context cultures? How do these concepts influence communication patterns within a particular culture? How might they influence communication between members of different cultures?

3. What is the relationship between the concept of political correctness and muted group theory? Does political correctness give voice to muted groups or does political correctness cause groups to be muted?

4. Mark Orbe argues that standpoint theory and muted group theory can usefully be expanded beyond their feminist roots to an analysis of a wide range of co-cultural groups. Do you agree? What are the differences between women as a cultural group and cultural groups based on other factors?

Bibliography

Abrams, P. (1982). *Historical sociology.* Somerset, UK: Open Books.

Afifi, W. A., & Burgoon, J. K. (1998). "We never talk about that": A comparison of cross-sex friendships and dating relationships on uncertainty and topic avoidance. *Personal Relationships, 5,* 255–272.

Afifi, W. A., & Burgoon, J. K. (1999). Reacting to nonverbal expressions of liking: A test of interaction adaptation theory. *Communication Monographs, 66,* 219–239.

Afifi, W. A., & Burgoon, J. K. (2000). The impact of violations on uncertainty and the consequences for attractiveness. *Human Communication Research, 26,* 203–233.

Afifi, W. A., & Metts, S. (1998). Characteristics and consequences of expectation violations in close relationships. *Journal of Social and Personal Relationships, 15,* 365–392.

Agassi, J. (1975). *Science in flux.* Boston Studies no. 28. Dordrecht, The Netherlands: Reidel.

Ajzen, I. (1985). From intentions to actions: A theory of planned behavior. In J. Kuhland & J. Beckman (Eds.), *Action-control: From cognitions to behavior* (pp. 11–39). Heidelberg, Germany: Springer.

Ajzen, I., & Fishbein, M. (1980). *Understanding attitudes and predicting social behavior.* Englewood Cliffs, NJ: Prentice Hall.

Ajzen, I., & Fishbein, M. (1983). Relevance and availability in the attribution process. In J. Jaspars, F. D. Fincham, & M. Hewstone (Eds.), *Attribution theory and research: Conceptual, developmental and social dimensions* (pp. 63–89). London: Academic.

Albrecht, T. L., & Adelman, M. B. (1987). *Communicating social support.* Beverly Hills, CA: Sage.

Allen, B. J. (1996). Feminist standpoint theory: A black woman's (re)view of organizational socialization. *Communication Studies, 47,* 257–271.

Allen, B. J. (2000). "Learning the ropes": A black feminist standpoint analysis. In P. M. Buzzanell (Ed.), *Rethinking organizational and managerial communication from feminist perspectives* (pp. 177–208). Thousand Oaks, CA: Sage.

Allen, M., & Reynolds, R. (1993). The elaboration likelihood model and the sleeper effect: An assessment of attitude change over time. *Communication Theory, 3,* 73–82.

Altheide, D. L., & Snow, R. P. (1988). Toward a theory of mediation. In J. A. Anderson (Ed.), *Communication yearbook 11* (pp. 194–223). Newbury Park, CA: Sage.

Altman, I., & Taylor, D. A. (1973). *Social penetration: The development of interpersonal relationships.* New York: Holt, Rinehart, & Winston.

Altman, I., Vinsel, A., & Brown, B. B. (1981). Dialectic conceptions in social psychology: An application to social penetration and privacy regulation. In L. Berkowitz (Ed.), *Advances in experimental social psychology* (Vol. 14, pp. 107–160). New York: Academic.

Andersen, P. A. (1985). Nonverbal immediacy in interpersonal communication. In A. W. Siegman & S. Feldstein (Eds.), *Multichannel integrations of nonverbal behavior* (pp. 1–36). Hillsdale, NJ: Erlbaum.

Andersen, P. A. (1987). Intentionality and communication: Is not communicating impossible? Paper presented to the International Communication Association, Montreal.

Andersen, P. A. (1991). When one cannot not communicate: A challenge to Motley's traditional communication postulates. *Communication Studies, 42,* 309–325.

Anderson, J. A. (1996). *Communication theory: Epistemological foundations.* New York: Guilford.

Anderson, L. R., & McGuire, W. J. (1965). Prior reassurance of group consensus as a factor in producing resistance to persuasion. *Sociometry, 28,* 44–56.

Arbib, M. A., Conklin, E. J., & Hill, J. (1987). *From schema theory to language.* Oxford: Oxford University Press.

Ardener, E. (1975). The "problem" revisited. In S. Ardener (Ed.), *Perceiving women* (pp. 19–27). London: Malaby.

Ardener, S. (1978). Introduction: The nature of women in society. In S. Ardener (Ed.), *Defining females* (pp. 9–48). New York: Wiley.

Asch, S. E. (1951). Effects of group pressure upon the modification and distortion of judgments. In H. S. Guetzkow (Ed.), *Groups, leadership, and men: Research in human relations* (pp. 177–190). New York: Russell & Russell.

Austin, J. L. (1962). *How to do things with words.* Oxford: Oxford University Press.

Ayer, A. J. (1960). *Language, truth, and logic.* London: Gollancz.

Babrow, A. S. (1992). Communication and problematic integration: Understanding diverging probability and value, ambiguity, ambivalence, and impossibility. *Communication Theory, 2,* 95–130.

Babrow, A. S. (1993). The advent of multiple-process theories of communication. *Journal of Communication, 43,* 110–118.

Babrow, A. S. (1995). Communication and problematic integration: Milan Kundera's "Lost Letters" in *The Book of Laughter and Forgetting. Communication Monographs, 62,* 283–300.

Babrow, A. S., & Kline, K. N. (2000). From "reducing" to "coping with" uncertainty: Reconceptualizing the central challenge in breast self-exams. *Social Science & Medicine, 51,* 1805–1816.

Babrow, A. S., & Swanson, D. L. (1988). Disentangling antecedents of audience exposure levels: Expectancy-value analyses of gratifications sought from television news. *Communication Monographs, 55,* 1–21.

Bakhtin, M. M. (1981). *The dialogic imagination: Four essays by M. M. Bakhtin* (M. Holquist, Ed.; C. Emerson & M. Holquist, Trans.). Austin: University of Texas Press.

Baldassare, M., & Katz, C. (1996). Measures of attitude strength as predictors of willingness to speak to the media. *Journalism & Mass Communication Quarterly, 73,* 147–158.

Bales, R. F. (1950). *Interaction process analysis.* Reading, MA: Addison-Wesley.

Bales, R. F. (1970). *Personality and interpersonal behavior.* New York: Holt, Rinehart, & Winston.

Ball-Rokeach, S. J. (1985). The origins of individual media system dependency: A sociological framework. *Communication Research, 12,* 485–510.

Ball-Rokeach, S. J. (1998). A theory of media power and a theory of media use: Different stories, questions, and ways of thinking. *Mass Communication & Society, 1,* 5–40.

Ball-Rokeach, S. J., & DeFleur, M. L. (1976). A dependency model of mass media effects. *Communication Research, 3,* 3–21.

Bandura, A. (1962). Social learning through imitation. In M. R. Jones (Ed.), *Nebraska Symposium on Motivation: Vol. 10.* Lincoln: University of Nebraska Press.

Bandura, A. (1969). *Principles of behavior modification.* Austin, TX: Holt, Rinehart, & Winston.

Bandura, A. (1977a). Self-efficacy: Toward a unifying theory of behavior change. *Psychological Review, 84,* 191–215.

Bandura, A. (1977b). *Social learning theory.* Englewood Cliffs, NJ: Prentice Hall.

Bandura, A. (1986). *Social foundations of thought and action: A social cognitive theory.* Englewood Cliffs, NJ: Prentice Hall.

Bandura, A. (1994). Social cognitive theory of mass communication. In J. Bryant & D. Zillmann (Eds.), *Media effects: Advances in theory and research* (pp. 61–90). Hillsdale, NJ: Erlbaum.

Bandura, A. (1995). *Self-efficacy in changing societies.* New York: Cambridge University Press.

Banks, S. P., & Riley, P. (1993). Structuration theory as an ontology for communication research. In S. A. Deetz (Ed.), *Communication yearbook 16* (pp. 167–196). Newbury Park, CA: Sage.

Bantz, C. R. (1980). *Organizing the news: Extending newswork theorizing through Weick's organizing formulation.* Paper presented at the annual meeting of the Speech Communication Association, New York.

Bantz, C. R. (1989). Organizing and *The social psychology of organizing. Communication Studies, 40,* 231–240.

Baran, S. J., & Davis, D. K. (2000). *Mass communication theory: Foundations, ferment, and future* (2nd ed.). Belmont, CA: Wadsworth.

Baranowski, T., Perry, C. L., & Parcel, G. S. (1997). How individuals, environments, and health behavior interact: Social cognitive theory. In K. Glanz, F. M. Lewis, & B. K. Rimer (Eds.), *Health behavior and health education: Theory, research, and practice* (2nd ed.) (pp. 153–178). San Francisco: Jossey-Bass.

Barker, J. R. (1993). Tightening the iron cage: Concertive control in self-managing teams. *Administrative Science Quarterly, 38,* 408–437.

Barker, J. R. (1999). *The discipline of teamwork: Participation and concertive control.* Thousand Oaks, CA: Sage.

Barker, J. R., & Cheney, G. (1994). The concept and the practices of discipline in contemporary organizational life. *Communication Monographs, 61,* 19–43.

Bastien, D., McPhee, R., & Bolton, K. (1995). A study and extended theory of the structuration of climate. *Communication Monographs, 62,* 87–109.

Bateson, G. (1958). *Naven.* Stanford, CA: Stanford University Press.

Bateson, G. (1966). Slippery theories. *International Journal of Psychiatry, 2,* 415–417.

Bavelas, J. B. (1990). Behavior and communicating: A reply to Motley. *Western Journal of Speech Communication, 54,* 593–602.

Bavelas, J. B. (1992). Research into the pragmatics of human communication. *Journal of Strategic and Systemic Therapies, 11,* 15–29.

Bavelas, J. B., Black, A., Chovil, N., & Mullett, J. (1990). *Equivocal communication.* Newbury Park, CA: Sage.

Baxter, L. A. (1988). A dialectical perspective on communication strategies in relationship development. In S. Duck (Ed.), *Handbook of personal relationships* (pp. 257–273). New York: Wiley.

Baxter, L. A. (1990). Dialectical contradictions in relationship development. *Journal of Social and Personal Relationships, 7,* 69–88.

Baxter, L. A. (1993). The social side of personal relationships: A dialectical perspective. In S. Duck (Ed.), *Understanding relationship processes, 3: Social context and relationships* (pp. 139–165). Newbury Park, CA: Sage.

Baxter, L. A., Mazanec, M., Nicholson, J., Pittman, G., Smith, K., & West, L. (1997). Everyday loyalties and betrayals in personal relationships. *Journal of Social and Personal Relationships, 14,* 655–678.

Baxter, L. A., & Montgomery, B. M. (1996). *Relating: Dialogues and dialectics.* New York: Guilford.

Baxter, L. A., & Simon, E. P. (1993). Relationship maintenance strategies and dialectical contradiction in personal relationships. *Journal of Social and Personal Relationships, 10,* 225–242.

Beach, W. A. (1990). On (not) observing behavior interactionally. *Western Journal of Speech Communication, 54,* 603–612.

Bem, D. J. (1967). Self-perception: An alternative interpretation of cognitive dissonance phenomena. *Psychological Review, 74,* 183–200.

Bem, D. J. (1972). Self-perception theory. In L. Berkowitz (Ed.), *Advances in experimental social psychology* (Vol. 6, pp. 1–62). New York: Academic.

Beninger, J. R. (1993). Communication—Embrace the subject, not the field. *Journal of Communication, 43* (3), 18–25.

Berger, A. A. (1989). *Signs in contemporary culture.* Salem, WI: Sheffield.

Berger, C. R. (1979). Beyond initial interaction: Uncertainty, understanding, and the development of interpersonal relationships. In H. Giles & R. St. Clair (Eds.), *Language and social psychology* (pp. 122–144). Oxford: Blackwell.

Berger, C. R. (1987). Communicating under uncertainty. In M. E. Roloff & G. R. Miller (Eds.), *Interpersonal processes: New directions in communication research* (pp. 39–62). Newbury Park, CA: Sage.

Berger, C. R. (1988). Planning, affect, and social action generation. In R. L. Donohew, H. Sypher, & E. T. Higgins (Eds.), *Communication, social cognition, and affect* (pp. 93–116). Hillsdale, NJ: Erlbaum.

Berger, C. R. (1991). Communication theories and other curios. *Communication Monographs, 58,* 101–113.

Berger, C. R. (1995). A plan-based approach to strategic communication. In D. E. Hewes (Ed.), *The cognitive bases of interpersonal communication* (pp. 141–179). Hillsdale, NJ: Erlbaum.

Berger, C. R. (1997). *Planning strategic interaction: Attaining goals through communicative action.* Mahwah, NJ: Erlbaum.

Berger, C. R., & Bradac, J. J. (1982). *Language and social knowledge: Uncertainty in interpersonal relations.* London: Arnold.

Berger, C. R., & Calabrese, R. J. (1975). Some exploration in initial interaction and beyond: Toward a developmental theory of interpersonal communication. *Human Communication Research, 1,* 99–112.

Berger, C. R., & DiBattista, P. (1993). Communication failure and plan adaptation: If at first you don't succeed, say it louder and slower. *Communication Monographs, 60,* 220–238.

Berger, C. R., Gardner, R. R., Clatterbuck, G. W., & Shulman, L. S. (1976). Perceptions of information sequencing in relationship development. *Human Communication Research, 3,* 29–46.

Berger, C. R., & Gudykunst, W. B. (1991). Uncertainty and communication. In B. Dervin & M. Voigt (Eds.), *Progress in communication sciences* (Vol. 10, pp. 21–66). Norwood, NJ: Ablex.

Berger, C. R., & Kellermann, K. (1994). Acquiring social information. In J. A. Daly & J. M. Weimann (Eds.), *Strategic interpersonal communication* (pp. 1–31). Hillsdale, NJ: Erlbaum.

Berger, P., & Luckmann, T. (1967). *The social construction of reality*. London: Penguin.

Berkowitz, L. (1964). The effects of observing violence. *Scientific American, 210*, 35–41.

Berlo, D. K. (1960). *The process of communication*. New York: Holt, Rinehart, & Winston.

Bernstein, B. (1971). *Class, codes, and control. Vol. 1: Theoretical studies toward a sociology of language*. London: Routledge & Kegan Paul.

Bernstein, B. (1973). *Class, codes, and control. Vol. 2: Applied studies toward a sociology of language*. London: Routledge & Kegan Paul.

Bernstein, B. (1975). *Class, codes, and control: Theoretical studies toward a sociology of language* (rev. ed.). New York: Schocken.

Bernstein, R. J. (1976). *The restructuring of social and political theory*. Philadelphia: University of Pennsylvania Press.

Berteotti, C. R., & Seibold, D. R. (1994). Coordination and role-definition problems in health-care teams: A hospice case study. In L. R. Frey (Ed.), *Group communication in context: Studies of natural groups* (pp. 107–131). Hillsdale, NJ: Erlbaum.

Billingsley, J. M. (1993). An evaluation of the functional perspective in small group communication. In S. A. Deetz (Ed.), *Communication yearbook 16* (pp. 615–622). Newbury Park, CA: Sage.

Blalock, H. M. (1969). *Theory construction: From verbal to mathematical formulations*. Englewood Cliffs, NJ: Prentice Hall.

Bochner, A. P. (1976). Conceptual frontiers in the study of communication in families: An introduction to the literature. *Human Communication Research, 2*, 381–397.

Bochner, A. P. (1984). The functions of human communication in interpersonal bonding. In C. C. Arnold & J. W. Bowers (Eds.), *Handbook of rhetorical and communication theory* (pp. 544–621). Boston: Allyn & Bacon.

Bochner, A. P. (1985). Perspectives on inquiry: Representation, conversation, and reflection. In M. L. Knapp & G. R. Miller (Eds.), *Handbook of interpersonal communication* (pp. 27–58). Newbury Park, CA: Sage.

Bochner, A. P., & Eisenberg, E. M. (1985). Legitimizing speech communication: An examination of coherence and cohesion in the development of the discipline. In T. Benson (Ed.), *Speech communication in the 20th century* (pp. 299–321). Carbondale: Southern Illinois University Press.

Bochner, A. P., & Eisenberg, E. M. (1987). Family process: System perspectives. In C. R. Berger & S. Chaffee (Eds.), *Handbook of communication science* (pp. 540–563). Beverly Hills, CA: Sage.

Bogart, L. (1991, August). The pollster and the Nazis. *Commentary*, 47–49.

Bormann, E. G. (1980). *Communication theory*. New York: Holt, Rinehart, & Winston.

Bormann, E. G. (1982). The symbolic convergence theory of communication and the creation, raising, and sustaining of public consciousness. In J. Sisco (Ed.), *The Jensen lectures: Contemporary communication studies* (pp. 71–90). Tampa: University of South Florida, Department of Communication.

Bormann, E. G. (1983). Symbolic convergence: Organizational communication and culture. In L. L. Putnam & M. E. Pacanowsky (Eds.), *Communication and organization: An interpretive approach* (pp. 99–122). Beverly Hills, CA: Sage.

Bormann, E. G. (1996). Symbolic convergence theory and communication in group decision-making. In R. Y. Hirokawa & M. S. Poole (Eds.), *Communication and group decision-making* (2nd ed.) (pp. 81–113). Thousand Oaks, CA: Sage.

Bormann, E. G., Cragan, J. F., & Shields, D. C. (1994). In defense of symbolic convergence theory: A look at the theory and its criticisms after two decades. *Communication Theory, 4*, 259–294.

Boster, F. J. (1995). Commentary on compliance-gaining message behavior research. In C. R. Berger & M. Burgoon (Eds.), *Communication and social influence processes* (pp. 91–113). East Lansing: Michigan State University Press.

Braithwaite, C. A. (1997). "Were YOU There?": A ritual of legitimacy among Vietnam veterans. *Western Journal of Communication, 61*, 423–447.

Braithwaite, D. O., & Baxter, L. A. (1995). 'I do' again: The relational dialectics of renewing marriage vows. *Journal of Social and Personal Relationships, 12*, 177–198.

Braybrooke, D. (1987). *Philosophy of social science*. Englewood Cliffs, NJ: Prentice Hall.

Brehm, J. W., & Cohen, A. R. (1962). *Explorations in cognitive dissonance*. New York: Wiley.

Brenders, D. A. (1987). Fallacies in the coordinated management of meaning: A philosophy of language critique of the hierarchical organization of coherent conversation and related theory. *Quarterly Journal of Speech, 73*, 329–348.

Brock, B. L. (Ed.) (1999). *Kenneth Burke and the 21st century*. Albany: State University of New York Press.

Brooks-Harris, J. E., Heesacker, M., & Mejia-Millan, C. (1996). Changing men's male gender-role attitudes by applying the elaboration likelihood model of attitude change. *Sex Roles, 35*, 563–580.

Brown, P., & Levinson, S. (1978). Universals in language usage: Politeness phenomena. In E. Goody (Ed.), *Questions and politeness* (pp. 56–323). Cambridge: Cambridge University Press.

Brown, P., & Levinson, S. C. (1987). *Politeness: Some universals in language use*. New York: Cambridge University Press.

Brummett, B. (Ed.) (1993). *Landmark essays on Kenneth Burke*. Davis, CA: Hermagoras.

Bryant, J., & Zillmann, D. (Eds.) (1991). *Responding to the screen: Reception and reaction processes*. Hillsdale, NJ: Erlbaum.

Bullis, C. (1991). Communication practices as unobtrusive control: An observational study. *Communication Studies, 42*, 254–271.

Bullis, C., & Stout, K. R. (2000). Organizational socialization: A feminist standpoint approach. In P. M. Buzzanell (Ed.), *Rethinking organizational and managerial communication from feminist perspectives* (pp. 47–75). Thousand Oaks, CA: Sage.

Bullis, C., & Tompkins, P. K. (1989). The forest ranger revisited: A study of control practices and identification. *Communication Monographs, 56*, 287–306.

Burgoon, J., Dillman, L., & Stern, L. A. (1993). Adaptation in dyadic interaction: Defining and operationalizing patterns of reciprocity and compensation. *Communication Theory, 4*, 293–316.

Burgoon, J., & Hale, J. L. (1988). Nonverbal expectancy violations: Model elaboration and application to immediacy behaviors. *Communication Monographs, 55*, 58–79.

Burgoon, J., & Jones, S. B. (1976). Toward a theory of personal space expectations and their violations. *Human Communication Research, 2*, 131–146.

Burgoon, J. K., LePoire, B. A., & Rosenthal, R. (1995). Effects of preinteraction expectancies and target communication on perceiver reciprocity and compensation in dyadic interaction. *Journal of Experimental Social Psychology, 31*, 287–321.

Burgoon, J. K., Stern, L. A., & Dillman, L. (1995). *Interpersonal adaptation: Dyadic interaction patterns*. Cambridge: Cambridge University Press.

Burgoon, J., & Walther, J. B. (1990). Nonverbal expectancies and the evaluative consequences of violations. *Human Communication Research, 17*, 232–265.

Burgoon, M., & Chase, L. J. (1973). The effects of differential linguistic patterns in messages attempting to induce resistance to persuasion. *Speech Monographs, 40*, 1–7.

Burgoon, M., Cohen, M., Miller, M. D., & Montgomery, C. L. (1978). An empirical test of a model of resistance to persuasion. *Human Communication Research, 5*, 27–39.

Burgoon, M., & Ruffner, M. (1978). *Human communication*. New York: Holt, Rinehart, & Winston.

Burke, K. (1935). *Permanence and change*. Indianapolis: Bobbs-Merrill.

Burke, K. (1945). *A grammar of motives*. Berkeley: University of California Press.

Burke, K. (1950). *A rhetoric of motives*. Berkeley: University of California Press.

Burke, K. (1966). *Language as symbolic action: Essays on life, literature and method*. Berkeley: University of California Press.

Burke, K. (1968). Dramatism. In D. L. Sills (Ed.), *The international encyclopedia of the social sciences* (Vol. 7, pp. 445–452). New York: MacMillan/Free Press.

Burke, K. (1976). The party line. *Quarterly Journal of Speech, 62*, 62–68.

Burleson, B. R. (1986). Attribution schemes and causal inferences in natural conversations. In D. G. Ellis & W. A. Donohue (Eds.), *Contemporary issues in language and discourse processes* (pp. 63–86). Hillsdale, NJ: Erlbaum.

Burleson, B. R. (1987). Cognitive complexity. In J. C. McCroskey & J. A. Daly (Eds.), *Personality and interpersonal communication* (pp. 305–349). Newbury Park, CA: Sage.

Burleson, B. R. (1989). The constructivist approach to person-centered communication: Analysis of a research exemplar. In B. A. Dervin, L. Grossberg, B. J. O'Keefe, & E. Wartella (Eds.), *Rethinking communication, Vol. 2: Paradigm exemplars* (pp. 29–46). Newbury Park, CA: Sage.

Burleson, B. R., & Caplan, S. E. (1997). Cognitive complexity. In J. C. McCroskey, J. A. Daly, & M. M. Martin (Eds.), *Communication and personality:*

Trait perspectives (pp. 230–286). Cresskill, NJ: Hampton.

Burnstein, E. (1982). Persuasion as argument processing. In H. Brandstatter, J. H. Davis, & G. Stocker-Kreichgauer (Eds.), *Group decision making* (pp. 103–124). New York: Academic.

Burrell, G., & Morgan, G. (1979). *Sociological paradigms and organisation analysis.* London: Heinemann.

Burrell, N. A., Buzzanell, P. M., and McMillan, J. J. (1992). Feminine tensions in conflict situations as revealed by metaphoric analyses. *Management Communication Quarterly, 6,* 115–149.

Buzzanell, P. (1994). Gaining a voice: Feminist organizational communication theorizing. *Management Communication Quarterly, 7,* 339–383.

Buzzanell, P. M., Burrell, N. A., Stafford, R. S., & Berkowitz, S. (1996). When I call you up and you're not there: Application of communication accommodation theory to telephone answering machine messages. *Western Journal of Communication, 60,* 310–336.

Byrne, D. (1971). *The attraction paradigm.* New York: Academic.

Cacioppo, J. T., & Petty, R. E. (1982). The need for cognition. *Journal of Personality and Social Psychology, 42,* 116–131.

Cacioppo, J. T., & Petty, R. E. (1984). The need for cognition: Relationship to attitudinal processes. In R. P. McGlynn, J. E. Maddux, C. D. Stoltenberg, & H. J. Harvey (Eds.), *Social perception in clinical and counseling psychology* (pp. 113–119). Lubbock: Texas Tech Press.

Canary, D. J., Brossman, B. G., & Seibold, D. R. (1987). Argument structures in decision-making groups. *Southern Speech Communication Journal, 53,* 18–37.

Cantor, J. (1991). Fright responses to mass media productions. In J. Bryant & D. Zillmann (Eds.), *Responding to the screen: Reception and reaction processes* (pp. 169–197). Hillsdale, NJ: Erlbaum.

Cantor, J., & Omdahl, B. (1991). Effects of fictional media depictions of realistic threats on children's emotional responses, expectations, worries, and liking for related activities. *Communication Monographs, 58,* 384–401.

Cantor, J., & Sparks, G. G. (1984). Children's fear responses to mass media: Testing some Piagetian predictions. *Journal of Communication, 34,* 90–103.

Cantor, J., & Wilson, B. J. (1988). Helping children cope with frightening media presentations. *Current Psychology: Research & Reviews, 7,* 58–75.

Cappella, J. N., & Greene, J. O. (1984). The effects of distance and individual differences in arousability on nonverbal involvement: A test of discrepancy-arousal theory. *Journal of Nonverbal Behavior, 8,* 259–286.

Carbaugh, D. (1989). Fifty terms for talk: A cross-cultural study. *International and Intercultural Communication Annual, 13,* 93–120.

Carbaugh, D. (1993). "Soul" and "self": Soviet and American cultures in conversation. *Quarterly Journal of Speech, 79,* 182–200.

Carbaugh, D. (1994). Personhood, positioning, and cultural pragmatics: American dignity in cross-cultural perspective. In S. Deetz (Ed.), *Communication yearbook 17* (pp. 159–186). Thousand Oaks, CA: Sage.

Carbaugh, D. (1995). The ethnographic communication theory of Philipsen and associates. In D. P. Cushman & B. Kovačić (Eds.), *Watershed research traditions in human communication theory* (pp. 269–297). Albany: State University of New York Press.

Carbaugh, D. (1999). "Just listen": "Listening" and landscape among the Blackfeet. *Western Journal of Communication, 63,* 250–270.

Carey, J. W. (1983). The origins of radical discourse on cultural studies in the United States. *Journal of Communication, 33,* 311–313.

Carlson, J. M. (1983). Crime show viewing by preadults: The impact of attitudes toward civil liberties. *Communication Research, 10,* 529–552.

Carnap, R. (1937). *Logical syntax of language.* London: Kegan Paul.

Cecil, D. W. (1998). Relational control patterns in physician-patient clinical encounters: Continuing the conversation. *Health Communication, 10,* 125–149.

Chaiken, S. (1987). The heuristic model of persuasion. In M. P. Zanna, J. M. Olson, & C. P. Herman (Eds.), *Social influence: The Ontario symposium* (Vol. 5, pp. 3–39). Hillsdale, NJ: Erlbaum.

Cheney, G., & Tompkins, P. K. (1988). On the facts of the text as the basis of human communication research. In J. A. Anderson (Ed.), *Communication yearbook 11* (pp. 455–501). Newbury Park, CA: Sage.

Cissna, K. N., Cox, D. E., & Bochner, A. P. (1990). The dialectic of marital and parental relationships within the stepfamily. *Communication Monographs, 57,* 44–61.

Clark, R. A., & Delia, J. G. (1977). Cognitive complexity, social perspective-taking, and functional persuasion skills in second-to-ninth grade children. *Human Communication Research, 3,* 128–134.

Clatterbuck, G. (1979). Attributional confidence and uncertainty. *Human Communication Research, 5,* 147–157.

Clevenger, T. (1991). Can one not communicate? A conflict of models. *Communication Studies, 42,* 340–353.

Cline, R. J. W. (1994). Groupthink and the Watergate cover-up: The illusion of unanimity. In L. R. Frey (Ed.), *Group communication in context: Studies of natural groups* (pp. 199–223). Hillsdale, NJ: Erlbaum.

Cody, M. J., & McLaughlin, M. L. (Eds.) (1990). *The psychology of tactical communication.* Clevedon, England: Multilingual Matters.

Cohen, B. C. (1963). *The press and foreign policy.* Princeton, NJ: Princeton University Press.

Cohen, B. P. (1994). Sociological theory: The half-full cup. In J. Hage (Ed.), *Formal theory in sociology: Opportunity or pitfall* (pp. 66–83). Albany: State University of New York Press.

Cohen, H. (1994). *The history of speech communication: The emergence of a discipline, 1914–1945.* Annandale, VA: Speech Communication Association.

Cohen, I. J. (1989). *Structuration theory: Anthony Giddens and the constitution of social life.* New York: St. Martin's.

Collin, F. (1985). *Theory and understanding: A critique of interpretive social science.* New York: Basil Blackwell.

Collins, B., & Guetzkow, H. (1964). *A social psychology of group processes for decision-making.* New York: Wiley.

Comte, A. (1970). *Introduction to positive philosophy.* (F. Ferre, Trans.). Indianapolis: Bobbs-Merrill.

Conquergood, D. (1991). Rethinking ethnography: Towards a critical cultural politics. *Communication Monographs, 58,* 179–194.

Conrad, C., & Macom, E. A. (1995). Re-visiting Kenneth Burke: Dramatism/logology and the problem of agency. *Southern Communication Journal, 61,* 11–28.

Contractor, N. S., & Seibold, D. R. (1993). Theoretical frameworks for the study of structuring processes in group decision support systems. *Human Communication Research, 19,* 528–563.

Contractor, N. S., Seibold, D. R., & Heller, M. A. (1996). Interactional influences in the structuring of media use in groups: Influence in members' perceptions of group decision support system use. *Human Communication Research, 22,* 451–481.

Conway, J. C., & Rubin, A. M. (1991). Psychological predictors of television viewing motivation. *Communication Research, 18,* 443–463.

Cook, T. D., & Campbell, D. T. (1979). *Quasi-experimentation: Design and analysis issues for field settings.* Chicago: Rand-McNally.

Cooper, J., & Fazio, R. H. (1984). A new look at dissonance theory. In L. Berkowitz (Ed.), *Advances in experimental social psychology* (Vol. 17, pp. 229–266). New York: Academic.

Cooren, F. (1999). Applying socio-semiotics to organizational communication: A new approach. *Management Communication Quarterly, 13,* 294–304.

Cooren, F., & Taylor, J. R. (1997). Organization as an effect of mediation: Redefining the link between organization and communication. *Communication Theory, 7,* 219–260.

Corbin, J., & Strauss, A. (1990). Grounded theory method: Procedures, canons, and evaluative criteria. *Qualitative Sociology, 13,* 3–21.

Corcoran, F. (1989). Cultural studies: From old world to new world. In J. Anderson (Ed.), *Communication yearbook 12* (pp. 601–617). Newbury Park, CA: Sage.

Corman, S. R., & Poole, M. S. (Eds.) (2000). *Perspectives on organizational communication: Finding common ground.* New York: Guilford.

Corman, S. R., & Scott, C. R. (1994). Perceived networks, activity foci, and observable communication in social collectives. *Communication Theory, 4,* 171–190.

Coupland, N., Coupland, J., Giles, H., & Henwood, K. (1988). Accommodating the elderly: Invoking and extending a theory. *Language in Society, 17,* 1–41.

Coupland, N., Coupland, J., Giles, H., & Henwood, K. (1991). Intergenerational talk: Goal consonance and intergroup dissonance. In K. Tracy (Ed.), *Understanding face-to-face interaction: Issues linking goals and discourse* (pp. 79–100). Hillsdale, NJ: Erlbaum.

Coupland, N., & Giles, H. (1988). Introduction: The communicative contexts of accommodation. *Language & Communication, 8,* 175–182.

Courtright, J. A., Millar, F. E., Rogers, L. E., & Bagarozzi, D. (1990). Interaction dynamics of relational negotiation: Reconciliation versus termination of distressed relationships. *Western Journal of Speech Communication, 54,* 429–453.

Cragan, J. F., & Shields, D. C. (1994). *Symbolic theories in applied communication research.* Cresskill, NJ: Hampton.

Cragan, J. F., & Wright, D. W. (1990). Small group communication research of the 1980s: A synthesis and critique. *Communication Studies, 41,* 212–236.

Craig, R. T. (1995). Book review of *A history of communication study* and *The history of speech communication. Communication Theory, 5,* 178–184.

Craig, R. T. (1999). Communication theory as a field. *Communication Theory, 9,* 119–161.

Crockett, W. H. (1965). Cognitive complexity and impression formation. In B. A. Maher (Ed.), *Progress in experimental personality research* (Vol. 2, pp. 47–90). New York: Academic.

Cronen, V. (1991). Coordinated management of meaning theory and postmodern ethics. In K. J. Greenberg (Ed.), *Conversations of communication ethics* (pp. 21–53). Norwood, NJ: Ablex.

Cronen, V., Chen, V., & Pearce, W. B. (1988). Coordinated management of meaning: A critical theory. *International and Intercultural Communication Annual, 12,* 66–98.

Cronen, V., Johnson, K., & Lannaman, J. (1982). Paradoxes, double binds, and reflexive loops: An alternative theoretical perspective. *Family Process, 20,* 91–112.

Cupach, W., & Imahori, T. T. (1993). Managing social predicaments created by others: A comparison of Japanese and American facework. *Western Journal of Communication, 57,* 431–444.

Cupach, W., & Metts, S. (1994). *Facework.* Thousand Oaks, CA: Sage.

Cushman, D. P., & Kunimoto, E. N. (1981). A symposium on "speech act theory in mainstream communication research": An introduction. *Communication Quarterly, 29,* 196–201.

Cutler, N. E., & Danowski, J. A. (1980). Process gratifications in aging cohorts. *Journalism Quarterly, 57,* 269–277.

Dance, F. E. X., & Larson, C. E. (1976). *The functions of human communication: A theoretical approach.* New York: Holt, Rinehart, & Winston.

D'Andrade, R. G., & Wish, M. (1985). Speech act theory in quantitative research on interpersonal behavior. *Discourse Processes, 8,* 229–259.

Davis, M. H. (1983). Measuring individual differences in empathy: Evidence for a multidimensional approach. *Journal of Personality and Social Psychology, 44,* 113–126.

Davison, W. P. (1983). The third-person effect in communication. *Public Opinion Quarterly, 47,* 1–15.

Deetz, S. A. (1973). Words without things: Toward a social phenomenology of language. *Quarterly Journal of Speech, 59,* 40–51.

Deetz, S. A. (1992). *Democracy in an age of corporate colonization: Developments in communication and the politics of everyday life.* Albany: State University of New York Press.

Deetz, S. A., & Kersten, S. (1983). Critical modes of interpretive research. In L. Putnam & M. Pacanowsky (Eds.), *Communication and organizations: An interpretive approach* (pp. 147–171). Beverly Hills, CA: Sage.

Deetz, S. A., & Mumby, D. K. (1990). Power, discourse, and the workplace: Reclaiming the critical tradition. In J. Anderson (Ed.), *Communication yearbook 13* (pp. 18–47). Newbury Park, CA: Sage.

DeFleur, M. L. (1998). Where have all the milestones gone? The decline of significant research on the process and effects of mass communication. *Mass Communication & Society, 1,* 85–98.

DeFleur, M. L., & Ball-Rokeach, S. (1982). *Theories of mass communication.* New York: Longman.

DeFleur, M. L., & Ball-Rokeach, S. (1989). *Theories of mass communication* (5th ed.). New York: Longman.

DeFleur, M. L., & Dennis, E. E. (1996). *Understanding mass communication* (6th ed.). Boston: Houghton Mifflin.

Delia, J. G., & Grossberg, L. (1977). Interpretation and evidence. *Western Journal of Speech Communication, 41,* 32–42.

Delia, J. G., O'Keefe, B. J., & O'Keefe, D. J. (1982). The constructivist approach to communication. In F. E. X. Dance (Ed.), *Human communication theory* (pp. 147–191). New York: Harper & Row.

Derlega, V. J. (1997). Creating a "big picture" of personal relationships: Lessons we can learn from 1970s-era theories. *Contemporary Psychology, 42,* 101–105.

Derlega, V. J., Metts, S., Petronio, S., & Margulis, S. T. (1993). *Self-disclosure.* Newbury Park, CA: Sage.

Dervin, B., Grossberg, L., O'Keefe, B., & Wartella, E. (Eds.) (1989). *Rethinking communication: Paradigm issues*. Newbury Park, CA: Sage.

DeSanctis, G., & Poole, M. S. (1994). Capturing the complexity in advanced technology use: Adaptive structuration theory. *Organization Science, 5*, 121–147.

Descartes, R. (1963). In E. Anscombe & P. Geach (Eds.), *Philosophical writings*. Edinburgh: Nelson.

Dewey, J., & Bentley, A. F. (1949). *Knowing and the known*. Boston: Beacon.

Diesing, P. (1991). *How does social science work? Reflections on practice*. Pittsburgh: University of Pittsburgh Press.

Dillard, J. P. (Ed.) (1990a). *Seeking compliance: The production of interpersonal influence messages*. Scottsdale, AZ: Gorsuch Scarisbrick.

Dillard, J. P. (1990b). A goal-driven model of interpersonal influence. In J. P. Dillard (Ed.), *Seeking compliance: The production of interpersonal influence messages* (pp. 41–57). Scottsdale, AZ: Gorsuch Scarisbrick.

Dillard, J. P. (1997). Explicating the goal construct: Tools for theorists. In J. O. Greene (Ed.), *Message production: Advances in communication theory* (pp. 47–69). Mahwah, NJ: Erlbaum.

Dillard, J. P., Segrin, C., & Harden, J. M. (1989). Primary and secondary goals in the production of interpersonal influence messages. *Communication Monographs, 56*, 19–38.

Dillard, J. P., & Solomon, D. H. (2000). Conceptualizing context in message-production research. *Communication Theory, 10*, 167–175.

Dindia, K. (1994). The intrapersonal-interpersonal dialectical process of self-disclosure. In S. Duck (Ed.), *Dynamics of relationships* (pp. 27–57). Thousand Oaks, CA: Sage.

Douglas, J. D. (1970). *Understanding everyday life*. Chicago: Aldine.

Dubin, R. (1978). *Theory building* (2nd ed.). New York: Free Press.

Duran, R. L., & Prusank, D. T. (1997). Relational themes in men's and women's popular nonfiction magazine articles. *Journal of Social and Personal Relationships, 14*, 165–189.

Edelstein, A. S. (1993). Thinking about the criterion variable in agenda-setting research. *Journal of Communication, 43*, 85–99.

Edwards, R. (1981). The social relations of production at the point of production. In M. Zey-Ferrell & M. Aiken (Eds.), *Complex organizations: Critical perspectives* (pp. 156–182). Glenview, IL: Scott Foresman.

Edwards, R., Honeycutt, J. S., & Zagacki, K. S. (1988). Imagined interaction as an element of social cognition. *Western Journal of Speech Communication, 52*, 23–45.

Eisenberg, E. M. (1991). Review of "Equivocal communication." *Communication Theory, 1*, 351–354.

Eisenberg, E. M., & Riley, P. (2001). Organizational culture. In F. M. Jablin & L. L. Putnam (Eds.), *The new handbook of organizational communication: Advances in theory, research, and methods* (pp. 291–322). Thousand Oaks, CA: Sage.

Ekman, P., & Friesen, W. (1975). *Unmasking the face*. Englewood Cliffs, NJ: Prentice Hall.

Ellis, D. G. (1991). Poststructuralism and language: Non-sense. *Communication Monographs, 58*, 213–224.

Ellis, D. G. (1995). Fixing communicative meaning: A coherentist theory. *Communication Research, 22*, 515–544.

Escudero, V., Rogers, E., & Gutierrez, E. (1997). Patterns of relational control and nonverbal affect in clinic and nonclinic couples. *Journal of Social and Personal Relationships, 14*, 5–29.

Eveland, W. P., Jr., McLeod, D. M., & Signorielli, N. (1995). Actual and perceived U.S. public opinion: The spiral of silence during the Persian Gulf War. *International Journal of Public Opinion Research, 7*, 91–109.

Evered, R., & Louis, M. (1981). Alternative perspectives in the organizational sciences: "Inquiry from the inside" and "inquiry from the outside." *Academy of Management Review, 6*, 385–396.

Fairhurst, G. T., Rogers, L. E., & Sarr, R. A. (1987). Manager-subordinate control patterns and judgments about the relationship. In M. McLaughlin (Ed.), *Communication yearbook 10* (pp. 395–415). Thousand Oaks, CA: Sage.

Farace, R. V., Monge, P. R., & Russell, H. M. (1977). *Communicating and organizing*. Reading, MA: Addison-Wesley.

Farrell, T. B. (1980). Critical modes in the analysis of discourse. *Western Journal of Speech Communication, 44*, 300–314.

Farrell, T. B., & Aune, J. A. (1979). Critical theory and communication: A selective literature review. *Quarterly Journal of Speech, 65*, 93–120.

Fay, B., & Moon, J. D. (1977). What would an adequate philosophy of social science look like? *Philosophy of Social Science, 7*, 209–227.

Festinger, L. (1957). *A theory of cognitive dissonance*. Stanford, CA: Stanford University Press.

Festinger, L., & Carlsmith, J. M. (1959). Cognitive consequences of forced compliance. *Journal of Abnormal and Social Psychology, 58*, 203–210.

Feyeraband, P. (1962). Explanation, reduction, and empiricism. In H. Feigl & G. Maxwell (Eds.), *Scientific explanation, space, and time* (pp. 28–97). Minneapolis: University of Minnesota Press.

Feyeraband, P. (1970). Against method: Outline of an anarchist theory of knowledge. In M. Radner & S. Winokur (Eds.), *Analyses of theories and methods of physics and psychology* (pp. 17–130). Minneapolis: University of Minnesota Press.

Finn, S., & Gorr, M. B. (1988). Social isolation and social support as correlates of television viewing motivations. *Communication Research, 15*, 135–158.

Fishbein, M. (Ed.) (1967). *Readings in attitude theory and measurement*. New York: Wiley.

Fishbein, M., & Ajzen, I. (1975). *Belief, attitude, intention, and behavior*. Reading, MA: Addison-Wesley.

Fisher, B. A. (1970). Decision emergence: Phases in group decision-making. *Communication Monographs, 37*, 53–66.

Fisher, W. R. (1978). Toward a logic of good reasons. *Quarterly Journal of Speech, 62*, 1–14.

Fisher, W. R. (1984). Narration as a human communication paradigm: The case of public moral argument. *Communication Monographs, 51*, 1–22.

Fisher, W. R. (1985). The narrative paradigm: An elaboration. *Communication Monographs, 52*, 347–367.

Fisher, W. R. (1987). *Human communication as narration: Toward a philosophy of reason, value, and action*. Columbia: University of South Carolina Press.

Fisher, W. R. (1988). The narrative paradigm and the interpretation and assessment of historical texts. *Journal of the American Forensic Association, 25*, 49–53.

Fisher, W. R. (1989). Clarifying the narrative paradigm. *Communication Monographs, 56*, 55–58.

Fisher, W. R. (1995). Narration, knowledge, and the possibility of wisdom. In R. F. Goodman & W. R. Fisher (Eds.), *Rethinking knowledge* (pp. 169–192). Albany: State University of New York Press.

Fiske, D. W., & Shweder, R. A. (Eds.) (1986). *Metatheory in social science: Pluralisms and subjectivities*. Chicago: University of Chicago Press.

Fiske, S. (1992). Thinking is for doing: Portraits of social cognition from daguerreotype to laserphoto. *Journal of Personality and Social Psychology, 63*, 877–889.

Fiske, S., & Taylor, S. (1984). *Social cognition*. Reading, MA: Addison-Wesley.

Fiske, S., & Taylor, S. (1991). *Social cognition*. New York: McGraw-Hill.

Fitch, K. (1991). The interplay of linguistic universals and cultural knowledge in personal address: Colombian *Madre* terms. *Communication Monographs, 53*, 254–272.

Flowerdew, J. (1990). Problems of speech act theory from an applied perspective. *Language Learning, 40*, 79–105.

Floyd, K., & Burgoon, J. K. (1999). Reacting to nonverbal expressions of liking: A test of interaction adaptation theory. *Communication Monographs, 66*, 219–239.

Ford, L. A., Babrow, A. S., & Stohl, C. (1996). Social support messages and the management of uncertainty in the experience of breast cancer: An application of problematic integration theory. *Communication Monographs, 63*, 189–207.

Forret, M. L., & Turban, D. B. (1996). Implications of the elaboration model for interviewer decision processes. *Journal of Business and Psychology, 10*, 415–428.

Forsdale, L. (1981). *Perspectives on communication*. Reading, MA: Addison-Wesley.

Foss, K. A., & Foss, S. K. (1991). *Women speak: The eloquence of women's lives*. Prospect Heights, IL: Waveland.

Foss, K. A., & Foss, S. K. (1994). Personal experience as evidence in feminist scholarship. *Western Journal of Communication, 58*, 39–43.

Foucault, M. (1976). *Discipline and punish: The birth of the prison* (A. Sheridan, Trans.). New York: Vintage.

Frey, L. R. (Ed.) (1994). *Group communication in context: Studies of natural groups*. Hillsdale, NJ: Erlbaum.

Frey, L. R. (1996). Remembering and "re-membering": A history of theory and research on communication and group decision making. In R. Y. Hirokawa & M. S. Poole (Eds.), *Communication and group decision making* (2nd ed.) (pp. 19–51). Thousand Oaks, CA: Sage.

Gadamer, H. (1975). *Truth and method*. New York: Seabury.

Gadamer, H. (1989). Text and interpretation. In D. Michelfelder & R. Palmer (Eds.), *Dialogue and deconstruction* (pp. 21–51). Albany: State University of New York Press.

Gallois, C., & Giles, H. (1998). Accommodating mutual influence in intergroup encounters. In M. T. Palmer & G. A. Barnett (Eds.), *Progress in communication sciences* (Vol. 14, pp. 135–162). Stamford, CT: Ablex.

Garfinkel, H. (1967). *Studies in ethnomethodology.* Englewood Cliffs, NJ: Prentice Hall.

Gastil, J. (1995). An appraisal and revision of the constructivist research program. In B. R. Burleson (Ed.), *Communication yearbook 18* (pp. 83–104). Thousand Oaks, CA: Sage.

Geertz, C. (1973). *The interpretation of cultures.* New York: Basic Books.

Geis, M. L. (1995). *Speech acts and conversational interaction.* Cambridge: Cambridge University Press.

Gerbner, G. (1966). On defining communication: Still another view. *Journal of Communication, 16,* 99–103.

Gerbner, G. (1990). Epilogue: Advancing on the path of righteousness (maybe). In N. Signorielli & M. Morgan (Eds.), *Cultivation analysis: New directions in media effects research* (pp. 249–262). Newbury Park, CA: Sage.

Gerbner, G., & Gross, L. (1976). Living with television: The violence profile. *Journal of Communication, 26,* 173–199.

Gerbner, G., & Gross, L. (1979). Editorial response: A reply to Newcomb's "humanistic critique." *Communication Research, 6,* 223–230.

Gerbner, G., Gross, L., Morgan, M., & Signorielli, N. (1981). A curious journey into the scary world of Paul Hirsch. *Communication Research, 8,* 39–72.

Gerbner, G., Gross, L., Morgan, M., & Signorielli, N. (1986). Living with television: The dynamics of the cultivation process. In J. Bryant & D. Zillmann (Eds.), *Perspectives on media effects* (pp. 17–40). Hillsdale, NJ: Erlbaum.

Gerbner, G., Gross, L., Morgan, M., Signorielli, N., & Jackson-Beeck, M. (1979). The demonstration of power: Violence profile no. 10. *Journal of Communication, 29,* 177–196.

Ghanem, S. (1997). Filling in the tapestry: The second level of agenda setting. In M. McCombs, D. L. Shaw, & D. Weaver (Eds.), *Communication and democracy: Exploring the intellectual frontiers in agenda-setting theory* (pp. 3–14). Mahwah, NJ: Erlbaum.

Giddens, A. (1976). *New rules of sociological method: A positive critique of interpretive sociologies.* New York: Basic Books.

Giddens, A. (1979). *Critical problems in social theory.* Berkeley: University of California Press.

Giddens, A. (1981). Agency, institution and time-space analysis. In K. Knorr-Cetina & A. V. Cicourel (Eds.), *Advances in social theory and methodology: Toward an integration of micro- and macro-sociologies* (pp. 161–174). Boston: Routledge & Kegan Paul.

Giddens, A. (1984). *The constitution of society: Outline of the theory of structuration.* Berkeley: University of California Press.

Giles, H. (1973). Accent mobility: A model and some data. *Anthropological Linguistics, 15,* 87–105.

Giles, H. (1980). Accommodation theory: Some new directions. *York Papers in Linguistics, 9,* 105–136.

Giles, H., Coupland, J., & Coupland, N. (Eds.) (1991a). *Contexts of accommodation: Developments in applied sociolinguistics.* Cambridge: Cambridge University Press.

Giles, H., Coupland, N., & Coupland, J. (1991b). Accommodation theory: Communication, context, and consequence. In H. Giles, J. Coupland, & N. Coupland (Eds.), *Contexts of accommodation: Developments in applied sociolinguistics* (pp. 1–68). Cambridge: Cambridge University Press.

Giles, H., Mulac, A., Bradac, J. J., & Johnson, P. (1987). Speech accommodation theory: The next decade and beyond. In M. McLaughlin (Ed.), *Communication yearbook 10* (pp. 13–48). Newbury Park, CA: Sage.

Giles, H., & Powesland, P. F. (1975). *Speech style and social evaluation.* London: Academic.

Giles, H., & Smith, P. M. (1979). Accommodation theory: Optimal levels of convergence. In H. Giles & R. St. Clair (Eds.), *Language and social psychology* (pp. 45–65). Oxford: Blackwell.

Giles, H., & Williams, A. (1992). Accommodating hypercorrection: A communication model. *Language & Communication, 12,* 343–356.

Gilligan, C. (1982). *In a different voice.* Cambridge, MA: Harvard University Press.

Gitlin, T. (1980). *The whole world is watching: Mass media in the making and unmaking of the New Left.* Berkeley: University of California Press.

Glaser, B., & Strauss, A. (1967). *The discovery of grounded theory.* Chicago: Aldine.

Glynn, C. J., Hayes, A. F., & Shanahan, J. (1997). Perceived support of one's opinions and willingness to speak out: A meta-analysis of survey studies on the "spiral of silence." *Public Opinion Quarterly, 61,* 452–463.

Glynn, C. J., & Park, E. (1997). Reference groups, opinion intensity, and public opinion expression. *International Journal of Public Opinion Research, 9,* 213–232.

Goffman, E. (1959). *Presentation of self in everyday life.* Garden City, NY: Doubleday.

Goffman, E. (1974). *Frame analysis: An essay on the organization of experience.* Cambridge, MA: Harvard University Press.

Goldsmith, D. (1989/1990). Gossip from the native's point of view: A comparative analysis. *Research on Language and Social Interaction, 23,* 163–194.

Gould, S. J. (1981). *The mismeasure of man.* New York: Norton.

Gouran, D. S. (1970). Response to "The paradox and promise of small group research." *Speech Monographs, 36,* 387–391.

Gouran, D. S. (1990). Exploiting the predictive potential of structuration theory. In J. A. Anderson (Ed.), *Communication yearbook 13* (pp. 313–322). Newbury Park, CA: Sage.

Gouran, D. S. (1999). Communication in groups: The emergence and evolution of a field of study. In L. R. Frey, D. S. Gouran, & M. S. Poole (Eds.), *The handbook of group communication theory and research* (pp. 3–36). Thousand Oaks, CA: Sage.

Gouran, D. S., & Hirokawa, R. Y. (1996). Functional theory and communication in decision-making and problem-solving groups: An expanded view. In M. S. Poole & R. Y. Hirokawa (Eds.), *Communication and group decision making* (pp. 55–80). Thousand Oaks, CA: Sage.

Gouran, D. S., Hirokawa, R. Y., Julian, K. M., & Leatham, G. B. (1993). The evolution and current status of the functional perspective on communication in decision-making and problem-solving groups: A critical analysis. In S. A. Deetz (Ed.), *Communication yearbook 16* (pp. 573–600). Newbury Park, CA: Sage.

Graham, E. E., Papa, M. J., & McPherson, M. P. (1997). An applied test of the functional communication perspective of small group decision-making. *Southern Communication Journal, 62,* 269–279.

Gramsci, A. (1971). *Selections from the prison notebooks* (Q. Hoare & G. Nowell Smith, Trans.). New York: International.

Grant, S. I., Guthrie, K. K., & Ball-Rokeach, S. J. (1991). Television shopping: A media system dependency perspective. *Communication Research, 18,* 773–798.

Gregory, D., & Urry, J. (Eds.) (1985). *Social relations and spatial structures.* London: Macmillan.

Greene, J. O. (1984). A cognitive approach to human communication: An action assembly theory. *Communication Monographs, 51,* 289–306.

Greene, J. O. (1989). Action assembly theory: Metatheoretical commitments, theoretical propositions, and empirical applications. In B. Dervin, L. Grossberg, B. J. O'Keefe, & E. Wartella (Eds.), *Rethinking communication, Vol. 2: Paradigm exemplars* (pp. 117–128). Newbury Park, CA: Sage.

Greene, J. O. (1990). Tactical social action: Toward some strategies for theory. In M. J. Cody & M. L. McLaughlin (Eds.), *The psychology of tactical communication* (pp. 31–47). Clevedon, UK: Multilingual Matters.

Greene, J. O. (1995). An action assembly perspective on verbal and nonverbal message production: A dancer's message unveiled. In D. E. Hewes (Ed.), *The cognitive bases of interpersonal communication* (pp. 51–85). Hillsdale, NJ: Erlbaum.

Greene, J. O. (1997a). A second generation action assembly theory. In J. O. Greene (Ed.), *Message production: Advances in communication theory* (pp. 151–170). Mahwah, NJ: Erlbaum.

Greene, J. O. (Ed.) (1997b). *Message production: Advances in communication theory.* Mahwah, NJ: Erlbaum.

Greene, J. O. (2000). Evanescent mentation: An ameliorative conceptual foundation for research and theory on message production. *Communication Theory, 10,* 139–155.

Greene, J. O., & Geddes, D. (1993). An action assembly perspective on social skill. *Communication Theory, 3,* 26–49.

Griffin, E. (2000). *A first look at communication theory* (4th ed.). New York: McGraw-Hill.

Griffin, R. J., & Sen, S. (1995). Causal communication: Movie portrayals and audience attributions for Vietnam veterans' problems. *Journalism & Mass Communication Quarterly, 72,* 511–524.

Gronbeck, B. E. (1980). Dramaturgical theory and criticism. The state of the art (or science?). *Western Journal of Speech Communication, 44,* 315–330.

Grossberg, L. (1984). Strategies in Marxist cultural interpretation. *Critical Studies in Mass Communication, 1,* 392–421.

Grove, T. G., & Werkman, D. L. (1991). Conversations with able-bodied and visibly disabled strangers: An adversarial test of predicted outcome value and uncertainty reduction theories. *Human Communication Research, 17,* 507–534.

Guba, E. G. (1990a). The alternative paradigm dialog. In E. G. Guba (Ed.), *The paradigm dialog* (pp. 17–27). Newbury Park, CA: Sage.

Guba, E. G. (Ed.) (1990b). *The paradigm dialog.* Newbury Park, CA: Sage.

Gudykunst, W. B. (1985). A model of uncertainty reduction in intercultural encounters. *Journal of Language and Social Psychology, 4,* 79–98.

Gudykunst, W. B. (1989). Culture and the development of interpersonal relationships. In J. Anderson (Ed.), *Communication yearbook 12* (pp. 315–354). Newbury Park, CA: Sage.

Gudykunst, W. B. (1993). Toward a theory of effective interpersonal and intergroup communication: An anxiety/uncertainty management perspective. In R. Wiseman & J. Koester (Eds.), *Intercultural communication competence.* Newbury Park, CA: Sage.

Gudykunst, W. B. (1995). The uncertainty reduction and anxiety-uncertainty management theories of Berger, Gudykunst, and associates. In D. P. Cushman & B. Kovacic (Eds.), *Watershed traditions in human communication theory* (pp. 67–100). Albany: State University of New York Press.

Gudykunst, W. B. (1997). Cultural variability in communication: An introduction. *Communication Research, 24,* 327–348.

Gudykunst, W. B., & Hammer, M. R. (1988). The influence of social identity and intimacy of interethnic relationships on uncertainty reduction processes. *Human Communication Research, 14,* 569–601.

Gudykunst, W. B., & Kim, Y. Y. (1997). *Communicating with strangers.* New York: McGraw-Hill.

Gudykunst, W. B., & Nishida, T. (1984). Individual and cultural influences on uncertainty reduction. *Communication Monographs, 51,* 23–36.

Gudykunst, W. B., & Ting-Toomey, S. (1996). Communication in personal relationships across cultures: An introduction. In W. B. Gudykunst, S. Ting-Toomey, & T. Nishida (Eds.), *Communication in personal relationships across cultures* (pp. 3–16). Thousand Oaks, CA: Sage.

Gunter, G. (1994). The question of media violence. In J. Bryant & D. Zillmann (Eds.), *Media effects: Advances in theory and research* (pp. 163–211). Hillsdale, NJ: Erlbaum.

Gunther, A. (1991). What we think others think: Cause and consequence in the third-person effect. *Communication Research, 18,* 355–372.

Gusfield, J. R. (1989). The bridge over separated lands: Kenneth Burke's significance for the study of human action. In H. W. Simons & T. Melia (Eds.), *The legacy of Kenneth Burke* (pp. 28–54). Madison: University of Wisconsin Press.

Habermas, J. (1971). *Knowledge and human interests* (J. Shapiro, Trans.). Boston: Beacon.

Habermas, J. (1979). *Communication and the evolution of society.* Boston: Beacon.

Habermas, J. (1984). *The theory of communicative action.* (T. McCarthy, Trans.). Boston: Beacon.

Hage, J. D. (1972). *Techniques and problems of theory construction in sociology.* New York: Wiley.

Haley, J. (1976). Development of a theory: A history of a research project. In C. E. Sluzki & D. C. Ransom (Eds.), *Double bind: The foundation of the communicational approach to the family* (pp. 59–104). New York: Grune & Stratton.

Hall, B. J. (1992). Theories of culture and communication. *Communication Theory, 2,* 50–70.

Hall, E. T. (1976). *Beyond culture.* New York: Doubleday.

Hall, E. T. (1983). *The dance of life: The other dimension of time.* Garden City, NY: Anchor Press/ Doubleday.

Hall, S. (1985). Signification, representation, ideology: Althusser and the post-structuralist debates. *Critical Studies in Mass Communication, 2,* 91–114.

Hamilton, J. A., Hunter, J. E., & Boster, F. J. (1993). The elaboration likelihood model as a theory of attitude formation: A mathematical analysis. *Communication Theory, 3,* 50–65.

Hample, D. (1981). The cognitive context of argument. *Journal of the American Forensic Association, 17,* 151–158.

Hanson, N. R. (1965). *Patterns of discovery.* Cambridge: Cambridge University Press.

Harding, S. (1987). The instability of the analytical categories of feminist theory. In S. Harding & J. O'Barr (Eds.), *Sex and scientific inquiry* (pp. 283–302). Chicago: University of Chicago Press.

Hardt, H. (1989). The return of the "critical" and the challenge of radical dissent: Critical theory, cultural studies, and American mass communication research. In J. Anderson (Ed.), *Communication yearbook 12* (pp. 558–600). Newbury Park, CA: Sage.

Harré, R. (1983). *An introduction to the logic of the sciences.* New York: St. Martin's.

Harrison, T. M. (1994). Communication and interdependence in democratic organizations. In S. Deetz (Ed.), *Communication yearbook 17* (pp. 247–274). Newbury Park, CA: Sage.

Hart, R. P., & Burks, D. M. (1972). Rhetorical sensitivity and social interaction. *Speech Monographs, 39*, 75–91.

Hartsock, N. C. M. (1983). The feminist standpoint: Developing the ground for a specifically feminist historical materialism. In S. Harding & M. B. Hintikka (Eds.), *Discovering reality: Feminist perspectives on epistemology, methodology, metaphysics and philosophy of science* (pp. 283–310). Boston: Reidel.

Hartsock, N. C. M. (1997). Standpoint theories for the next century. In S. J. Kenney & H. Kinsella (Eds.), *Politics and feminist standpoint theory* (pp. 93–101). New York: Haworth.

Hartsock, N. C. M. (1998). *The feminist standpoint revisited and other essays.* Boulder, CO: Westview.

Hawkins, R. P., & Pingree, S. (1980). Some processes in the cultivation effect. *Communication Research, 7*, 193–226.

Hawkins, R. P., & Pingree, S. (1982). Television's influence on social reality. In D. Pearl, L. Bouthilet, & J. Lazar (Eds.), *Television and behavior: Ten years of scientific progress and implications for the 80's, Vol. 2: Technical reviews* (pp. 224–247). Rockville, MD: National Institute of Mental Health.

Hawkins, R. P., & Pingree, S. (1990). Divergent psychological processes in constructing social reality from mass media content. In N. Signorielli & M. Morgan (Eds.), *Cultivation analysis: New directions in media effects research* (pp. 35–50). Newbury Park, CA: Sage.

Hawkins, R. P., Pingree, S., & Adler, I. (1987). Searching for cognitive processes in the cultivation effect. *Human Communication Research, 13*, 553–577.

Haynes, W. L. (1989). Shifting media, shifting paradigms, and the growing utility of narrative as metaphor. *Communication Studies, 40*, 109–126.

Heath, R. L. (1986). *Realism and relativism: A perspective on Kenneth Burke.* Macon, GA: Mercer University Press.

Hebb, D. O. (1955). Drives and the C. N. S. (conceptual nervous system). *Psychological Review, 62*, 243–254.

Heider, F. (1958). *The psychology of interpersonal relations.* New York: Riley.

Held, D., & Thompson, J. B. (Eds.) (1989). *Social theory of modern societies: Anthony Giddens and his critics.* Cambridge: Cambridge University Press.

Hempel, C. G. (1966). *Philosophy of natural science.* Englewood Cliffs, NJ: Prentice Hall.

Herzog, H. (1941). Professor Quiz: A gratification study. In P. F. Lazarsfeld & F. N. Stanton (Eds.), *Radio research, 1941.* New York: Duell, Sloan, & Pearce.

Herzog, H. (1944). What do we really know about day-time serial listeners? In P. F. Lazarsfeld & F. N. Stanton (Eds.), *Radio research, 1942–43.* New York: Duell, Sloan, & Pearce.

Higgins, E. T., & King, G. A. (1981). Accessibility of social constructs: Information-processing consequences of individual and contextual variability. In N. Cantor & J. F. Kihlstrom (Eds.), *Personality, cognition, and social interaction* (pp. 69–122). Hillsdale, NJ: Erlbaum.

Hindeman, E. B. (1999). "Lynch-mob journalism" vs. "Compelling human drama": Editorial responses to coverage of the pretrial phase of the O. J. Simpson case. *Journalism & Mass Communication Quarterly, 76*, 499–515.

Hines, S. C., Babrow, A. S., Badzek, L., & Moss, A. H. (1997). Communication and problematic integration in end-of-life decisions: Dialysis decisions among the elderly. *Health Communication, 9*, 219–235.

Hirokawa, R. Y. (1983). Group communication and problem-solving effectiveness II: An exploratory investigation of procedural functions. *Western Journal of Speech Communication, 47*, 59–74.

Hirokawa, R. Y. (1985). Discussion procedures and decision-making performance: A test of a functional perspective. *Human Communication Research, 12*, 203–224.

Hirokawa, R. Y. (1987). Why informed groups make faulty decisions: An investigation of possible interaction-based explanations. *Small Group Behavior, 18*, 3–29.

Hirokawa, R. Y. (1988). Group communication and decision-making performance: A continued test of the functional perspective. *Human Communication Research, 14*, 487–515.

Hirokawa, R. Y., & Keyton, J. (1995). Perceived facilitators and inhibitors of effectiveness in organizational work teams. *Management Communication Quarterly, 8*, 424–446.

Hirokawa, R. Y., & Pace, R. C. (1983). A descriptive investigation of possible communication-based reasons for effective and ineffective group decision-making. *Communication Monographs, 50,* 363–379.

Hirokawa, R. Y., & Salazar, A. J. (1999). Task-group communication and decision-making performance. In L. R. Frey, D. S. Gouran, & M. S. Poole (Eds.), *The handbook of group communication theory and research* (pp. 167–191). Thousand Oaks, CA: Sage.

Hirokawa, R. Y., Salazar, A. J., Erbert, L., & Ice, R. J. (1996). Small group communication. In M. B. Salwen & D. W. Stacks (Eds.), *An integrated approach to communication theory and research* (pp. 359–382). Mahwah, NJ: Erlbaum.

Hirsch, P. M. (1980). The "scary world" of the non-viewer and other anomalies: A reanalysis of Gerbner et al.'s findings of cultivation analysis, Part I. *Communication Research, 7,* 403–456.

Hirsch, P. M. (1981). Distinguishing good speculation from bad theory: Rejoinders to Gerbner et al. *Communication Research, 8,* 73–95.

Hirschmann, N. J. (1997). Feminist standpoint as postmodern strategy. In S. J. Kenney & H. Kinsella (Eds.), *Politics and feminist standpoint theory* (pp. 73–92). New York: Haworth.

Hitchon, J. C., & Chang, C. (1995). Effects of gender schematic processing on the reception of political commercials for men and women candidates. *Communication Research, 22,* 430–458.

Ho, D. (1976). On the concept of face. *American Journal of Sociology, 81,* 867–884.

Hoffner, C., & Cantor, J. (1991). Factors affecting children's enjoyment of a frightening film sequence. *Communication Monographs, 58,* 41–62.

Hofstede, G. (1980). *Culture's consequences: International differences in work-related values.* Beverly Hills, CA: Sage.

Hofstede, G. (1991). *Culture and organizations: Software of the mind.* London: McGraw-Hill.

Hofstede, G., & Bond, M. (1984). Hofstede's culture dimensions. *Journal of Cross-Cultural Psychology, 15,* 417–433.

Hollihan, T. A., & Riley, P. (1987). The rhetorical power of a compelling story: A critique of a "Toughlove" parental support group. *Communication Quarterly, 35,* 13–25.

Holstein, J. A., & Gubrium, J. F. (2000). *The self we live by.* New York: Oxford University Press.

Honeycutt, J. M. (1990). A functional analysis of imagined interaction in everyday life. In J. E.

Shorr, P. Robbins, J. A. Connella, & M. Wolpin (Eds.), *Mental imagery: Current perspectives* (pp. 13–25). New York: Plenum.

Honeycutt, J. M., & Cantrill, J. G. (1991). Using expectations of relational actions to predict number of intimate relationships: Don Juan and Romeo unmasked. *Communication Reports, 4,* 14–21.

Honeycutt, J. M., Cantrill, J. G., & Greene, R. W. (1989). Memory structures for relational escalation: A cognitive test of the sequencing of relational actions and stages. *Human Communication Research, 16,* 62–90.

Honeycutt, J. M., Zagacki, K. S., & Edwards, R. (1990). Imagined interaction and interpersonal communication. *Communication Reports, 3,* 1–8.

Hoover, S. M. (1990). Television, religion, and religious television: Purposes and cross purposes. In N. Signorielli & M. Morgan (Eds.), *Cultivation analysis: New directions in media effects research* (pp. 123–140). Newbury Park, CA: Sage.

Hopper, R. (1981). How to do things without words: The taken-for-granted as speech-action. *Communication Quarterly, 29,* 228–236.

Horton, D., & Wohl, R. R. (1956). Mass communication and para-social interaction. *Psychiatry, 19,* 215–229.

Houston, M., & Kramarae, C. (1991). Speaking from silence: Methods of silencing and of resistance. *Discourse and Society, 2,* 387–399.

Hovland, C. J., Janis, I. L., & Kelley, H. H. (1953). *Communication and persuasion.* New Haven, CT: Yale University Press.

Howard, G. S. (1985). The role of values in the science of psychology. *American Psychologist, 40,* 255–265.

Howard, L. A., & Geist, P. (1995). Ideological positioning in organizational change: The dialectic of control in a merging organization. *Communication Monographs, 62,* 110–131.

Hu, H. C. (1944). The Chinese concept of "face." *American Anthropologist, 46,* 45–64.

Huebner, J., Fan, D. P., & Finnegan, J., Jr. (1997). "Death of a thousand cuts": The impact of media coverage on public opinion about Clinton's health security act. *Journal of Health Communication, 2,* 253–270.

Hugel, R., Degenhardt, W., & Weiss, H. (1989). Structural equation models for the analysis of the agenda-setting process. *European Journal of Communication, 4,* 191–210.

Hughes, M. (1980). The fruits of cultivation analysis: A re-examination of the effects of television watching on fear of victimization, alienation, and the approval of violence. *Public Opinion Quarterly, 44*, 287–302.

Hui, C., & Triandis, H. (1986). Individualism-collectivism: A study of cross-cultural researchers. *Journal of Cross-Cultural Psychology, 17*, 225–248.

Huspek, M. (1991). Taking aim on Habermas's critical theory: On the road toward a critical hermeneutics. *Communication Monographs, 58*, 225–233.

Huspek, M. (1993). Dueling structures: The theory of resistance in discourse. *Communication Theory, 3*, 1–25.

Huspek, M. (1997). Toward normative theories of communication with reference to the Frankfurt school: An introduction. *Communication Theory, 7*, 265–276.

Hymes, D. (1962). The ethnography of speaking. In T. Gladwin & W. Sturtevant (Eds.), *Anthropology and human behavior* (pp. 13–53). Washington, DC: Anthropological Society of Washington.

Hymes, D. (1972). Models of the interaction of language and social life. In J. Gumperz & D. Hymes (Eds.), *Directions in sociolinguistics: The ethnography of communication* (pp. 35–121). New York: Holt, Rinehart, & Winston.

Iyengar, S., & Kinder, D. R. (1987). *News that matters*. Chicago: University of Chicago Press.

Jablin, F. M., & Kramer, M. W. (1998). Communication-related sense-making and adjustment during job transfers. *Management Communication Quarterly, 12*, 155–182.

Jackson, D. D. (1957). The question of family homeostasis. *Psychiatric Quarterly Supplement, 31*, 79–90.

Jackson, S., & Jacobs, S. (1983). The collaborative production of proposals in conversational argument and persuasion: A study of disagreement regulation. *Journal of the American Forensic Association, 18*, 77–90.

Jacobs, S., & Jackson, S. (1982). Conversational argument: A discourse analytic approach. In J. R. Cox & C. A. Willard (Eds.), *Advances in argumentation theory and research* (pp. 205–237). Carbondale: Southern Illinois University Press.

Jacobs, S., & Jackson, S. (1983). Speech act structure in conversation: Rational aspects of pragmatic coherence. In R. T. Craig & K. Tracy (Eds.), *Conversational coherence: Form, structure, and strategy* (pp. 47–66). Beverly Hills, CA: Sage.

Jacobson, T. L. (1991). Theories as communication. *Communication Theory, 1*, 145–159.

Janis, I. L. (1972). *Victims of groupthink: Psychological studies of foreign policy decisions and fiascoes*. Boston: Houghton Mifflin.

Janis, I. L. (1982). *Groupthink* (2nd ed.). Boston: Houghton Mifflin.

Janis, I. L. (1989). *Crucial decisions: Leadership in policy making and crisis management*. New York: Free Press.

Jaspars, J., Hewstone, M., & Fincham, F. D. (1983). Attribution theory and research: The state of the art. In J. Jaspars, M. Hewstone, & F. D. Fincham (Eds.), *Attribution theory and research: Conceptual, developmental and social dimensions* (pp. 3–36). London: Academic.

Jones, E. E. (1976). How do people perceive the causes of behavior? *American Scientist, 64*, 300–305.

Jones, E. E., & Nisbett, R. E. (1972). The actor and observer: Diverging perceptions of the causes of behaviour. In E. E. Jones, D. Kanouse, H. H. Kelley, R. E. Nisbett, S. Valins, & B. Weiner (Eds.), *Attribution: Perceiving the causes of behavior* (pp. 79–94). Morristown, NJ: General Learning Press.

Katriel, T. (1986). *Talking straight: "Dugri" speech in Israeli Sabra culture*. Cambridge: Cambridge University Press.

Katriel, T., & Philipsen, G. (1981). "What we need is communication": "Communication" as a cultural category in some American speech. *Communication Monographs, 48*, 301–317.

Katz, C., & Baldassare, M. (1994). Popularity in a freefall: Measuring a spiral of silence at the end of the Bush presidency. *International Journal of Public Opinion Research, 6*, 1–12.

Katz, D., & Kahn, R. L. (1966). *The social psychology of organizations*. New York: Wiley.

Katz, E. (1957). The two-step flow of communication: An up-to-date report. *Public Opinion Quarterly, 21*, 61–78.

Katz, E. (1983). Publicity and pluralistic ignorance: Notes on "The spiral of silence." In E. Wartella & C. Whitney (Eds.), *Mass communication review yearbook 4* (pp. 89–99). Beverly Hills, CA: Sage. (Reprinted from *Public opinion and social change: For Elisabeth Noelle-Neumann*, pp. 28–38, by H. Baier, H. M. Kepplinger, & K. Reumann, Eds., 1981, Wiesbaden: Westdeutscher Verlag.

Katz, E., Blumler, J., & Gurevitch, M. (1974). Utilization of mass communication by the individual. In J. G. Blumler & E. Katz (Eds.), *The uses of mass* communications: *Current perspectives on gratifications research* (pp. 19–32). Beverly Hills, CA: Sage.

Kellermann, K. (1986). Anticipation of future interactions and information exchange in initial interaction. *Human Communication Research, 13,* 41–75.

Kellermann, K. (1992). Communication: Inherently strategic and primarily automatic. *Communication Monographs, 59,* 288–300.

Kellermann, K., Broetzmann, S., Lim, T-S., & Kitao, K. (1989). The conversation MOP: Scenes in the stream of discourse. *Discourse Processes, 12,* 27–61.

Kellermann, K., & Cole, T. (1994). Classifying compliance gaining messages: Taxonomic disorder and strategic confusion. *Communication Theory, 4,* 3–60.

Kellermann, K., & Reynolds, R. (1990). When ignorance is bliss: The role of motivation to reduce uncertainty in uncertainty reduction theory. *Human Communication Research, 17,* 5–75.

Kelley, H. H. (1967). Attribution in social psychology. In D. Levine (Ed.), *Nebraska Symposium on Motivation: Vol. 15* (pp. 192–238). Lincoln: University of Nebraska Press.

Kelley, H. H., & Michela, J. L. (1980). Attribution theory and research. *Annual Review of Psychology, 31,* 457–501.

Kellner, D. (1995). Media communications vs. cultural studies: Overcoming the divide. *Communication Theory, 5,* 162–177.

Kellow, C. L., & Steeves, H. L. (1998). The role of radio in the Rwandan genocide. *Journal of Communication, 48,* 107–128.

Kelly, G. A. (1955). *The psychology of personal constructs* (2 vols.). New York: Norton.

Kennamer, D. (1990). Self-serving biases in perceiving the opinions of others: Implications for the spiral of silence. *Communication Research, 17,* 393–404.

Kenney, S. J., & Kinsella, H. (Eds.)(1997). *Politics and feminist standpoint theories.* New York: Haworth.

Kerlinger, F. N. (1979). *Behavioral research: A conceptual approach.* New York: Holt, Rinehart, & Winston.

Kielwasser, A. P., & Wolf, M. A. (1992). Mainstream television, adolescent homosexuality, and significant silence. *Critical Studies in Mass Communication, 9,* 350–373.

Kim, J., & Rubin, A. M. (1997). The variable influence of audience activity on media effects. *Communication Research, 24,* 107–135.

Klumpp, J. F. (1995). "Dancing with tears in my eyes": Celebrating the life and work of Kenneth Burke. *Southern Communication Journal, 61,* 1–10.

Knapp, M. L. (1978). *Social intercourse: From greeting to goodbye.* Boston: Allyn & Bacon.

Kosicki, G. M. (1993). Problems and opportunities in agenda-setting research. *Journal of Communication, 43,* 100–127.

Kramarae, C. (1978). Male and female perception of male and female speech. *Language and Speech, 20,* 151–161.

Kramarae, C. (1981). *Women and men speaking: Frameworks for analysis.* Rowley, MA: Newbury House.

Kramer, M. W. (1993). Communication and uncertainty reduction during job transfers: Leaving and joining processes. *Communication Monographs, 60,* 178–197.

Krassa, M. A. (1988). Social groups, selective perception, and behavioral contagion in public opinion. *Social Networks, 10,* 109–136.

Kreps, G. (1980). A field experimental test and re-evaluation of Weick's model of organizing. In D. Nimmo (Ed.), *Communication yearbook 4* (pp. 389–398). New Brunswick, NJ: Transaction Books.

Kreps, G. (1990). *Organizational communication: Theory and practice.* New York: Longman.

Kuhn, T. (1997). The discourse of issues management: A genre of organizational communication. *Communication Quarterly, 45,* 188–210.

Kuhn, T. S. (1962). *The structure of scientific revolutions.* Chicago: University of Chicago Press.

Kuhn, T. S. (1977). *The essential tension: Selected studies in scientific tradition and change.* Chicago: University of Chicago Press.

Lakatos, I. (1970). Falsification and the methodology of scientific research programmes. In I. Lakatos & A. Musgrave (Eds.), *Criticism and the growth of knowledge* (pp. 91–195). Cambridge: Cambridge University Press.

Lakatos, I. (1978). *The methodology of scientific research programmes.* Cambridge: Cambridge University Press.

Lambert, B. L., & Gillespie, J. L. (1994). Patient perceptions of pharmacy students' hypertension compliance-gaining messages: Effects of message design logic and content themes. *Health Communication, 6,* 311–325.

Lammers, J., & Krikorian, D. (1997). Theoretical extension and operationalization of bona fide group construct with an application to surgical teams. *Journal of Applied Communication Research, 25,* 17–38.

Lang, K., & Lang, G. E. (1993). Perspectives on communication. *Journal of Communication, 43,* 92–99.

Langellier, K. M., & Peterson, E. E. (1993). Family storytelling as a strategy of social control. In D. K. Mumby (Ed.), *Narrative and social control: Critical perspectives* (pp. 49–76). Newbury Park, CA: Sage.

Langer, E. J. (1978). Rethinking the role of thought in social interaction. In J. H. Harvey, W. J. Ickes, & R. F. Kidd (Eds.), *New directions in attribution research* (Vol. 2). Hillsdale, NJ: Erlbaum.

Langer, E. J. (1989). Minding matters: The consequences of mindlessness-mindfulness. In L. E. Berkowitz (Ed.), *Advances in experimental social psychology* (Vol. 22, pp. 137–173). New York: Academic.

Langer, S. (1942). *Philosophy in a new key.* Cambridge, MA: Harvard University Press.

Lannaman, J. W. (1991). Interpersonal communication research and ideological practice. *Communication Theory, 1,* 179–203.

Lasorsa, D. L. (1991). Political outspokenness: Factors working against the spiral of silence. *Journalism Quarterly, 68,* 131–140.

Lasswell, H. (1927). *Propaganda techniques in the world war.* New York: Knopf.

Lasswell, H. (1964). The structure and function of communication in society. In L. Bryson (Ed.), *The communication of ideas* (pp. 37–51). New York: Cooper Square. (Original work published 1948)

Laudan, L. (1977). *Progress and its problems.* Berkeley: University of California Press.

Laudan, L. (1982). *Science and values.* Berkeley: University of California Press.

Layder, D. (1994). *Understanding social theory.* Thousand Oaks, CA: Sage.

Leeds-Hurwitz, W. (1992). Forum introduction: Social approaches to interpersonal communication. *Communication Theory, 2,* 131–139.

Leeds-Hurwitz, W. (1993). *Semiotics and communication: Signs, codes, cultures.* Hillsdale, NJ: Erlbaum.

LePoire, B. A., & Burgoon, J. K. (1996). Usefulness of differentiating arousal responses within communication theories: Orienting response or defensive arousal within nonverbal theories of expectancy violation. *Communication Monographs, 63,* 208–230.

LePoire, B. A., & Yoshimura, S. M. (1999). The effect of expectancies and actual communication on nonverbal adaptation and communication outcomes. A test of interaction adaptation theory. *Communication Monographs, 66,* 1–30.

Lesch, C. L. (1994). Observing theory in practice: Sustaining consciousness in a coven. In L. R. Frey (Ed.), *Group communication in context: Studies of natural groups* (pp. 57–82). Hillsdale, NJ: Erlbaum.

Levinson, S. C. (1979). Activity types and language. *Linguistics, 17,* 365–399.

Levinson, S. C. (1981). Some pre-observations on the modelling of dialogue. *Discourse Processes, 4,* 93–116.

Levinson, S. C. (1983). *Pragmatics.* Cambridge: Cambridge University Press.

Lewin, K. (1951). *Field theory in social science: Selected theoretical papers* (D. Cartwright, Ed.). New York: Harper & Row.

Lim, T.-S. (1994). Facework and interpersonal relationships. In S. Ting-Toomey (Ed.), *The challenge of facework: Cross-cultural and interpersonal issues* (pp. 209–229). Albany: State University of New York Press.

Lim, T.-S., & Bowers, J. W. (1991). Facework: Solidarity, approbation, and tact. *Human Communication Research, 17,* 415–450.

Lincoln, Y. S., & Guba, E. G. (1985). *Naturalistic inquiry.* Newbury Park, CA: Sage.

Lippmann, W. (1922). *Public opinion.* New York: Harcourt Brace.

Littlejohn, S. W. (1996). *Theories of Human Communication* (5th ed.). Belmont, CA: Wadsworth.

Loges, W. E., & Ball-Rokeach, S. J. (1993). Dependency relations and newspaper readership. *Journalism Quarterly, 70,* 602–614.

Lopez-Escobar, E., Llamas, J. P., McCombs, M., & Lennon, F. R. (1998). Two levels of agenda setting among advertising and news in the 1995 Spanish elections. *Political Communication, 15,* 225–238.

Louis, M. R. (1980). Surprise and sense-making: What newcomers experience when entering unfamiliar organizational settings. *Administrative Science Quarterly, 23,* 225–251.

Lyne, J. R. (1981). Speech acts in a semiotic frame. *Communication Quarterly, 29,* 202–208.

MacIntyre, A. (1981). *After virtue: A study in moral theory.* Notre Dame: University of Notre Dame Press.

Madden, T. J., Ellen, P. S., & Ajzen, I. (1992). A comparison of the theory of planned behavior and the theory of reasoned action. *Personality and Social Psychology Bulletin, 18,* 3–9.

Mael, F., & Ashforth, B. E. (1992). Alumni and their alma mater: A partial test of the reformulated model of organizational identification. *Journal of Organizational Behavior, 13,* 103–123.

Mandler, J. M. (1984). *Stories, scripts, and scenes: Aspects of schema theory.* Hillsdale, NJ: Erlbaum.

Manusov, V. (1990). An application of attribution principles to nonverbal behavior in romantic dyads. *Communication Monographs, 57,* 104–118.

Manusov, V., Winchatz, M. R., & Manning, L. M. (1997). Acting out our minds: Incorporating behavior into models of stereotype-based expectancies for cross-cultural interactions. *Communication Monographs, 64,* 119–139.

Markham, A. N. (1998). *Life online: Researching real experience in virtual space.* Walnut Creek, CA: Altamira.

Martin, J. N., Nakayama, T. K., & Flores, L. A. (1998). A dialectical approach to intercultural communication. In J. N. Martin, T. K. Nakayama, & L. A. Flores (Eds.), *Readings in cultural contexts* (pp. 5–15). Mountain View, CA: Mayfield.

Martin, M., & McIntyre, L. C. (Eds.) (1994). *Readings in the philosophy of social science.* Cambridge, MA: MIT Press.

Martin, W. (1986). *Recent theories of narrative.* Ithaca, NY: Cornell University Press.

Marwell, G., & Schmitt, D. R. (1967). Dimensions of compliance-gaining behavior: An empirical analysis. *Sociometry, 30,* 350–364.

Marx, K. (1967). *Writings of the young Marx on philosophy and society* (L. D. Easton & K. H. Guddat, Eds. & Trans.). New York: Anchor.

Masheter, C., & Harris, L. M. (1986). From divorce to friendship: A study of dialectic relationship development. *Journal of Social and Personal Relationships, 3,* 177–189.

McCombs, M., Einsiedel, F., & Weaver, D. H. (1991). *Contemporary public opinion: Issues and the news.* Hillsdale, NJ: Erlbaum.

McCombs, M., & Shaw, D. (1972). The agenda-setting function of mass media. *Public Opinion Quarterly, 36,* 176–185.

McCombs, M., Shaw, D. L., & Weaver, D. (Eds.) (1997). *Communication and democracy: Exploring the intellectual frontiers of agenda-setting theory.* Mahwah, NJ: Erlbaum.

McCroskey, J. C. (1984). The communication apprehension perspective. In J. A. Daly & J. C. McCroskey (Eds.), *Avoiding communication: Shyness, reticence, and communication apprehension* (pp. 13–38). Beverly Hills, CA: Sage.

McGuire, W. J. (1961). Resistance to persuasion conferred by active and passive prior refutation of the same and alternative counterarguments. *Journal of Abnormal and Social Psychology, 63,* 326–332.

McGuire, W. J. (1962). Persistence of the resistance to persuasion induced by various types of prior belief defenses. *Journal of Abnormal and Social Psychology, 64,* 241–248.

McGuire, W. J. (1964). Inducing resistance to persuasion. Some contemporary approaches. In L. Berkowitz (Ed.), *Advances in experimental social psychology* (Vol. 1, pp. 191–229). New York: Academic.

McGuire, W. J., & Papageorgis, D. (1961). The relative efficacy of various types of prior belief-defense in producing immunity against persuasion. *Journal of Abnormal and Social Psychology, 62,* 327–337.

McLaughlin, M. L. (1984). *Conversation: How talk is organized.* Beverly Hills, CA: Sage.

McPhee, R. D. (1985). Formal structure and organizational communication. In R. D. McPhee & P. Tompkins (Eds.), *Organizational communication: Traditional themes and new directions* (pp. 149–178). Beverly Hills, CA: Sage.

McPhee, R. D. (1989). Organizational communication: A structurational exemplar. In B. Dervin, L. Grossberg, B. O'Keefe, & E. Wartella (Eds.), *Rethinking communication: Paradigm exemplars* (pp. 199–212). Beverly Hills, CA: Sage.

McQuail, D. (1983). *Mass communication theory: An introduction.* London: Sage.

McQuail, D. (1984). With the benefit of hindsight: Reflections on uses and gratifications research. *Critical Studies in Mass Communication, 1,* 177–191.

McQuail, D. (1994). *Mass communication theory: An introduction* (Rev. ed.). London: Sage.

McQuail, D., Blumler, J. G., & Brow, J. R. (1972). The television audience: A revised perspective. In D. McQuail (Ed.), *Sociology of mass communications* (pp. 135–165). Harmondsworth, England: Penguin.

Mead, G. H. (1934). *Mind, self, and society.* Chicago: University of Chicago Press.

Mead, G. H. (1956). *The social psychology of George Herbert Mead* (A. M. Strauss, Ed.). Chicago: University of Chicago Press.

Meltzer, B. N., & Petras, J. W. (1970). The Chicago and Iowa schools of symbolic interactionism. In

T. Shibutani (Ed.), *Human nature and collective behavior.* Englewood Cliffs, NJ: Prentice Hall.

Merskin, D. (1999). Media dependency theory: Origins and directions. In D. Demers & K. Viswanath (Eds.), *Mass media, social control, and social change* (pp. 77–98). Ames: Iowa State University Press.

Merskin, D. L., & Huberlie, M. (1996). Companionship in the classifieds: The adoption of personal advertisements by daily newspapers. *Journalism and Mass Communication Quarterly, 73,* 219–229.

Meyers, R. A. (1989). Testing persuasive argument theory's predictor model: Alternative interactional accounts of group argument and influence. *Communication Monographs, 56,* 112–132.

Meyers, R. A., & Brashers, D. E. (1999). Influence processes in group interaction. In L. R. Frey, D. S. Gouran, & M. S. Poole (Eds.), *The handbook of group communication theory and research* (pp. 288–312). Thousand Oaks, CA: Sage.

Meyers, R. A., & Seibold, D. R. (1987). Interactional and noninteractional perspectives on interpersonal argument: Implications for the study of decision-making. In F. H. Van Emeron, P. Grootendorst, J. A. Blair, & C. A. Willard (Eds.), *Argumentation: Perspectives and approaches* (pp. 205–214). Dordrecht, The Netherlands: Foris.

Meyers, R. A., & Seibold, D. R. (1990). Perspectives on group argument: A critical review of persuasive arguments theory and an alternative structurational view. In J. Anderson (Ed.), *Communication yearbook 13* (pp. 268–302). Newbury Park, CA: Sage.

Milgram, S. (1961). Nationality and conformity. *Scientific American, 205,* 45–51.

Millar, F. E., Rogers, L. E., & Bavelas, J. B. (1984). Identifying patterns of verbal conflict in interpersonal dynamics. *Western Journal of Speech Communication, 48,* 231–246.

Miller, G. R. (1966). On defining communication: Another stab. *Journal of Communication, 16,* 92.

Miller, G. R. (1980). On being persuaded: Some basic distinctions. In M. E. Roloff & G. R. Miller (Eds.), *Persuasion: New directions in theory and research* (pp. 11–28). Beverly Hills, CA: Sage.

Miller, G. R. (1995). "I think my schizophrenia is better today," said the communication researcher unanimously: Some thoughts on the dysfunctional dichotomy between pure and applied communication research. In K. N. Cissna (Ed.), *Applied communication in the 21st century* (pp. 47–55). Mahwah, NJ: Erlbaum.

Miller, G. R., Boster, F. B., Roloff, M. E., & Seibold, D. R. (1977). Compliance-gaining message strategies: A typology and some findings concerning effects of situational differences. *Communication Monographs, 44,* 37–51.

Miller, G. R., & Burgoon, M. (1973). *New techniques of persuasion.* New York: Harper & Row.

Miller, G. R., & Nicholson, H. E. (1976). *Communication inquiry: A perspective on a process.* Reading, MA: Addison-Wesley.

Miller, G. R., & Steinberg, M. (1975). *Between people: A new analysis of interpersonal communication.* Chicago: Science Research Associates.

Miller, K. I. (1999). *Organizational communication: Approaches and processes* (2nd ed.). Belmont, CA: Wadsworth.

Miller, K. I. (2000). Common ground from the postpositivist perspective: From "straw person" argument to collaborative coexistence. In S. R. Corman & M. S. Poole (Eds.), *Perspectives on organizational communication: Finding common ground* (pp. 46–67). New York: Guilford.

Miller, K. I. (2001). Quantitative research methods. In F. M. Jablin & L. L. Putnam (Eds.), *The new handbook of organizational communication: Advances in theory, research, and methods* (pp. 137–160). Thousand Oaks, CA: Sage.

Miller, K. I., Joseph, L., & Apker, J. (2000). Strategic ambiguity in the role development process. *Journal of Applied Communication Research, 28,* 193–214.

Miller, K. I., Stiff, J. B., & Ellis, B. H. (1988). Communication and empathy as precursors to burnout among human service workers. *Communication Monographs, 55,* 250–265.

Miller, N. E., & Dollard, J. (1941). *Social learning and imitation.* New Haven, CT: Yale University Press.

Miller, R. W. (1987). *Fact and method.* Princeton, NJ: Princeton University Press.

Miller, V. D., & Jablin, F. M. (1991). Information seeking during organizational entry: Influences, tactics, and a model of the process. *Academy of Management Review, 16,* 92–120.

Mohrmann, G. P. (1980). Elegy in a critical graveyard. *Western Journal of Speech Communication, 44,* 265–274.

Monge, P. R., & Contractor, N. S. (2001). Emergence of communication networks. In F. M. Jablin & L. L. Putnam (Eds.), *The new handbook of organizational communication: Advances in theory, research, and methods* (pp. 440–502). Thousand Oaks, CA: Sage.

Mongeau, P. A., & Carey, C. M. (1996). Who's wooing whom II? An experimental investigation of date-initiation and expectancy violation. *Western Journal of Communication, 60,* 195–213.

Mongeau, P. A., & Stiff, J. B. (1993). Specifying causal relationships in the elaboration likelihood model. *Communication Theory, 3,* 65–72.

Monson, T. C., & Snyder, M. (1977). Actors, observers, and the attribution process: Toward a reconceptualization. *Journal of Experimental Social Psychology, 13,* 89–111.

Morgan, G. (1986). *Images of organization.* Newbury Park, CA: Sage.

Morgan, G. (1997). *Images of organization* (2nd ed.). Newbury Park, CA: Sage.

Morgan, M., & Shanahan, J. (1997). Two decades of cultivation research: An appraisal and meta-analysis. In B. Burleson (Ed.), *Communication yearbook 20* (pp. 1–45). Thousand Oaks, CA: Sage.

Morgan, M., & Signorielli, N. (1990). Cultivation analysis: Conceptualization and methodology. In N. Signorielli & M. Morgan (Eds.), *Cultivation analysis: New directions in media effects research* (pp. 13–34). Newbury Park, CA: Sage.

Morley, D., & Chen, K.-H. (1996). *Stuart Hall: Critical dialogues in cultural studies.* New York: Routledge.

Morris, C. W. (1938). *Foundations of the theory of signs.* Chicago: University of Chicago Press.

Morrow, R. A. (1994). *Critical theory and methodology.* Thousand Oaks, CA: Sage.

Motley, M. T. (1990). On whether one can(not) not communicate: An examination via traditional communication postulates. *Western Journal of Speech Communication, 54,* 1–20.

Motley, M. T. (1991). How one may not communicate: A reply to Andersen. *Communication Studies, 42,* 326–339.

Mumby, D. K. (1987). The political function of narrative in organizations. *Communication Monographs, 54,* 113–127.

Mumby, D. K. (1989). Ideology and the social construction of meaning: A communication perspective. *Communication Quarterly, 37,* 291–304.

Mumby, D. K. (1997). Modernism, postmodernism, and communication studies: A rereading of an ongoing debate. *Communication Theory, 7,* 1–28.

Mumby, D. K. (2000). Common ground from the critical perspective: Overcoming binary opposi-

tions. In S. R. Corman & M. S. Poole (Eds.), *Perspectives on organizational communication: Finding common ground* (pp. 68–86). New York: Guilford.

Mumby, D. K. (2001). Power and politics. In F. M. Jablin & L. L. Putnam (Eds.), *The new handbook of organizational communication: Advances in theory, research, and methods* (pp. 585–623). Thousand Oaks, CA: Sage.

Nakagawa, G. (1990). "What are we doing here with all these Japanese?": Subject-constitution and strategies of discursive closure represented in stories of Japanese American internment. *Communication Quarterly, 38,* 388–402.

Natale, M. (1975). Convergence of mean vocal intensity in dyadic communication as a function of social desirability. *Journal of Personality and Social Psychology, 32,* 790–804.

Natanson, M. (1966). *Essays in phenomenology.* The Hague, The Netherlands: Martinus Nijhoff.

Newcomb, H. (1978). Assessing the violence profile of Gerbner and Gross: A humanistic critique and suggestion. *Communication Research, 5,* 264–282.

Nichols, M. H. (1952). Kenneth Burke and the "new rhetoric." *Quarterly Journal of Speech, 38,* 133–134.

Nisbett, R. E., & Ross, L. (1980). *Human inference: Strategies and shortcomings of social judgment.* Englewood Cliffs, NJ: Prentice Hall.

Noelle, E. (1940). *Amerikanische Massenbefragungen über Politik und Presse.* Frankfurt, Germany: Verlag Moritz Diesterweg.

Noelle-Neumann, E. (1984). *The spiral of silence.* Chicago: University of Chicago Press.

Noelle-Neumann, E. (1991). The theory of public opinion: The concept of the spiral of silence. In J. A. Anderson (Ed.), *Communication yearbook 14* (pp. 256–287). Newbury Park, CA: Sage.

Noelle-Neumann, E. (1993). *The spiral of silence* (2nd ed.). Chicago: University of Chicago Press.

Ogden, C. K., & Richards, I. A. (1946). *The meaning of meaning.* New York: Harcourt Brace & World.

O'Keefe, B. J. (1988). The logic of message designs: Individual differences in reasoning about communication. *Communication Monographs, 55,* 80–103.

O'Keefe, B. J. (1990). The logic of regulative communication: Understanding the rationality of message designs. In J. P. Dillard (Ed.), *Seeking compliance: The production of interpersonal influence strategies* (pp. 87–104). Scottsdale, AZ: Gorsuch Scarisbrick.

O'Keefe, B. J. (1993). Against theory. *Journal of Communication, 43* (3), 75–82.

O'Keefe, B. J. (1997). Variation, adaptation, and functional explanation in the study of message design. In G. Philipsen & T. L. Albrecht (Eds.), *Developing communication theories* (pp. 85–118). Albany: State University of New York Press.

O'Keefe, B. J., & Delia, J. G. (1982). Impression formation and message production. In M. E. Roloff & C. R. Berger (Eds.), *Social cognition and communication* (pp. 33–72). Beverly Hills, CA: Sage.

O'Keefe, B. J., & Lambert, B. L. (1995). Managing the flow of ideas: A local management approach to message design. In B. R. Burleson (Ed.), *Communication yearbook 18* (pp. 54–82). Thousand Oaks, CA: Sage.

O'Keefe, B. J., & McCornack, S. A. (1987). Message design logic and message goal structure: Effects on perceptions of message quality in regulative communication situations. *Human Communication Research, 14,* 68–92.

O'Keefe, B. J., & Shepherd, G. J. (1987). The pursuit of multiple objectives in face-to-face persuasive interactions: Effects of construct differentiation on message organization. *Communication Monographs, 54,* 396–419.

O'Keefe, D. J. (1990). *Persuasion: Theory and research.* Newbury Park, CA: Sage.

O'Keefe, D. J., & Sypher, H. E. (1981). Cognitive complexity measures and the relationship of cognitive complexity to communication: A critical review. *Human Communication Research, 8,* 72–92.

Oliver, M. B. (1994). Contributions of sexual portrayals to viewers' responses to graphic horror. *Journal of Broadcasting & Electronic Media, 38,* 1–17.

Orbe, M. P. (1995). African American communication research: Toward a deeper understanding of interethnic communication. *Western Journal of Communication, 59,* 61–78.

Orbe, M. (1996). Laying the foundation for co-cultural theory: An inductive approach to studying "non-dominant" communication strategies and the factors that influence them. *Communication Studies, 47,* 157–176.

Orbe, M. P. (1998). *Constructing co-cultural theory: An explication of culture, power, and communication.* Thousand Oaks, CA: Sage.

Orona, C. J. (1990). Temporality and identity loss due to Alzheimer's disease. *Social Science and Medicine, 30,* 1247–1256.

Oshagan, H. (1996). Reference group influence on opinion expression. *International Journal of Public Opinion Research, 8,* 335–354.

Outhwaite, W., & Bottomore, T. (Eds.) (1993). *The Blackwell dictionary of twentieth-century social thought.* Oxford: Basil Blackwell.

Palmgreen, P. (1984). Uses and gratifications: A theoretical perspective. In R. N. Bostrom (Ed.), *Communication yearbook 8* (pp. 20–55). Beverly Hills, CA: Sage.

Papa, M. J., Auwal, M. A., & Singhal, A. (1997). Organizing for social change within concertive control systems: Member identification, empowerment, and the masking of discipline. *Communication Monographs, 64,* 219–249.

Park, J-W., & Hastak, M. (1995). Effects of involvement on on-line brand evaluations: A stronger test of the ELM. *Advances in Consumer Research, 22,* 435–439.

Parks, M. R. (1982). Ideology in interpersonal communication: Off the couch and into the world. In M. Burgoon (Ed.), *Communication yearbook 5* (pp. 79–108). New Brunswick, NJ: Transaction Books.

Parks, M. R., & Adelman, M. B. (1983). Communication networks and the development of romantic relationships: An expansion of uncertainty reduction theory. *Human Communication Research, 10,* 55–79.

Patterson, M. L. (1982). A sequential function model of interpersonal intimacy. *Psychological Review, 89,* 231–249.

Pearce, W. B. (1976). The coordinated management of meaning: A rules-based theory of interpersonal communication. In G. R. Miller (Ed.), *Explorations in interpersonal communication* (pp. 17–36). Beverly Hills, CA: Sage.

Pearce, W. B. (1995). A sailing guide for social constructionists. In W. Leeds-Hurwitz (Ed.), *Social approaches to communication* (pp. 88–113). New York: Guilford.

Pearce, W. B., & Cronen, V. (1980). *Communication and meaning: The creation of social realities.* New York: Praeger.

Pearce, W. B., Cronen, V. E., & Conklin, F. (1979). On what to look at when analyzing communication: A hierarchical model of actors' meanings. *Communication, 4,* 195–220.

Pearce, W. B., & Foss, K. A. (1990). The historical context of communication as a science. In G. L. Dahnke & G. W. Clatterbuck (Eds.), *Human communication: Theory and research.* Belmont, CA: Wadsworth.

Pearce, W. B., & Pearce, K. A. (2000). Extending the theory of the coordinated management of meaning (CMM) through a community dialogue process. *Communication Theory, 10*, 405–423.

Penelope, J. (1990). *Speaking freely: Unlearning the lies of the fathers' tongues*. New York: Pergamon.

Perry, S. D., Jenzowsky, S. A., Hester, J. B., King, C. M., & Yi, H. (1997). The influence of commercial humor on program enjoyment and evaluation. *Journalism & Mass Communication Quarterly, 74*, 388–399.

Petty, R. E., & Cacioppo, J. T. (1981). *Attitudes and persuasion: Classic and contemporary approaches*. Dubuque, IA: Brown.

Petty, R. E., & Cacioppo, J. T. (1983). Central and peripheral routes to persuasion: Application to advertising. In L. Percy & A. Woodside (Eds.), *Advertising and consumer psychology* (pp. 3–23). Lexington, MA: Heath.

Petty, R. E., & Cacioppo, J. T. (1986). *Communication and persuasion: Central and peripheral routes to attitude change*. New York: Springer-Verlag.

Petty, R. E., Cacioppo, J. T., & Kasmer, J. A. (1988). The role of affect in the elaboration likelihood model of persuasion. In L. Donohew, H. E. Sypher, & E. T. Higgins (Eds.), *Communication, social cognition, and affect* (pp. 117–146). Hillsdale, NJ: Erlbaum.

Petty, R. E., Cacioppo, J. T., & Schumann, D. (1983). Central and peripheral routes to advertising effectiveness: The moderating role of involvement. *Journal of Consumer Research, 10*, 135–146.

Petty, R. E., Heesacker, M., & Hughes, J. N. (1997). The elaboration likelihood model: Implications for the practice of school psychology. *Journal of School Psychology, 35*, 107–136.

Petty, R. E., Kasmer, J. A., Haugtvedt, C. P., & Cacioppo, J. T. (1987). Source and message factors in persuasion: A reply to Stiff's critique of the elaboration likelihood model. *Communication Monographs, 54*, 233–249.

Petty, R. E., Wegener, D. T., Fabrigar, L. R., Priester, J. R., & Cacioppo, J. T. (1993). Conceptual and methodological issues in the elaboration likelihood model of persuasion: A reply to the Michigan State critics. *Communication Theory, 3*, 336–362.

Pfau, M. (1992). The potential of inoculation in promoting resistance to the effectiveness of comparative advertising messages. *Communication Quarterly, 40*, 26–44.

Pfau, M. (1995). Designing messages for behavioral inoculation. In E. Maibach & R. L. Parrott (Eds.), *Designing health messages: Approaches from communication theory and public health practice* (pp. 99–113). Thousand Oaks, CA: Sage.

Pfau, M. (1996). Innoculation model of resistance to influence. In F. J. Boster & G. Barnett (Eds.), *Progress in communication sciences* (Vol. 12, pp. 133–171). Norwood, NJ: Ablex.

Pfau, M., & Burgoon, M. (1988). Inoculation in political campaign communication. *Human Communication Research, 15*, 91–111.

Pfau, M., Kenski, H. C., Nitz, M., & Sorenson, J. (1990). Efficacy of inoculation strategies in promoting resistance in political attack messages: Application to direct mail. *Communication Monographs, 57*, 1–12.

Pfau, M., Tusing, K. J., Koerner, A. F., Lee, W., Godbold, L. C., Penaloza, L. J., Yang, V. S-H., & Hong, Y-H. (1997). Enriching the inoculation construct: The role of critical components in the process of resistance. *Human Communication Research, 24*, 187–215.

Pfau, M., & Van Bockern, S. (1994). The persistence of inoculation in conferring resistance to smoking initiation among adolescents: The second year. *Human Communication Research, 20*, 413–430.

Pfau, M., Van Bockern, S., & Kang, J. G. (1992). Use of inoculation to promote resistance to smoking initiation among adolescents. *Communication Monographs, 59*, 213–230.

Philipsen, G. (1975). Speaking "like a man" in Teamsterville: Culture patterns of role enactment in an urban neighborhood. *Quarterly Journal of Speech, 61*, 13–22.

Philipsen, G. (1976). Places for speaking in Teamsterville. *Quarterly Journal of Speech, 62*, 15–25.

Philipsen, G. (1987). The prospect for cultural communication. In L. Kincaid (Ed.), *Communication theory: Eastern and Western perspectives*. New York: Academic.

Philipsen, G. (1992). *Speaking culturally: Explorations in social communication*. Albany: State University of New York Press.

Philipsen, G. (1995). The coordinated management of meaning theory of Pearce, Cronen, and associates. In D. P. Cushman & B. Kovacic (Eds.), *Watershed traditions in human communication theory* (pp. 13–43). Albany: State University of New York Press.

Philipsen, G. (1997). A theory of speech codes. In G. Philipsen & T. L. Albrecht (Eds.), *Developing communication theories* (pp. 119–156). Albany: State University of New York Press.

Philipsen, G., & Carbaugh, D. (1986). A bibliography of fieldwork in the ethnography of communication. *Language in Society, 15,* 387–398.

Phillips, D. C. (1987). *Philosophy, science, and social inquiry.* Oxford, UK: Pergamon.

Phillips, D. C. (1990). Postpositivistic science: Myths and realities. In E. G. Guba (Ed.), *The paradigm dialog* (pp. 31–45). Newbury Park, CA: Sage.

Phillips, D. C. (1992). *The social scientist's bestiary: A guide to fabled threats to, and defences of, naturalistic social science.* Oxford, UK: Pergamon.

Piaget, J. (1926). *The language and thought of the child.* London: Routledge & Kegan Paul.

Planalp, S., & Honeycutt, J. M. (1985). Events that increase uncertainty in personal relationships. *Human Communication Research, 11,* 593–604.

Pollock, D., & Cox, J. R. (1991). Historicizing "reason": Critical theory, practice, and postmodernity. *Communication Monographs, 58,* 170–178.

Poole, M. S. (1983a). Book review of "Communication, action, and meaning: The creation of social realities." *Quarterly Journal of Speech, 69,* 223–224.

Poole, M. S. (1983b). Decision development in small groups II: A study of multiple sequences in decision-making. *Communication Monographs, 50,* 206–232.

Poole, M. S. (1985). Communication and organizational climates: Review, critique, and a new perspective. In R. McPhee & P. Tompkins (Eds.), *Organizational communication: Traditional themes and new directions* (pp. 79–108). Beverly Hills, CA: Sage.

Poole, M. S. (1990). Do we have any theories of group communication? *Communication Studies, 41,* 237–247.

Poole, M. S. (1999). Group communication theory. In L. R. Frey, D. S. Gouran, & M. S. Poole (Eds.), *The handbook of group communication theory and research* (pp. 37–70). Thousand Oaks, CA: Sage.

Poole, M. S., & DeSanctis, G. (1992). Microlevel structuration in computer-supported group decision making. *Human Communication Research, 19,* 5–49.

Poole, M. S., & Doelger, J. A. (1986). Developmental processes in group decision-making. In R. Y. Hirokawa & M. S. Poole (Eds.), *Communication and group decision-making* (pp. 35–61). Beverly Hills, CA: Sage.

Poole, M. S., Holmes, M., & DeSanctis, G. (1991). Conflict management in a computer-supported meeting environment. *Management Science, 37,* 926–953.

Poole, M. S., & Lynch, O. H. (2000). Reflections on finding common ground. In S. R. Corman & M. S. Poole (Eds.), *Perspectives on organizational communication: Finding common ground* (pp. 211–227). New York: Guilford.

Poole, M. S., & McPhee, R. (1983). A structurational theory of organizational climate. In L. Putnam & M. Pacanowsky (Eds.), *Communication and organizations: An interpretive approach* (pp. 195–219). Beverly Hills, CA: Sage.

Poole, M. S., & Roth, J. (1989a). Decision development in small groups IV: A typology of group decision paths. *Human Communication Research, 15,* 323–356.

Poole, M. S., & Roth, J. (1989b). Decision development in small groups V: Test of a contingency model. *Human Communication Research, 15,* 549–589.

Poole, M. S., Seibold, D. R., & McPhee, R. D. (1986). A structurational approach to theory-building in group decision-making research. In R. Y. Hirokawa & M. S. Poole (Eds.), *Communication and group decision making* (pp. 237–264). Beverly Hills, CA: Sage.

Poole, M. S., Seibold, D. R., & McPhee, R. D. (1996). The structuration of group decisions. In M. S. Poole & R. Y. Hirokawa (Eds.), *Communication and group decision making* (2nd ed.) (pp. 114–146). Thousand Oaks, CA: Sage.

Popper, K. (1959). *The logic of scientific discovery.* London: Hutchinson.

Popper, K. (1962). *Conjectures and refutations: The growth of scientific knowledge.* New York: Basic Books.

Popper, K. (1976). The logic of the social sciences. In T. Adorno et al. (Eds.), *The positivist dispute in German sociology.* New York: Harper & Row.

Poster, M. (1989). *Critical theory and poststructuralism.* Ithaca, NY: Cornell University Press.

Potter, W. J. (1991a). The linearity assumption in cultivation research. *Human Communication Research, 18,* 562–584.

Potter, W. J. (1991b). The relationships between first and second order measures of cultivation. *Human Communication Research, 18,* 92–113.

Potter, W. J. (1993). Cultivation theory and research: A conceptual critique. *Human Communication Research, 19,* 564–601.

Potter, W. J. (1997). The problem of indexing risk of viewing television violence. *Critical Studies in Mass Communication, 14,* 228–248.

Price, V., & Allen, S. (1990). Opinion spirals, silent and otherwise: Applying small-group research to public opinion phenomena. *Communication Research, 17,* 369–392.

Procter, D. E. (1995). Placing Lincoln and Mitchell counties: A cultural study. *Communication Studies, 46,* 222–233.

Propp, K. M., & Nelson, D. (1996). Problem-solving performance in naturalistic groups: A test of the ecological validity of the functional perspective. *Communication Studies, 47,* 35–45.

Protess, D. L., Cook, F. L., Doppelt, J. C., Ettema, J. S., Gordon, M. T., Leff, D. R., & Miller, P. (1991). *The journalism of outrage: Investigative reporting and agenda building in America.* New York: Guilford.

Psathas, G. (1995). *Conversation analysis: The study of talk-in-action.* Thousand Oaks, CA: Sage.

Putman, W., & Street, R. (1984). The conception and perception of noncontent speech performance: Implications for speech accommodation theory. *International Journal of Sociology and Language, 46,* 97–114.

Putnam, H. (1981). *Reason, truth, and history.* Cambridge: Cambridge University Press.

Putnam, L. L. (1983). The interpretive perspective: An alternative to functionalism. In L. L. Putnam & M. E. Pacanowsky (Eds.), *Communication in organizations: An interpretive approach* (pp. 31–54). Beverly Hills, CA: Sage.

Putnam, L. L. (1989). Negotiating and organizing: Two levels within the Weickian model. *Communication Studies, 40,* 249–257.

Putnam, L. L., & Stohl, C. (1990). Bona fide groups: A reconceptualization of groups in context. *Communication Studies, 41,* 248–265.

Putnam, L. L., & Stohl, C. (1996). Bona fide groups: An alternative perspective for communication and small group decision making. In M. S. Poole & R. Y. Hirokawa (Eds.), *Communication and group decision making* (2nd ed.) (pp. 147–178). Thousand Oaks, CA: Sage.

Putnam, L. L., Van Hoeven, S. A., & Bullis, C. A. (1991). The role of rituals and fantasy themes in teachers' bargaining. *Western Journal of Speech Communication, 55,* 85–103.

Putnam, R. (2000). *Bowling alone: The collapse and revival of American community.* New York: Simon & Schuster.

Radnitzky, G. (1970). *Contemporary schools of meta-science* (2 vols.). Goteborg, Sweden: Akademiforlaget.

Rawlins, W. K. (1983). Negotiating close friendships: The dialectic of conjunctive freedoms. *Human Communication Research, 9,* 255–266.

Rawlins, W. K. (1989). A dialectical analysis of the tensions, functions and strategic challenges of communication in young adult friendships. In J. A. Anderson (Ed.), *Communication yearbook 12* (pp. 157–189). Newbury Park, CA: Sage.

Rawlins, W. K. (1992). *Friendship matters: Communication, dialectics, and the life course.* New York: Aldine de Gruyter.

Rawlins, W. K., & Holl, M. (1988). Adolescents' interactions with parents and friends: Dialectics of temporal perspective and evaluation. *Journal of Social and Personal Relationships, 5,* 27–46.

Rayburn, J. D., & Palmgreen, P. (1984). Merging uses and gratifications and expectancy-value theory. *Communication Research, 11,* 537–562.

Real, M. (1984). The debate on critical theory and the study of communications. *Journal of Communication, 34,* 72–80.

Richards, I. A. (1936). *The philosophy of rhetoric.* London: Oxford University Press.

Rickford, J. (1986). The need for new approaches to social class analysis in sociolinguistics. *Language & Communication, 6,* 215–221.

Ricoeur, P. (1981). *Hermeneutics and the human sciences: Essays on language, action and interpretation.* (J. B. Thompson, Ed. & Trans.). New York: Cambridge University Press.

Ricoeur, P. (1986). *From text to action: Essays in hermeneutics II.* (K. Blamey & J. B. Thompson, Trans.). Evanston, IL: Northwestern University Press.

Roberts, C. V., & Watson, K. W. (Eds.) (1989). *Intrapersonal communication processes: Original essays.* Scottsdale, AZ: Gorsuch Scarisbrick.

Roberts, M., & McCombs, M. (1994). Agenda setting and political advertising: Origins of the news agenda. *Political Communication, 11,* 249–262.

Rogers, E. M. (1994). *A history of communication study: A biographical approach*. New York: Free Press.

Rogers, E. M., & Dearing, J. W. (1988). Agenda-setting research: Where has it been, where is it going? In J. A. Anderson (Ed.), *Communication yearbook 11* (pp. 555–594). Newbury Park, CA: Sage.

Rogers, E. M., Dearing, J. W., & Bregman, D. (1993). The anatomy of agenda-setting research. *Journal of Communication, 43*, 68–84.

Rogers, L. E., Millar, F. E., & Bavelas, J. B. (1985). Methods for analyzing marital conflict discourse: Implications of a systems approach. *Family Process, 24*, 175–187.

Rogers, L. E., & Farace, R. V. (1975). Analysis of relational communication in dyads: New measurement procedures. *Human Communication Research, 1*, 222–239.

Rorty, R. (1979). *Philosophy and the mirror of nature*. Princeton, NJ: Princeton University Press.

Rosenberg, A. (1986). Philosophy of science and the potentials for knowledge in the social sciences. In D. W. Fiske & R. A. Shweder (Eds.), *Metatheory in social science: Pluralisms and subjectivities* (pp. 339–346). Chicago: University of Chicago Press.

Rosengren, K. E. (1993). From field to frog ponds. *Journal of Communication, 43*, 6–17.

Rowland, R. C. (1989). On limiting the narrative paradigm: Three case studies. *Communication Monographs, 56*, 39–54.

Rubin, A. M. (1984). Ritualized and instrumental television viewing. *Journal of Communication, 34*, 67–77.

Rubin, A. M., & Perse, E. M. (1987). Audience activity and soap opera involvement: A uses and effects investigation. *Human Communication Research, 14*, 249–268.

Rubin, A. M., & Rubin, R. B. (1982). Older persons' TV viewing patterns and motivations. *Communication Research, 9*, 287–313.

Rubin, A. M., & Windahl, S. (1986). The uses and dependency model of mass communication. *Critical Studies in Mass Communication, 3*, 184–199.

Ryan, E. B., Giles, H., Bartolucci, G., & Henwood, K. (1986). Psycholinguistic and social psychological components of communication by and with the elderly. *Language & Communication, 6*, 1–24.

Saeki, M., & O'Keefe, B. J. (1984). Refusals and rejections: Designing messages to serve multiple goals. *Human Communication Research, 21*, 67–102.

Salmon, C. T., & Moh, C. Y. (1992). The spiral of silence: Linking individual and society through communication. In J. D. Kennamer (Ed.), *Public opinion, the press, and public policy* (pp. 145–161). Westport, CT: Greenwood.

Samovar, L., Porter, R., & Jain, N. (1981). *Understanding intercultural communication*. Belmont, CA: Wadsworth.

Schacter, S. (1964). The interaction of cognitive and physiological determinants of emotional state. In L. Berkowitz (Ed.), *Advances in experimental social psychology* (Vol. 1, pp. 49–80). New York: Academic.

Schank, R. C. (1982). *Dynamic memory: A theory of reminding and learning*. New York: Cambridge University Press.

Schegloff, E. A. (1980). Preliminaries to preliminaries: "Can I ask you a question?". *Sociological Inquiry, 50*, 104–152.

Schegloff, E. A. (1984). On some questions and ambiguities in conversation. In J. M. Atkinson & J. Heritage (Eds.), *Structures of social action: Studies in conversation analysis* (pp. 28–53). Cambridge: Cambridge University Press.

Schegloff, E. A. (1988). Presequences and indirection: Applying speech act theory to ordinary conversation. *Journal of Pragmatics, 12*, 55–62.

Schutz, A. (1962). *Collected papers* (Vol. 1). The Hague, The Netherlands: Martinus Nijhoff.

Schutz, A. (1964). The stranger: An essay in social psychology. In *Collected papers* (Vol. 2, pp. 91–105). The Hague, The Netherlands: Martinus Nijhoff.

Scott, C. R. (1997). Identification with multiple targets in a geographically dispersed organization. *Management Communication Quarterly, 10*, 491–522.

Scott, C. R., Corman, S. R., & Cheney, G. (1998). Development of a structurational model of identification in the organization. *Communication Theory, 8*, 298–336.

Scott, C. R., Quinn, L., Timmerman, C. E., & Garrett, D. M. (1998). Ironic uses of group communication technology: Evidence from meeting transcripts and interviews with group decision support system users. *Communication Quarterly, 46*, 353–374.

Searle, J. R. (1969). *Speech acts: An essay in the philosophy of language*. Cambridge: Cambridge University Press.

Searle, J. R. (1975). Indirect speech acts. In P. Cole & J. Morgan (Eds.), *Syntax and semantics. Vol. 3: Speech acts* (pp. 59–82). New York: Academic.

Searle, J. R. (1979). *Expression and meaning.* New York: Cambridge University Press.

Searle, J. R. (1992). Conversation. In J. R. Searle et al. (Eds.), *(On) Searle on conversation* (pp. 7–29). Amsterdam: Benjamins.

Seibold, D. R. (1995). *Theoria* and *Praxis*: Means and ends in applied communication research. In K. N. Cissna (Ed.), *Applied communication in the 21st century* (pp. 23–38). Mahwah, NJ: Erlbaum.

Seibold, D. R., Cantrill, J. G., & Meyers, R. A. (1985). Communication and interpersonal influence. In M. L. Knapp & G. R. Miller (Eds.), *Handbook of interpersonal communication* (pp. 551–614). Beverly Hills, CA: Sage.

Seidman, S. (1994). *Contested knowledge: Social theory in the postmodern era.* Cambridge, MA: Blackwell.

Shamir, J. (1997). Speaking up and silencing out in face of a changing climate of opinion. *Journalism & Mass Communication Quarterly, 74,* 602–714.

Shaw, D. L., & McCombs, M. E. (1977). *The emergence of American political issues: The agenda-setting function of the press.* St. Paul, MN: West.

Sheppard, B. H., Hartwick, J., & Warshaw, P. R. (1988). The theory of reasoned action: A meta-analysis of past research with recommendations for modifications and future research. *Journal of Consumer Research, 15,* 325–343.

Sherif, C. W., Sherif, M., & Nebergall, R. E. (1965). *Attitude and attitude change.* Philadelphia: Saunders.

Sherif, M., & Hovland, C. I. (1961). *Social judgment: Assimilation and contrast effects in communication and attitude change.* New Haven, CT: Yale University Press.

Shields, S. (1975). Functionalism, Darwinism and the psychology of women: A study in social myth. *American Psychologist, 30,* 739–754.

Sias, P. M. (1996). Constructing perceptions of differential treatment: An analysis of coworker discourse. *Communication Monographs, 63,* 171–187.

Simons, H. W. (1989). Introduction: Kenneth Burke and the rhetoric of the human sciences. In H. W. Simons & T. Melia (Eds.), *The legacy of Kenneth Burke* (pp. 3–27). Madison: University of Wisconsin Press.

Simons, H. W., & Melia, T. (Eds.) (1989). *The legacy of Kenneth Burke.* Madison: University of Wisconsin Press.

Simpson, C. (1996). Elisabeth Noelle-Neumann's "spiral of silence" and the historical context of communication theory. *Journal of Communication, 46,* 149–173.

Skumanich, S. A., & Kintsfather, D. P. (1998). Individual media dependency relations within television shopping programming: A causal model reviewed and revised. *Communication Research, 25,* 200–219.

Slater, M. D. (1999). Integrating application of media effects, persuasion, and behavior change theories to communication campaigns: A stages-of-change framework. *Health Communication, 11,* 335–354.

Smith, J. D. (1990). Goodness criteria: Alternative research paradigms and the problem of criteria. In E. G. Guba (Ed.), *The paradigm dialog* (pp. 167–187). Newbury Park, CA: Sage.

Smith, L. D. (1989). A narrative analysis of the party platforms: The Democrats and Republicans of 1984. *Communication Quarterly, 37,* 91–99.

Smith, R. C. (1992). *Images of organizational communication: Root-metaphors of the organization-communication relation.* Paper presented at the meeting of the International Communication Association, Washington, DC, June.

Stewart, J. (1986). Speech and human beings: A complement to semiotics. *Quarterly Journal of Speech, 76,* 282–299.

Stiff, J. B. (1986). Cognitive processing of persuasive message cues: A meta-analytic review of the effects of supporting information on atittudes. *Communication Monographs, 53,* 75–89.

Stiff, J. B. (1994). *Persuasive communication.* New York: Guilford.

Stiff, J. B., & Boster, F. J. (1987). Cognitive processing: Additional thoughts and a reply to Petty, Kasmer, Haugtvedt, and Cacioppo. *Communication Monographs, 53,* 75–89.

Stiff, J. B., Dillard, J. P., Somera, L., Kim, H., & Sleight, C. (1988). Empathy, communication, and prosocial behavior. *Communication Monographs, 55,* 198–213.

Stohl, C., & Holmes, M. E. (1993). A functional perspective for bona fide groups. In S. A. Deetz (Ed.), *Communication yearbook 16* (pp. 601–614). Newbury Park, CA: Sage.

Stohl, C., & Putnam, L. L. (1994). Group communication in context: Implications for the study of bona fide groups. In L. R. Frey (Ed.), *Group communication in context* (pp. 285–292). Hillsdale, NJ: Erlbaum.

Strauss, A., & Corbin, J. (Eds.) (1997). *Grounded theory in practice.* Thousand Oaks, CA: Sage.

Sunnafrank, M. (1986). Predicted outcome value during initial interactions. *Human Communication Research, 13*, 3–33.

Sunwolf, & Seibold, D. R. (1998). Jurors' intuitive rules for deliberation: A structurational approach to communication in jury decision making. *Communication Monographs, 65*, 282–307.

Suppe, F. (1977). The search for philosophic understanding of scientific theories. In F. Suppe (Ed.), *The structure of scientific theories* (pp. 3–232). Urbana: University of Illinois Press.

Surber, J. P. (1998). *Culture and critique: An introduction to the critical discourses of cultural studies.* Boulder, CO: Westview.

Swanson, D. (1992). Understanding audiences: Continuing contributions of gratifications research. *Poetics, 21*, 305–328.

Swanson, D., & Babrow, A. S. (1989). Uses and gratifications: The influence of gratification-seeking and expectancy-value judgments on the viewing of television news. In B. Dervin, L. Grossberg, B. J. O'Keefe, & E. Wartella (Eds.), *Rethinking communication. Vol 2: Paradigm exemplars* (pp. 361–375). Newbury Park, CA: Sage.

Tajfel, H. (Ed.) (1978). *Differentiation between social groups.* London: Academic.

Tajfel, H., & Turner, J. C. (1979). An integrative theory of intergroup conflict. In W. G. Austin & S. Worchel (Eds.), *The social psychology of intergroup relations* (pp. 33–47). Monterey, CA: Brooks/Cole.

Takeshita, T. (1997). Exploring the media's roles in defining reality: From issue-agenda setting to attribute-agenda setting. In M. McCombs, D. L. Shaw, & D. Weaver (Eds.), *Communication and democracy: Exploring the intellectual frontiers in agenda-setting theory* (pp. 15–27). Mahwah, NJ: Erlbaum.

Tamborini, R. (1996). A model of empathy and emotional reactions to horror. In J. B. Weaver & R. Tamborini (Eds.), *Horror films: Current research on audience preferences and reactions* (pp. 103–123). Mahwah, NJ: Erlbaum.

Tamborini, R., & Choi, J. (1990). The role of cultural diversity in cultivation research. In N. Signorielli & M. Morgan (Eds.), *Cultivation analysis: New directions in media effects research* (pp. 157–180). Newbury Park, CA: Sage.

Taylor, D. A. (1968). The development of interpersonal relationships: Social penetration processes. *Journal of Social Psychology, 75*, 79–90.

Taylor, D. A., & Altman, I. (1987). Communication in interpersonal relationships: Social penetration processes. In M. Roloff & G. R. Miller (Eds.), *Interpersonal processes: New directions in communication research* (pp. 257–277). Newbury Park, CA: Sage.

Taylor, J. R. (1993). *Rethinking the theory of organizational communication: How to read an organization.* Norwood, NJ: Ablex.

Taylor, J. R. (1995). Shifting from a heteronomous to an autonomous worldview of organizational communication: Communication theory on the cusp. *Communication Theory, 5*, 1–35.

Taylor, J. R. (1999). The other side of rationality: Socially distributed cognition. *Management Communication Quarterly, 13*, 317–326.

Taylor, J. R., Cooren, F., Giroux, N., & Robichaud, D. (1996). The communicational basis of organization: Between the conversation and the text. *Communication Theory, 6*, 1–39.

Taylor, S. E. (1981). The interface of cognitive and social psychology. In J. Harvey (Ed.), *Cognition, social behavior, and the environment* (pp. 189–211). Hillsdale, NJ: Erlbaum.

Therborn, G. (1980). *The ideology of power and the power of ideology.* London: Verso.

Thibaut, J. W., & Kelley, H. H. (1959). *The psychology of groups.* New York: Wiley.

Tice, T. N., & Slavens, T. P. (1983). *Research guide to philosophy.* Chicago: American Library Association.

Ting-Toomey, S. (1988). Intercultural conflict styles: A face-negotiation theory. In Y. Y. Kim & W. Gudykunst (Eds.), *Theories in intercultural communication* (pp. 213–235). Newbury Park, CA: Sage.

Ting-Toomey, S. (Ed.) (1994). *The challenge of facework.* Albany: State University of New York Press.

Ting-Toomey, S., & Cocroft, B.-A. (1994). Face and facework: Theoretical and research issues. In S. Ting-Toomey (Ed.), *The challenge of facework: Cross-cultural and interpersonal issues* (pp. 307–340). Albany: State University of New York Press.

Ting-Toomey, S., Gao, G., Trubisky, P., Yang, Z., Kim, H. S., Lin, S.-L., & Nishida, T. (1991). Culture, face maintenance, and styles of handling interpersonal conflict: A study in five cultures. *International Journal of Conflict Management, 2*, 275–296.

Tompkins, P. K. (1997). How to think and talk about organizational communication. In P. Y. Byer (Ed.), *Organizational communication: Theory and behavior* (pp. 361–373). Boston: Allyn & Bacon.

Tompkins, P. K., & Cheney, G. E. (1985). Communication and unobtrusive control in contemporary organizations. In R. D. McPhee & P. K. Tompkins (Eds.), *Organizational communication: Traditional themes and new directions* (pp. 179–210). Beverly Hills, CA: Sage.

Tracy, K. (1990). The many faces of facework. In H. Giles & W. P. Robinson (Eds.), *Handbook of language and social psychology* (pp. 209–226). New York: Wiley.

Trigg, R. (1985). *Understanding social science.* Oxford, UK: Blackwell.

Tuchman, G. (1988). Mass media institutions. In N. Smelser (Ed.), *Handbook of sociology* (pp. 601–626). Newbury Park, CA: Sage.

Turner, E. H., & Cullingford, R. E. (1989). Using conversation MOPs in natural language interfaces. *Discourse Processes, 12,* 63–90.

Van Lear, C. A. (1987). The formation of social relationships: A longitudinal study of social penetration. *Human Communication Research, 13,* 299–322.

Van Lear, C. A. (1991). Testing a cyclical model of communicative openness in relationship development: Two longitudinal studies. *Communication Monographs, 58,* 337–361.

van Rees, M. A. (1992). The adequacy of speech act theory for explaining conversational phenomena: A response to some conversation analytic critics. *Journal of Pragmatics, 17,* 31–47.

Vangelisti, A. L. (1992). Communication problems in committed relationships: An attributional analysis. In J. H. Harvey, T. L. Orbuch, & A. L. Weber (Eds.), *Attributions, accounts, and close relationships* (pp. 144–164). New York: Springer-Verlag.

Vendler, Z. (1972). *Res cogitans: An essay in rational psychology.* Ithaca, NY: Cornell University Press.

Vocate, D. R. (1994). *Intrapersonal communication: Different voices, different minds.* Hillsdale, NJ: Erlbaum.

Waldron, V. R. (1997). Toward a theory of interactive conversational planning. In J. Greene (Ed.), *Message production: Advances in communication theory* (pp. 195–220). Mahwah, NJ: Erlbaum.

Wanta, W. (1997). The messenger and the message: Differences across news media. In M. McCombs, D. L. Shaw, & D. Weaver (Eds.), *Communication and democracy: Exploring the intellectual frontiers in agenda-setting theory* (pp. 137–151). Mahwah, NJ: Erlbaum.

Watt, J. H., & van den Berg, S. A. (1995). *Research methods for communication science.* Boston: Allyn & Bacon.

Watzlawick, P., Beavin, J. H., & Jackson, D. D. (1967). *Pragmatics of human communication.* New York: Norton.

Weaver, D. H. (1977). Political issues and voter need for orientation. In D. L. Shaw & M. E. McCombs (Eds.), *The emergence of American political issues: The agenda-setting function of the press* (pp. 107–119). St. Paul, MN: West.

Weaver, W. (1949). Recent contributions to the mathematical theory of communication. In C. Shannon & W. Weaver, *The mathematical theory of communication.* Urbana: University of Illinois Press.

Weber, M. (1968). *Economy and society* (G. Roth & C. Wittich, Eds. & Trans.). New York: Bedminster.

Weber, R., & Crocker, J. (1983). Cognitive processing in the revision of stereotypic beliefs. *Journal of Personality and Social Psychology, 45,* 961–977.

Weick, K. E. (1969). *The social psychology of organizing.* Reading, MA: Addison-Wesley.

Weick, K. E. (1979). *The social psychology of organizing* (2nd ed.). Reading, MA: Addison-Wesley.

Weick, K. E. (1985). Sources of order in underorganized systems: Themes in recent organizational theory. In Y. S. Lincoln (Ed.), *Organizational theory and inquiry* (pp. 106–136). Beverly Hills, CA: Sage.

Weick, K. E. (1988). Enacted sensemaking in crisis situations. *Journal of Management Studies, 25,* 305–317.

Weick, K. E. (1989). Organized improvisation: 20 years of organizing. *Communication Studies, 40,* 241–248.

Weick, K. E. (1990). The vulnerable system: An analysis of the Tenerife air disaster. *Journal of Management, 16,* 571–593.

Weick, K. E. (1993). The collapse of sensemaking in organizations: The Mann Gulch disaster. *Administrative Science Quarterly, 38,* 626–652.

Weick, K. E. (1995). *Sensemaking in organizations.* Thousand Oaks, CA: Sage.

Weiner, B. (1986). *An attributional theory of motivation and emotion.* New York: Springer-Verlag.

Welton, K. (1997). Nancy Hartsock's standpoint theory: From content to "concrete multiplicity." In S. J. Kenney & H. Kinsella (Eds.), *Politics and feminist standpoint theory* (pp. 7–24). New York: Haworth.

Werner, C. M., & Baxter, L. A. (1994). Temporal qualities of relationships: Organismic, transactional and dialectical views. In M. L. Knapp & G. R. Miller (Eds.), *Handbook of interpersonal communication* (2nd ed.) (pp. 323–379). Newbury Park, CA: Sage.

Werner, H. (1957). The concept of development from a comparative and organismic point of view. In D. B. Harris (Ed.), *The concept of development*. Minneapolis: University of Minnesota Press.

White, R. W. (1972). *The enterprise of living: Growth and organization in personality.* New York: Holt, Rinehart, & Winston.

Wicks, R. H. (1992). Schema theory and measurement in mass communication research: Theoretical and methodological issues in news information processing. In S. A. Deetz (Ed.), *Communication yearbook 15* (pp. 115–145). Newbury Park, CA: Sage.

Wilder, C. (1979). The Palo Alto group: Difficulties and directions of the interactional view for human communication research. *Human Communication Research, 5,* 171–186.

Wilke, J. (1995). Agenda-setting in an historical perspective: The coverage of the American revolution in the German press (1773–83). *European Journal of Communication, 10,* 63–86.

Williams, A., Giles, H., Coupland, N., Dalby, M., & Manasse, H. (1990). The communicative contexts of elderly social support and health: A theoretical model. *Health Communication, 2,* 123–143.

Williams, R. (1977). *Marxism and literature.* Oxford: Oxford University Press.

Willnat, L. (1997). Agenda setting and priming: Conceptual links and differences. In M. McCombs, D. L. Shaw, & D. Weaver (Eds.), *Communication and democracy: Exploring the intellectual frontiers in agenda-setting theory* (pp. 51–66). Mahwah, NJ: Erlbaum.

Wilson, B. J. (1994). A challenge to communication empiricists: Let's be more forthcoming about what we do. *Western Journal of Communication, 58,* 25–31.

Wilson, B. J., Cantor, J., Gordon, L., & Zillmann, D. (1986). Affective responses of nonretarded and retarded children to the emotions of a protagonist. *Child Study Journal, 16,* 77–93.

Wilson, S. R. (1990). Development and test of a cognitive rules model of interaction goals. *Communication Monographs, 57,* 81–103.

Wilson, S. R. (1995). Elaborating the cognitive rules model of interaction goals: The problem of accounting for individual differences in goal formation. In B. R. Burleson (Ed.), *Communication yearbook 18* (pp. 3–25). Thousand Oaks, CA: Sage.

Wilson, S. R. (1997). Developing theories of persuasive message production: The next generation. In J. O. Greene (Ed.), *Message production: Advances in communication research* (pp. 15–43). Mahwah, NJ: Erlbaum.

Wilson, S. R. (2000). Developing planning perspectives to explain parent-child interaction patterns in physically abusive families. *Communication Theory, 10,* 210–220.

Wilson, S. R., Cruz, M. G., Marshall, L. J., & Rao, N. (1993). An attributional analysis of compliance-gaining interactions. *Communication Monographs, 60,* 352–371.

Wittgenstein, L. (1953). *Philosophical investigations.* Oxford: Basil Blackwell.

Witmer, D. F. (1997). Communication and recovery: Structuration as an ontological approach to organizational culture. *Communication Monographs, 64,* 324–349.

Wolfram, W. (1973). *Sociolinguistic aspects of assimilation: Puerto Rican English in East Harlem.* Arlington, VA: Center for Applied Linguistics.

Wood, J. T. (1997). *Communication theories in action: An introduction.* Belmont, CA: Wadsworth.

Wood, J. T., & Duck, S. (1995). Off the beaten track: New shores for relationship research. In J. T. Wood & S. Duck (Eds.), *Understanding relationship processes. 6: Understudied relationships: Off the beaten track* (pp. 1–21). Thousand Oaks, CA: Sage.

Wyer, R. S., & Srull, T. K. (1981). Category accessibility: Some theoretical and empirical issues concerning the processing of social stimulus information. In E. T. Higgins, C. P. Herman, & M. P. Zanna (Eds.), *The Ontario symposium* (Vol. 1, pp. 161–197). Hillsdale, NJ: Erlbaum.

Yagoda, B. (1980). Kenneth Burke: The greatest literary critic since Coleridge? *Horizon, 23,* 66–69.

Yates, J. (1989). The emergence of the memo as a managerial genre. *Management Communication Quarterly, 2,* 485–510.

Yates, J., & Orlikowski, W. J. (1992). Genres of organizational communication: A structurational approach to studying communication and media. *Academy of Management Review, 17,* 299–326.

Yerby, J. (1995). Family systems theory reconsidered: Integrating social construction theory and dialectical process. *Communication Theory, 5,* 339–365.

Zagacki, K. S., Edwards, R., & Honeycutt, J. M. (1992). The role of mental imagery and emotion in imagined interaction. *Communication Quarterly, 40,* 56–68.

Zhu, J. H. (1992). Issue competition and attention distraction: A zero-sum theory of agenda-setting. *Journalism Quarterly, 69,* 825–836.

Zhu, J. H., & Blood, D. (1997). Media agenda-setting theory: Telling the public what to think about. In D. P. Cushman & G. Kovacic (Ed.), *Emerging theories of human communication* (pp. 88–114). Albany: State University of New York Press.

Zhu, J. H., Watt, J. H., Snyder, L. B., Yan, J., & Jiang, Y. (1993). Public issue policy formation: Media agenda-setting and social interaction. *Journal of Communication, 43,* 8–29.

Zillmann, D. (1971). Excitation transfer in communication-mediated aggressive behavior. *Journal of Experimental Social Psychology, 7,* 419–434.

Zillmann, D. (1980). Anatomy of suspense. In P. H. Tannenbaum (Ed.), *The entertainment functions of television* (pp. 133–163). Hillsdale, NJ: Erlbaum.

Zillmann, D. (1983). Transfer of excitation in emotional behavior. In J. T. Cacioppo & R. E. Petty (Eds.), *Social psychophysiology: A sourcebook* (pp. 215–240). New York: Guilford.

Zillmann, D. (1991a). Television viewing and physiological arousal. In J. Bryant & D. Zillmann (Eds.), *Responding to the screen: Reception and reaction processes* (pp. 103–133). Hillsdale, NJ: Erlbaum.

Zillmann, D. (1991b). Empathy: Affect from bearing witness to the emotions of others. In J. Bryant & D. Zillmann (Eds.), *Responding to the screen: Reception and reaction processes* (pp. 135–167). Hillsdale, NJ: Erlbaum.

Zillmann, D. (1994). Mechanisms of emotional involvement with drama. *Poetics, 23,* 33–51.

Zillmann, D. (1996). The psychology of suspense in dramatic exposition. In P. Vorderer, H. J. Wulff, & M. Friedrichsen (Eds.), *Suspense: Conceptualizations, theoretical analyses, and empirical explorations* (pp. 199–231). Hillsdale, NJ: Erlbaum.

Zillmann, D., & Cantor, J. R. (1976). A disposition theory of humor and mirth. In A. J. Chapman & H. C. Foot (Ed.), *Humour and laughter: Theory, research, and applications* (pp. 93–115). London: Wiley.

Zillmann, D., Taylor, K., & Lewis, K. (1998). News as nonfiction theater: How dispositions toward the public cast of characters affect reactions. *Journal of Broadcasting & Electronic Media, 42,* 153–169.

Zillmann, D., & Weaver, J. B. (1996). Gender-socialization theory of reactions to horror. In J. B. Weaver and R. Tamborini (Eds.), *Horror films: Current research on audience preferences and reactions* (pp. 81–101). Mahwah, NJ: Erlbaum.

Zillmann, D., Weaver, J. B., Mundorf, N., & Aust, C. F. (1986). Effects of an opposite-gender companion's affect to horror on distress, delight, and attraction. *Journal of Personality and Social Psychology, 51,* 586–594.

Zucker, H. G. (1978). The variable nature of news media influence. In B. Ruben (Ed.), *Communication yearbook 2* (pp. 225–246). New Brunswick, NJ: Transaction Books.

Credits

Table 5.1 From G. Burrell and G. Morgan, *Sociological Paradigms and Organisation Analysis*, Heinemann, 1979, pp. 298-299. Reprinted by permission of Heinemann Educational Publishers. **Fig. 8.2** From R. E. Petty and J. T. Cacioppo, *Communication and Persuasion: Central and Peripheral Routes to Attitude Change*, Springer-Verlag, 1986, p. 4. Reprinted with permission from the publisher. **Table 9.1** From J. K. Burgoon, L. A. Stern, and L. Dillman, *Interpersonal Adaptation: Dyadic Interaction Patterns*, Cambridge University Press, 1995, p. 271. Reprinted with the permission of Cambridge University Press. **Fig. 9.2** From C. Gallois and H. Giles, "Accomodating Mutual Influence in Intergroup Encounters," in M. T. Palmer and G. A. Barnett, eds., *Progress in Communication Sciences*, volume 14, Ablex, 1998, pp. 135, 162. Reprinted with permission. **Fig. 11.1** From L. E. Rogers and R. V. Farace, "Analysis of Relational Communication in Dyads: New Measurement Procedures," *Human Communication Research*, volume 1, number 3, p. 232. Reprinted with permission from International Communication Association. **Fig. 14.1**

From M. L. DeFleur and S. Ball-Rokeach, *Theories of Mass Communication*, fifth edition, Longman, 1989, p. 196. Copyright © 1989 by Allyn & Bacon. Reprinted by permission. **Fig. 14.2** From D. Merskin, "Media Dependency Theory: Origins and Directions," in D. Demers and K. Viswanath, eds., *Mass Media, Social Control, and Social Change*, Iowa State University Press, 1999, pp. 77-98. Reprinted by permission of the publisher. **Fig. 15.1** From E. M. Rogers and J. W. Dearing, "Agenda-Setting Research: Where Has It Been, Where Is It Going?" in J. A. Anderson, ed., *Communication Yearbook 11*, Sage, 1988, pp. 555-594. Copyright © 1988 Sage Publications, Inc. Reprinted by permission of Sage Publications, Inc. **Table 16.1** From W. B. Gudykunst and S. Ting-Toomey, "Communication in Personal Relationships Across Cultures: An Introduction," in W. B. Gudykunst, S. Ting-Toomey, and T. Nishida, eds., *Communication in Personal Relationships Across Cultures*, Sage, 1996, pp. 3-16. Copyright © 1996 Sage Publications, Inc. Reprinted by permission of Sage Publications, Inc.

Index

Abrams, P., 90
abstraction, 20
accommodation, 141, 145–146
acting-together, 92
action
  as dramatic, 90–91
  felicity conditions criteria
    applied to speech, 134–135
  language as, 89–90
  as rhetorical, 91–92
  See also behavior
action assembly theory, 101–106,
  104*t*
activation processes, 104–105
actual behavior (A), 150
adaptive structuration theory,
  227–229*t*
Adorno, T. W., 63
affection-instrumentality dialectic,
  187
affective exchange stage, 154
agency, 202–203
agenda setting process, 258, 259*f*,
  260
agenda setting theory, 257–264
aggressive behavior, 251
Ajzen, I., 115, 116
Alcoholics Anonymous, 205
alienation, 61–62, 63
Allen, B., 291
Altman, I., 154, 155, 157, 158, 161
ambiguity, 128
ambivalence, 128
American Revolution (German
  press coverage), 264
analogic communication syntax,
  177–178
analogic messages, 10–11
Andersen, P., 10, 11
Anderson, J. A., 15
Annenberg School, 269

anomalies, 44
antithesis, 183
Apel, K.-O., 48
appropriateness meta-goal, 107
appropriation moves (adaptive
  structuration theory),
  227–229*t*
Arbib, M. A., 77
Ardener, Edwin, 291
Ardener, Shirley, 291
Aristotle, 2, 61
arousal, 147–148, 251
arousal management goals, 107
Asch, Solomon, 265
Ashby, Ross, 175
assembly processes, 104–105
assimilation, 117
attribution theory, 81–83
attuning, 141
Aust, C., 254
Austin, J. L., 133, 134
autonomy face, 287
Auwal, M. A., 214
axiology
  critical theory, 67–69
  interpretive theory, 53
  overview of, 27–29
  post-positivism, 36–37
axioms
  of particularity, 278
  Pragmatics, 177–178
  uncertainty reduction theory,
    164, 165*t*, 166
Ayer, A., 33

Babrow, A. S., 125, 126, 127, 128
Bakhtin, M., 183–185
Bales, R. F., 218, 230, 232
Ball-Rokeach, S., 236, 237, 246,
  247, 248, 249, 250, 255
Bandura, A., 239, 240, 241

Banks, S. P., 202, 203, 204
Baranowski, T., 240
Barker, J. R., 210, 211, 212, 213
Bateson, G., 174, 175, 176, 178,
  179
Bavelas, J. B., 10, 177, 179–180,
  181
Baxter, L. A., 183, 184, 185, 186,
  187, 188, 189, 192
Beach, W., 10
Beavin, J. H., 9
behavior
  attributional judgments on
    interpersonal, 82*t*–83
  excitation transfer theory on,
    251–252
  intentionality of, 9–10
  internal and external attribution
    for, 81–82
  meta-goals regulation of, 107
  operant conditioning and, 239
  Palo Alto system view of,
    175–182
  self-efficacy and, 241, 268
  social cognitive theory on,
    239–242
  subjective norms and, 115–116
  symptomatic vs. analogic, 10–11
  theory of planned, 116*f*
  See also action
behavioral complexity, 99
behavioral intention, 115
Bem, D. J., 115
Beninger, J. R., 15
Benjamin, W., 63
Berger, C. R., 44, 106, 108, 110,
  163, 164, 166, 167, 168, 169,
  170, 171, 172
Berger's theory of planning,
  108–109
Berkowitz, L., 241

Berlo, D., 5
Bernstein, B., 69, 98, 279, 280
"be spontaneous" paradox, 140
Between People (Miller & Steinberg), 160
Billingsley, J. M., 223
Black, A., 180
black box of mental system, 103
Blalock, H., 164
Blood, D., 261
Blumer, H., 50
Blumler, J. G., 242, 243
Bochner, A. P., 161, 179, 182
bona fide group perspective, 233–234
Book of Laughter and Forgetting, The (Kundera), 130
booster messages, 125
Bormann, E., 230, 231, 232
Boster, F. B., 95, 96
boundaries, 38
boundary conditions, 220–221t
Bowers, J., 287
Braithwaite, C. A., 190, 284
Bregman, D., 258
British cultural studies tradition, 70
Broetzmann, S., 78
Brown, B. B., 154
Brown, J. R., 242
Brown, P., 100, 287
Brummett, B., 89
Bullis, C., 214, 232
bureaucratic control, 210–211
Burgoon, J. K., 6, 147, 148, 149
Burgoon, M., 123
Burke, K., 88–90, 91, 92, 212
Burleson, B. R., 97, 98, 99
Burrell, G., 24, 47, 61
Burrell, N. A., 291
Bush, G. W., 263
Buzzanell, P. M., 291
Byrne, D., 143

Cacioppo, J., 118, 121
Calabrese, R., 163, 164, 165, 170, 172
Cantor, J., 253
Caplan, S. E., 97, 99
Carbaugh, D., 278, 284
Carey, J. W., 70

Carnap, R., 33
Cartesian dualism, 47
catharsis function, 80
central route to persuasion, 118
Centre for Contemporary Cultural Studies (University of Birmingham), 70
certainty-uncertainty dialectic, 186–187
Chaiken, S., 121, 122
Chang, C., 81
change
    first-order vs. second-order, 179
    reframing and, 179
Cheney, G., 48, 205, 210, 212
Chicago school, 50, 53
Chinese culture, 286–287
Chovil, N., 180
Cissna, K. N., 182, 190, 191
classical positivism, 33
Clevenger, T., 10
climate concept, 204
Clinton, B., 3
CMM hierarchy of meaning, 138–139f
CMM. *See* coordinated management of meaning theory (CMM)
co-cultural communication, 292–294, 295t
co-cultural groups theories, 289–294t
coding interaction sequences, 180
cognitive complexity, 97
cognitive dissonance theory, 114–115
cognitive-informational tradition, 226
cognitive miser metaphor, 77
cognitive rules model of goals, 107
Cohen, B., 21–22, 258
Cole, T., 96
collectivistic culture, 286
Collin, F., 55
Collins, B., 217
Columbine High School shooting (1999), 262–263
combination appropriation, 228, 229t

communication
    classic models on persuasive, 114–117
    co-cultural, 292–294, 295t
    considering perspectives of, 1
    convergent conceptualizing of, 5–8
    defining, 3–5t, 4t
    dialectical tensions in, 162
    divergent conceptualizing of, 8–11
    dysfunctional, 178–179
    failure of, 2
    identification and, 92
    problematic integration implications for, 128–130
    structuration theory in organizational, 204–205
    theory in the discipline of, 29–31
    See also conversation; group communication
communication accommodation theory, 141–146, 144f
Communication, Action and Meaning: (Cronen & Pearce), 136
communication competence, 24
Communication and the Evolution of Society (Habermas), 64
communication interaction
    CMM coordination of, 140
    CMM on rules in, 137–138
    coding sequences of, 180
    communication accommodation theory on, 141–146
    formative research in group, 216–218
    functions of imagined, 80
    goals of, 107
    laws of, 38
    parasocial, 245
    plans for, 108
    predictive and explanatory components of, 163–164
    Rogers-Farace coding scheme for, 180, 182f
    schemas on mass, 80–81
    self-disclosure and reciprocity in, 156
    text and conversation and, 207–210
communication process
    agenda setting, 258–260f

defining, 5–6
study of, 2
communication research
   Burkean analysis in, 92
   concertive control theory
      application to, 213–214
   narrative theory in, 87–88
   post-positivism in, 44–45
   speech codes tradition used in,
      284
communication studies
   attribution theory in, 83
   conceptual domains of, 11–12
   critical approaches in, 69–72
   developments of Palo Alto
      Group, 179–182
   disciplinary domains of, 12–15
   emic and etic approaches to
      culture and, 277t–278
   interpretive theory used in,
      51–53
   organizational, 196–197
   schema theory in, 79–81
   social penetration theory used
      in, 158–160
   subdisciplinary domains in, 14t
communication theory
   conceptual domains of, 13t
   on culture and communication,
      278–296
   in developing relationships,
      163–172
   of discourse and interaction,
      132–152
   diverse roots of, 2
   in ongoing relationships,
      174–193
   organizational, 197–215
   as pluralistic enterprise, 29–31
   relationship development and,
      153–172
   on small group communication,
      216–234
communicative competence, 68
communicator reward valence, 149
comparison level (CL), 157–158
comparison level of alternatives
   (CL$_{alt}$), 157–158
competence face, 287
complementary interaction, 178
complex cyclic path, 217

compliance gaining research,
   95–96
Comte, A., 33
conceptualizing communication
   intention and, 9–11
   as process, 5–6
   as social activity, 8–9
   as symbolic, 7–8
   as transactional, 6–7
conceptual problem, 22
concertive control theory,
   210–214
conjecture and refutation
   procedure, 43
Conklin, E. J., 77
connection-autonomy dialectic,
   186
Conrad, C., 90
consciousness, 63
consistency seeker metaphor, 77
Constitution of Society, The
   (Giddens), 64, 204
constitutive meaning, 282
constitutive model of
   communication, 11
constitutive rules, 137
construct differentiation, 97
constructivist theory
   linking constructs/
      communication, 98–99
   message design logics of,
      99–101, 100t
   message production construct
      system, 97
   metatheoretical foundations of,
      96–97
   on person-centered
      communication, 97–98
   protective belt of, 111
construct systems
   linking person-centered
      communication and, 98–99
   of message production, 97
consubstantial, 92
consubstantiation, 92
container metaphor, 205
content function, 177
context of discovery, 28
context of justification, 28
Contexts of Accommodation: (Giles,
   Coupland, & Coupland), 146

context theories, 57
contradictions
   defining dialectics, 185
   major relational, 186–187
   praxis patterns and, 188–189t
contrast process, 117
control
   post-positivism, 40
   theory of concertive, 210–214
   unobtrusive, 212–213
conventional design logic, 101
convergence process, 141–142,
   143–145
conversation
   Nacirema, 280–281, 284
   Teamsterville study on,
      280–281, 283, 284
   text and, 207–210
   See also utterances
conversational MOPs, 80
Cool Hand Luke (film), 2
coordinated management of
   meaning theory (CMM)
   central concepts of, 137–140
   described, 136
   evidence for and critiques of,
      140–141
   metatheoretical foundations of,
      136–137
coordination of interaction
   processes, 140
Cooren, F., 205
Corcoran, F., 70
Corman, S. R., 205
Coupland, N., 141
Cox, D. E., 182
Craig, R., 11, 12, 13
critical-emancipatory cognitive
   interest, 67
critical perspectives on theory
   development
   compared to interpretivists/
      post-positivists, 60–61
   overview of, 61–69
Critical Problems in Social Theory
   (Giddens), 64
critical theory
   communication studies using,
      69–72
   contemporary, 64–69
   Frankfurt School, 63–64t

critical theory *(continued)*
 historical roots of, 61–64
 Marxism, 61–63
 perspective of, 60–61
critiques
 agenda setting theory, 263–264
 CMM, 140–141
 communication accommodation
  theory, 146
 critical theory, 62, 69
 elaboration likelihood model,
  119–122
 social penetration theory,
  161–162
 speech act theory, 135–136
 spiral of silence theory, 268–269
 uncertainty reduction theory,
  168–170, 171–172
Cronen, V., 136
Cruz, M. G., 83
Cuban missile crisis, 218
cultivation effect, 271, 273–274
cultivation theory, 269–274
cultural indicators, 271–272
cultural information, 160
cultural metaphor, 197
cultural patterns, 139
culture
 as code/community, 276
 conceptualizing notion of,
  276–277
 critical approach to study of,
  69–71
 dimensions of variability in,
  285–286
 emic and etic approaches to,
  277t–278
 facework and, 288–289
 individualistic vs. collectivistic,
  285–286
 juxtaposition of Teamsterville
  and Nacirema, 284
 low-context vs. high-context, 286
 speech codes in Teamsterville,
  280–281, 283, 284
 speech codes theory on,
  278–284
 theories of face and, 284–289
Cupach, W., 288

Dance, F. E. X., 3

Dearing, J. W., 257, 258
decision making
 group communication and
  effective, 221–222
 group decision support system
  (GDSS) and, 227
 groupthink and, 219–220
deductive approach, 21
Deetz, S. A., 49, 62
"definition of man" (Burke), 89
DeFleur, M. L., 236, 237, 246, 247,
  249
degrees of separation, 208–209t
Delia, J., 96, 99
dependency relationships, 247
Derlega, V. J., 156, 158
Dervin, B., 23
DeSanctis, G., 227
Descartes, R., 46
desired (D) factors, 150
Dewey, J., 70
dialectic of control, 203
dialectics
 central concepts in, 185–186
 contradictions in relational,
  186–188
 described, 182–183
 philosophical roots of, 183–185
 praxis of relational, 188–189t
 research on, 189–191
 social penetration theory on
  tensions of, 162
Diesing, P., 34, 48
digital communication syntax,
  177–178
Dillard, J. P., 38, 107
Dilthey, W., 47–48, 61
direct appropriation, 227, 229t
discipline, 212–213
disinhibitory effect, 240
distanciation, 208
divergence
 communication accommodation
  theory on, 142–143, 145
 as problematic integration,
  127–128
Dollard, J., 239
Donahue talk show (TV), 284
double binds, 178–179
double hermeneutic of social life, 65
double interacts, 181

dramatic action, 90–91
dramatism theory, 88–92
dramatistic pentad, 91
"dramatizes" group function, 230
dualism
 Cartesian, 47
 dialectical concept vs., 185
 of structure, 65, 202, 224
Dubin, R., 37, 38
dysfunctional communication,
  178–179

Edelstein, A. S., 263
Edwards, R., 210, 212
efficiency meta-goal, 107
Einsiedel, F., 263
Eisenberg, E. M., 179, 180
Ekman, P., 8
elaborated coding principles, 279
elaboration likelihood model,
  118–122, 120f
Ellis, D. G., 38
emic approach, 277t–278
empathic communication "mini-
  theory," 38, 39t
empathy, 252–253
empirical-analytical cognitive
  interest, 66
empirical indicators, 38
empirical problem, 22
empirical support
 of social penetration theory,
  160–161
 of uncertainty reduction theory,
  167–169
empirical validity criticism, 135
enactment event, 198
enhance understanding function,
  80
Enlightenment theory
  development, 46–47
epistemology
 critical theory, 66–67
 interpretive theory, 52–53
 overview of, 25–27t
 post-positivism, 36–37
Époche method, 49–50
equifinality, 175–176
equivocality concept, 199
etic approach, 277t–278
evaluative judgments, 126

evolutionary growth of theory, 43–44
excitation transfer theory, 251–252
expectancies
  described, 147
  impact of violation of, 148–149
  violations of, 147–148
expectancy violation theory, 146–150
expected (E) factors, 150
exploratory affective exchange stage, 154
expressive design logic, 101
external attribution for behavior, 81–82
external dialectics, 187–188
Exxon Valdez oil spill, 91

face and culture theories, 284–289
face metaphor, 286–287
face threats, 288
facework, 288–289
faithful appropriation, 228, 229t
falsification goal of science, 34
family systems
  dialectics in, 190–191
  double binds impact on, 179
  Palo Alto applications to, 180–181
fantasy chain, 231
fantasy theme, 231, 232–233
fantasy type, 231
Farace, V., 180
Fay, B., 30
Fayol, H., 196
fear of isolation, 264–265
feasibility criticism, 135
feedback
  Palo Alto group on, 175–176
  Pragmatics axiom on, 178
Feigl, H., 33
felicity conditions criteria, 134–135
fellowship face, 287
feminist standpoint, 290
feminist studies
  critical approach to, 71–72
  major approaches to, 72–73t
  Marxist theory used in, 289–290
"Ferment in the Field" issue (*Journal of Communication*), 69

Festinger, L., 114
Feyeraband, P., 30
Fincham, F. D., 81
first-level agenda setting, 262
first-order change, 179
first-order cultivation effects, 273–274
Fishbein, M., 115
Fisher, B. A., 217
Fisher, W., 84, 86, 87, 88
Fiske, S., 78
Flowerdew, J., 135
Ford, L. A., 129
Foss, K. A., 2
Foucault, M., 212
framing, 262–263
Frankfurt School, 61, 63–64t
Freud, S., 68
friendship
  dialectics in, 190
  ideal-real dialectic of, 188
  See also relationships
Friendship Matters (Rawlins), 190
Fromm, E., 63
Frost, R., 32, 119
functional theory, 218–224, 222t
fundamental attribution error, 82
"Future of the Field" issue (*Journal of Communication*), 15

Gadamer, H., 49
Gastil, J., 111
Geertz, C., 278
Geis, M. L., 135, 136
Geist, P., 205
gender differences
  media effects and, 254
  muted group theory on, 291–292
  television content patterns and, 271
general interpretive theories, 54–56
generalized other, 51
Generative realism school, 103
genre concept, 204
"genuine-because" motives, 55
Gerbner, G., 269, 270, 271, 272
German idealism, 47, 49
Ghanem, S., 262
Giddens, A., 61, 64, 65, 66, 68, 69, 70, 201, 202, 203, 205, 224, 229

Giles, H., 141, 142, 143, 144, 146
Glaser, B., 56, 57
Glynn, C. J., 267
goal construct, 107
Godel, K., 33
Goffman, E., 286, 287
Gore, A., 263
Gould, S. J., 28
Gouran, D., 216, 218, 219, 220, 221, 223
Graham, E. E., 223
Grameen Bank Cooperation, 214
Grant, S. I., 250
gratification sought/obtained, 244t
Greene, J., 101, 102, 103, 105, 106, 110
Griffin, E., 164, 265
Gronbeck, B., 88
Gross, L., 269
Grossberg, L., 23, 71, 96
grounded theory, 56–58t
Grounded Theory in Practice (Strauss & Corbin), 58
group communication
  formative research on, 216–218
  functional theory on, 218–224
  speech codes theory on, 278–284
  structuration of arguments and, 226–227
  symbolic convergence theory on, 229–233
  theories of co-cultural, 289–294t
  See also communication
group decision support system (GDSS), 227, 228
group development model, 217
group fantasy, 231
groupthink, 219–220
Guba, E. G., 28–29, 37
Gubrium, J. F., 51
Gudykunst, W., 168, 170–171
Guetzkow, H., 217
guilt process, 90–91
Gunter, G., 241

Habermas, J., 61, 64, 66, 67, 68, 69
Hale, J. L., 147
Hall, E., 286
Hall, S., 70
Hanson, N. R., 28

Harding, S., 28
Hardt, H., 70
Harris, L. M., 190
Harrison, T. M., 203
Hartsock, N., 290
health communication, 241–242
Health Security Act (1993), 264
Heath, R. L., 92
Hebb, D. O., 251
Hegel, G. W. F., 61, 66, 183, 289
hegemony concept, 67
Heidegger, M., 49
Heider, F., 81
Hempel, C., 33
hermeneutic-historical cognitive
    interest, 66–67
hermeneutic school, 47–49
Herzog, H., 242
Hester, J. B., 251
Heuristic Model of Persuasion, 121
heuristic processing, 121–122
Hewstone, M., 81
hierarchical notion, 25
hierarchy of meaning (CMM),
    138–139f
hierarchy principle, 108
high-context culture, 286
Hill, J., 77
Hindeman, E. B., 83
Hirokawa, R. Y., 218, 219, 222,
    223
Hirsch, P. M., 272
Hirschmann, N. J., 290
Hitchon, J. C., 81
Ho, D., 286, 287
Hofstede, G., 285
Hoggart, R., 70
Holl, M., 190
Holstein, J. A., 51
Honeycutt, J., 80
Hopper, R., 136
Horkheimer, M., 63
Hovland, C. J., 3, 5
Howard, G. S., 27–28
Howard, L. A., 205
How to Do Things with Words
    (Austin), 133
Hu, H. C., 286
Huberlie, M., 250
human-as-scientist view, 81
Huspek, M., 68–69

Husserl, E., 49, 61
Hymes, D., 279–280, 282
hypercorrection, 146
hypodermic needle effect, 237
hypotheses
    muted group theory, 294t
    post-positivism on, 38
    See also theories

ideal-real dialectic, 188
ideal speech situation, 68
ideational representation, 104
identification
    communication and, 92
    concertive control and, 212
    rhetoric as creating, 91–92
identity goals, 107
ideology
    American life, 71
    described, 67
    dominant behaviors and
        organization, 197
illocutionary act, 134
Images of Organization (Morgan),
    196
imagined communication
    interactions, 80
impossibility, 128
individualistic culture, 285–286
individual model metaphor, 77
inductive approach, 21
information
    cultural/psychological/
        sociological, 160
    organizational socialization and
        seeking, 171
    uncertainty reduction theory on
        seeking, 167–168
information-seeking strategies,
    166–167
inhibitory effect, 240
inoculation theory, 122–125
"in-order-to" motives, 55
"inquiry from the inside," 53
institutionalization process,
    203–204
institutional structure, 203–204
intentionality of communication,
    9–11
interaction. *See* communication
    interaction

interaction adaptation theory,
    149–150, 151t
interactional representation, 104
interaction position (IP), 150
Interaction Process Analysis (Bales),
    218
interacts, 181
internal attribution for behavior,
    81–82
internal dialectics, 187–188
Internet, 243–244
interpersonal communication,
    95–96
interpersonal construct system, 97
interpersonal relationship, 160
interpretive perspective on theory
    development
    communication study and,
        51–53
    general, 54–56
    grounded, 56–58t
    hermeneutics position of, 47–49
    historical background of, 46–47
    phenomenology position of,
        49–50
    structure/function of, 53–54
    symbolic interactionism position
        of, 50–51
intrapersonal communication, 8–9
Iowa school, 50
ironic appropriation, 228, 229t
issue obtrusiveness, 262
Iyengar, S., 263

Jablin, F. M., 171
Jackson, S., 133, 135, 136, 226
Jacobs, S., 133, 135, 136, 226
Jacobson, T. L., 30
James, W., 70
Janis, I. L., 3
Jaspars, J., 81
Jenzowsky, S. A., 251
Jones, E. E., 81, 82, 147
Journal of Communication, 15, 69

Kant, I., 47, 61
Katriel, T., 280
Katz, E., 238, 243
Kellermann, K., 11, 78, 79, 80, 96,
    107, 169
Kelley, H. H., 3, 81, 157

Kellner, D., 13
Kellow, C. L., 249
Kelly, G. A., 97
Kennedy, Bobby, 269
"kernel climates," 204
Kielwasser, A. P., 275
Kim, J., 38, 244
Kinder, D. R., 263
King, C. M., 251
King, M. L., Jr., 269
Kitao, K., 78
Klumpp, J. F., 92
Knapp, M., 158–160, 162
Knowledge and Human Interests
    (Habermas), 64
Kraft, V., 33
Kramarae, C., 292, 294
Krammer, M., 171
Krassa, M. A., 267
Kreps, G., 201
Kuhn, T. S., 23, 40, 41, 44, 85, 110
Kundera, M., 130

Lakatos, I., 43, 111
Lambert, B. L., 101
Langer, E. J., 7
language
    felicity conditions criteria
        applied to, 134–135
    as form of action, 89–90
    speech codes theory on,
        278–284
Larson, C. E., 3
Lasswell, H., 6, 237
latitude of acceptance, 117
latitude of noncommitment, 117
latitude of rejection, 117
Laudan, L., 21–22
laws of interaction, 38
Layder, D., 202, 203
learning
    observational, 239–240
    reinforcement, 240–241
    social cognitive theory on,
        239–242
    social learning theory on, 240
Lebenswelt, 50
Leeds-Hurwitz, W., 24
LePoire, B. A., 149, 150
Levinson, S., 100, 135, 287
Lewin, K., 22

liberal feminist approach, 72
lien, 286
life script level, 138–139
Lim, T.-S., 78, 287
limited effects model, 238
Lippmann, W., 274, 275
Loges, W. E., 247, 255
logical positivism, 33–34
low-context culture, 296
Lyne, J. R., 136

machine metaphor, 196
Macom, E. A., 90
Macy Foundation cybernetics
    conference (1942), 175
magic bullet effect, 237
mainstreaming, 273
maintenance (communication), 142
Manusov, V., 81, 83
Marcuse, H., 63
Margulis, S. T., 156
Marshall, L. J., 83
Martin, J. N., 293–294
Marx, Karl, 60–62, 65, 66, 67, 183,
    289
Marxism, 61–63, 289–291
Masheter, C., 190
mass media communication
    agenda setting theory on,
        257–264
    cultivation theory on, 269–274
    media and emotion theories on,
        250–254
    media systems dependency
        theory on, 246–250
    O. J. Simpson case covered by,
        83, 253
    research and schemas on, 80–81
    school violence issue and,
        262–263
    social cognitive theory and,
        241–242
    spiral of silence theory on,
        264–269, 265t, 270t
    uses and gratifications theory on,
        242–246
    See also media effects
material dialectics, 183
material life, 290–291
McCombs, M. E., 258, 259, 260,
    261, 262, 263, 264

McCulloch, W., 175
McGee, M., 88
McGuire, W., 122, 123, 130
McPhee, R. D., 204
McPherson, M. P., 223
McQuail, D., 242
Mead, G. H., 50, 89
meaning
    CMM hierarchy of, 138–139f
    distanciation from, 208
    intentionality of, 9
    phenomenology on, 49
    of science vs. metaphysical
        statements, 33–34
    speech code constitutive,
        282
    symbolic interactionism on,
        51
    symbols and shared, 7–8
means of production, 62
media agenda, 258, 260–261
media effects
    alternatives to strong, 238–239
    early research on, 236–237
    gender differences in, 254
    magic bullet and hypodermic
        needle, 237
    selective influence theories on,
        238f
    theories on emotion and,
        250–254
    See also mass media
        communication
media information dependence
    theory, 250
media systems dependency theory
    (MSD), 246–250
Megill, A., 88
memory organization packets
    (MOPs), 78, 79, 80
mental illness, 175–176
Merleau-Ponty, M., 49
Merskin, D. L., 247, 250
message design logics model,
    99–101, 100t
message processing
    classic models of persuasion on,
        114–117
    elaboration likelihood model,
        118–122
    inoculation theory on, 122–125

message production
action assembly theory on, 101–106
comparison of theories on, 109–111
constructivism on, 97
planning/goals considerations in, 106–109
scholarship on, 95–96
messages
as central to relationships, 158–160
content and relational functions of, 177
inoculation booster, 125
verbal vs. analogic, 10–11
metacommunication, 282, 284
meta-goals, 107
metaphors
container, 205
cultural, 197
losing face, 286–287
meteorological, 204
organizational machine, 196
organization as instruments of domination, 197
social life, 76–77
metaphysical statements, 33–34
metatheory, 23–24
meteorological metaphor, 204
Metts, S., 156, 288
Meyers, R., 226
Michigan State critics, 121
mien-tzu, 286
Milgram, S., 265
Millar, F., 180
Miller, G. R., 10, 22, 96, 114, 160
Miller, K. I., 38
Miller, N. E., 239
Miller, R., 21
Miller, V. D., 171
Mind, Self, and Society (Mead), 50
modalities (structuration theory), 225t
models of persuasion
cognitive dissonance theory, 114–115
social judgment theory, 116–117
theory of reasoned action, 115–116
modes of production, 62

Moh, C. Y., 268
Montgomery, B. M., 183, 185, 188, 189, 192
Moon, J. D., 30
Morgan, G., 24, 47, 61, 196
Morgan, M., 269, 272
Morris, C., 133
Morrow, R. A., 61, 63, 67
mortification, 90
mother/motherhood meaning, 51
motivations reducing uncertainty, 168
Motoley, M., 9, 10
Mullett, J., 180
multiple sequence model, 217
Mumby, D. K., 62, 67
Mundorf, N., 254
muted group theory, 291–292, 293t

Nacirema talk, 280–281, 284
Nakayama, G., 293
narrative coherence, 87
narrative fidelity, 87
narrative paradigm
comparing rational world and, 86t–87
overview of, 84–87
narrative theory
analysis of narrative rationality using, 87
in communication research, 87–88
world view of, 84–87
National Commission on the Causes and Prevention of Violence (1967–1968), 269
National Enquirer, The, 80
need for orientation, 261
negative esteem compliance strategies, 95
negative face, 287
Neurath, O., 33
Newman, P., 2
New Rules of Sociological Method (Giddens), 64
newspaper readership, 249–250
Nichols, M. H., 89
Nisbett, R. E., 82
Nixon, R., 218
Noelle-Neumann, E., 264, 265, 266, 267, 268, 269

nominalist ontology, 24, 52
norms (subjective), 115–116

objectivist epistemology, 26, 27t
objectivist ontology, 24
observational learning, 239–240
Ogden, C. K., 7
O. J. Simpson case, 83
O'Keefe, B. J., 15, 23, 96, 99, 100, 101
O'Keefe, D. J., 96, 113
"On Defining Communication: Still Another View" (Gerbner), 3
"On Defining Communicaton: Another Stab" (Miller), 3
one-across utterances, 180
one-down utterances, 180
one-up utterances, 180
onion model of communication, 155f
ontology
critical theory, 65–66
described, 24–25
interpretive theory, 52
post-positivism, 35–36
openness-closedness dialectic, 1887
operant conditioning processes, 239
oppressed groups, 291
Orbe, M., 289, 292, 293, 294
organizational communication, 13
defining, 205
overview of, 196–197
structuration theory in, 204–205
text and conversation of, 205–210
unobstrusive and concertive control theory of, 210–214
organization as instruments of domination metaphor, 197
orientation stage, 154
Orona, C. J., 57
Oshagan, H., 267
outcome expectancies, 240–241
outcome expectations, 240
outcomes of relationship, 157
output representations, 104t

Palmgreen, P., 243
Palo Alto Group
communication developments from, 179–182

described, 174–175
from individual to system focus
of, 175–179
influence of *Pragmatics* on,
176–179
Papa, M. J., 214, 223
paradigm
comparing rational
world/narrative, 86t–87
defining, 44
narrative, 84–87
parasocial interaction, 245
parent/child communication
process of, 6–7
transactional nature of, 6–7
Park, E., 267
Parks, M. R., 161
Patterns of Discovery (Hanson), 28
Pearce, B., 2, 136, 137
Peirce, C., 70
pentadic ratio, 91
performative verbs concept, 134
peripheral route to persuasion, 118
perlocutionary acts, 134
Perry, C. L., 240, 251
Persian Gulf War, 267
personal resource goals, 107
person-centered communication,
97–98
perspectives
bona fide group, 233–234
defining, 1
post-positivist, 32–45
theory development using
interpretive, 46–58t
persuasive communication
central and peripheral routes to,
118–119
classic models of, 114–117
described, 114
Petronio, S., 156
Petty, R. E., 118, 121
Pfau, M., 123, 124, 125
phase models, 217
phenomenology, 49–50
Philbin, R., 249
Philipsen, G., 278, 279, 280, 281, 283
Phillips, D. C., 19, 27, 32, 33, 35,
36, 37
Phillipsen, G., 137, 140
philosophy of anthropology, 96

Philosophy in a New Key (Langer), 7
philosophy of science, 96
Piaget, J., 98
Planning Social Interaction (Berger),
108
planning theory, 108–109
Plato, 2, 48
policy agenda, 258
politeness theory, message design
logics of, 100
Poole, S. M., 30, 140, 204, 221,
227, 228, 232
Popper, Sir K., 18, 28, 43, 172
positive altercasting compliance
strategies, 95
positive face, 287
positivism
classical, 33
demise of, 34–35
logical, 33–34
usage of, 33
postmodern feminists, 72
post-positivism perspective
in communication research,
44–45
epistemology and axiology,
36–37
on evaluating/comparing
theories, 40–41
on function of theory, 38–40
implications of, 32–33
ontology, 35–36
philosophical roots of, 33–35
in social research, 35–44
structure of theory, 37–38
theoretical development, 41–44
Potter, W. J., 271, 273, 274
power
Marxist theory on, 289–291
muted group theory on,
291–292
tripartite media dependency
relationship and, 247f–249
Weber on bureaucratic, 211
power distance, 285
Powesland, P. F., 143
practical problems, 22–23
*Practical Wisdom Reconfigured: The
Other Side of the Narrative
Paradigm* (Fisher), 85
pragmatic master analogue, 231

pragmatics, 133
*Pragmatics of Human
Communication, The*
(Watzlawick, Beavin, &
Jackson), 9, 176–179
praxis
defining, 186
relational dialectics and patterns
of, 188-189t
predictability-novelty dialectic,
186–187
predicted outcome value theory,
169–170
*Presentation of Self in Everyday Life,
The* (Goffman), 286
primary goals, 107
priming, 263
Principles of Philosophy (Descartes),
46
probabilistic judgments, 126
problematic integration theory,
125–130, 129t
problem of induction, 43
problem solving, 22–23
procedural record, 103–104
processes
agenda setting, 258–260f
communication, 2, 5–6
dialectical contradictions as part
of, 186
institutionalization, 203–204
operant conditioning, 239
of organizing, 198–201
retention, 200–201
selection, 198–200
process theories, 57
promising compliance strategies, 95
*Propaganda Techniques in the World
War* (Lasswell), 237
proposition 6 (Berger's planning
theory), 108, 109t
propositional act, 134
propositions of Berger's planning
theory, 109t
psychological information, 160
public agenda, 258, 260–261
public opinion
assessing, 265
during Persian Gulf War, 267
spiral of silence theory on,
264–269

Public Opinion (Lippmann), 257
Putnam, L. L., 52, 201, 232, 233

Quarterly Journal of Speech, 92

radical feminist approach, 72
Rao, N., 83
rational world paradigm, 86t–87
Rawlins, W. K., 187, 188, 191
realism/realists, 24, 35–36
realist ontology, 24
Real, M., 69
reasoned action theory, 115–116
recipes of organizing process, 199
reciprocity, 156
redemption process, 90–91
RED factors, 150
reference, 7
referents, 7, 8, 133
reflexive agents, 225
reflexivity, 202–203
refutational preemption, 123–125
regulative rules, 137–138
rehearsal function, 80
Reichenbach, H., 33
reinforcement, 240–241
relational dialectics, 188–189
relational function, 177
relational resource goals, 107
relationship development
  social penetration theory on,
    153–163
  uncertainty reduction theory on,
    163–172
relationships
  dialectics of, 182–191
  dialectics in romantic, 190
  double binds impact on,
    178–179
  messages as central to, 158–160
  social penetration theory on,
    154–160
  tripartite media dependency,
    247f–249
  trust and interpersonal, 160
  uncertainty in continuing,
    170–171
required (R) factors, 150
resonance, 273
resources, 203
retention processes, 200–201

revelation-concealment dialectic,
  187–188
revolutionary growth of theory, 44
Reynolds, R., 169
rhetorical action, 91–92
rhetorical design logic, 101
rhetorical vision, 231
Richards, I. A., 7
Ricoeur, P., 48
righteous master analogue, 231
right Hegelians, 61
Riley, P., 88, 202, 203, 204
Robert's Rules of Order, 203
Rogers, E. M., 180, 257, 258
Rogers-Farace coding scheme,
  180f, 181
Rogers, L. E., 180
role category question (RCQ), 97,
  98, 111
role taking, 51
Roloff, M. E., 95
romantic relationship dialectics,
  190
Rosenberg, A., 30
Rosenthal, R., 149
Rowland, R. C., 88
Rubin, A. M., 244
Ruffner, M., 6
rules
  CMM on interaction, 137–138
  cognitive rules model of goals,
    107
  constitutive, 137
  functions of, 203
  Palo Alto orientation on,
    176
  regulative, 137–138
ruling groups, 291

Salazar, A. J., 222, 223
Salmon, C. T., 268
scapegoats, 90–91
Schank, R. C., 79
Schegloff, E. A., 135
schemas
  communication research using,
    79–81
  typology of, 77–78t
schema theory
  in communication discipline,
    79–81

overview of, 77
what and how of, 77–79
Schlick, M., 33
school violence issues, 262–263
Schumann, D., 118
Schutz, A., 49, 50, 89, 199
science
  falsification vs. verification goal
    of, 34
  metaphysics vs., 33–34
  positivism philosophy of,
    33–35
scientific method
  compared to naive observation,
    42t
  described, 32
  post-positivist, 41–43
scientific statements, 33
Scott, C. R., 205
Searle, J., 133, 134
secondary goals, 107
second-level agenda setting, 262
second-order change, 179
second-order cultivation effects,
  274
Seibold, D. R., 95, 226
selection processes, 198–200
self-disclosure, 156
self-efficacy, 241, 268
semantics, 133
semiotics, 7
Sensemaking in Organizations
  (Weick), 197
sensemaking properties, 199t,
  199–200
sensorimotor representation, 104
Shanahan, J., 272
Shaw, D., 258, 259, 260, 261, 262,
  264
Sherif, C., 116
Sherif, M., 116
Shields, S., 28
"shows tension release" group
  function, 230
significant others, 51
significant symbols, 51
signified, 7
signifier, 7
Signorielli, N., 269, 272
signs, 7, 8, 133
Simon, E. P., 187

Simons, H., 92
simple control, 210
Simpson, C., 268
Simpson, O. J., 83, 253
Singhal, A., 214
Smith, J. D., 35
Smith, L. D., 88
Smith, R. C., 205
social activity
    communication as, 8–9
    theory as abstraction of, 20
social classes, 67
social cognitive theory, 239–242
social constructionist ontology,
    35–36, 52
social constructionist position,
    24–25
social dramas, 282
social exchange
    four situations of, 157f
    social penetration theory on,
        156–157
social exchange theory, 157
Social Intercourse (Knapp), 158
social-international tradition, 226
social judgment theory, 116–117
social learning theory, 240
social life
    double hermeneutic of, 65
    dramatistic pentad of, 91
    metaphors of, 76–77
social master analogue, 231
Social Penetration (Altman &
    Taylor), 154
social penetration theory
    communication application of,
        158–162
    described, 153–154
    developments/critiques of,
        160–162
    onion model of, 155f
    original statements of,
        154–158
    summary/evaluation of,
        162–163
social phenomenology, 49
*Social Psychology of Organizations,
    The* (Katz & Kahn), 198
Social Psychology of Organizing, The
    (Weick), 197
social realists, 24

social schemata typology, 78t
social scientific approaches
    attribution theory used in,
        81–83
    schema theory used in, 77–81
social systems, 203
social world
    Cartesian dualism of, 47
    epistemological considerations
        of, 25–27
    identification with others in, 92
    metatheoretical considerations
        of, 23–24
    ontological considerations of,
        24–25
    television cultivation effect on,
        271–272
    transcendental phenomenology
        on, 49–50
    verstehen understanding of, 47,
        49
society
    manufactured consent of power
        structure in, 67
    substructure and superstructure
        of, 62
sociological information, 160
solution-oriented path, 217
S-O-R models, 238, 239
SPEAKING mnemonic, 282,
    283t
speech act theory
    applications/challenges of,
        135–136
    described, 132–133
    original formulations of, 133–135
    on text and conversation, 207
speech codes theory, 278–284
spiral of silence theory, 264–269,
    265t, 270t
S-R models, 238, 239
stable exchange stage, 154
standpoint feminist approach, 72
standpoint theory, 289–291
Steeves, H. L., 249
Steinberg, M., 160
Stiff, J., 38, 117, 121
stimulus discrimination, 160
stimulus generalization, 160
Stohl, C., 220, 223, 233
Strauss, A., 56, 57

strong effects model, 238–239
structurational approach to group
    communication, 224–229t
structuration theory
    adaptive, 227–229t
    on group arguments, 226–227
    modalities in, 225t
    overview of, 201–205, 224–226
structure
    described, 203–204
    duality of, 65, 202, 224
*Structure of Scientific Revolutions,
    The* (Kuhn), 23, 43
subjective norms, 115–116
subjectivist epistemology, 26–27t,
    52–53
subjectivist ontology, 24
substance conception, 91–92
substructure of society, 62
Sunnafrank, M., 169
superstructure of society, 62
Suppe, F., 96
Surber, J. P., 62, 68
Surgeon General's Scientific
    Advisory Committee on
    Television and Social
    Behavior (1972), 269
Swanson, D., 242, 243, 245, 246
symbolic communication, 7–8
symbolic convergence theory,
    229–233
symbolic interactionism, 50–51
symbolic organization
    attribution theory on, 81–83
    humanistic approaches to,
        84–92
    narrative theory of, 84–88
    schema theory on, 77–81
    social life metaphors and, 76–77
    social scientific approaches to,
        76–84
symbols
    semantic triangle of, 7
    significant, 51
    sign vs., 7
symmetrical interaction, 178
symptomatic behavior, 10–11
syntactics, 133
syntax (digital vs. analogic),
    177–178
synthesis, 183

systematic processing, 121

Takeshita, T., 262
"talking to yourself," 8–9
Tamborini, R., 273
Taylor, D. A., 154, 155, 157, 158, 161
Taylor, F., 196
Taylor, J. R., 205–206, 207–208, 209, 210
Taylor, S. E., 76, 78
Teamsterville code study, 280–281, 283, 284
technological control, 210
television
    content patterns of, 271
    cultivation theory on, 269–274
    excitation transfer theory applied to, 251–252
    gender differences in response to, 254
    nature of, 270, 273
    nature of viewing, 270–271
    speech codes of *Donahue* talk show on, 284
    subjectivist approach to children and, 26–27
    Who Wants to Be a Millionaire show on, 242, 243, 245, 248–249
    See also mass media communication
terministic screen, 91
Texas A&M University, 213
text concept, 48, 207–210
theorems (uncertainty reduction theory), 164–165, 166t–167t
theories
    assessing quality of, 22–23
    common-sense, 18–19
    context vs. process, 57
    criteria for evaluating/ comparing, 40–41
    defining function of, 21–23
    defining nature of, 19–21
    evolutionary growth of, 43–44
    ontological considerations of, 24–25
    post-positivism on, 35–45
    revolutionary growth of, 44

theories of communication in developing relationships
    comparison and commentary on, 172
    social penetration, 153–163
    uncertainty reduction, 163–172
theories of communication in ongoing relationships
    comparison and commentary on, 191–193
    relational dialectics, 182–191
    relational systems theory: Palo Alto group, 174–182
theories of culture and communication
    co-cultural groups, 289–294t
    comparison and commentary on, 294–296
    face and culture, 284–289
    speech codes, 278–284
theories of discourse and interaction
    communication accommodation, 141–146
    comparison and commentary on, 150–152
    coordinated management of meaning, 136–141
    expectancy violation and interaction adaptation, 146–150, 151t
    speech act, 132–136, 207
theories of media processing and effects
    comparison and commentary on, 254–256
    media effects research and, 236–239
    of media and emotion, 250–254
    media systems dependency, 246–250
    social cognitive, 239–242
    uses and gratifications, 242–246
theories of media and society
    agenda setting, 257–264
    comparison and commentary on, 274–275

cultivation, 269–274
    spiral of silence, 264–269, 265t, 270t
theories of message processing
    classic models of persuasion, 114–117
    comparison and commentary on, 130–131
    elaboration likelihood model, 118–122
    inoculation, 122–125
    overview of, 113
    problematic integration, 125–130, 129t
theories of message production
    action assembly, 101–106
    comparison and commentary on, 109–111
    constructivist, 96–101
    historic scholarship on, 95–96
    planning and goals, 106–109
theories of organizational communication
    comparison and commentary of, 214–215
    structuration, 201–205
    unobtrusive concertive control, 210–214
    Weick's, 197–201
theories of relational dialectics
    central concepts of, 185–186
    contradictions of, 186–188
    overview of, 182–183
    philosophical roots of, 183–185
    praxis of, 188–189
    research on, 189–191
theories of small group communication
    comparison and commentary on, 233–234
    formative research in group interaction and, 216–218
    functional, 218–224
    structurational approaches, 224–229t
    symbolic convergence, 229–233
theories of symbolic organization
    attribution, 81–83
    comparison/commentary on, 92–93

dramatism, 88–92
narrative, 84–88
schema theory, 77–81
Theory Building (Dubin), 37
theory of bureaucracy, 47
Theory of Communication Action, The (Habermas), 64
Theory Construction (Blalock), 164
theory development
  axiological considerations of, 27–29
  critical perspectives on, 60–74
  deductive vs. inductive approach to, 21
  epistemological considerations of, 25–27t
  interpretive perspectives of, 46–59
  metatheoretical considerations of, 23–24
  post-positivist, 32–45
theory of empathic communication, 38, 39t
theory function
  general interpretive, 53–54
  grounded, 56–57
  post-positivism on, 38–40
theory of logical types, 176
theory of planned behavior, 116f
theory of reasoned action, 115–116
theory structure
  general interpretive, 54–55
  grounded, 56–57
  post-positivism on, 37–38
theory verification, 43
Thibaut, J., 157
Thompson, E. P., 70
threat/inoculation process, 123
Ting-Toomey, S., 287, 288, 289
Tompkins, P. K., 36, 48, 210, 212
totality, 63, 185–186
totemizing ritual, 282
toughlove story, 88
Tracy, K., 287
train test, 266
transactional communication, 6–7
transcendental phenomenology, 49–50

transmission model of communication, 11
tripartite media dependency relationship, 247f–249
trust, 160

uncertainty avoidance, 285
uncertainty reduction theory
  axioms and theorems of, 164–165, 166t–167t
  Berger's extensions to, 165, 167–168
  expanding/evaluation of, 170–172
  original statement of, 163–165
  testing/critiques of, 168–170
unitary sequence path, 217
unobtrusive control, 212–213
uses and gratifications theory, 242–246
U.S. Forest Service identification, 214
utterances
  act of, 133
  coding sequences of, 180
  representation of, 104
  See also conversation

values
  axiology (study) of, 27–29
  post-positivism on bias of, 37
Van Bockern, S., 125
Vangelisti, A. L., 83
Van Lear, Arthur, 162
van Rees, M. A., 135
Vendler, Z., 134
verbal messages, 10
verification goal of science, 34
verisimilitude state, 43
verstehen understanding, 47, 49
victimage, 90–91
Vienna Circle, The, 33–34
Vinsel, A., 154
von Neumann, John, 175

Waismann, Friedrich, 33
Walther, J. B., 149
Wartella, E., 23

Washington Post, The, 80
Watergate break-in, 218
Watzlawick, P., 9
Weaver, D. H., 262, 263
Weaver, J. B., 254
Weber, M., 47, 61, 196, 210–211
Weick, K., 197, 198, 199, 200, 201
Weick's theory of organizing, 197–201
Weiner, B., 82
Welton, K., 290
Wentanschauungen, 96–97
Werner, C. M., 186
Werner, H., 97
Who Wants to Be a Millionaire (TV show), 242, 243, 245, 248–249
Wicks, R. H., 77, 79
Wiener, N., 175
Wilder, C., 174, 175–176
Williams, A., 146
Williams, R., 70
Willnat, L., 263
Wilson, B., 36
Wilson, S. R., 83, 95, 107, 109
Witmer, D. F., 205
Wittgenstein, L., 133
Wizard of Oz, The (film), 121
Wolf, M. A., 275
Wolfram, W., 144
women
  media effects on, 254
  muted group theory on, 291–292
  television content patterns of, 271
  See also feminist studies
Wood, J. T., 161

Yagoda, Ben, 92
Yerby, J., 190
Yi, H., 251
Yoshimura, S. M., 150

Zhu, J. H., 261, 263
Zillmann, D., 250, 251, 252, 253, 254
Zucker, H. G., 262